The American Pre-Raphaelites

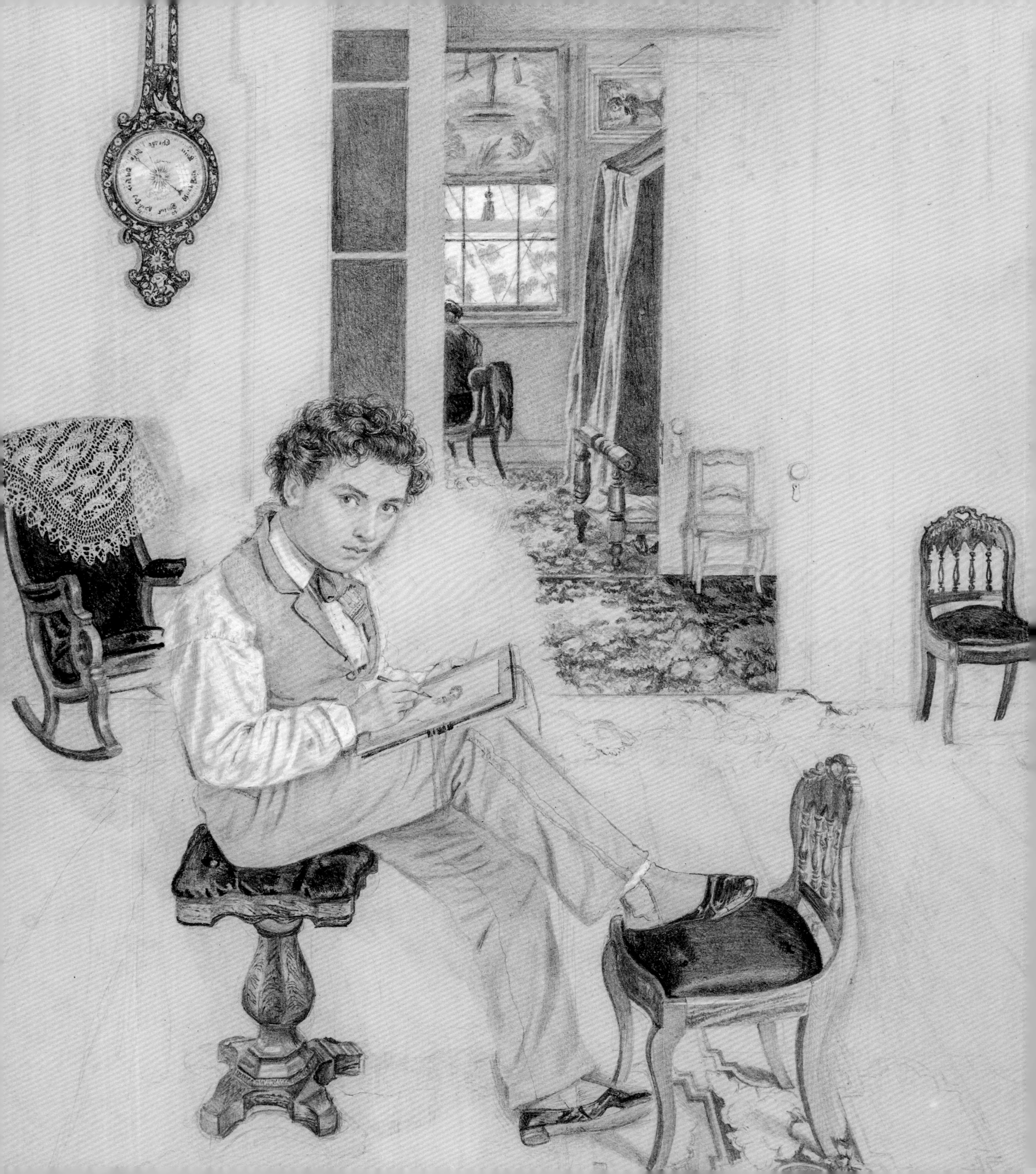

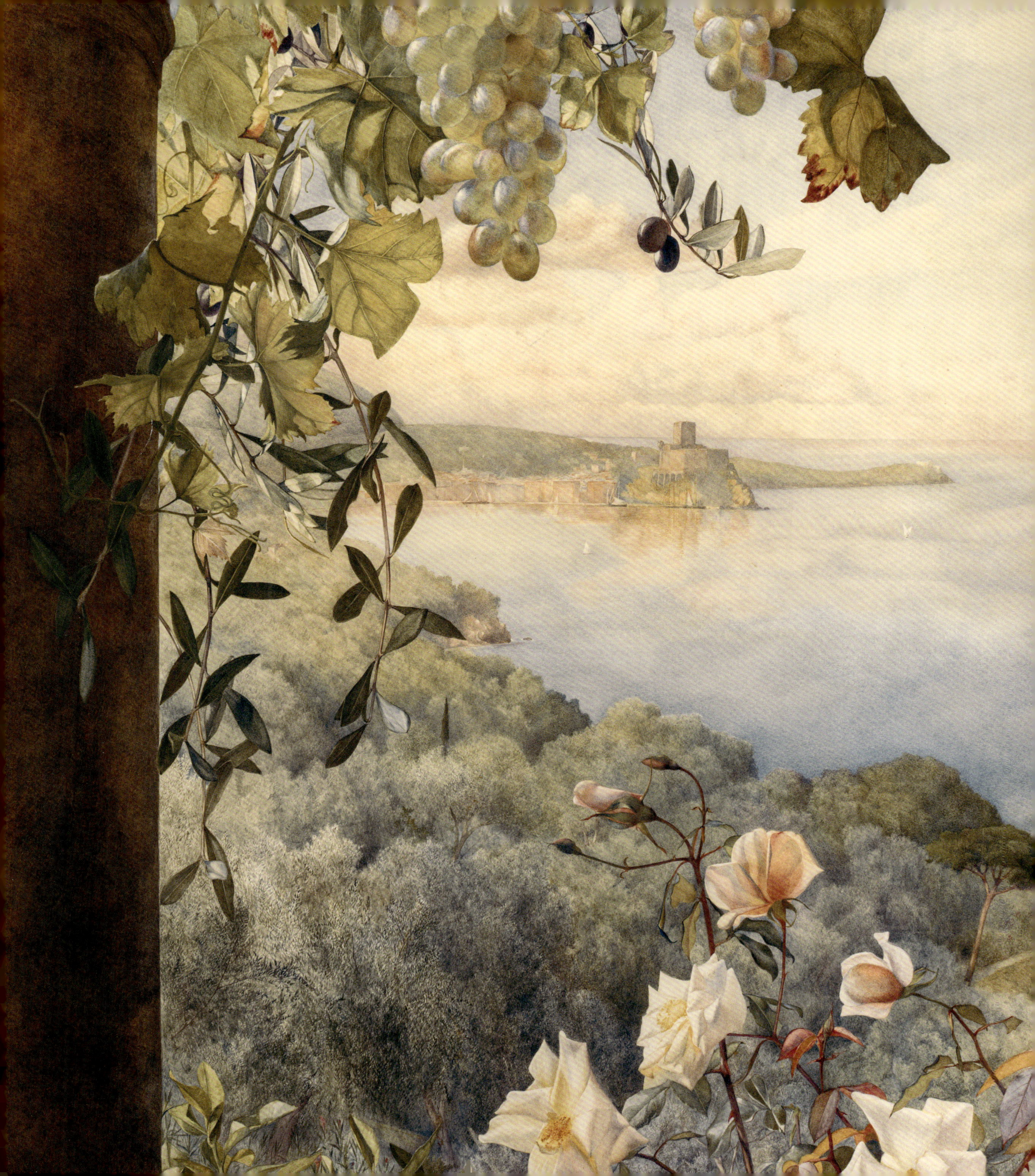

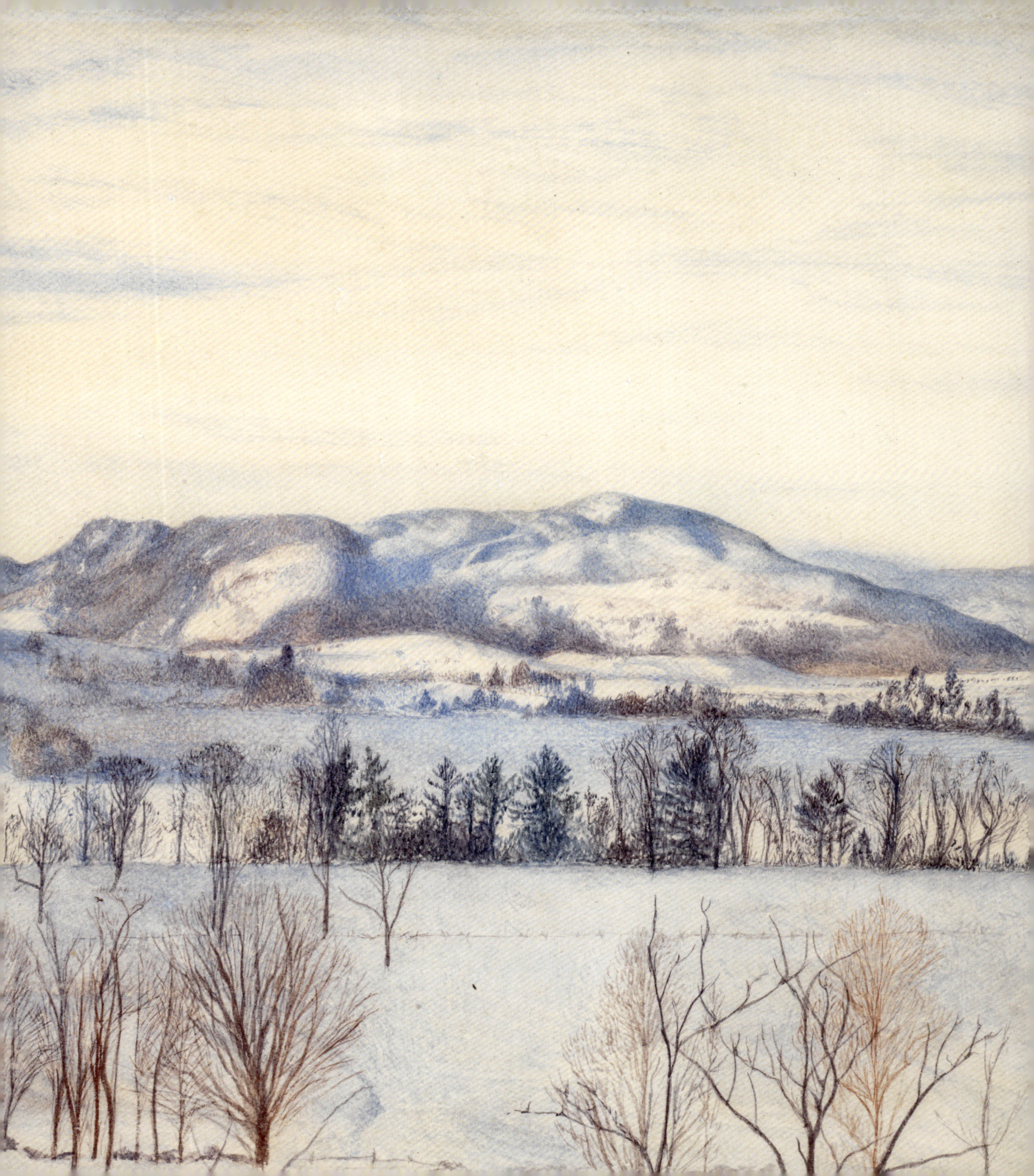

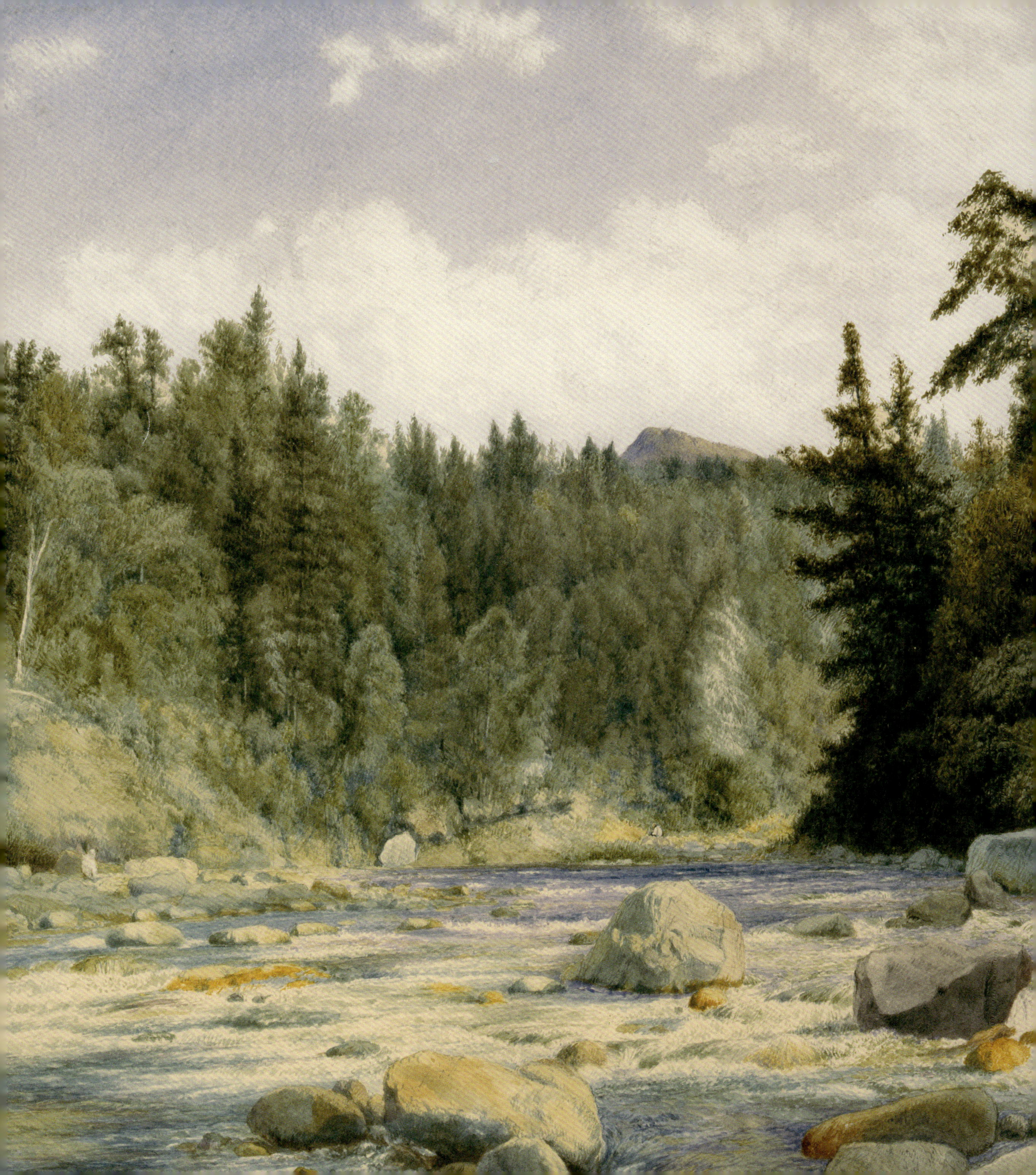

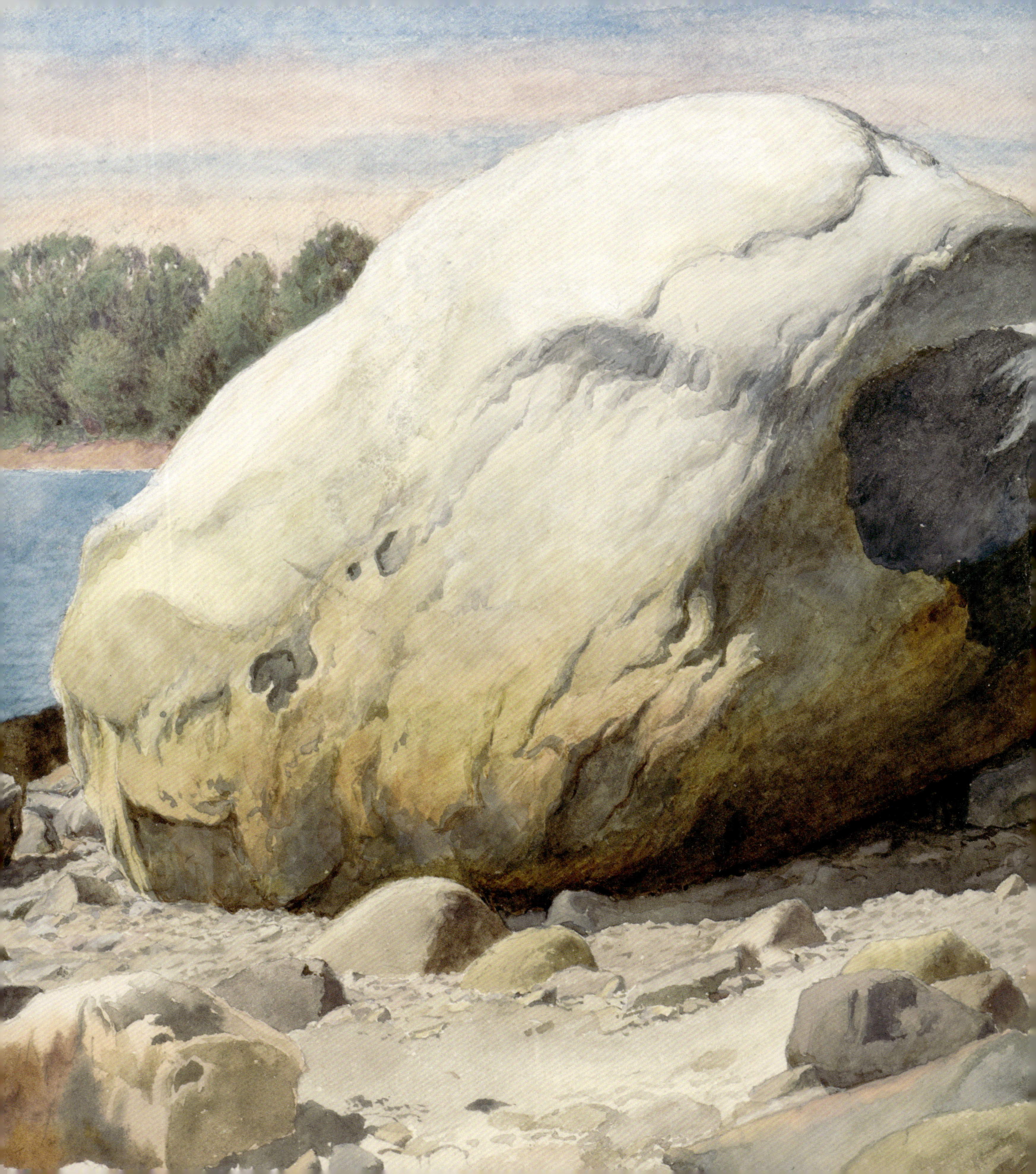

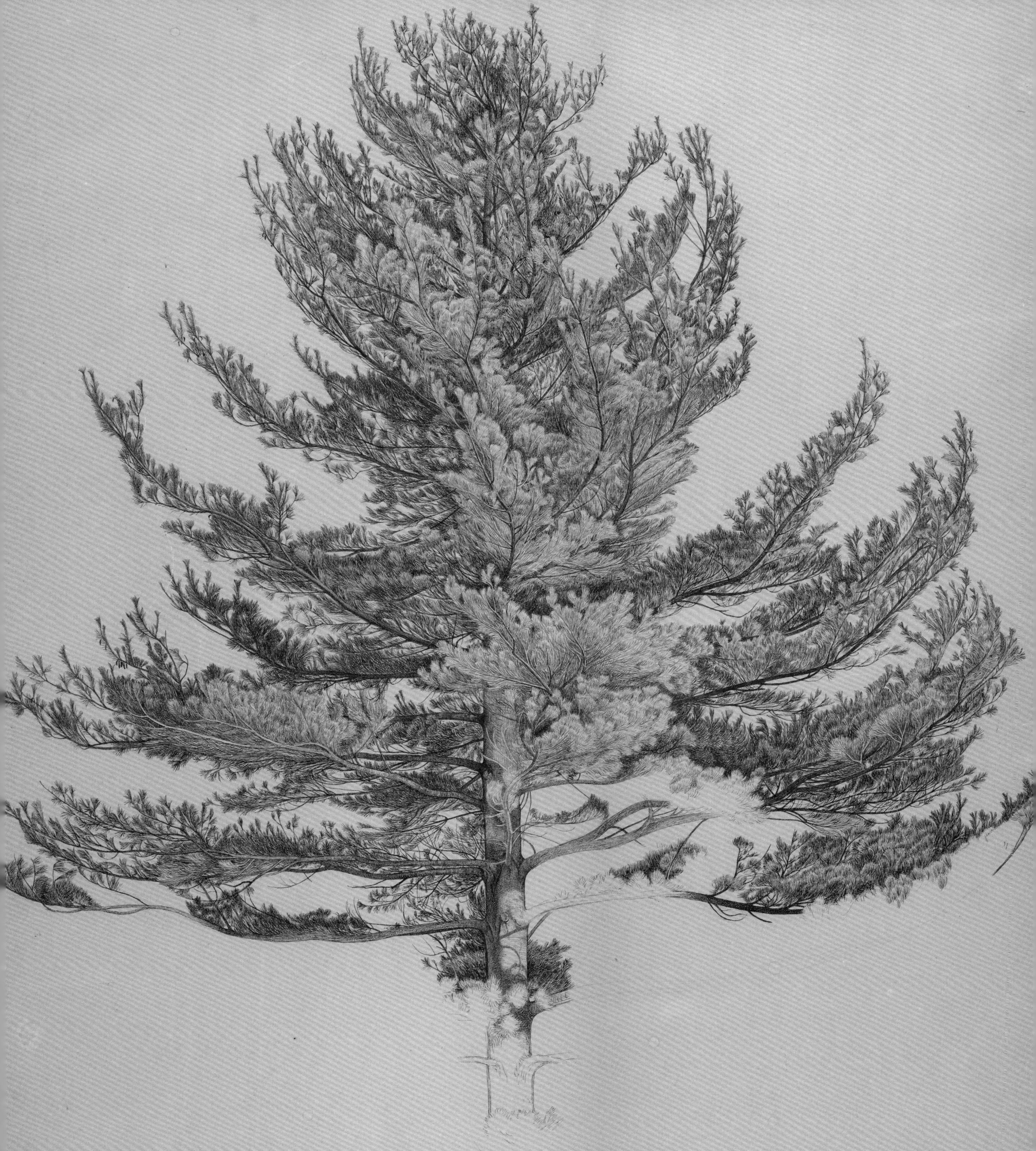

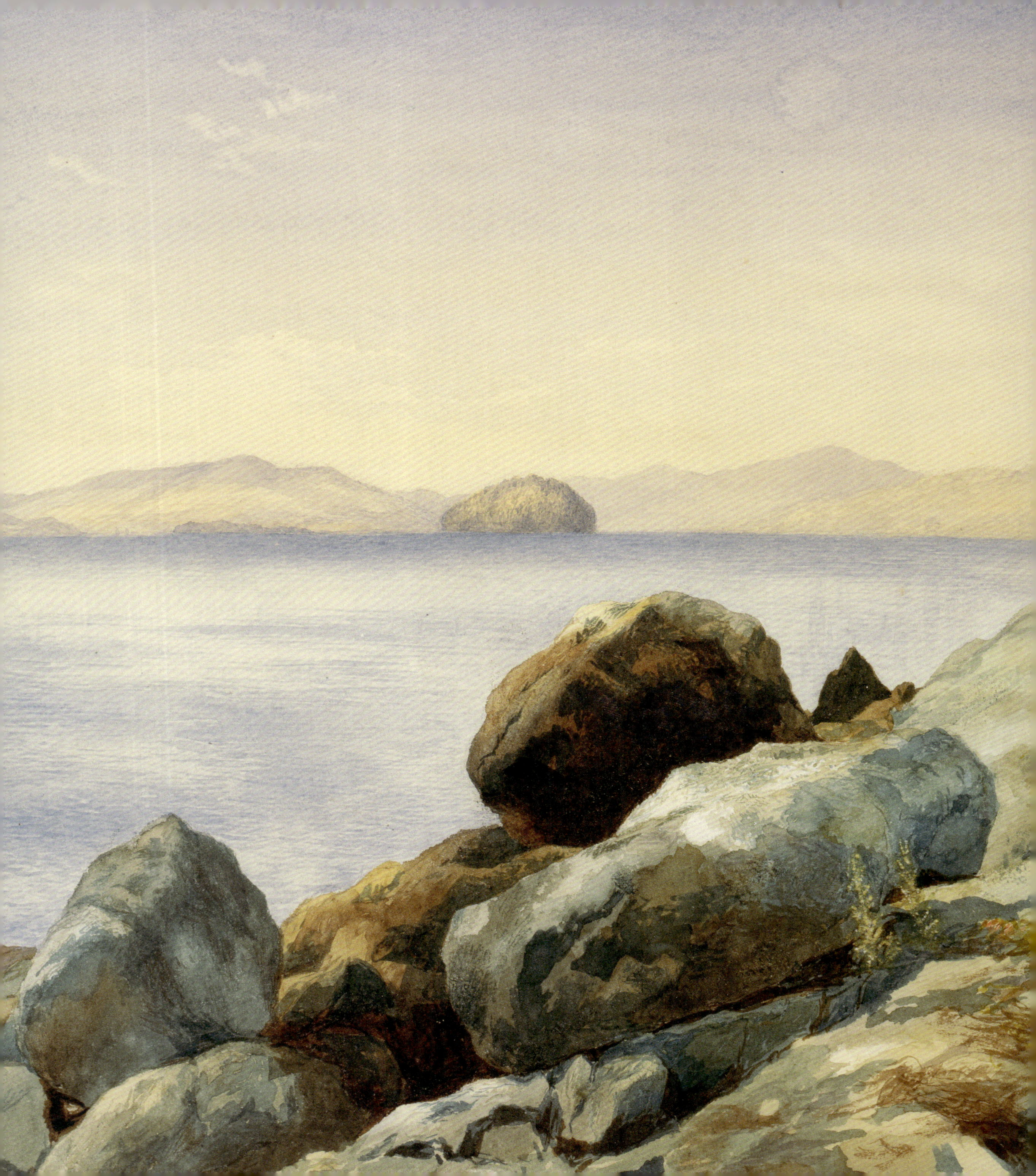

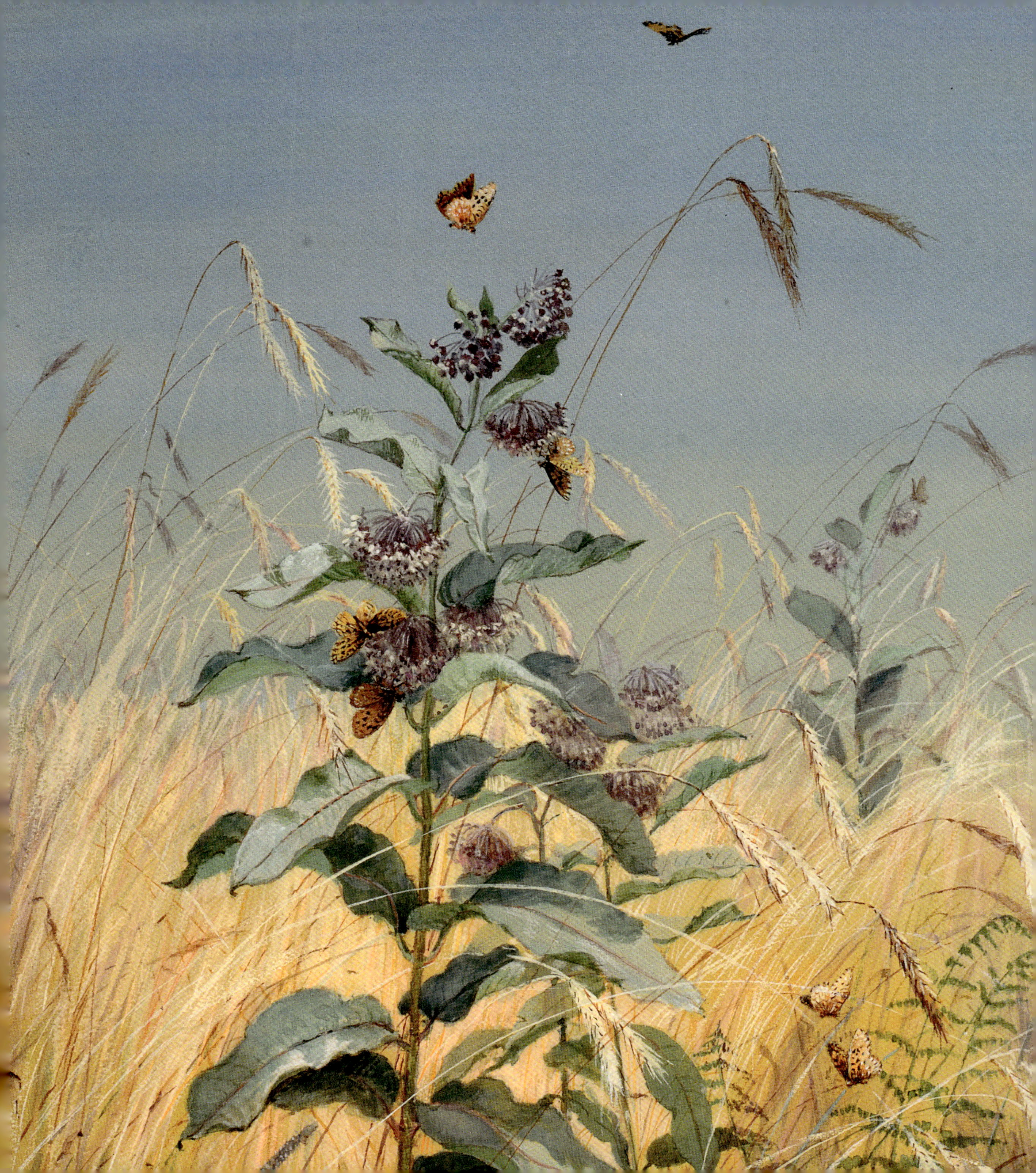

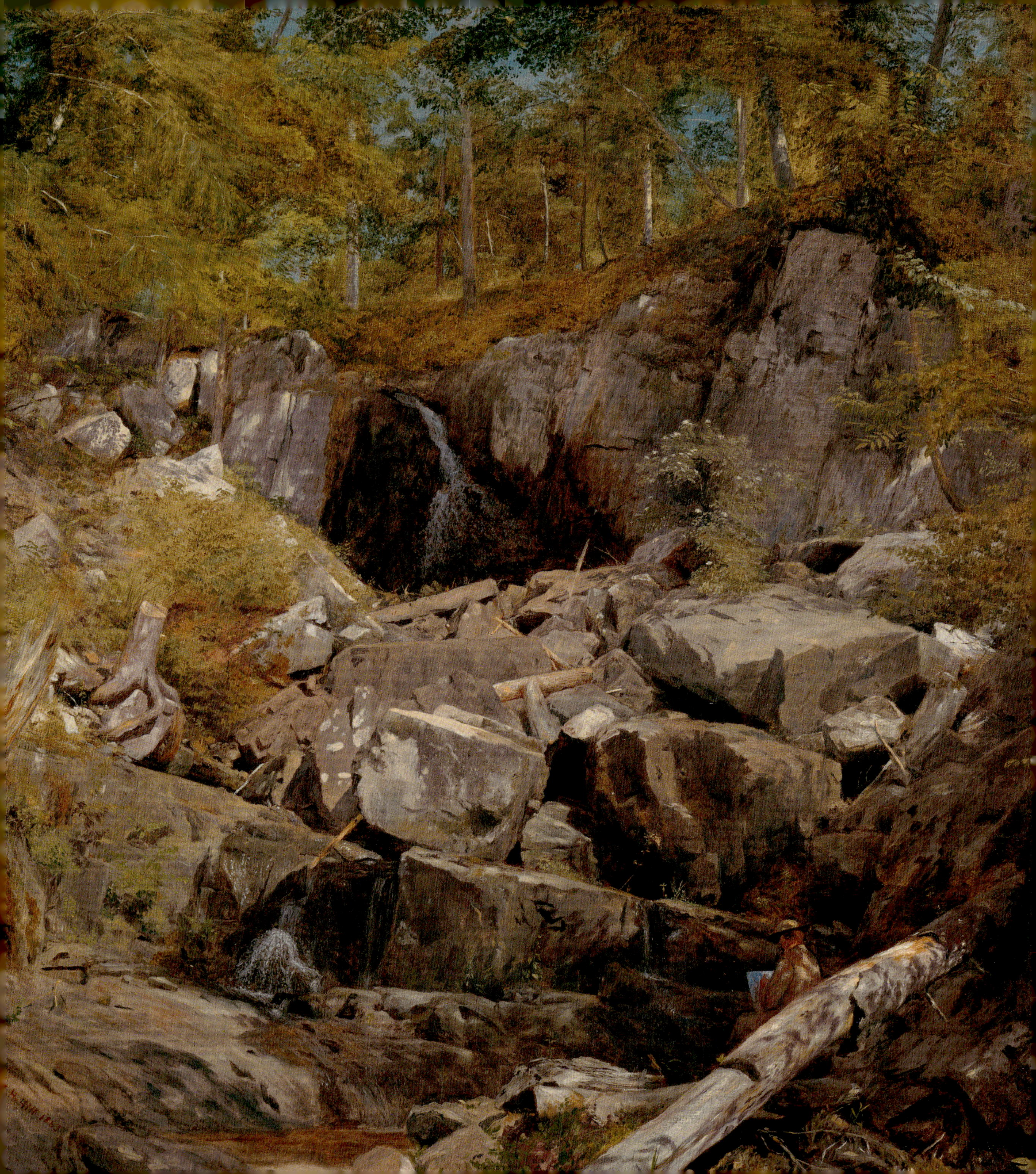

The American Pre-Raphaelites

Radical Realists

LINDA S. FERBER
and NANCY K. ANDERSON

with
TIM BARRINGER
BARBARA DAYER GALLATI
SOPHIE LYNFORD
MARK D. MITCHELL
JANICE SIMON
DIANE WAGGONER

National Gallery of Art
Washington

in association with
Yale University Press
New Haven and London

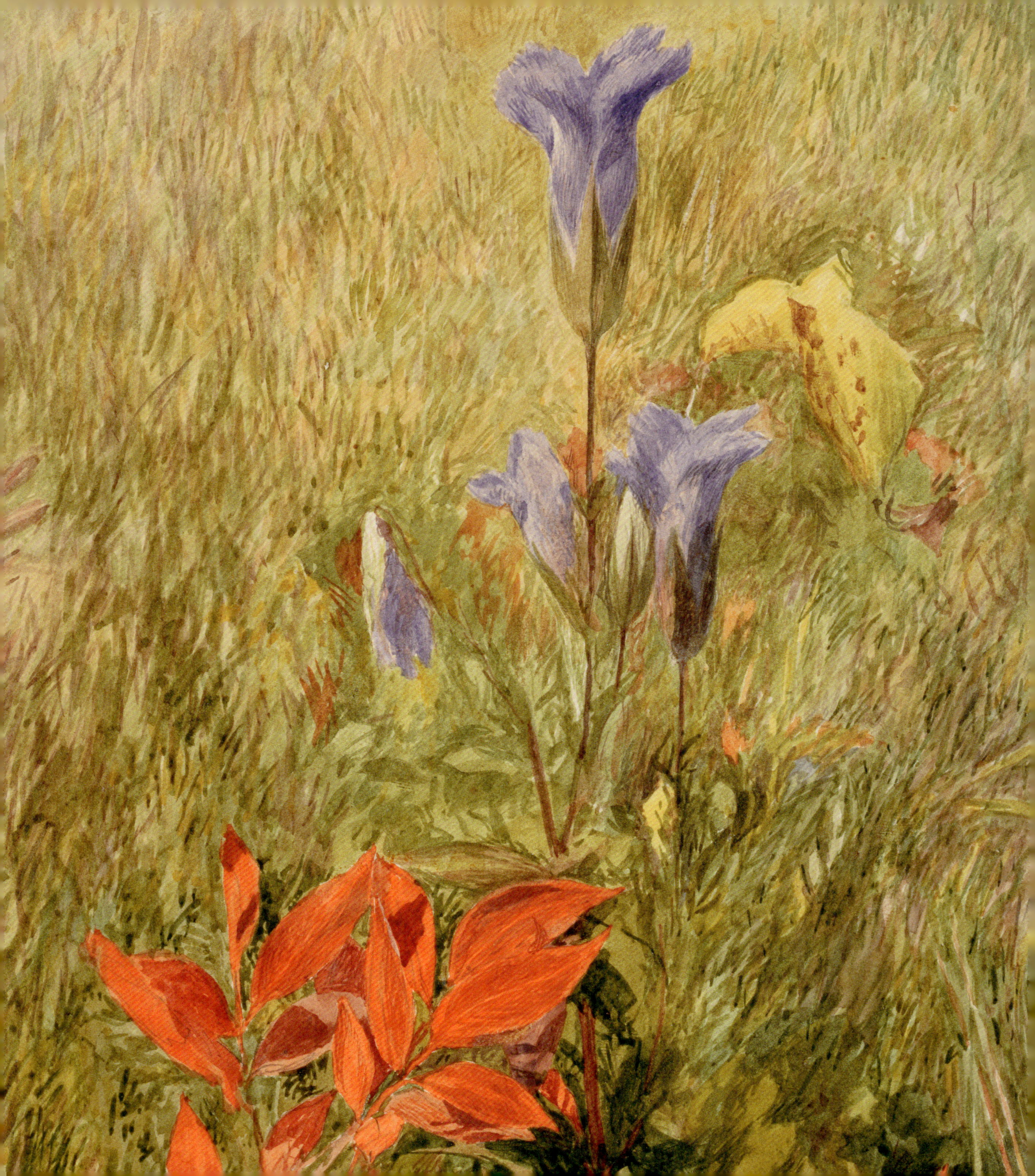

Contents

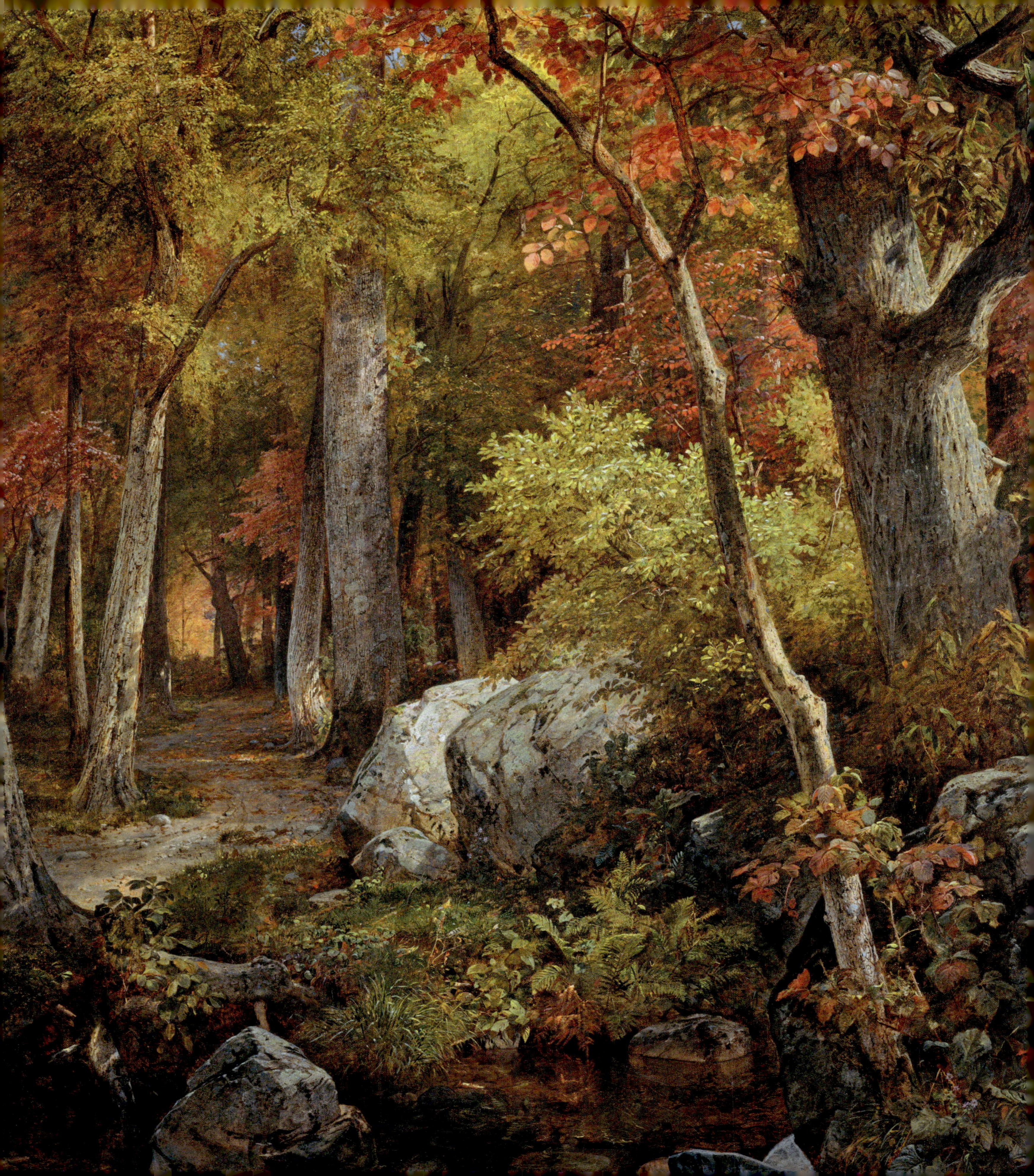

Director's Foreword

William Trost Richards, *October*, 1863 (detail, plate 78)

In celebration of the two-hundredth anniversary of the birth of John Ruskin (1819–1900), the most influential art critic of the Victorian era, the National Gallery of Art presents an exhibition of paintings, watercolors, drawings, and photographs created by American artists profoundly influenced by Ruskin's call for revolutionary change in the practice of art. Although Ruskin never traveled to the United States, his appeal for radical reform reached American shores through his many publications and reviews, including those in which he championed the reformist agenda of the British Pre-Raphaelite artists. Ruskin's rejection of traditional academic art and his plea for works that reflected a deep reverence for both the spiritual and scientific qualities of the natural world found a sympathetic audience in America among a group of like-minded artists, architects, scientists, critics, and collectors.

Thomas Charles Farrer, a young British expatriate who had studied with Ruskin and Pre-Raphaelite painter Dante Gabriel Rossetti in London, became the leader of this eclectic group. In January 1863, Farrer and several other American Ruskinians gathered in the artist's studio to channel their shared admiration for Ruskin's teachings into a formal organization—the Association for the Advancement of Truth in Art. Although the Association was short-lived (as was their radical journal, *The New Path*), a remarkable number of stunningly beautiful works were created during the period when Association members were actively following Ruskin's admonition that they leave tradition behind, exit the studio, work outdoors, and reproduce nature's "truth" with exacting detail.

In 1985, Linda S. Ferber, guest curator of *The American Pre-Raphaelites: Radical Realists*, and Professor William H. Gerdts introduced this group of artists in a landmark exhibition, *The New Path: Ruskin and the American Pre-Raphaelites*, organized by the Brooklyn Museum. More than thirty years have now passed since that pioneering exhibition. In the interim, many additional works by artists associated with the group have come to light, and scholarship in nineteenth-century American art has advanced significantly. New research has revealed that the Association members' desire for reform extended beyond the practice of art to include, as well, the urgent political debate about slavery. The organizational meeting convened in January 1863 took place at the height of the Civil War, just days after Abraham Lincoln had issued the Emancipation Proclamation. Most members of the Association were abolitionists — Farrer himself served in the Union army. Coded references to the war are present in a number of exquisitely detailed landscape paintings that do not appear, initially, to carry symbolic meaning. Members of the group followed Ruskin's directive to record the natural world with strict attention to detail, but they also created works that often include a rich political subtext.

The American Pre-Raphaelites: Radical Realists features more than ninety paintings, watercolors, drawings, and photographs including a number of recently discovered works never before exhibited publicly. In addition to contributions by Linda S. Ferber, guest curator and senior art historian at the New-York Historical Society, and Nancy K. Anderson, curator and head of American and British Paintings at the National Gallery of Art, the exhibition catalog includes revealing and wide-ranging essays by Tim Barringer, Barbara Dayer Gallati, Sophie Lynford, Mark D. Mitchell, Janice Simon, and Diane Waggoner. We are deeply grateful for the contributions of these scholars whose new research places these beautiful and provocative works of art within the larger cultural and political context of their historical moment. We also wish to acknowledge the foundational scholarship on the American Pre-Raphaelites by William H. Gerdts.

All important loan exhibitions depend on the generosity of lenders. We extend our profound thanks to the institutions and private collectors who responded so generously to our loan requests. We extend our deep appreciation as well to the Terra Foundation for American Art and the Henry Luce Foundation for their generous support of the exhibition and catalog.

Earl A. Powell III
National Gallery of Art

Lenders to the Exhibition

Amon Carter Museum of American Art, Fort Worth
Bowdoin College Museum of Art, Brunswick
Brooklyn Museum, New York
The Cleveland Museum of Art
Jeff and Betsey Cooley
Crystal Bridges Museum of American Art, Bentonville
Peter A. Feld
Mr. and Mrs. Stuart P. Feld
Elizabeth Feld-Herzberg
The Hon. William Gibson
Harvard Art Museums, Cambridge
High Museum of Art, Atlanta
Rob and Mary Joan Leith
The Metropolitan Museum of Art, New York
Leonard and Ellen Milberg
The Morgan Library & Museum, New York
Munson-Williams-Proctor Arts Institute, Utica
Museum of Fine Arts, Boston
National Gallery of Art, Washington
New Britain Museum of American Art
The New-York Historical Society
Amy and Robert Poster
Princeton University Art Museum
Private Collections
Smith College Museum of Art, Northampton
The State University of New York at Geneseo
Susan and Ted Stebbins
Virginia Museum of Fine Arts, Richmond
The Walters Art Museum, Baltimore
Washburn Gallery, New York
Paul Worman Fine Art, Worcester

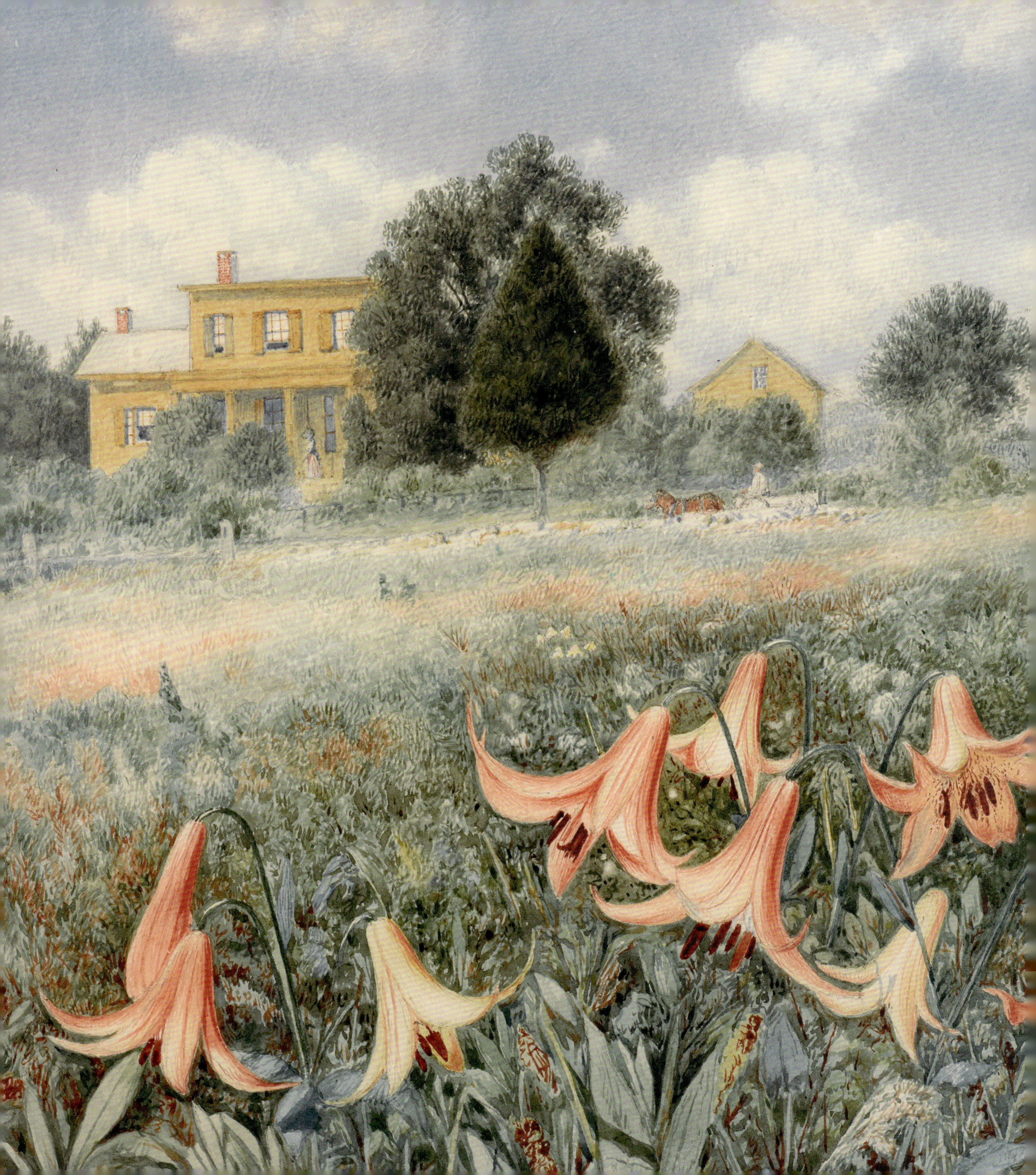

Who Were the American Pre-Raphaelites?

LINDA S. FERBER

John William Hill, *West Nyack, New York (The Lilies of the Field)*, 1868 (detail, plate 46)

> By the mercy of God, Ruskin has been sent to open our eyes.
>
> —Charles Herbert Moore, "Fallacies of the Present School," *The New Path*, 1863

John Ruskin never visited the United States but his ideas sparked a revolt. As the most important art critic of the Victorian era, Ruskin (fig. 1) enjoyed tremendous influence, including in America where his books were eagerly read and discussed. His *Modern Painters* (1843–1860) was begun as a defense of the British artist J. M. W. Turner and evolved into an extended critique of landscape painting. It was in this work that, he declared, "every class of rock, earth and cloud must be known by the painter, with geologic and meteorologic accuracy."[1] Ruskin was also a brilliant draftsman whose works provided powerful models of drawing and watercolor as tools with which to observe and understand the natural world. In the United States, his influence was most profound through the 1860s, when his ideas and opinions inspired an organized Ruskinian reform of American art and architecture. The Association for the Advancement of Truth in Art, the organization inspired by his teachings, was launched in New York during the Civil War.[2] Although short-lived, this outspokenly progressive movement proved to be an important catalyst for the founding of the American Watercolor Society and a potent harbinger of the American Aesthetic movement.

In the first volume of *Modern Painters*, Ruskin had urged artists to reject academic studio convention, instead drawing and painting out of doors directly from nature: "rejecting nothing, selecting nothing and scorning nothing."[3] He inspired and championed the painters of the English Pre-Raphaelite Brotherhood (PRB), which was founded in 1848 by Dante Gabriel Rossetti, John Everett Millais, and William Holman Hunt (figs. 2, 10, 3, 6, 5, 8 in Barringer essay;

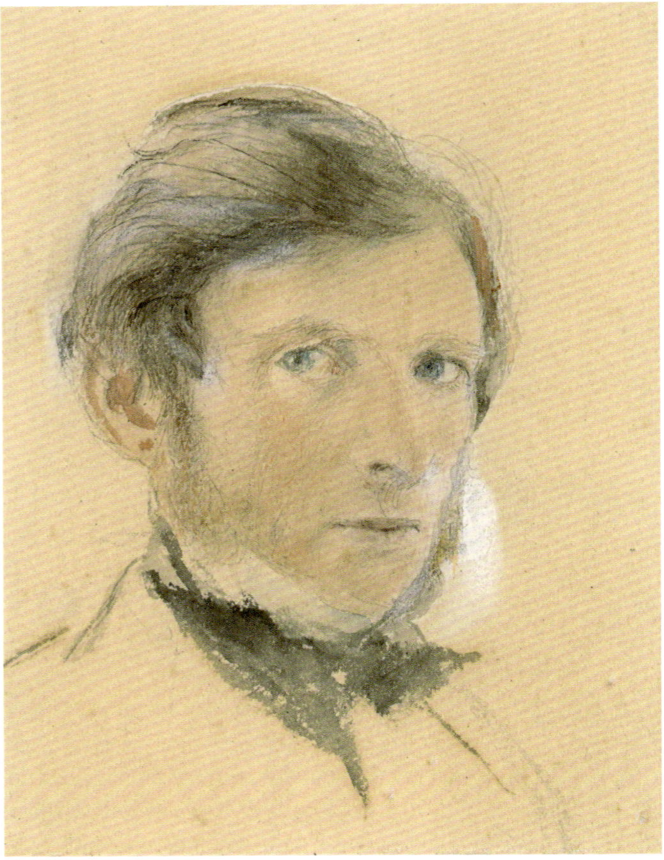

fig. 1 in Lynford essay; figs. 5, 2 in Gallati essay). He also argued for the historical importance of Gothic art and architecture in subsequent publications. Ruskin was among those who advocated for reviving the style in modern times, in part as an earnest effort to address the dehumanizing impact of industrial production on English artisans and workers.[4]

In America, as Ruskin scholar Roger Stein has written, the fundamental importance of Ruskin's writings was "his identification of the interest in art with morality and religion as well as with the love of nature, his ability to build a loose but convincing system where art, religion and nature were inextricably intertwined."[5] Contemporaneous responses confirm Stein's insight. Future American Pre-Raphaelite Clarence Cook captured the eloquence that enchanted so many American readers: "We love Ruskin's glowing style," he wrote, "we love his love of nature, we love his love of God. He carries us along with him by his enthusiasm."[6] In 1855, Asher B. Durand, then president of the National Academy of Design, redelivered Ruskin's messages about "truth to nature" to American artists in his

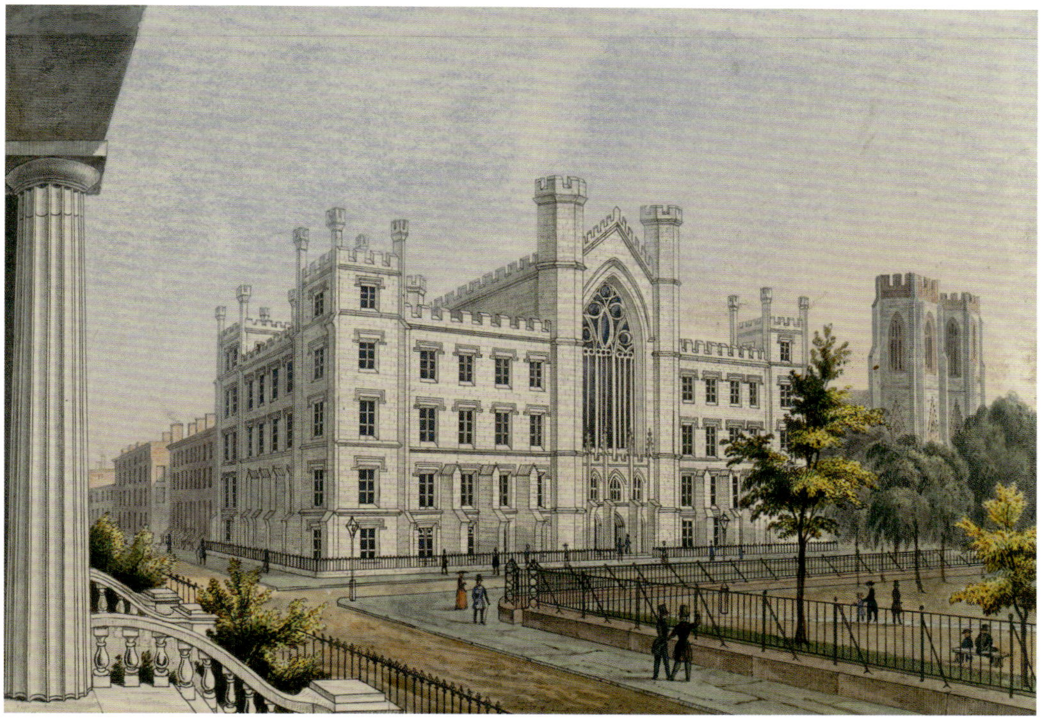

1. John Ruskin, *Self-Portrait*, 1861, watercolor over pencil, The Morgan Library & Museum, New York, Purchased as the gift of the Fellows

2. *University of the City of New York, Washington Square*, 1850, watercolor, The New York Public Library, I. N. Phelps Stokes Collection of American Historical Prints, The Miriam and Ira D. Wallach Division of Art, Prints and Photographs: Print Collection

"Letters on Landscape Painting." Durand positioned Ruskin's advocacy for plein-air painting and close attention to detail not only as the path to artistic and spiritual enlightenment, but also as the key to the emergence of a national school.[7]

The New York art world was small then. Durand's "Letters" were published in the first issue of *The Crayon*, an art journal founded in 1855 by his son John Durand and artist William James Stillman. A letter to Stillman from Ruskin himself was published in an early issue. "I have much to thank America for," the eminent critic claimed, "—heartier appreciation and a better understanding of what I am and mean, than I have ever met in England."[8] The most famous work of art by Ruskin in the United States was *Fragment of the Alps* (c. 1854–1856, plate 84), a watercolor belonging to Charles Eliot Norton, Ruskin's longtime friend and a champion of the American movement.[9] This spectacular study of an alpine boulder would beget a large progeny (for example, plates 34, 37, 55).

An Organized Revolt

On January 27, 1863, Thomas Charles Farrer, an English expatriate artist, ardent abolitionist, and recent veteran of the Union army, convened the first meeting of the Association for the Advancement of Truth in Art at his Waverly Place studio in

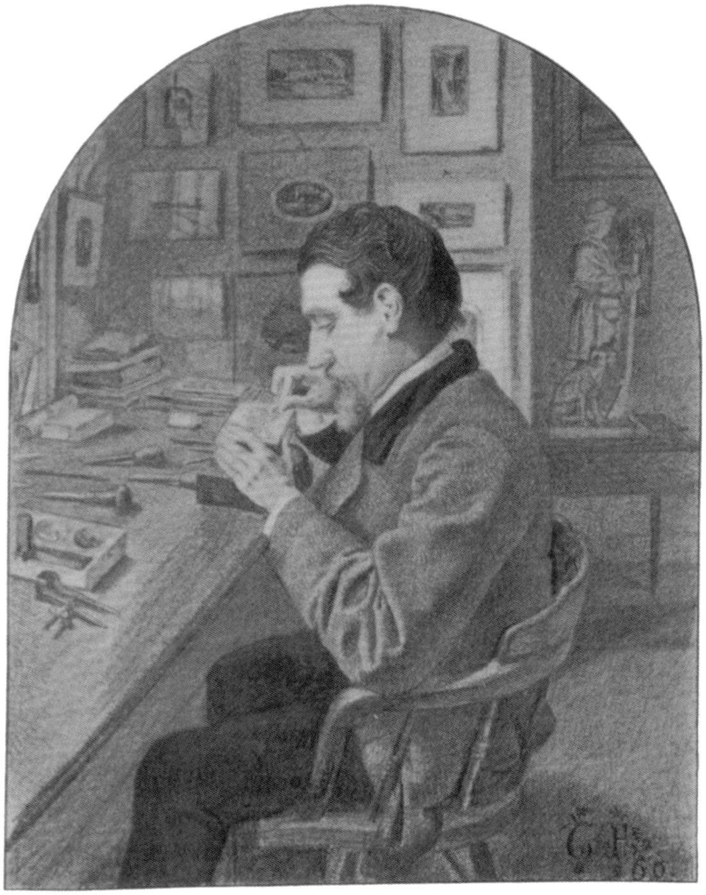

the New York University Building on Washington Square (fig. 2).[10] The Association (also called the Society) was a crusading organization of men and women from many walks of American life. They were united by a patriotic commitment to the preservation of the Union and to the abolition of slavery. They would publish *The New Path*, a radical journal voicing their dedication as well to the reform of American art, architecture, criticism, manufacture, and design. Some member artists named themselves "realists," while others preferred the Pre-Raphaelite label. In the press, they were dubbed the American Pre-Raphaelites. Many other Ruskinians unaffiliated with the Association, but equally committed, would also be called by that name.[11]

Farrer had arrived in New York late in 1858, fresh from studying drawing with Ruskin and Dante Gabriel Rossetti at the Working Men's College in London.[12] Connecting with a network of American Ruskin advocates, Farrer portrayed a number of them in a series of informal portraits executed early on. The iconographical content of these small, exquisitely detailed drawings alludes to the sitters' vocations as well as their Ruskinian allegiance. Sitters include John William Hill and his son John Henry Hill of Nyack, longtime admirers of Ruskin (plates 23, 20, 21). The Hills extended hospitality and opportunities to work out of doors at their homestead in Rockland County, New York (plate 46; detail, essay frontispiece opposite p. 1). Farrer's densely detailed likenesses of critic and abolitionist Cook and engraver and soon-to-be art dealer Samuel P. Avery document other early friendships (fig. 1 in Gallati essay; fig. 3). The nineteen-year-old Farrer also recorded himself at work on a self-portrait (plate 22; detail, book frontispiece).

Counted among the other men and women who were members and supporters were not only artists, architects, and critics, but an assembly of concerned citizens eager for Union victory and for social and political as well as artistic reform. They included scientists, journalists, lawyers, engineers, manufacturers, businessmen, collectors, and subscribers to *The New Path*; some are well known today and others obscure. While the names of nine women (seven of them Association members) are recorded in the minutes, the lives of most of them remain to be more fully documented.[13] Farrer offers a few clues in two drawings of women artists at work. One portrays a young woman braving the chill to sketch in the open air. Seated on the ground, she leans against a large (Ruskinian) boulder, making a careful drawing of the plants and rocks before her (plate 24). The other portrays Farrer's student and Association member Sarah Strong Tuthill at her easel (fig. 4).

America's Modern Painters

These radical realists were hailed by *The New Path* as America's modern painters. They included Farrer (plate 14), Charles Herbert Moore (plates 52, 56), the Hills (plates 26, 30, 38, 39, 44, 50), and William Trost Richards (plates 78, 79), as well as Henry Roderick Newman (plates 60, 61, 62) and Robert J. Pattison (plate 71). Nonmember artists who were attracted by Ruskin's ideas and felt the Association's influence are also represented: Fidelia Bridges, the best known among Ruskinian women artists (plates 2, 6); Robert B. Brandegee, Sarah Tuthill's nephew, whom she taught (plate 1); Henry Farrer, Thomas's brother, who emigrated around 1862 (plates 9, 11); Aaron Draper Shattuck (plate 87); and William John Hennessy (plate 25). William James Stillman was mentored as a painter by Ruskin, whom he met in 1850. Active more than a decade before the founding of the Association, Stillman was hailed by them as the earliest of the American Pre-Raphaelites (plate 89).[14]

3. Print after Thomas Charles Farrer, *Samuel P. Avery in His Engraving Room*, 1860, location of original watercolor unknown, Thomas J. Watson Library, The Metropolitan Museum of Art, New York

While far less well known today than their English counterparts, the American Pre-Raphaelites produced a distinctive body of work. Ruskin's influence united them in an enterprise of close observation of nature wedded to methods of careful

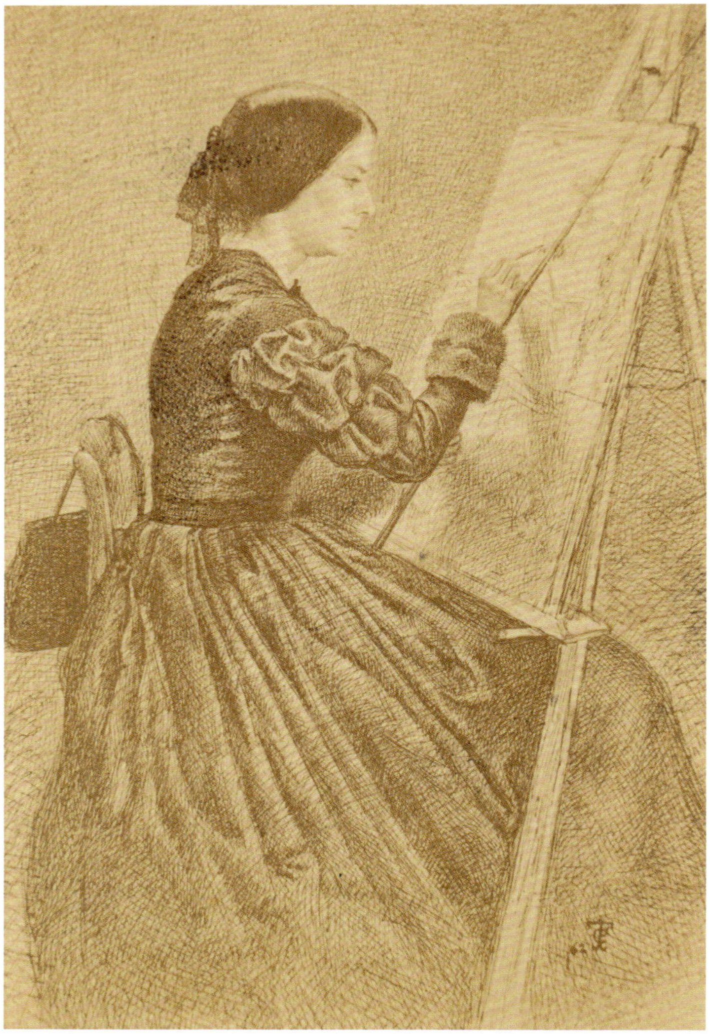

recording in both watercolor and oil. In their landscapes and still-life paintings, picturesque conventions gave way to quasi-scientific precision and strong color, producing an intense particularization (sometimes verging on the surreal) that seemed all the more startling in the context of more painterly and muted mainstream artistic production.

During the heyday of the movement in the mid-1860s, the realists' oil paintings and watercolors—obsessively detailed and vivid in color—were interpreted by the partisan critical voices of *The New Path* as vibrant agents promoting reform when displayed among conventional works. "They will NOT be passed by," noted one observer.[15] The brilliance of the American Pre-Raphaelite watercolor was produced in large part by stippled and hatched application of saturated colors over washes or white paper with a miniaturist's touch (plates 29, 40, 81, 82).[16] Over time, although these bright and detailed still-life and flower subjects—executed precisely in what was still considered a minor medium—would appeal to a growing taste for the intimate and the decorative, they were still well beyond the pale of conventional taste in watercolors.[17] Conservative audiences and critics saw few or no redeeming qualities in the realists' landscapes in oil, protesting their paintings as "repulsive" and "hard and harsh," as well as devoid of both atmosphere and poetry (plates 13, 15, 53). Any praise was always conditional. While Henry Tuckerman might "enjoy" Richards's Pre-Raphaelite landscapes as "miracles of special study," he nevertheless questioned "the principle upon which they are executed" (plates 77, 80).[18]

Modern Gothic: The Architects

The Association's founding architect members were Peter Bonnett Wight and Russell Sturgis Jr.[19] Their projects were among the earliest significant American monuments of the modern Gothic revival. Following Ruskin's tenets, they interpreted the Gothic not as a fashionable revival style but as a "renewal of the way of building which prevailed in former glorious times for art."[20] As in England, modern Gothic developed as a progressive style that was promoted as a response to the downgrading of workers in the face of standardized manufacturing methods.

Both young architects were early on in their careers dedicated to the style, especially as advocated by Ruskin in *The Stones of Venice* (1851–1853), his study of Venetian art and architecture. Both Wight and Sturgis contributed long articles to *The New Path* on the history of architecture and the importance of the Gothic revival for America. Both were perceptive and knowledgeable architectural critics, as was Clarence Cook. The entire June 1864 issue, for example, was devoted to Sturgis's discussion of Wight's National Academy of Design building then under construction on the corner of Twenty-Third Street and Fourth Avenue in New York City. Wight's design for the Academy was in the Venetian Gothic style advocated by Ruskin (figs. 2, 4 in Lynford essay). This remarkable though sadly short-lived building was erected during the Civil War. Construction was suspended during the 1863 New York City draft riots; when it finally opened, the building was draped in mourning for recently assassinated President Lincoln.[21]

4. Thomas Charles Farrer, *Portrait of Sarah Strong Tuthill*, 1862, drawing photographed by Maurice Stadtfeld, carte-de-visite albumen print, Paul Worman Fine Art, Worcester

Wight would go on to design Street Hall, the fine-arts building at Yale—the first American edifice to house a collegiate art school and art galleries.[22] Those galleries would be, in 1867, the locus for the first (and only) collective presentation of works by the American Pre-Raphaelites. Sturgis would review the building and the exhibition for *The New Path* and *The Nation*.[23] As a practicing architect, he would also design several buildings at Yale between 1865 and 1880, all in the collegiate Gothic style.[24]

Critics and Teachers

Cook, Sturgis, and Wight were articulate critics in the Ruskinian mode, so it is not surprising that the Association assigned a lofty status to the critic as equal, if not at times superior, to the artist. The artist, Sturgis explained, "[only] feels.... He can affirm, but he cannot reason." Therefore the critic must make "cool, considered, moderate judgments." He must speak with "independence and boldness" and be above influence.[25] The "true" critic's duty, he believed, was to educate the American public about ancient and modern art (including the decorative arts and household furnishings) and to encourage development of a discerning taste in readers that would lead to progress in the arts. "We must all think more about Art," Sturgis asserted, "before Art will give us much that is worth thinking about."[26]

Indeed, the "true" critic would be cast as a powerful instrument in the "systematic effort" of "the great Reformation" outlined in the Association's Articles of Organization, a manifesto that opened with a Ruskinian credo: "We hold that the primary object of Art is to observe and record truth." Stressing the unity of all arts, the Articles declared that once established, this "faithful study of nature" would motivate the improvement of American architecture, sculpture, and painting, as well as "every decorative art" including "glass, painting, mosaic, metal working, pottery, furniture, and drapery."[27] The United States, then engaged in the great reformation of a wrenching civil war to preserve the Union and end slavery, must have seemed ripe for such an ambitious program of cultural and artistic reform.

The first issue of *The New Path* appeared in May 1863; it was America's first radical art journal dedicated to the elevation of national cultural production and American taste through the Ruskinian critique of art and architecture, as well as the decorative and manual arts. Clarence Cook's editorial in the first issue opened with a clarion call that set the provocative tone for the militant magazine's subsequent twenty-four issues (published between May 1863 and December 1865): "The future of Art in America," Cook declared, "is not without hope if looked at from certain points of view."[28]

These "certain points of view" included the candid critical opinions that appeared in *The New Path's* exhibition reviews. Cook, especially, was feared for his severe critiques of both historic and current American art; Thomas Cole and Asher Durand, he declared, "belong[ed] to a past age and a dead system."[29]

One critic quipped that the magazine had been "baptized the 'New Wrath' by its enemies." Another, however, found *The New Path* "as refreshing in its fearless art-criticism as ice water on a hot day."[30]

Indeed, the magazine's editorial mission was not only to inform and educate its readership but also to professionalize the current practice of art criticism in America, which they judged as offering little but indiscriminant praise of mostly inferior works. In "Art Criticism" Sturgis proposed, instead, a disciplined criticism that would be a "science of art." Close scrutiny, accurate documentation, and truthful evaluation were to be its foundation; the critic's duty was to teach the public as well as the artist whose work was critiqued.[31]

While Cook, Sturgis, and Wight carried out the Association's didactic agendas through art criticism, artist-members were committed to implementing "the great Reformation" through art instruction, especially the teaching of drawing and watercolor. Their pedagogical model was twofold. First, there was Ruskin's system at the Working Men's College, where Farrer had been educated and whose ideals he put into practice in America when he was appointed in 1861 as drawing instructor at the recently opened Cooper Union's innovative School of Design for Women, where he used natural objects such as single leaves or stuffed birds as models, rather than casts.[32] Second, Association artist-members drew on Ruskin's *Elements of Drawing* (1857), a best-selling manual that offered detailed instruction on drawing and watercolor. His essay "On First Practice" brought nature indoors: "Go out into your garden," Ruskin commanded, "and pick up the first round or oval stone you can find, . . . put the stone . . . on the table in front of you. . . . Now if you can draw that stone, you can draw anything."[33] Richards's *Corner of the Woods* (1864, plate 83) and Moore's *Pine Tree* (1868, plate 58) present paradigms of this Ruskinian ideal. The Association's Articles of Organization declared that not only was it the artist's "duty to strive for the greatest attainable power of drawing," following the Ruskinian method (plate 86), but that it was also the artist's duty to teach others.[34]

The pedagogical energy of the realists would continue in some quarters long after the formal organization had disbanded. One of them was the Hill homestead at Nyack.[35] In 1867 the younger Hill, John Henry, made his contribution to the Ruskinian system with *Sketches from Nature*, which reproduced his etchings of twenty-five landscape and still-life subjects as models for the student. (Farrer's 1859 portrait drawing of Hill etching [plate 21] testifies to Hill's skill as a printmaker.) The introduction advised "beginners in landscape art" to consult Ruskin's *Elements of Drawing* and *Modern Painters*, and Hill himself continued to seek Ruskin's guidance.[36] (Two small Hill watercolors of Lake George bear Ruskin's critiques in the margins: plates 32, 33.) Hill's etched models include

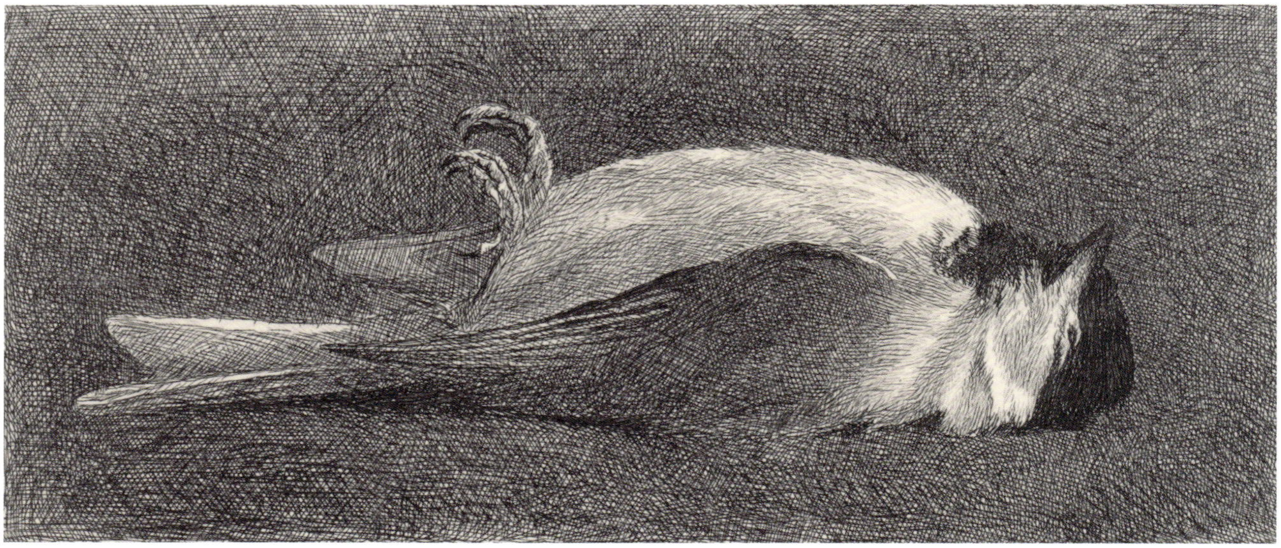

Thrush's Nest (plate 36), a favorite motif. The poignant *Black Capped Titmouse* recapitulates Farrer's use of "small stuffed birds" as models, an exercise that initiated a popular Ruskinian theme (fig. 5; plates 8, 28, 43).[37]

All Association artist-members taught the fundamentals of *Elements of Drawing* at some time in their career. Newman substituted for Farrer at Cooper Union's School of Design for Women. Sarah Tuthill taught daughters of the progressive elite at Miss Porter's School. Richards promoted the Ruskinian way in Philadelphia. Pattison moved to Brooklyn around 1889, where he was professor of drawing at the Boys' High School, a prestigious public school.[38] Moore, ultimately, would take the Ruskinian curriculum to the realm of American higher education, teaching first at Harvard's Lawrence School of Engineering and then at Harvard College in a famous partnership with professor of art history Charles Eliot Norton.[39]

Wartime

The Civil War was not an unpropitious time for launching a reform movement. Nor did it seem to be an unpropitious moment for the art market. Cook commented that a "kind of picture mania" had taken over since the war began.[40] In fact, the American Ruskinian movement itself was a creature of wartime fervor. Saving the Union and abolishing slavery were mighty campaigns of political and social reform. Association members were outspoken abolitionists and unionists who believed that they were in the vanguard of shaping postwar American culture and society. Cook's bellicose language in reviews for *The New Path* and

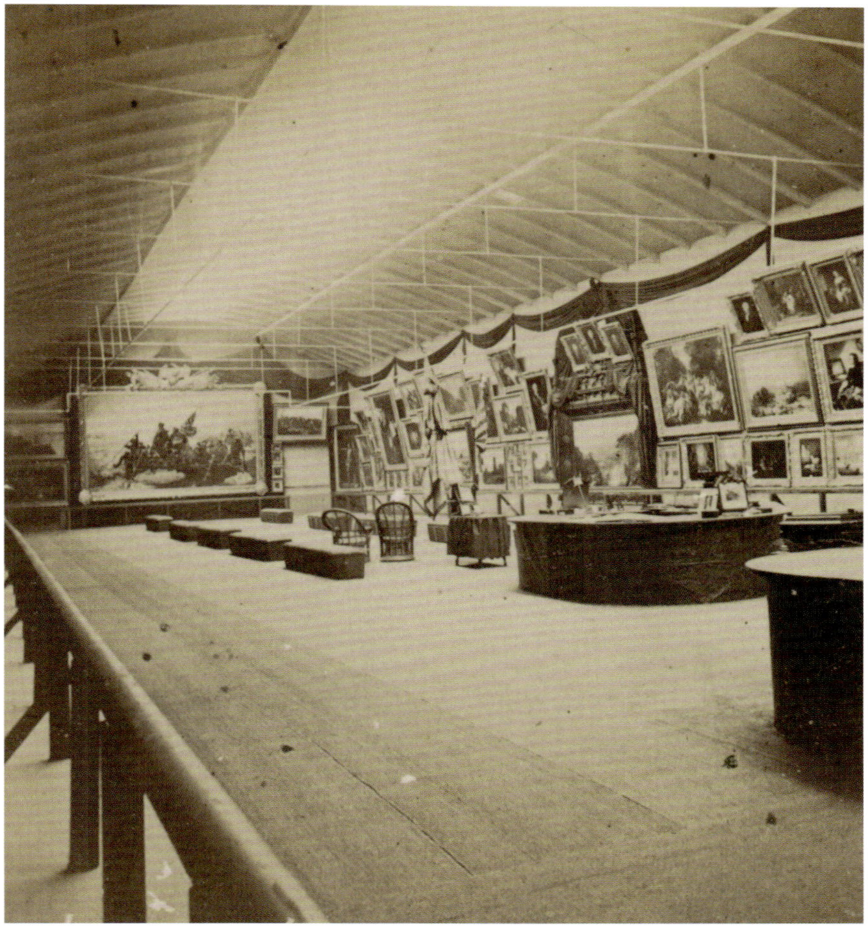

5. John Henry Hill, *Black Capped Titmouse*, plate 7 in *Sketches from Nature*, c. 1866, etching on white paper, The New York Public Library, The Miriam and Ira D. Wallach Division of Art, Prints and Photographs: Print Collection

6. Bierstadt Brothers (Charles and Edward), *Picture Gallery, Metropolitan Fair, N. Y.* (detail), 1864, stereoscopic albumen print, Library of Congress, Prints and Photographs Division, Washington, DC

New-York Daily Tribune consistently put forth a revolutionary narrative for the radical realists signaling the Association's high degree of historical consciousness. Their antislavery position was not only documented in the pages of *The New Path* but also embedded in the iconography of certain drawings and paintings. Wight contributed architectural and engineering services to the United States Sanitary Commission (USSC), a forerunner of the Red Cross, designing a field hospital and the temporary structure that housed the art exhibition organized for the Great Metropolitan Fair that opened in April 1864.[41] The exhibition of some 360 works (including four by Association members) was an event that mobilized the cultural power of New York's institutions and private collectors to benefit the USSC.[42]

The scale and scope of the exhibition offered Cook (and the Association) the opportunity to present an extended critique of American art, past and present. There were nods to historical American art; a trio of Founding Fathers by Gilbert Stuart and Rembrandt Peale were present, as well as iconic landscapes by Thomas Cole. Emmanuel Leutze's mammoth *Washington Crossing the Delaware* (1851) occupied the place of honor at the gallery's north end, while Frederic Church's *Heart of the Andes* (1859) and Albert Bierstadt's *The Rocky Mountains, Lander's Peak* (1863) squared off on each side of the long walls (fig. 6). Cook's appraisal in his *Tribune* reviews was unsparing, calculated to foment public outrage. In the first of two reviews, he dismissed Leutze's massive patriotic panorama as "a [theatrical] drop scene with the mythical Washington striking an attitude," demanding instead "something more real and smacking of the time." As if to drive home his point, Cook's next review opened with a lavish paean of praise for T. C. Farrer's diminutive nocturnal wartime farewell *Twilight* (fig. 7).[43] Castigated as unseemly and unpatriotic, Cook's "savage" attack is still referenced in histories of American art.[44]

Postwar: The 1867 Exhibition at Yale

The radical realists had won the war but lost the battle to influence postwar American art; young American artists as well as collectors looked instead to Barbizon, Munich, and Paris. Although the Association's organized reform had ended with the final issue of *The New Path* in December 1865, the realists and their fellow architects and critics enjoyed a rather high profile in the immediate postwar years, especially in the exhibitions that were the run-up to the public debut of the American Watercolor Society in 1867.[45] This landmark display took place in Wight's new National Academy even as his building at Yale was under construction. Cook and Sturgis kept the realists' works in both oil and watercolor before the public in the *Tribune* and *The Nation*.

Wight's modern Gothic fine-arts building at Yale officially opened in July 1867 with an exhibition inaugurating the space. The Yale School of Fine Arts was the first professional art school on an American campus and the only school in Yale College to admit women.[46] The recently closed National Academy Annual and Yale's own collections provided a majority of paintings. In recognition of Wight's Ruskinian affiliations, Farrer was tapped to secure additional works by former Association members and their unaffiliated Ruskinian colleagues.[47] As a result, sixty-nine of nearly three hundred works loaned to the exhibition were by realist painters. These were sympathetically and innovatively installed in two coherent groups: oil paintings in the South Gallery, watercolors and drawings in the Corridor.[48] Thus the exhibition provided a splendid venue for the first and only retrospective of the Ruskinian realists.

The occasion offered an opportunity to reflect upon the impact of Ruskinian reform in America. A historically conscious narrative about the movement, first manifested in exhibition reviews, began to take shape. Cook and Sturgis were

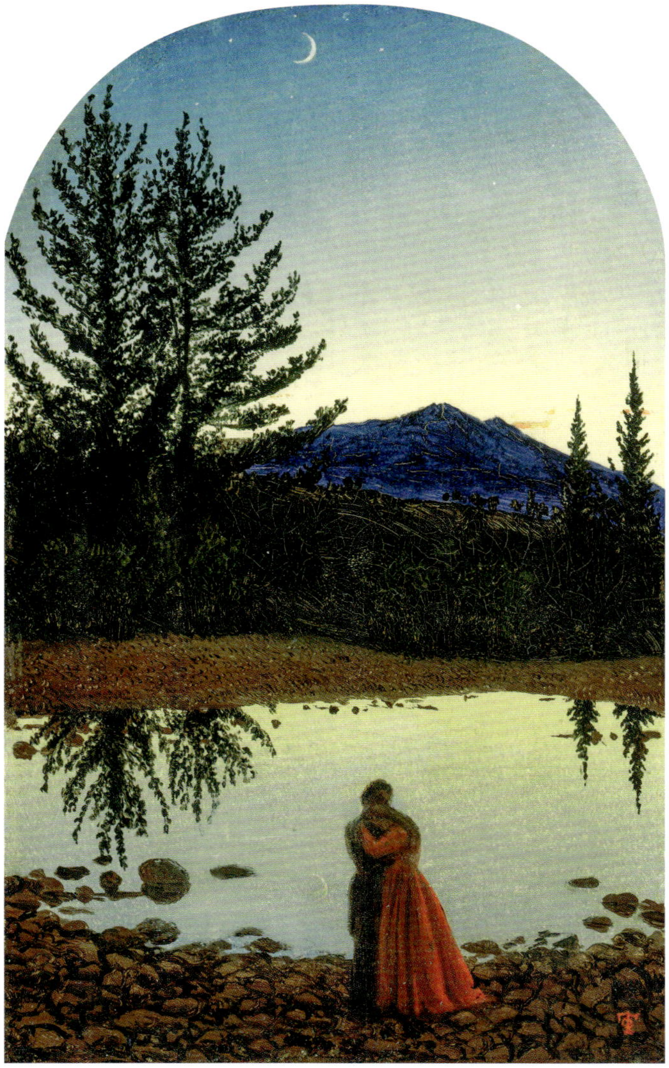

7. Thomas Charles Farrer, *Twilight*, c. 1864, oil on academy board, Museum of Fine Arts, Boston, James E. Neill Memorial Fund

keenly aware that the largest collective display of Ruskinian realists was taking place in a modern Gothic building designed by one of their own members for the teaching of fine art on the campus of one of the nation's oldest institutions of higher learning. In the *Tribune*, Cook proclaimed a ringing valedictory for "this coterie of young men and women": "Here, for the first time," he wrote, "is a movement in American Art, not merely original and peculiar, but springing from an enthusiasm, a belief in something higher than the mercantile spirit that has thus far animated us; an independent movement clear of the Old World . . . careless of criticism, careless of applause, and only bent on solving its own problems in its own way."[49]

Local reviewers recognized the occasion as well. "[Our] American pre-Raphaelites," wrote the *Hartford Daily Courant*, "look at first so repulsive, so hard and harsh and real are their every feature, but after an half an hour's study . . . I begin to wonder whether, after all these men and this school have not a future, and whether revolutions in art are not as necessary as revolutions in politics."[50]

What Has Become of the Pre-Raphaelites?

Ironically, the Association artists, architects, and critics had never seemed to have so public a presence and coherent a message as during the several years right after the war. Yet the moment was a passing one, especially for the artists. By 1870, they had mostly gone their separate ways, some of them exhausted by the strenuous Ruskinian regimen and weary of the still-hostile reception of their works.[51] Farrer returned to England. Newman settled in Florence. Richards, a Philadelphian and perhaps the best known of the realists to the general public, was somehow peripheral to the Association itself—he never attended a meeting, nor did he exhibit at Yale.[52] By 1870, he had redirected his attention from landscape to marine subjects in oil and watercolor. Pattison submitted five paintings to the 1867 Yale exhibition; few of his works are now known, however.[53] His recently located *Mountain View* (c. 1867, plate 71), an impressive exhibition watercolor, hopefully portends other discoveries.

Unaffiliated Ruskinians Henry Farrer and Fidelia Bridges successfully pursued specialties as watercolorists and both were regulars at the American Watercolor Society exhibitions, as was Richards (and occasionally the Hills). Brandegee's Ruskinian phase was a youthful one; his mature style, as a figure and portrait painter, was formed in Paris. In 1881 he succeeded his aunt, Sarah Tuthill, as art instructor at Miss Porter's School. Hennessy moved abroad in 1870, and Shattuck's early Ruskinian intensity mellowed into a successful mainstream landscape career ending in 1888 following an illness that affected his vision.

The 1880s were a time of collective recollection. Wight possessed the Association's Minutes, perhaps inspiring a sense of duty to set the record straight in what amounted to an invaluable firsthand account of the Association's founding and subsequent activities, published in 1884. Wight, like Cook, saw the youthful reformers of the Society of American Artists as spiritual descendants of the radical realists of 1863.[54]

John William Hill pursued the Ruskinian way at Nyack, only occasionally exhibiting in New York. John Henry Hill served as staff artist on a government survey of the Far West in 1868 led by geologist Clarence King, a former Association member; eventually John Henry, too, returned to Nyack for life.[55] The senior Hill, John

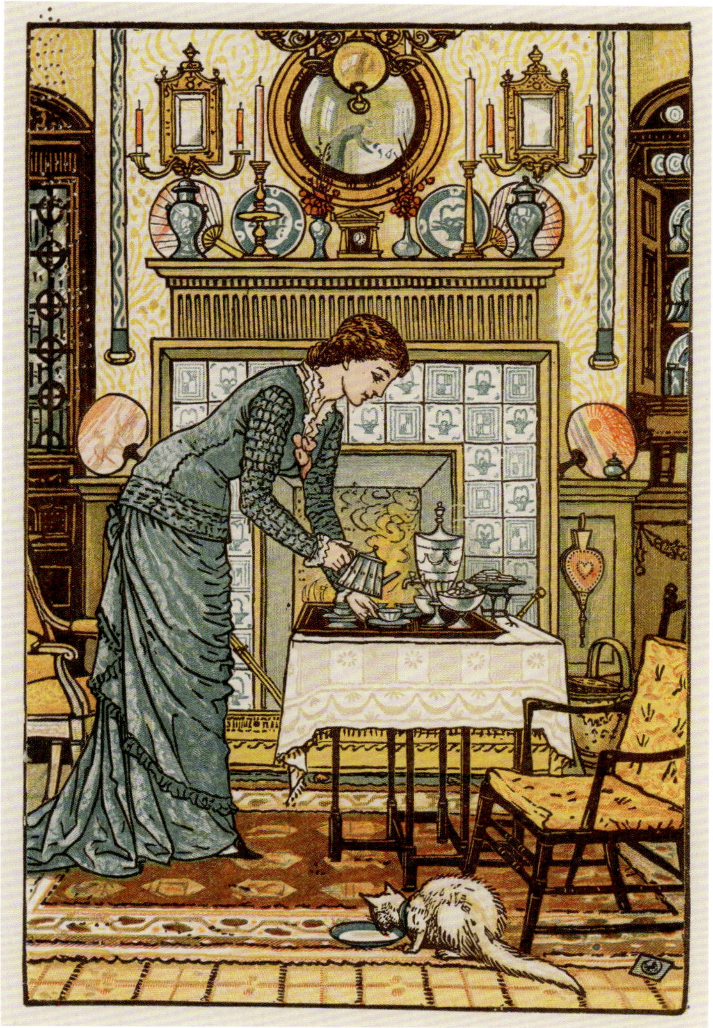

8. Walter Crane, "My Lady's Chamber," frontispiece to Clarence Cook's *The House Beautiful: Essays on Beds and Tables, Stools and Candlesticks*, New York, 1878

William, the Association's elder and founding president, died there in September 1879—a catalyst, perhaps, for the stock-taking testaments of the 1880s. An article by Cook in the *Princeton Review*, "Art in America in 1883," places him still very much in the fray as a scourge of the establishment and defender of the progressive. Cook located the most promising signs of art-world vitality in the secession from the National Academy by the young artists who formed the Society of American Artists. Cook was their immediate and outspoken champion.[56] He was also deeply involved in the reform of American design. His beautifully produced books *The House Beautiful* (1878, fig. 8) and *What Shall We Do with Our Walls?* (1880) are seminal documents of the American Aesthetic movement, which counted a number of former Association members among early advocates.[57]

At his father's death, John Henry organized memorial tributes at the Brooklyn Art Association and the American Watercolor Society.[58] During the following decade he undertook another tribute to his father: *An Artist's Memorial*, a folio volume privately published in 1888. Moore, then teaching at Harvard, provided a biography and appreciation, narrating the elder Hill's life as the true parable of an artist trained in all the old landscape methods, whose eyes had been opened to nature in midlife by reading the first volume of *Modern Painters*.[59]

Epilogue: Into the Twentieth Century

The early canon-building academic surveys of American art dismissed the movement, if they mentioned it at all. For example, Samuel Isham's *History of American Painting* (1905) acknowledged Ruskin's influence on American landscape painting but failed to appreciate the American Pre-Raphaelite movement as anything more than an aberration. "These principles as transplanted into American soil brought forth fruits hardly to be recognized by the P. R. B."[60] On the other hand, art critic Elisabeth Luther Cary, an admirer of the English Pre-Raphaelites who had grown up among her father Edward L. Cary's paintings by T. C. Farrer and John William Hill, knew these strange "fruits" well. In 1904, her magazine *The Scrip* would publish Edward Cary's early recollections of the Association.[61] Elisabeth had a better understanding than Isham about parallels between the two schools. She will have the last word: "Thus in America as in England the name Pre-Raphaelitism stood for sincere methods and personal ideas, and the Pre-Raphaelites were the 'men of progress' in their respective countries."[62]

Charles Herbert Moore, *Autumn Landscape*, 1865–1868 (detail, plate 52)

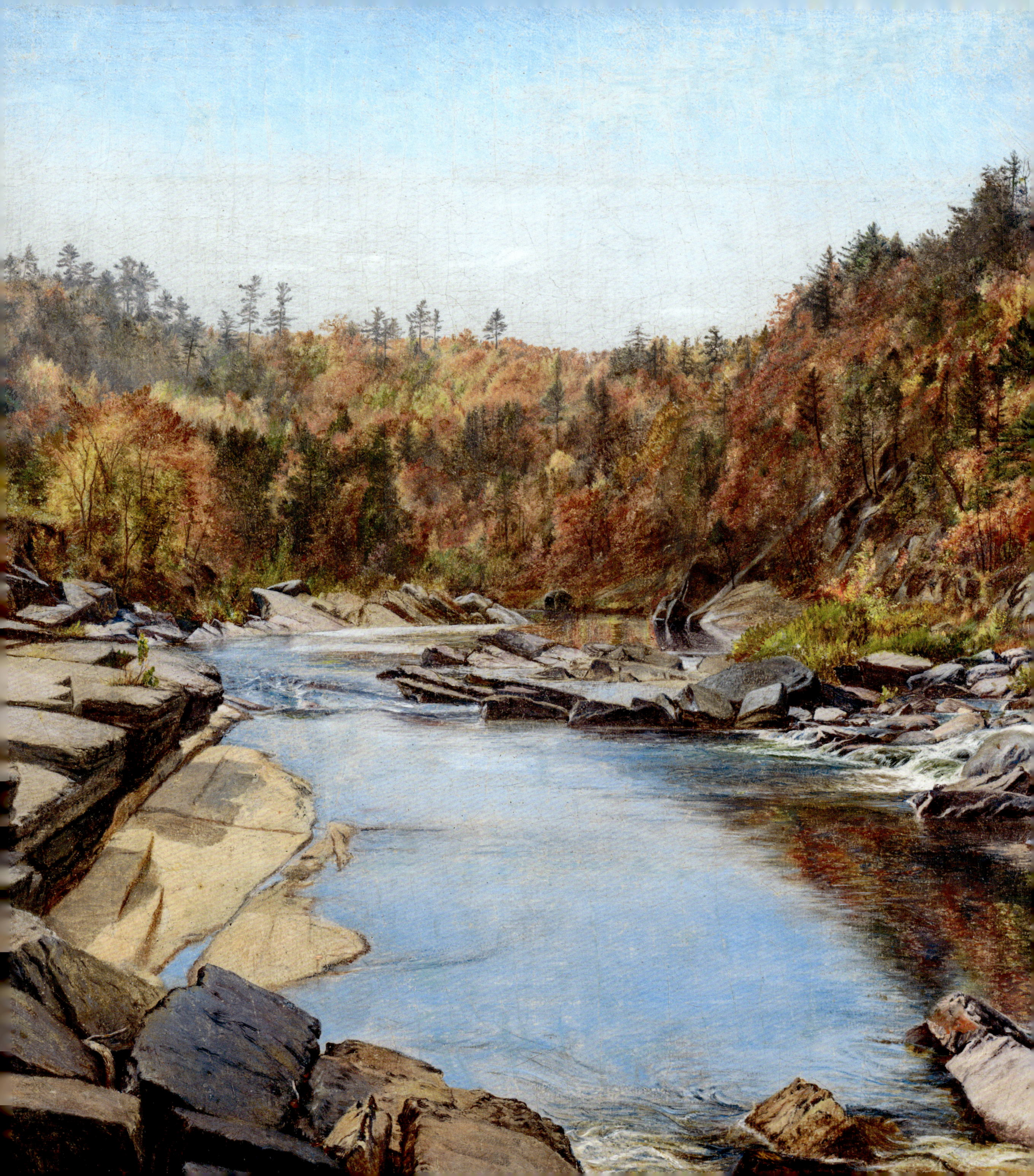

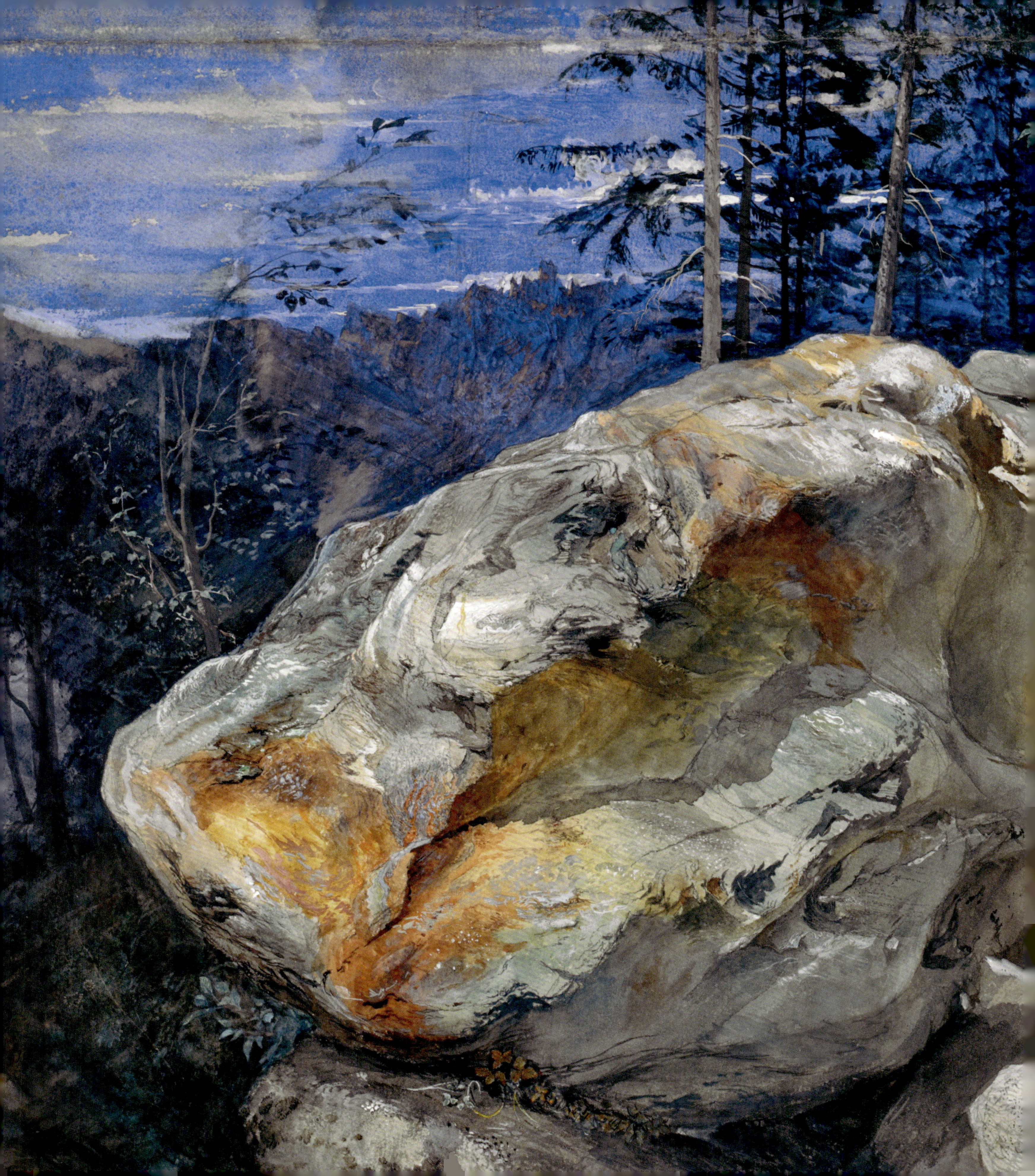

A Radical Legacy: The British Pre-Raphaelites and Global Pre-Raphaelitism

TIM BARRINGER

John Ruskin, *Fragment of the Alps*, c. 1854–1856 (detail, plate 84)

Founded in London in 1848, the Pre-Raphaelite Brotherhood initiated the Victorian era's most influential avant-garde art movement, whose international legacy lasted beyond the First World War. The essential nature of Pre-Raphaelitism, however, remains a matter for debate: revivalist or realist, reactionary or radical, insular or cosmopolitan, academic or secessionist? Derided by modernist critics after 1900, the movement never fell out of popular favor and lies in the ancestry of the Aesthetic movement, symbolism, art nouveau, and even the Bauhaus. Following the demise of Franco-American modernism, the Pre-Raphaelites have, since the 1990s, reemerged as a significant force in the history of European art and culture, and the international ramifications of the Pre-Raphaelite movement have come to the fore as a subject for new research.[1] So, who were the British Pre-Raphaelites, what was the Pre-Raphaelitism that emerged from it, and why did this initially insular vanguard movement exert, for a half century, a gravitational pull in New York, Antwerp, Munich, Warsaw, Saint Petersburg, Melbourne, Tokyo, and beyond?

Radical Historicism and the Origins of the Victorian Avant-Garde

The Pre-Raphaelite Brotherhood had three leading members—Dante Gabriel Rossetti, William Holman Hunt, and John Everett Millais—who had all been students at the Royal Academy Schools. They were joined by the aspiring painters James Collinson and Frederic George Stephens, the sculptor Thomas Woolner, and Rossetti's younger brother William Michael, who served as the Brotherhood's secretary from 1849 to 1853. The members of the Brotherhood were character-

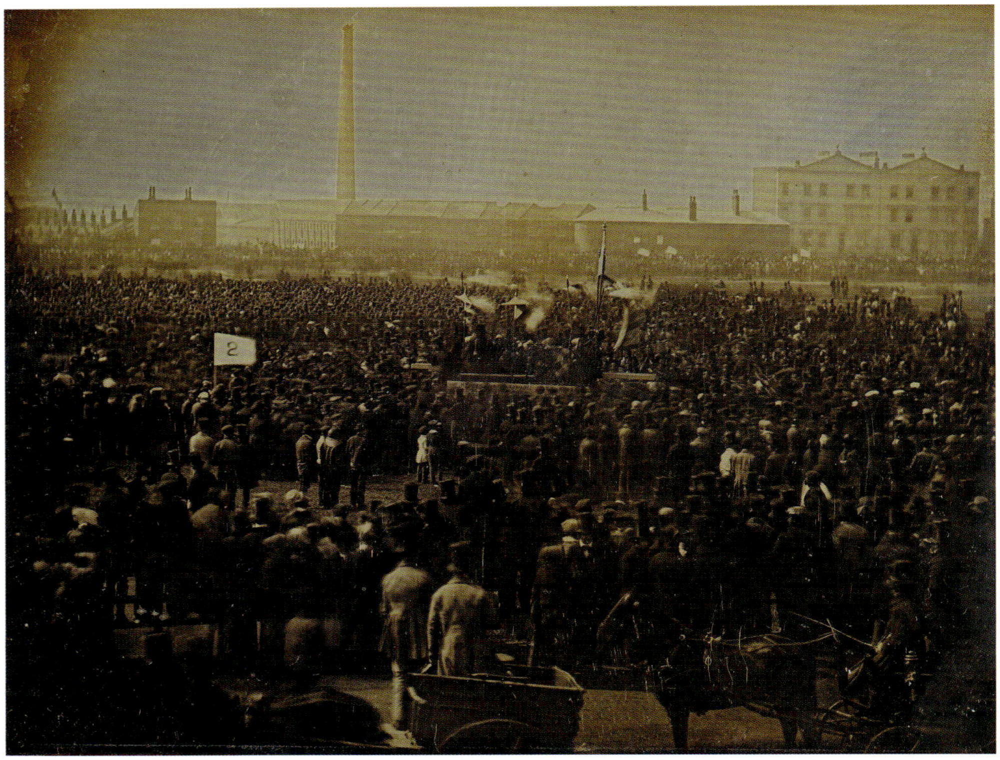

ized by their youth and precocity—Millais, at only nineteen, was a superbly accomplished draftsman and painter, while Dante Gabriel Rossetti was a published poet, well read and abundantly talented in literature and art, at just twenty. William Holman Hunt, from a more modest background, was already experimenting with compositions that challenged orthodox prescriptions. These friends shared a dissatisfaction with the condition of contemporary art, as manifested in the education offered by the Royal Academy's schools and in its annual summer exhibitions, which seemed either sleazy and commercialized or dull and unduly awed by the work of the old masters.

These young artists' impetus to challenge the status quo resonated with the larger political climate in the year of European revolutions: Hunt and Millais had witnessed in person the great Chartist meeting on Kennington Common, in an industrial district of South London, on April 10, 1848. William Kilburn's daguerreotype of that event (fig. 1) indicates the broader context for Pre-Raphaelitism's avant-garde intervention: Britain was the world's first industrial nation, dominating the production of textiles and machinery. The social cost of rapid industrialization was seen in environmental despoliation, class tension between an emerging trade union movement and an entrenched capitalist elite commit-

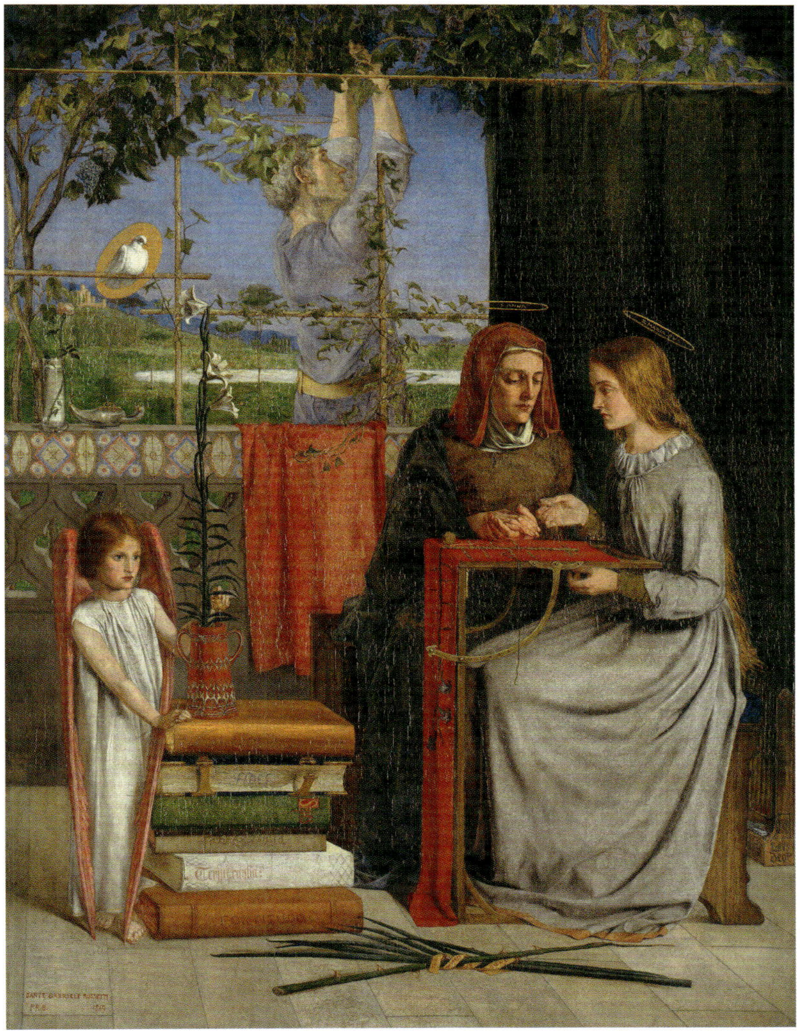

1. William Edward Kilburn, *The Chartist Meeting on Kennington Common, 10 April 1848*, 1848, daguerreotype, Royal Collection Trust

2. Dante Gabriel Rossetti, *The Girlhood of Mary Virgin*, 1848–1849, oil on canvas, Tate, London, Bequeathed by Lady Jekyll 1937

ted to free trade, and an exploitative, deregulated model of economic organization. Traditional craft skills and traditional rhythms of work were being lost as mechanization came to the fore. A major triumph for the industrial bourgeoisie was the Great Exhibition of the Industry of All Nations, held in the prefabricated glass-and-iron Crystal Palace designed by Joseph Paxton and installed in Hyde Park, London, in 1851. After the market revolution of the 1830s, the United States followed suit with the Exhibition of the Industry of All Nations, which took place in its own Crystal Palace in New York in 1853–1854. The dominance of industrial production and the social model, described by Thomas Carlyle as the "cash nexus," was challenged by British artists and intellectuals who looked back to earlier times as a model of social harmony and creative labor. The archi-

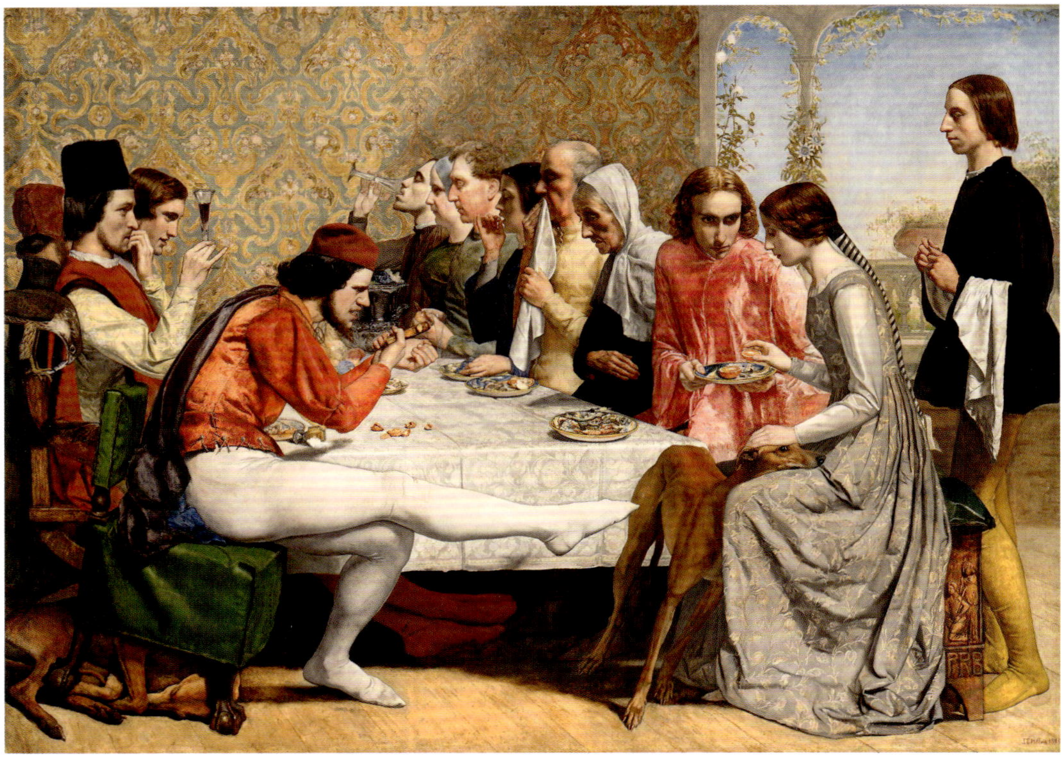

tect Augustus Welby Northmore Pugin, for example, espoused a return to the Middle Ages — not merely its buildings, but its cultural and social forms. In 1836, he published *Contrasts, or A Parallel between the Noble Edifices of the Fourteenth and Fifteenth Centuries, and Similar Buildings of the Present Day; Shewing the Present Decay of Taste*, whose polemical tone may be judged from its title. A second edition was issued in 1841 with a new frontispiece that demonizes the liberal state, urbanism, secularism, and ultimately capitalism itself, all of them judged against the organic unity and aesthetic beauty of the medieval city.[2] The Gothic revival, as envisaged by Pugin, was not a matter of style so much as a full-blown critique of modernity with a utopian promise of social and visual change.

It was against this background that the mysterious initials PRB were seen for the first time in March 1849 at the Free Exhibition in London. The portentous letters were meticulously inscribed in red paint beneath the signature in the lower left corner of Dante Gabriel Rossetti's painting *The Girlhood of Mary Virgin* (fig. 2). The following year the meaning of the initials was revealed: Pre-Raphaelite Brotherhood. The Brothers aimed to return art to the condition of freshness and honesty that they perceived in works from before the time of Raphael (1483–1520), which they knew from newly acquired early Italian and Netherlandish paintings

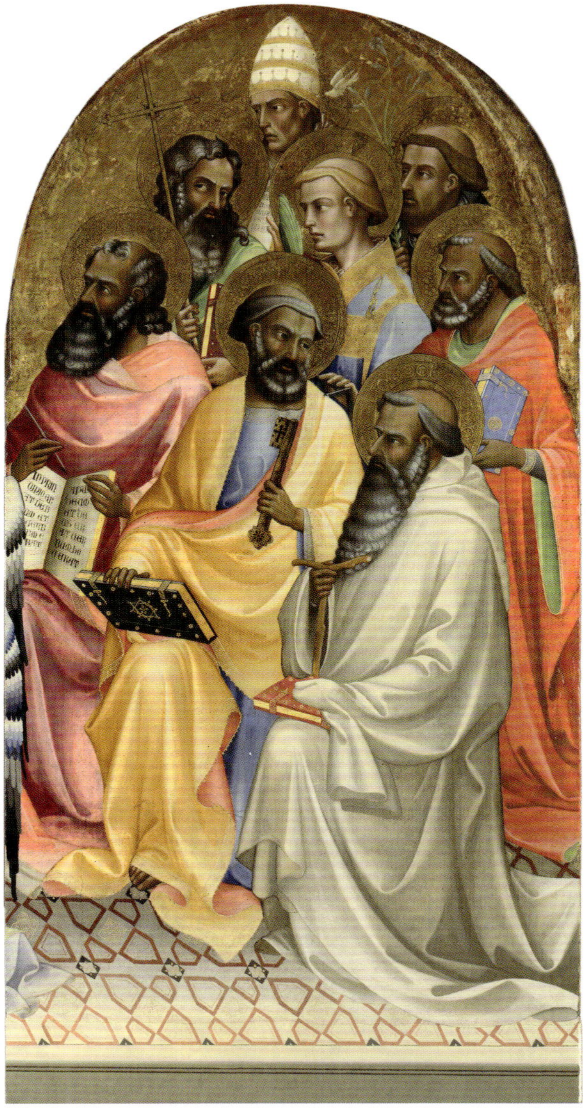

3. John Everett Millais, *Isabella*, 1848–1849, oil on canvas, National Museums Liverpool, Walker Art Gallery

4. Lorenzo Monaco, *Adoring Saints,* right panel of the *San Benedetto Altarpiece*, 1407–1409, egg tempera on wood, National Gallery, London, Presented by William Coningham, 1848

at the National Gallery, London, and print series such as Carlo Lasinio's line engravings reproducing frescoes by Benozzo Gozzoli at Pisa. To challenge the status of Raphael—long considered (with Michelangelo) to represent the apogee of the fine arts, and central to the teachings of the Royal Academy—implied a radical critique of the institution and its hierarchies of value and authority. In *The Girlhood of Mary Virgin* the careful observation of nature, echoed by Mary's own meticulous transcription in her embroidery of the lilies before her, stood alongside the use of gold for haloes and inscriptions as in a medieval manuscript or a quattrocento panel painting.

The first masterpiece of Pre-Raphaelitism, Millais's *Isabella* (fig. 3), exhibited at the Royal Academy in 1849, presented the new style at its most provocative. The drawing was sharply angular, the conventional rules of perspective were ignored, and the young artist employed brilliant colors and startlingly precise details to create a hypnotically vivid effect. The inventiveness of Millais's work lay in his ability to look both backward into history for a cleansing, fresh historical example, and to assert, at the same time, a vivid contemporaneity—for despite the Renaissance garb, these were modern teenagers, beset with love, lust, and jealousy. In *Isabella,* Millais responded specifically to Lorenzo Monaco's *San Benedetto Altarpiece* of 1407–1409 (fig. 4), which was acquired and placed on view in the National Gallery, then sharing its Trafalgar Square premises with the Royal Academy, in 1848. Resonances of the Italian panels can be detected in the deliberate compression of pictorial space, in the use of crisply etched profiles piled one upon another, in the representation of everyday people rather than professional models, and in the vibrant patches of decorative color. Yet the faces have the insistent, preternatural sharpness of photography and surely derived from Millais's awareness of daguerreotype portraits. Professional models were eschewed, and the young painter refused to reproduce ideal types: instead, each head was painstakingly studied from an individual who was close at hand, such as the two Rossetti brothers and Millais's father. *Isabella* is at once intensely historical and unmistakably modern.

A key figure in the PRB's formation was Ford Madox Brown, born in 1821, a deeply serious painter of historical subjects, a querulous figure with anti-establishment leanings who veered toward socialism. Well versed in history painting owing to his training in the Ghent and Antwerp academies, he acted as a mentor, briefly taking on Rossetti as his pupil. Brown's work of the late 1840s prefigures many of the major tenets of Pre-Raphaelitism and his works of the 1850s are masterpieces in the Pre-Raphaelite style. He may have been asked to join the Brotherhood in 1848 and refused; he was never formally a member.

The literary and the visual were imbricated in British Pre-Raphaelitism. Rossetti's first successes came through poetry and his paintings often grew from his literary conceptions. In 1850, under William Michael Rossetti's editorship, the group produced *The Germ: Thoughts towards Nature in Poetry, Literature and Art,* a short-lived literary periodical that stood as a manifesto for the PRB. It included poetry, short stories, and factual articles by members of the circle. This journal provided an important model for American followers of Ruskin and the Pre-Raphaelites who published the ambitious periodicals *The Crayon* and *The New Path*.

Critical hostility to the PRB reached a peak in 1850, when Millais's *Christ in the House of His Parents* (1849–1850, Tate, London) was denounced, notably by Charles

Dickens, for its allegedly disrespectful characterization of the Holy Family. For Dickens, Millais's Christ resembled "a blubbering red-headed boy in a bed-gown."[3] Though there were signs of interest from some sympathetic members of the press, it seemed at times as if the avant-garde gambit of the seven young men would end in obloquy.

John Ruskin, Ford Madox Brown, and Radical Realism

The critical fortunes of the Pre-Raphaelite Brotherhood changed dramatically in 1851, however, when John Ruskin, the most eminent critic of the day, wrote to the London *Times* in defense of the Pre-Raphaelites. Ruskin's fame derived from his vividly phrased and passionate defense of the work of J. M. W. Turner, published as *Modern Painters* (five volumes, 1843–1860). So compelling was Ruskin's prose that Charlotte Brontë wrote, in response, "this book seems to give me eyes."[4] Widely read in America, it was remembered by William James Stillman as "one of the sensation-books of the day like a thunderbolt from the clear sky."[5] Although he had not yet met the Pre-Raphaelites, Ruskin wrote sagely in a letter to the London *Times* in May 1851:

> They intend to return to early days in this one point only—that, as far as in them lies, they will draw either what they see, or what they suppose might have been the actual facts of the scene they desire to represent, irrespective of any conventional rules of picture-making.[6]

With this dramatic intervention, Ruskin transformed the movement from a revivalist trajectory, following the insights of Pugin, to adopt a realist approach in which science and photography, more than the efforts of early painters, would provide benchmarks of achievement. Ruskin's brilliance lay in his ability to unite these two seemingly contradictory projects: "They know very little of ancient paintings," he chided, "who suppose the works of these young artists to resemble them. As far as I can judge of their aim . . . the Pre-Raphaelites intend to surrender no advantage which the knowledge or inventions of the present time can afford to their art." Unlike artists from after the time of Raphael, who strove to produce only "fair pictures," the London avant-gardists had bravely decided to "represent stern facts."[7] The Pre-Raphaelites were not making facsimiles of Renaissance works: rather, like the painters of the fifteenth century (so the argument runs), they saw the world with fresh eyes unencumbered by tradition.

This brought Pre-Raphaelitism into line with Ruskin's own thinking, as developed in the first volume of his *Modern Painters,* published in 1843. Ruskin espoused a radical realism in which young artists, taking the early works of Turner as their model, should be "humble and earnest in following the steps

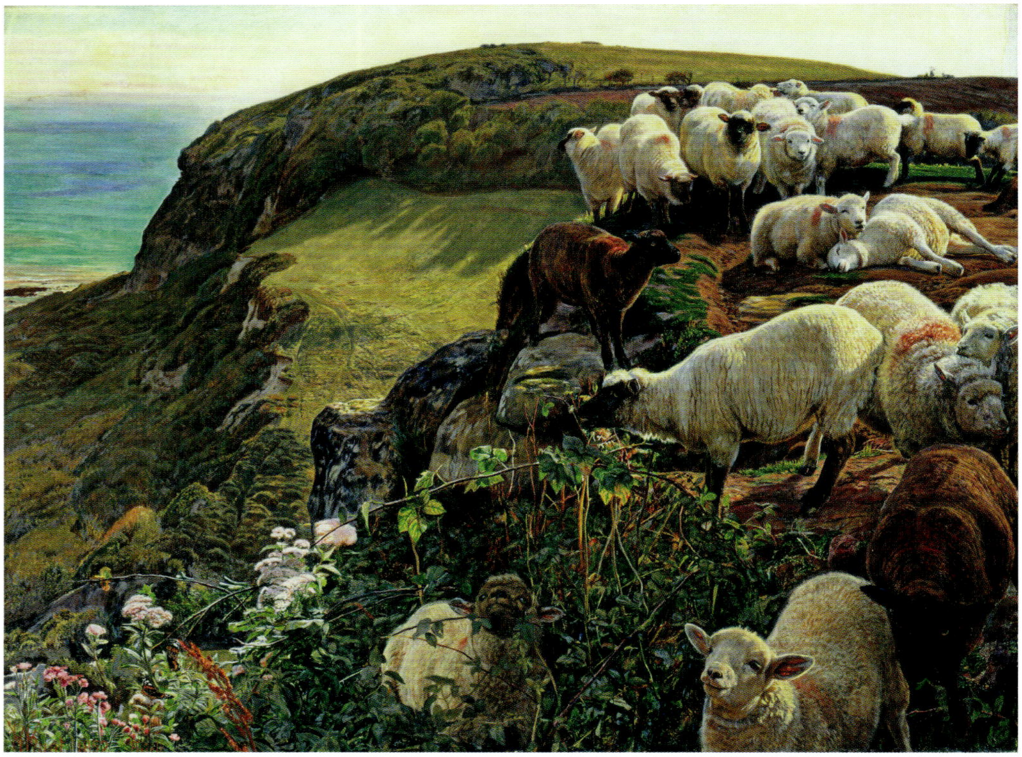

of nature, and tracing the finger of God.... [They should] go to Nature in all singleness of heart, and walk with her laboriously and trustingly, having no other thoughts but how best to penetrate her meaning, and remember her instruction; rejecting nothing, selecting nothing and scorning nothing...and rejoicing always in the truth."[8] Ruskin put this manifesto into practice in his own drawings. While he was never a professional artist and did not attempt to produce finished works for exhibition or sale, he was a master of observed detail in nature, with a special interest in geology. Among his most spectacular works, *Fragment of the Alps* (plate 84) (later bought from Ruskin by his American devotee, Charles Eliot Norton) demonstrates Ruskin's fearless use of saturated color, his geological understanding and attentiveness to the fall of light on stone, and his ability to paint foliage with botanical precision, but also with a sense of awe, so inspired was he by the sheer profusion of creation. It was Ruskin's writings, as much as the works of the Pre-Raphaelites themselves, which would resonate across the English-speaking world and beyond. In the 1850s, Ruskin developed relationships with two Americans who would play central roles in importing both his critical doctrines and Pre-Raphaelite principles to the United States. William James Stillman, who had read *Modern Painters* while a student of Frederic Edwin Church and met Ruskin on a trip to London in 1850, founded *The Crayon*

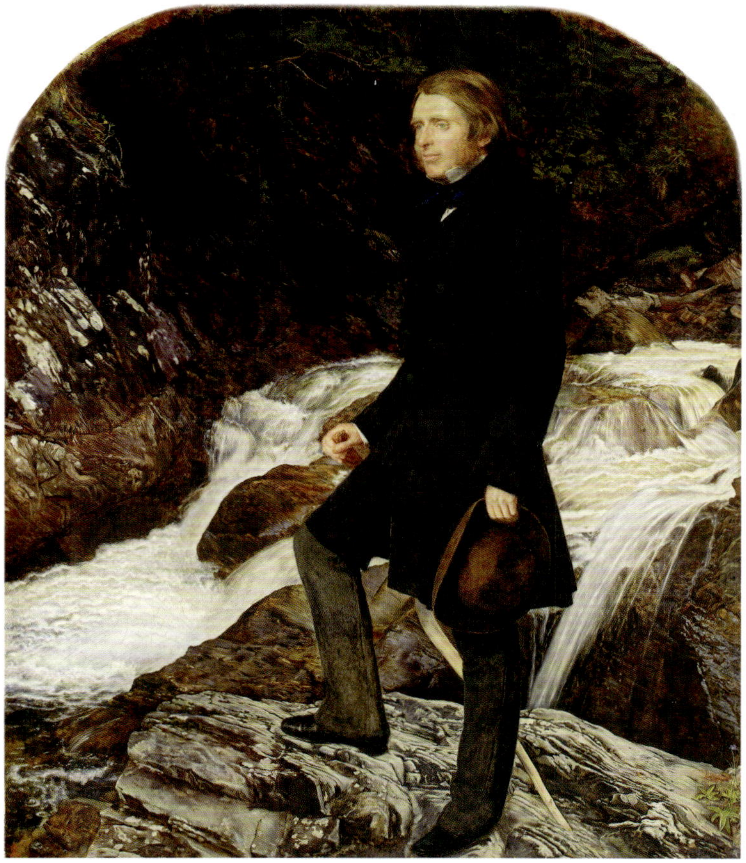

with John Durand in 1855.[9] This journal introduced excerpts from Ruskin's writings to an American audience. Norton, who would become the first professor of the history of art at Harvard, was Ruskin's closest friend and, later, his executor, and would become one of the most steadfast supporters of the American Pre-Raphaelite project in the 1860s. American painters from Church to Asher Brown Durand (John's father) embraced Ruskin's teachings, but it was the American Pre-Raphaelites, more than Ruskin's English contemporaries, who would explore the potential of Ruskin's creed and methods in his own chosen medium of watercolor, pursuing the goal of truth to nature in their works on paper with fervid enthusiasm. The American Pre-Raphaelites' dedication to the watercolor medium, as mandated by Ruskin in his practical guide *The Elements of Drawing* (1857), was a catalyst in the launch of watercolor painting in America.[10]

5. William Holman Hunt, *Our English Coasts*, 1852, oil on canvas, Tate, London, Presented by the Art Fund 1946

6. John Everett Millais, *John Ruskin*, 1853–1854, oil on canvas, Ashmolean Museum, University of Oxford

Many of the most original effects of early Pre-Raphaelite painting were achieved by painting outdoors in oil directly onto a canvas prepared with brilliant white ground, rejecting the use of preparatory sketches and studies. Whether or not

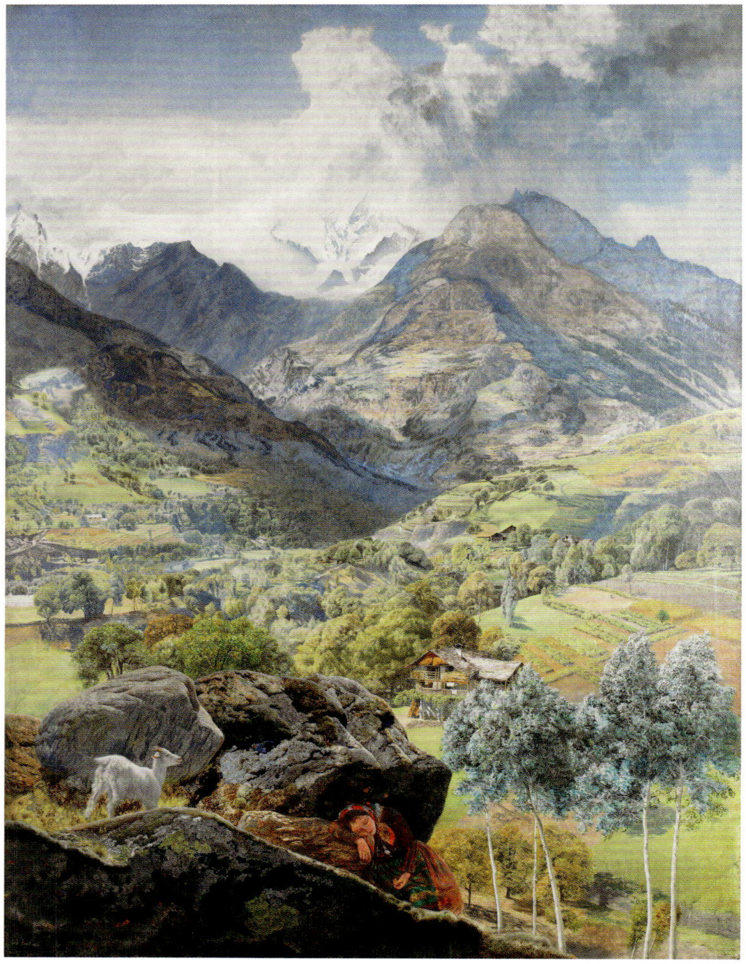

this was solely inspired by Ruskin's writings remains a matter of contention. Two works exhibited at the Royal Academy in 1852, Millais's *Ophelia* (1851–1852, Tate, London) and Hunt's *The Hireling Shepherd* (1851–1852, Manchester Art Gallery), demonstrated an unprecedented brilliance of color and fidelity of natural detail, while Hunt's pure landscape exhibited the following year, *Our English Coasts,* is the apotheosis of this approach (fig. 5). Hunt fearlessly matches the local color of the viewed object with the paint applied to the canvas. The effect is richly chromatic, brazen in its disregard for those conventions of composition, tone, and chiaroscuro, which even such daring painters as Turner and John Constable had respected. No detail is too trivial to be recorded with painstaking—even religious—fervor; Hunt expended vast labor, for example, on the ears of the sheep, so that the veins can clearly be seen, the thin flesh becoming transparent owing to the intensity of evening light.

While Hunt pushed painting from nature to new extremes, it was John Everett Millais, with his effortless virtuosity and swift assimilation of advice and influence, whom Ruskin identified as a potential successor to Turner after the master's death in December 1851. In 1853, Ruskin commissioned Millais to paint his portrait in a landscape setting, which would be painted from nature at Glenfinlas, near Brig o'Turk in the Trossachs, a remote region of Scotland (fig. 6). "Millais has chosen his place," wrote the critic to his father: a "lovely piece of worn rock, with foaming water, and weeds, and moss, and a noble overhanging bank of dark crag—and I am to be standing looking quietly down the stream."[11] Ruskin believed that the portrait would "make a revolution in landscape painting."[12] Painted with the utmost fidelity, the portrait provides an authoritative application of Ruskin's artistic theory.

Ruskin found other figures to champion in the coming years, among them John William Inchbold and John Brett, whose alpine painting *Val d'Aosta* (fig. 7) seemed to follow Ruskin's instructions to the letter. Every detail of the landscape is meticulously inscribed, its local color preserved in chromatic splendor in the finished canvas. Yet Ruskin's critique of Brett's *Val d'Aosta* was withering, and the artist never really recovered from it: "It has a strange fault, considering the school to which it belongs—it seems to me wholly emotionless. I cannot find from it that the painter loved, or feared, anything in all that wonderful piece of the world.... I never saw the mirror so held up to Nature—but it is Mirror's work, not Man's."[13] The geology was brilliant, but the elements of love and fear were missing—Brett was one of the greatest naturalists ever to wield a brush, but, like the impassive gaze of the camera, he seemed to have no sense of the sublime. Having encouraged artists to study the world with a scientist's eye, Ruskin was in the end horrified by work that seemed closer in approach to the publications of a geologist like Sir Charles Lyell (1797–1875) than to the Romantic works of an artist like Turner.

7. John Brett, *Val d'Aosta*, 1858, oil on canvas, Private Collection

Ruskin's work as a critic ran parallel to his art-historical projects. In 1851, just as he began to champion the Pre-Raphaelites, he was at work on a three-volume study, *The Stones of Venice,* an architectural history that tracks the rise and fall of Venice as parable, in which artistic style acts as a barometer of the moral health of the state. The exquisite illustrations to *The Stones of Venice,* based on Ruskin's own drawings, some of them guided by daguerreotypes he had purchased, exerted a powerful influence on architecture in the 1850s. By 1872 he was complaining bitterly that "I have had an indirect influence on nearly every cheap villa-builder between [Denmark Hill] and Bromley; and there is scarcely a public-house near the Crystal Palace but sells its gin and bitters under pseudo-Venetian capitals copied from the Madonna of Health or of Miracles."[14] Despite his disavowal of modern architecture, in the mid-1850s he supported, and participated in, the construction of the Oxford Museum, designed by Benjamin Woodward. Ruskin's campaign to encourage contemporary architects to use natural forms in the adornment of buildings, in part as a riposte to the kinds of machine-cut stone and prefabricated iron and glass typical of mid-Victorian buildings, was widely taken up in institutional and domestic contexts. Ruskin's architectural influence was carried to the United States by the American Pre-Raphaelite architects Peter Bonnett Wight and Russell Sturgis Jr., who created major Gothic revival buildings with a distinctly Ruskinian appearance in New York and New Haven, Connecticut. The American Pre-Raphaelite painter Charles Herbert Moore, who taught drawing at Harvard's Lawrence Scientific School, served as Ruskin's traveling companion in 1876–1878, studying and recording architecture and paintings in company with the critic. Moore also produced copies of Italian works both for Ruskin and for Norton. Moore introduced Ruskin to the work of Henry Roderick Newman, who also traveled with Ruskin in Italy, making closely observed architectural studies, some of which were used to illustrate Ruskin's late works, and eventually settled in Florence.

Painters of Modern Life and Labor

The Pre-Raphaelites represented everyday life with the same unflinching verisimilitude that distinguished their paintings of nature. An article in *The Germ* by the sculptor John Lucas Tupper asked why artists turned to the past for serious subjects when the modern world contained fine examples of both virtue and vice:

> If, as every poet, every painter, every sculptor will acknowledge, his best and most original ideas are derived from his own time: if his great lessonings to piety, truth, charity, love, honour, honesty, gallantry, generosity, courage, are derived from the same source; why transfer them to distant periods, and make them *not things of to-day*? Why teach us to revere saints of old, and not our own family-worshippers? Why to admire the lance-armed knight and not the patience-armed hero of misfortune? Why to draw a sword we do not wear to aid an oppressed damsel, and not a purse which we do wear to rescue an erring one? . . . Why teach us to hate a Nero or an Appius, and not an underselling oppressor of workmen and betrayer of women and children?[15]

In fact, scenes of modern life—genre paintings—were popular fare at early Victorian exhibitions; they often presented a rose-tinted vision of the world and glossed over the social problems of the day. The Pre-Raphaelites, however, confronted the thorniest issues in contemporary society head on.

A key figure in this regard was the prostitute, the unmarried woman who represented the very opposite of the Victorian ideal of womanhood embodied in the

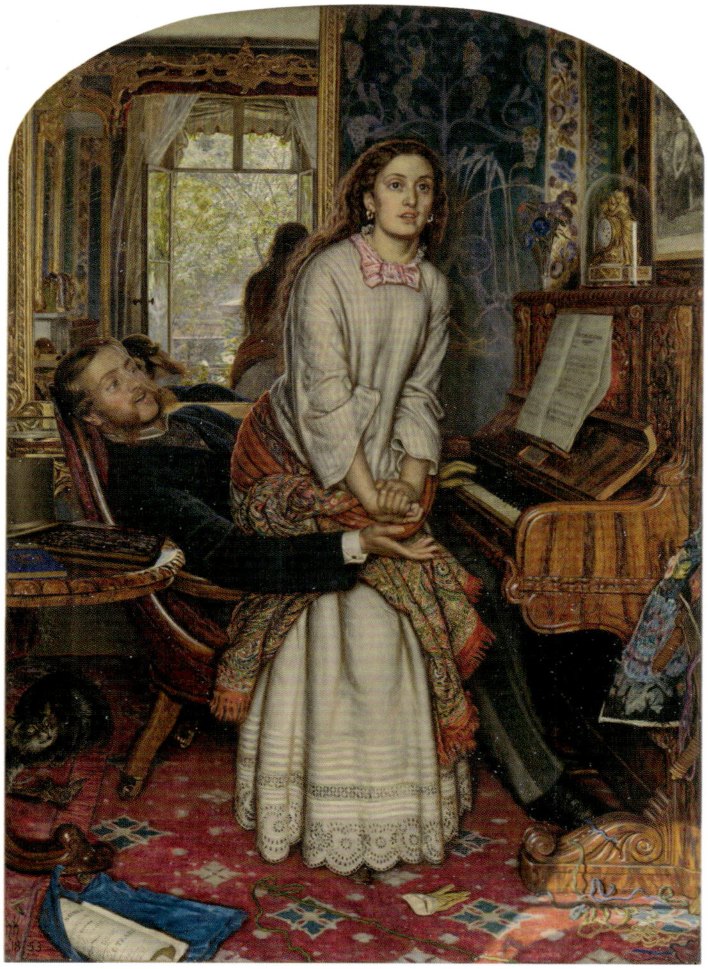

8. William Holman Hunt, *The Awakening Conscience*, 1853–1854, oil on canvas, Tate, London, Presented by Sir Colin and Lady Anderson through the Friends of the Tate Gallery 1976

dutiful wife and mother. It was not the men who frequented prostitutes who stood condemned by society; rather, by a widely accepted double standard, it was the prostitute herself who was held responsible and blamed for the spread of disease and the destruction of families. A strikingly critical engagement with this cluster of beliefs can be found in Hunt's *The Awakening Conscience* (1853–1854, fig. 8), a painting at once elaborately symbolic and obsessively realistic. A kept woman is seen with her lover in the interior of a garishly furnished apartment in St John's Wood, a bourgeois area in northwest London. We see the fallen woman at the moment when, inspired by the sun shining through the trees in front of her (and reflected in the mirror), she realizes the errors of her ways: her conscience is awakening. A wealth of visual clues provides commentary on the characters; for example, the song on the piano, "Oft in the Stilly Night"—clearly legible to any viewer who (as Ruskin advised) had brought a magnifying glass to the exhibi-

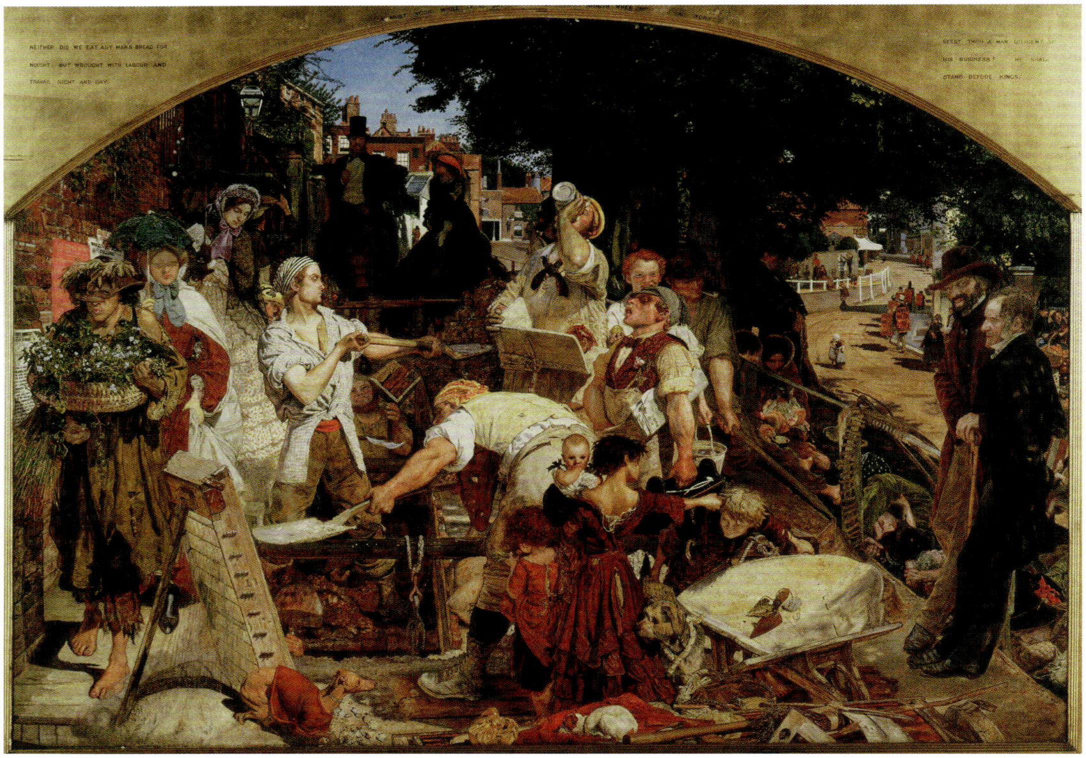

tion—might also have been a cause of her revelation. The lyrics recall a happier, and purer, past in contrast with the present situation, where she is caught like the wounded bird in the painting, attempting to escape from the predatory cat under the table. Symbols abound, too, of the woman's fall from domestic righteousness, among them the unfinished embroidery, left untidily in the foreground. Ruskin was acutely aware that the interior itself betrayed many levels of corruption: "There is not a single object in all that room, common, modern, vulgar... but it becomes tragical, if rightly read," he noted. "That furniture so carefully painted, even to the last vein of rosewood—is there nothing to be learnt from the terrible lustre of it, from its fatal newness?"[16] (The influence of Hunt's painting is discussed in Barbara Gallati's essay in this volume.)

Ford Madox Brown, now indelibly associated with the Pre-Raphaelites, began in 1852 two compositions that would stand among the greatest achievements of Pre-Raphaelite modern-life painting: *The Last of England* (1852–1855, City Art Gallery, Birmingham), a study of emigrants leaving for Australia, and *Work* (fig. 9). In the latter, Brown radically departs from convention by presenting as his heroes a group of manual laborers digging a trench for new water pipes in Heath Street, Hampstead. In the right foreground of *Work* appear two intellectuals: the critic Thomas Carlyle, whose analysis of the "Condition of England" decried the industrial world as lacking in idealism and purpose, and the Anglican clergyman Frederick Denison Maurice, a central figure in the Christian socialist movement. The most radical pronouncements of Christian socialism were contained in the short-lived newspaper *Politics for the People*, which was founded in response to the last great Chartist meeting in 1848. Another leading Christian socialist, Charles Kingsley—more of a demagogue than his friend, the erudite Maurice—addressed the "Workmen of England" on a placard displayed at the 1848 Chartist demonstration: "You have more friends than you think... Englishmen! Saxons! Workers of the great, cool-headed, strong-handed nation of England, the workshop of the world and the leader of freedom for 700 years... a nobler day is dawning for England, a day of freedom, science, industry... be wise and then you *must* be free, for you will be *fit* to be free!"[17] The Christian socialists created an institution in which such wisdom could be acquired through the process of education. This was the Working Men's College in Red Lion Square, London, of which Maurice was the principal and where Brown himself taught drawing alongside Ruskin and Rossetti.[18] A poster on the brick wall to the left of Brown's *Work* advertises the college, suggesting that in its classrooms may be found the solution to the difficulties experienced by working men present in the painting—from the flower seller in the left foreground with his battered hat, through the navvies and the pub potman in the center, to the orphans and unemployed haymakers to the right. The presence of Brown, Ruskin, and Rossetti at the Working Men's College indicates the status of Pre-Raphaelitism as a politically, as well as aesthetically, radical movement. As Sophie Lynford notes (pp. 41–42), it was in the Working Men's College that Thomas Farrer, the son of a glazier given to radical views, received an education in drawing, in an environment where questions of equality and a model of brotherly relations between men of different classes were pioneered. Farrer carried the reforming zeal of the college, as well as Ruskin's creed of radical realism, to the United States when he emigrated in 1858.

PRB to Pre-Raphaelitism

9. Ford Madox Brown, *Work*, 1852–1863, oil on canvas, Manchester Art Gallery

The Pre-Raphaelites gained the support of a small but active group of patrons—mainly members of the industrial middle class, such as Thomas Plint, the evangelical Leeds stockbroker, and Thomas Fairbairn, the owner of a large Manchester engineering concern. Paradoxically, these men embodied the very values that Carlyle, Maurice, Ruskin, and the Pre-Raphaelites subjected to harsh critique. But even as some of its members experienced mounting financial success, the original Brotherhood had begun to fragment. James Collinson left as early as 1850; Thomas Woolner emigrated from Britain to Australia in 1852. In the spring of 1854, Hunt departed for an extended painting trip in Palestine, effectively bringing the Brotherhood to an end. He left behind two related works that were exhibited at the Royal Academy after his departure: *The Awakening Conscience* and *The Light of the World* (1854, Keble College, Oxford; see fig. 2 in Gallati essay), an emblematic representation of Christ knocking at the door of the human soul, which became perhaps the most widely circulated religious image of the nineteenth century.

After 1854, the founders continued to pursue their individual artistic careers. Millais gradually abandoned the sharp focus of early Pre-Raphaelite work: he experimented instead with atmospheric tone-poems such as *Autumn Leaves* (1855, Manchester Art Gallery) and historical narrative subjects notable for their psychological complexity. Popular with a wide audience, he ended his life as president of the Royal Academy. Hunt returned from the Holy Land as something of a celebrity. *The Finding of the Saviour in the Temple* (1860, Birmingham Museums and Art Gallery) was an elaborate historical painting that offered a reconstruction of a scene from Christ's childhood based on extensive ethnographic and archaeological research. Exhibited in London at the German Gallery, owned by the celebrated dealer Ernest Gambart, the painting scored a popular triumph and embarked on a national tour. Hunt received £5,500 for the work from Gambart, a vast sum that the dealer recouped within six months from ticket receipts and the sale of engravings. In this form, Hunt's work attained widespread international acclaim.

Aesthetes and Socialists

The Pre-Raphaelite movement, however, was far from extinguished. Although Rossetti had ceased to exhibit his work publicly by the mid-1850s, he produced a series of exquisite watercolors on medieval themes, and in 1859 began a series of evocative oil paintings of female sitters in luxurious interior settings with enigmatic titles such as *The Blue Bower* (fig. 10). During the 1860s, Rossetti became the lodestar of a bohemian group centered on his residence, Tudor House, Chelsea, which included the poet Algernon Swinburne and the American painter James McNeill Whistler. Their experimentation with artistic form was decisively influential for a generation of artists and designers in Britain and the United States. Bound together by a shared joy in flouting convention, they collected Chinese and Japanese ceramics and explored the relationship between the sister arts of painting and music. Rossetti's model, lover, and housekeeper at Tudor House, Fanny Cornforth (born Sarah Cox, daughter of a Sussex blacksmith), appears in many of his works of the 1860s, including *The Blue Bower*. Rather as an actress develops a role in a play, Cornforth seems to have played a role in shaping Rossetti's artistic choices, as he moved toward more opulent and sensuous productions during the 1860s. After 1863, the pioneering photographer Julia Margaret Cameron developed a distinctive idiom in dialogue with Rossetti's work, utilizing the focal length of the camera to create sumptuous visual effects. Like Rossetti, she often created images with a single female sitter.

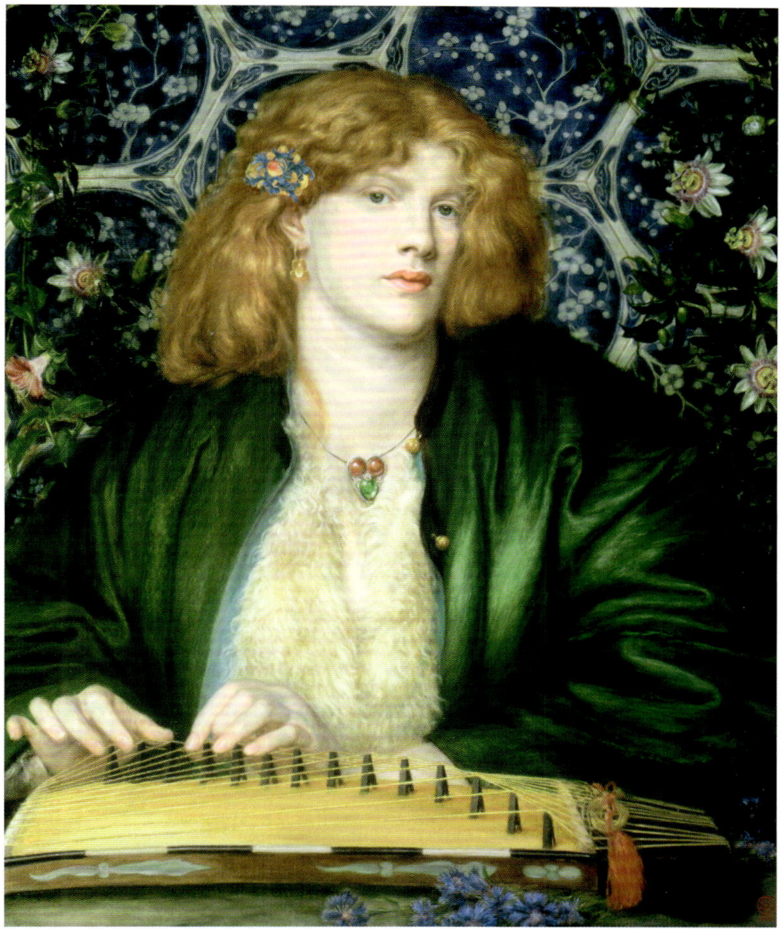

10. Dante Gabriel Rossetti, *The Blue Bower*, 1865, oil on canvas, The Barber Institute of Fine Arts, University of Birmingham

Even before his move to Tudor House, Rossetti had already acquired an ardent circle of younger admirers. Commissioned in 1856 to decorate the Oxford Union building with frescoes, Rossetti could command the talents of what amounted to a new brotherhood. The group was joined by two young men whom he had met when they were Oxford undergraduates: Edward Burne-Jones and William Morris. In their hands, Pre-Raphaelitism entered a new phase in which distinctions between the fine and decorative arts were entirely collapsed, and the implicit political radicalism of the earlier movement, directly inspired by Ruskin's social criticism, was eventually transformed into a revolutionary socialist politics.

Although the Oxford frescoes were something of a failure, owing to Rossetti's incomplete technical knowledge, the creative partnership with Morris and Burne-Jones would be of global significance. The three joined with Ford Madox Brown, the architect Philip Webb, and two business partners, Peter Paul Marshall and Charles Faulkner, to form Morris, Marshall, Faulkner & Co., a pioneering enterprise in the decorative arts. With Morris and Burne-Jones as its primary designers, the firm pioneered the revival of craft techniques in the production of textiles, wallpaper, furniture, and stained glass. Their stand at the 1862 International Exhibition in London was widely admired. The explicitly anti-industrial methods of production led, ironically, to high retail prices, but Morris and Burne-Jones's distinctive reinvention of medieval motifs and media influenced artists and designers across the world, playing a significant role in the emergence, for example, of the Arts and Crafts movement in Britain and the United States, art nouveau in France, and Jugendstil in the German-speaking lands: as Nikolaus Pevsner revealed, Morris's ideas even lie in the ancestry of the Bauhaus.[19]

Morris, who had also achieved considerable distinction as a Pre-Raphaelite poet, moved decisively toward politics, as leader of the Socialist League from December 1884 to 1889. Some of his final collaborations with Burne-Jones, such as the exquisitely typeset illustrated books they created for their Kelmscott Press, put forth a socialist message in a visual language derived, in the Pre-Raphaelite manner, from the Middle Ages. Toward the end of his career, Burne-Jones created large-scale oil paintings in a distinctive, richly decorative idiom, such as the vast upright canvas *King Cophetua and the Beggar Maid*. Surrounded by decadent material splendor, the king is transfixed by the honest beauty of a simply dressed pauper. When shown at the Exposition Universelle in Paris in 1889, the painting was understood as a socialist parable. Widely reproduced in photogravure and other print media, Burne-Jones's work exerted influence on artists from the Americans Edwin Austin Abbey, John Singer Sargent, and Elihu Vedder, to the young Spanish painter Pablo Picasso.

Epilogue

While the Pre-Raphaelites were derided by modernist critics from Roger Fry to Clement Greenberg, a significant revival of interest in Pre-Raphaelite painting began with centenary exhibitions and publications in 1948. Revelatory exhibitions reassessed Brown (1964), Millais (1967), Hunt (1969), Rossetti (1973), and Burne-Jones (1975). These shows won popular and critical acclaim in the "Swinging Sixties" and psychedelic early seventies. The Tate Gallery's massive survey exhibition of 1984, with scholarly catalog, precipitated a tide of revisionist academic activity and popular interest that continues to this day. A parallel exhibition at the Institute of Contemporary Arts, *William Morris Today*, insisted on the contemporary relevance of the group's ideas in the neoliberal world of Margaret Thatcher and Ronald Reagan, while *Ruskin, Turner and the Pre-Raphaelites* (2000) at the newly founded Tate Britain explored the critic's radical thinking. *The New Path: Ruskin and the American Pre-Raphaelites* at the Brooklyn Museum in

1985 provided a first, illuminating account of the American Pre-Raphaelites—a theme further explored in *The Last Ruskinians: Charles Eliot Norton, Charles Herbert Moore, and Their Circle* at Harvard University Art Museum in 2007. The Tate's *Pre-Raphaelite Vision: Truth to Nature* (2004) was the first survey exhibition of the whole movement to include American artists Henry Roderick Newman and expatriate Englishman Thomas Charles Farrer. A new interpretation was proposed in *Pre-Raphaelites: Victorian Avant-Garde* (2012–2013), making explicit claims for the quality and importance of the group's work and its status within the history of modern art. The present exhibition is the first of what may become a series of revisionist endeavors charting the worldwide impact of the avant-garde movement begun by seven young men in the febrile London of 1848.

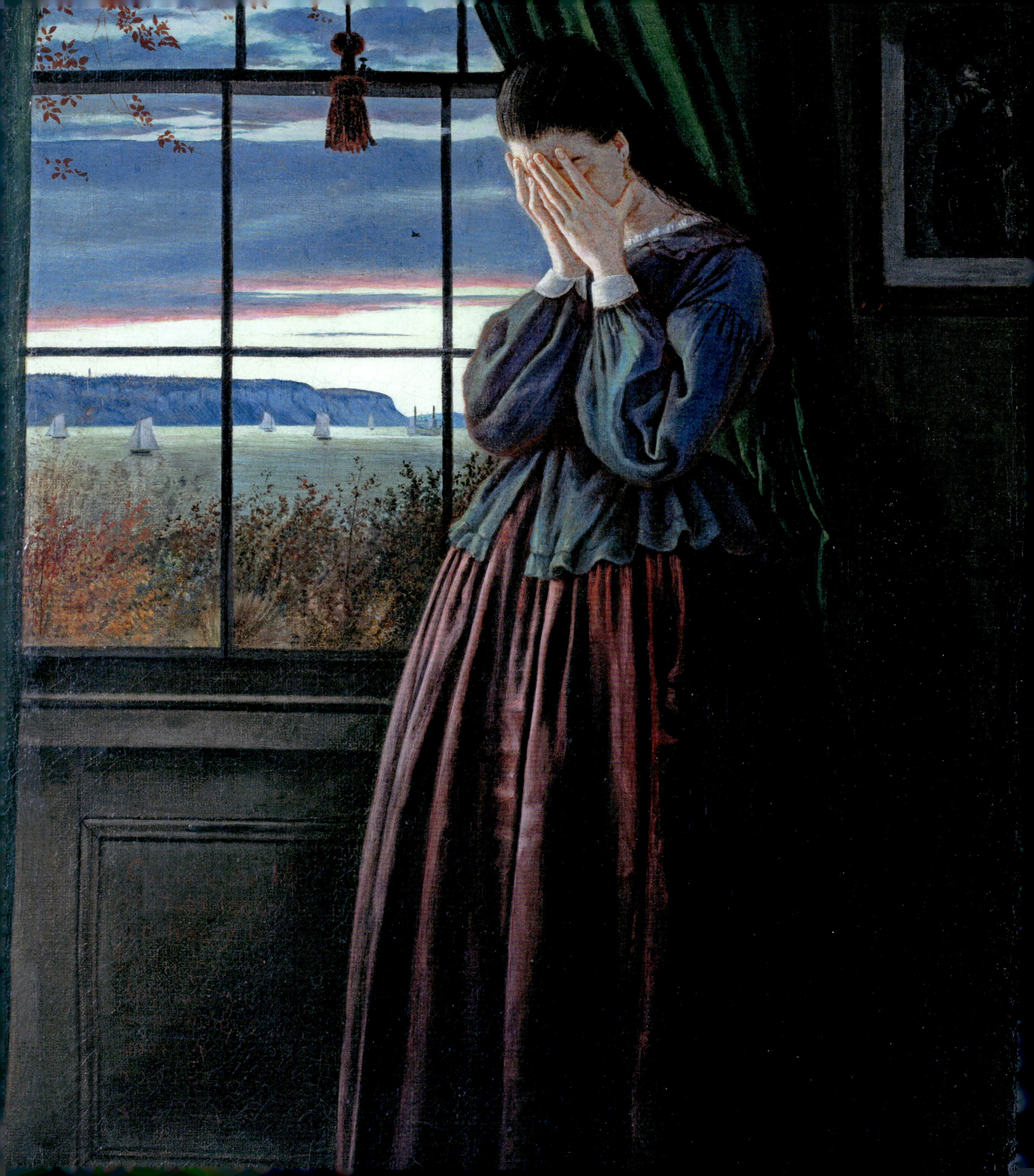

Abolitionism and the American Pre-Raphaelite Experiment

SOPHIE LYNFORD

Thomas Charles Farrer, *Gone! Gone!*, 1860 (detail, plate 12)

"Art in America has been pursued on wrong principles . . . never to this day has an American painted a line that could be construed into a reproach to American Slavery. . . . And yet, what a work of Art might have been accomplished if there had been a man with a warm heart, and a clear brain, and a skillful pencil, to seize the golden opportunity!" The American Pre-Raphaelites published these words in their journal, *The New Path*, in January 1864 as the Civil War raged. Titled "A Letter to a Subscriber," the editorial is unique as a collective political statement by a group of American artists, architects, and critics. The letter indicts the nation's painting, sculpture, and architecture—which the group viewed as uniformly debased—as having both reflected and fostered a culture "infected" by the "sin of slavery" and "moral cowardice."[1] During the years of their collaborative association, the American Pre-Raphaelites executed paintings and designed buildings that embodied principles of social equity, civil conduct, and beauty, and that they believed could herald lasting social and political reform.

Because the painted output of the American Pre-Raphaelites is not overtly preoccupied with images of slavery, manumission, or war, and appears almost insistently apolitical, it is difficult to isolate political messaging within their works. But assessing the American Pre-Raphaelites' legacy through an examination of only the paintings produced by its members does not tell the complete story of the group's reformist aspirations. The full dimension of the American Pre-Raphaelites' pictorial and political rebellion can only be understood in the context of the group's comprehensive, multipronged agenda—which aimed at nothing less than a radical displacement of established modes of landscape painting, in addition to a reformation of American architecture and criticism.

The American Pre-Raphaelites founded the Association for the Advancement of Truth in Art in 1863, authoring the Articles of Organization—a de facto manifesto—and establishing mechanisms of governance, a publishing arm, and a platform that sought to influence painting, sculpture, and architecture, as well as to educate the taste of the American public. Attracting painters, architects, critics, scientists, and patrons, the Association eventually assembled nearly thirty members.[2] The core group, however, comprised the founders and their close associates: architects Peter Bonnett Wight and Russell Sturgis Jr.; critic and writer Clarence Cook; and painters Thomas Charles Farrer, Charles Herbert Moore, John William and John Henry Hill (father and son), William Trost Richards, and Henry Roderick Newman. They were united by their mutual commitment to promulgating the aesthetic doctrines of the British critic John Ruskin and to extending the Pre-Raphaelite experiment onto American soil. Believing the "union of the Arts is necessary for the full development of each," the Association argued that the "close connection between Architecture, Sculpture and Painting" allowed those arts to find "their highest perfection" and "greatest glory."[3]

The American Pre-Raphaelites were inspired not only by Ruskin's aesthetic prescriptions, which demanded that art serve as visual records of geologic, natural, and human history, but also by his increasingly pointed societal and economic critiques that linked the condition of a nation to the condition of its art. Imbibing the British critic's theories on the ethical relationship between art, labor, and society, the American Pre-Raphaelites pursued aggressive reform, their priorities including the abolition of slavery and reverence for the working man. The group was convinced that mainstream antebellum art and architecture, executed by "men who did not strike slavery when strokes were needed," had produced a society "beset on all sides by old-time prejudice and obstinate ignorance."[4] In response, the American Pre-Raphaelites waged a "most uncompromising war against all deception and untruth."[5] For the group's painters, their protest was expressed through their repudiation of idealized landscape representation, which they believed disguised the moral corruption at the heart of their nation's democratic experiment. In their devotion to direct observation, with compositional arrangements, facture, and palettes that rejected the traditions of picturesque landscape, the American Pre-Raphaelites abstained from both the thematics and techniques associated with their predecessors and contemporaries, artists later labeled the Hudson River School. Those painters found it culturally resonant and commercially rewarding to present America as a new Eden. The American Pre-Raphaelites, skeptical of artistic conventions that extolled the New World's paradisiacal status, instead pursued an arduous mimesis that they understood as the sole means to unleash the spiritual and liberative energies that inhered in the natural world.

The radicalism of American Pre-Raphaelite painting lay in the violation of conventional spatial relationships and the destabilization of the landscape genre induced by a hyperrealist style. The Pre-Raphaelite movement's architects, by contrast, could more palpably articulate their group's reformist agenda by employing the materials, ornamentation, and redemptive influence of Gothic forms, and by directly incorporating elements of nature into architectural designs. The American Pre-Raphaelites believed there was a direct linkage between the imperatives to depict landscape realistically and to construct naturalistic forms in architecture: both traced back to the teachings of Ruskin. Beauty in both arts, he argued in *Modern Painters,* vol. 3 (1856), depended on the apprehension and imitation of the unified forms apparent everywhere in nature, and not on a display of the artist's subjectivity.[6]

The American Pre-Raphaelite architects had also internalized Ruskin's faith in the socially recuperative benefits of Gothic architecture and particularly in how it could blunt the pernicious effects of mechanization on the arts. They promoted Gothic revivalism as a model that could nurture the creative impulse of the artisan-craftsman and, by extension, the laborer who would otherwise fall victim to the anonymous and alienating effects of industrialization. Within half a decade, the Association members had permeated a wide array of American cultural spheres, including art collecting, exhibition design, public and private architectural commissions, nationally and internationally circulated newspapers and journals, and higher education.[7] When these projects are viewed as part of a broad interartistic initiative, the American Pre-Raphaelites' provocations and accomplishments in painting, architecture, and criticism can be reclaimed from the periphery of nineteenth-century culture and positioned at the center of key transatlantic artistic, pedagogical, and political discourses.

British Precedents and Proselytes: The Politicization of Thomas Charles Farrer

Any attempt to view the American Pre-Raphaelites through the lens of their political ideology generally, and specifically with respect to their ardent abolitionism, must confront the education and canon of the group's leader, Thomas Charles Farrer. During his childhood and adolescence in London, British-born Farrer studied commercial draftsmanship at the Government School of Design, later enrolling in drawing classes at the Working Men's College taught by Ruskin himself and the British Pre-Raphaelite painter Dante Gabriel Rossetti. For the group of artists and architects he befriended after arriving in New York in late 1858, Farrer served as an ambassador of the British models of landscape painting and Gothic revivalism they believed would allow them to "produce pictures, statues, and buildings worthy of the age and country in which we live."[8]

Farrer's progressive sense of moral and political justice was inculcated at the Working Men's College, an educational endeavor founded by a group of churchmen and intellectuals associated with Christian socialism. Distressed by the failure of the Chartist movement, which had fought to extend full manhood suffrage throughout England, the college's leaders advocated on behalf of the working man by offering educational opportunities previously reserved for the wealthy.[9] As the leading art critic in England, Ruskin was tasked with inaugurating the school's drawing class. Ruskin's idealized view of the social structure and labor practices of the medieval workshop made him a particularly apposite choice to teach the "cabinet-makers, tailors, printers, engravers, pianoforte makers, woodworkers, watchmakers, gilders, coach-builders, bookbinders, and instrument makers who were the [school's] first students."[10] Farrer himself was the son of a glazier, "a radical of the extreme type"—likely with Chartist sympathies.[11]

Farrer would have been exposed to fervent political debate about progressive causes, including abolition, while at the Working Men's College. During the 1840s and 1850s, there was an active lecture circuit in England for African American abolitionists, whom Chartists and other British radicals believed shared a common purpose with their own movements. Farrer brought these values with him when he arrived in the United States, encountering the heated polemics over the extension of slavery, which had been abolished in the United Kingdom and throughout much of the British Empire in 1834.[12] Farrer's advocacy of abolition appears in his earliest American productions. Known today largely for his landscapes, Farrer was the only member of the American Pre-Raphaelites who produced a significant body of figurative work, a talent he developed in Rossetti's classroom. Mostly drawings in pencil and in pen and ink, executed around 1859, as well as a few surviving figurative oil paintings from the early 1860s, these works evince Farrer's interest in suggestive narratives and the psychological dimensions of his subjects. Further, they confirm the intensity of Farrer's commitment to the extirpation of slavery and the convergence of his emerging passion for the most pressing issue on the American political scene with representational strategies he imported from his English training. In drawings and paintings he produced shortly after his arrival in New York and subsequent to his enlistment in the Union army in May 1862, Farrer directly treated, with an obsessive realism, subjects related to the mobilization of Union troops, Union war heroes, and scenes redolent of parting and loss—as well as, most critically, references to three leading abolitionists.

The only located oil painting that Farrer completed during this period is *Gone! Gone!* (plate 12). In her essay in this volume Barbara Gallati argues that, though the work is dated to 1860, preceding the outbreak of the war, Farrer incorporated symbols and references into his compositions that suggest a purposely

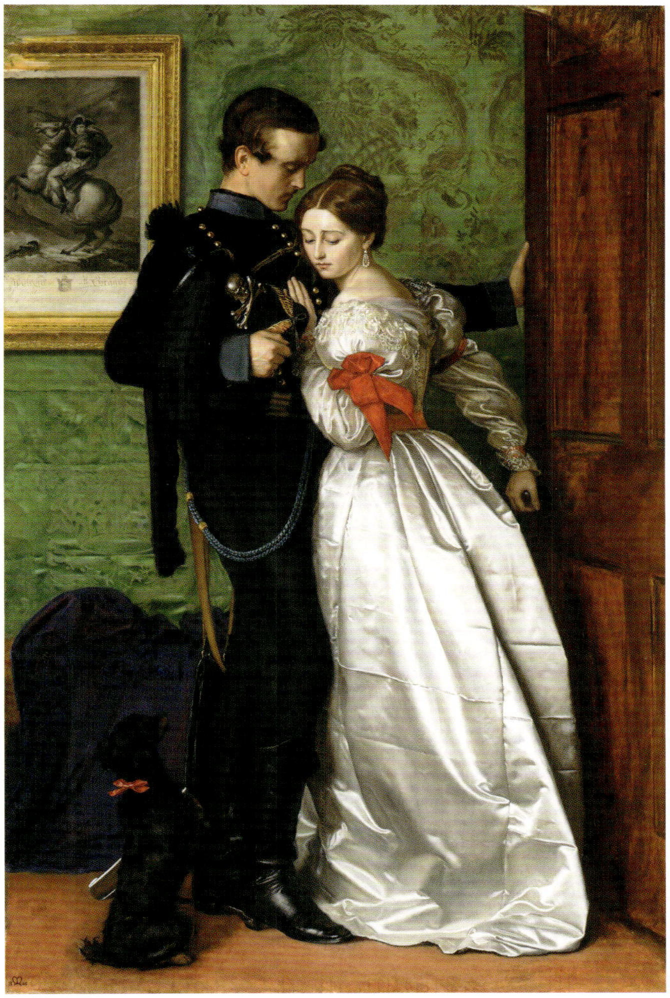

1. John Everett Millais, *The Black Brunswicker*, 1860, oil on canvas, National Museums Liverpool, Lady Lever Art Gallery, Port Sunlight

cryptic—if not prescient—narrative for *Gone! Gone!* Gallati points specifically to the engraving Farrer inserts after John Everett Millais's *The Huguenot Lover* (1851–1852, fig. 5 in Gallati essay) as an especially persuasive visual cue that Farrer is building upon Millais's engagement with the foreboding associated with imminent war (see detail at top right, p. 38). Further supporting this reading is Millais's own description of *The Huguenot Lover* as "a perfect pendant" to *The Black Brunswicker* (1860, fig. 1), which Farrer saw at the Royal Academy during a visit to London in 1860.[13] *The Black Brunswicker* and *The Huguenot Lover* are part of a series of paintings, including *The Proscribed Royalist, 1651* (1853, Birmingham Museum and Art Gallery) and *The Order of Release, 1746* (1852, Tate, Britain), that gave visual expression to a single theme set within the distinct historical contexts of the sixteenth, seventeenth, eighteenth, and nineteenth centuries. In *The Black*

Brunswicker, the soldier, a member of the Brunswick Ducal Corps unit in the Napoleonic Wars, prepares to fight in the Battle of Quatre Bras in 1815. On the wall behind the Brunswicker, Millais includes a framed print of Jacques-Louis David's famous *Napoleon Crossing the Alps* (1800–1801), its presence presaging both the French victory at Quatre Bras and the certain death of the English soldier in battle. Millais's son, John Guille Millais, noted that his father's series embodied "unselfish love, in which the sweetness of woman shines conspicuous," but each work also assumes ambitious formal challenges of integrating rich, if not conventionally graceful, representations of the human figure and keenly observed objects, costumes, and natural details into disparate historical settings.[14] In *Gone! Gone!* Farrer extends Millais's project of dramatizing eternal motifs, such as the sacrifices demanded by war and the courage required to survive crisis, separation, and the death of loved ones, but transposes these issues onto an American landscape: the Hudson River and Palisades are visible through the window. Importing the British Pre-Raphaelite practice of iterating a single theme across historical periods, and emulating Millais's practice of visual quotation by representing *The Huguenot Lover* in miniature, Farrer processed and interpreted the sectional tensions that would inflame the nation.[15]

Farrer's increasing artistic engagement with American progressive politics and abolitionism was explicit in another work he exhibited at the National Academy of 1861, *Evening Thoughts*. While the painting remains unlocated, a review in *The Crayon* describes "the portraits of Washington and John Brown associated together on the mantelpiece."[16] Farrer likely linked the two American luminaries due to their respective connections to the arsenal at Harpers Ferry (where Farrer would be stationed just a year later after enlisting in the Union army). Farrer's interest in John Brown had likely been piqued in England, where the abolitionist's exploits were widely reported. The British Pre-Raphaelite Ford Madox Brown, who was also an instructor at the Working Men's College during Farrer's enrollment, twice considered painting the subject "John Brown Assisting the Escape of Runaway Slaves," though he never realized the work.[17] Farrer, though, returned multiple times to John Brown's iconic presence, inserting Brown's image into portraits to indicate the commitment of both sitter and artist to the radical antislavery platform. In Farrer's *Portrait of Clarence C. Cook* (1861, fig. 1 in Gallati essay), a likeness of Brown hangs on the wall behind the critic. If there was any lingering question of Cook's allegiances, Farrer noticeably placed the calling card of another abolitionist, Wendell Phillips, atop the table on which Cook writes.[18]

Scenes related to mobilization and the struggle to preserve the Union, gleaned from personal experience, became subjects for Farrer's future paintings. He would take up the suggestion of Louisa Cook, Clarence's wife, who wrote to Farrer a month after the outbreak of war and a year prior to Farrer's own enlistment:

I wish you would seize some of the beautiful subjects—the grand drama now enacting in America offers for an artist—I was delighted with a picture drawn by a newspaper correspondent a little while ago of the arrival of the Seventh Regiment at Annapolis... they arrived on a beautiful Sunday... in the rich morning sunshine resting from their fatigues, they would have to wade knee deep in clover blossoms to apply the match to their cannon if needed.... Could there be a more picturesque subject?[19]

One year later, Farrer would enlist in the Union army, assembling on Seventh Street in Manhattan for his departure with the Twenty-Second Regiment of the National Guard of the State of New York. One of "550 Strong," Farrer and his regiment were sent off with great fanfare, "The Battle Hymn of the Republic" resounding in the background: "About 9 o'clock the band, after playing a few airs, finally struck up 'John Brown's Body,' the regiment and the crowd around them took it up again in a vast swell of sound that peaked like a great organ, and as the song ended, all burst into a deafening uproar of cheers, in the midst of which the column started."[20]

Although Farrer's enlistment lasted only three months, the experience of marching off to battle would reverberate in his imagination through the end of the war. In the first months of 1865, he would paint *April, 1861* (unlocated), which, according to Russell Sturgis, pictured "the Seventh Regiment marching, on its way to war, through the street without, while a lady within turns away from the window through which the street and the soldiers are seen."[21] Echoing the imagery and sense of loss that occupied him in *Gone! Gone!*, and likely recalling Louisa Cook's description of the Seventh Regiment of four years earlier, Farrer's *April, 1861* would inaugurate the period—the summer and fall of 1865 spent in Northampton, Massachusetts—marked by intense production and experimentation in both oils and watercolors, landscapes and still lifes. Though the war had concluded, Farrer sought out connections among local residents that allowed him to process both the national and his personal trauma. Farrer and his wife stayed in the home of Colonel Joseph B. Parsons, the last commander of the Tenth Massachusetts Volunteers, which "participated in almost every major battle fought by the Army of the Potomac, beginning with the Peninsula campaign through Antietam and Fredericksburg in 1862."[22] The colonel would have been more than a landlord to Farrer, and bonds of camaraderie were likely formed as both men shared their experiences of the Peninsula campaign, which included the protracted battles at Harpers Ferry. Parsons publicly displayed his support of his tenant when he opened his residence at summer's end for an exhibition of the paintings Farrer had completed in Northampton that season.

During these months following the war's conclusion, Farrer developed his signature style, characterized by a controlled distribution of natural elements executed with relentless verism. While *Mount Tom* (1865, plate 14) appears to adhere more closely to picturesque conventions than other paintings by Farrer, the work suggests he was productively exploring multiple styles in order to come to terms with his personal experience of war, as well as with the grievous wound inflicted on the nation by the bullet fired at Ford's Theatre. Featuring Farrer's characteristic "painstaking attention to minute details," as one reviewer complained—particularly visible in the foreground's foliage, where each leaf is rendered individually—*Mount Tom* also possesses a darker ambiguity.[23] In the quietude of this painting is a sense of mourning; Farrer inserts only a single human figure, a fisherman whose hat immediately signaled his status as a Union veteran. He wears a kepi, standard issue to Union soldiers for fatigue duty.[24] This veteran angler is the lone human presence in an otherwise depopulated landscape, grieving lost comrades, and the viewer too is reminded of those who will never return but still haunt Farrer's imagination.

Censure in Stone: The American Pre-Raphaelites' Architectural Intervention

Just a few months after Farrer's return to New York in fall 1862, he and seven colleagues cofounded the Association. Central to the heterogeneous assembly, which included painters, lawyers, and scientists, were architects Peter Bonnett Wight and Russell Sturgis Jr. Boyhood friends from their years at New York's Free Academy, they were devoted members of the group, helping to write the Association's Articles of Organization, serving as elected officers, and actively contributing to, and later editing, *The New Path*. Wight and Sturgis had, since their school years, been steeped in contemporary discourse on the most urgent social concerns of the day. As one Free Academy classmate remembered, the adolescents "waxed warm, in the debating societies and out of them, about the Union and slavery, and the possible extension of slavery into the territories, and the threats of the dissolution of the Union."[25] The political leanings of the American Pre-Raphaelites cannot be fully grasped without recognizing the critical contributions, both ideological and architectural, of Wight and Sturgis.

For the Association, architecture—Gothic revival architecture, in particular—was an especially powerful conduit of political ideas, owing in large measure to the salutary associations Ruskin had bound to medieval guilds in his writings over the previous decade. Ruskin's sixth chapter of *The Stones of Venice* (1851), "The Nature of Gothic," was one of the critic's earliest forays into blending his aesthetic concerns with his broader cultural and social interests. It was in this text that Ruskin presented his idealized view of the Gothic workshop, where both collaborative labor and self-expression were encouraged. Such cooperative arrangements allowed craftsmen freedom to execute designs they had conceived themselves, which often displayed distortion and irregularities, expressive elements that Ruskin hoped would be introduced to contemporary architecture, and would serve to combat the pernicious effects of the spiritless uniformity of machine-produced objects.[26]

The American Pre-Raphaelite architects were early converts to Ruskinian doctrine. In fact, it was their mutual affinity for the British critic's architectural writings that had brought the teenagers together. Wight recalled: "Our friendship was cemented by the study of... architecture. We read all the books on the subject to be found in the college library, including a set of Ruskin's 'Seven Lamps' and 'Stones of Venice,' which had just come out."[27] Over the course of their early careers, the friends followed Ruskin and the British Pre-Raphaelites in identifying the republicanism of the late Middle Ages in Italy as having been prerequisite for the production of powerfully evocative art. Ruskin argued that Venice in particular had sustained a culture that generated highly naturalistic and animated poses and facial features both in painted figures and sculptural carving. Decorated capitals such as those at the Doge's Palace allowed for displays of greater naturalism in depictions of flora and fauna. These ideas were to percolate for over a decade before Wight and Sturgis would design some of the first Ruskinian buildings in the United States in the 1860s.

Wight and Sturgis found in Gothic revival architecture a potent medium for promoting the egalitarian values they believed were absent elsewhere in American culture. In Ruskin's famous formulation, the symmetrical proportions of classical architecture as well as the mechanical repetition utilized in modern designs denigrated the worker while foreclosing his opportunity for individual expression. Gothic architecture, by contrast, was built by craftsmen whose guilds guaranteed devoted workmanship, granted workers autonomy, and conferred status and respect. As Linda Dowling observes, "invoking history, especially medieval history, thus became for [the] mid-century generation neither an 'aristocratic' flourish nor a 'nostalgic' appeal but a fervent gesture of sympathy and solidarity with humanity."[28]

As the country went to war, Wight and Sturgis sought their first major architectural commissions, which became laboratories to test Ruskin's theories on how medieval building practices could elevate the laborer within their own country's flawed and polarized democracy. As heightening sectional tensions led to civil war, the young architects adapted ideas on medieval craftsmanship and the politics of the Middle Ages to the present American moment, becoming further convinced that nineteenth-century Gothic revivalism could extend Gothic architec-

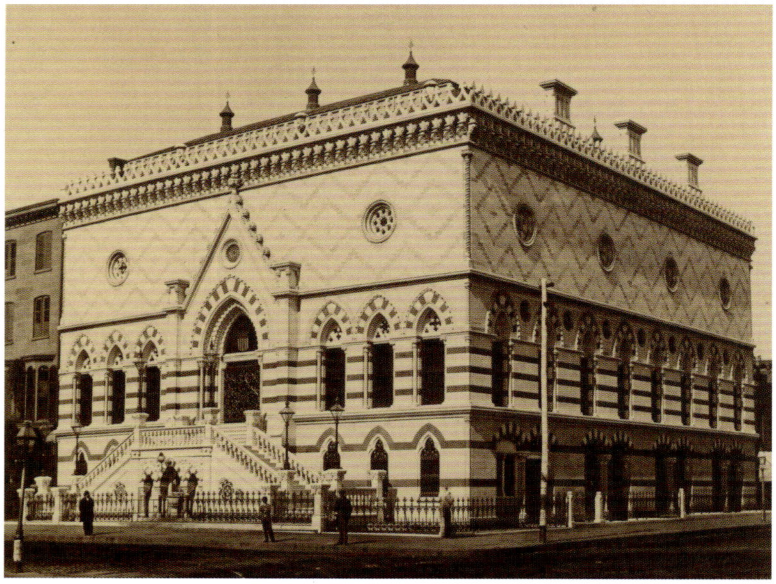

ture's legacy of spiritual populism. As Wight wrote in *The New Path*: "There is no reason therefore to doubt that if one is thoroughly acquainted with the needs of the present time, and masters the principles of the medievalists, he will be able to commence at a point only a little anterior to where they left off and his work will approach perfection according to the skill and knowledge of the mind that controls it."[29] The invocation of the Middle Ages, for the American Pre-Raphaelites, constituted an assertion of the best properties of aesthetic imagination, including heightened perception and the privileging of bold color and natural forms. Medieval history offered a living past, characterized by a profusion of artistic expression made possible by communal bonds that represented at once a stark contrast and censure of the paucity of spirit, commercial aggrandizement, and social alienation that the group feared had beset the American experiment.

The American Pre-Raphaelites positioned Gothic revival architecture as a vehicle to address issues of enforced servitude, the disaffected laborer, and widespread cultural illiteracy that they believed plagued the nation. The architects' first prominent opportunity to prove the salubrious benefits of the Gothic style occurred in 1861, when Wight's proposal for an Italian Gothic polychrome structure won the competition for the new National Academy of Design building, to be erected at the corner of East Twenty-Third Street and Fourth Avenue (fig. 2).[30] Wight followed Ruskin in his belief that the Gothic was the architectural form most functionally adaptable, ornamentally expressive, and supportive of collective enterprise and the integrity of labor. A central principle of the Gothic revival, Ruskin explained, "is that all architectural ornamentation should be executed by the men who design it, and should be of various degrees of excellence, admitting, and therefore exciting, the intelligent co-operation of various classes of workmen."[31]

Erected "in the years of angry strife," the Academy cannot be separated from its historical moment.[32] Although Wight had won the building's commission in 1861, his design was not officially accepted until April 1863—the delay due, in part, to diversions caused by the conflict, as well as to requested revisions to Wight's initial plans. Once construction began, it "carried on in spite of every discouragement," according to Wight, including the "draft for the army during the progress of the work."[33] The opening was finally expected to be a celebratory occasion, scheduled for April 15, 1865, just days after General Lee's surrender. But instead, the building was "draped in mourning; the American colors on a shield, covered in crape, was placed on a doorway... on the occasion of the passage through the city of the mortal remains of the late President."[34]

Although Wight did not serve in the Union army, he viewed the architectural commissions he accepted during the war years as important contributions to the Northern effort.[35] Following the selection of his plan for the National Academy, Wight was employed twice by the United States Sanitary Commission: to design the North's first army field hospital to treat wounded soldiers and, later, to design and oversee the construction of the Union Square Annex of New York's Sanitary Fair in 1864. But it was the National Academy, "designed in the mediaeval spirit," that was Wight's boldest declaration of his wartime allegiances.[36] Sturgis praised the building in his review in *The New Path* as "designed in entire accordance with the views concerning Architecture which have always been set forth in this journal."[37] Borrowing elements of Ruskin's preferred Italian Gothic aesthetic, the National Academy featured polychrome stone mined from the region: gray and white marble from Westchester, New York, North River bluestone from the Hudson Valley, and red marble from Vermont.[38] These selections were consistent with Ruskin's view of the associative and historical resonance of locally sourced materials, studied firsthand and carved by worker-craftsmen. By choosing to build with stone from nearby quarries, Wight sought to imbue civic architecture with ideals that at once promoted individual freedom and broader moral instruction.

2. Peter Bonnett Wight, architect; Maurice Stadtfeld, photographer. *National Academy of Design* (detail), albumen print, in *National Academy of Design. Photographs of the New Building with an Introductory Essay and Description by P. B. Wight, Architect*, New York, 1866

Wight put into practice many of Ruskin's prescriptions in the design and building of the National Academy. Following the example set by architects Thomas Newenham Deane and Benjamin Woodward, who had worked with Ruskin in their plan and construction of the Oxford Museum, Wight hired carvers whom he granted total freedom in the design and ornamentation of columns and capitals. He provided his workmen with photographs, live plants, and botanical studies—likely influenced by the works of his friends in the Association and partic-

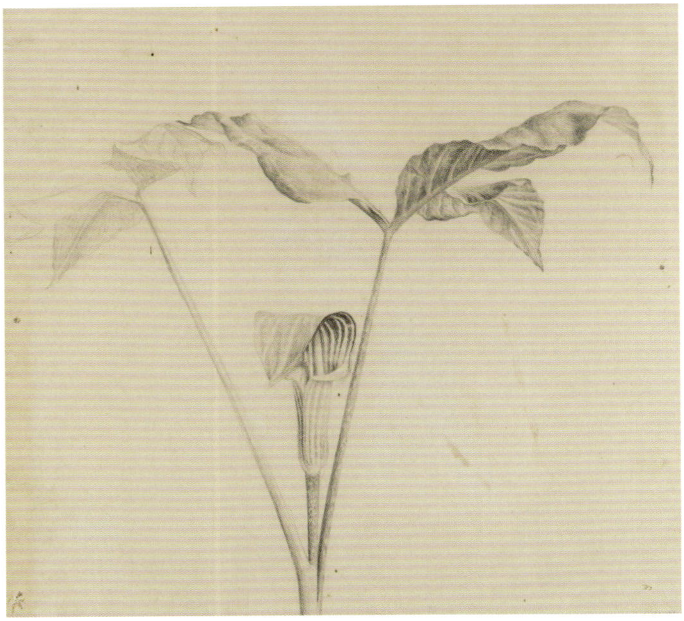

ularly by Farrer's meticulous pencil drawings, which Wight personally collected (fig. 3)—encouraging craftsmen to carve extemporaneously their ornamentation, using the images and flora only as inspiration (fig. 4).[39] For Wight, "the carved capitals on that building, designed by the workmen from nature" were central to his "attempt to revive the system of decoration derived from nature... an example that I would set for all future work."[40] But Wight also viewed his methods as not only espousing the very values that the North was fighting to protect but as an affirmation that manual labor, when practiced under the right conditions and even within a stratified society, could be a rewarding and honored profession, "giving the workmen an opportunity to THINK."[41]

Wight's design, construction, and adornment reflected the naturalism that Ruskin had invoked in "The Nature of Gothic" to describe how Gothic ornamentation both "resembled" nature and channeled the spiritual commitment of the carver.[42] Naturalism for Wight elicited multiple expressive strengths from the craftsman, including emotional intensity, idiosyncrasies of personal style, and a pleasing variation that was the inevitable result of imperfect execution. But Wight's and his colleagues' vision of the egalitarian role of architecture was far more radical in its implications than Ruskin would endorse. Ruskin did believe in the social value of ornament, and asserted that if executed appropriately according to what he viewed as the sanguine principles of the medieval guilds, such ornament would serve worthy didactic purposes. But despite the radical implications of some of Ruskin's arguments, his political and social views were far from

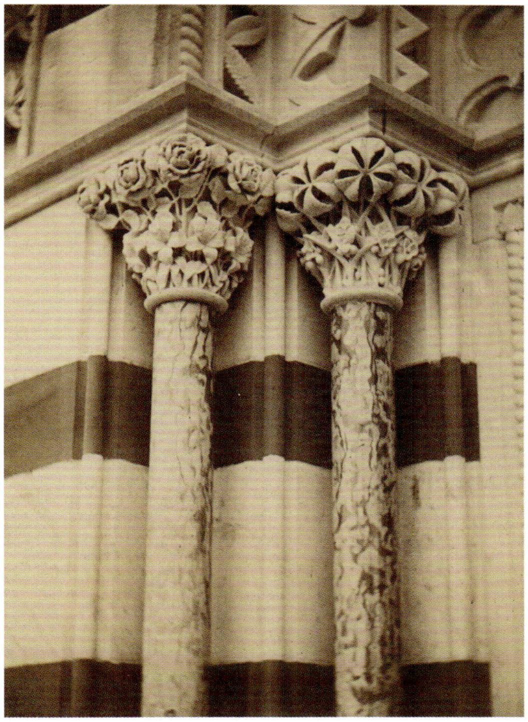

democratic: he held that unequal labor relations do not fundamentally disadvantage one class above another or lead to political suppression, authoritarianism, or slavery. In fact, in Ruskin's view, any dilution of the social stratifications conferred by birth and privilege would result in a further undermining of England's national culture and polity.[43] Such a retrograde political philosophy could not be sustained by the American Pre-Raphaelites in a nation that was being sundered by slavery and civil war. Wight understood the design and construction of the National Academy as a revolutionary aesthetic and political statement that would ramify and transform not only the nation's future architecture, but also the status, dignity, and freedom that must be granted to all laborers if the nation was to fulfill its social compact and nurture a flourishing culture.

3. Thomas Charles Farrer, *Jack-in-the-Pulpit*, c. 1860, pencil on paper, The Art Institute of Chicago

4. Peter Bonnett Wight, architect; Maurice Stadtfeld, photogapher. *Columns at the National Academy of Design*, 1866, albumen print, Historic Architecture and Landscape Image Collection, Ryerson & Burnham Archives, The Art Institute of Chicago

The National Academy, constructed according to "the principle that the workman should have to do with the design of what he executes," was, for Wight, a symbol of "hope for art in the future."[44] As the architect wrote of the building after it was completed: "I believe it will be one of the results of unseen regenerative influences which have been felt throughout the world, to a greater or less extent, during this generation, and of which modern wars, and especially our civil war, have been no small part."[45] Wight understood that a revival of Gothic architecture and medieval building practices was only one of a cluster of "regenerative influences" required to induce a total reformation of American art and culture. Key among those influences was the invigoration of American painting by his colleagues in the Association as they eschewed established landscape conventions and pursued their own alternative vision. Wight was aware that his National Academy building, together with the Pre-Raphaelite paintings it would showcase, could not only "advance the cause" but could ensure the "permanent success of this great reformation."[46]

Dissent in Facture and Message: The American Pre-Raphaelite Landscape

In the years following the opening of the new Academy building in 1865, American Pre-Raphaelite painters received significant attention in the critical coverage of the Academy's annual exhibitions. The 1865 exhibition brought mixed reviews. Cook lamented in the *New-York Daily Tribune* that Farrer's work had been the subject of "jokes, sneers, epithets, ridiculous explanations [that] fill the air in the galleries where they hang, and overflow into the newspapers with a terrible unanimity."[47] On occasion, individual efforts and artists received praise. Charles Herbert Moore was lauded in *The Round Table* as "steadily pursuing a course of discipline that will, in time, carry him far in advance of all landscape painters on this side of the water."[48]

Over the course of the war, the Association's painters had refined their own contribution to the group's pro-Union and abolitionist agenda. Where the American Pre-Raphaelite architects faulted mechanized methods of construction as responsible for "homes of ugliness" and the "utter lack of feeling and of knowledge of art," the painters' reformist stance was located in both their stylistic innovations and their repudiation of the idealized landscape norms found in the work of "old King Cole and his school."[49] The Association condemned Thomas Cole, Asher Durand, Frederic Church, Albert Bierstadt, and their followers as condoning an expansionist and militarist ethos in landscape paintings that celebrated or tacitly supported the policy of Manifest Destiny. The American Pre-Raphaelites, by contrast, renounced traditional spatial configurations, formulaic entry points, and pathways that lured the eye through a composition—devices upon which their predecessors consistently relied. The American Pre-Raphaelites viewed such visual paradigms as an inherited schema that sustained the illusion that the viewer could inhabit and take cognitive possession of the pictured, and, by extension, the physical landscape.

Charles Herbert Moore's *Hudson River, Above Catskill* (plate 51), painted in 1865, demonstrates the ability of American Pre-Raphaelites to complicate their mimesis through the selection of modest subjects that, in concert with their mimetic detail, evoke contemporary events. In Moore's depiction of a small strip of the Hudson riverfront, painted the month the war ended, he records "every beautiful pebble" "with equal exactness" while responding to the inconsolable grief and anxieties imposed by the national conflict.[50] Moore presents the river's rocky bank littered with anti-picturesque detritus. With the precision of a geologist, he renders fragments of rocks with such specificity that they are identifiable as the shales and carbonates that underlie the Hudson River at Catskill. Scattered bones and the remnants of an equine skull have been deposited next to a rib bone, and, next to that, a red apple. A small rowboat, emptied of its oars, appears as if it has recently been dragged on shore. This unusual assemblage privileges the Pre-Raphaelite allegiance to faithful transcription over the aesthetic and moral compromises that Moore and his colleagues found in grandiose, idealized landscapes and viewed as the price of a false compositional harmony.

The trope of the stranded boat has received scholarly attention, most notably by David C. Miller. In Miller's view, the wrecked or stranded boat was emblematic of a foundered ship of state and the associated "fears for and even a loss of faith in the American corporate enterprise during and following the Civil War."[51] Patricia Junker extends this argument to her reading of Moore's work, which she interprets as a "private memorial" to Lincoln, assassinated that April.[52] She asks: "Is that haunting absence of an oarsman that we feel in Moore's painting the dead Lincoln, and the oar-less boat the ship of state?"[53] Such a reading is not at odds with the American Pre-Raphaelites' aversion to overt narratives and conventional allegory. Moore's binding commitment to realism did not exempt him from mourning the war's human carnage. Nor do these responses undermine Moore's primary endeavor of treating his chosen Catskill landscape as still life, as a collection of disparate objects, rather than unified into a grand Claudean or Turnerian vision. The profusion of botanical, biological, and geologic residua, each the product of a discrete observation, conflates the generative act of the artist with the taxonomic discipline of the scientist. While endowing his work with psychological freight, while selecting and painting landscapes that were permeable to political readings, Moore remained steadfast to the American Pre-Raphaelite project, pursued with messianic intensity, of rendering seemingly uncomposed natural settings with unwavering mimetic fidelity.

John Henry Hill viewed the "faithful and loving representations of Nature" he completed during the war years as his own contribution to the North's campaign.[54] His *A Study of Trap Rock (Buttermilk Falls)* (1863, plate 26) was, he wrote, "the most elaborately literal study from nature I ever made. It was done in July and occupied me every afternoon in the month while our civil war was going on."[55] Another detail that must be considered in reading this work is the critical fact that the artist sketching in the lower right corner is not a self-portrait, as has long been presumed, but rather Hill's friend and colleague Thomas Farrer, less than one year returned from the front.[56] While Hill described the setting as "a pleasant rocky dell," the painting has been interpreted as an allegorical treatment of the slaughter and sacrifice of war. The power of the piece resides in the tension between this "pleasant dell," hewn by millions of years of volcanic rifting, and the immediacy of the stone outcroppings outlined in the bright air of midsummer, each block cleaved and angled, each individuated through the precision of Hill's draftsmanship. May Brawley Hill likens these "broken... blocks and boulders that jumbled together with the trunks of dead trees like so many fallen bodies... [and] the sundered rock as an emblem of the several states, once strong and unified, now torn apart by civil war."[57] In the case of *A Study of Trap Rock*, Hill participates in a program of perceptual and cultural reform as set forth by Ruskin but reconstituted with a new politics in the American northeast. He captures the artist's confrontation—his own and Farrer's—with "The Stones" of Nyack, New York, but his objective is not unlike Ruskin's on behalf of the modern traveler to Venice: to provide in America an experience of looking at landscape as a means to a reformation of contemporary culture.

The American Pre-Raphaelites' unconventionally composed landscapes carry a potent emotional charge when such painstakingly rendered exertions are invested in comparatively quotidian elements of nature. William Trost Richards's Pre-Raphaelite oeuvre presents a range of both explicit and oblique engagement with war themes, as Linda S. Ferber has demonstrated. Richards's oil sketch *John Brown's Grave* (1863/1864, private collection) and the landscape *Recruiting Station (Bethlehem)* (1861/1862, Pennsylvania Academy of the Fine Arts) directly treat subjects that had narrative resonance for all viewers. But Richards also executed landscapes and still lifes that, while remaining faithful to Ruskin's exactions, could *also* sustain the burden of being apprehended metaphorically. *A Neglected Corner of the Wheatfield* (1865, plate 80) includes the American Pre-Raphaelites' signature effect of the obstructed foreground, and multiple botanical species—including field bindweed, wild grape vine, and red clover—competing for space and light with an apparently untended field of wheat. Between these representations of good husbandry and negligence stand what appears to be a gate, overgrown and abandoned, a last remnant of a dilapidated wall. The gate's weathered posts and crosspieces suggest not only neglect and loss but also ineffective efforts to impose human order, an inattention that implies moral decay. Focusing on the imagery's effect upon the viewer, Ferber isolates the work's narrative potential and posits that *A Neglected Corner of the Wheatfield* and Richards's *And Some Fell Among Thorns* (c. 1863, oil unlocated, see fig. 5) "may be read as moral allegories of the contrast between good and poor husbandry that could not fail to be interpreted as political by an American audience at a time when the Union cause was often symbolized in the popular press by wheat and the Confederate cause by cotton plants."[58]

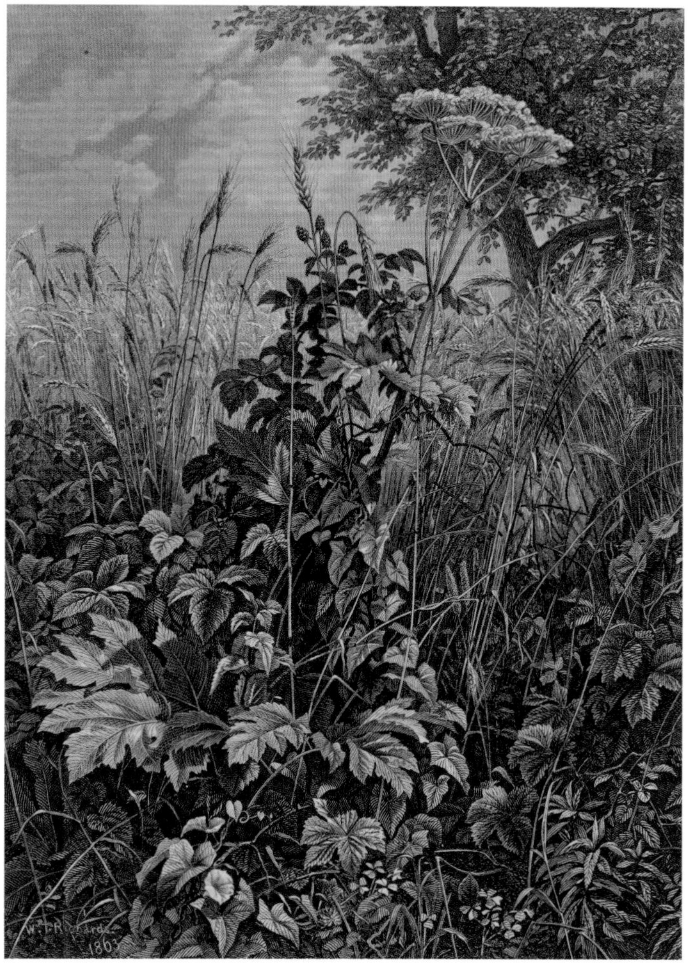

5. Samuel Valentine Hunt after William Trost Richards, *And Some Fell Among Thorns*, c. 1863, etching and engraving, Courtesy of the Pennsylvania Academy of the Fine Arts, Philadelphia, John S. Phillips Collection

These works by Moore, Hill, and Richards demonstrate that the American Pre-Raphaelites' mimetic imagery could also perform metaphorically, an attribute more typically associated with idealized landscapes predicated upon a poeticized pictorial vocabulary. The group's opposition to the grandiosity of mainstream academic landscapes aligns with Ruskin's declaration that a "showy work will always be found, on stern examination of it, to have been done by some conventional rule;—some servile compliance with directions which the student does not see the reason for; and representations of truths which he has not himself perceived."[59] Rebelling against inherited hierarchical principles of composition, the landscapes of the American Pre-Raphaelites depend on acts of discrete and quickened perception and resonate with the quality that Ruskin, invoking an Old Testament passage, described when he wrote that "God is not in the earthquake, nor in the fire, but in the still, small voice."[60]

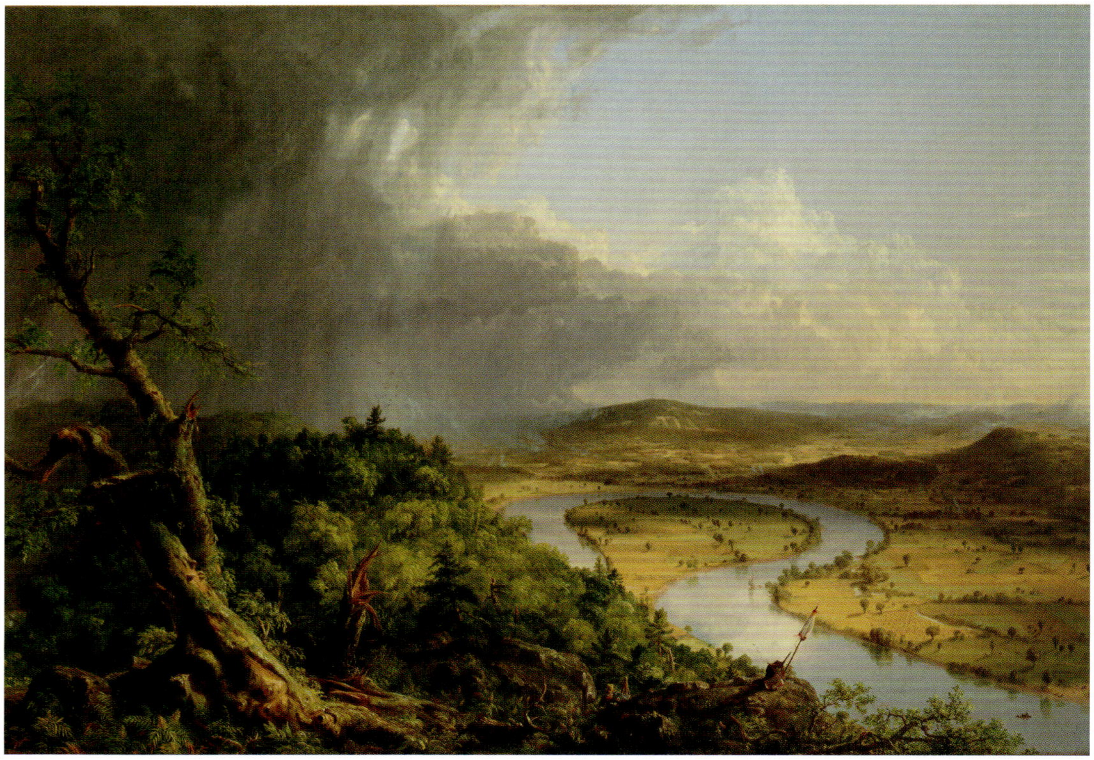

That still, small voice finds visual articulation in Farrer's most ambitious landscape, *View of Northampton from the Dome of the Hospital* (1865, plate 15). Emptied of repoussoir trees, undulating hills, and winding paths—picturesque markers that arrest the viewer's gaze and endorse a regime of pictorial and, by extension, physical possession—*View of Northampton* is Farrer's most assertive statement of aesthetic dissent. Through its confrontation with the legacy of Thomas Cole, Farrer's painting dismantles the exhausted tropes of idealized composition that the American Pre-Raphaelites believed produced landscapes of subjugation. Farrer pictures the same landscape as does Cole in his famous *View from Mount Holyoke, Northampton, Massachusetts, after a Thunderstorm—The Oxbow* (1836, fig. 6). But Farrer captures the Northampton meadows from the opposite direction, from a site northwest of Cole's vantage point at Mount Holyoke's summit. Farrer's version depicts the region as he viewed it in 1865: bustling with settlement and industry, evidenced by residential neighborhoods, institutions for education and religion, and commercial and leisure activities tied to the river. *The Oxbow*, by contrast, shows a landscape reticulated by its initial parceling. The painting served as Cole's "manifesto for an American sublime," a pronouncement of disapprobation that wilderness had been cleared in the name of cultivation and progress.[61]

Where Cole manipulated his composition, framing the geographical features of Northampton within preexisting tropes of the picturesque and sublime, Farrer rejected the visual hierarchies of both modes of representation and depicted the vicinity as he directly apprehended it. Further spurning the practices associated with idealized landscape productions, Farrer understood that the touristic view from the top of Mount Holyoke was not consonant with his project, instead choosing as his vantage the dome of the State Hospital for the Insane. Farrer's decision was imbued with a democratic impulse: just a few months after the war's conclusion, planning his most ambitious landscape to date, he selected a viewpoint that he shared with the hospital's patients, many of whom were fellow former Union soldiers.[62] More significantly, however, Farrer's egalitarian disposition also suffused his representational vision. Every element pictured in *View of Northampton*, both organic and manmade, is in compositional equilibrium, a precise and seemingly uninflected rendition of nature. In this he far exceeded the realist mandate of Ruskin's *Modern Painters*, which presupposed a hierarchy of beauty in which wild scenery was preferred to any landscape of cultivation. Astringent in execution and message, Farrer's panorama rejects not only the practice of representing hierarchy in nature, but repudiates the expansionist political narratives found in the work of Cole's successors. Instead of the attempt at allegorical truth in the work of Cole, Durand, or Church, Farrer offers a form of truth uniquely available from a sustained act of attention—both his, in the presence of his subject, and that asked of the viewer. Presenting no feature as more or less deserving of the viewer's perceptual attention, Farrer, in solidarity with the hospital's patients, offers viewers a postbellum Northampton that visually embodies values of equality for which he himself had fought.

The American Pre-Raphaelites shared the conviction that works of art forged by acts of devoted, even fanatical, mimesis could alter both perception and consciousness through the revelation—observable in direct proportion to its truthful depiction—of divinity in nature. Denouncing their predecessors, the American Pre-Raphaelites attributed to them the collective failure of perpetuating an idealized—and thus, sanitized—vision of America. Those artists, argued the American Pre-Raphaelites, who participated in promoting the national mythos of Manifest Destiny, whose false and overwrought landscapes precluded the recognition of the Creator's design, elevated a morally compromised vision of the American narrative. Instead, the Association's painters and architects cultivated an acuity of vision sustained by unstinting exertions that they understood were prerequisite to truth, in which the arts of realistic painting and sculptural naturalism could converge. Defiant in their refusal to be implicated in the moral evasions of artistic precedent, the American Pre-Raphaelites believed that the triangle of faith, art, and polity could only be nourished in painting and architecture by a righteous and unyielding realism.

6. Thomas Cole, *View from Mount Holyoke, Northampton, Massachusetts, after a Thunderstorm—The Oxbow*, 1836, oil on canvas, The Metropolitan Museum of Art, New York, Gift of Mrs. Russell Sage, 1908

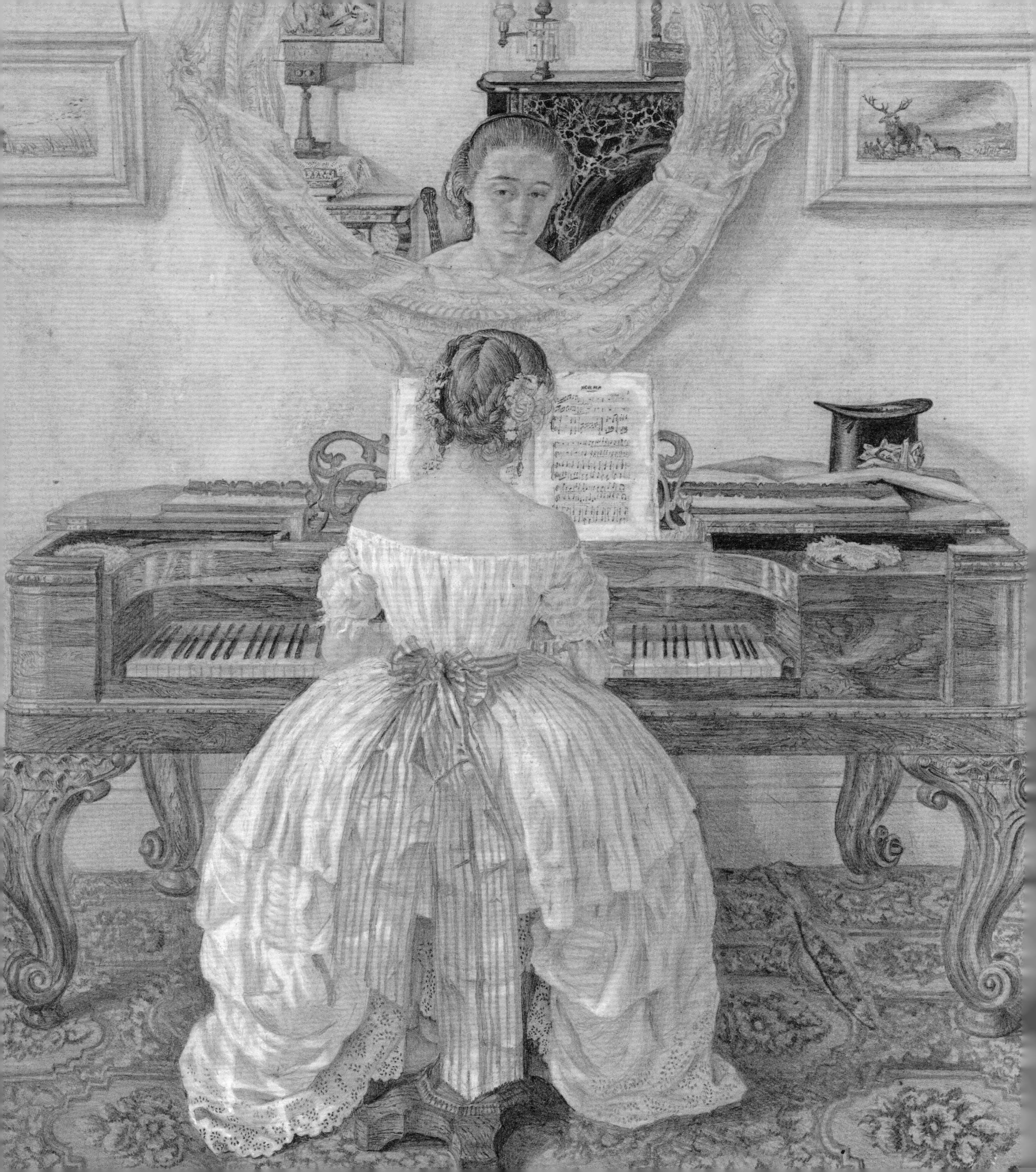

Thought on Canvas: American Pre-Raphaelite Iconography

BARBARA DAYER GALLATI

Thomas Charles Farrer, *Practicing Her Lesson*, 1859 (detail, plate 19)

"A painter of pictures should be a thinker on canvas or paper, and a picture should be thought on canvas or paper." So wrote Russell Sturgis Jr. in "Pictures and Studies," an article published in the July 1864 issue of *The New Path*. It seems contradictory that this long article in the official publication of the Association for the Advancement of Truth in Art (hereafter referred to as the Association) should conclude that even the Association's leading artist, Thomas Charles Farrer, "has, so far, never tried to make a picture out of his work, but has chosen what he would paint, and has then painted it faithfully."[1] Such an opinion corresponds to the conclusion drawn by the art critic and collector James Jackson Jarves (1818–1888), who complained that the "exact literalists" (Farrer and Charles Herbert Moore, in particular) were guilty of "rendering the little and great with equal love and patience, irrespective of ideas and imagination."[2] Jarves repeated his claims throughout the 1860s, pronouncing that the American Ruskinians achieved little more than "barren externalism and dry-bones literalism."[3] His attacks resonated with the views of other of the movement's detractors who deemed the Association's credo of truth superficial. Indeed, most of the commentary on the American Pre-Raphaelites, with its emphasis on technique, has perpetuated this perception and generally ignored the existence of thematic content that did, in fact, engage the "ideas and imagination," as desired by Jarves.

Although their rationale for absolute truth was repeatedly presented in *The New Path*, the American Ruskinians continued to gather critical opprobrium based on the perceived lack of imaginative content in their art. This can be accounted for in part by the stridently evangelical tone adopted by the Association's spokesmen, whose hair-splitting tracts likely predisposed the art audience to judge their art only on virtuoso demonstrations of nature's minutiae. Then, too, the more widely read newspaper critiques rarely accorded rapturous praise to the work of Ruskin and his followers; as one reviewer complained about Ruskin's *Water, Rock, and Foliage*, exhibited at the National Academy of Design in 1856, "With all our admiration for Mr. Ruskin as a critic, we must still pronounce this drawing of his pure trumpery. There is nothing in it." In the end, the writer concluded that the work was an "elaborate but worthless drawing."[4]

Such criticism notwithstanding, the American Pre-Raphaelites did, indeed, create "pictures" designed to communicate ideas derived from considered and imaginative thought. The method used to substantiate this depends on iconographic readings of the art itself. (The word iconography derives from the Greek *ikon*, or image.) Iconography (or iconology) is a system of looking used to interpret works of art by studying imagery separately from style. Thus, the following interpretations rely primarily on discovering content through the relationships of the objects depicted, which are then supported by ancillary facts and texts.

Key to deciphering the major strains of American Pre-Raphaelite content is Thomas Farrer's intriguing *Portrait of Clarence C. Cook* (fig. 1), which provides vital information about Farrer's thematic concerns, proving him a maker of "pictures" and not simply "studies."[5] The drawing depicts the art critic, and a principal contributor to *The New Path,* as he writes in a cramped script that is frustratingly illegible to the viewer. The obsessively tight scrawl, perhaps a metaphor for the intense thought flowing from Cook's mind to the page, finds its equivalent throughout the crowded composition in which Cook himself is left barely enough space to wield the pen. Farrer's use of light to emphasize Cook's forehead enlists the familiar iconographic convention linking the intellect with creative production, as do the objects that surround him. Given Cook's espousal of Ruskinian theory, it is not surprising to discover references to Ruskin's ideals within this claustrophobic chamber—for instance, the names of Dante Gabriel Rossetti and J. M. W. Turner and images of William Holman Hunt's *The Light of the World* (fig. 2) and Albrecht Dürer's *Melencolia*—all of which insinuate that everything else packed into the composition has a role in conveying meaning. Thus, the seemingly anomalous portrait of the abolitionist John Brown at the upper right, and the small bone on the writing table, must surely carry some weight in discussing thematic substance.[6] Since, for example, Farrer's drawing of Cook (technically a *portrait d'apparat*) includes Brown's portrait, it may be assumed that the image alludes to Cook's support for the Union cause in the Civil War conflict.[7] Farrer, however, is known to have included Brown's portrait in another of his works, the unlocated *Evening Hours* that was shown at the National Academy of Design in 1861 and described as "imaginative" partly because it depicted portraits of Brown and

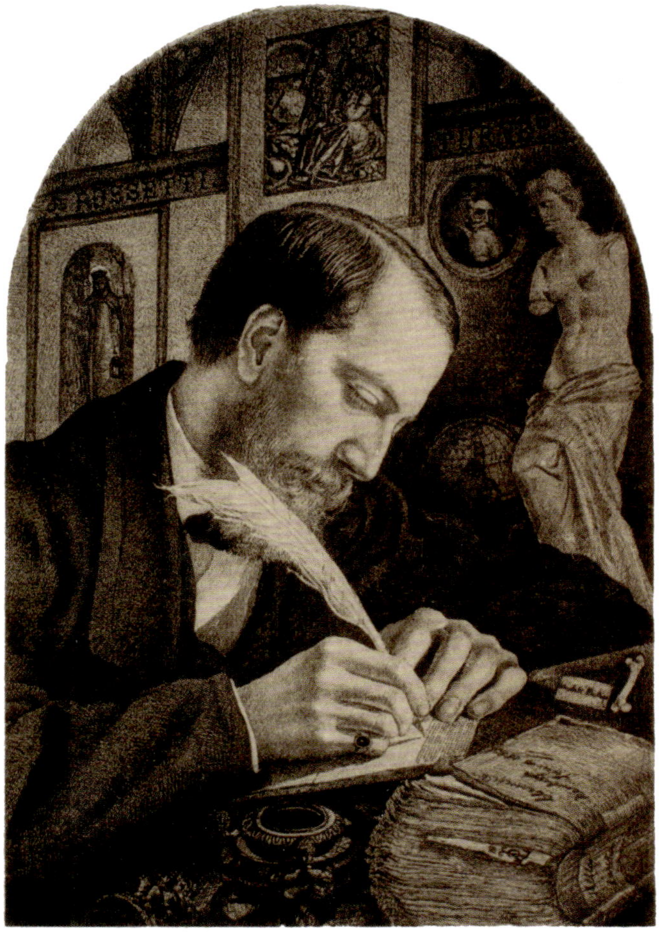

1. Thomas Charles Farrer, *Portrait of Clarence C. Cook*, 1861, pen and ink, reproduced as frontispiece to *Poems by Clarence Cook*, New York, 1902

George Washington in a domestic interior.[8] Thus in both works Brown's portrait may refer to Farrer's own politics, as later manifested in his service in the Union army in 1862. With such particulars in mind, Farrer's portrait of Cook may be interpreted as a visual manifesto that catalogs the aesthetic, thematic, and political concerns at the root of American Pre-Raphaelite production.

The "Work" of Art

Farrer's portraits of Cook and other members of his inner circle document his embrace of the concept of labor as a fundamental theme. This opinion is buttressed by Farrer's reading of a poem, "Work," at one of the Association's early meetings, in a didactic performance of sorts that may be interpreted as a reflection of Ruskin's fiercely moralizing views on the virtues of industrious and honest occupation.[9] As Ruskin wrote: "It is only by labour that thought can be made healthy, and only by thought that labour can be made happy, and the two cannot be separated with impunity."[10] Of primary relevance in this respect was the intensely laborious technique required by Ruskinian teaching. Truth was in the technique regardless of the subject portrayed. Beyond this, however, Farrer seems to have felt it especially necessary to underscore the ideal of toil by often depicting his artist and writer friends bent over their work, as in his portraits of Cook, John Henry Hill (plate 21), and Samuel Putnam Avery (fig. 3 in Ferber essay). Farrer's close relationship with the Hill family is well documented, but his long association with the engraver, collector, and influential art dealer Avery is less so and deserves closer examination.[11]

The preoccupation with the theme of work is reflected to a lesser extent in the art of others, as in Robert J. Pattison's *Portrait of John Henry Hill* (plate 72) and particularly in Robert Brandegee's precisely executed *Writing to Mother* (plate 1), which portrays his younger brother Henry deeply absorbed in drafting a letter, echoing a compositional format that reiterates those of Farrer's portraits of Cook, Avery, and John Henry Hill. Brandegee received his early art training from his aunt, Association member Sarah S. Tuthill, and then from either John William or John Henry Hill, and Thomas Farrer. The watercolor's meticulous stippling technique bespeaks Brandegee's labor and reinforces the sensibility of intense thought and practiced manual dexterity on the part of his young sitter. Moreover, the prominently placed apple at the table's edge may be an oblique reference to the carefully wrought still-life subjects of his instructors.

Yet another thread of consonant imagery is the subject of music making, a theme that arises primarily in the art of Farrer, whose *The Fiddler* (plate 20) and *Practicing Her Lesson* (plate 19; detail on p. 58) involve musicianship demanding practice and dedication. In this context work is defined as exertion, be it physical or mental, the results of which are either intellectual or material products. Similar imagery evoking mental absorption and/or manual skill prevails in works featuring women, as in Farrer's *Sketching from Nature* (plate 24) and *Woman Sewing* (plate 18) and Fidelia Bridges's *Laura Brown in a Wingchair* (plate 3). Even John William Hill, who did not ordinarily focus on the human figure, created a tender portrayal of his daughter at her needlework in the outdoors.[12]

A subtler take on the work motif appears in John William Hill's *West Nyack, New York* (plate 46), an eccentrically composed worm's-eye view across a lush, sunlit field leading to the artist's home and studio.[13] Carefully delineated Canada lilies dominate the foreground, forming the friezelike band that contributed to the painting's original title, *The Lilies of the Field*, under which it was exhibited at the American Watercolor Society in 1871. The initial title is taken from Matthew 6:28, which reads, "Consider the lilies of the field, how they grow; they toil not, neither

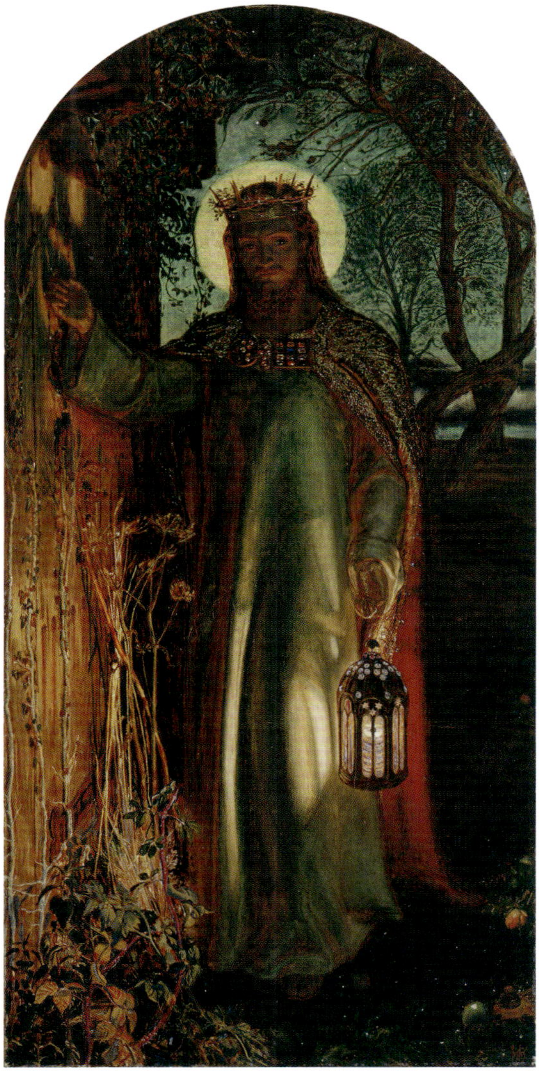

2. William Holman Hunt, *The Light of the World*, 1851–1853, oil on canvas, Manchester Art Gallery

do they spin." As Kathleen Foster has observed, the painting afforded Hill the opportunity to unite his two favored genres, still life and landscape.[14] What is more, its title invited viewers to assume that Hill had endowed the image with a level of symbolism beyond that which his work ordinarily suggested. Indeed, just the year before this watercolor was painted, both John William and John Henry Hill had been rebuked by the critic Stillman S. Conant, who praised their technical skills but nevertheless maintained that "both men are deficient in imagination; they draw the outward forms of what they see, but rarely interpret for us the spiritual import. The work of Mr. J. W. Hill is thus the perfection of imitation."[15] By juxtaposing the wildflowers with his working studio, Hill invested the image with notions of work and nature's beauty and inserted the "spiritual import" that Conant had found lacking in his art.

The Language of Flowers

Floral symbolism was commonly understood in Victorian culture, and this "language of flowers" was known on both sides of the Atlantic through poetry, prose, and numerous publications devoted to the subject.[16] The American Pre-Raphaelites do not seem to have used a specific set of symbolic floral meanings that would separate their truth-to-nature message from the standard floral symbolism of the era; nonetheless, there were particular flowers that seem to have been preferred by the group, such as fringed gentians (plates 27, 29, 30). The particular species portrayed (*Gentianopsis crinita*) is native to North America and blooms late in the year, usually from September through November. William Cullen Bryant had praised it in his 1832 poem "To the Fringed Gentian," in which the solitary flower's appearance when "the aged year is near his end" is likened to the coming of death. More pertinent, however, is Clarence Cook's sonnet "To the Fringed Gentian," published in the October 1865 issue of *The New Path*, which describes the flower's "maiden solitude" and "cloistered life" that prevail until the blue blossoms are discovered "between the pine-wood boughs." Similar to Bryant's poem, Cook's verses associate the flower with death—although, in this case, the flower triumphs: "Thine azure flowers should never fade nor die / But bloom, exhale and gain their native sky."[17] Henry Roderick Newman depicted the fringed gentian in a now-unlocated work that was published as a chromolithograph by Prang & Co. in 1868 (fig. 3). The chromo was highlighted in the company's Boston-based promotional journal in September 1868, in which it was described as "one of the careful and faithful representations of vegetable life in which the pre-Raphaelite school of artists in New York excel." The passage closed with a quotation from the *Chicago Republican*: "The whole is a sermon, — nay, better, a poem, — teaching of the presence of abounding life amid the ever-visible tokens of mortality. Artistically, nothing could be more perfect than the contrast of colors, — the living blue and green set off against the sober shades of the dead, decaying wood and leaves."[18] Here, again, the fringed gentian is interpreted as a vital sign of life that persists in the face of the dying year.

For the most part, the American Pre-Raphaelites portrayed humble wildflowers as evidence that the beauty of divine creation could be found in the most unassuming places. Once he settled in Florence in 1874, Newman concentrated on depicting Tuscan wildflowers, with special attention given to the anemone (plate 65).[19] Although no proof exists as to what specific meaning Newman may have attached to the anemone, the flower had enjoyed a long tradition as a symbol for sorrow and, in the Christian era, was associated particularly with the

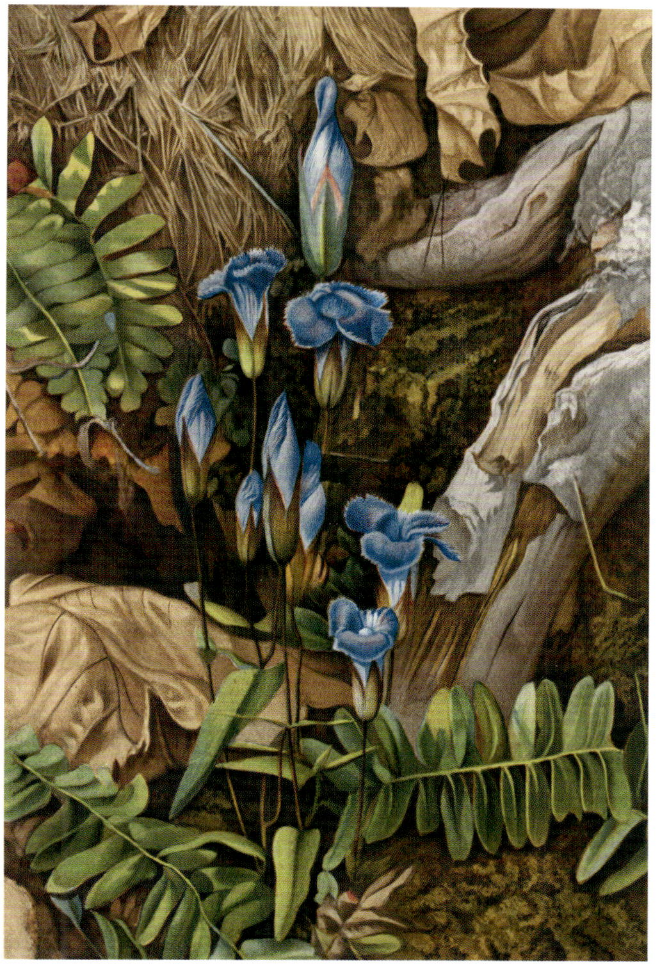

3. Henry Roderick Newman, *Fringed Gentian*, c. 1868, chromolithograph, Boston Public Library, Louis Prang & Company Collection

mourning Virgin Mary at the Crucifixion.[20] Royal W. Leith has suggested that Newman may have intended viewers to recognize this same meaning, noting that Newman's attention to Italian floral subjects may have derived from the fact that Florence's famed Duomo (itself a symbol of the city) is formally called Saint Mary of the Flower (Cattedrale di Santa Maria del Fiore).[21] Such veiled symbolism may also have extended to Newman's images of grapes and olives (plate 63), which call to mind the Christian signs of the Eucharist, the Annunciation, and peace.

The Metaphor of the Unweeded Garden

Yet another manner of constructing meaning is found in the American Pre-Raphaelites' occasional reliance on well-known works of art to create their own, a practice that closely relates their work to that of their British forerunners.

The prominent position of William Holman Hunt's *The Light of the World* (fig. 2) in Thomas Farrer's *Portrait of Clarence C. Cook* (fig. 1) indicates Farrer's likely familiarity with the first version of the painting that was shown at London's Royal Academy of Arts in 1854, where it inspired Ruskin to declare it "one of the very noblest works of sacred art ever produced in this or any other age."[22] The American art audience was primed to receive the painting favorably. *The Crayon* published John Lucas Tupper's poem in praise of it in 1855, and an 1856 article devoted lengthy passages to it.[23] The painting's esteem in America was reinforced by the display of a smaller version (Manchester Art Gallery) in the American Exhibition of British Art in New York in 1857 and Philadelphia in 1858, where it was generally admired by the public and received variously by the critics. It soon garnered additional celebrity when it was purchased by the noted New York collector John Wolfe (1821–1894).[24]

Apart from eliciting a large measure of respect for its religious significance, *The Light of the World* apparently attracted Ruskin's American followers because of its exquisite botanical detail. The 1856 article in *The Crayon* allotted considerable space to describing the setting in which Jesus is shown: "The scene is a waste orchard, the branches of the wild fruit-trees stand ghastly . . . ; while among the long grass, sprinkled with frosty spiculae, which shows the night has been keen, lies the unripe and abortive produce of the trees."[25] The writer's emphasis on barren fields coincides with a number of works in which the unproductive character of the landscape elements invokes metaphors equating a disorderly, unweeded garden with an uncultivated mind or spirit. This sensibility is plainly revealed in the titles of several works by William Trost Richards: *A Neglected Garden* (plate 73), *A Neglected Corner of the Wheatfield* (plate 80), and *And Some Fell Among Thorns* (fig. 5 in Lynford essay). Richards's religious intent is revealed in the title of the last-mentioned work, taken from the parable of the sower in Matthew 13:1–23 ("And others fell among thorns; and the thorns grew up and choked them").[26] In addition to the biblical references, it seems likely that the plays of William Shakespeare were fundamental to the understanding of this imagery.[27] Take, for instance, Hamlet's lament about the world, "tis an unweeded garden, / That grows to seed; things rank, and gross in nature, / Possess it merely" (*Hamlet*, act 1, scene 2), or Lear's crown of weeds that signifies his madness (*King Lear*, act 4, scene 4). Perhaps more relevant for the American audience of the 1860s, however, is the likelihood that such imagery recalled the untended, battle-scarred fields of both the North and South and thus was a metaphor for the disorder of war.

Hidden Symbolism Unveiled

William Holman Hunt's influence was also strongly felt with regard to hidden symbolism, through published descriptions of *The Awakening Conscience* (fig. 8 in

Barringer essay) and firsthand knowledge—as in the case of Thomas Farrer, who likely saw it at the 1854 London Royal Academy of Arts exhibition. Hunt's visual account of a fallen woman redeemed is orchestrated through a domestic setting overflowing with common household objects whose symbolic aggregate explicates her sinful status and the spiritual awakening of the painting's title. Farrer's finely detailed drawing *Practicing Her Lesson* (plate 19; detail on p. 58) demonstrates that his devotion to the symbolism of household minutiae is comparable to that found in Hunt's famous painting, an opinion supported by May Brawley Hill's comprehensive catalog of the contents of the room shown in the drawing.[28] General consensus holds that the parlor displayed is that of Edward Meek, the English cabinetmaker who lived on West Fifty-Second Street in Manhattan, where both Thomas Farrer and his brother Henry stayed shortly after their respective arrivals in the United States. The two brothers maintained close ties with the Meeks over the years; in 1877 Henry married the elder Meek daughter, Amelia Sarah.[29]

Unlike Hunt's *The Awakening Conscience*, a visual narrative focusing on a kept woman, Farrer's *Practicing Her Lesson* adopts a tamer approach and only hints at the presence of a visiting suitor (signified by the top hat and gloves resting on the piano). Both artists conveyed meaning through the sheet music in their respective works. Hunt signals that the "awakening" is prompted by Thomas Moore's "Oft in the Stilly Night"; Farrer imparts a trace of unease with an allusion to Vincenzo Bellini's popular opera *Norma*, a tale of the heroine's transcendence over thoughts of infanticide, suicide, and the murder of her lover.[30] The glum expression of the woman in Farrer's drawing, reflected in the circular mirror above the piano, conveys a sense of disquiet; it is frustratingly impossible to determine if this is a fictive narrative or if it relates to actual relationships Farrer observed in the Meek household. Moreover, the drawing's title raises the question about what lesson the woman really practices: is it merely the music at hand, or a lesson of significant moral concern? The two prints hanging on either side of the mirror, reproductions of Edwin Landseer's *Sanctuary* (left) and *At Bay* (right), add to the impression of female vulnerability in the context of romantic pursuit and resolution.

The significance of mirrors resurfaces in Farrer's *Self-Portrait, Sketching*, a drawing that presents a reversed view of the artist at work in the Meek household (plate 22). Although it is unseen, the mirror into which Farrer looks is nonetheless central to the composition inasmuch as it produces an alternative or inverted reality and is thus reminiscent of Hunt's use of a mirror image in *The Awakening Conscience*, which, in turn, is believed to have been influenced by Jan van Eyck's *Arnolfini Portrait* (fig. 4), where the artist (presumably) is reflected in a convex mirror that extends the pictorial space.[31] Having entered the London National Gallery's collection in 1842, the highly acclaimed Van Eyck panel has also been cited as a possible influence on Farrer (as well as Hunt), who had likely seen the painting.

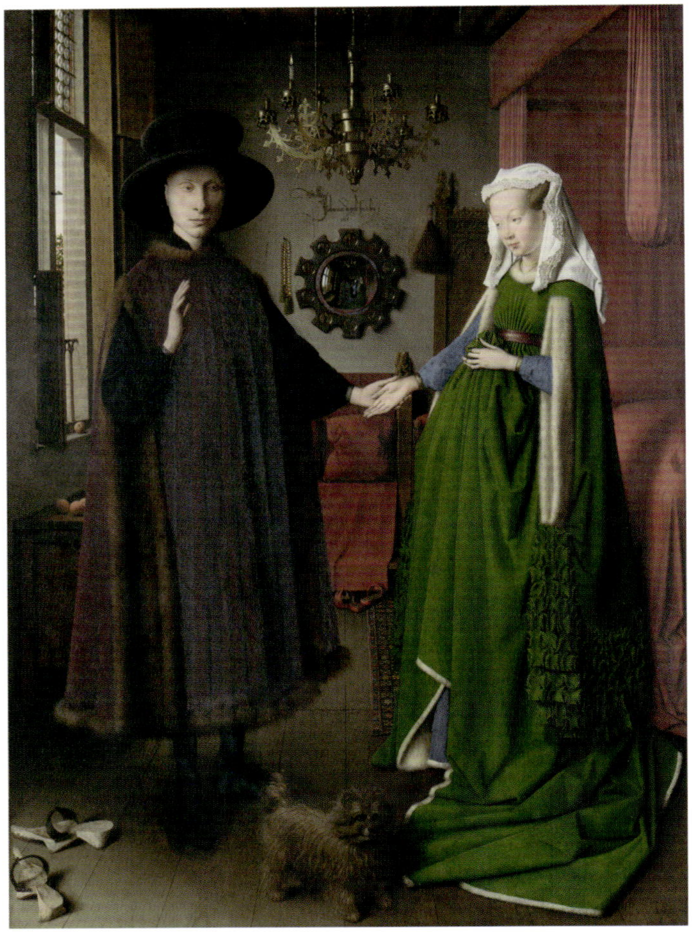

Indeed, the meticulously detailed interior, steeply slanted floor plane, and distortions caused by Farrer's acutely angled point of view replicate characteristics of the fifteenth-century Flemish paintings admired by the British Pre-Raphaelites. With this, the true nature of perceived reality is interrogated, for the mirror image that we see is really a reversed version of the truth, a product of reflected light and then set down on paper.[32]

In addition, and by implication, the hidden symbolism so deeply associated with the *Arnolfini Portrait* is inevitably bound up in current assessments of Farrer's aesthetics, as demonstrated by interpretations of his *Woman Sewing*, a drawing that invites comparison with Eyckian forerunners (plate 18).[33] The sitter has again been identified as one of the Meek sisters, who sews in the same bedroom that is seen in reverse in the background of Farrer's *Self-Portrait, Sketching*. Each object resonates with meaning, especially the reproduction of Raphael's *Madonna della*

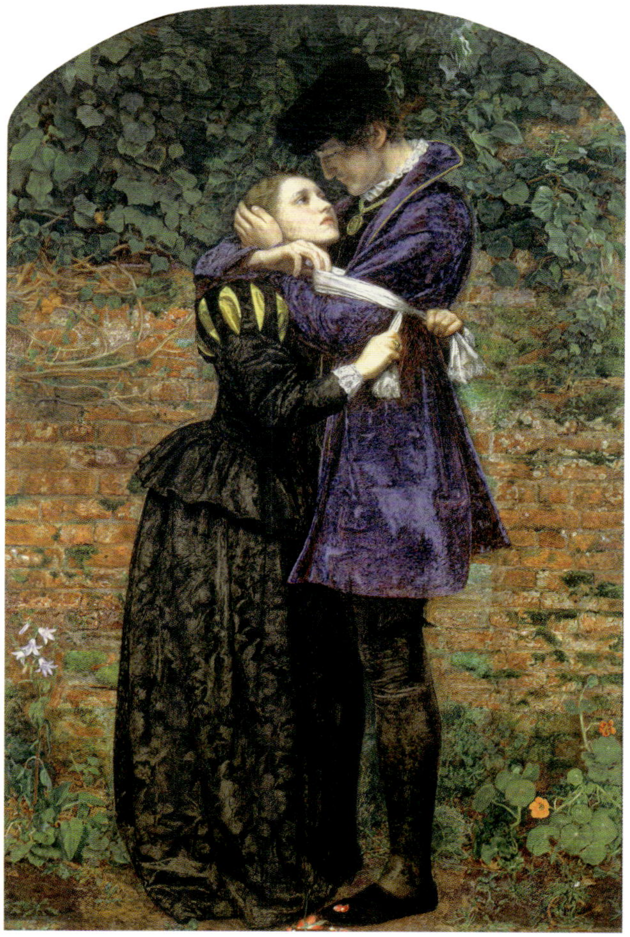

Sedia (c. 1514, Palatine Gallery, Palazzo Pitti, Florence) and the grapevines framing the window, which lend a Christian sensibility to the image of the young woman.

Images of Separation and Loss

4. Jan van Eyck, *The Arnolfini Portrait (Portrait of Giovanni[?] Arnolfini and His Wife)*, 1434, oil on oak, National Gallery, London, Bought, 1842

5. John Everett Millais, *A Huguenot, on Saint Bartholomew's Day, Refusing to Shield Himself from Danger by Wearing the Roman Catholic Badge*, 1851–1852, oil on canvas, The Makins Collection

Just as he did with the Landseers in *Practicing Her Lesson* and the Raphael in *Woman Sewing*, Farrer used the "picture-within-a-picture" device to augment content in *Gone! Gone!* (plate 12). Here the pain of loss is underscored at the upper right by a print after John Everett Millais's *A Huguenot, on Saint Bartholomew's Day, Refusing to Shield Himself from Danger by Wearing the Roman Catholic Badge*, hereafter referred to as *The Huguenot Lover* (fig. 5).[34] Millais's art, like Hunt's, received considerable attention in the United States in the 1850s and 1860s despite the fact that none of his major works had yet crossed the Atlantic by that time.[35] Millais's painting was, however, available in print form and that, in tandem with the painting's fame, supports the opinion that many Americans were familiar with the image and its meaning.[36] Inspired by Giacomo Meyerbeer's opera *Les Huguenots*, the painting shows a young Catholic woman entreating her Protestant (Huguenot) beloved to wear a white band on his arm, falsely indicating his Catholic faith, in order to escape death at the hands of French Catholics in an infamous massacre that took place in Paris on Saint Bartholomew's Day in 1572.[37] The image elicits a sense of impending tragedy as the doomed lovers gaze into each other's eyes with the knowledge that his refusal to betray his faith will likely result in his death. Although *Gone! Gone!* eschews such narrative specificity, several elements—the woman's obvious sorrow, the twilight hour, the autumnal season, the Millais print, and, of course, the painting's title—indicate separation and loss. The comforting Bible verses from Matthew 11:28 inscribed on the frame reinforce the impression of bereavement.[38]

Although it is tempting to conclude that the grief portrayed in *Gone! Gone!* relates to the Civil War, the painting was displayed the month before Fort Sumter was fired upon, at the National Academy of Design annual exhibition that opened in March 1861. Nonetheless, the painting does appear to refer to the national divisions that led to the war. Farrer likely painted the work after he returned to the United States from England in November or December 1860, fresh from seeing British paintings that may have inspired him to turn to the oil medium. The final weeks of 1860 were eventful ones; Americans witnessed the secession of South Carolina in December, a fateful move that precipitated the secession of Mississippi, Florida, Alabama, Georgia, Louisiana, and Texas over the next two months. By February 9, 1861, the Confederate States of America were established, thus officially sundering the nation. In this context, *Gone! Gone!*, with its powerful message of separation and loss, must be considered to be Farrer's artistic response to the political ruptures that ultimately steered the country to war.[39]

Other artists in the American Pre-Raphaelite orbit also addressed the issue of war, often opting to use the female figure rather than more straightforward military scenes. The landscape specialist Aaron Draper Shattuck adopted a conversation-piece format to portray his wife, firstborn child (William), and mother in the parlor of the Shattucks' summer home in Great Barrington, Massachusetts (plate 88).[40] Through a variety of strategies—hidden symbolism, pictures-within-the-picture, and a group portrait of three generations of his family—Shattuck created a pictorial essay extolling the sanctity of the home and its enduring importance during the Civil War. Major indicators of this theme are the prints hanging on the wall: Achille-Louis Martinet's *Virgin and Child* (after Paul Delaroche, c. 1850s) and the Barlow mezzotint after Millais's *The Huguenot Lover*, which sets the tone for a Civil War interpretation.[41]

Shattuck's use of *The Huguenot Lover* at a time when so many men were away from home establishes the theme of separation that is tacitly reiterated by the absence of the husband/father/son in the Shattuck family group.[42] More germane to a specific Civil War reading, however, is the rosary on the table beneath the Millais print, a curious object to be found in a Protestant household, but one which is thought to refer to Shattuck's close friend, the poet Fitz-James O'Brien (1828–1862), who died of wounds received when fighting in the Union army and to whom the rosary is believed to have belonged.

William John Hennessy offered a more overt statement about the losses suffered by those who remained at home during the war. He first addressed the subject in 1866 in a work titled *Mon Brave*, described in *The American Art Journal* as a "beautiful conceit" depicting "the widow of a soldier kissing his portrait which is hanging on the wall."[43] Hennessy's American career ended in 1870 when he settled in London.[44] In January 1871 he displayed another painting titled *Mon Brave* (plate 25) in an exhibition benefiting French peasants, this time placing the image in the context of the Franco-Prussian War. If the mourning dress and the woman's gesture were not enough to convey the grim narrative of loss, then one has only to examine Hennessy's exploitation of floral symbolism to validate this idea; the laurel leaves atop the portrait confirm the soldier's heroism, the white roses signify chastity and love, the forget-me-nots are emblems of lasting devotion, and the iris (*fleur-de-lis*) symbolizes France. The model, with her flowing golden hair and trancelike state (reinforcing the underlying necrophilic mood), bears close resemblance to the women in the works of Millais and Dante Gabriel Rossetti. The composition also shares specific connections with George Scharf's (1788–1860) 1854 illustration for John Keats's poem "Isabella; or The Pot of Basil," in which the mourning Isabella is shown similarly posed at a prie-dieu against the backdrop of a curtained bedstead.[45]

Antediluvian Histories

A previously unexplored aspect of American Pre-Raphaelite iconography is rooted in the burgeoning interest in the sciences that swept through Europe and the United States in the nineteenth century.[46] Geology and paleontology were especially popular as scientists, philosophers, and clerics alike attempted to solve the mysteries surrounding the history of creation, while simultaneously endeavoring to reconcile religious belief with scientific discovery. Ruskin himself was devoted to the study of geology from early childhood and firmly believed that the secrets of divine creation were contained in the rocky crevices and fissures of the earth.[47] The fascination with geology was manifested in several works exhibited in the 1857–1858 American Exhibition of British Art, most notably Ruskin's *Fragment of the Alps* (plate 84) and John Brett's *Glacier of Rosenlaui* (fig. 6), the latter of which

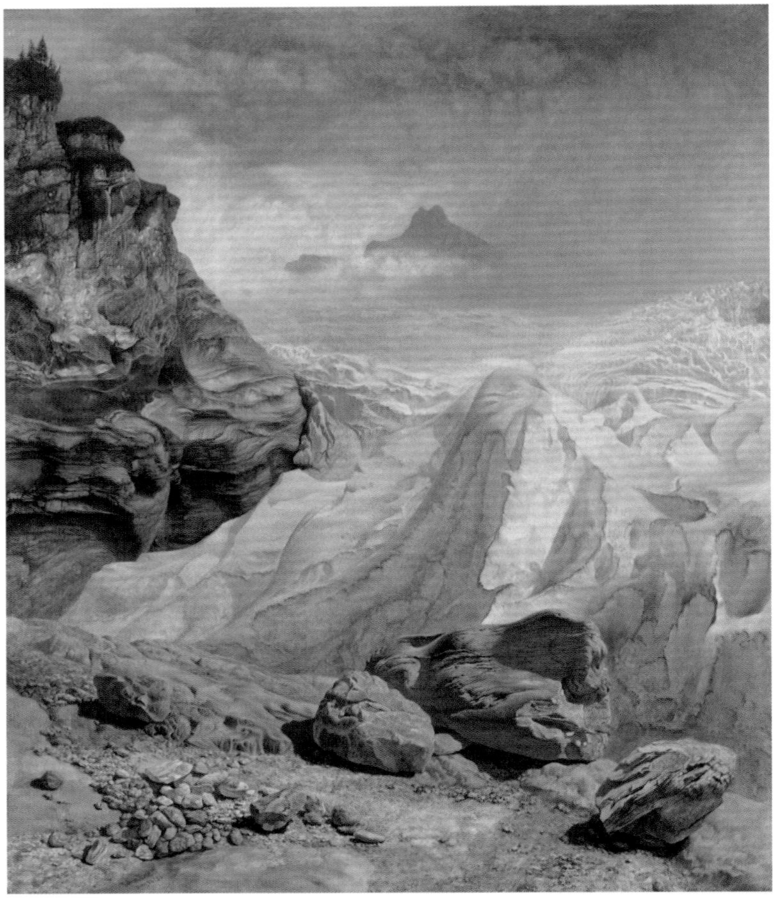

roused a Boston critic to maintain that "if we only knew the language in which time and the elements write, we could surely find here not only 'sermons in stones' but whole antediluvian histories, maybe, in the cerulean cells of the glacier and upon the cold and expressive faces of its adamantine walls."[48]

Perhaps the most compelling testimony to the importance of scientific investigation within the American Pre-Raphaelite circle is that two geologists, Clarence King and James Terry Gardner, were charter members of the Association. Despite King's position as secretary of the group, his (and Gardner's) activity was brief; the two joined the California Geological Survey in the spring of 1863, a move that marked the beginning of illustrious careers for each. King, who had also studied with the internationally renowned scientist Louis Agassiz (1807–1873), was appointed US Geologist for the Geological Exploration of the Fortieth Parallel in 1868, and was the first director of the United States Geological Survey. Gardner was chief topographer for the Fortieth Parallel Survey and, later, director of the

State Survey of New York. Even though King and Gardner were rarely in direct contact with their fellow members of the Association after 1863, King's subsequent fame doubtless acted as a persuasive reminder of the scientific component attached to Ruskin's theories. What is more, art itself was integral to documenting the findings of the geological surveys. John Henry Hill was a staff artist for King's Fortieth Parallel Survey and painted *Shoshone Falls* (private collection) on the spot, from the campsite overlooking the falls on the Snake River in Idaho where the survey team spent ten days.[49] Hill's attention to rock formations persisted, as shown in the treatment of the boulders in the foreground of *Lake George* (plate 34) and in *Natural Bridge, Virginia* (plate 35), in which the towering geologic structure stands in testimony to the powerful movement of ancient waters over the centuries.

Prior to joining King's survey, Hill's geological interests had already materialized in his art, occasionally revealing the Ruskinian tendency to allegorize landscape elements. In *Modern Painters* Ruskin had devoted lengthy passages to rocks, which he called the "materials of mountains," and, after classifying them according to three types, he concluded: "It can hardly be necessary to point out how these natural ordinances seem to be intended to teach us the great truths which are the basis of all political science; . . . and how, even if the knowledge of these processes [formation] be denied to us, that present aspect may in itself seem no imperfect image of the various states of mankind."[50] The trap rock of the title of Hill's *A Study of Trap Rock (Buttermilk Falls)* (plate 26) refers not to a place-name but to a type of igneous rock that, according to Ruskin, represented the "perfect state of brotherhood and strength in which each character is clearly distinguished, separately perfected, and employed in its proper place and office."[51] In this context an additional meaning can be proposed based on Hill's inclusion of the small figure of an artist at the lower right who has been identified as Thomas Charles Farrer. Both Hill and Farrer were admirers of Ruskin; theirs was a brotherhood devoted to truth to nature, and it seems likely that Hill intended to liken Farrer to that solid rock surrounding him as he works from nature, "employed in [his] proper place and office."

6. John Brett, *Glacier of Rosenlaui*, 1856, oil on canvas, Tate, London, Purchased 1946

Ruskin also proposed that the earth's past and future could be ascertained from studying its contemporary appearance. Accordingly, he instructed his readers to "try always, whenever you look at a form, to see the lines in it which have the power over its past fate and will have power over its futurity."[52] This idea registers strongly in John William Hill's *Fawn's Leap, Catskill Mountains* (plate 38). Situated in Kaaterskill Clove in the heart of the Catskills, Fawn's Leap was a popular site for such Hudson River School artists as Asher B. Durand and John F. Kensett and was an attraction for a growing number of tourists whose interests often focused on exploring geologic formations. Here, the rushing torrent of water at the center of the composition is an instrument of change as it carves through the rock, shaping and reshaping it over time. And, while the two small figures in the foreground may refer to tourism, Hill's ultimate intention may have been to emphasize mankind's powerlessness in the face of the ever-changing forces of nature. In this light, it can be imagined that Hill selected the scene with Ruskin's words sounding in his mind and may also have taken a cue from Thomas Farrer, who had painted the same subject a year earlier.

The ineluctable sovereignty of time is a fundamental concept that unifies the geologic imagery in the works of the American Pre-Raphaelites. The notion of time exerts significant impact in several works by Charles Herbert Moore, whose conversion to Ruskinian methods doubtless came under the influence of Farrer.[53] Before then, however, Moore had already embarked on a promising career in New York, where he very likely saw Ruskin's *Fragment of the Alps* (plate 84) and Brett's *Glacier of Rosenlaui* (fig. 6) in the American Exhibition of British Art. By 1863 Moore had officially declared his allegiance to Ruskin's theories when he became a member of the Association, and with the publication of an important article in *The New Path*.[54] It is reasonable to assume that Moore's attention would have been drawn to "Naturalism and Genius," an article that appeared immediately after his in the same issue of *The New Path* and devoted lengthy commentary to Ruskin's *Study of a Block of Gneiss* (as *Fragment of the Alps* was then known). The author, identified as William James Stillman, had unreserved praise for the watercolor and concluded that "there is no American landscapist, living or dead, whose work would be at all an equivalent."[55] In a manner of speaking, Stillman posed a challenge that Moore willingly accepted, for his small watercolor *Rocks by the Water* (plate 55) must be seen as the American reply to Ruskin's boulder.

Both Ruskin's and Moore's watercolors feature large rocks known as erratic boulders—massive, isolated chunks of stone that have no material relation to the bedrock on which they sit. Long thought to be evidence of the biblical flood, erratic boulders were later understood as proof of glacial movement, a theory generally credited to the British geologist Charles Lyell and promoted by Louis Agassiz and Clarence King.[56] Moore's boulder, unlike Ruskin's, possesses a strange, unnerving quality. It registers (perhaps intentionally, perhaps not) as an ancient relic, possibly the huge skull of a long-extinct animal that once roamed the antediluvian earth. Such an association gains credence if Moore's Swedenborgian upbringing is considered. A member of the "New Church," Moore was trained from childhood to find correspondences between the worldly and spiritual spheres. In light of the growing scholarly and popular interest in geology and paleontology, and a desire to reconcile religion with science, it is not difficult to understand the conception of rocks as "bones of the earth" in theories of creation. Ruskin alludes to this idea in *Modern Painters*: "The keenness of the artist's eye may almost precisely be tested by the degree in which he perceives the curves that give them [mountain peaks] their strength and grace, and in harmony with which the flakes of granite are bound together, *like the bones of the jaw of a saurian* [emphasis added]."[57]

Even more curious than Moore's *Rocks by the Water* is his *Hudson River, Above Catskill* (plate 51), a scene that has been identified as the same shoreline that appears in Thomas Farrer's *A Buckwheat Field on Thomas Cole's Farm* (plate 13).[58] From this fact and the strange conjunction of the oarless boat, the pristine apple, and the horse's skull, Patricia Junker has argued that *Hudson River, Above Catskill* is not only an allusion to Cole's famed four-part series *The Voyage of Life* (1842, National Gallery of Art, Washington) but also a memorial to the recently assassinated Abraham Lincoln, whose death occurred only days after Lee's surrender at Appomattox in the shade of an apple tree. Such an interpretation is temptingly convincing and is persuasive enough to confirm that there is more to Moore's Ruskinian dedication to nature than meets the eye. Indeed, it is yet another instance of hidden symbolism, albeit symbolism expressed in a distinctly American vernacular.

The horse's skull and other bones scattered along the shore in Moore's painting are telling reminders of the tiny bone that sits on Clarence Cook's writing table in the Farrer portrait (fig. 1, above). The presence of that seemingly incidental thing is a potent indicator of the layers of meaning embedded in even the simplest of objects in the art of the American Pre-Raphaelites. Their commitment to Ruskin's call for truth to nature took priority in their aesthetics, yet their motives were also guided by the events and beliefs of their time and place. Whether in the context of the Civil War, in the sciences attached to the exploration of the American continent, or in the imperative to redirect the course of American art, theirs was certainly an art of thought and imagination.

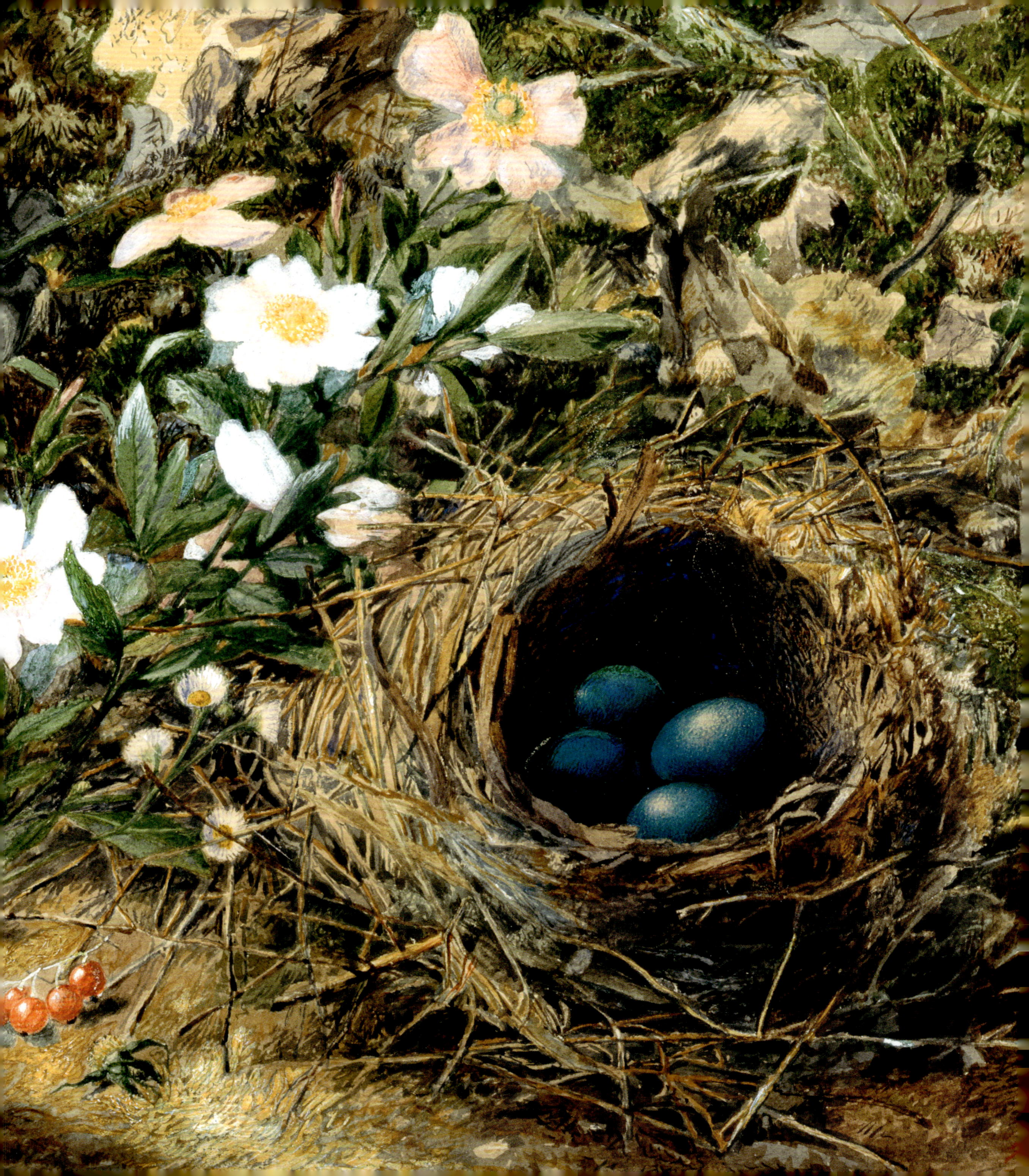

A Knowing Look: The American Pre-Raphaelite Still Life

MARK D. MITCHELL

John William Hill, *Bird's Nest and Dog Roses*, 1867 (detail, plate 45)

John Ruskin's most distinct contribution to American art came in still life, a field that the English Pre-Raphaelites—forerunners of the American movement—barely considered, but that preoccupied Ruskin himself. In this most empirical of genres, Ruskin invited a fresh, intimate appreciation of nature, a subject that had been interwoven with American identity since the beginning of the nineteenth century.

To define Ruskin's impact on mid-nineteenth-century American art more broadly can feel like an exercise in futility, because his influence was diverse and seemingly ubiquitous. In the 1850s, his name became a byword for the direct and detailed study of nature, ranging from the expansive mandate to look carefully at real objects, to very specific directives about style and subject matter. Within any one of Ruskin's many books, his ideas can appear inconsistent or even contradictory. Greater understanding of Ruskin's meaning for American artists may be discovered by the study of their work—what they actually created—in response to his vision as a critic, teacher, and artist. Still life offers an ideal forum for such comparison and one that was uniquely meaningful in the American context.

And yet, Ruskin's was not the only current running through American still life at midcentury, nor was it the primary one. A second dimension of American Pre-Raphaelite still life was its selective interaction with mainstream practice. In particular, around 1848—roughly the same moment that Ruskin's ideas gained recognition in the United States—a new school of colorful, sensual still life ascended that was inspired by popular German Romanticism and accelerated

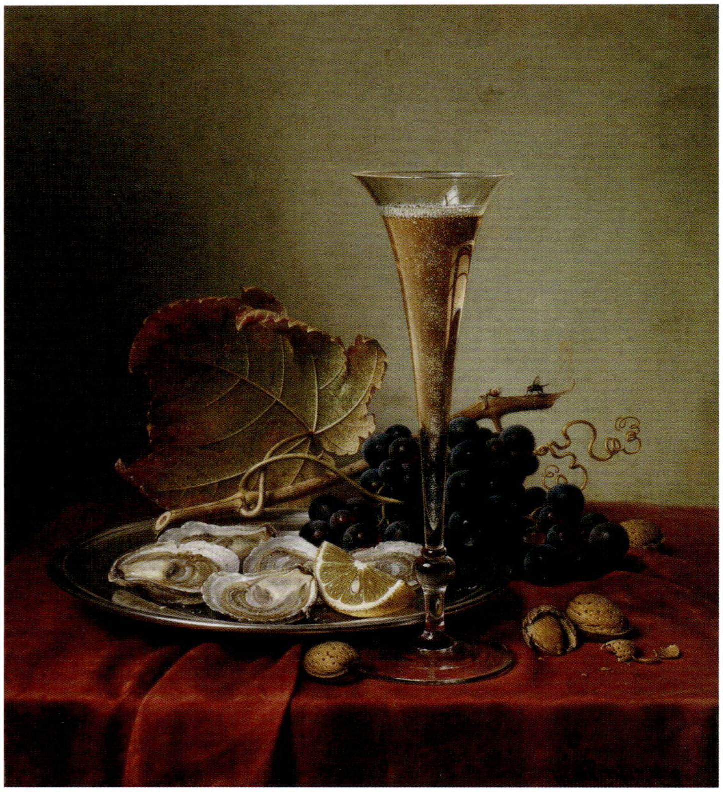

by a massive wave of German immigration. Artists such as Johann Wilhelm Preyer were widely admired in America during midcentury, and works such as his *Still Life* (fig. 1), owned by the leading Baltimore collector William T. Walters, shaped the prevailing culture against which the Ruskinian artists rebelled. Both groups shared commitments to detail and colorism, and yet their underlying principles were vastly different: consumption versus contemplation. Their uneasy cohabitation in the realms of taste and criticism defined American still life of the period. The practice of American Pre-Raphaelite still life was therefore not simply that of a small, like-minded brotherhood in isolation, but rather an assortment of interpretations of Ruskin's ideas that were in constant negotiation with the era's prevailing taste for lush sensuality.[1]

Ruskin's influence on American still life came in three primary forms, categorized here as Word, Image, and Model. Word refers to Ruskin's widely read books *Modern Painters* (1843–1860) and *The Elements of Drawing* (1857), which offered Americans compelling explanations of the ideal relationship between an artist and nature with anecdotes and examples to emulate. The second category, Image, encompasses Ruskin's own watercolors and drawings, which were intermittently available to Americans either in printed reproductions or in person in collections and exhibitions, including the revelatory 1857–1858 American Exhibition of British Art that toured eastern cities and featured Ruskin's *Fragment of the Alps* (plate 84).[2] The third, Model, refers to how Ruskin directed his readers to specific artists and artworks as samples of the attributes he admired. In this last category, alongside his primary inspiration, the landscapist Joseph Mallord William Turner, Ruskin held up still-life and watercolor specialist William Henry Hunt as a template of best practice. The remarkable disparity of appearance, technique, and subject between the works of the many American artists inspired by Ruskin may best be explained by these differing sources of inspiration, not least in the genre of still life.

Word: Reading Ruskin in America

American artists first knew Ruskin through his books. Works such as John Henry Hill's watercolor *Fringed Gentians* (plate 29) and *Gentians* (plate 30)—gentians being a recurring synonym Ruskin used in his writing for the color blue—may be read like passages from Ruskin translated into an American vernacular, an American edition.[3] Educated by his father, John William Hill, in Nyack, New York—notably outside of New York City, though not far—at the family homestead where he resided for most of his life (and which is the subject of the elder Hill's *West Nyack, New York*, plate 46), John Henry was immersed in art and Ruskinian aesthetics from a young age and already exhibiting at the National Academy of Design's annual exhibition at sixteen. In 1860, he wrote to the already loyal Ruskinian Thomas Charles Farrer, with remarkable precocity three years before the founding of their Association for the Advancement of Truth in Art, "I am confident the Preraphaelites school will make steady progress, and every succeeding exhibition will show marked advance on all former effort."[4] Like Farrer, John Henry Hill would become a founding and active member of the Association. A primary exponent of American Pre-Raphaelite practice in both watercolor and oil, young Hill adapted Ruskin's text in a work that offers a useful example to understand the kind of active reading manifested in American Pre-Raphaelite still life.

1. Johann Wilhelm Preyer, *Still Life*, 1859, oil on canvas, The Walters Art Museum, Baltimore

Fall has arrived in Hill's *Fringed Gentians* (plate 29) watercolor of around 1867. The late-blooming gentian has peaked, the sumac has turned bright red, and the field grasses behind them begin to dry yellow.[5] Hill's low gentian, seen from above, is framed in full, setting its saturated flowers against the busy, hatched, more muted tapestry of the grassy hillside.[6] "In general, all banks are beautiful things," Ruskin instructed.[7] Dislocation of space crops the branches of the sumac in the foreground along the bottom edge, setting it below the relatively low-growing gentian, but contrasting their forms and dense primary colors to frame a satisfying composition.

The climbing perspective of the watercolor's grassy background reinforces the work as a Ruskinian paean to gentians (two engravings of which are found in Ruskin's "rudimentary" series at the Ruskin School of Drawing, now in the collection of the Ashmolean Museum at Oxford, and discussion of which appears in *Modern Painters*), but transfers it to an American context with the distinction of the American-native fringed variety. Hill respects, equally, Ruskin's guidance on the twisting forms of leaves in his instructional *The Elements of Drawing* and the sensation of exploring a field in the Swiss Alps where the grass grows "deep and free." "And we may, perhaps, at last know the meaning of those quiet words of the 147th Psalm, 'He maketh grass to grow upon the mountains.'"[8] Such religiosity was a cardinal aspect of Ruskin's precepts, and underlay his artistic philosophy.

Ultimately, Ruskin's teachings manifest in Hill's painting in medium and method, as well as subject. Although Hill also painted an oil version of the subject (plate 27), watercolor was Ruskin's preferred medium, admired for its control and capacity to convey detail. The qualities of discipline and technical rigor are evident in the masterful watercolor *Three Eggs* (plate 17), recently reattributed to Thomas Charles Farrer, that embodies one of Ruskin's challenges to artists in *The Elements of Drawing*: the depiction of round forms in three dimensions.[9] Natural, living context was Ruskin's directive, however, for sustaining objects' connection to divine creation—evident in Hill's meticulous and delicate *Waterlilies* (plate 31)—rather than presenting them indoors on a domestic tabletop, long a convention of still life. In both cases, Ruskin's words provided a map to his ideas that could be followed closely, and often were.

Image: Translating Ruskin's Art

As John Henry Hill relied on Ruskin's text, so Charles Herbert Moore relied on his art. Only Farrer seems to have followed Ruskin's example more closely, and yet so little of Farrer's still-life work remains that we struggle to appreciate his contribution to the field. Moore's art, on the other hand—combined with his long service as an instructor and, later, professor and museum director at Harvard (which paralleled Ruskin's teaching and collection development at Oxford), and his personal relationship with Ruskin—presents a strong record of just how closely one could emulate the British critic.[10] At the time, most Americans read Ruskin's writings fairly loosely, as a source of general inspiration and validation for the primacy of visual perception over artistic convention, but Moore hewed to Ruskin's own art as his model and was heralded as a savior in the pages of the American Pre-Raphaelites' official mouthpiece, *The New Path*.[11] For such uncompromising zeal, however, Moore suffered poverty during the 1860s and would later rely on his teaching salary and directorship of Harvard's museum.[12]

The similarity of Moore's watercolor *Rocks by the Water* (plate 55) to Ruskin's *Fragment of the Alps* offers a prominent instance of direct emulation of Ruskin's artistic example. The inclusion of *Fragment* in the 1857–1858 exhibition of British paintings that toured the United States—the show that introduced Pre-Raphaelitism to American audiences—and the painting's acquisition by the young scholar Charles Eliot Norton render it an important, documented example for admirers such as Moore.[13] Ruskin's boulder of metamorphic gneiss describes the formative powers of nature to create stone and raise mountains, as well as those of erosion and gravity to bring them down. Ruskin felt that in describing an object, the artist must convey its past, present, and future.[14] His *Fragment* does just that, witnessing the geological forces that formed the gneiss, recording its precariously balanced present, and suggesting its future erosion with fractures and wear.

Moore chose a strikingly similar subject for *Rocks by the Water*—evidently an homage to Ruskin's *Fragment*—yet its granite is more durable than Ruskin's gneiss.[15] Moore created *Rocks by the Water* at the time when he was in communication with Norton, who owned Ruskin's work, and also around when Norton invited Moore to join the Harvard faculty.[16] He could hardly have conceived a better means to explore Ruskin's method than to emulate one of the British critic's most famous works in the United States, and yet he appears to explore a different aspect, translating Ruskin's ideas from his art, as John Henry Hill did from his writing, to a discernibly American context.

The relationship between the two watercolors is no less overt for Moore's variations from Ruskin's example, as if he were deliberately illuminating the format's range of expressive potential by contrasting the type and character of stone, landscape, weather, perspective, technique, and palette. Likely located along the coast of New York or Connecticut, Moore's boulder was deposited at this site by a retreating glacier during the last ice age, seemingly immutable and immobile, rather than balancing precariously after tumbling down a mountainside as Ruskin's has. In seemingly every aspect, Moore set his practice and his national landscape apart, even as he paid tribute to Ruskin with a watercolor that would have specifically evoked *Fragment of the Alps* in the minds of American viewers. Moore's project was therefore as much an exploration or extension of Ruskin's vision as it was an homage.

Model: Looking with Ruskin

As a gentleman and a critic, Ruskin did not want to be perceived as a self-interested professional artist, so he instead directed his readers' attention to the works of other artists whom he admired. In still life, that meant William Henry Hunt, whose watercolors Ruskin's father had collected and which may have helped to

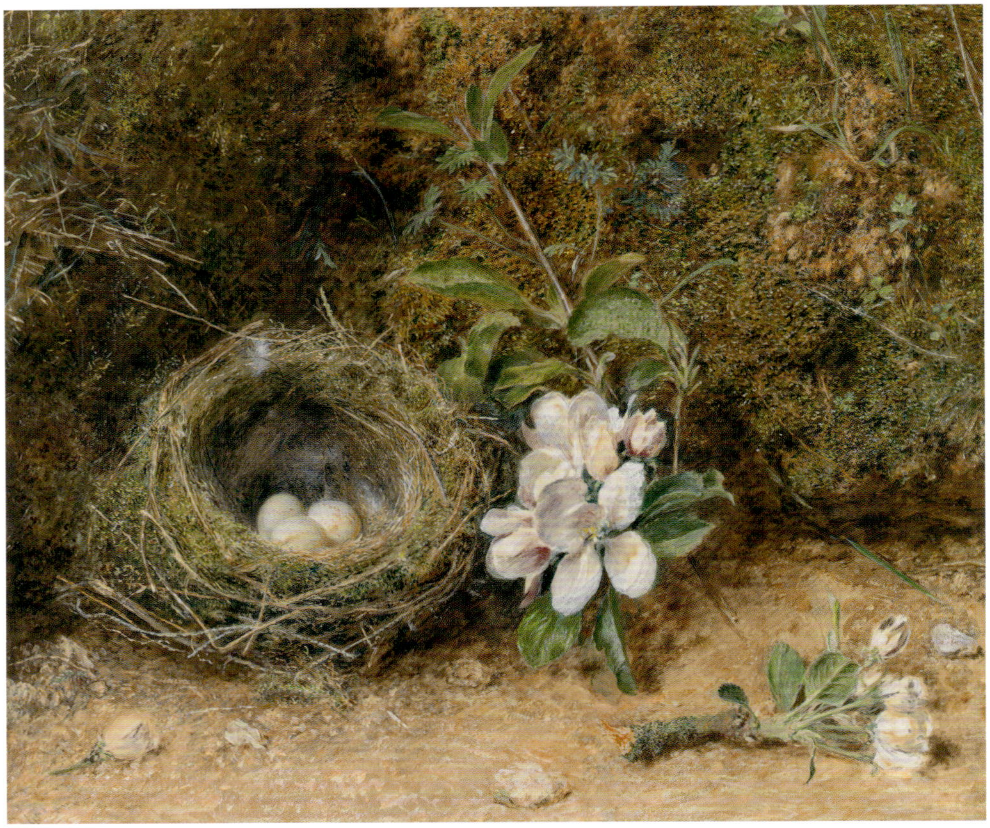

shape his sensibility.[17] Even late in life, Ruskin displayed one of Hunt's still lifes over the mantel in his bedroom, granting it remarkable prominence amid his large holding of J. M. W. Turner landscapes. Ruskin assessed Hunt as "the best painter of still life, I believe, that ever existed."[18]

It is remarkable, then, that John William Hill, whose works often emulate Hunt's, reportedly stood apart from his country's Pre-Raphaelites, as Hunt had from the English brotherhood.[19] Like Hunt, Hill was Ruskin's senior, if only by seven years, but a generation older than his peers in the Association for the Advancement of Truth in Art. Hill's *Bird's Nest and Dog Roses* (plate 45) is nearly a copy of one of Hunt's works, and yet Hill's work is bright and lively when compared with Hunt's emphasis on texture and refinement.[20] In most other contexts, Hill would play the role of the disciplined describer, but when compared with Hunt's work, his watercolor appears comparatively dynamic in handling and brilliant in color. In drawing, his son John Henry Hill's works, such as *Thrush's Nest* (plate 36), more closely approximate Hunt's fine orchestration of lines. That both father and son looked so closely to Hunt's example speaks volumes about Ruskin's impact.

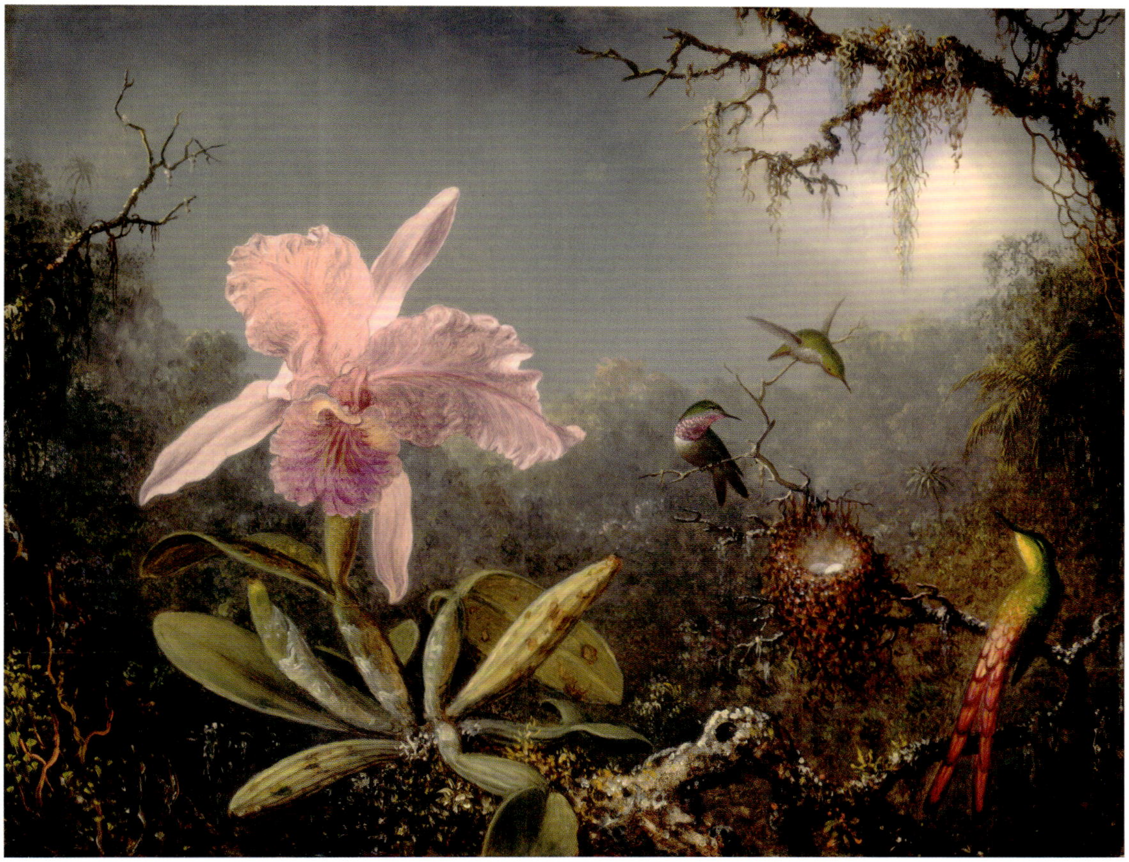

To spend time with Hunt's finest watercolors, such as *Bird's Nest with Sprays of Apple Blossoms* (fig. 2), is to marvel at his meticulous process and control of his medium, the pillars of Ruskinism, and his ideal of delicacy. Charles Herbert Moore would later credit John William Hill's influence for the widespread use of similar compositions by the other artists in their circle.[21] The affectation of Hunt's still-life formula, however, is a striking violation of Ruskin's tenets: this gathering of a bird's nest with flowers and fruits along the edge of a path or roadway that rises in the background into the mossy bank. Despite its impression as a study from nature, Hunt's practice was far more elaborate than it seems, including in-studio reconstructions and confabulations of miscellaneous substitute materials into the scenes from which he actually painted indoors—and, yes, on a tabletop.[22]

2. William Henry Hunt, *Bird's Nest with Sprays of Apple Blossoms*, c. 1847, watercolor, pen and black ink, gouache, and graphite on paper, Yale Center for British Art, New Haven, CT, Paul Mellon Collection

3. Martin Johnson Heade, *Cattleya Orchid and Three Hummingbirds*, 1871, oil on wood, National Gallery of Art, Washington, Gift of The Morris and Gwendolyn Cafritz Foundation

Most often, however, Hunt's compositions are smaller and simpler, usually contrasting just two central forms (a "contrastive harmony," in the artist's terms)—typically, different kinds of fruit—to vary colors, textures, and morphology, a model followed by Hill's *Apples and Plums* (plate 47).[23] Hunt's *Bird's*

Nest with Sprays of Apple Blossoms, however, is larger and more ambitious, and its forcefulness and sophistication command greater consideration of its visual analogies and implied narrative. Hill's *Bird's Nest and Dog Roses* does not seem to reach a similar level of metaphor; neither, in fairness, do most of Hunt's smaller compositions. Instead, they concentrate the viewer's attention on a single juxtaposition of texture, color, and form that collectively gratifies the senses and dramatizes their differences. Even in these artists' smaller scenes, however, such as Henry Farrer's early *Pink Rose* (plate 10), which echoes Hunt's *Study of a Rose* (1835, Fitzwilliam Museum, Cambridge University), their subjects' symbolic aspects are at times more prominent: here, the fleeting life of beauty.

Hunt's legacy is evident in works such as the American Martin Johnson Heade's depictions of tropical hummingbirds with their eggs or young in their nests, as seen in *Cattleya Orchid and Three Hummingbirds* (fig. 3). At the intersection of art and scientific knowledge and description, Heade's compositions seem to offer a specific expansion of Hunt's project, transferred to a new, (South) American geography. Heade incorporates the active surfaces seen in Hunt's paintings while also alluding to ornithological specificity that, for Hunt, is evident only indirectly in his attention to the intricate construction of a chaffinch's nest. No Pre-Raphaelite, Heade was nevertheless one of the many artists influenced by Ruskin during the later decades of the nineteenth century.

A Studied Nature: Staging Reality

As John Henry Hill's gentian, Charles Herbert Moore's boulder, and John William Hill's bird's nest all suggest, each of Ruskin's main avenues of influence encouraged still-life artists to portray natural objects in natural settings rather than in domestic interiors. Ruskin went further, however, to advocate for specific designs, such as plants growing in the underbrush or framed against a blue sky. These configurations at times suggest landscape foregrounds more than conventional still lifes. American interpretations of such "nature studies"—a term Ruskin adapted from earlier precedents—often leaned on the poetics of still life even as they sought liberation from its conventions through the ostensibly direct study of nature in situ. Moreover, during the 1860s, a hybrid and increasingly prevalent practice emerged that related to Hunt's typical format: composing objects—both natural and manmade—in confected, but still outdoor, arrangements, which scholar William H. Gerdts has dubbed "still life in a natural setting."[24]

Models of Ruskin's method include John William Hill's delicate, fresh *Peach Blossoms* (plate 48) and Ruskin's own *Twig of Peach Bloom* (plate 85). The attention to new growth and opening energy in these watercolors manifest Ruskin's characterization (in *Modern Painters*) of the unlimited poetic potential of flower buds.[25]

The works also echo the lessons Ruskin sets for his students in *The Elements of Drawing*, establishing the primary movements and forms of trees and their growth.[26] While the contrasting backdrop of a blue wall—as its visible shadows define—in *Twig of Peach Bloom* may have struck Ruskin as coloristically felicitous, it also served to highlight the abstract designs of the branches and leaves, which related to other progressive aesthetic developments later in the century.

Fidelia Bridges was among those who took up Ruskin's call to nature studies with a remarkably modern sensibility that was influenced by Japanese aesthetics.[27] Bridges was a student and longtime friend of the Philadelphia painter William Trost Richards, whose *A Neglected Corner of the Wheatfield* (plate 80) and *And Some Fell Among Thorns* (see fig. 5 in Lynford essay) her anecdotal *Milkweeds* (plate 6) closely follows. She likely knew her neighbor George Cochran Lambdin, whose themes and approach echo her refined and allusive *Calla Lily* (plate 5) and *Wisteria on a Wall* (plate 7). Over time, Bridges would help to advance Ruskinian nature studies toward more mainstream aestheticism.[28] Her elegant, attenuated watercolor *Pink Roses* (plate 4) anticipates such abstraction. Even as Bridges and her peers continued to experiment and test the formal possibilities of Ruskin's silhouettes, however, they preserved the naturalism of detailed description that defined the Pre-Raphaelite sensibility more broadly.

And yet perhaps the most forthright of these compositions emerge not from nature but from the conservatory, where plants are cultivated in close foregrounds that mimic the shallow forest undergrowth. In Richards's early *The Conservatory* (plate 75), or even the vestigial blooms in *A Neglected Garden* (plate 73), we observe a model analogue for the subtle but complete control exercised in Ruskinian forest interiors such as Aaron Draper Shattuck's *Leaf Study with Yellow Swallow Tail* (plate 87) and Richards's own *Ferns in a Glade* (plate 74). The overall fullness of the compositions and their apparent lack of visual priority echo one of Ruskin's tenets often cited by the American Pre-Raphaelites: to neither privilege nor exclude anything in nature, as if God has created everything of equal value, weight, and interest. Individual elements become overall textures and even Shattuck's titular butterfly, despite its bright yellow color, is nearly indiscernible in the lower right corner of the composition. Such a scene in nature would be unlikely, but it very neatly invokes the sense of space and display of urban conservatories.

Such decentralized attention is a hallmark of the design sensibility associated with the dawning Aesthetic movement. It also relates to the busy, overall compositions of John William Hill's *Apple Blossoms* (plate 49) and Joseph Decker's *Ripening Pears* (fig. 4), which balance vivid detail with broad effect, thus rewarding close looking as much as first impression. Only rarely, however, did artists tip their

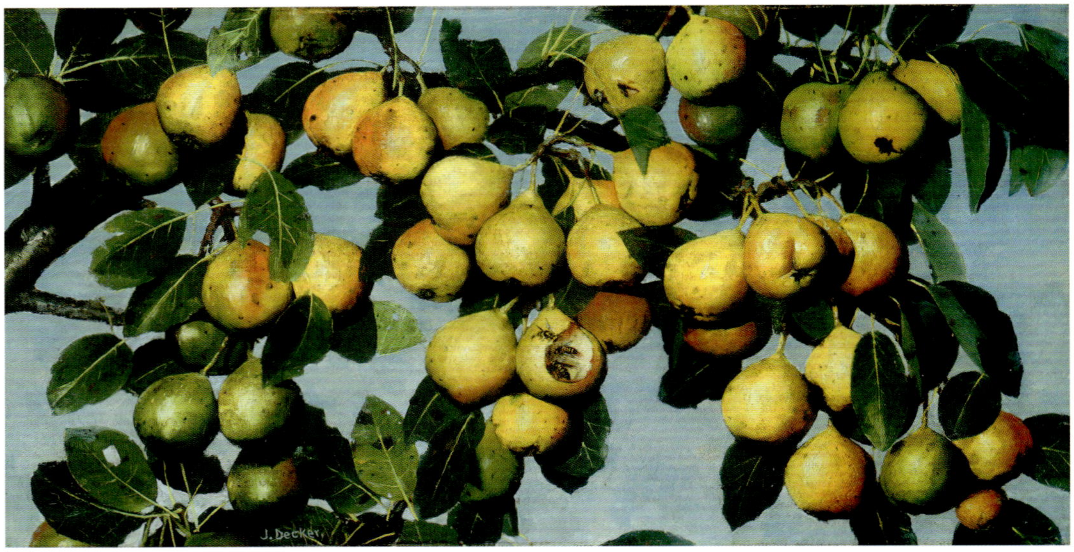

hands to disclose the extent of their affectation, as Richards did in *The Conservatory*. Ruskin must have known physical disability prevented Hunt from the kind of rustic rambles that he portrayed, and yet he sustained both his appreciation of Hunt and the discipline of his principles that unsuspecting American readers, and artists, were more likely to embrace literally.

Engaging the Senses: Intersections with Mainstream Practice

The American Pre-Raphaelite artists' preference for landscape and still life over the medieval figural subjects of their English peers reflected different priorities for American patrons and for the painters themselves, although certain stylized compositions—Thomas Charles Farrer's *June* (plate 16) and Charles Herbert Moore's *Lilies of the Valley* (plate 54) and *Dog Tooth Violet* (plate 57), for example—reveal a related spirit. During midcentury, as industrialization accelerated, American artists responded to an ascendant culture of consumption in which still life resonated across the fine, decorative, vernacular, and even popular arts, such as mass-produced lithography. Still life was everywhere, packed with vivid colors, lustrous finery, perfectly ripe fruits and flowers, and abundant sensuality. This was the mainstream culture of still life at the midcentury moment in which the Ruskinian artists worked, and interaction was inevitable.

Characteristic of the time, the bright tabletop confection of flowers from all seasons seen in Severin Roesen's large *Flower Still Life with Bird's Nest* (fig. 5) reflects the influence of the seventeenth-century Dutch Golden Age of still-life painting, and

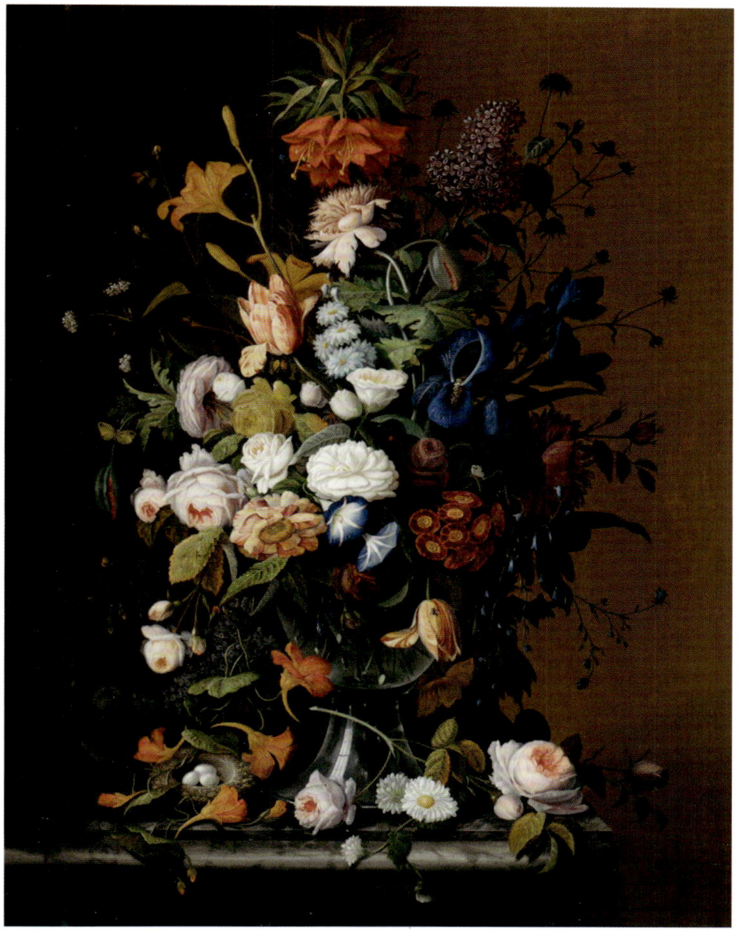

4. Joseph Decker, *Ripening Pears*, c. 1884/1885, oil on canvas, National Gallery of Art, Washington, Gift of Ann and Mark Kington/The Kington Foundation and the Avalon Fund

5. Severin Roesen, *Flower Still Life with Bird's Nest*, 1853, oil on canvas, Philadelphia Museum of Art, Purchased with support from the Henry P. McIlhenny Fund in memory of Frances P. McIlhenny, Mr. and Mrs. Robert L. McNeil, Jr., the Edith H. Bell Fund, Mrs. J. Maxwell Moran, Marguerite and Gerry Lenfest, the Center for American Art Fund, Donna C. and Morris W. Stroud II, Dr. and Mrs. Robert E. Booth, Jr., Frederick LaValley and John Whitenight, Mr. and Mrs. John A. Nyheim, Charlene Sussel, Penelope P. Wilson, the American Art Committee, and with the gift (by exchange) of Theodore Wiedemann in memory of his wife, Letha M. Wiedemann, 2010

more recent interpreters of that tradition included the Flemish master Jan Frans van Dael and German Johann Wilhelm Preyer during the early nineteenth century. Preyer taught at the Royal Academy in Düsseldorf—where both landscape and still life enjoyed unusual prominence—and gained an American audience for his own work in still life at the same moment that many young Americans traveled there for training.[29] Anticipating Ruskin, the Düsseldorf Academy's director, Wilhelm Schadow, proclaimed that art's "subject should be imbued with palpable life and that its representation would remain an incomplete work of art without the basis of natural reality."[30]

The early nineteenth-century German petit bourgeois sensibility known as Biedermeier had dominated that nation's culture early in the century and asserted itself in the United States as well during midcentury, led by a wave of immigration due to greater economic opportunities in New York during the

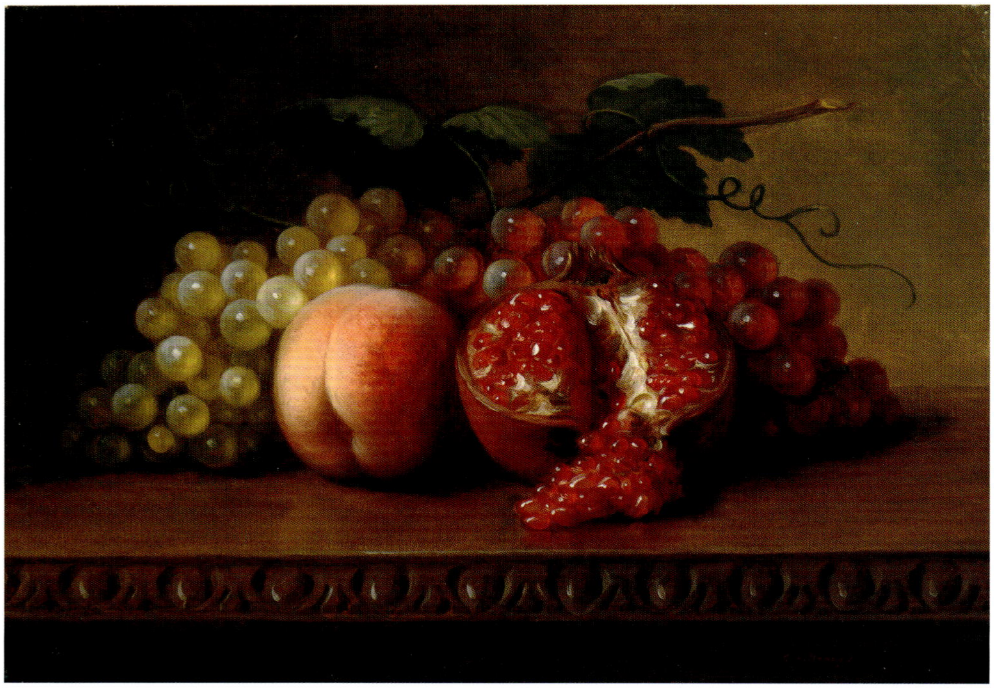

second quarter of the century and exacerbated by Germany's March Revolution of 1848.[31] Biedermeier offered an accessible, populist style of painting and decorative design that appealed to the emerging American middle class. The aesthetic translated readily to the burgeoning, increasingly affluent American cities of midcentury, especially New York, with only moderate changes that, in still life, manifested as a simplified and amplified sense of colorism. In this period, many leading American artists in both landscape and still life had either trained in Germany or were themselves German immigrants (such as Severin Roesen), and so they were already well acquainted with Biedermeier culture. Roesen is believed to have trained in Cologne as a porcelain painter before emigrating in late 1847. His scenes of natural abundance have come to be identified in surveys of American art with still-life practice of this period, but they stand in for the work of less-known artists, such as Charles Baum and Peter Baumgras, who shared related aesthetics and personal histories. For many Americans, German painting was "believed to be the epitome of contemporary artistic achievement" and Ruskin lamented their similar prominence among the British.[32]

The American Pre-Raphaelites admired Ruskin for his assertion of the common man's capacity for aesthetic response to nature based on individual perception, his appeal to the working man rather than to connoisseurs with received knowledge.[33] The indifference of German (and French, Flemish, and Dutch) still-life

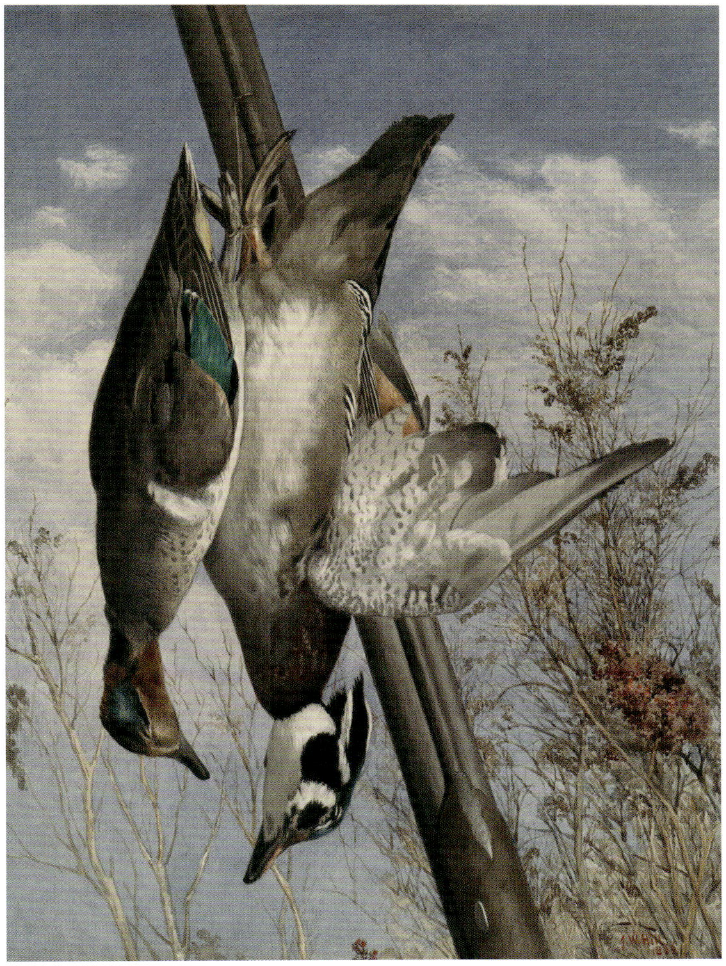

artists to the cycles of nature made them vulnerable to Ruskin's criticism, which reached all the way back to the Dutch Golden Age; yet, contemporary critics often admired these same works in terms similar to Ruskinian naturalism, even as they differentiated their practices. For example, one 1857 essay on the Düsseldorf school states that it "aims at truthfulness to Nature and Life" and that "adherence to truth and nature has produced no mere formalism, nor barrenness in language and conception, as is apt to be the case with those who rigidly reproduce Nature," voicing a common critique of Ruskin-inspired literalism.[34]

6. George Henry Hall, *Still Life with Grapes, Peach and Pomegranates*, 1862, oil on canvas, Colby College Museum of Art, Waterville, ME, Gift of Willard W. Cummings

7. John William Hill, *Hanging Game Birds*, 1866, watercolor on paper, Yale University Art Gallery, New Haven, CT, Gift of Theodore E. Stebbins, Jr., B. A. 1960

In the United States, the two practices of Biedermeier and Ruskinian realism coexisted but the Pre-Raphaelites were the later, fewer, and lesser. According to Henry T. Tuckerman, German-trained painter George Henry Hall enjoyed particular financial success in still life, reportedly earning $12,000 from a single auction of seventy-five "small but carefully elaborated" fruit and flower compositions (fig. 6), a striking contrast to the financial hardships endured by the Pre-Raphaelite painters. It seems only natural that many American still-life painters on the edges of the Pre-Raphaelite movement would integrate aspects of both aesthetics. Even John William Hill painted tabletops, including *Plums, Pears, Peaches, and a Grape* (plate 41), and implausible exotics, such as *Pineapples* (plate 42), staged by a shady roadside.[35] The adaptation of certain themes to Pre-Raphaelite still life likely tested their potential appeal to prevailing American tastes. Colorful songbird compositions, such as Henry Farrer's *Two Birds: Canary and Robin* (plate 8), John William Hill's *Dead Blue Jay* (plate 43), and John Henry Hill's *Golden Robin (Northern Oriole)* (plate 28), are an instance of the artists' exploration of saturated colorism without breaching Ruskin's principles and commitment to morality in their expressive portrayal of life's brevity. Moreover, still-life painters such as John William Hill (in his *Hanging Game Birds*, fig. 7) and Henry Farrer deployed a form of hunt scene with hanging game that was already popular in Germany and would later crystallize in the United States in the trompe l'oeil illusionism of the 1870s.

Brightly colored birds, like flowers, offered an excuse to create a lively composition that displayed its most dramatic side to the viewer in a show of the exhibitionism characteristic of wider still-life practice during the period.[36] Despite Ruskin's respect for more mundane content, vibrant flowers and lustrous fruit remained the primary subjects of the American still-life painters he influenced. Recall Hill's *Fringed Gentians* with its pyramidal composition of dynamic color forms rising upward in front of a largely neutral backdrop. The gentian flowers turn away from the viewer to show their brightest blue aspect (which age and light exposure appear to have yellowed slightly toward purple in the present day), as do the foreground sumacs with their red leaves.[37] Even in this most seemingly naturalistic presentation of growing flowers, a format Ruskin specifically endorsed, Hill configures his subjects to maximize their impact in both color and design, much as Roesen did. Intense, even amplified colorism was as significant to and characteristic of American Pre-Raphaelite painting as it was for the German immigrant painters such as Roesen. Wrote one critic in *The New Path* in 1863: "Do not let us be afraid of Nature's brilliant color, it is one of the noblest things she does for us."[38]

Afterlife: Ruskin's Lingering Influence

The American Pre-Raphaelite movement peaked during the mid-1860s and had dispersed by the end of the decade. The artists' revolutionary zeal abated with the end of the Civil War. And yet, Ruskin's influence was evident in some artists' work into the twentieth century. What of the afterlife, then, of Pre-Raphaelite still life?

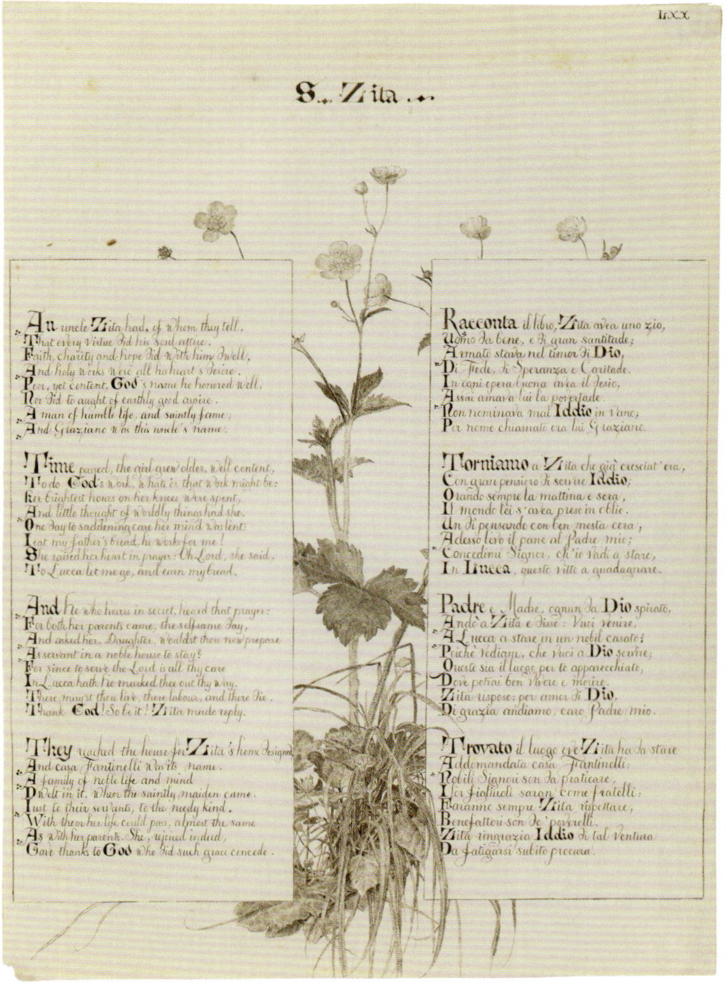

8. Esther Frances (Francesca) Alexander, *S. Zita*, 1874–1882, brown ink on paper, Brooklyn Museum, Dick S. Ramsay Fund

By the end of the century, the Anglo-American loop had closed and Ruskin himself came to patronize and uphold the Americans Henry Roderick Newman, Charles Herbert Moore, and Francesca Alexander as paragons of practice. During the 1880s, he wrote about and enthusiastically collected Newman's Italian subjects, having first been introduced to his work by Moore in 1877—including buying four still lifes as models for his own teaching. Newman, in turn, introduced Ruskin to Alexander, whose works Ruskin would collect and later edit as *Roadside Songs of Tuscany* for publication in 1884–1885 (fig. 8).[39] Despite public obscurity, several of the original members of the Association for the Advancement of Truth in Art—especially John William and John Henry Hill, Moore, and Newman—carried on individually and even sought closer ties to Ruskin himself through correspondence and personal visits.

Newman, however, became Ruskin's bridge to a new age. Color was perhaps Newman's signature attribute, especially in his vibrant scenes of spring anemones, such as *Anemones and Daffodils* (plate 65), on the hills around Florence, where he had settled in 1874. Ruskin admired and collected those subjects (which invoke John Henry Hill's *Fringed Gentians*), as well as architectural watercolors by Newman (plate 66) and Moore, placing them among the rare artists to whom Ruskin looked in multiple genres. Newman and Moore followed the models of both still-life painter William Henry Hunt and architectural painter Samuel Prout, whose works Ruskin featured together in a shared retrospective in 1879. Similarly, Newman's elegant visions of light-washed grape vines and olive trees framing gracious, rolling Italian landscapes—seen in *Grapes and Olives* (plate 63) and *Italy* (plate 64)—advance and embellish earlier, more demure models including John William Hill's *Grapes* (plate 40), with its vivid but narrow view of blue sky. The above influences notwithstanding, Newman's vivid colorism and perspectival contrivance are at times more evocative of Asian aesthetics, documented by his dramatic *Sasanqua, Wild Tea, Yokohama* (plate 69), than of English realism. His travels in Egypt and Asia yielded new subjects that he depicted in works such as *Ramleh* (plate 67), *Wall Enclosing the Mausoleum of Ieyasu at Nikko, Japan* (plate 68), and *The Temple Door at Abu Simbel* (plate 70), which better illustrate the virtuosity and eclecticism of the Aesthetic movement than Ruskinian discipline.

Why still life? Why would such a significant portion of Ruskin's influence on American art manifest in this seemingly marginal genre? The answer is manifold. Partly because of its promise of intimacy with nature; partly because of its unassuming, democratic quality, with a keen resonance in the young American republic; and partly because it so well manifested an extreme interpretation of Ruskinism: to select nothing and reject nothing in nature—in other words, to recognize the beauty and power of divine creation in all things found in the natural world.[40] This would be the American Pre-Raphaelites' rallying cry, effectively inverting the hierarchy of genres and bringing still life from the background to the fore.[41]

Fidelia Bridges, *Pink Roses*, 1875 (detail, plate 4)

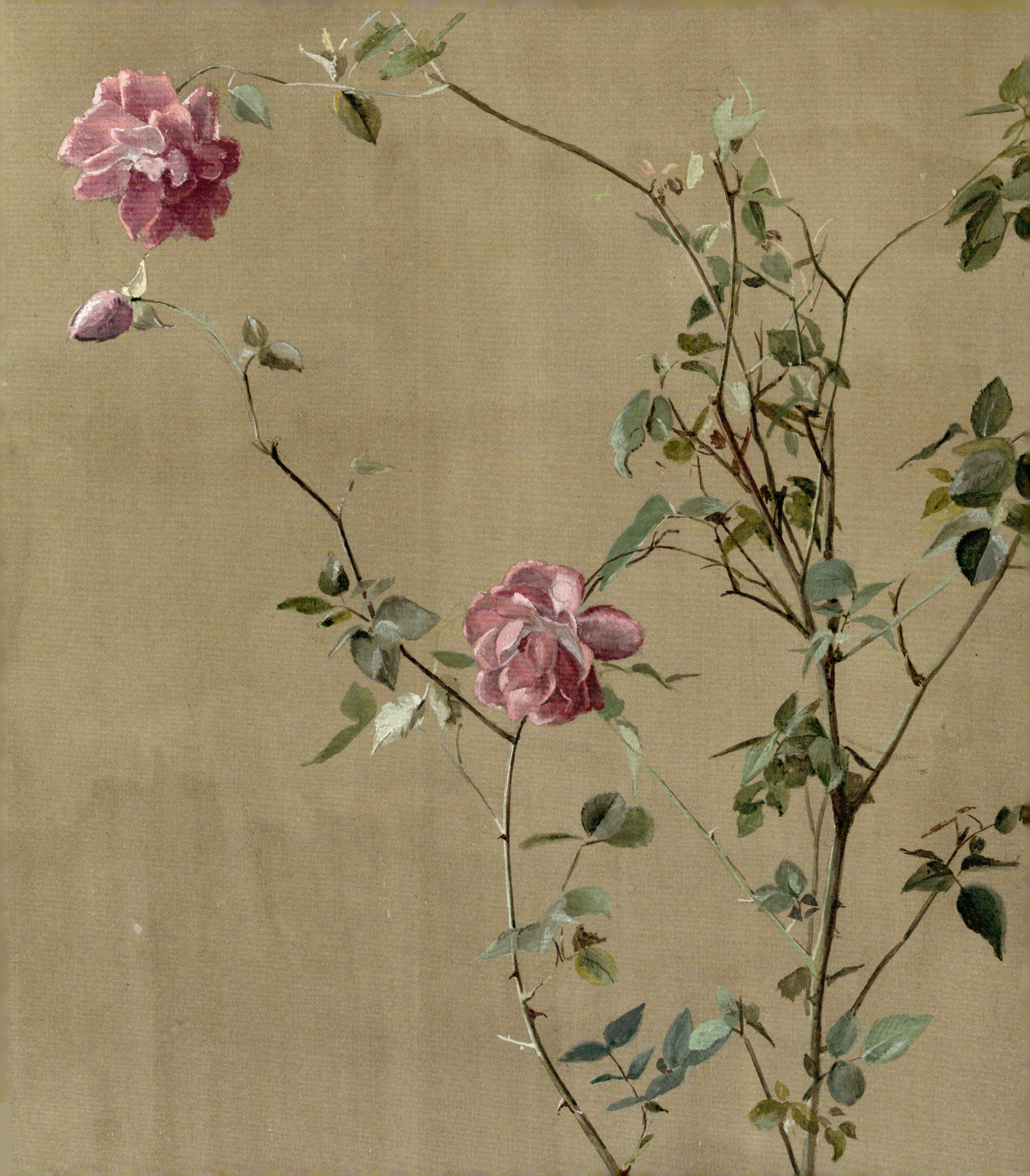

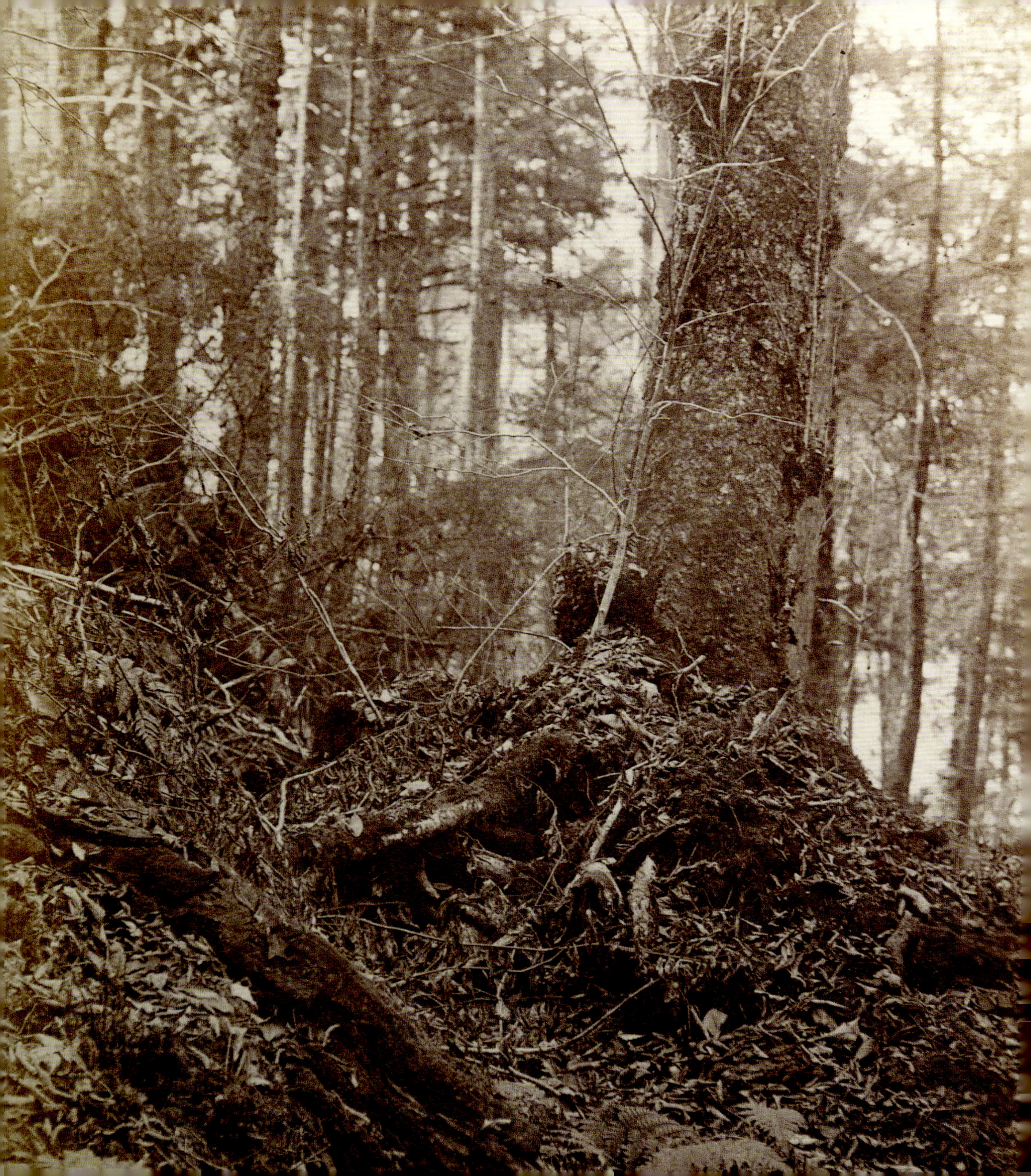

“The Perfect Observance of Truth”: Photography and American Pre-Raphaelitism

DIANE WAGGONER

> Direct copying of nature could not be carried further. The great boulder is, as it were, photographed in color, every hue of its wonderfully varied colors, every irregular split and crack and broken surface, every substance inlaid in its mass, like a precious stone in Florentine mosaic, every incrustation is given with faultless mirror-like accuracy.
>
> —J. S., “Naturalism and Genius,” *The New Path*, 1863

William James Stillman, *Photographic Study*, 1859 (detail, plate 91)

In his vibrant watercolor *Fragment of the Alps* (plate 84), John Ruskin intricately rendered contours of stone in delicate grays and vivid coppers, foregrounding them against the deep emerald green of trees and cobalt blue of sky conveyed by more broadly applied wash. Described in the journal *The New Path* in 1863 as the pinnacle of “direct copying of nature,” the work was an exemplar to the American Pre-Raphaelites, embodying Ruskin’s exhortation that artists observe nature closely and transcribe it faithfully. Owned from 1858 by Bostonian Charles Eliot Norton, a prominent man of letters and, later, an influential art historian at Harvard, the watercolor had been displayed in the American Exhibition of British Art that toured New York, Boston, and Philadelphia in 1857 and 1858. The author of the *New Path* article was “J. S.,” identified as William James Stillman—a friend of Norton, a writer pivotal to bringing Ruskin’s ideas to the United States, and a seminal artist who worked in both landscape painting and photography. His description of Ruskin’s study as “photographed in color” highlights the creative shift in artistic practice and style toward a precise realism that Ruskin’s writings had inspired: first in British artists, with the radical rebellion of Pre-Raphaelitism, and then among American artists, with their subsequent adoption of Ruskinian tenets—especially Stillman and the artists who joined together in 1863 to form the Association for the Advancement of Truth in Art and published *The New Path*.

The link between photography and painting made by Stillman was, however, unusual. Contemporary commentators seldom articulated the significance that photography held for this new emphasis on realism. Yet just as photography had inevitably influenced British Pre-Raphaelitism, it played a vital role in the evolution of American art onward from 1839, the year the medium was announced to the world.[1] While the advent of photography sparked lengthy debates concerning whether it should be considered a merely technical, scientific instrument or, instead, a potential vehicle for artistic expression, the medium's very existence posed an inherent challenge to art-making. The work of artists associated with American Pre-Raphaelitism was dramatically informed by this simultaneous emergence of Ruskin's call for truth to nature and the acknowledged capacity of photography to record the observable world.

Delineating Nature

The opening editorial of the first issue of *The New Path,* by Clarence Cook, proclaims: "These artists [of the Association] are nearly all young men; they are not hampered by too many traditions; and they enjoy the almost inestimable advantage of having no past, no masters and no schools."[2] Cook's comment echoes some of the earliest writers on photography, who often described the pictures it made as generated by nature; because photography recorded what was visible through the lens of the camera, it too could offer "perceptions naturally direct and true."[3] The daguerreotype, the dominant process used in the United States during the first decade and a half of photography's existence, was praised for its crystalline clarity and ability to capture the minutiae of faces, nature, and architecture in a way that the hand of the artist could not. By the time of the formation of the Association in 1863, the daguerreotype had been superseded by the wet collodion glass negative and the albumen print, which combined sharp exactitude and a rich range of tonal gradations. A thriving community of photographers, in both large cities and small towns, was firmly established. And while landscape photography had been slower to flourish in the United States than in Europe, by the late 1850s and 1860s a number of American photographers were beginning to actively cultivate the genre and experiment with new strategies of composition that impelled the genre forward aesthetically.[4] Photography—at least conceptually, if not visually—exerted an undeniable influence on American artists' ways of seeing and their attempts to find a fresh visual language. The medium sharpened artistic handling and endowed the role of description and detail with a new importance, contributing to the rise of realism as an aesthetic mode. The peculiarities of photographic vision—such as flattened forms and an abruptly cropped visual field—began to make their way into painting, serving as a marker of fidelity to observation and propelling artists like the young Ruskinians toward a microcosmic focus on the myriad details of nature. Indeed, in *The New Path*, photography was invoked as a guarantor of realism, as in Stillman's description of the "faultless mirror-like accuracy" of Ruskin's watercolor painting of a boulder.[5]

The connection between photography's ability to record details and Pre-Raphaelitism was also at times explicitly recognized in other outlets. For example, in 1856, even before the American Exhibition of British Art raised the profile of Pre-Raphaelitism in the United States, H. H. Snelling, editor of one of the earliest American photography periodicals, noted of photographer and painter Franklin White's photographic view of a cliff face in New Hampshire's White Mountains:

> This picture shows the capabilities of the photographic art in delineating nature truthfully better than any other we have published, and affords a field for study, under the magnifying glass, which no pencil can possibly give; presenting to the view many remarkable points which could not possibly be detected by the eye in looking upon this remarkable work of nature itself. It also furnishes a forcible argument in favor of the pre-Raffael principle of painting.[6]

While Snelling's writing reinforced his goal to foster an artistic sensibility among the country's growing numbers of photographers, he also highlighted the noticeable emphasis on minute, legible detail that photography could achieve and that Pre-Raphaelite practice nurtured, creating images that invited close scrutiny.

William James Stillman

The convergence of these new visual codes in photography and painting was first evident in the art of Stillman, whom the younger members of the Association claimed as their forebear.[7] "Less than ten years ago there was but one man in America, W. J. Stillman," *The New Path* stated, "who practically understood and believed in the new art."[8] In 1848, after he graduated from college, Stillman settled in New York, seeking to find his way as an artist. He had read Ruskin's first volume of *Modern Painters*, published in America in 1847, and he later recalled he had "absorbed the views of Ruskin in large draughts. . . . The art-loving public was full of Ruskinian enthusiasm, and what strength I had shown was in that vein."[9] He traveled to London for the first time in 1850 and a second time in 1853, where he met Ruskin and other British artists, viewed the works of J. M. W. Turner, and had his first sight of paintings by Dante Gabriel Rossetti and John Everett Millais, noting that the "latter impressed me very strongly; in fact it determined me in the manner in which I should follow art on my return home."[10] Back in the United States, he spent the next several years "given to hard and monotonous painting from nature while the weather permitted. . . . My larger studies from nature (25 × 30 inches) had attracted attention and had been hung on the line, getting for me the election to the Associateship of Design, and the appellation of the 'American Pre-Raphaelite.'"[11]

Suffering from bouts of illness and depression, Stillman spent time in the White Mountains and the Adirondacks, places that became the chief subjects of his landscape paintings. During these sojourns, he discovered a profound love for solitude and nature infused with a strong sense of spirituality. Though few of his paintings survive, *Saranac Lake, Adirondack Mountains* (plate 89) from 1854 was completed after his first trip to the Adirondacks. In this view of the lake through trees, Stillman lavished his attention on the foreground, endeavoring to precisely capture not only the mottled tones and textures of the tree trunks and rocks, the soil and plant cover of the forest floor, but also the complex play of shade and sunlight over these forms. Though he adopted a darker palette—more akin to the paintings of Asher B. Durand and other American artists who had studied in Düsseldorf than to the brilliant luminosity of British Pre-Raphaelite painting—Stillman demonstrated his Ruskinian bona fides by his intensely faithful adherence to his subject.

Stillman described another painting from this period, *The Forest Spring* (no longer extant), as picturing "a little spring under a branching beech and surrounded by mossy boulders" that "was absolutely unconventional." While it was accepted for the National Academy of Design exhibition, the "old stagers did not know what to say of a picture which was all foreground." Stillman noted that Durand had said of it, "The stones seemed to be, not painting, but the real thing."[12] This mimetic realism was equated with photography when Stillman further recounted, "As the negative photographic process had just then been introduced in America, I had the picture photographed, and a friend took a print of it to the head of the old school, without any explanation. My antagonist and critic looked at it carefully and exclaimed, 'what is the use of Stillman making his pre-Raphaelite studies when we can get such photographs from nature as this!'"[13] Stillman had carried out photography's challenge to achieve what he would call "the perfect observance of truth" in his own paintings, to the extreme, so that determining what was a photograph and what was a painting could be difficult and confusing. In a bold statement, Stillman described the way in which photography newly tested painters:

> Studies from nature that would once have been considered satisfactory, when placed by the side of a photograph become poor things, and their artist must improve or be neglected. [Photographs] are a standard, infallible so far as they go, and [artists] must either give something which the daguerreotype cannot attain, or do something which can approach it in fidelity. . . . This effect cannot be otherwise than beneficial, since on the perfect observance of truth all other qualities of Art are based, and in truth it would seem that as our powers of observation become microscopic they become telescopic also, *i.e.* the more minutely we see, the *more* we see.[14]

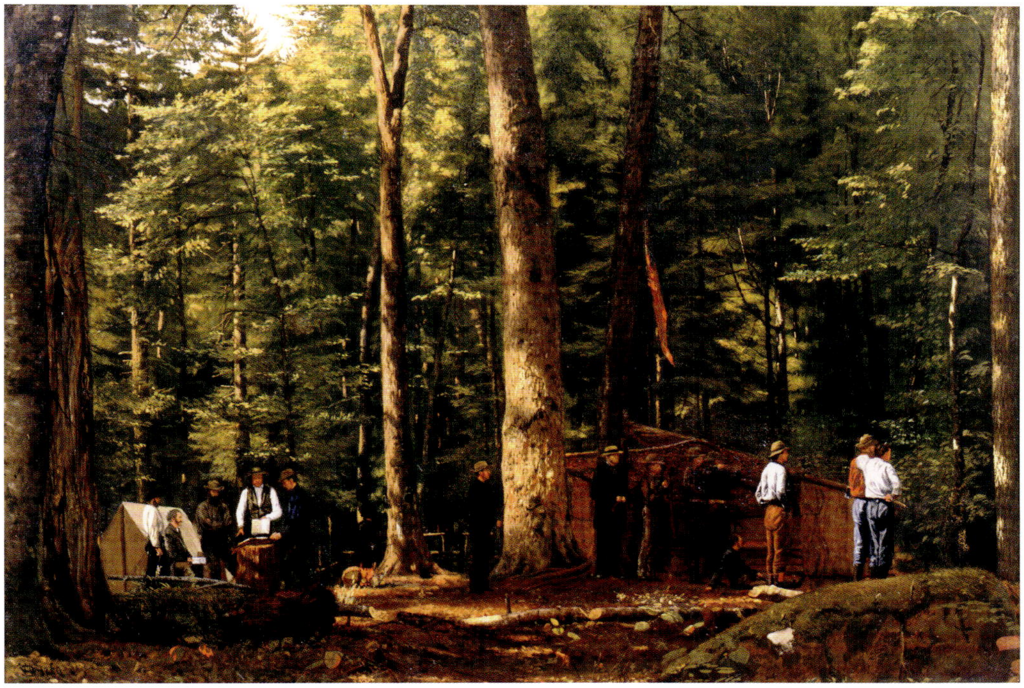

1. William James Stillman, *The Philosophers' Camp in the Adirondacks*, 1858, oil on canvas, Courtesy Concord Free Public Library, MA

This remark, highlighting the sharpening of vision that photography made essential, was published in *The Crayon*, the journal Stillman cofounded in 1855 with Durand's son, John. *The Crayon* was a precursor to *The New Path*, and was instrumental in bringing Ruskin's writings and ideas to an American audience. An ambitious publication for two young men to undertake, the journal quickly earned praise. The editors secured writings from prominent literati such as James Russell Lowell and William Cullen Bryant, and also published Ruskin and William Michael Rossetti, who served as an English correspondent. Stillman left the editorship of *The Crayon* in 1856, citing mental and physical exhaustion, but his important contribution as editor left his mark on the American art world, laying the groundwork for the ardent followers of Ruskin who would eventually form the Association.

Stillman, more than any other painter working at the time, paved the way for a distinctly American branch of Pre-Raphaelitism in both painting and photography by bringing together Ruskinian philosophy and American transcendentalism. He intensely admired the poet, essayist, and editor Lowell, with whom he became acquainted in the early 1850s. Lowell introduced him to Norton, who became a close friend and financial supporter, and to others in his circle of Boston intellectuals, including Ralph Waldo Emerson and Louis Agassiz. In his letters to Norton, Stillman ruminates expansively on the divine presence he felt in nature.

Later, he wrote, "It has been my habit for many years, at all times when I found myself broken down by fatigue, to resort to the wilderness for recuperation; and I have lured wiser men and better workers to follow me and find renewal, ... In the wilderness are silence and oblivion, which bring repose and render recreation possible."[15] Many of those "wiser men" were "lured" to an extraordinary camping expedition with Stillman as guide in 1858 at Follansby Pond in the Adirondacks, dubbed the Philosophers' Camp and leading to the founding of the so-called Adirondack Club, whose members included Lowell, Emerson, and Agassiz.

Looking Through the Phenomena

Stillman painted a study of the historic gathering of these men who critically shaped the way that America valued the natural environment. *The Philosophers' Camp in the Adirondacks* (fig. 1) is set in the forest clearing where the men built shelter:

> In my study the party is divided in the habit of the morning occupations: Lowell, Hoar, Binney, Woodman, and myself engaged in firing at the target; Agassiz and Wyman dissecting a trout on a tree-stump, while Holmes and Dr. Howe watch the operation; but Emerson, recognizing himself as neither a marksman or a scientist, choosing a position between the two groups, pilgrim-staff in hand, watches the marksmen, with a slight preference as between the two groups. My own figure I painted from a photograph, the company insisting on my putting myself in; but it was ill done, for I could never paint from a photograph.[16]

Not only was Stillman guiding these men's experience of nature, he also pictorially represented their physical and mental exertions as they studied and immersed themselves in the forest. In the painting, sunlight streams through the trees, bathing the figures with bright light to conjure a sense of their communion with nature. After the party departed for Boston, Stillman stayed on by himself, rapturously "rowing, hunting, fishing and exploring new recesses of that marvellous forest which buries me deeper each time I enter it."[17]

Though Stillman avowed that he could not paint from a photograph, his declaration did not keep him from taking up photography itself. He was the first to bring this philosophical and spritual sensbility to the practice of photography. The following year, in 1859, he traveled to Florida to recuperate from a bout of pneumonia and made his first documented photographs there.[18] That fall, Stillman returned to the Adirondacks, camping again on this trip with a smaller group on a tract of land at Ampersand Pond that he had purchased the previous winter on behalf of the Adirondack Club with the intention (never realized) that the prop-

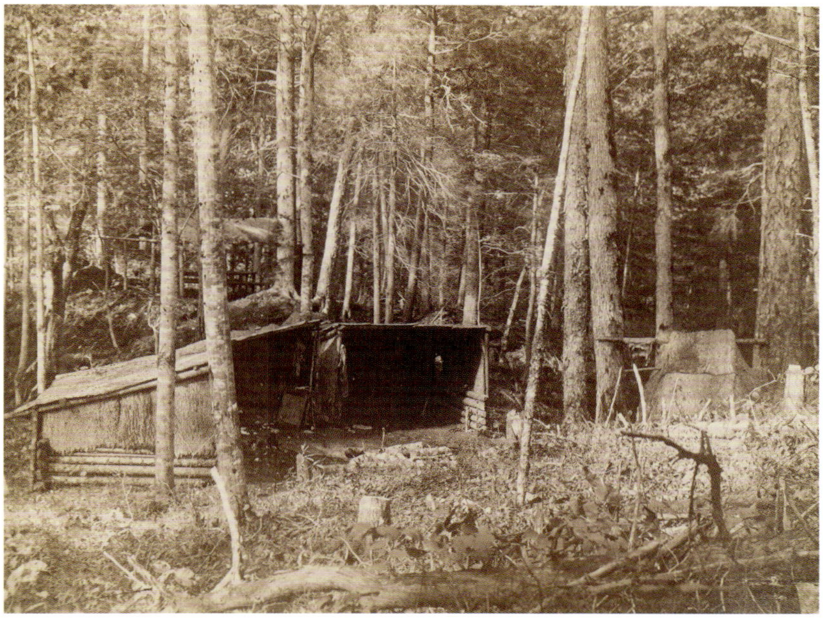

2. William James Stillman, *Photographic Study*, 1859, albumen print, from *Photographic Studies by W. J. Stillman. Part 1. The Forest. Adirondac Woods*, Amon Carter Museum of American Art, Fort Worth

erty would serve as the club's permanent camping site. After the other men left, Stillman remained by himself as he had the year before, in hopes of improving his fatigue and low spirits. He wrote to Norton that "I have not done much on my picture but I have chopped wood[,] rowed, taken photographs about the camp in the intervals of the showers, sketched some and hunted more," closing the letter by noting, "I have made some very nice little photographs of forest subjects."[19] Stillman assembled these "forest subjects" as a portfolio, titled *Photographic Studies by W. J. Stillman. Part 1. The Forest. Adirondac Woods* (part 2 never materialized). These photographs were unprecedented within American photography, with Stillman employing Ruskinian art theory and practice in his choice of subject and compositions (plates 90–93). Few copies of the portfolio survive and each contains a slightly different number of photographs; it is uncertain how many were in the original, but fifteen images are extant. In *The Philosophers' Camp in the Adirondacks*, Stillman had shown the party of wilderness seekers ensconced in their camp, the material necessities of tent and lean-to shelter combined with the figures as evidence of their communal gathering. Humans are absent in the *Forest* photographs, but Stillman alluded to their presence with the inclusion of a lean-to in one of the photographs and a hut in another (fig. 2).

Stillman's strategies of composition included several vignetted scenes in which the round shape of the photographic image evokes both the circular camera lens and the human eye. In one—a snow scene, showing how late into the year Stillman remained in the Adirondacks—the pictorial viewpoint corresponds to

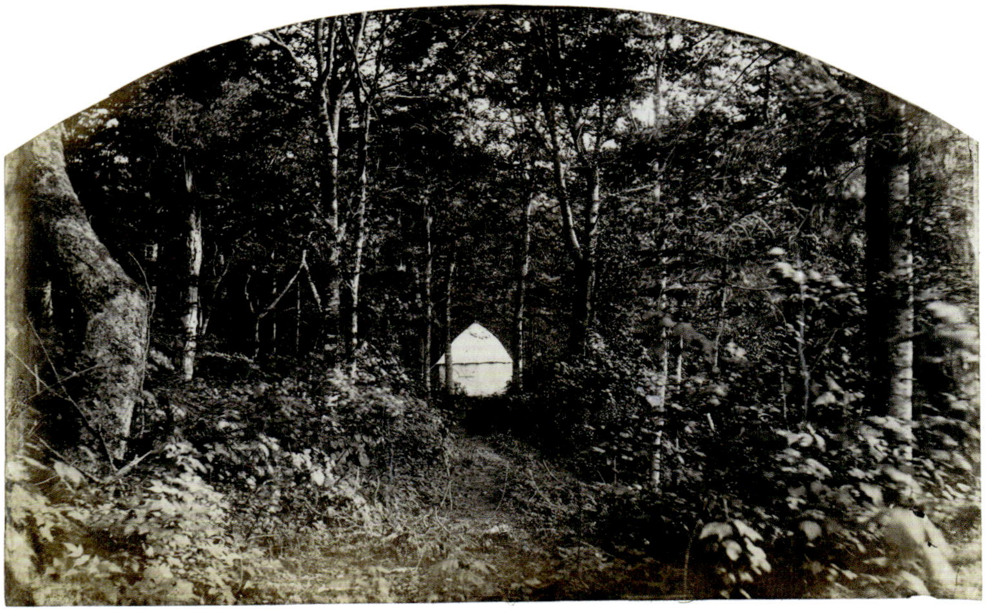

the camera's height on a tripod, pointed straight into the forest, as a keyhole into an untouched world (plate 92). In another vignette, a glimpse of forest floor packs the foreground while the remainder of the pictorial plane is occupied by the slope of a rock covered in mosses or lichen, thin branches, and sparse leaves, and the diagonal line of a tree trunk on the left (plate 90). In one image without the vignette format, Stillman fills the frame vertically, from forest floor to the sunlight shining through the treetops (plate 91). Another offers an off-kilter perspective, capturing a vertical slope with a tree growing out of it, where the viewer's only point of orientation is the group of trees in the background at left (plate 93). Each of the photographs invokes the microscopic seeing Stillman had described earlier in *The Crayon*, and the destabilizing, dizzying effect imparts the sense of full immersion in the woods, just as Stillman recounted in his letters to Norton. These close-up views echoed Stillman's own painting *Saranac Lake* as well as those by Durand and William Trost Richards (plate 76), but they are even more unorthodox than their painted counterparts: there is no far vista in the photographs as there is in the paintings. Instead, nature crowds around and encroaches, with only glimpses of light visible.

Stillman never resided permanently in the United States after 1860, when he sailed for London and reconnected with Ruskin and the British art community, but he did come back periodically. Eventually, after suffering under Ruskin's criticism, he gave up painting and became a diplomat and journalist, but continued to write photography and art criticism and make photographs.[20] In extant

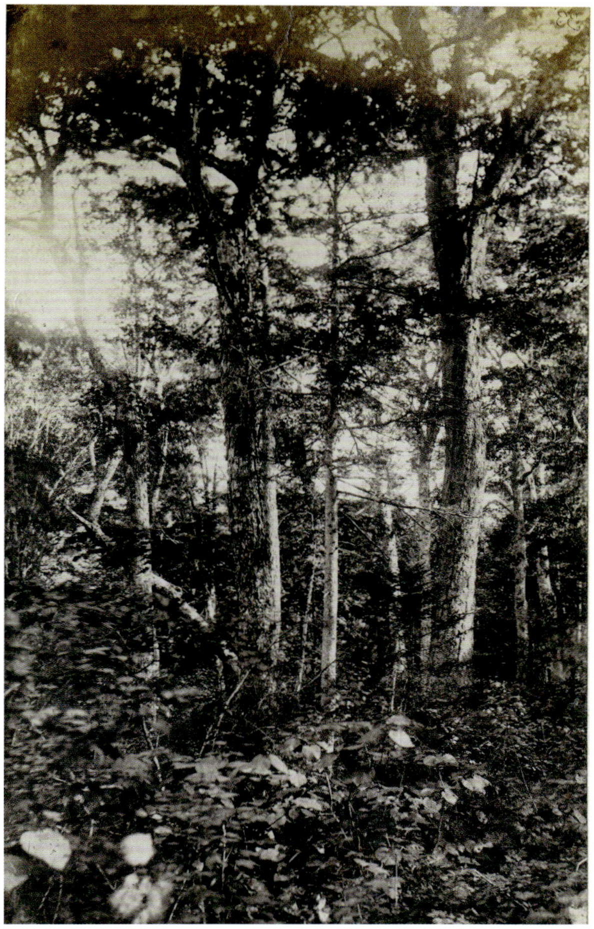

3. William James Stillman, *White Mountains*, probably 1860s, albumen print, Courtesy of Special Collections, Schaffer Library, Union College

4. William James Stillman, *White Mountains*, probably 1860s, albumen print, Courtesy of Special Collections, Schaffer Library, Union College

photograph albums, Stillman included pictures he made in the White Mountains that exhibit the same hallmarks as his *Forest* pictures. It is not clear when he made them: he had not yet acquired a camera by the time of his first documented trip there in 1856, but he visited the White Mountains during at least one subsequent sojourn in America from Europe.[21] One of the photographs presents a view teeming with forest undergrowth in the foreground, a perfectly centered tent glowing through the trees in the middle ground, and a small glimpse of sky visible through the treetops at the top (fig. 3).[22] Others employ similar compositions, with foreground vegetation leading back to light shining through trees (fig. 4).[23]

Stillman's photographs of the Adirondacks and the White Mountains suggest that the artist was searching for a way to express his own spirituality as well as the transcendentalism of Emerson, fostered by his time with the author in the woods at the Philosophers' Camp:

> Emerson and I had many hours alone on the lake and in the wood. He seemed to be a living question, perpetually interrogating his impression of all that there was to be seen. The rest of us were always at the surface of things, —even the naturalists were only engaged with their anatomy; but Emerson in the forest, or looking at the sunset from the lake, seemed to be looking through the phenomena, studying them by their reflections on an inner speculum.[24]

While in *The Philosophers' Camp in the Adirondacks* Stillman evokes Emerson's powers of observation, in his photographs he seems to search for a means to communicate beyond "the surface of things," incorporating glimpses of light to make his photographs of nature serve as emblems of immanence. Despite this, Stillman's photographs were primarily interpreted—as were his paintings—as models of Ruskinian realism: the *Forest* portfolio received one mention in the press, in the *Atlantic Monthly* (then under the editorship of Lowell). The *Atlantic* critic emphasizes the Pre-Raphaelite qualities of the photographs, rather than their Emersonian ideals: "The points of view are chosen with the fine feeling of an artist, and the tangled profusion and grace of the forest, with the moment's whim of sunfleck and shadow, are given with exquisite delicacy.... One may study these pictures till he becomes as familiar as a squirrel with fern and tree-bark and moose-wood and lichen, till he knows every trunk and twig and leaf as intimately as a sunbeam."[25] Stillman thus laid the groundwork for the realist and observational turn in American art in the middle decades of the century. As he proudly stated in his autobiography, "I influenced some of my contemporaries and gave a jog to the landscape painting of the day."[26]

Photographic Reproductions

When the short-lived Association formed in 1863 to formalize their devotion to Ruskinian principles, their journal, *The New Path*, occasionally discussed photography, but the editors also cannily used the medium to publicize the Association's work. The April 1864 issue announced a series of ten photographic reproductions of a number of pen and pencil drawings and two oil paintings by artist members that would allow readers to see the kind of works advocated in its pages.[27] The photographs were produced by Maurice Stadtfeld, who operated a studio on Broadway not far from the Tenth Street studio building where Stillman, Charles Herbert Moore, and John Henry Hill had each briefly worked. Stadtfeld had arrived in New York in 1860 and offered all manner of photography, including art reproductions. Other than Thomas Charles Farrer's *Gone! Gone!* and a reproduction of his drawing *May in the Woods*, none of the drawings listed are extant and no sets of these photographs are known to survive.

A lengthy *New Path* article, however, noted that the reproduced works illustrated "what we say about working from nature" and explained that all but one of them were made entirely in front of the subject at hand rather than in the studio. The author distinguishes between a *study* and a *picture*; in the *study*, the artist works faithfully in nature, and, echoing Stillman's description of Ruskin's watercolor, undertakes "careful, weeklong work to be done in painting that rock fissure by fissure, lichen by lichen, making of it a photograph in color."[28] The *picture*, then, can only be properly achieved by having conducted conscientious study of the visual world. Making it clear that the photographed works should be understood as studies, the essay describes the drawings of "determined realists" Thomas Charles Farrer, Moore, Henry Roderick Newman, and John Henry Hill, emphasizing their minute details as well as remarking upon the specificity of location and date for each work. Presumably chosen to demonstrate the artists' dedication to faithful observation as clearly as possible, the essayist emphasized the small size of the drawings—in most cases, the photographs were described as only marginally smaller than the studies themselves, while in the case of Moore's *Cedar Tree*, both photograph and study were the same size. Farrer—as evident in the intricate close-up *May in the Woods*, picturing "a tangle of last year's old blackberry vine stems, with sharp briers, and among these a wealth of the new-sprung wild flowers"—is described as holding "up a mental frame before him," having "drawn with fidelity and patient skill everything which it enclosed," echoing the conditions of making a photograph.[29] The author, however, notes the photographic reproductions display greater shortcomings in suggesting the colors and gradation of shades in the two oil paintings (Robert J. Pattison's *Dog's Head* and Farrer's *Gone! Gone!*, plate 12) than in accurately representing the detailed pen, pencil, or sepia drawings of the other works. He furthermore remarks of Moore's *Cedar Tree* that a photograph never quite achieves the perfection in rendering "tree forms and foliage" that the hand of the artist did.[30]

Studies of Foreground Only

Though none of the artists associated with the Association are known to have practiced photography themselves during the 1860s, there was a synchrony between the nature motifs chosen by them and by the rising generation of photographers that included Stillman. One of the most significant, John Moran, photographed side by side with his artist brothers Thomas and Edward. He tellingly labeled many of his photographs *Landscape Studies*, which—as with Stillman's use of the term—staked a claim for his photographs to be understood as functioning within the same artistic sphere as paintings. Indeed, John Moran became America's earliest and strongest advocate for photography's place among the fine arts, an argument that Stillman ultimately resisted: despite having his own photographic practice, Stillman generally saw photography as inferior when measured against

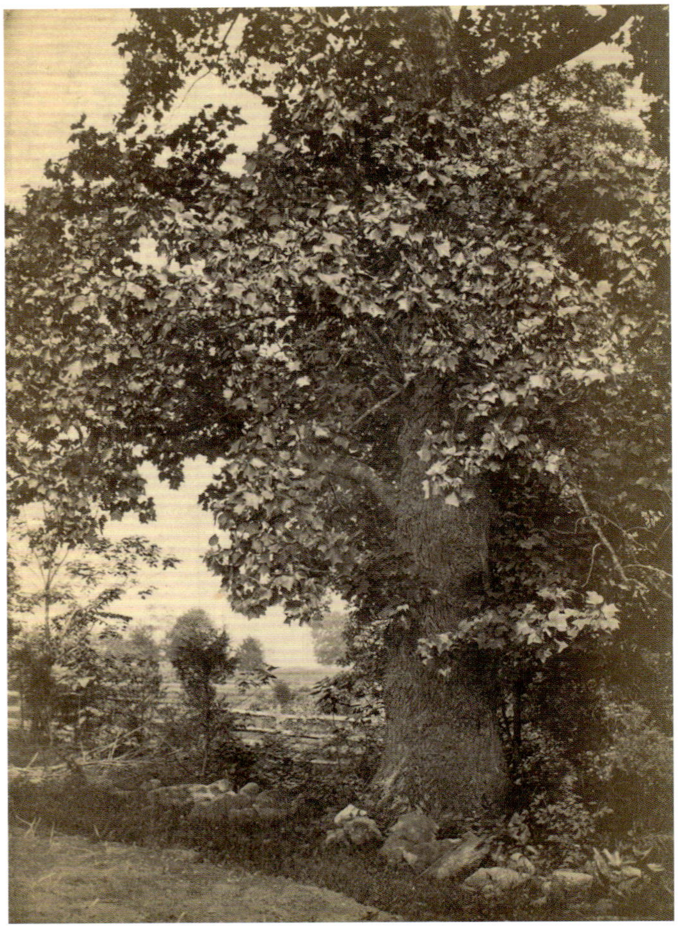

the imagination of the artist. In 1862, Moran photographed in the Allegheny Mountains along the route of the Pennsylvania Railroad, producing both stereographs and larger prints, many of which he compiled into two albums.[31] Combining views of the landscape and railroad tracks, as well as the mining industries and other settlements that were rapidly altering the terrain, Moran brought a meticulous eye for composition to his work with the camera. Included among the photographs were several close-up studies of nature that clearly employed a Ruskinian approach and were explicitly compared to Pre-Raphaelite painting by Coleman Sellers, a Philadelphia engineer and amateur photographer:

> Some show us glimpses of far-off mountains and rugged foregrounds, while a great many are studies of foreground only, rocks, weeds, and fallen trunks. One gem is the American tulip tree, so perfect in every detail that the shape and structure of its broad leaves can be studied,

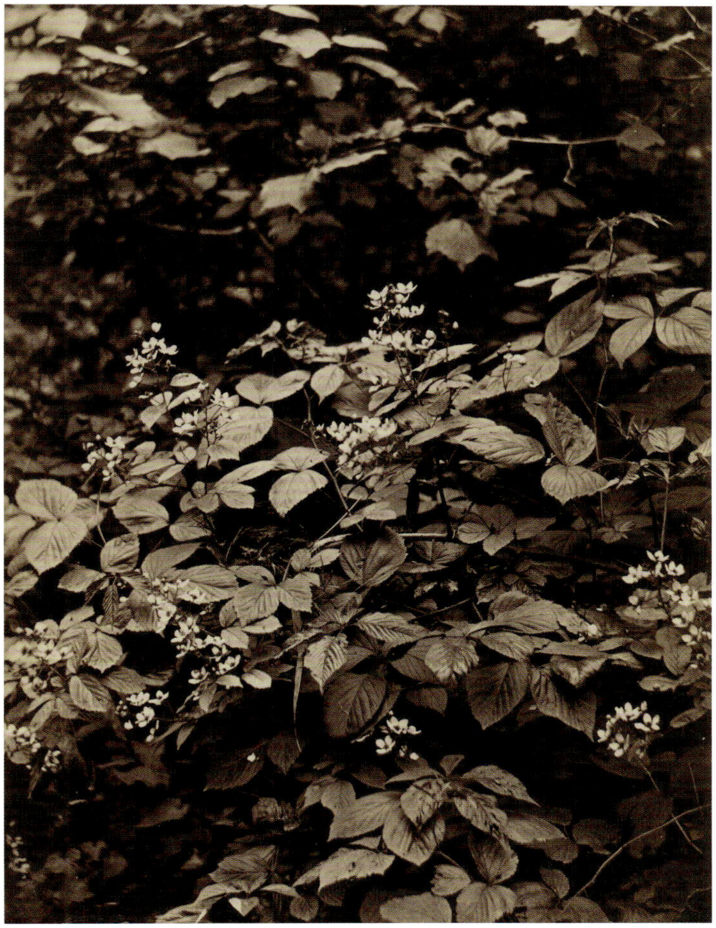

while its rough but regular bark is given with a pre-Raphaelite distinctness. It is a picture to be lingered over, and does full justice to the pride of the American forest.[32]

5. John Moran, *Tulip Tree*, 1862, albumen print, William L. Clements Library, University of Michigan, Ann Arbor

6. John Moran, *Blackberry Bushes*, c. 1862, albumen print, Collection of William L. Schaeffer

Moran's tulip tree (fig. 5) has a more objective quality than Stillman's forest subjects, eschewing the latter's fragmentary cropping and representing the specificities of its subject more broadly situated in the landscape. Moran's photograph, as Sellers asserts, imparts information, inviting the viewer to learn, through its clarity of representation, the particularities of the tulip-shaped leaves and contours of the tree bark under sunlight and shadow.

In addition to the tulip tree singled out by Sellers, among John Moran's *Landscape Studies* are photographs of blackberry bushes (fig. 6). Both the tulip tree and the blackberry bushes show a marked similarity not only to the paintings of his

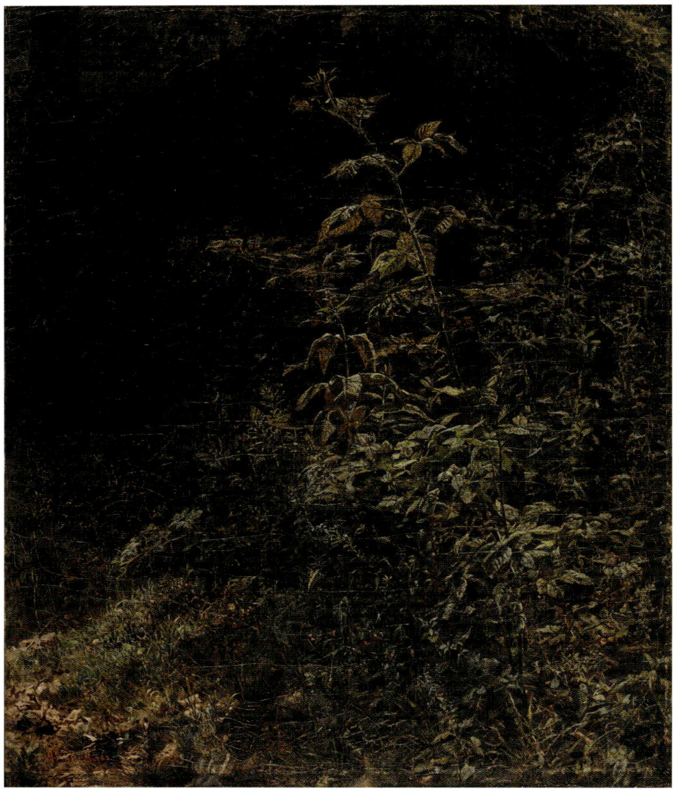

brother, Thomas, but also to the contemporaneous paintings of their fellow Philadelphian, and Association member, William Trost Richards. The two men would have undoubtedly been aware of each other's work. Richards had begun making Ruskinian nature studies in 1858, including his own oil of a blackberry bush, painted outdoors over the summer after the American Exhibition of British Art was shown in Philadelphia early that year, where he would have seen Ruskin's watercolor. He painted this small canvas in a markedly subdued palette, using multiple layers of thin washes over a dark ground, described by John Henry Hill as "painted in black and white with a little color."[33] *Blackberry Bush* (fig. 7) was exhibited at the National Academy of Design the following year and in London in 1860. Richards then produced the more colorful *Tulip Trees* (fig. 8) in 1859, which was exhibited at the Pennsylvania Academy of the Fine Arts in 1862, the same year Moran made his photograph. Richards continued producing several intensely detailed, close-up nature studies through 1865 in drawing, watercolor, and oil, later prompting Henry T. Tuckerman to declare that "so carefully finished in some of them are the leaves, grasses, grain-stalks, weeds, stones, and flowers, that we seem not to be looking at a distant prospect, but lying on the ground with herbage and blossoms directly under our eyes" (plates 83, 81, 80).[34]

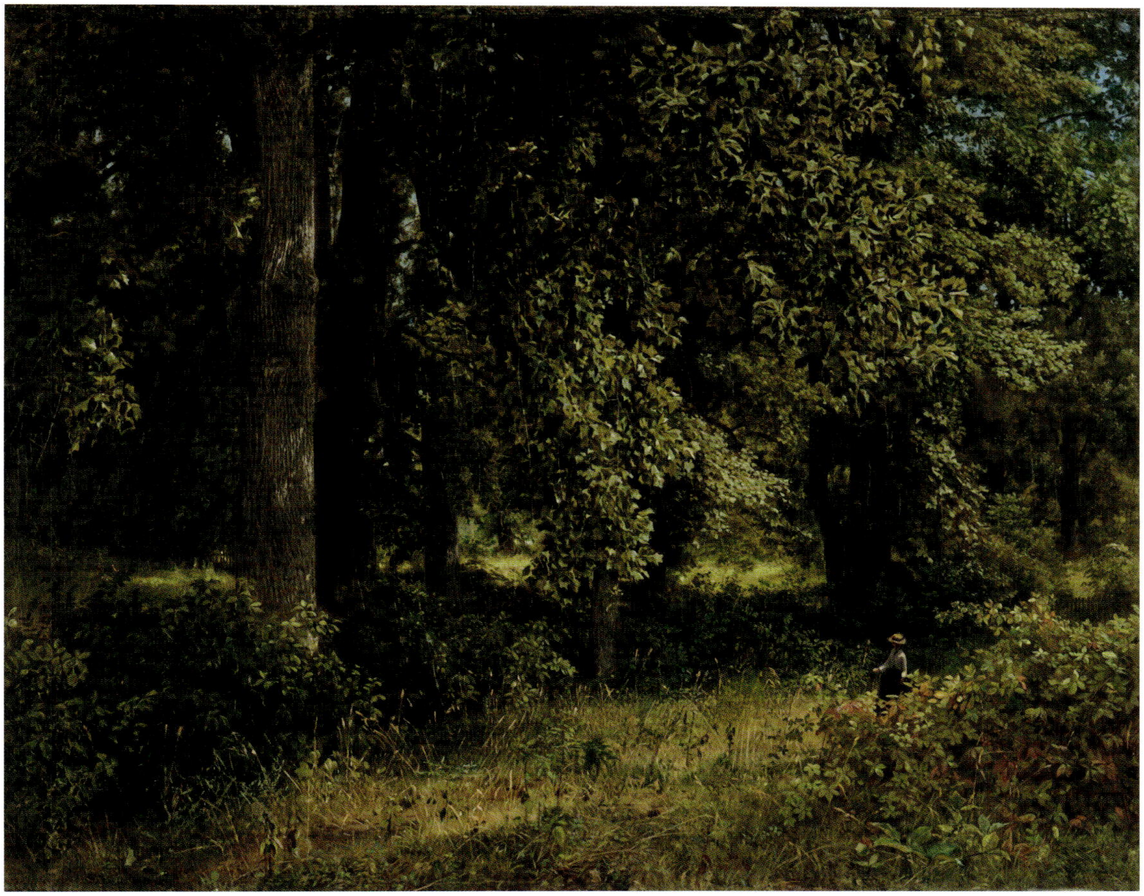

While Richards spent months observing the blackberry bushes or the tulip tree to paint his canvases, Moran would have spent only hours at the location; his photographs nevertheless demonstrate the camera's ability to achieve the same intense focus on the motif. The responses to all of these works by Stillman, Moran, and Richards emphasize the ability of these pictures not only to magnify details and sharpen powers of observation but also to place the embodied eye in close-up positions that amplify and heighten the process of looking.

7. William Trost Richards, *Blackberry Bush*, 1858, oil on canvas, Brooklyn Museum, Gift of Mrs. Theodore Conant

8. William Trost Richards, *Tulip Trees*, 1859, oil on canvas, Brooklyn Museum, Gift of Nancy Carey

The New Path

These contemporaneous efforts in painting and photography expressed ideals that would soon be more coherently expounded in *The New Path* between 1863 to 1865, asserting that images of nature should be legible not only to the aesthete but also to the scientist so that they could inform the botanist or the geologist as well as the art lover. Sellers was already attuned to such a fusion of ideas when he described some stereoscopic photographs of Niagara Falls in 1862 as "particularly interesting to geologists; for the huge masses of rock laid bare by the wearing back of the falls, through countless ages, is given with all the pre-Raffaelite perfection in detail that the camera only can give."[35] Art and science were joined in the writings of Ruskin and in the abilities of the new medium of photography; it followed that geologists Clarence King and James T. Gardner were members of the Association. When King organized the United States Geological Survey of the Fortieth Parallel in the late 1860s and early 1870s, former Association compatriot John Henry Hill and photographer Timothy O'Sullivan accompanied him, utilizing both drawing and photography to represent the exploration of the western landscape.[36] And Gardner later served as the director of the New York State Survey, joining with Frederick Law Olmsted to advocate for the preservation of Niagara Falls: in 1880, he published the results of the survey in a book that included photographs by George Barker showing the degraded state of the landscape.[37]

In the last issue of *The New Path*, an essay on art and photography commented that "Photography has reached such perfection of late, that evident confusion has arisen in the minds of many persons respecting the relative difference in value between it and Fine Art; and, in mere rendering of facts of external nature, at least, they think it may supersede Art."[38] Though the author praises photography for its abilities to render detail, he defends the painter by arguing that only an artist could imbue a picture with feeling. This was a common contemporary refrain on the limitations of photography, as well as a prejudice that photographers faced throughout the nineteenth century. Regardless of its status as an accepted aesthetic mode, however, photography had an irrefutable effect on painting. The anxiety that the author expressed regarding photography's capacity to surpass the artist was surely a factor contributing to the demise of the organized American Pre-Raphaelite movement by 1867, though it was not the only cause. Changes were already afoot that more directly generated the resistance to the Ruskinian manifesto of the American Pre-Raphaelites. During the 1860s, American artists began looking to European influences, moving away from the tight handling and strict detail encouraged by Ruskin toward a more painterly handling that emphasized light, effect, color, and gesture. As Stillman had argued, painters, when faced with photography, had to compete with its exactitude. The heyday of American Pre-Raphaelitism would be short-lived, as most artists chose a different path, embarking on an exploration of the material possibilities that painting offered and photography could not ostensibly accomplish.

William James Stillman, *Photographic Study*, 1859 (detail, plate 90)

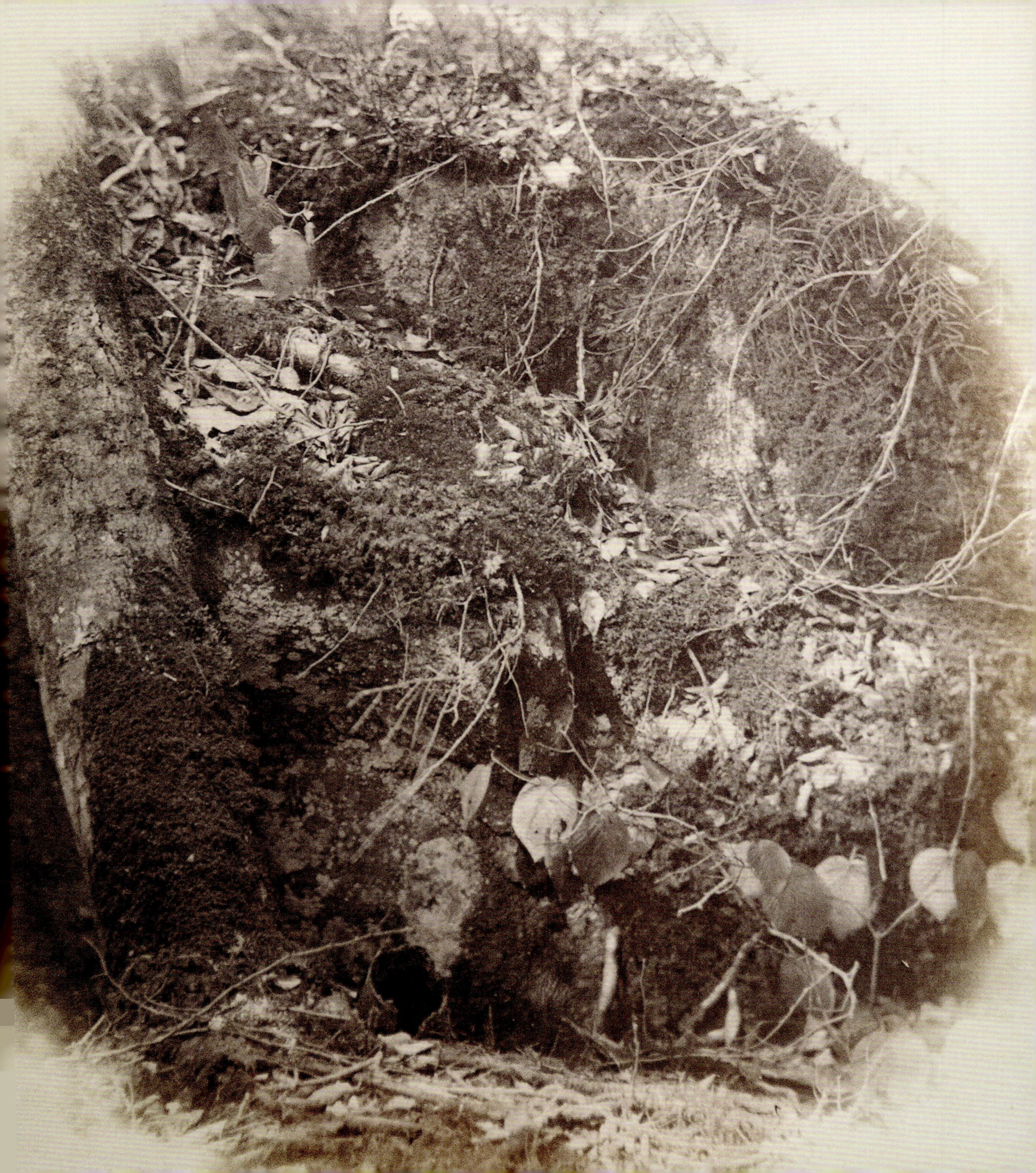

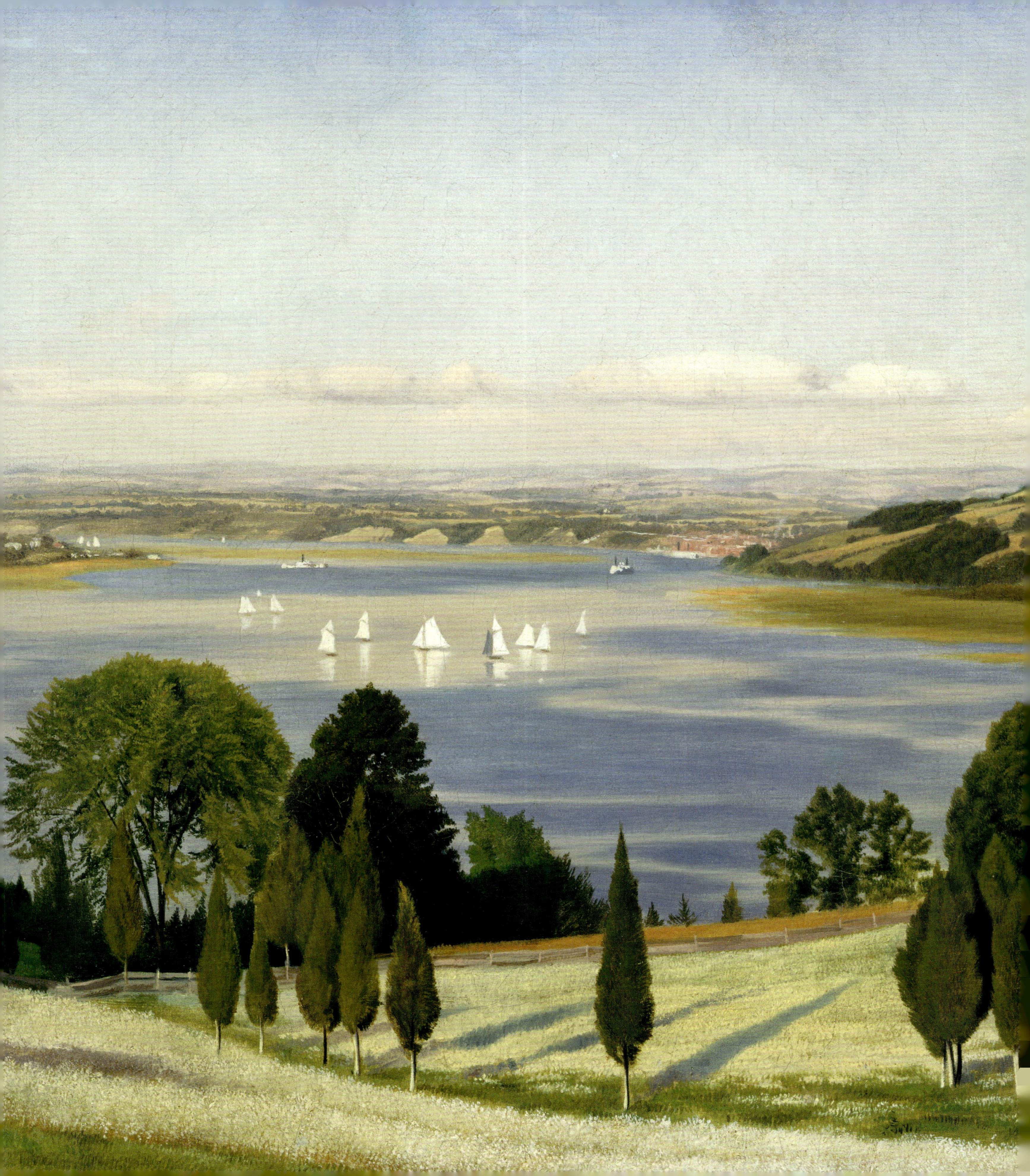

The New Path 1863–1865: "He Serves All, Who Dares Be True"

JANICE SIMON

Readers of the inaugural issue of *The New Path*, which appeared in May 1863, found no cover, no images, no fancy script, no advertisements (fig. 1). What they did find, however, was a motto as masthead—"Write the things which thou hast seen, and the things which are, and the things that shall be hereafter"—that would appear in every issue of the first volume's twelve-month run through April 1864. This directive comes from the King James Bible, Revelation 1:19, citing the words of Jesus Christ to Saint John on Patmos. With these words, Clarence Cook, editor of *The New Path*, pronounced an ultimate authority to the new critical journal of the Association for the Advancement of Truth in Art, lending all that followed in its pages the weight of divine revelation. Vision and material existence as the sources of unvarying truth would continue to be voiced throughout the journal's twenty-four issues as primary to art creation, understanding, and appreciation. So too would the journal's authors ordain its prescriptions for the future of American art with all the certainty of its biblical maxim.

Thomas Charles Farrer, *A Buckwheat Field on Thomas Cole's Farm*, 1863 (detail, plate 13)

Two art journals that provided the precedents and models for *The New Path* featured their own literary mastheads: *The Germ* (London, January 1850–May 1850, skipping April issue) and *The Crayon* (New York, 1855–1861; first year biweekly and then monthly). They claimed their intellectual origins, as did *The New Path*, with the writings of John Ruskin and allegiance to the art of the British Pre-Raphaelites. *The Germ: Thoughts towards Nature in Poetry, Literature and Art*—edited by William Michael Rossetti, who contributed twelve of its fifty-one offerings (and who would also write for *The Crayon*)—prefaced its contents with a sonnet in Gothic script: "When whoso merely hath a little thought / Will plainly think the thought which is in him . . . Ask: 'Is this truth?' For it is still to tell / That, be the theme a point or the whole earth, / Truth is a circle, perfect, great or small?" Rossetti later explained that he intended the sonnet to express how a writer or painter "ought to think out his subject honestly and personally, not imitatively, and ought to express it with directness and precision."[1] This emphasis on earnestness against imitation was a guiding principle of *The New Path* and would be repeated in its pages throughout its existence. *The Germ*'s subtitle, *Thoughts towards Nature in Poetry, Literature and Art,* indicated (according to Rossetti) "that an artist, whether painter or writer, ought to be bent upon defining and expressing his own personal thoughts, and that these ought to be based on a direct study of Nature, and harmonized with her manifestations."[2] This concept of an immediate vision of nature as central to art production shaped the aesthetics put forth by *The New Path*.

The Crayon, edited by William James Stillman and John Durand (son of painter Asher B. Durand, president of the National Academy of Design 1845–1861), borrowed the motto on its cover from Ruskin's *Modern Painters*, volume 2, chapter 12, "Of Vital Beauty. First as Relative": "Whence, in fine, looking to the whole kingdom of organic nature, we find that our full receiving of its beauty depends first on the sensibility and then on the accuracy and touchstone faithfulness of the heart in its moral judgments." Nature's truth is once again extolled as the foundation of what is beautiful, moral, and expressive; Ruskin's sentence continues for a full page with an assertion that "we should not only love all creatures well, but esteem them in that order which is according to God's laws and not according to our own human passions and predilections."[3] An emphasis on the divine continued through the journal to the point that, when Stillman left the editorship in June 1856, Durand replaced Ruskin's pronouncement with that of Saint Paul's to the Philippians (verse 8) for volume 4: "Whatsoever things are true, whatsoever things are just, whatsoever things are pure, whatsoever things are lovely, whatsoever things are of good report; if there be any virtue, and if there be any praise, think on these things." Whether voiced biblically or poetically, a Platonic concern with beauty as truth united all three journals in their aesthetic positions.

"We *Are* Iconoclasts": *The New Path,* a Radical Departure

The New Path, like its British precursor, began as a group idea arising from an association of like-minded individuals who were more diverse in occupation than *The Germ*'s Pre-Raphaelite painters and poets. The Association for the Advancement of the Cause of Truth in Art, as it was officially named in its minutes, met on January 27, 1863, at Thomas Charles Farrer's studio in Waverly Place, New York

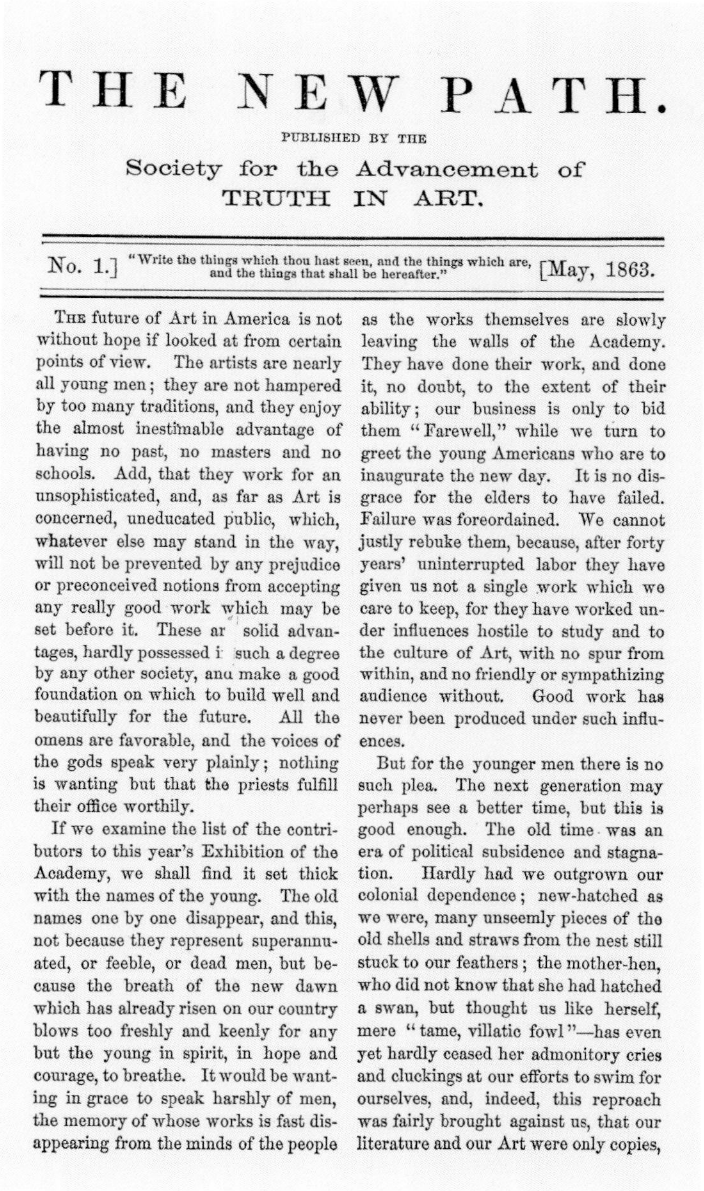

THE NEW PATH.

PUBLISHED BY THE

Society for the Advancement of
TRUTH IN ART.

No. 1.] "Write the things which thou hast seen, and the things which are, and the things that shall be hereafter." [May, 1863.

THE future of Art in America is not without hope if looked at from certain points of view. The artists are nearly all young men; they are not hampered by too many traditions, and they enjoy the almost inestimable advantage of having no past, no masters and no schools. Add, that they work for an unsophisticated, and, as far as Art is concerned, uneducated public, which, whatever else may stand in the way, will not be prevented by any prejudice or preconceived notions from accepting any really good work which may be set before it. These ar solid advantages, hardly possessed i such a degree by any other society, anu make a good foundation on which to build well and beautifully for the future. All the omens are favorable, and the voices of the gods speak very plainly; nothing is wanting but that the priests fulfill their office worthily.

If we examine the list of the contributors to this year's Exhibition of the Academy, we shall find it set thick with the names of the young. The old names one by one disappear, and this, not because they represent superannuated, or feeble, or dead men, but because the breath of the new dawn which has already risen on our country blows too freshly and keenly for any but the young in spirit, in hope and courage, to breathe. It would be wanting in grace to speak harshly of men, the memory of whose works is fast disappearing from the minds of the people as the works themselves are slowly leaving the walls of the Academy. They have done their work, and done it, no doubt, to the extent of their ability; our business is only to bid them "Farewell," while we turn to greet the young Americans who are to inaugurate the new day. It is no disgrace for the elders to have failed. Failure was foreordained. We cannot justly rebuke them, because, after forty years' uninterrupted labor they have given us not a single work which we care to keep, for they have worked under influences hostile to study and to the culture of Art, with no spur from within, and no friendly or sympathizing audience without. Good work has never been produced under such influences.

But for the younger men there is no such plea. The next generation may perhaps see a better time, but this is good enough. The old time was an era of political subsidence and stagnation. Hardly had we outgrown our colonial dependence; new-hatched as we were, many unseemly pieces of the old shells and straws from the nest still stuck to our feathers; the mother-hen, who did not know that she had hatched a swan, but thought us like herself, mere "tame, villatic fowl"—has even yet hardly ceased her admonitory cries and cluckings at our efforts to swim for ourselves, and, indeed, this reproach was fairly brought against us, that our literature and our Art were only copies,

1. Excerpt from *The New Path* 1, no. 1, May 1863, Courtesy University of Wisconsin Digital Collections, Madison

City, with artists, architects, geologists, and lawyers as the original group. Others joined, so that by the third meeting on February 11, the Articles of Organization were adopted with the Second Article specifying that education of the public was central to the Association's aims and that a journal would be established. By the April 3 meeting, held in architect Peter B. Wight's rooms, the members enumerated the specifics of the journal—its publication on the first day of the month, its subscription cost, its contents (including "articles on art, having for their principal purpose the education of the public to the true perception of Nature, and understanding of Art"), as well as art criticism, poetry, correspondence, and excerpts from the Association's meetings. They unanimously elected Clarence Cook editor; on April 7 his wife suggested the chosen title of the journal.[4] As Linda Ferber has suggested, the title may have been sparked by Ruskin's lectures published in 1859 as *The Two Paths*.[5] In his preface Ruskin asserted the principal law that "all noble design" depended on "the sculpture or painting of Organic Form." The way of life divides itself into two paths: "one way leading to the Olive mountains—one to the vale of the Salt Sea.... Let him pause at the parting of The Two Paths."[6] It is nature that paves the truthful, new path espoused in the journal, one divinely ordained.

When readers flipped through the pages of that inaugural issue, they found content obsessively focused on the aims of artists and critics determined to mark their creations as a radical departure from the nation's cultural history. "We hold that the primary object of Art is to observe and record truth, whether of the visible universe or of emotion," declared one author. "All great Art results from an earnest love of the beauty and perfectness of God's creation, and is the attempt to tell the truth about it."[7] From the journal's first issue to its last, these ideals of truth, faithfulness, and the supreme authority of God the Creator reigned. An insistence on the accurate seeing of nature's facts, combined with earnest feeling and an imaginative sensitivity to beauty, undergirded virtually all the commentary and poetry in *The New Path*. Didactic articles, art reviews, and some verse compose the journal. The fine arts—painting, sculpture, architecture, even furniture—were the primary focus of articles by Cook, Wight, Russell Sturgis Jr., Charles Herbert Moore, Farrer, and (likely) William James Stillman. *The New Path* proudly refrained from reporting on artist comings and goings, recent studio displays and sales, or extensive correspondence from afar.

The Germ, by contrast, openly displayed its literary origins, primarily featuring poetry with handsome full-page engravings. Some art theory and art history peppered the journal. Not art but book reviews closed each issue. *The Crayon*, the physically largest (with its 8 ½" × 11 ½" folio pages) and the longest-lasting of the Ruskin-inflected journals, featured the most diverse content, with articles not only by its editors and regular contributors on a range of art, literature, and nature subjects, but also extensive excerpts from magazines and books including Ruskin, German philosophers, and sociology. It regularly recounted studio gatherings and displays, artists' travels, and correspondence.

Cook made no apologies for the independent, even strident tone of *The New Path*. In the ninth issue, for example, he and his fellow editors reminded a subscriber that the publication was not produced to please or to make money, but rather "for the purpose of stirring up strife; of breeding discontent . . . we *are* iconoclasts."[8]

"The Moving Spirit of the Age": Freedom and the Redemption of Art

Clarence Cook's unsigned inaugural essay for *The New Path* established the tone and the language to follow in its twenty-four issues.[9] Claiming for the journal nothing less than a manifesto for the redemption of art in America, Cook challenged American artists to reject the traditions of the past—inauthentic, idealized renditions of nature and blind copying of European models among them—for their own self-reliant vision based on the truth to be seen and known, firsthand, from nature. Citing the advantage of youth unencumbered by the burdens of the past, Cook prophesied a fundamental "revolution" of art "worthy of the age and country in which we live." The nation's cultural and artistic naïveté protected these emerging artists from preconceptions that would hinder their development toward greatness. America possessed an innocent ignorance of art matters that made it much more open to the artist-revolutionary than was England's "very ignorant" and "unsympathetic" public. A case in point was the English opposition to the Pre-Raphaelites and the Gothic revival, two artistic causes that *The New Path* championed in its pages. America could take heart, however, because its "free land" promised an air unburdened by England's entrenched traditions and prejudices. In fact, Cook encouraged the nation's new artists "to leap with the strength of youth into this unfenced acre and take full possession." He also noted that the current National Academy exhibition resonated with the "names of the young" as older artists disappeared from the sight and memory of viewers. Claiming that failure of past artists and writers was inevitable because they only copied from European models, Cook counseled the new artists to "turn their backs deliberately and without ceremony upon the rubbish of the past."

As Sophie Lynford argues in this volume, the Civil War and abolitionism pushed Cook and the American Pre-Raphaelites to adopt such a radical rejection of convention and the past. Members of the Association were ardent supporters of the Union cause; as the Civil War took an increasingly bloody turn, Cook employed apocalyptic language, at once religious and of the battlefield, in order to declare that American independence of thought had truly arrived: "In literature, in religion, in society, in art—we are fast sweeping into the glad new year when America shall sound the trumpet-call, and marshal her children to do her work in her own free way."[10] As of January 1863, just months before the publication of the first issue of *The New Path*, there came a new national freedom to aspire to, the Emancipation Proclamation, ostensibly freeing slaves in the rebellious states. Cook framed this national situation as one of artistic opportunity and cultural duty.

Freedom from tyranny, then, consisted not only in the abolition of slavery but also, for these new artists, in a rejection of outmoded artistic conventions, an intuitive and conscientious turning to nature, and a faithful dedication to art not for material gain but as a means of enjoyment and "love of God's work." Education of the public to a proper taste would occur through exposure to the new artists' persistent allegiance to the principles of great art based on fidelity to the natural world: ideal truth conveyed in paint. The words *true* and *truth*, along with *faithful*, *earnest*, *conscientious*, *nature*, and *God* appear in Cook's introductory essay and throughout the pages of the journal:

> The new path into which the best minds of the present day summon the young to enter, is the earnest loving study of God's work of nature. This is not only taught to the artist, but to the Writer, the Poet, and the Teacher. It is the moving spirit of the age in which we live; an age greater in all essentials than any that has preceded it, second to none in the purity and strength of its religious ideas; in its love of man, which is the best fruit of its love of God; in its tolerance, its enthusiasm, its energy, and in the widespread diffusion of wealth and education, which are saving it from selfishness and dillettanteelism [*sic*].[11]

With this optimistic assessment of the moment at hand, Cook recounts utopian reforms for a future postwar cultural millennium. Linking the aspirations of this "moving spirit of the age" to those of *The New Path*, Cook finally concluded his essay by assuring his new audience of an unprecedented level of critical honesty and persuasion not found in the often-obsequious newspapers.

"The American Scholar": The Emersonian Ideal and *The New Path*

Foreshadowing Cook's call for American artistic independence was a work written twenty-six years earlier by a fellow graduate of Harvard University, Ralph Waldo Emerson: "The American Scholar: An Oration Delivered before the Phi Beta Kappa Society, at Cambridge, August 31, 1837," which Oliver Wendell Holmes Sr. called "our intellectual Declaration of Independence." Emerson first published this monumental address as a pamphlet in 1837; significantly, it reappeared under the title "The American Scholar" in his *Nature; Addresses, and Lectures* published in September 1849.[12] As Kenneth Sacks argues, the essay would have a profound influence on Emerson's own development as well as on that of his cultural contemporaries and successors.[13] Putting faith in the ordinary and in an original relationship with nature, Emerson extolled the "Man Thinking," a biblical Adam reborn. The American Scholar would not be "an unthinking bookworm" but an "active soul" who obtained fresh insight in his free engagement with the world, unburdened by "the courtly muses of Europe" or by "the book, the college, the school of art, the institution of any kind." Cook's independent young men, free from the tyranny of schools, have their origins in Emerson's call for a nation of men who "will walk on our own feet; we will work with our own hands; we will speak our own minds" because each will believe "himself inspired by the Divine Soul." Cook shares Emerson's faith in nature as the ultimate influence upon the mind, whether of the scholar, the artist, or the viewer. Emerson's declaration in "The American Scholar"—that nature's laws and beauty are that of one's own mind, exhorting readers to "Know thyself" and "Study nature"—would resonate throughout the pages of *The New Path* and in the art it championed.[14]

In the journal's fourth issue (August 1863), the author of "Art as a Record," signed as J. S., reaffirms the same principles voiced by Cook in the first issue. He addresses the duty of the artist, just as Emerson had articulated the duties of the American Scholar in the acts of observation and feeling. Emerson is invoked alongside fellow poets James Russell Lowell, John Greenleaf Whittier, Holmes, Henry Wadsworth Longfellow, William Cullen Bryant, and Henry David Thoreau as models of pleasure and instruction, of observation and truthfulness. The Romantic subjectivity of Emersonian creativity is downplayed, however, in favor of the manual exactitudes required by the realities of art production. J. S. challenges artists "to go out into the woods and fields" in all seasons, not just the summer, in order to capture in paint Emerson's Rhodora or Thoreau's Poke Berry. What emerges, again, is an unwavering insistence on truth and the nobility of faithfully recording what is seen "minutely and completely" in order to convey a "humble love of God's work." The dutiful artist, J. S. asserts, restrains fancy in favor of observing and recording truth: even among "the great imaginative painters or poets there is not one who is not eminent as an observer." The good and the true become one, and "the greater the man the more accurate his observation."[15]

In "Naturalism and Genius," published in issue 6 (October 1863), J. S. continues his assertion that character and work are one, with the mind revealed in the details of nature. Contrasting the generalist painter with the painter of "perception and grasp," the author declares that the latter man is able to reveal to the viewer the nature uncommonly seen—the inner workings of nature, the processes of a higher order, the microcosm unveiling the macrocosm. As in John Ruskin's highly detailed *Fragment of the Alps* (plate 84), previously on display in New York in the winter of 1858, "the truth is told about each square inch, and therefore the truth is told about the whole." J. S. invokes Emerson once more in a defense of comparisons between painters and poets and the labor involved in the truthfulness of each: "If a painter sees nature as Emerson sees her," he writes, "he will surely try and tell us what he sees; and not reason that it is impossible for him to describe as many scenes in the same time and with the same labor, and that therefore he won't try."[16] Emerson, along with Ruskin, remained the prophetic visionary who inspired the new generation of *The New Path*.

J. S.'s explicit invocation of Emerson in the two articles discussed above, and the Emersonian inflections embedded in *The New Path* as a whole, raises the question as to the identity of this pseudonym. As Sophie Lynford argues, J. S. is most likely William James Stillman, who had returned from Rome in early July of 1863 to fetch his wife Laura and son Russie (named after Ruskin).[17] The many references to the literary figures Stillman was close to, including Lowell, Holmes, and Emerson—with whom he spent time in the Adirondacks as participants in the Philosophers' Camp as well as in Cambridge—implies his authorship.[18] Even more convincing, however, are the same familiarity and easy movement from literature to art to philosophy that characterize Stillman's previous writings for *The Crayon*. In Stillman's "The Art of the Present" from May 9, 1855, he quotes Longfellow and Lowell on the imperative of the individual to engage with the world of the present, extending that directive to the artist whose "utility" depends on searching out and seeing the beauty and spiritual worth in nature's moments, not furnishing "us with phantasies." The artist's duty is to convey truth and to teach us "to see for ourselves" the "seal of Divinity in His works" by using our eyes and opening our hearts so that we "may understand the sign in which it is written."[19] This Emersonian vision reverberates throughout *The Crayon*, and subsequently, as we have seen, in *The New Path*.

"The Artist's Business": Duty Not Commerce

Above all others, it is Emerson who gets the last word in *The New Path*. Closing the last page of the journal's last issue (December 1865) is an excerpt from his 1847 poem "Initial, Daemonic, and Celestial Love": "He who feeds men serveth few; / He serves all, who dares be true."[20] That the last word of the journal is *true* is indeed fitting for a publication "founded by a Society devoted to the advancement of truth in art," in which references to the *true*, the *faithful*, the *factual*, and the *earnest* occupy almost every page, essay, and even sentence. But Emerson's words also resonate with the plea at the end of *The New Path*'s final essay, "Art and Photography." The author addresses the rise of the mechanism of photography as artistic competition but states emphatically that it will "never supersede Fine Art." The artist, unlike the photographer, can economize the gradations and subtleties of nature, merging them with a deep feeling toward "God's work." The easy means, and by implication financial gains, of the photograph must not fool the artist into giving up the hard labor of diligent seeing and the manual recording of nature. The writer implores artists to heed their duty to serve society with a higher spiritual purpose: "It is the artist's business, by harmoniously associated representations of truth and loveliness, to quicken love and gratify and inform the mind concerning the Creator's work, and to lead it to contemplate and dwell upon those things which is good for human souls to heed."[21] With this appeal, *The New Path*'s constant concern about monetary ambitions soiling the transcendent duties of the artist, introduced in its first pages, comes full circle, as do ties to its predecessor *The Crayon*.[22]

"The Poet and the Artist": Literary Influences on the American Pre-Raphaelites

Echoes of Emerson's poetic voice resonated throughout the pages of *The New Path* with excerpts from other poets, particularly the Romantics and Victorians, and especially in the journal's first year of publication. Although the journal did not employ literary figures as contributors or editors, as did *The Germ* (William M. Rossetti with his famous poetic family) and *The Crayon* (Justin Winsor and J. G. Brownlee Brown, among others), Cook's own literary background afforded him connections and awareness for applicable inclusions.[23] In "A Letter to a Subscriber," Cook and his fellow editors reasserted the journal's governing principles and conception of art, connecting the visual and literary arts in their purpose. "The Poet and the Artist have the same errand in the world," they wrote, "and while one sings his message to the ear, the other paints his to the eye." Both "draw lessons for the teaching of the race" from human experience through the processes of deep observation and truthful reporting.[24]

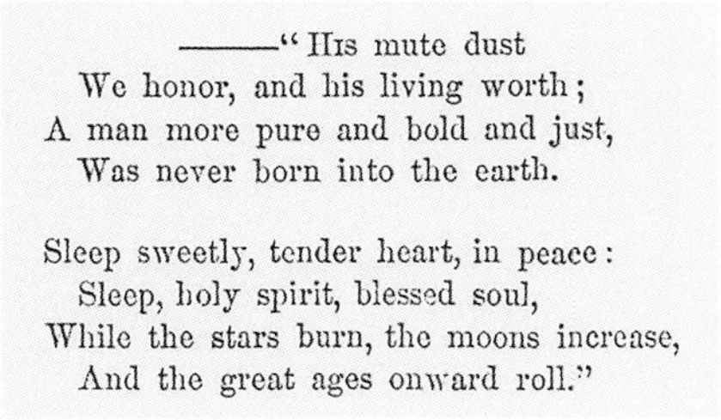
——"His mute dust
We honor, and his living worth;
A man more pure and bold and just,
Was never born into the earth.

Sleep sweetly, tender heart, in peace:
Sleep, holy spirit, blessed soul,
While the stars burn, the moons increase,
And the great ages onward roll."

2. "In Memory of Abraham Lincoln," *The New Path* 2, no. 5, May 1865, Courtesy University of Wisconsin Digital Collections, Madison

One of the first quotations of the poetic to aid in understanding the visual appears in Russell Sturgis's analysis of the power of Gothic architecture, published in the July 1863 issue. Sturgis includes lines from the prologue to Alfred, Lord Tennyson's *Princess, A Medley* (1847), in which the ruins of a medieval abbey suggest a wildness amid the passage of time, appealing to the current taste for the Gothic.[25] A year later, Sturgis revisits the poet—a favorite of the period and of *The New Path*—in "Pictures and Studies" of July 1864, in which Tennyson's "Charge of the Light Brigade" (1854) is framed as a model of what the painter can do to evoke experience if rightly armed with facts and in command of his medium.[26] Tennyson also received praise from Stillman, who marveled at the "accuracy of perception somewhat beyond that of a common observer" imaginatively coalesced with musical rhythms in the poem "The Eagle."[27] Tennyson's poetic lines for his friend James Spedding after the death of his brother Edward, "To J. S." (1833), are repurposed in *The New Path*'s May 1865 memorial to Abraham Lincoln (fig. 2), offering solace to a nation in mourning.[28] Appropriately, the selected characteristics of "a man more pure and bold and just" emphasize not only the qualities of Lincoln's leadership as he faced down those who would sever the Union, but also those values *The New Path* sought in its ideal artists and their creations.

Verse from William Wordsworth and John Keats closes the issues of September and October 1863, with substantial excerpts from Wordsworth's *Lines Written a Few Miles above Tintern Abbey* (1798) and Keats's *Endymion* (1818). Both poems evoke the power of nature to instill love, truth, faith, and spirit into its admirer. Wordsworth's selection begins with the line "Nature never did betray / The heart that loved her," reminding the reader of the natural world's capacity to elevate the mind, for "all that which we behold / Is full of blessings." *Tintern Abbey* offers a concrete example of what Cook, in his article "Advance" on the previous page, presents as the importance of the Romantic break from the rules of classicism so that the true representations of "life and nature" prevail, whether in literature, music, or art.[29] In the journal's next issue, an excerpt from Keats asserts that "A thing of beauty is a joy forever. . . . Some shape of beauty moves away the pall / From our dark spirits," illustrating in poetic verse the sentiments voiced for the redemptive primacy of naturalism in art by Charles Herbert Moore ("Fallacies of the Present School") and Stillman ("Naturalism and Genius"). According to Moore,

> The world has had enough morbid fiction, it now needs healthy fact. God's truth must come in and take the place of vanity. Now in the present school, what there is of love for God and nature, and reverence for, and careful rendering of truth, will live, and we believe there is much of it; but it must purge itself from falsehood or it will die.[30]

Other poetry echoing the Romantics appeared in *The New Path,* including, notably, John Ruskin's "Mount Blanc Revisited, July 1845" and Clarence Cook's sonnet "To the Fringed Gentian," which refashioned William Cullen Bryant's "To the Fringed Gentian" (1832) with a greater emphasis on the present moment than on Bryant's heavenly destination.[31] In each of these poems nature offers lessons for those who truly heed her through the eye and the heart, aligning the journal's critical and ideological aims with its literary references.

"The Artist's Singular Perception": Naturalism and Imagination

From its inception *The New Path* promised to speak a revelatory truth about the art of the present day and past traditions. Its various articles, addressing aesthetic theories, criticism, literary references, and the visual arts, harnessed the revolutionary spirit of Emersonian self-reliance and Romantic attention to nature's truths. Current exhibition reviews, as well as evaluation of recent architectural monuments, allowed readers to find out if theory and practice corresponded and whether the new American art that had been prophesied was actually anywhere in sight. On the whole, the exhibition reviews, most presumably written by Cook (at

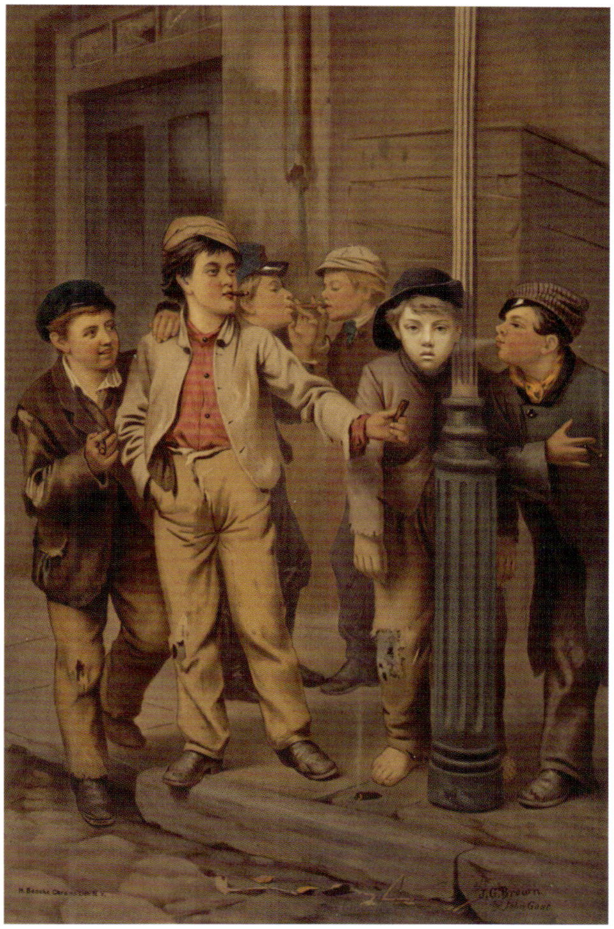

3. John Gast after John George Brown; Herman Bencke, lithographer, *The First Cigar*, c. 1870, chromolithograph, Library of Congress, Prints and Photographs Division, Washington, DC

least until May 1864 when Sturgis took over the editorship), relentlessly measured artists against the Ruskinian truth-to-nature realism advocated in the journal's pages. Impatience and even disgust with established artists were not unusual. The article "The Humorous in Art" attached the words *vulgar*, *beastiality* [*sic*], *disgusts*, *sickens*, *mistake*, and *dangerous* to William H. Beard's anthropomorphic *Jealous Rabbits* and John George Brown's urchin story *The First Cigar* (fig. 3). For the author, the subject matter was even more offensive because it was painted naturalistically. Neither depiction possessed the reformative qualities of proper genre painting; Beard's was salacious, and Brown's denigrated poor youth. Thomas Farrer's *Gone! Gone!* (plate 12), with its empathy and biblical references, provided a noble example, as did the paintings of Eastman Johnson.[32] A review titled "The Artist's Fund Society, Fourth Annual Exhibition" sparked brutal attacks on deceased artists Thomas Cole and Washington Allston, characterizing them as members of the American old school that the new naturalist artists in the Pre-Raphaelite vein would best ignore. Deeming three works by Cole "pieces of hopeless imbecility," the author, "Lionel," wished that there were more on view so that everyone would "learn, once for all, how empty are this man's much vaunted claims to high rank. They cannot stand in the light of today," he wrote, "and in twenty-five years will not be worth the canvas they are painted on."[33] Artists who followed Cole's lead, like Jasper Cropsey in his *Corfe Castle,* could be accused of never painting "a stroke out of doors" and were advised to never paint again. Yet Cropsey's Greenwood Lake paintings, on view at the National Academy of Design's thirty-ninth annual exhibition, did receive praise, depending on the earnestness of their naturalism and how close they corresponded to plein-air painting. The *Homestead* version seemed to convey an experience equal to an actual journey to the countryside.[34]

Cropsey could not compete, however, with the exhibition's newer artists John Henry Hill (who "studies Nature, and Nature only") and C. C. Griswold, whose *December* garnered praise for "accuracy of perception... delicate and complete drawing of form... and faithful transcript of color, —a complete insight into the whole winter landscape, and a tender and artistic delineation of it quite beyond praise."[35] Farrer's Catskill paintings and drawings epitomized the journal's value of vision, especially *A Buckwheat Field on Thomas Cole's Farm* (1863, plate 13; detail on p. 112). In descriptive prose Sturgis led the viewer's eye through the space of the canvas, remarking on the "golden yellow" tinges of the buckwheat field "crossed by pale purple shadows": "So lovely a chord of color it is not often our good fortune to see. And all this beauty comes of copying Nature! The theorizers about color have as yet hardly reached such a result." Sturgis reminded his readers that the painting's importance comes not only from its plethora of facts but also from "the artist's singular perception of and feeling for color."[36]

Albert Bierstadt and Frederic Church, among others, annoyed Cook as much for how their too-large canvases were displayed as for what was painted on them. Railing against the business of selling pictures with elaborate spectacle displays of drapery, lighting, viewing tubes, and descriptive pamphlets, Cook evaluated Bierstadt's *The Rocky Mountains, Lander's Peak* (1863, fig. 4) as both impressive (in its detailed scene of Indian life in the foreground) and lacking (in its generalization of geology with wasted, and all-too-evident, brush marks). Bierstadt's *Mount Hood, Oregon,* on sale at the Mutual Art Association in spring of 1865, failed miserably in Sturgis's estimation in following the realities of nature, descending into mannerism in the depiction of trees and mountain silhouettes. Sturgis feared Bierstadt's style has "lost him to nature, lost to good art." Yet he offered hope that Bierstadt would once "again walk with nature, seeking in all reverence and humility to discover her truths."[37] It was a practice that Sturgis perceived in Moore's small landscapes, especially *Winter Study in the Catskills,* which had "more faithful rendering of all the facts of nature taken together... than in any landscape picture of the

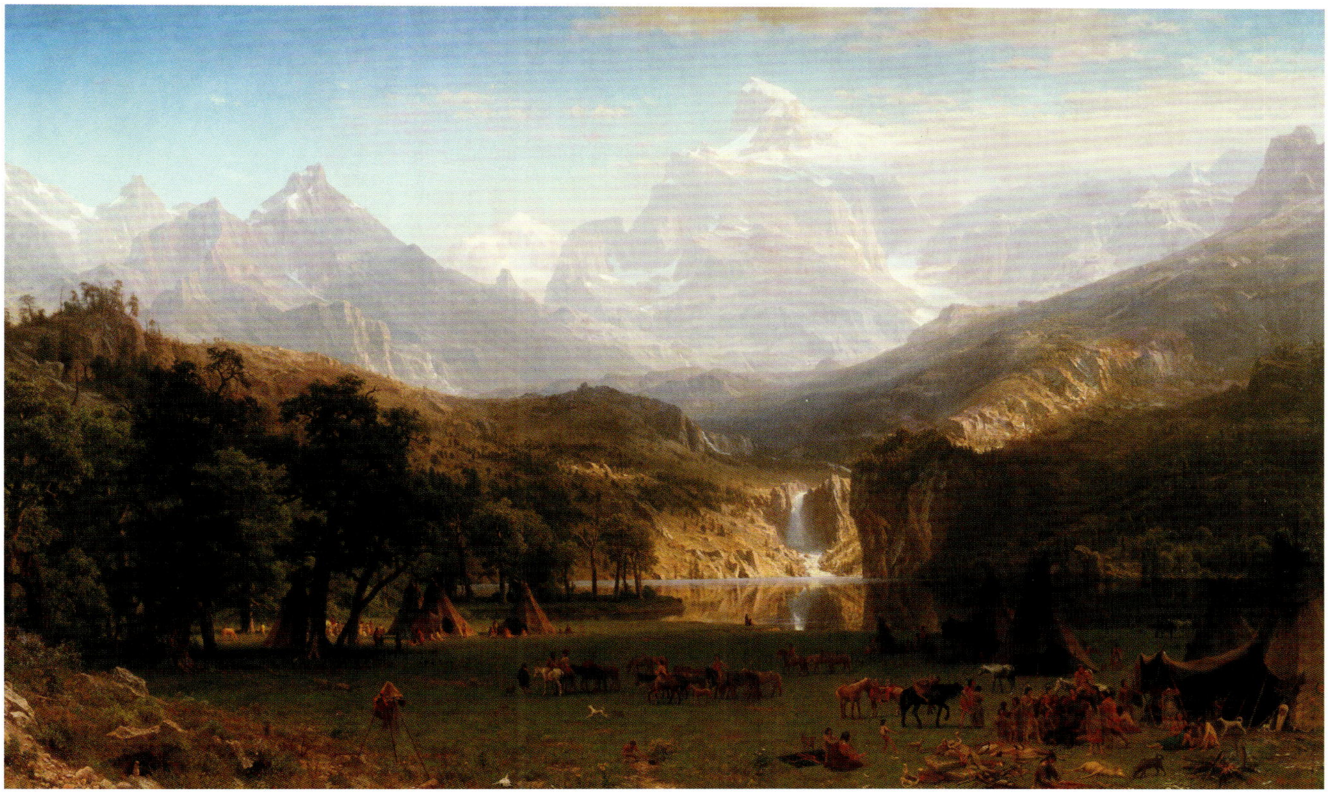

4. Albert Bierstadt, *The Rocky Mountains, Lander's Peak*, 1863, oil on canvas, The Metropolitan Museum of Art, New York, Rogers Fund, 1907

past year by any American artist." Although *Winter Study* is unlocated, *High Peak and Round Top (Catskill) in Winter* (1866, plate 53) depicts a similar scene and shares qualities Sturgis found so admirable. Indeed, Moore's achievement prompted Sturgis to articulate, in what would be the last issue of *The New Path,* his (and Cook's) true ideal of landscape painting:

> The ideal of landscape is not the submitting of special truths to general truths, but the full realization of all the truths in perfect harmony with each other . . . not a correcting of nature, but a stopping short of the whole truth of nature, just so far as is made necessary by the physical limitations of art, and a stopping short in the best (i.e., the least injurious) way. This ideal is, so far as we know, yet to be reached.[38]

Charles Moore aspired to this Emersonian ideal of synthesizing nature's multiplicity not only in his painting but also in his theoretical writing for *The New Path*. His "Fallacies of the Present School," published in October 1863, posited that "the true ideal is based upon, and grows out of, the real" and placed faith that God would reveal truth to the receptive eye and receiving heart.[39] The following month, *The New Path* opened with Moore's evangelical "The Office of Imagination,"[40] in which he elaborated on a component of artistic creativity that might have seemed antithetical to the Association's advocation of an all-seeing naturalism. As Stillman argued in "Naturalism and Genius," however, the imagination sees with the eye, illuminating as a lamp what the eye cannot physically see.[41] Significantly, Moore aligned this special seeing with the weight of religious enlightenment by connecting his espoused theories to the revolutionary voice and revelatory tone of the journal's masthead quotation and subsequent pages. Moore prefaced his comparison of the "healthy imagination" of the true, deep seer against the ignoble imagination of superstitious contrivance with a New Testament passage from John 7:18 about seeking the glory of God in one's teachings: "He that speaketh of himself seeketh his own glory, but he that seeketh His glory that sent Him, the same is true, and no unrighteousness is in him." Other biblical references include Jeremiah and two passages from Saint Paul to the Corinthians (2:3:6; 1:15:46), with mention of the "Spirit which giveth life."[42] These passages reiterated the role of spiritual inspiration in guiding the inner and outer eye of both artist and critic as they sought to know the truth, and therefore the beauty, of the world. As Moore stated:

> Form is the cup which bears the essence of spiritual realities to us. This truth, proves the truth of the Realistic principles, — namely, that absolute truth is the necessary basis of all true beauty and imagination. . . . True imagination is that power which can show us the inherent beauty in things that to a superficial eye appear ugly.[43]

The artist, therefore, revealed the spirit in all things with an Emersonian eye. The seemingly unexceptional became extraordinary; a single, simple leaf commanded the viewer's attention (plate 59). In closing, Moore expressed excitement that a new path was truly being forged, that at that moment in 1863 there were "mental wars . . . shaking the dogmas of men to their very foundations." As the Civil War continued to rage, Moore alluded to the apocalyptic imagery used by Cook in his introductory essay: "The 'days of the dragon are numbered,' and the battles will not cease till Babylon is utterly destroyed. Hereafter all that can endure must be built upon the rock of TRUTH."[44]

Charles Herbert Moore, *High Peak and Round Top (Catskill) in Winter*, 1866 (detail, plate 53)

The New Path did not conclude with those powerful words; there would be seventeen more issues, in fact, where the ideal of truth, and all its variants, would be repeated relentlessly. As the product of one of the young artists Cook heralded as the promise of America's artistic revolution, Moore's essay serves as an apt summary of the goals of the Association for the Advancement of Truth in Art and the voice of its journal. In the end, to paraphrase Emerson, *The New Path* sought to serve all humanity by daring to embrace the truth.

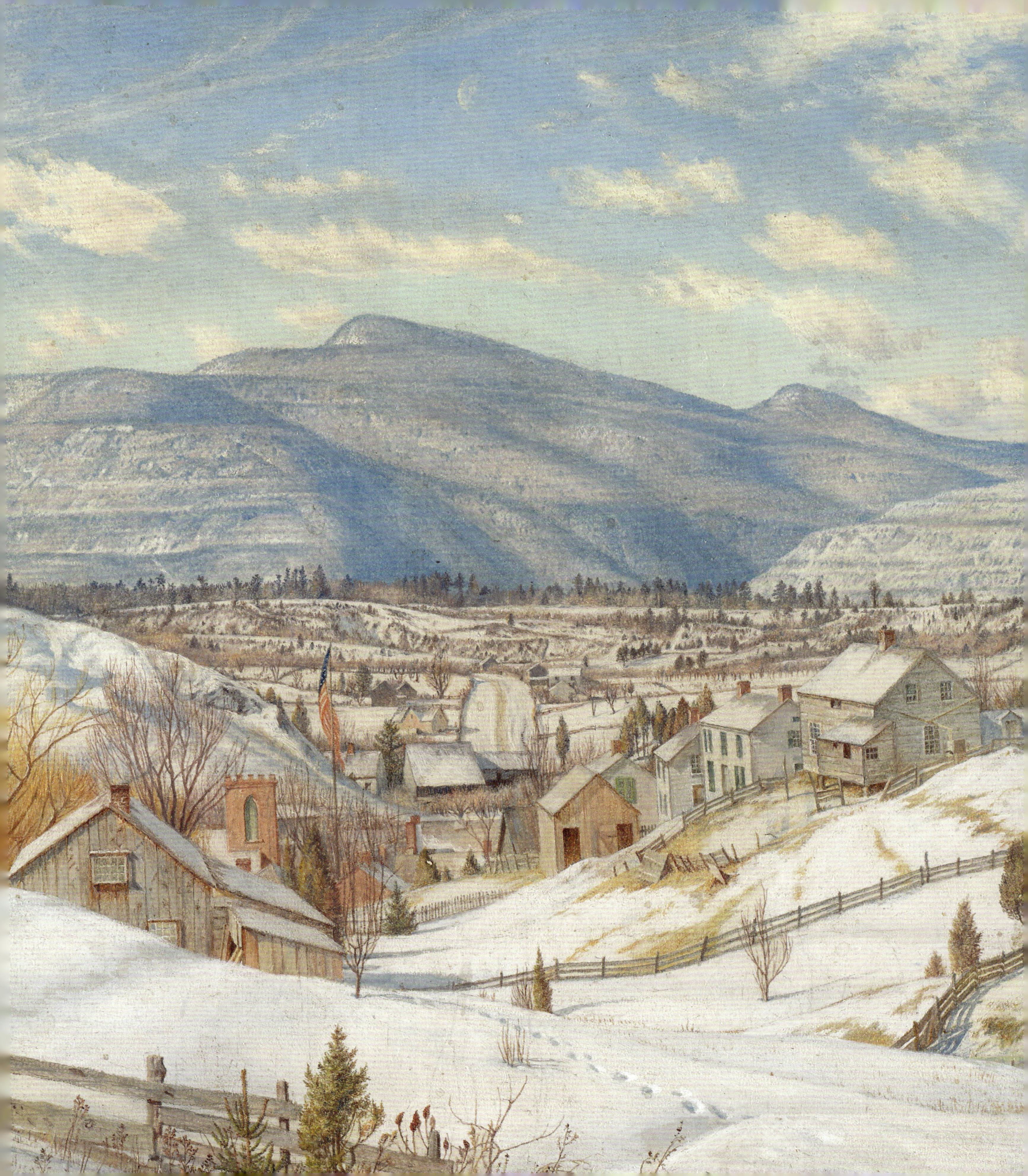

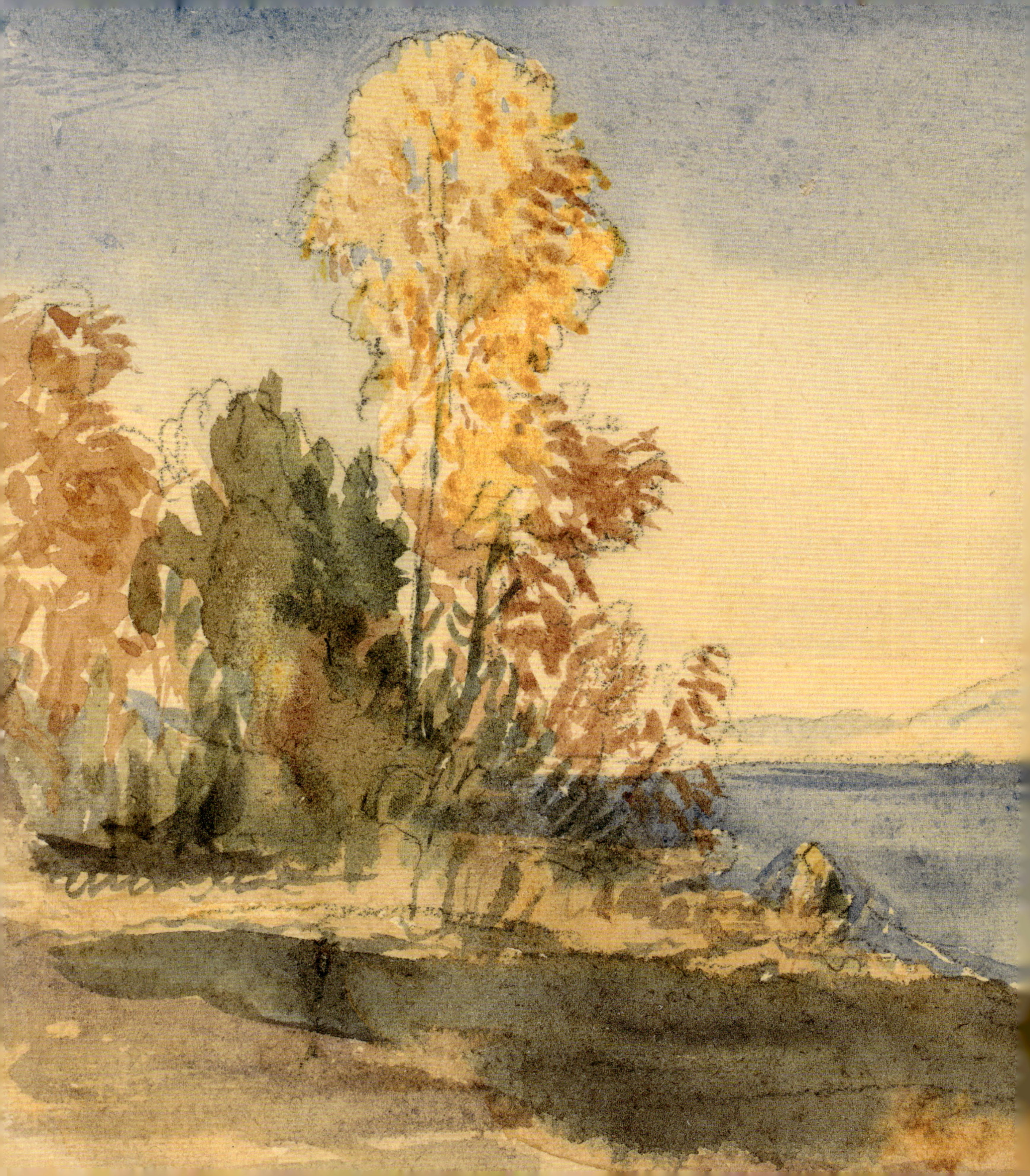

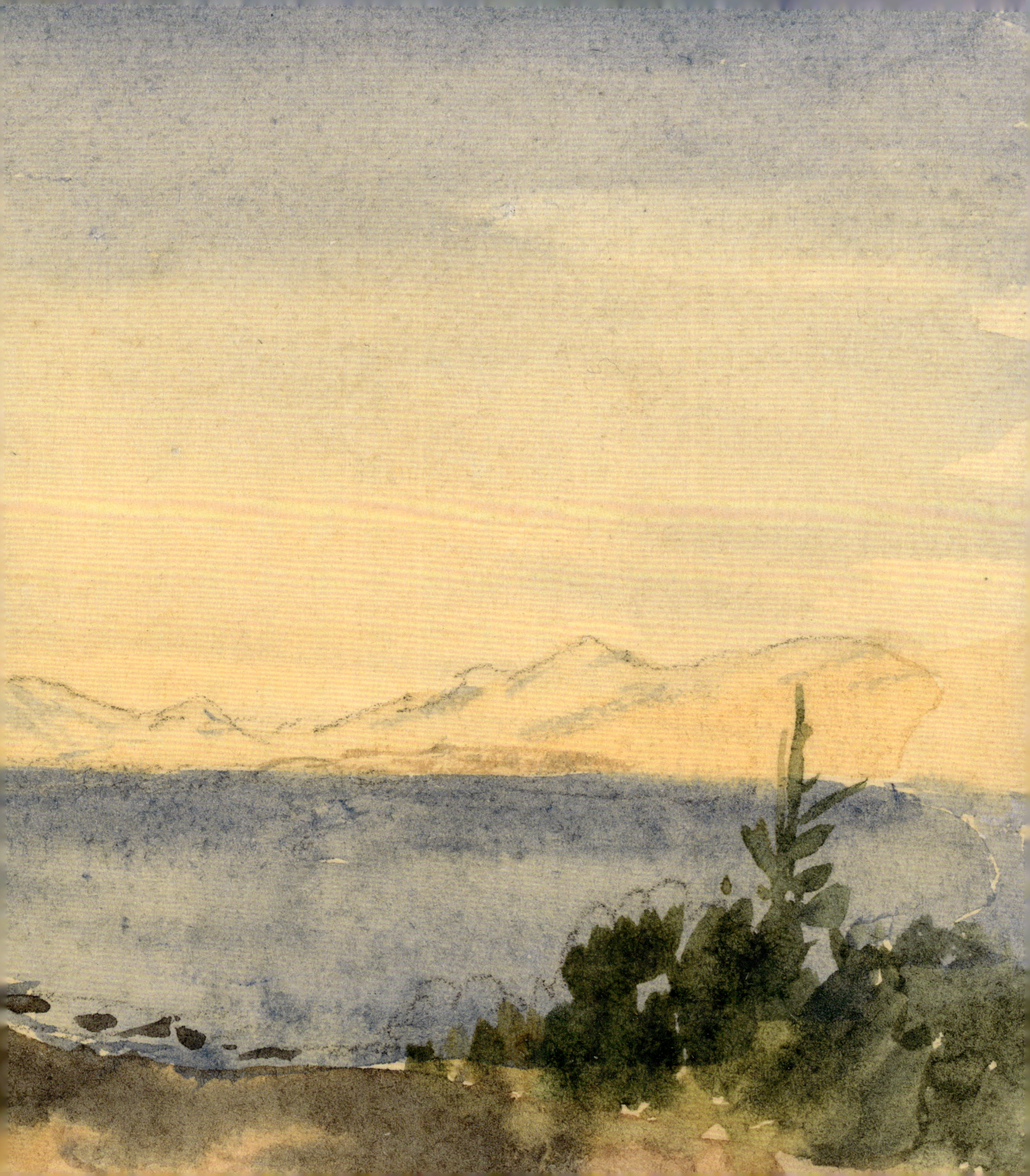

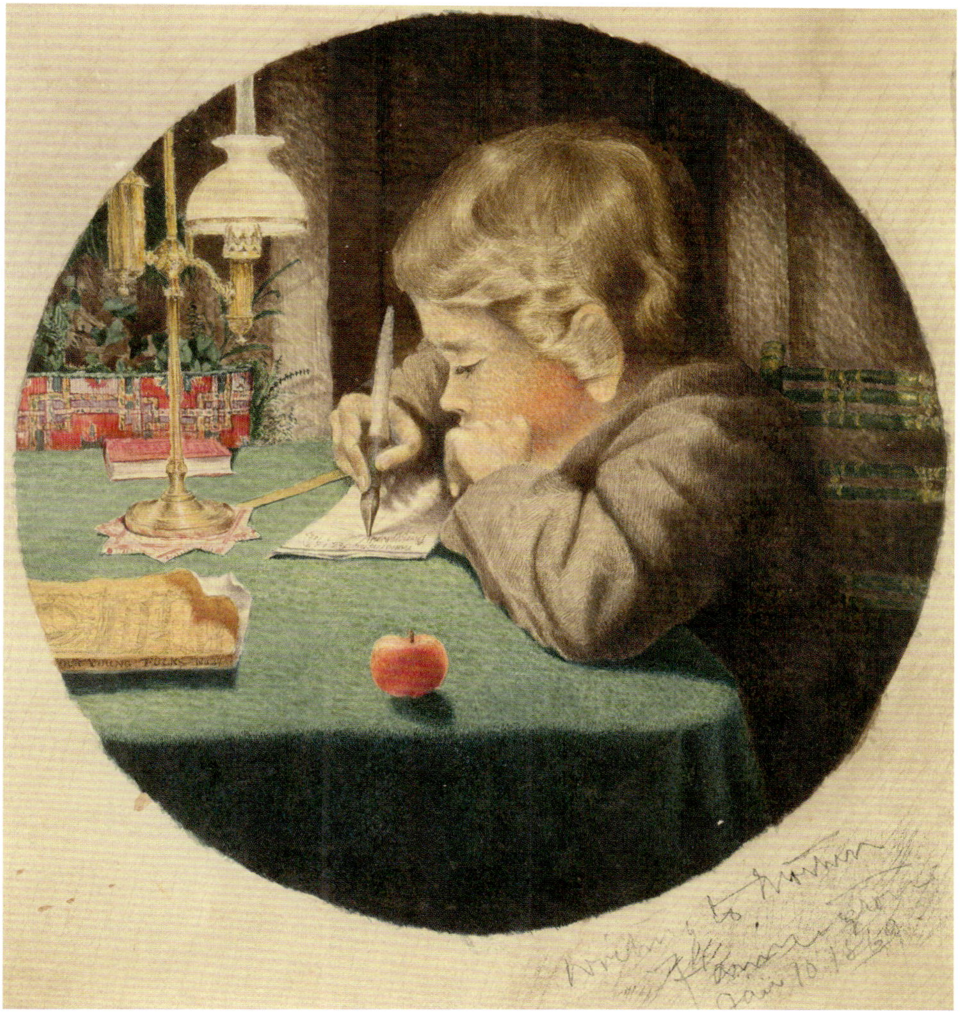

1
ROBERT BOLLING BRANDEGEE
Writing to Mother, 1869

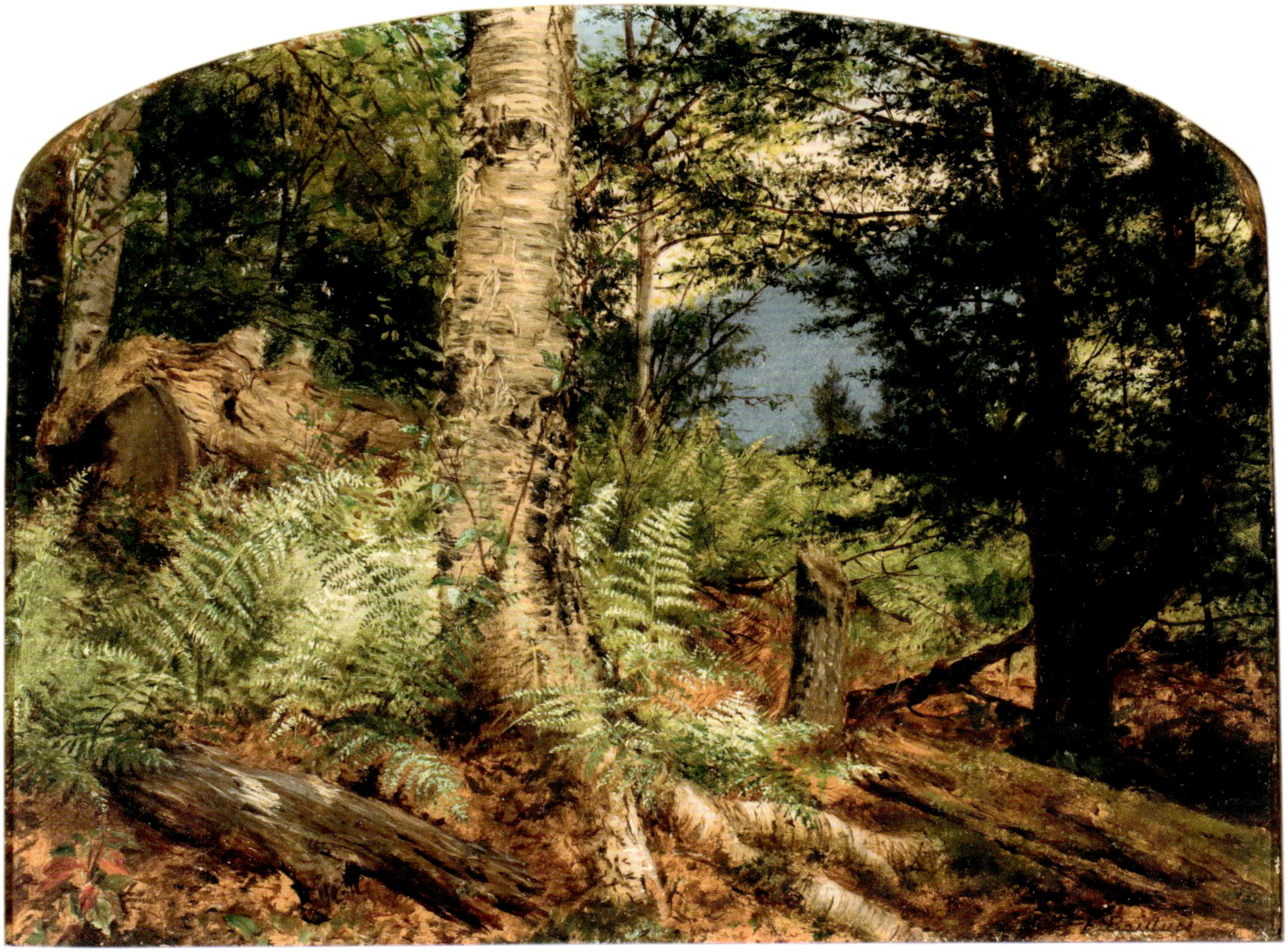

2

FIDELIA BRIDGES

Study of Ferns, 1864

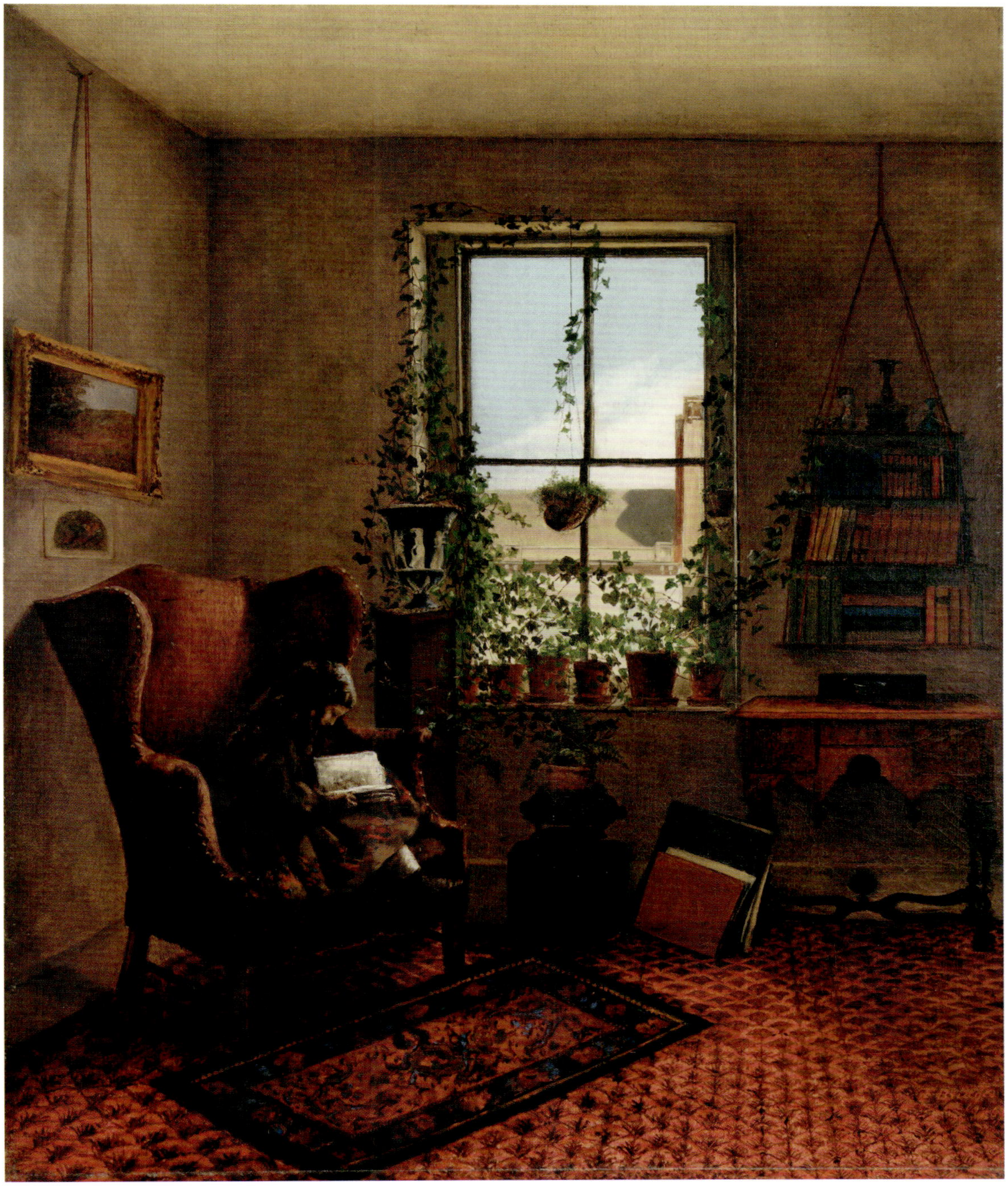

3
FIDELIA BRIDGES
Laura Brown in a Wingchair, 1867

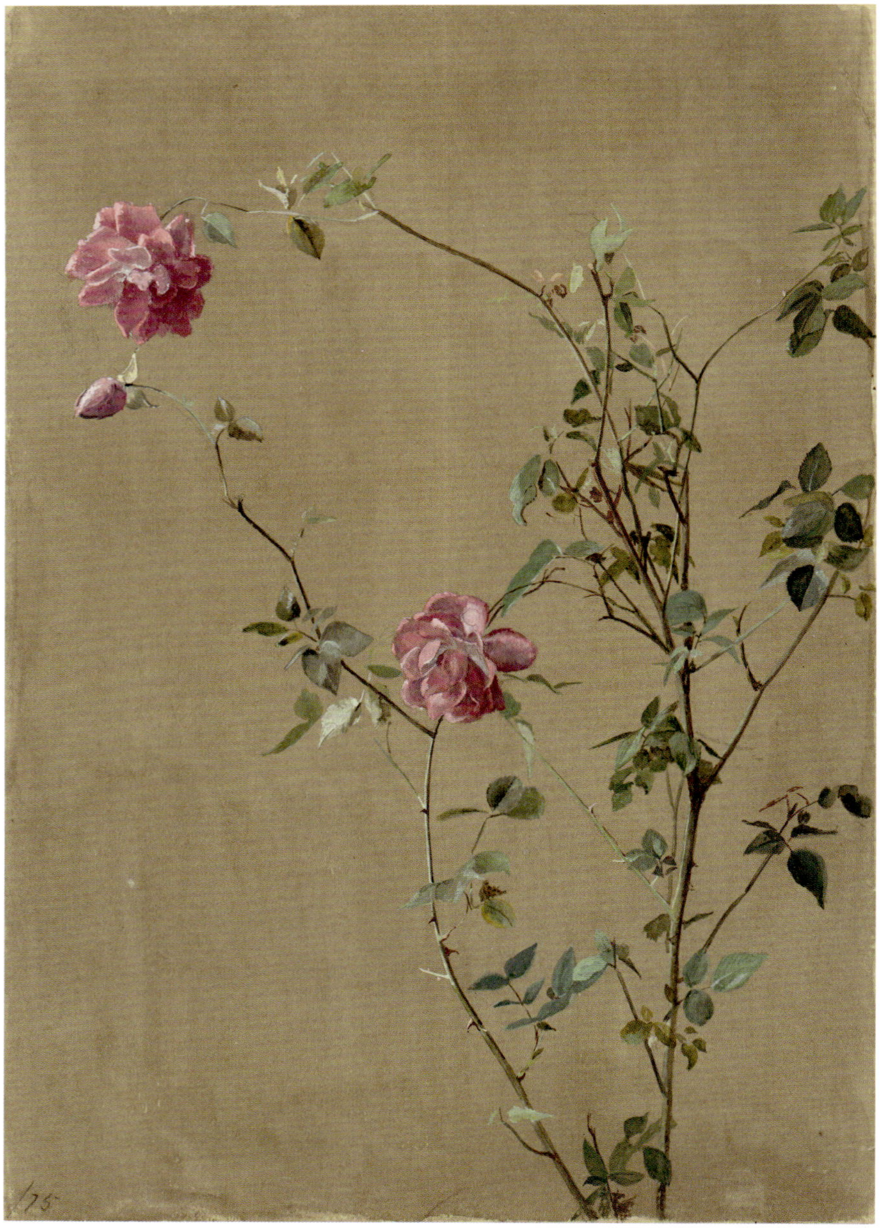

4
FIDELIA BRIDGES
Pink Roses, 1875

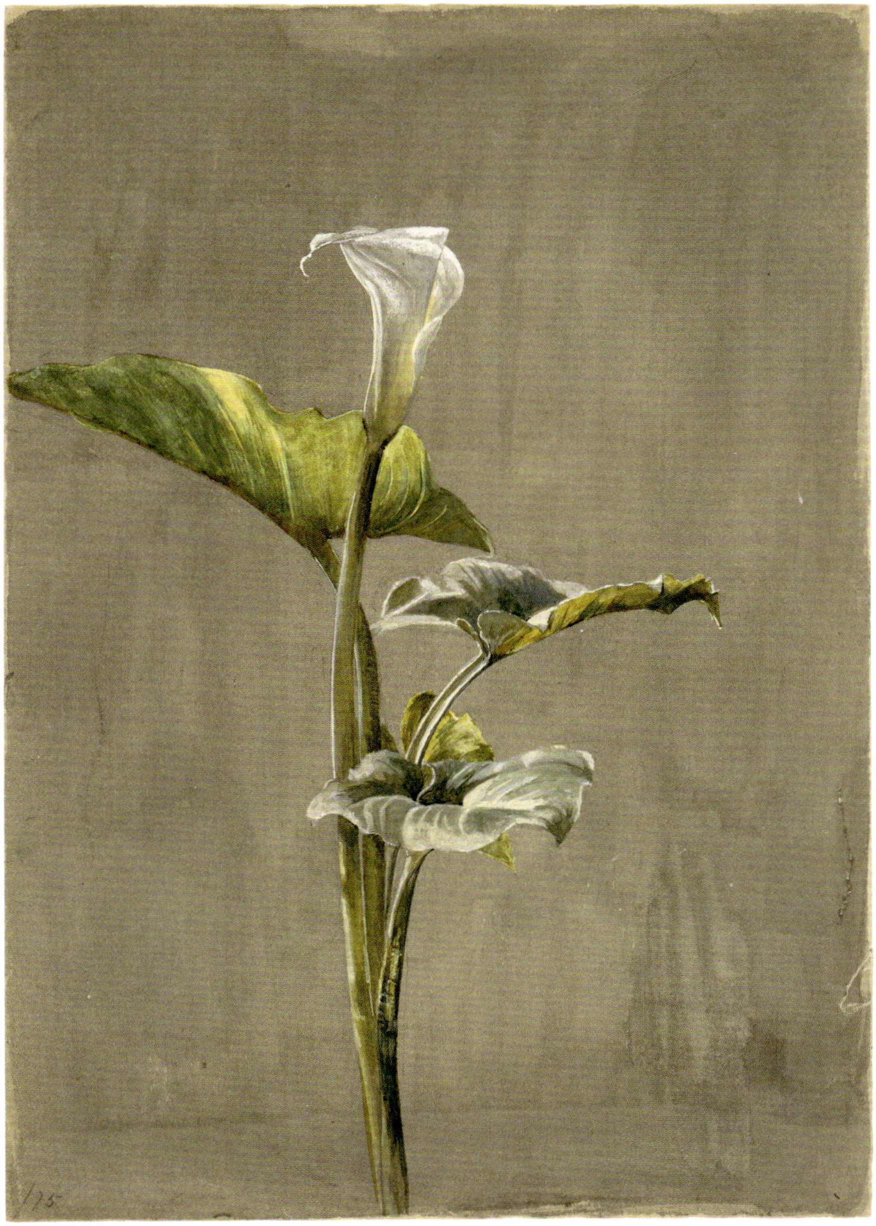

5
FIDELIA BRIDGES
Calla Lily, 1875

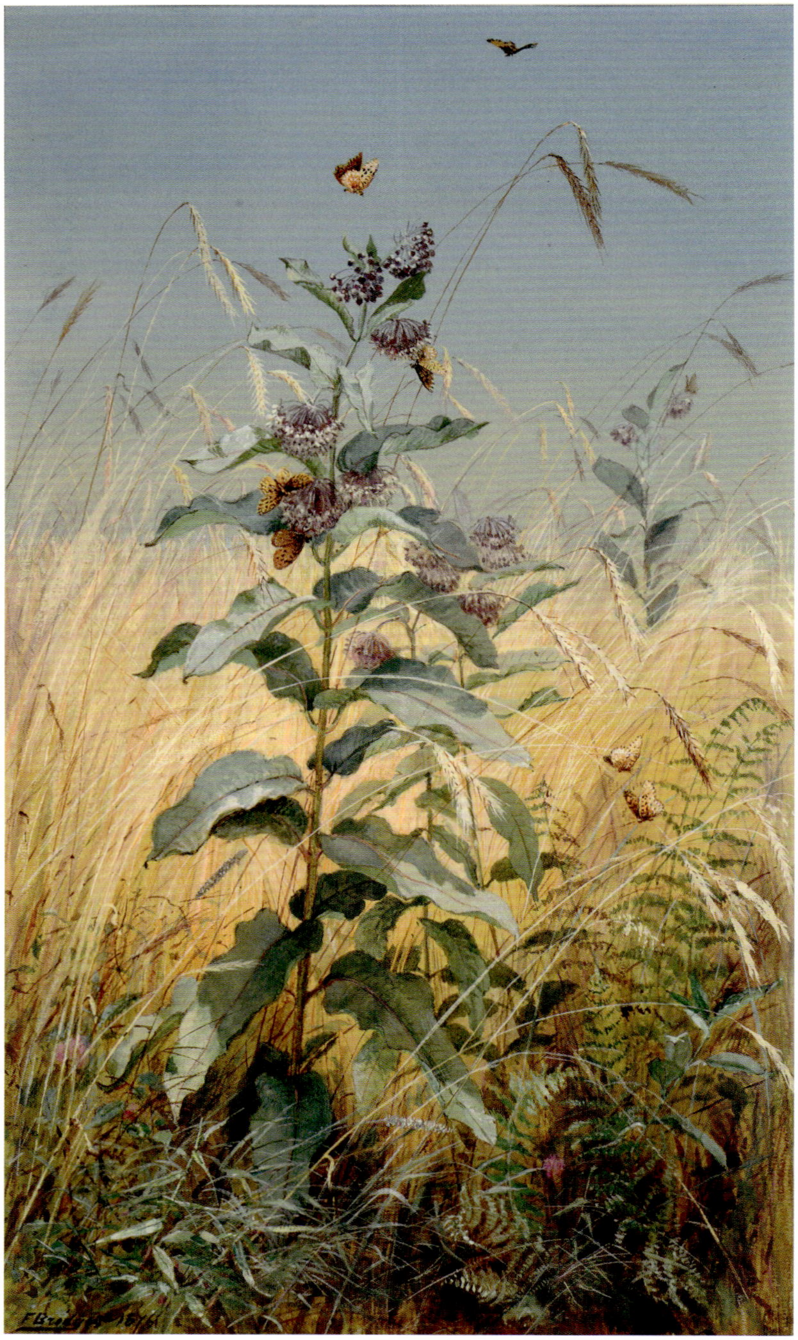

6
FIDELIA BRIDGES
Milkweeds, 1876

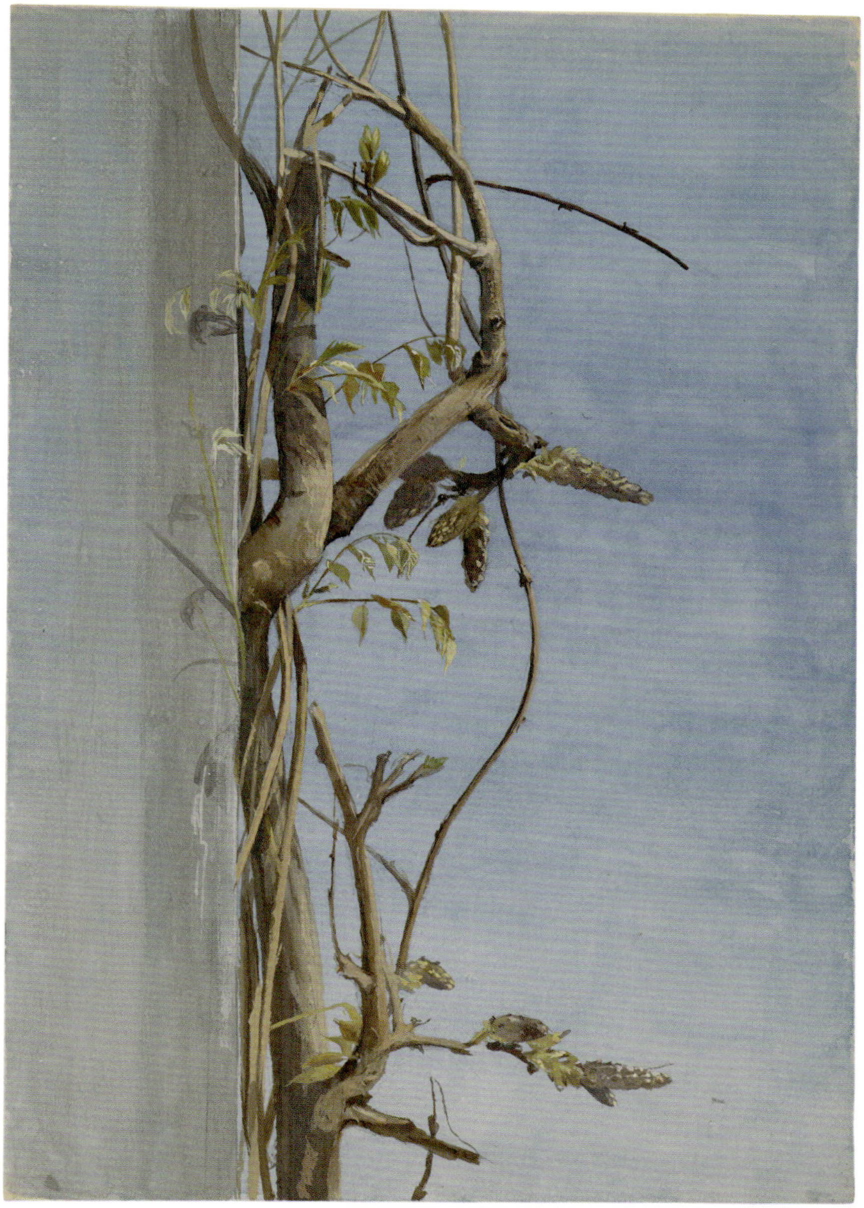

7
FIDELIA BRIDGES
Wisteria on a Wall, 1870s

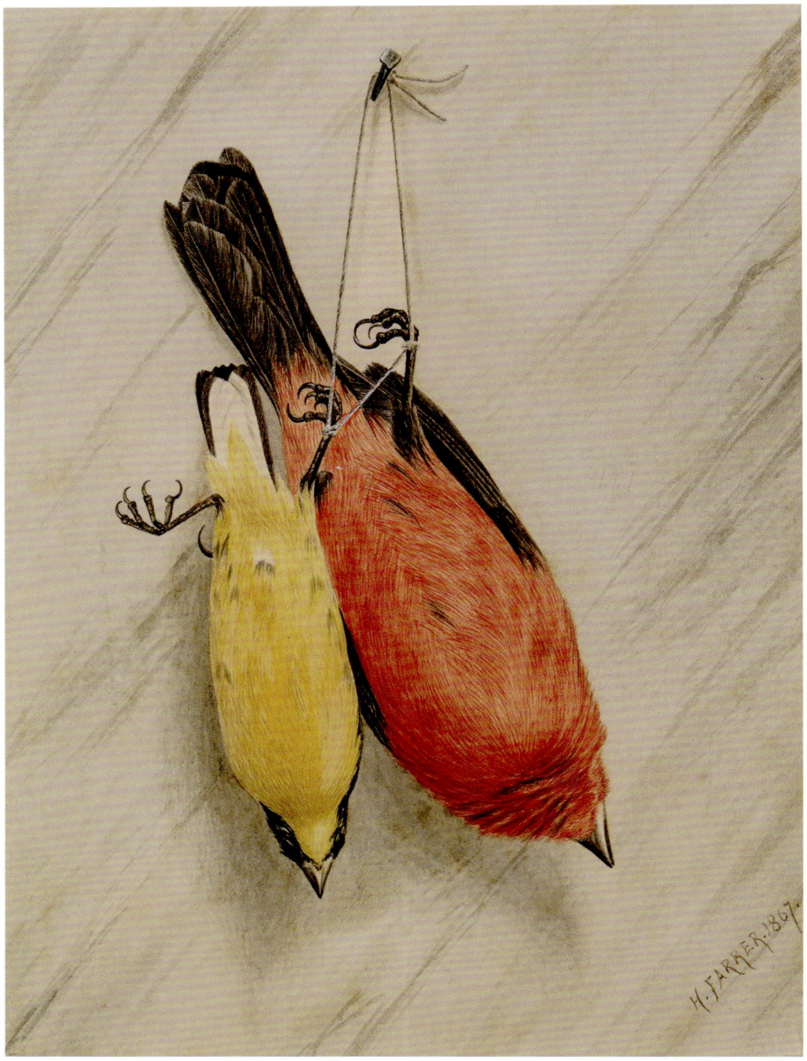

8

HENRY FARRER

Two Birds: Canary and Robin, 1867

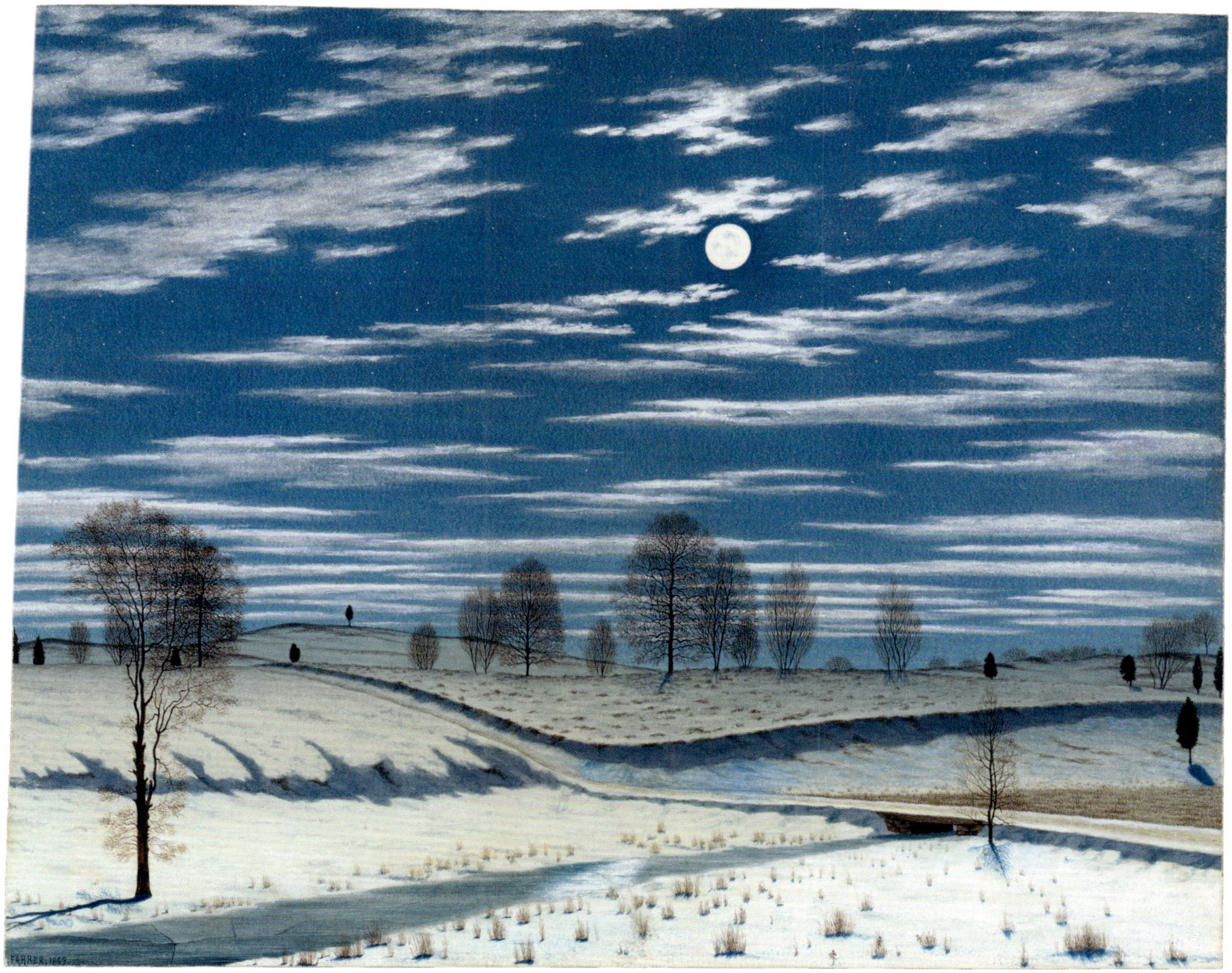

9
HENRY FARRER
Winter Scene in Moonlight, 1869

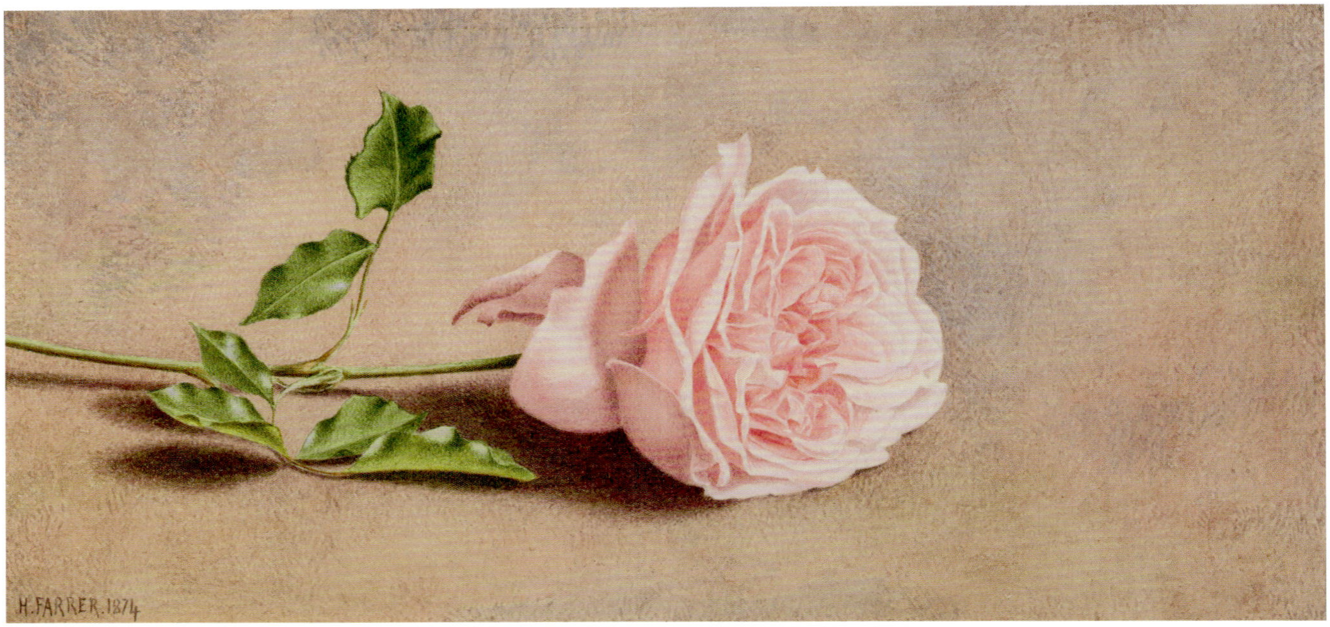

10
HENRY FARRER
Pink Rose, 1874

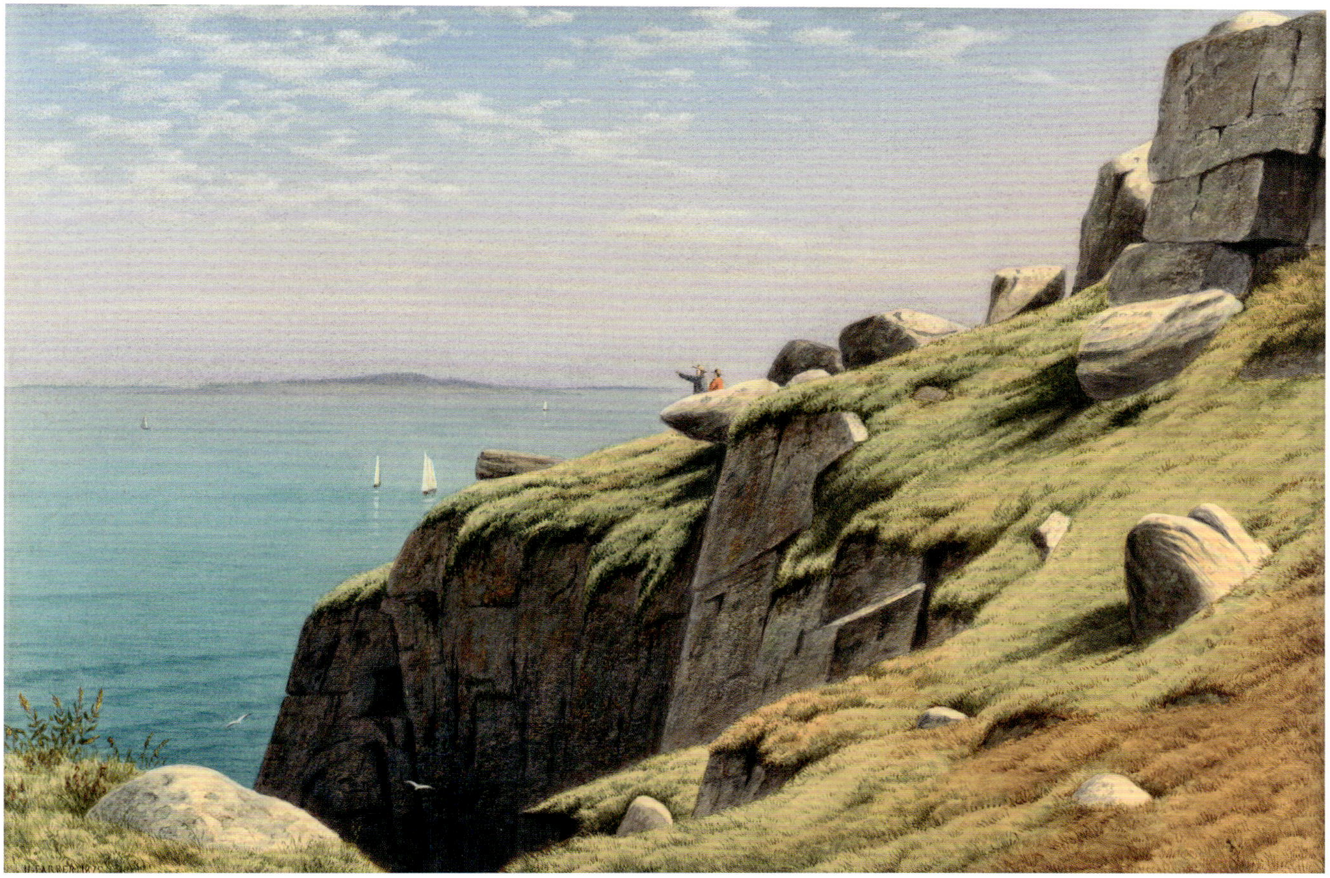

11
HENRY FARRER
On Whitehead, Coast of Maine, 1875

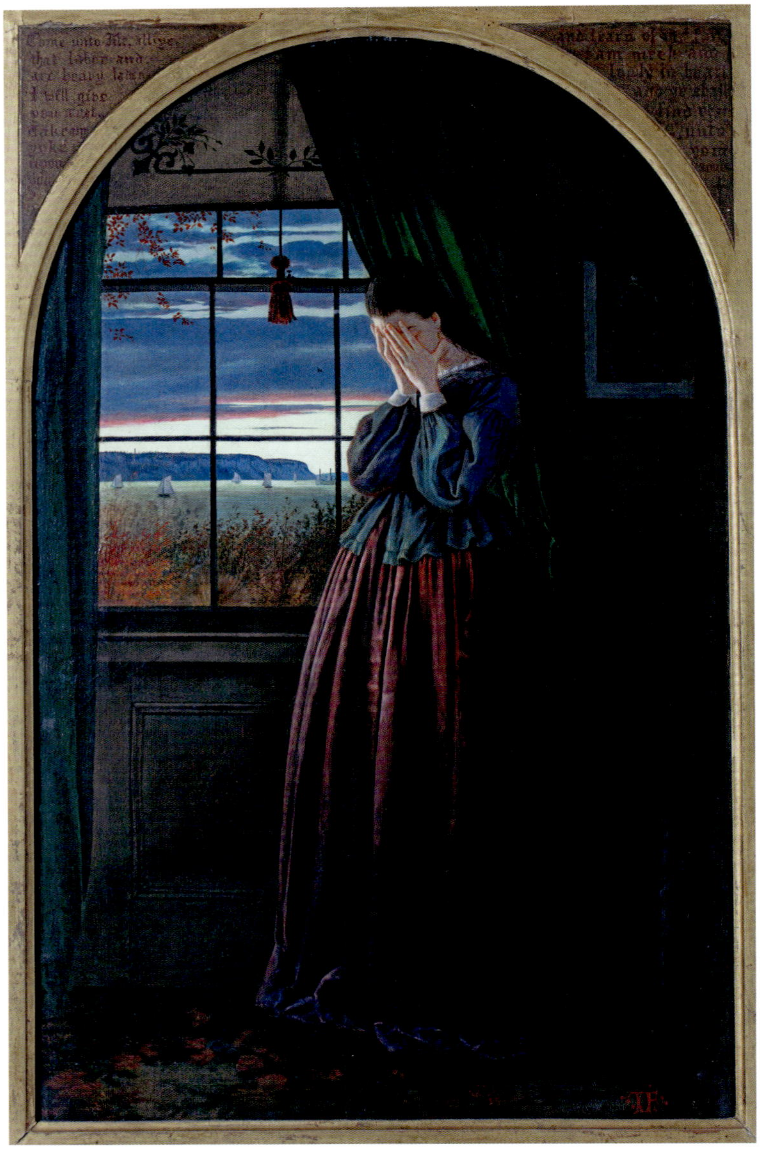

12

THOMAS CHARLES FARRER

Gone! Gone!, 1860

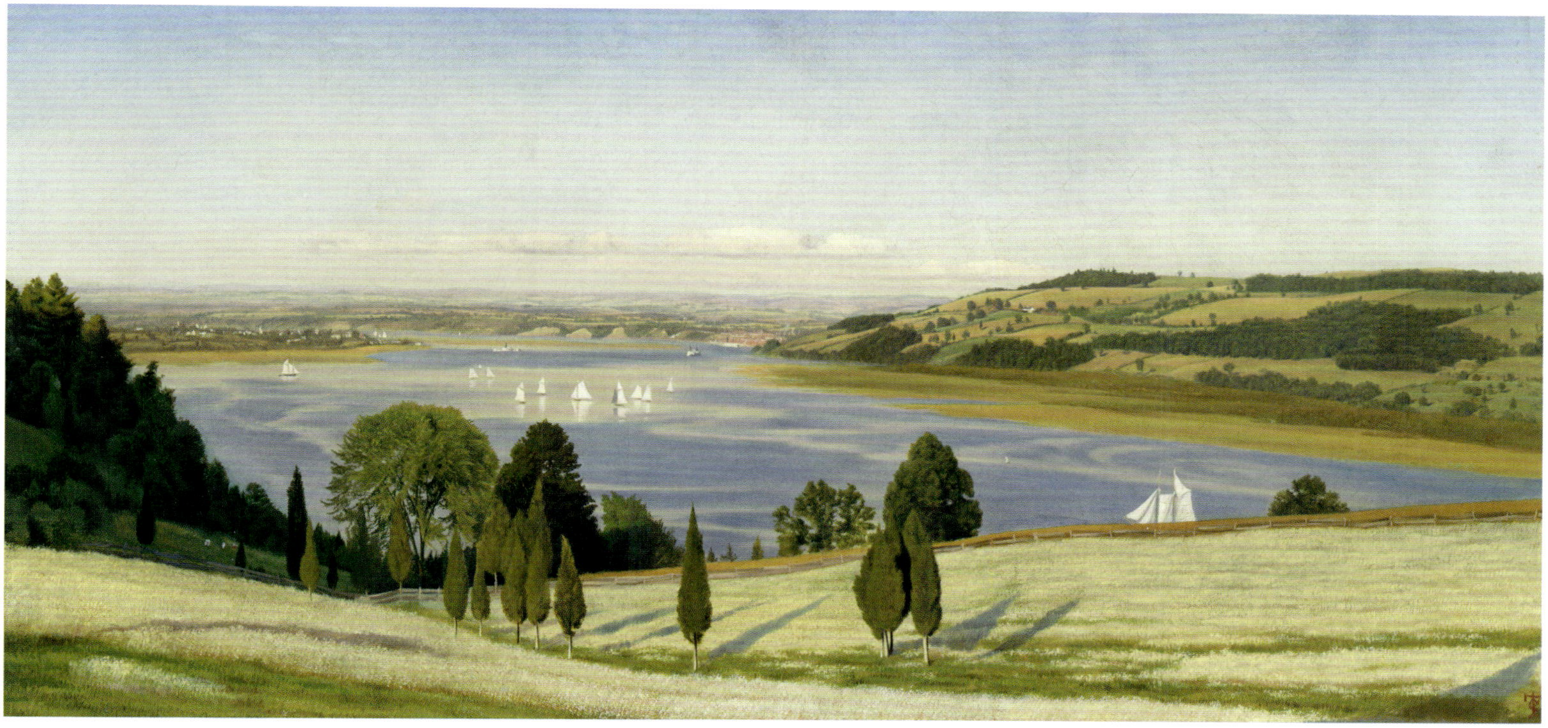

13
THOMAS CHARLES FARRER
A Buckwheat Field on Thomas Cole's Farm, 1863

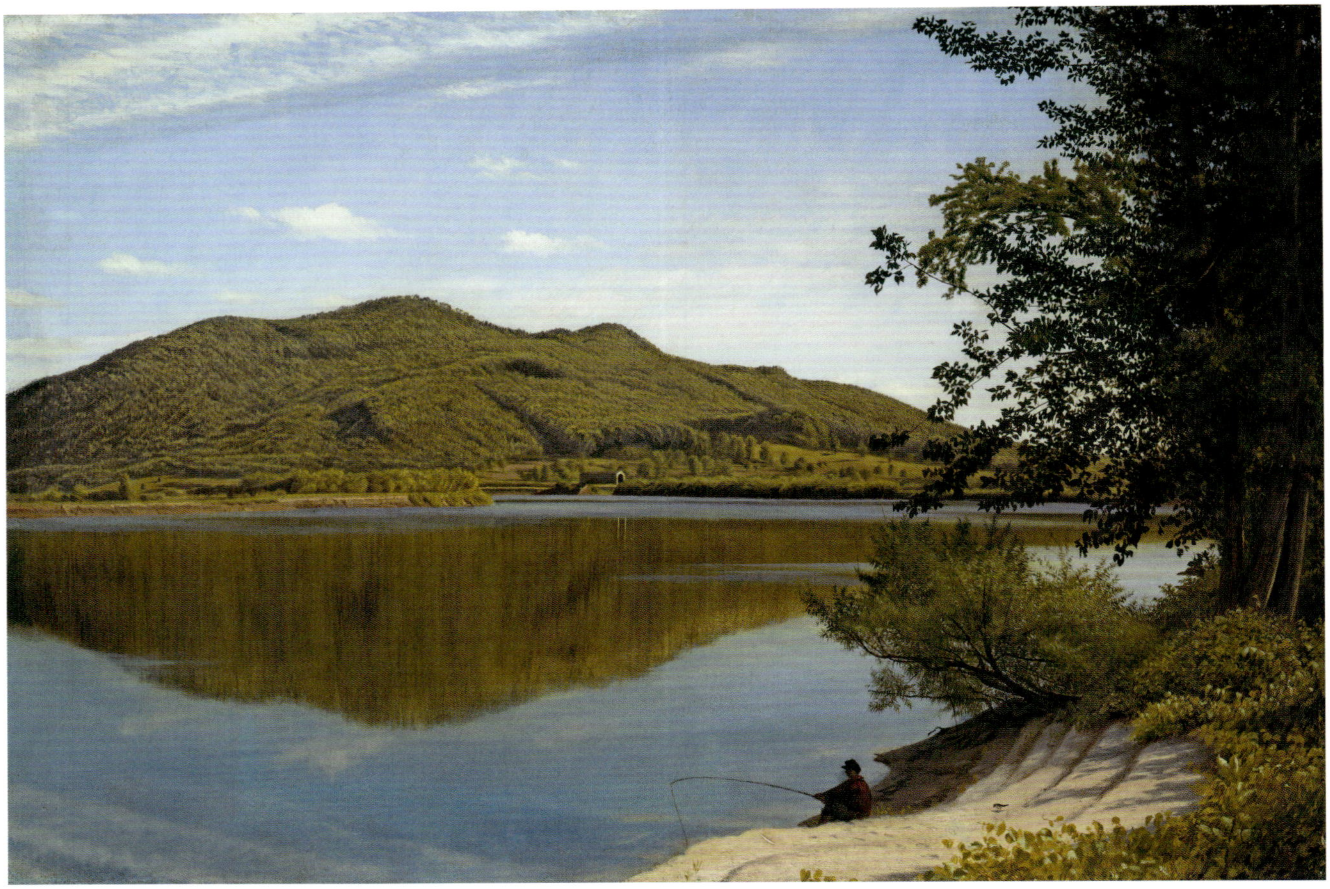

14
THOMAS CHARLES FARRER
Mount Tom, 1865

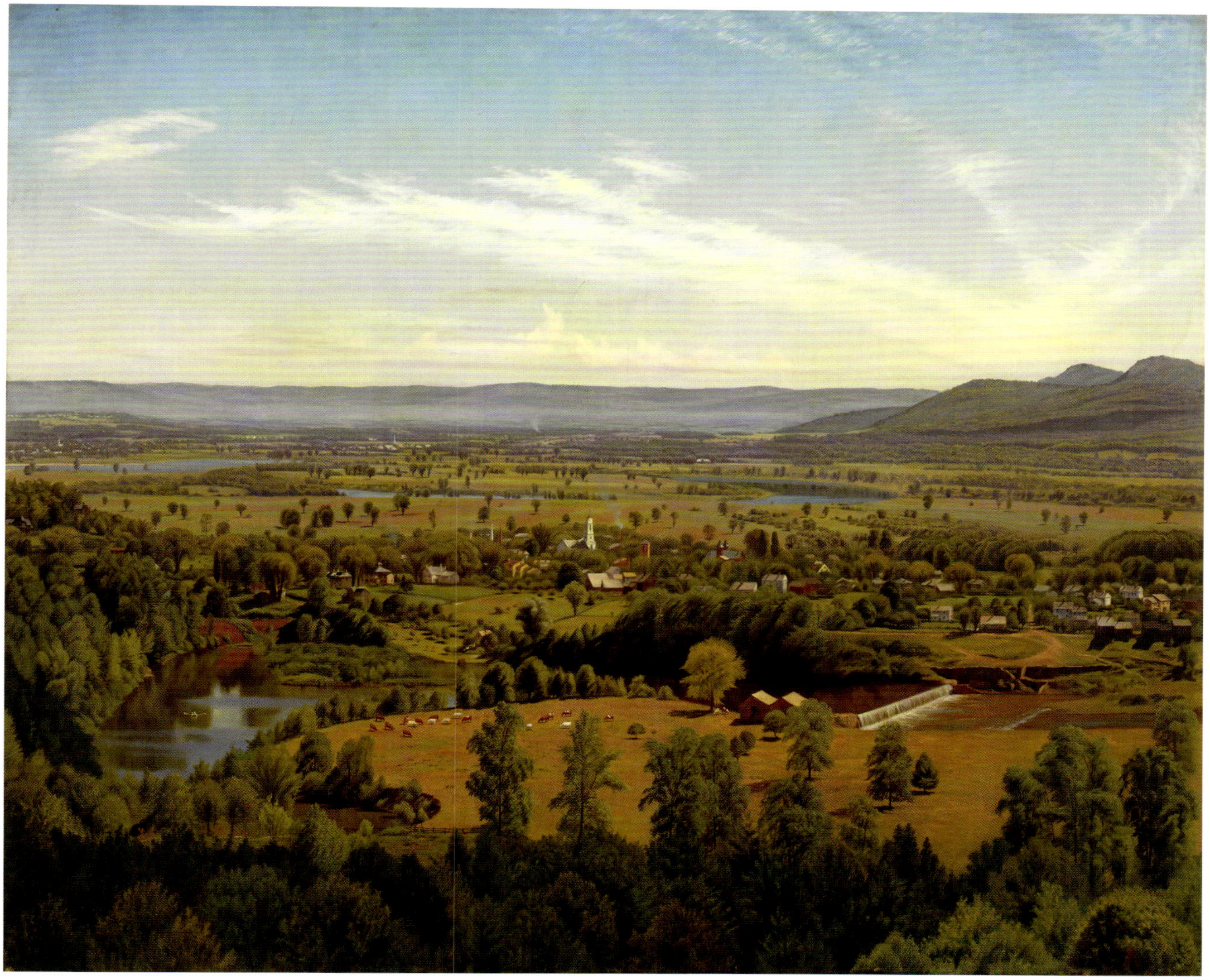

15
THOMAS CHARLES FARRER
View of Northampton from the Dome of the Hospital, 1865

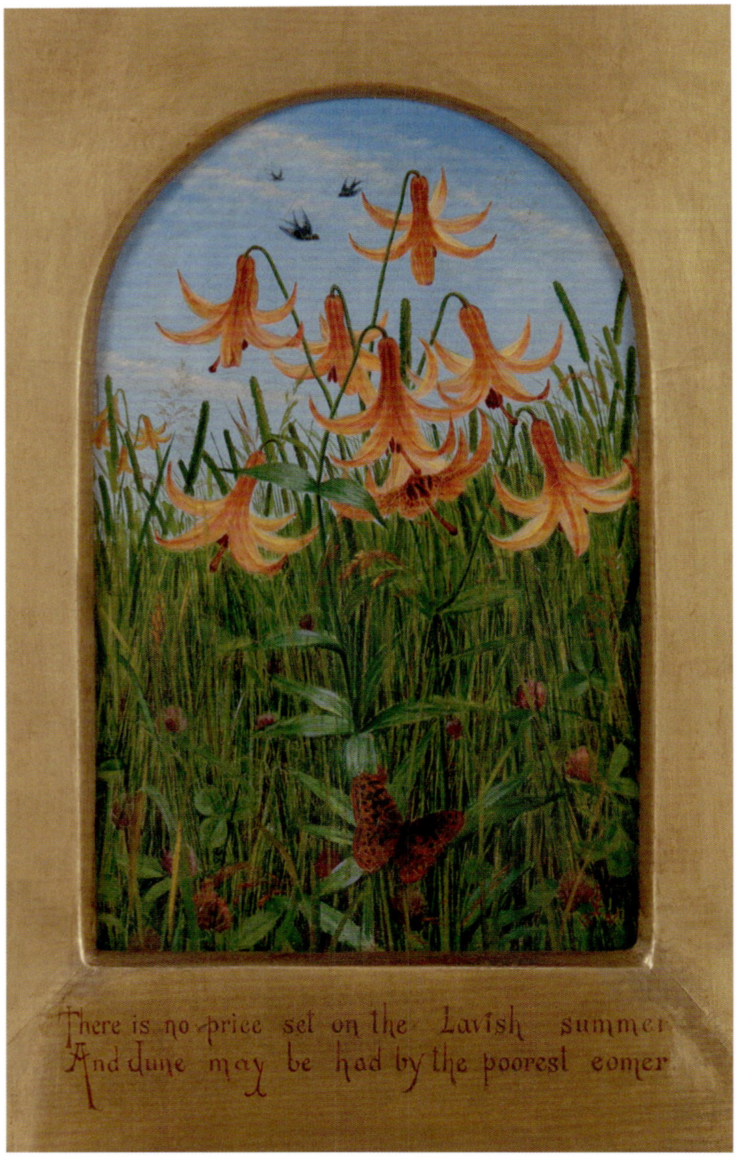

16
THOMAS CHARLES FARRER
June, 1867

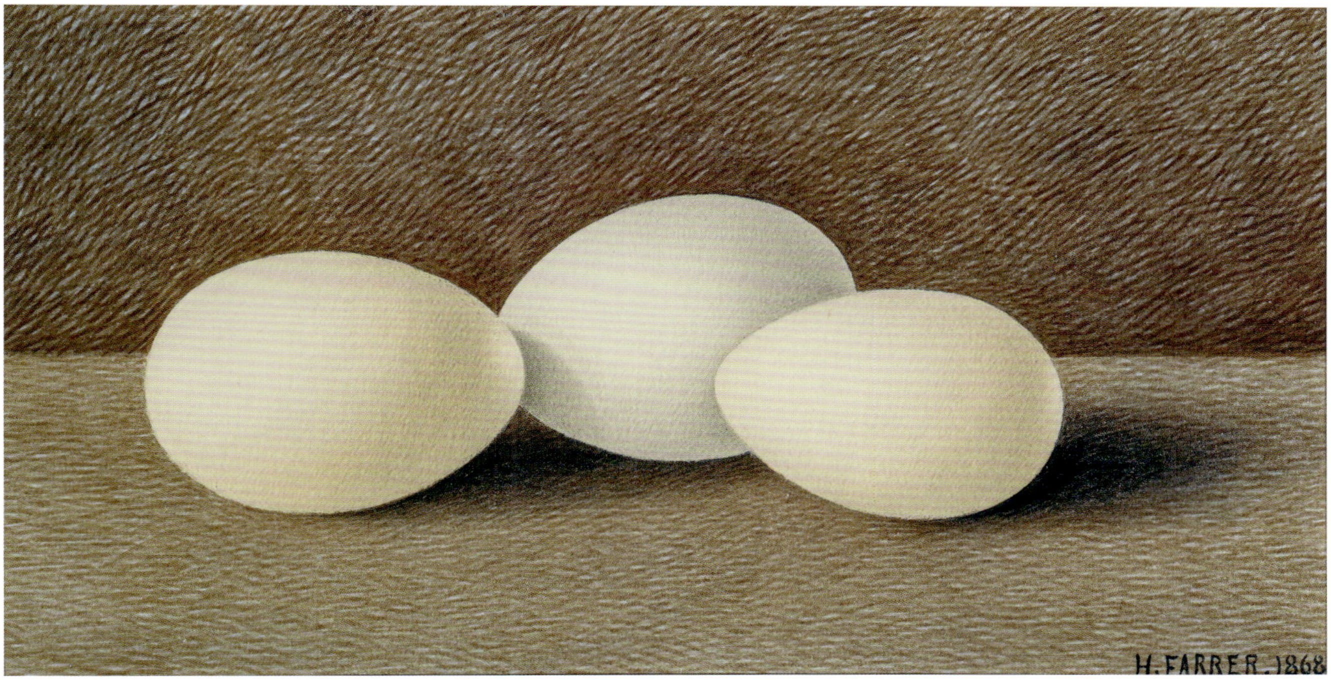

17
THOMAS CHARLES FARRER
Three Eggs, 1868

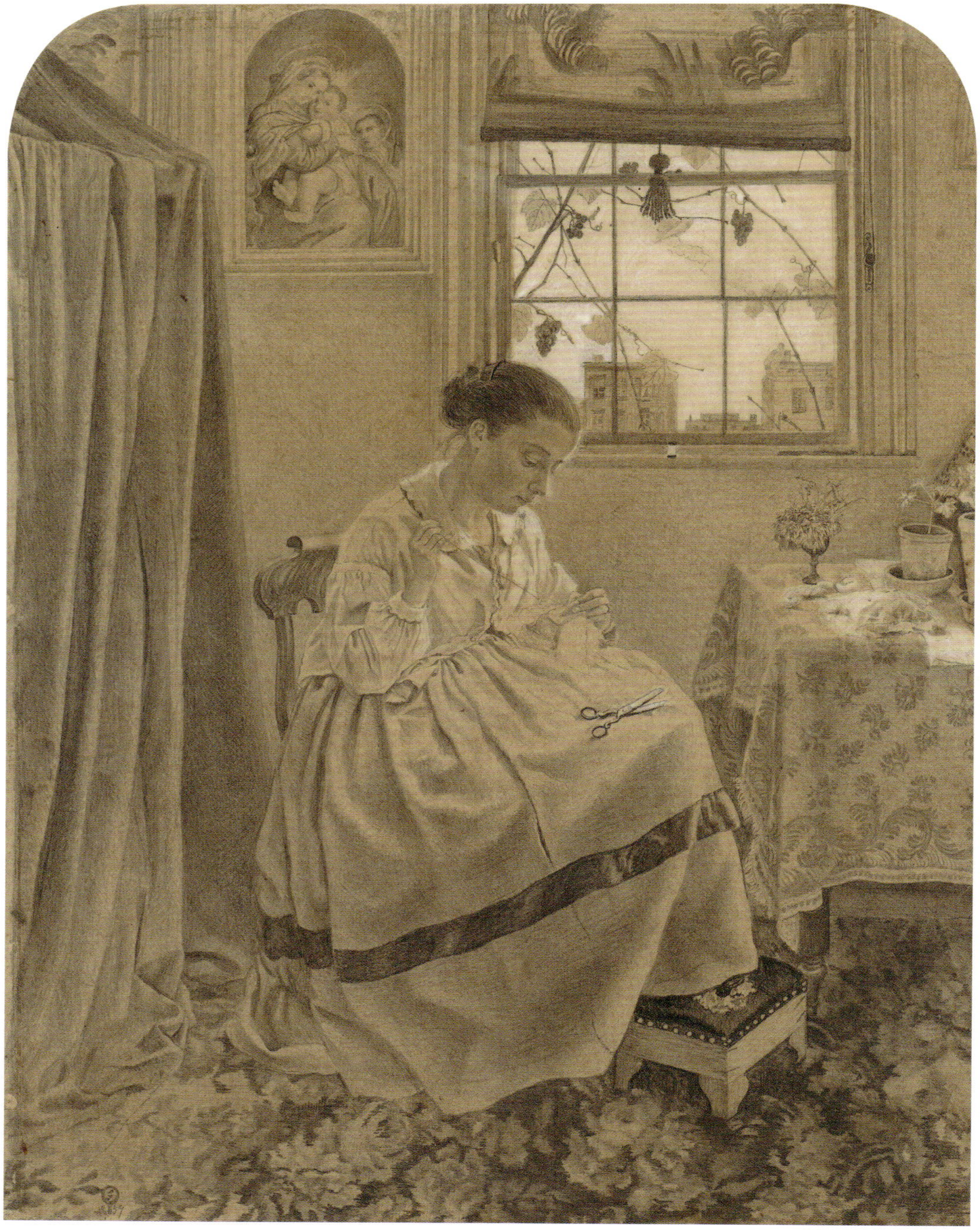

18
THOMAS CHARLES FARRER
Woman Sewing, 1859

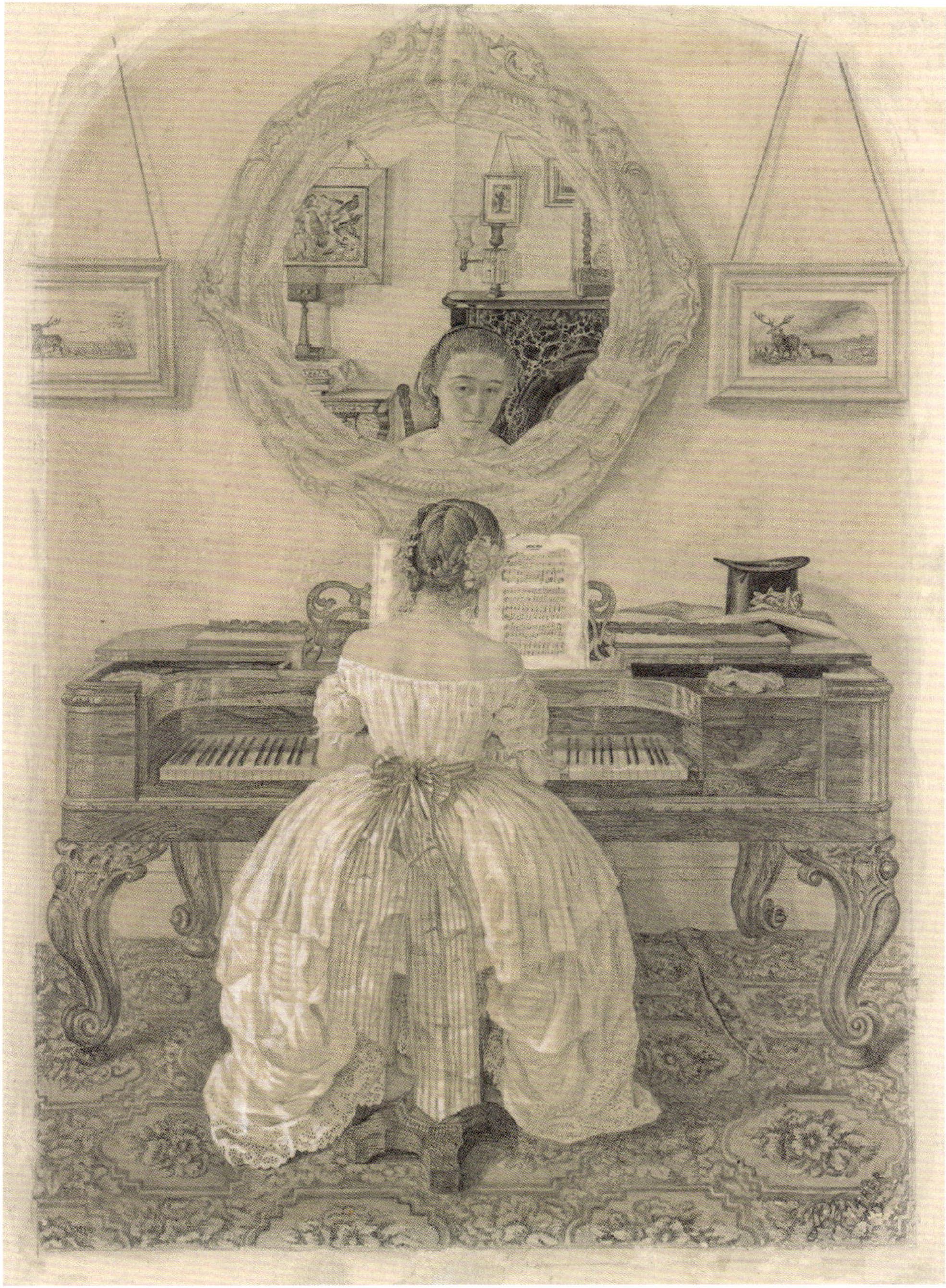

19
THOMAS CHARLES FARRER
Practicing Her Lesson, 1859

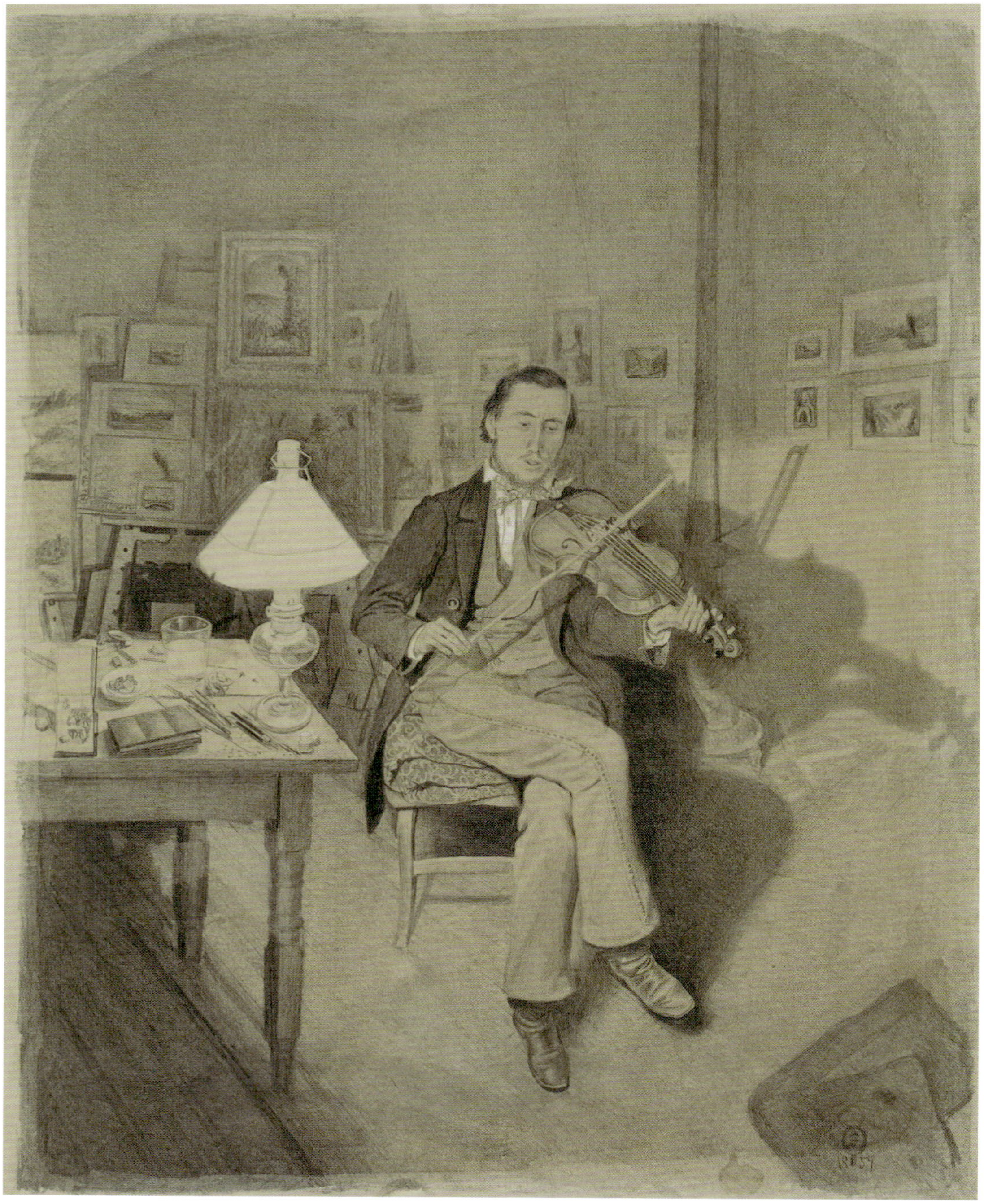

20
THOMAS CHARLES FARRER
The Fiddler, 1859

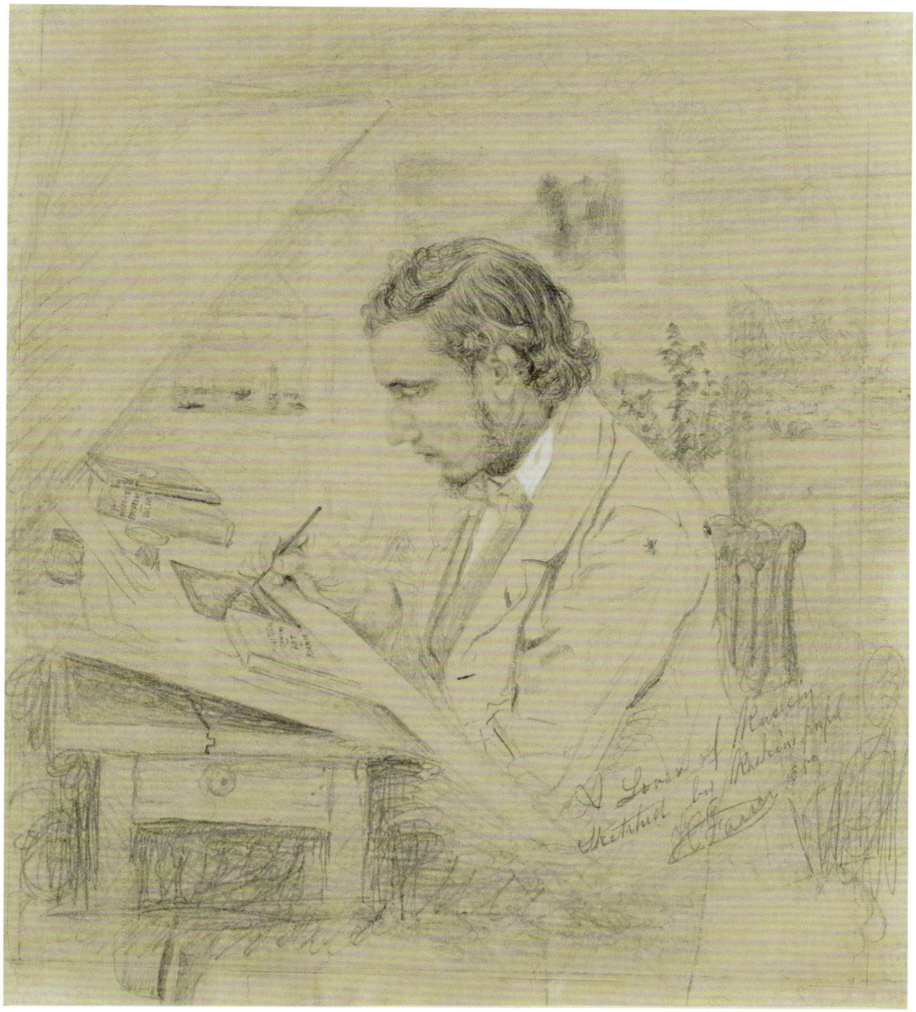

21
THOMAS CHARLES FARRER
John Henry Hill in the Studio Etching, 1859

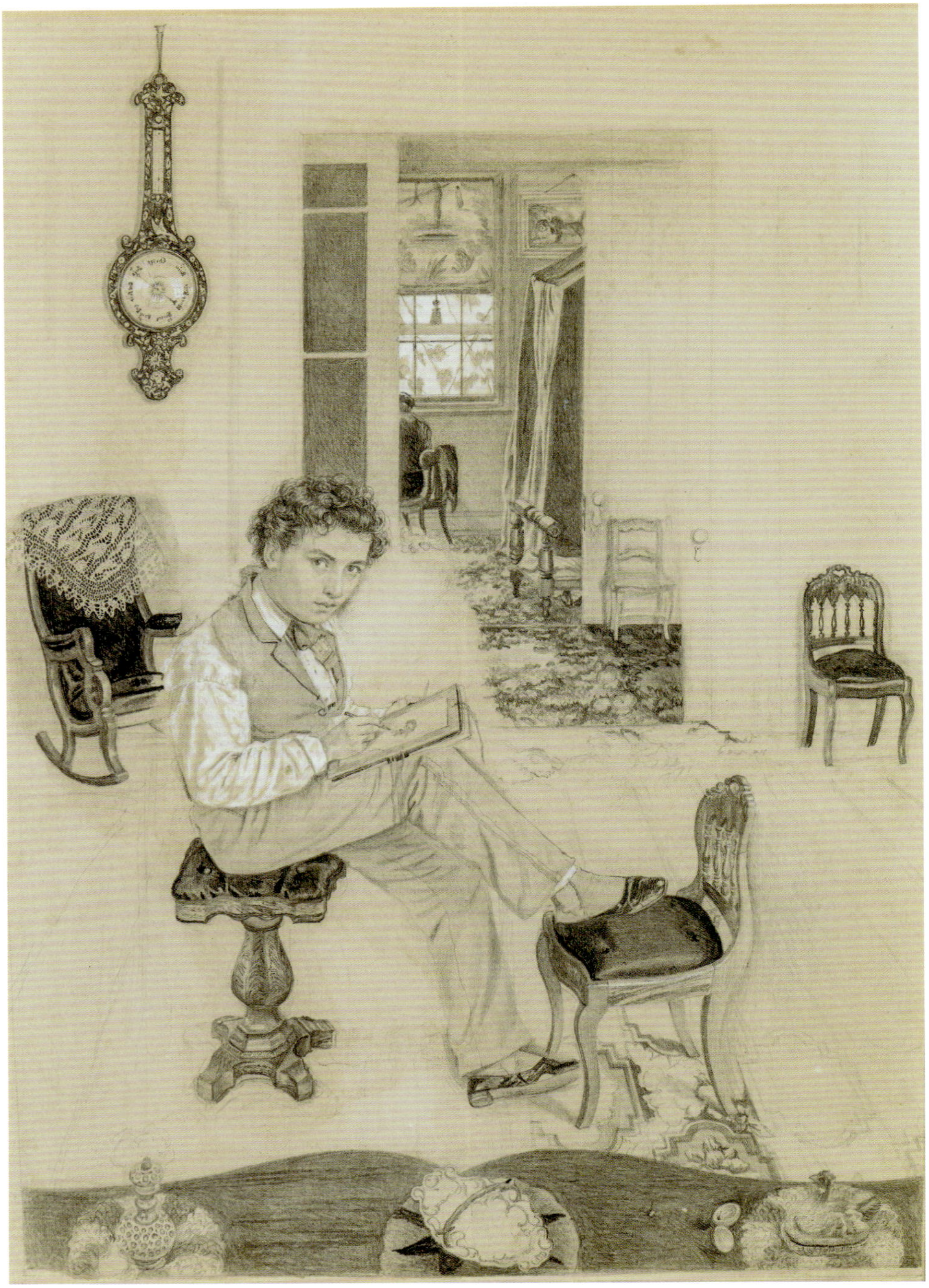

22

THOMAS CHARLES FARRER

Self-Portrait, Sketching, c. 1859

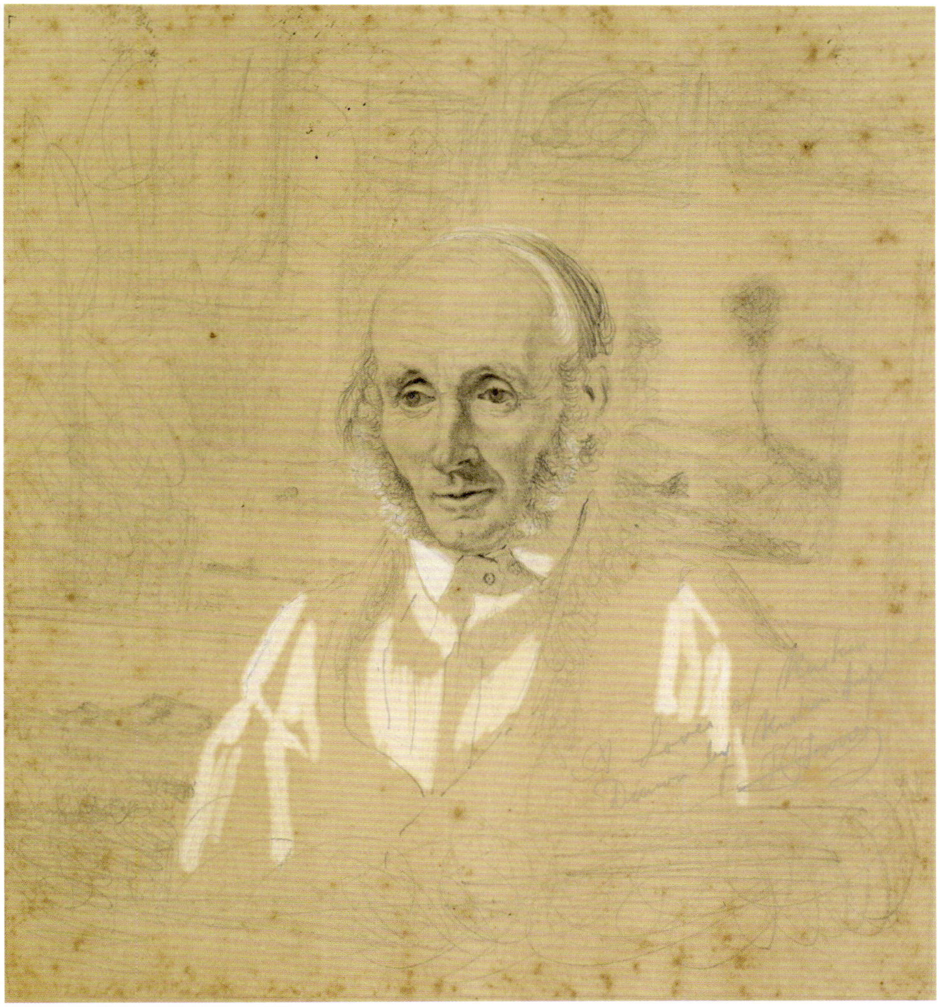

23
THOMAS CHARLES FARRER
Portrait of John William Hill, c. 1859

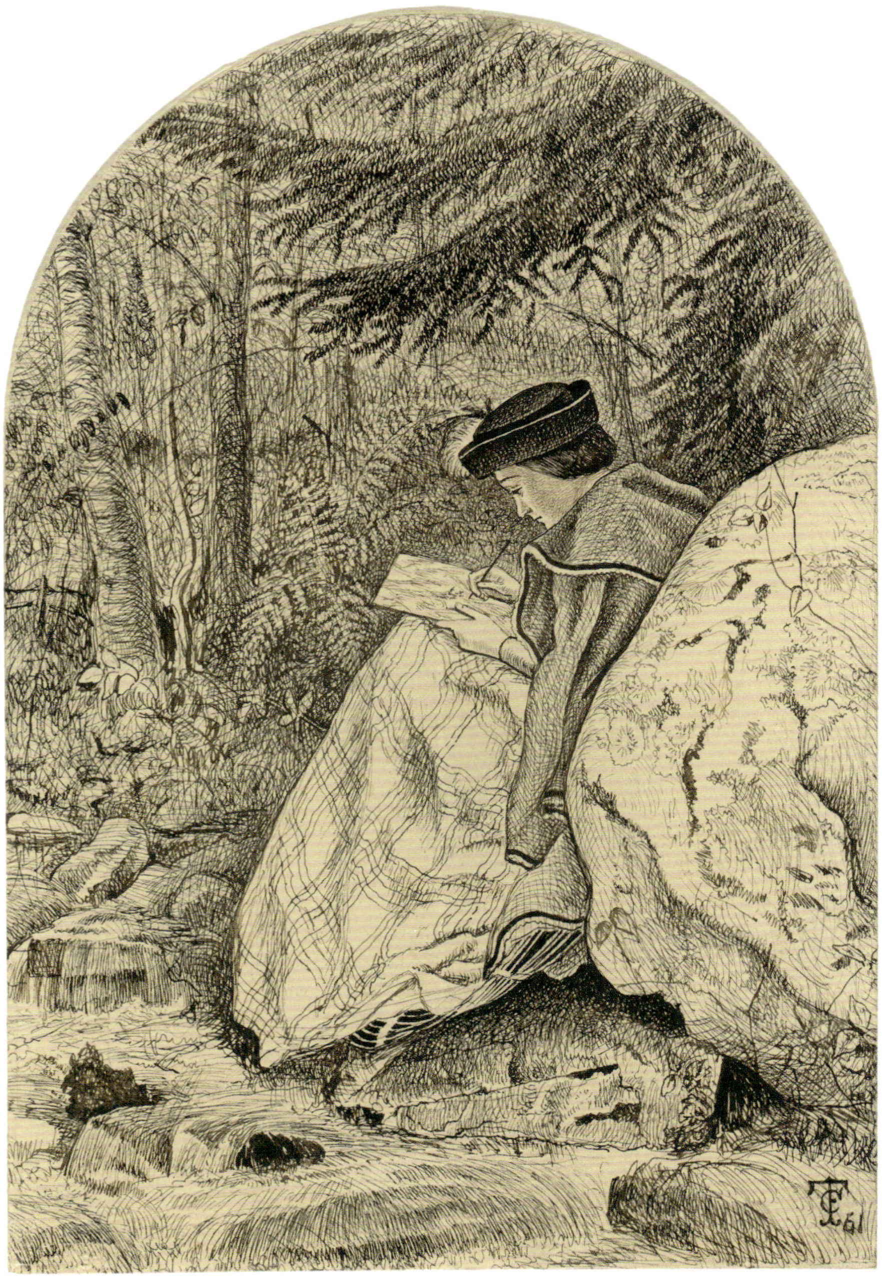

24
THOMAS CHARLES FARRER
Sketching from Nature, 1861

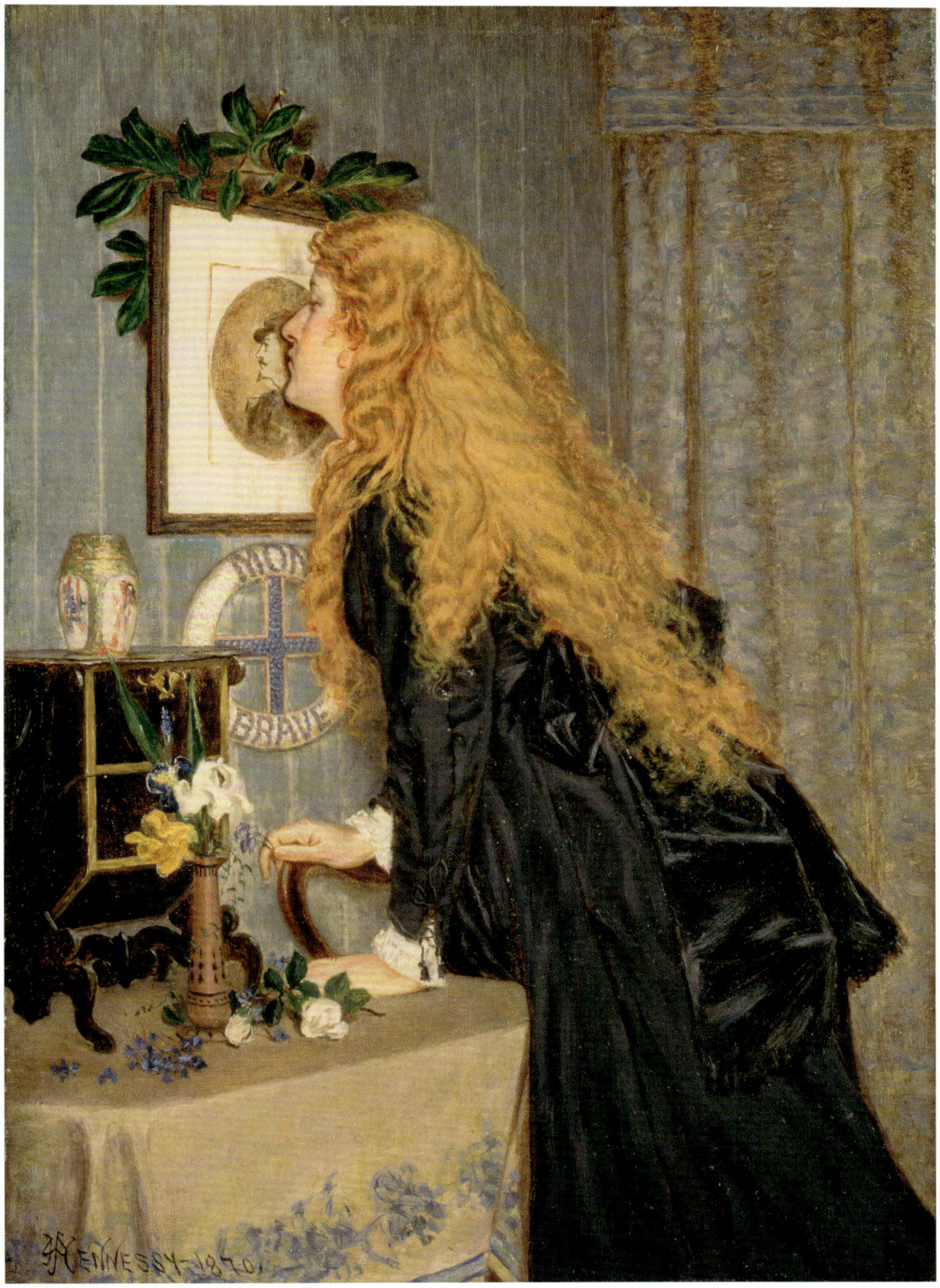

25
WILLIAM JOHN HENNESSY
Mon Brave, 1870

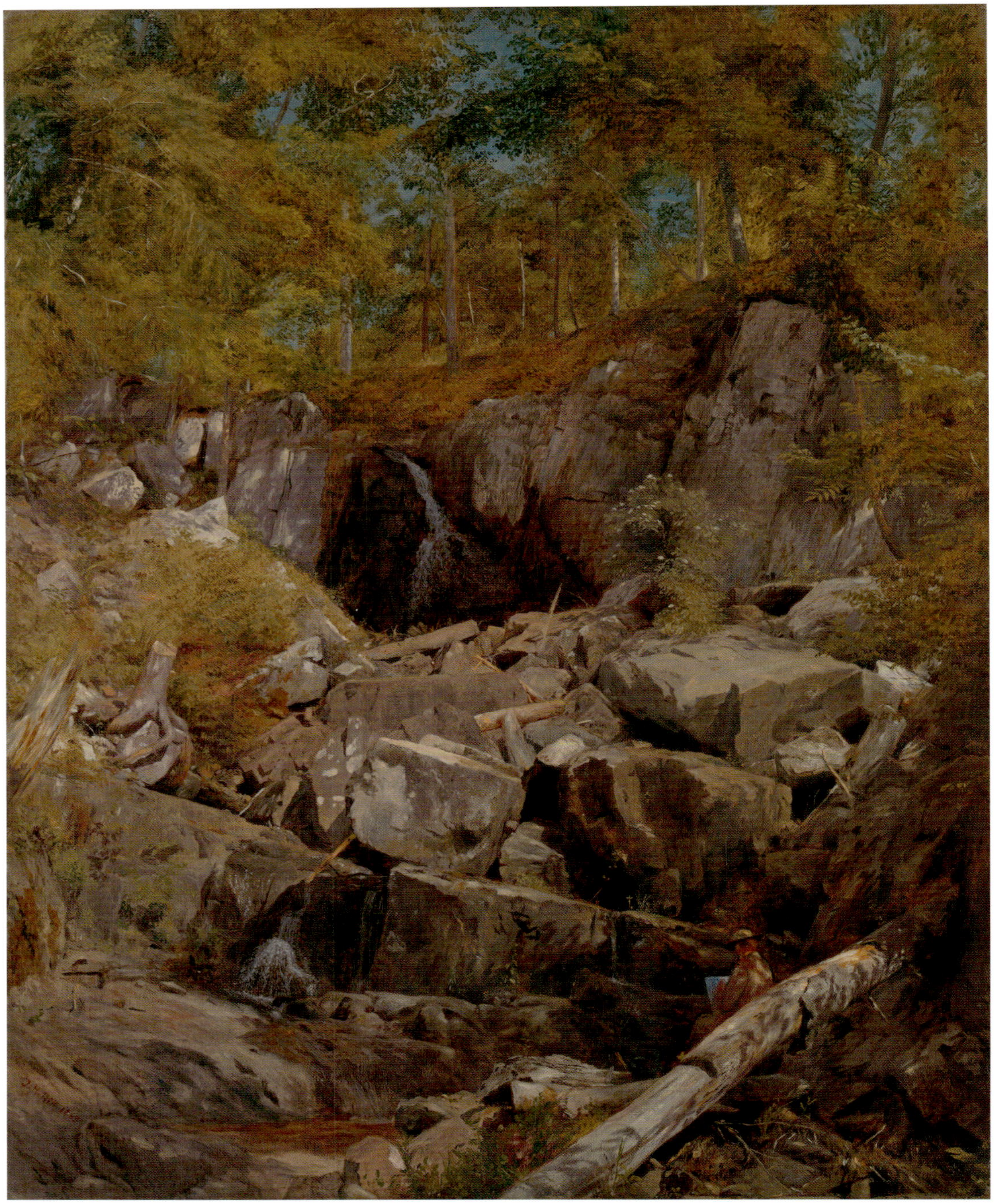

26

JOHN HENRY HILL

A Study of Trap Rock (Buttermilk Falls), 1863

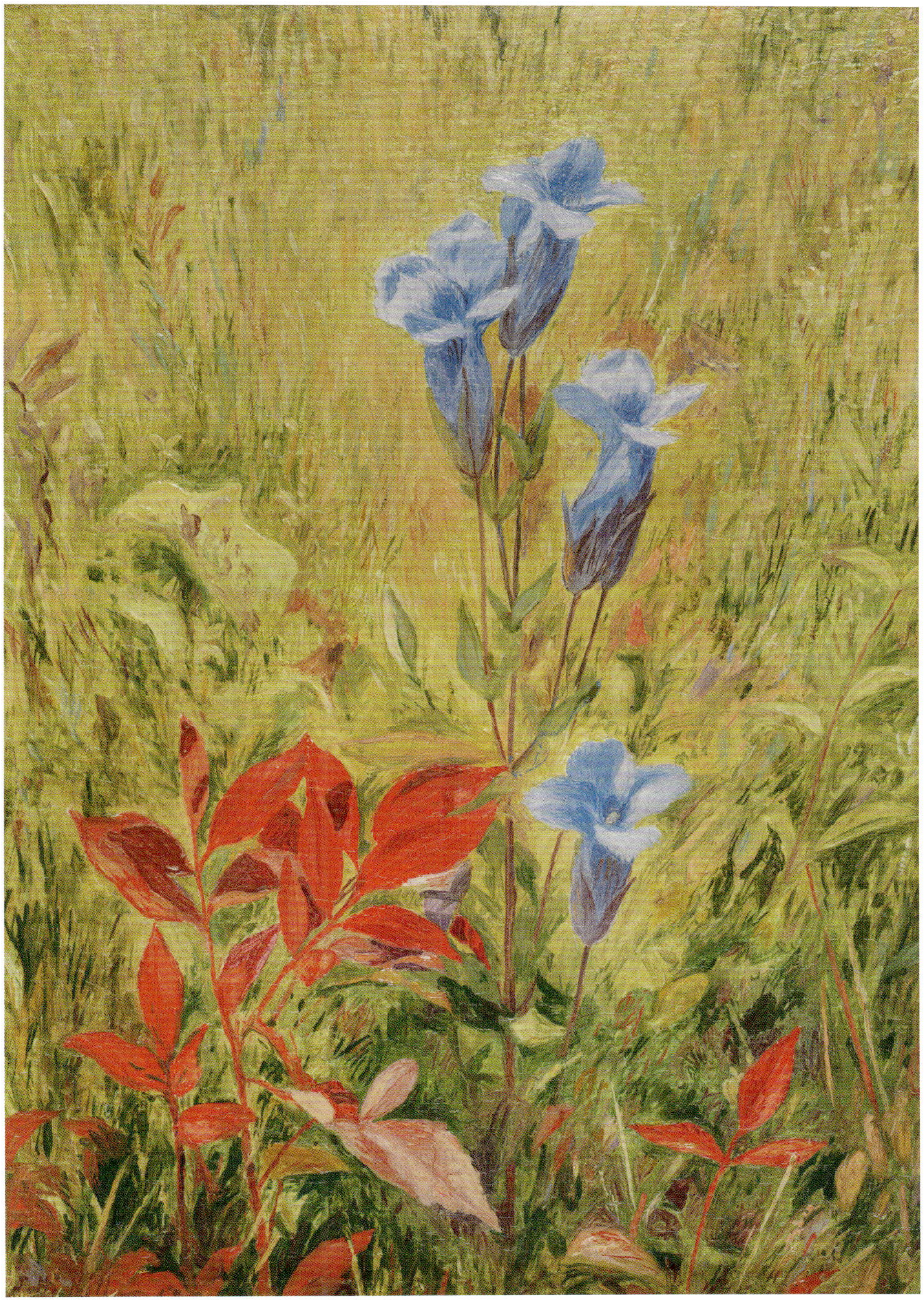

27
JOHN HENRY HILL
Fringed Gentians, c. 1867

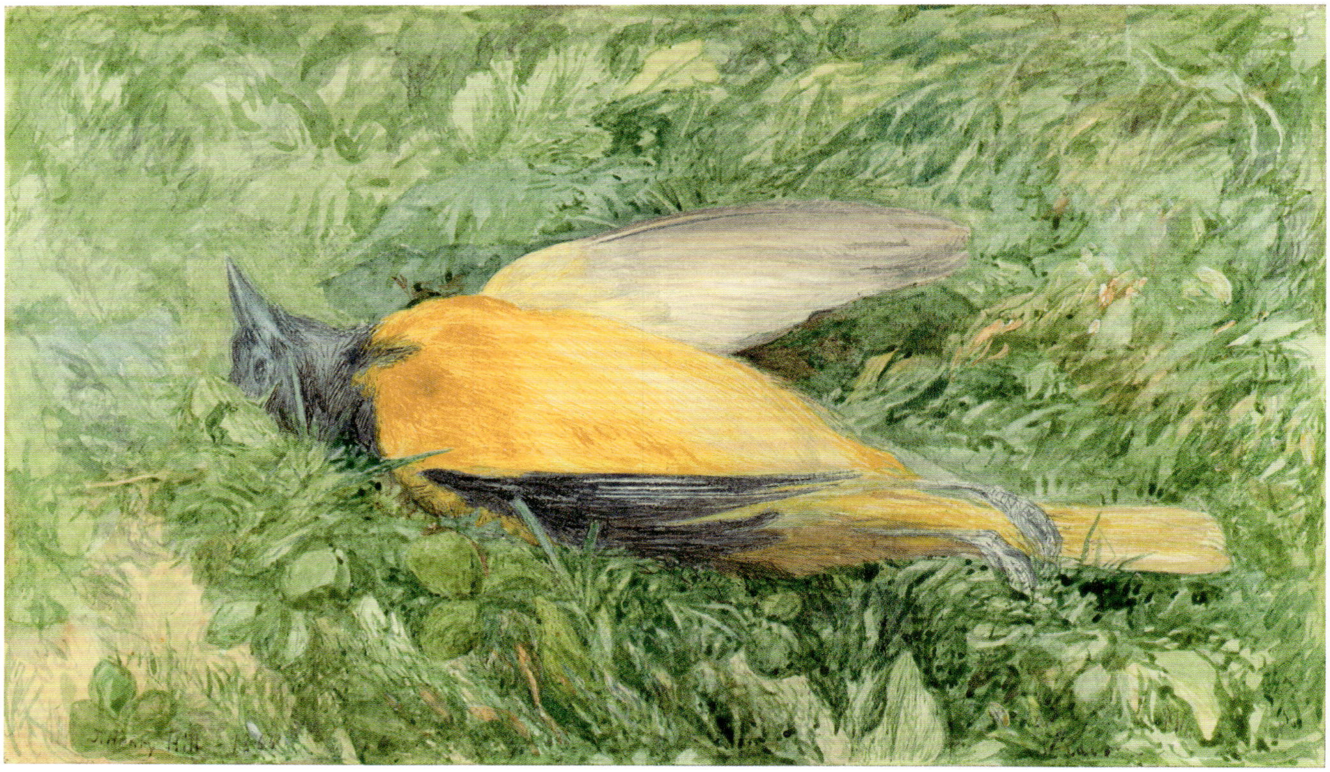

28
JOHN HENRY HILL
Golden Robin (Northern Oriole), 1866

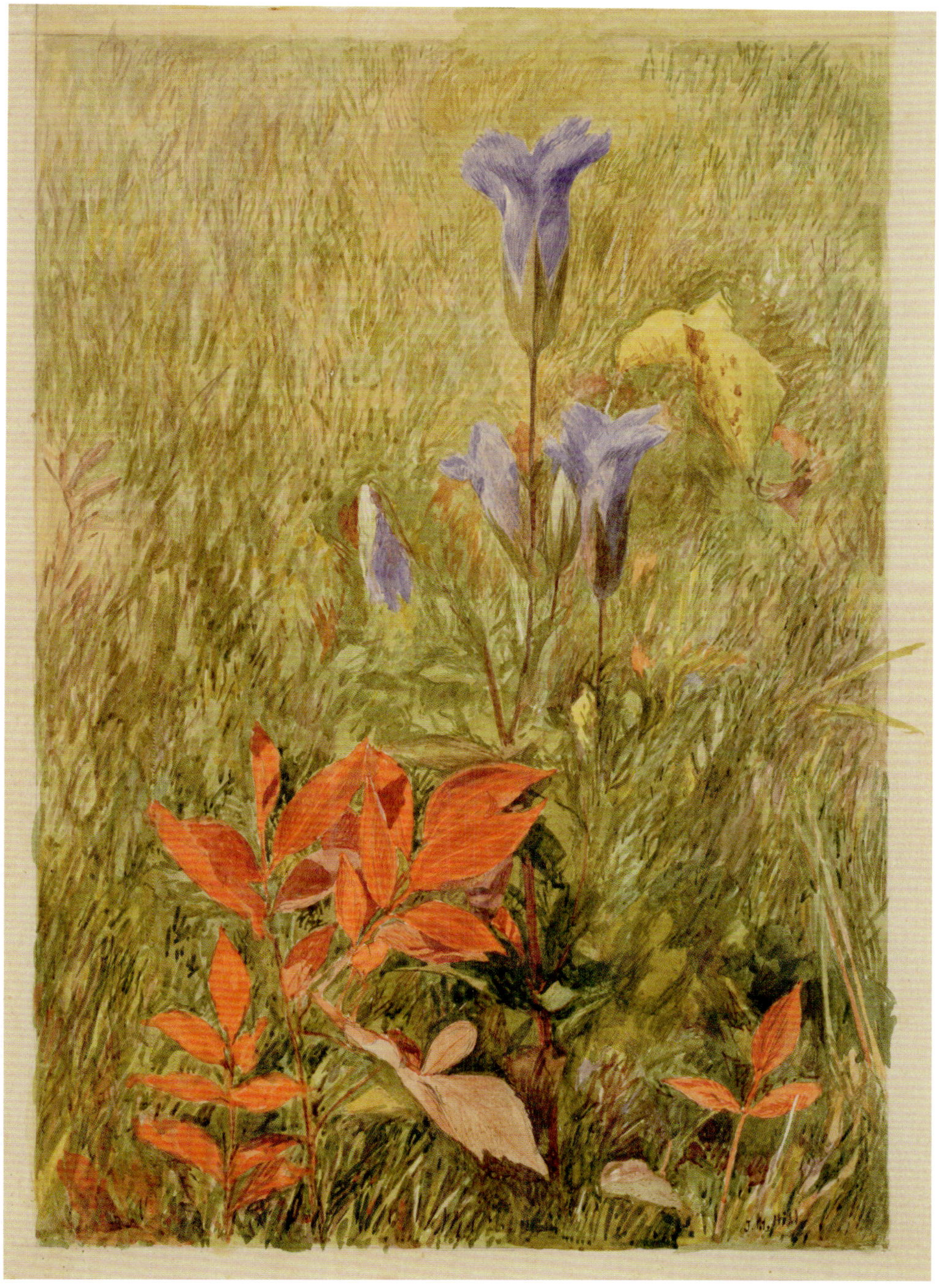

29
JOHN HENRY HILL
Fringed Gentians, c. 1867

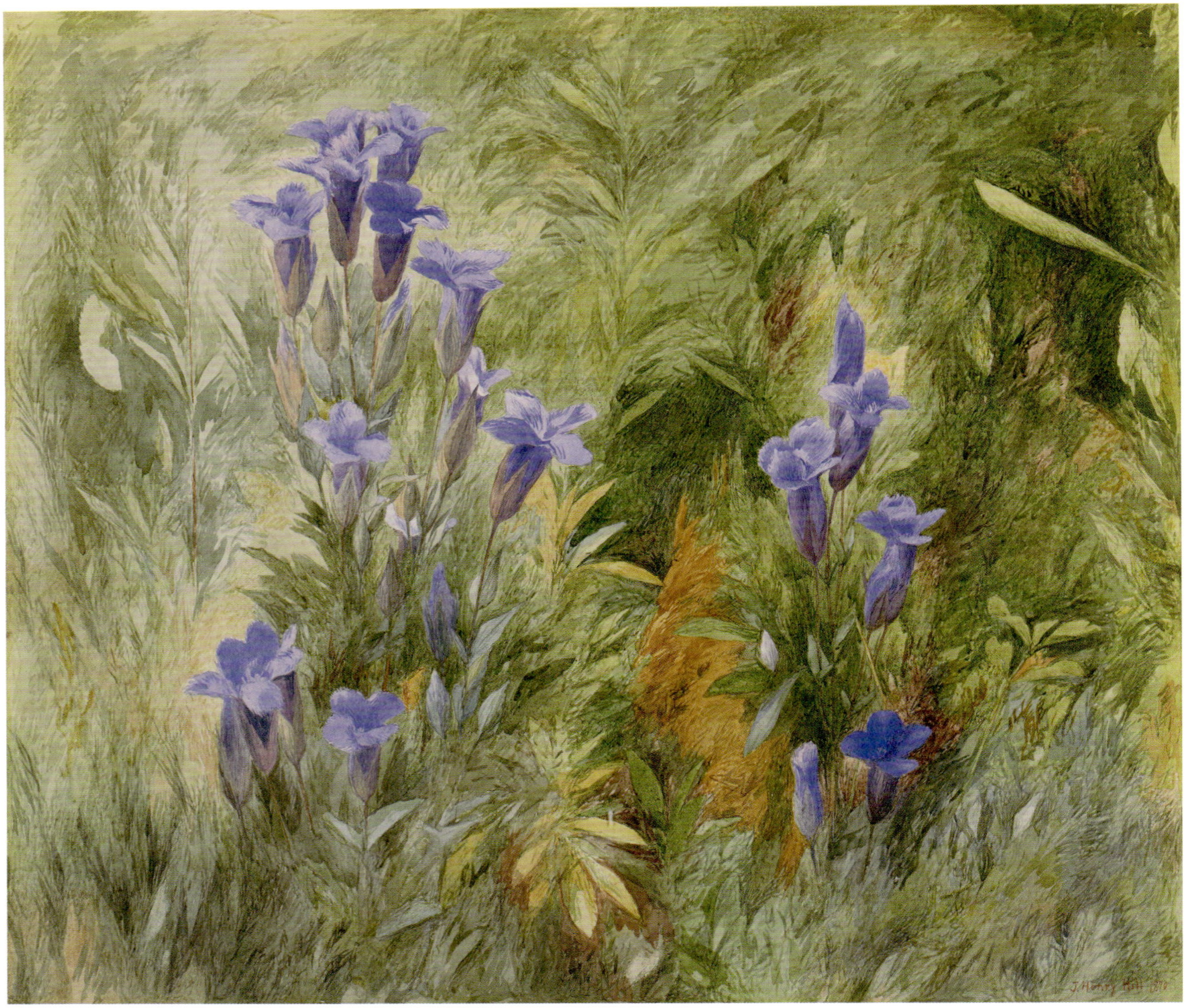

30
JOHN HENRY HILL
Gentians, 1870

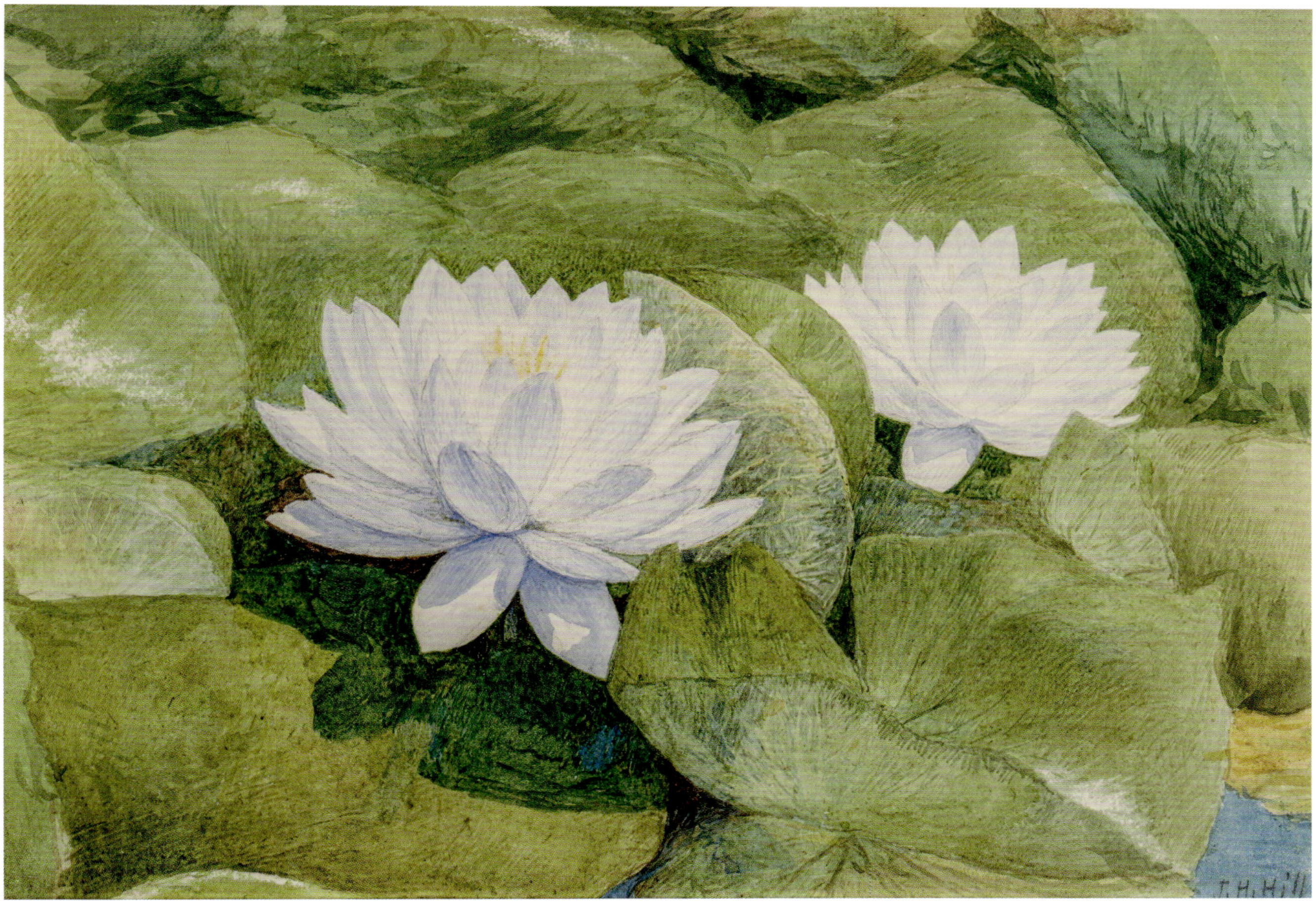

31
JOHN HENRY HILL
Waterlilies, c. 1870

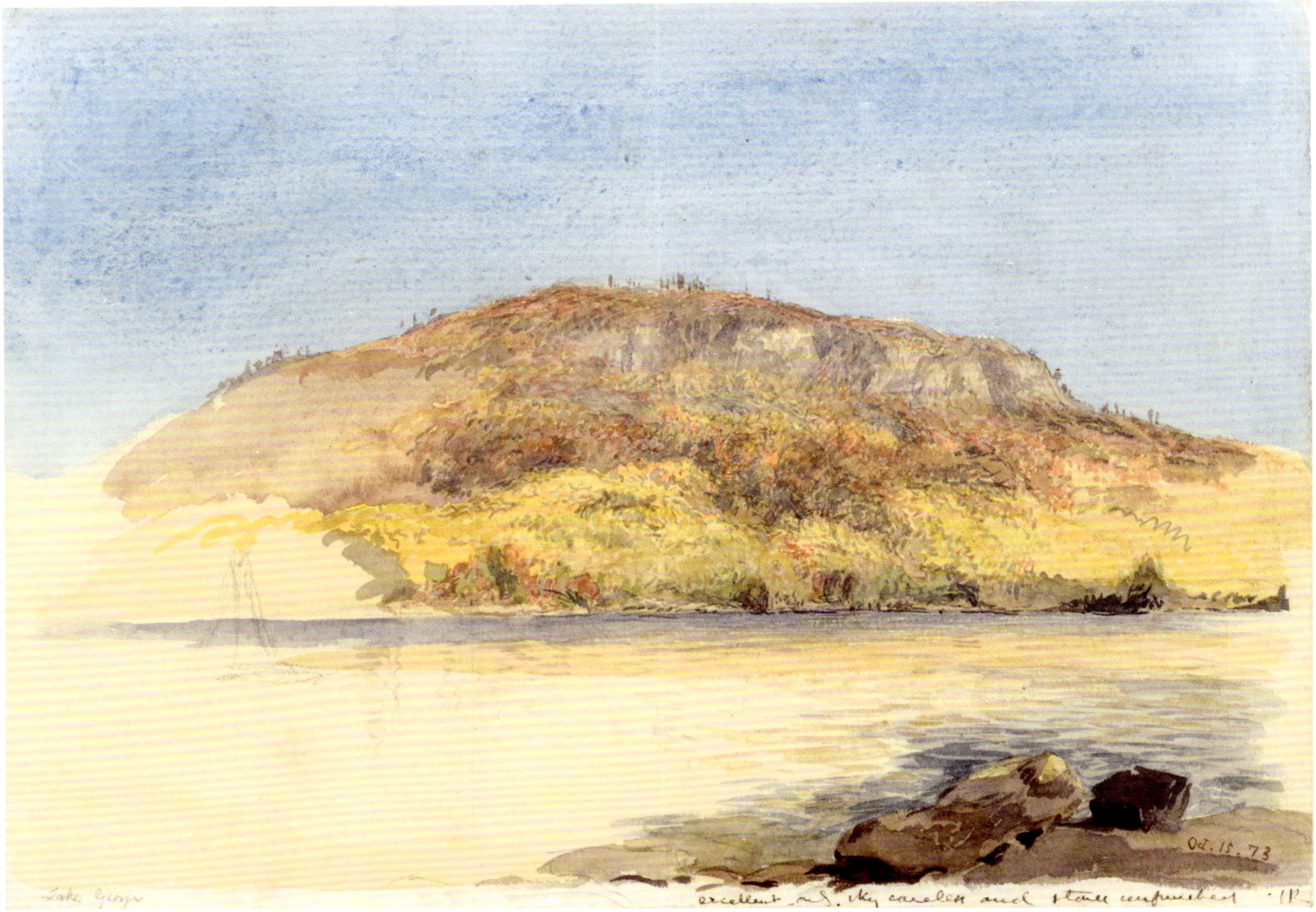

32

JOHN HENRY HILL

Lake George, 1873

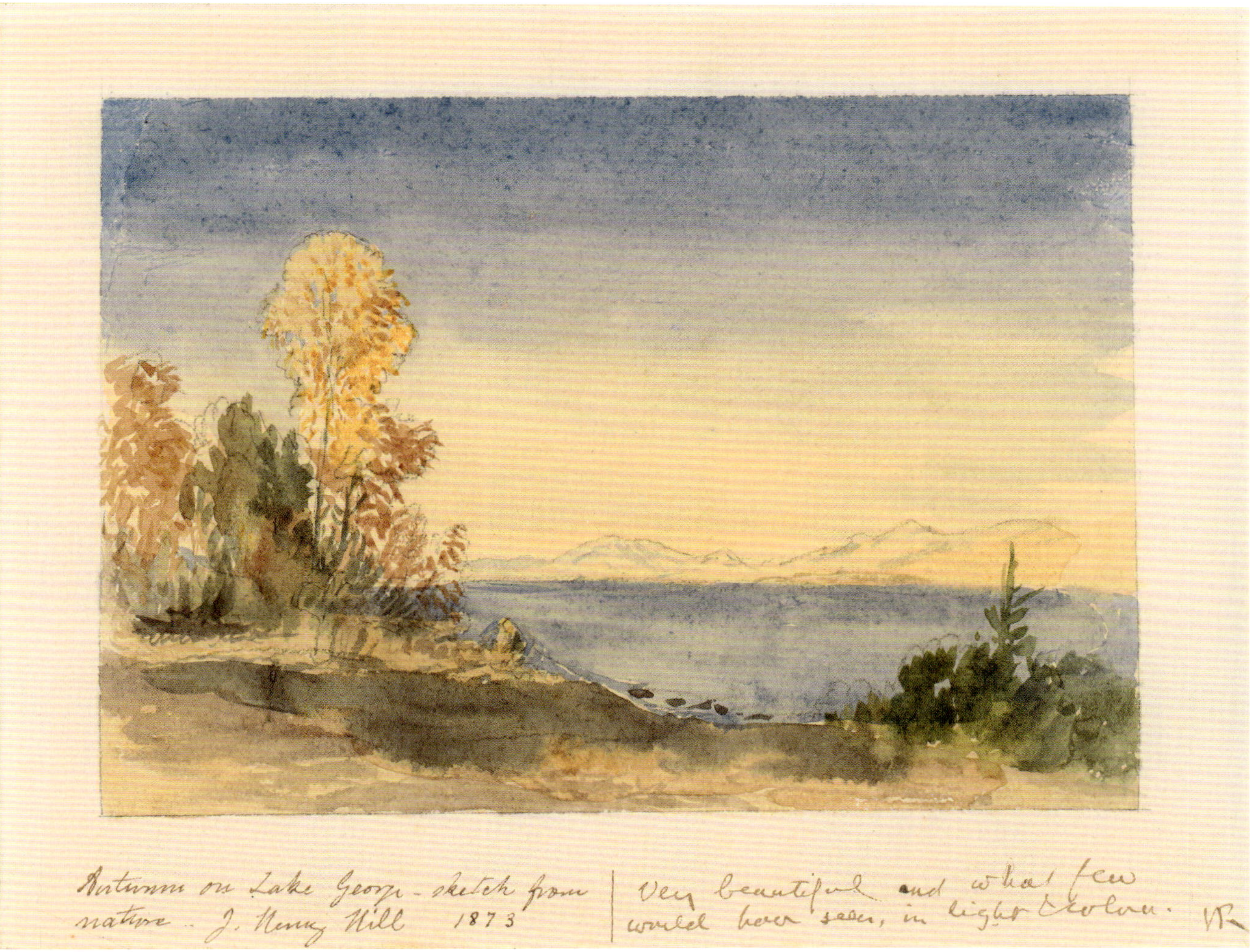

33
JOHN HENRY HILL
Autumn on Lake George, 1873

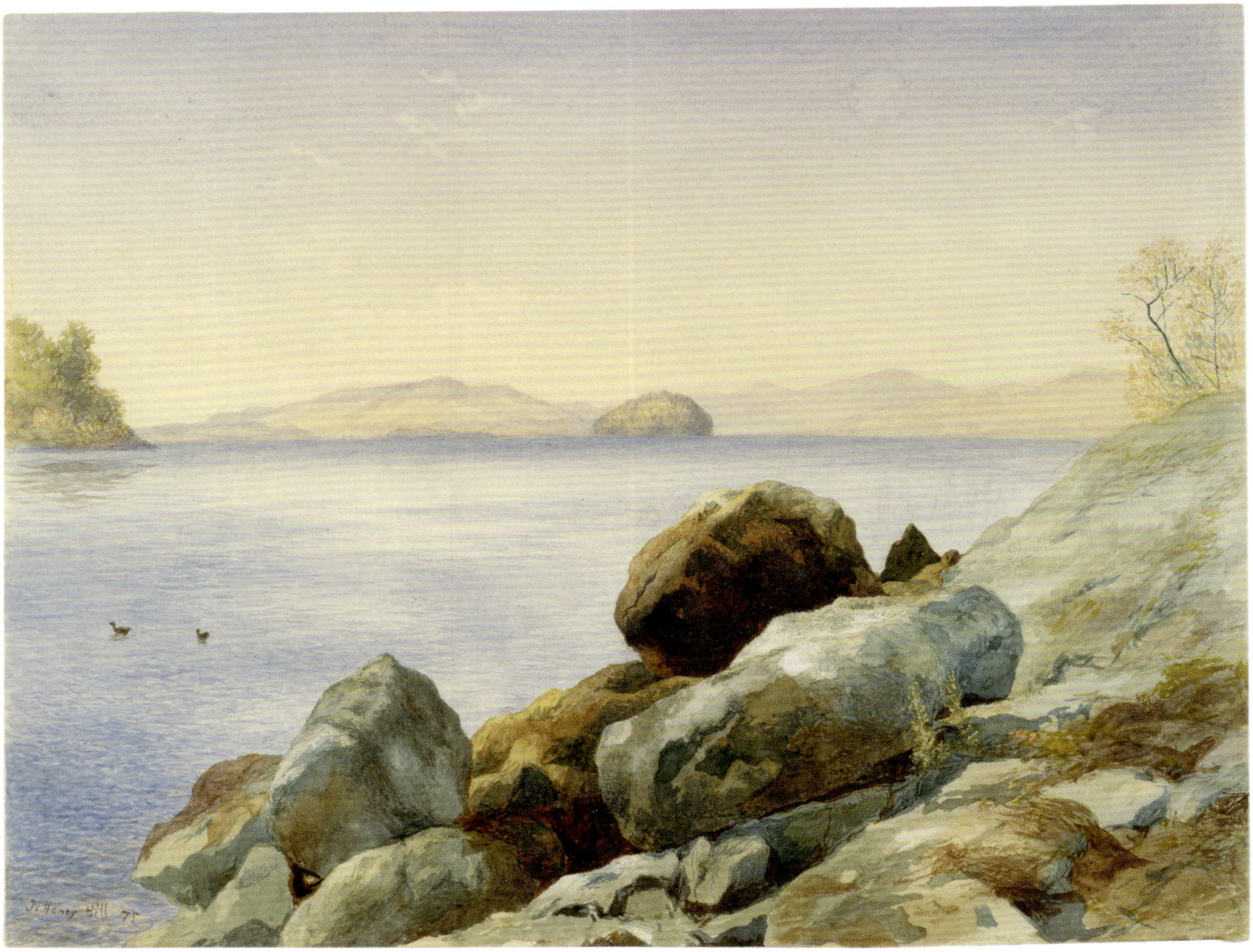

34
JOHN HENRY HILL
Lake George, 1875

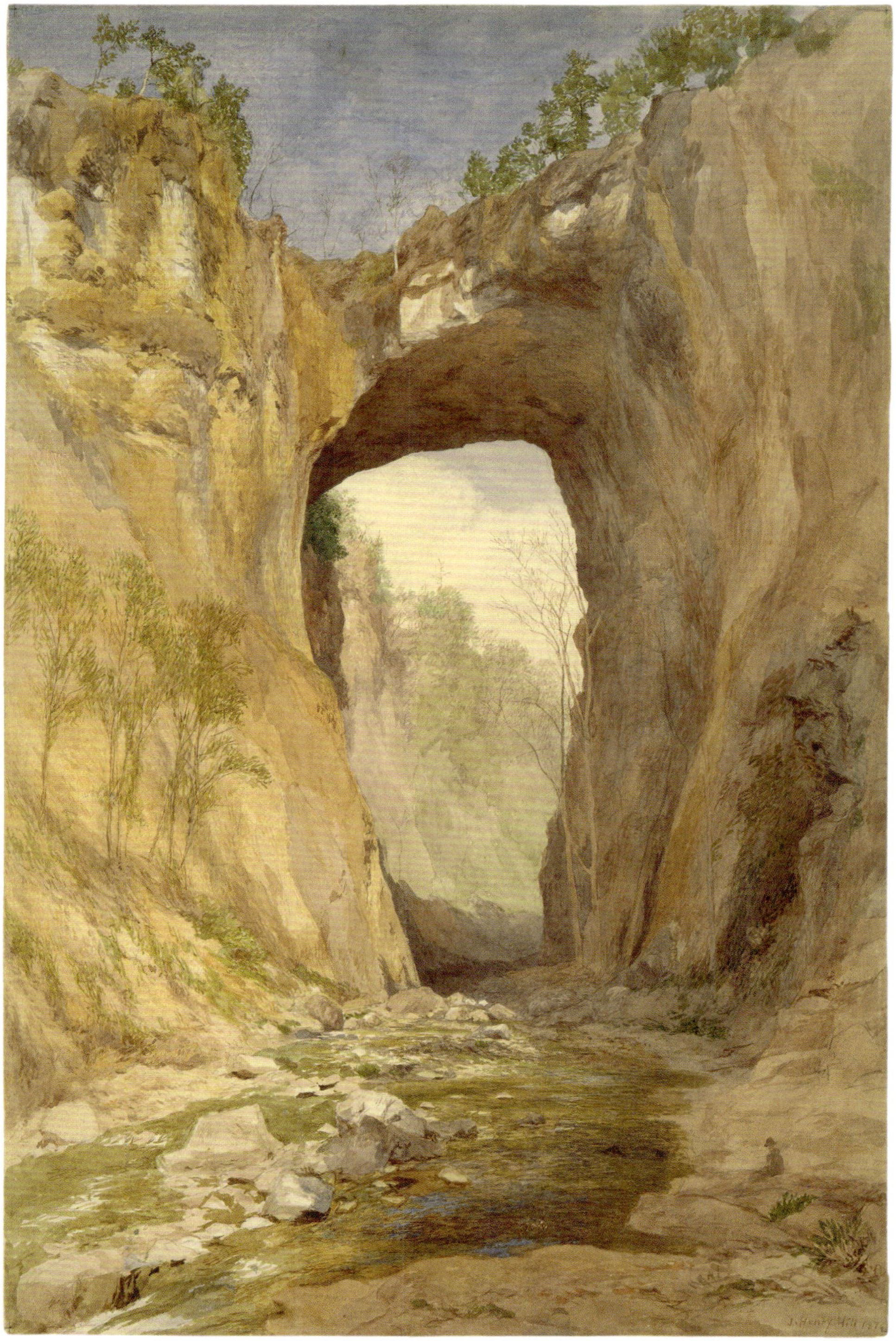

35
JOHN HENRY HILL
Natural Bridge, Virginia, 1876

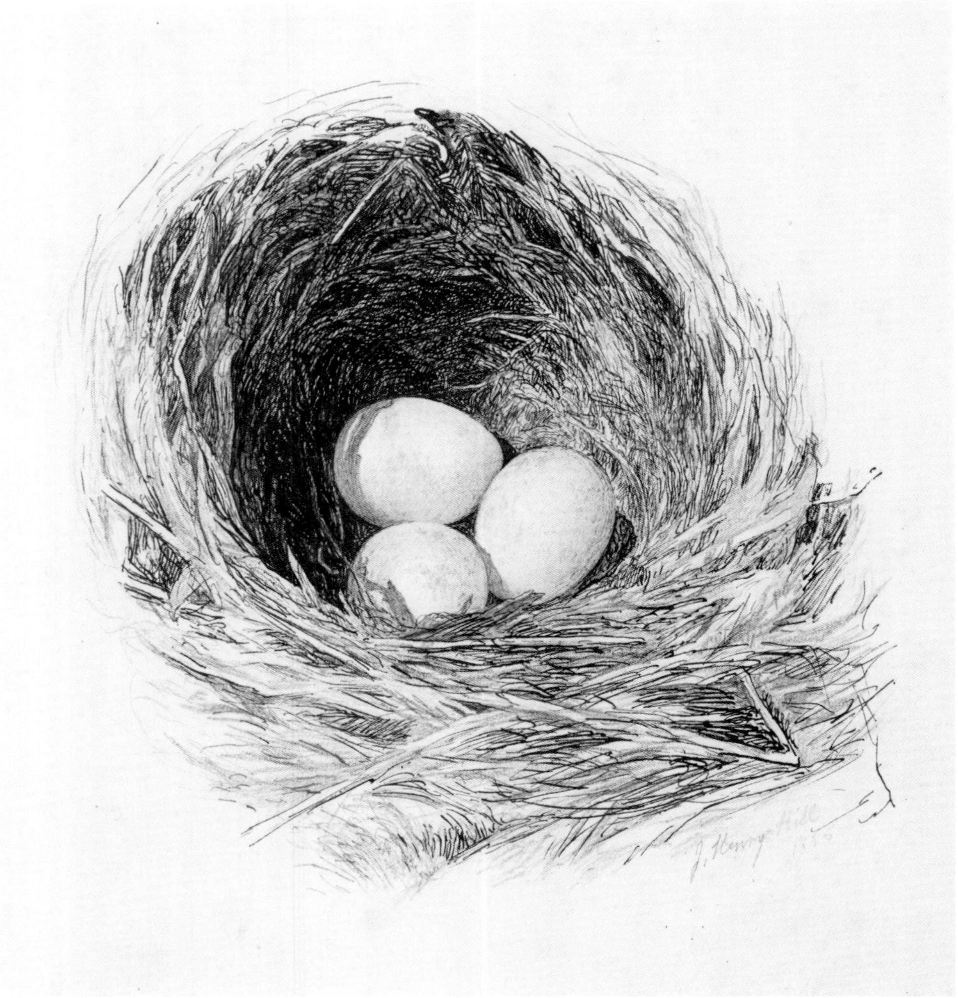

36
JOHN HENRY HILL
Thrush's Nest, 1866

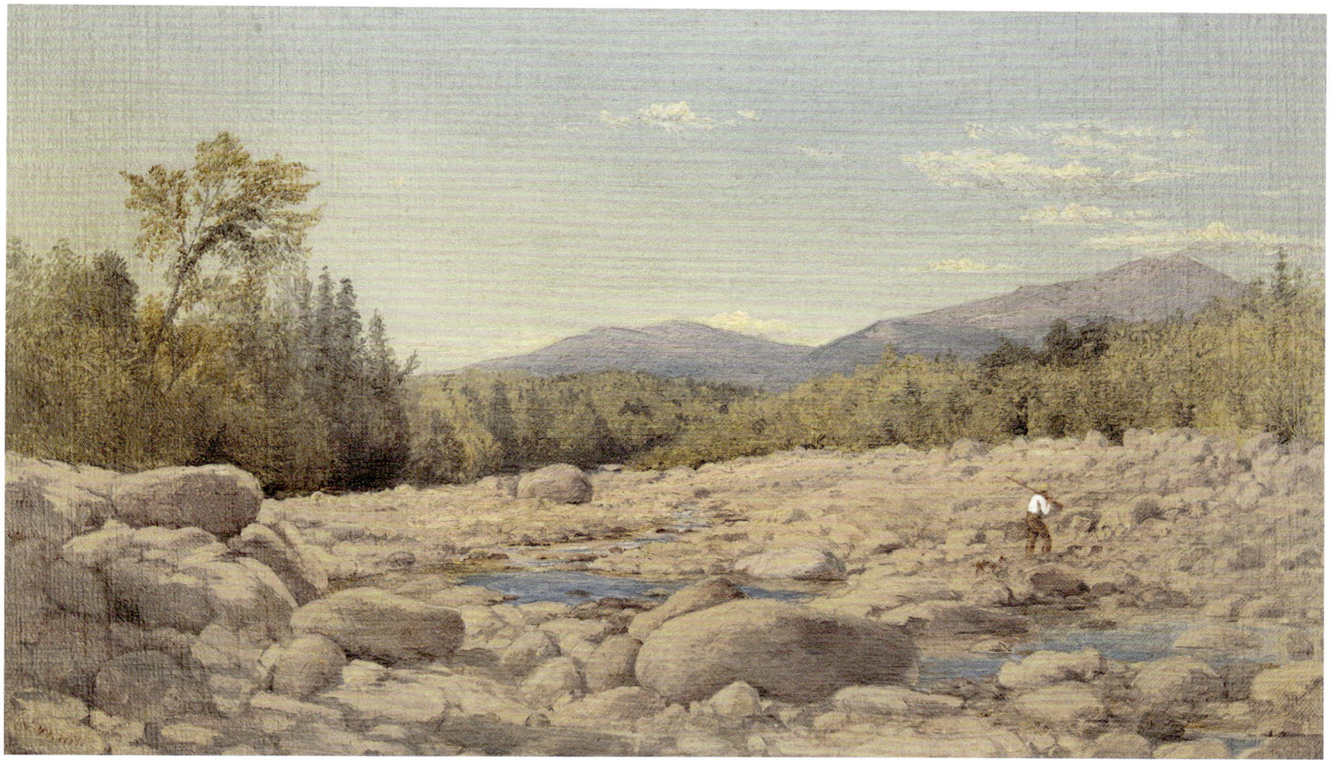

37
JOHN WILLIAM HILL
Hunter and Dog, c. 1867

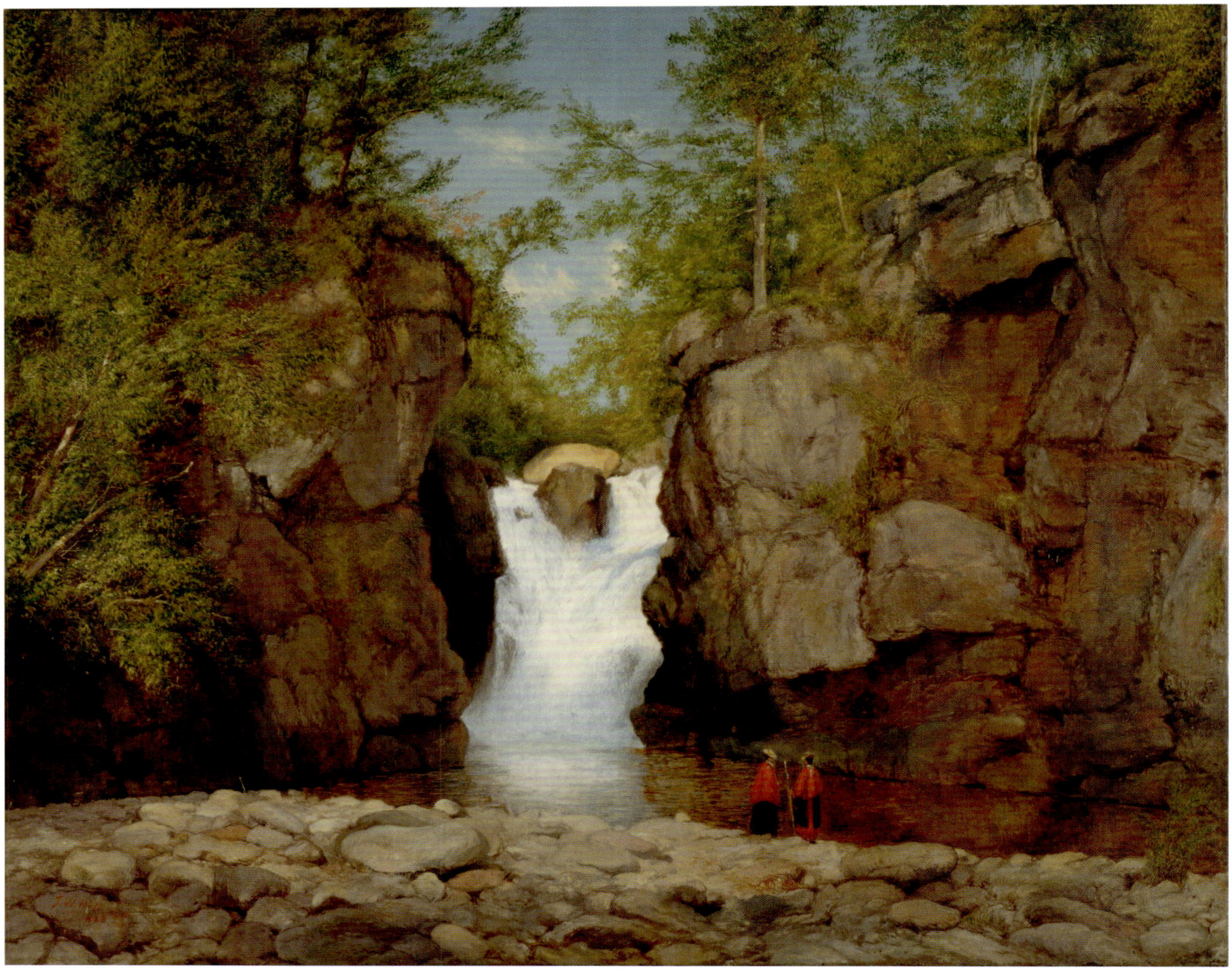

38
JOHN WILLIAM HILL
Fawn's Leap, Catskill Mountains, 1868

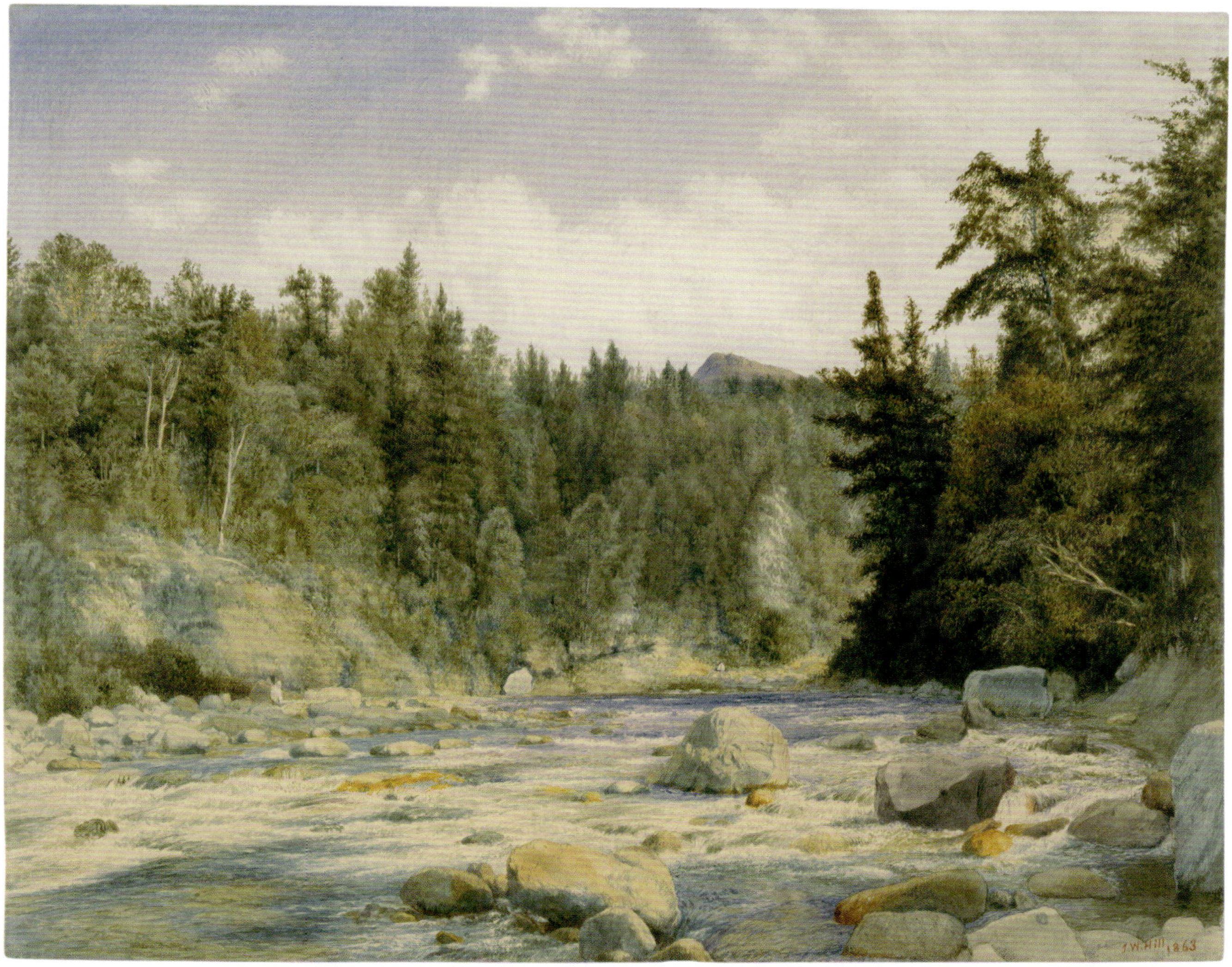

39
JOHN WILLIAM HILL
Mountain Stream (Catskill Creek), 1863

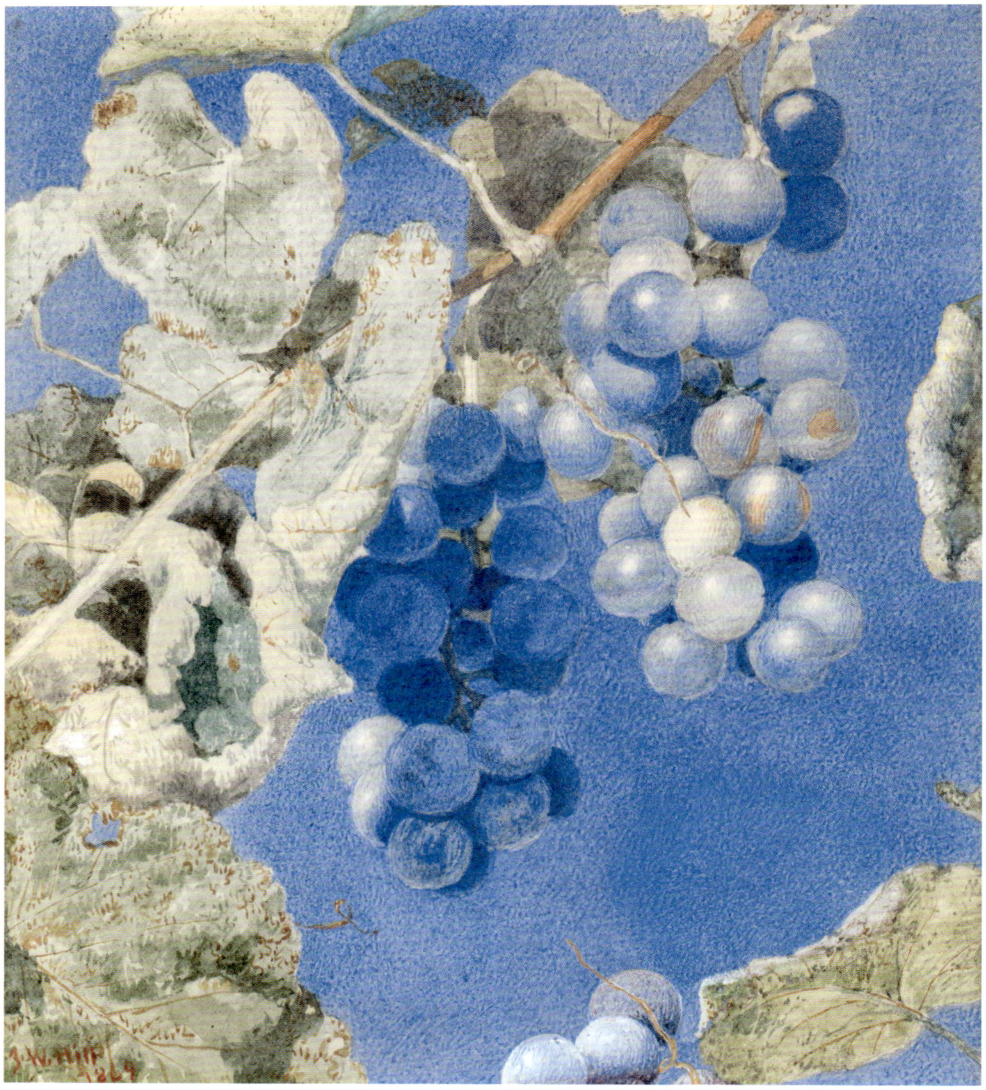

40
JOHN WILLIAM HILL
Grapes, 1864

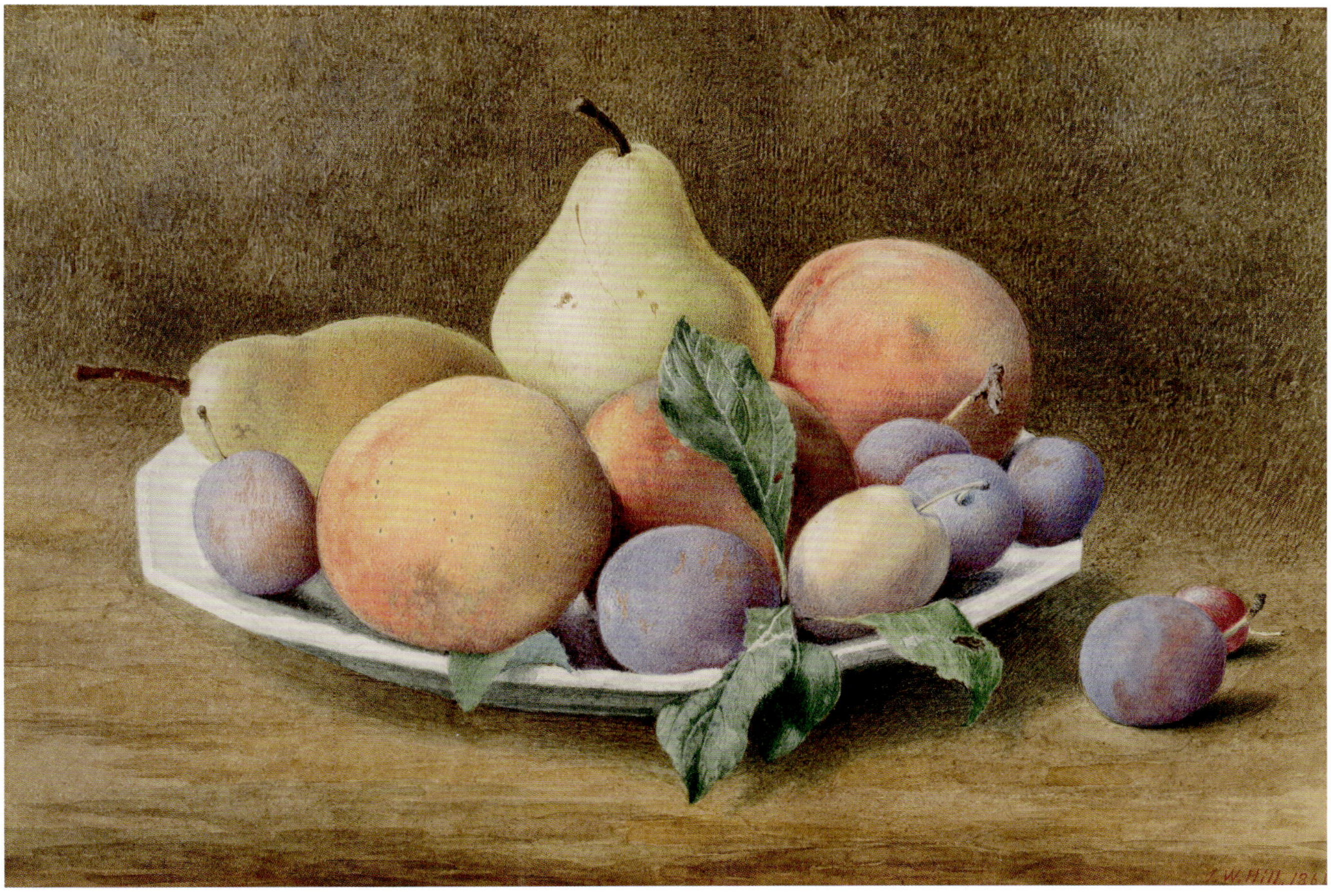

41
JOHN WILLIAM HILL
Plums, Pears, Peaches, and a Grape, 1864

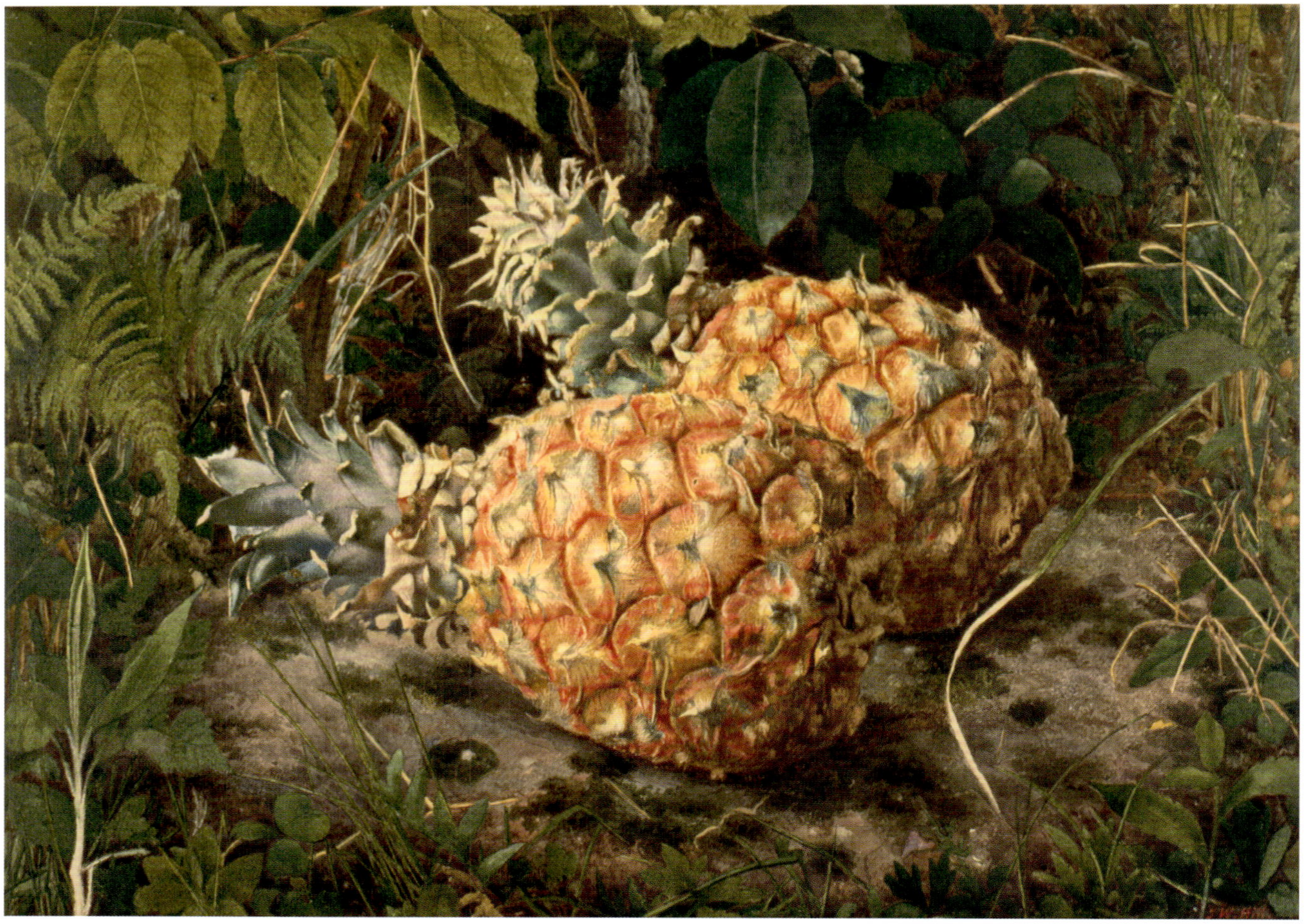

42
JOHN WILLIAM HILL
Pineapples, c. 1864

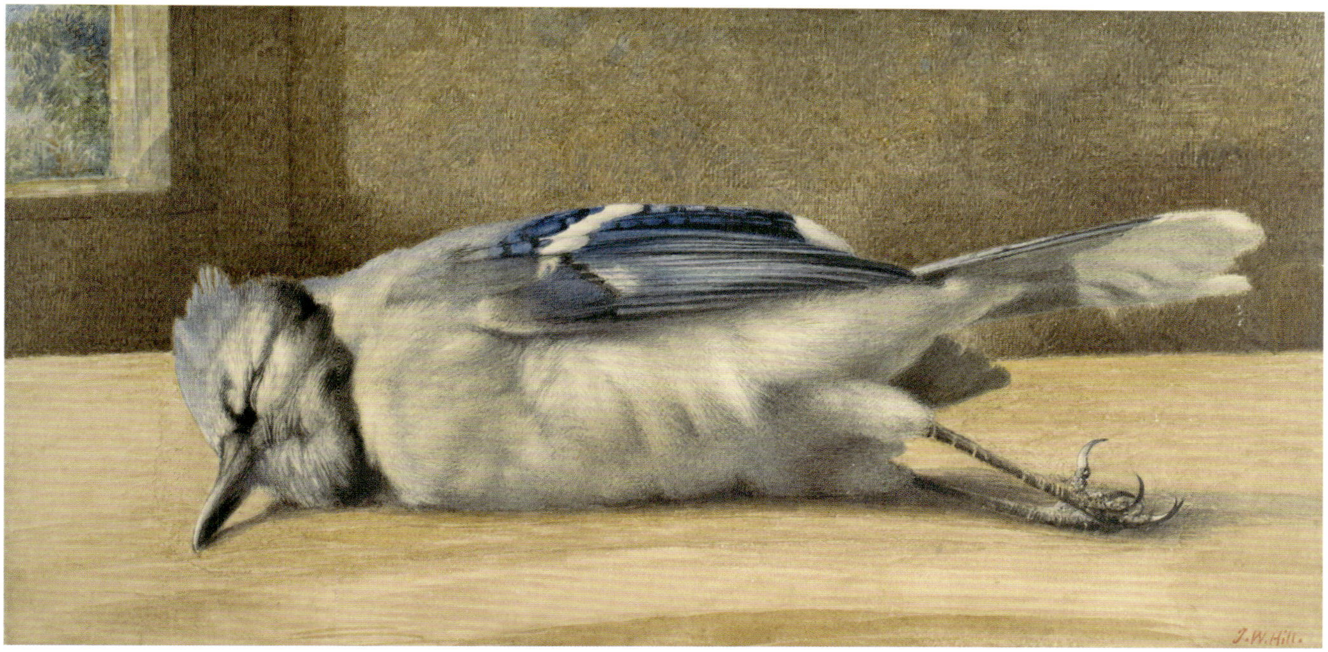

43
JOHN WILLIAM HILL
Dead Blue Jay, c. 1865

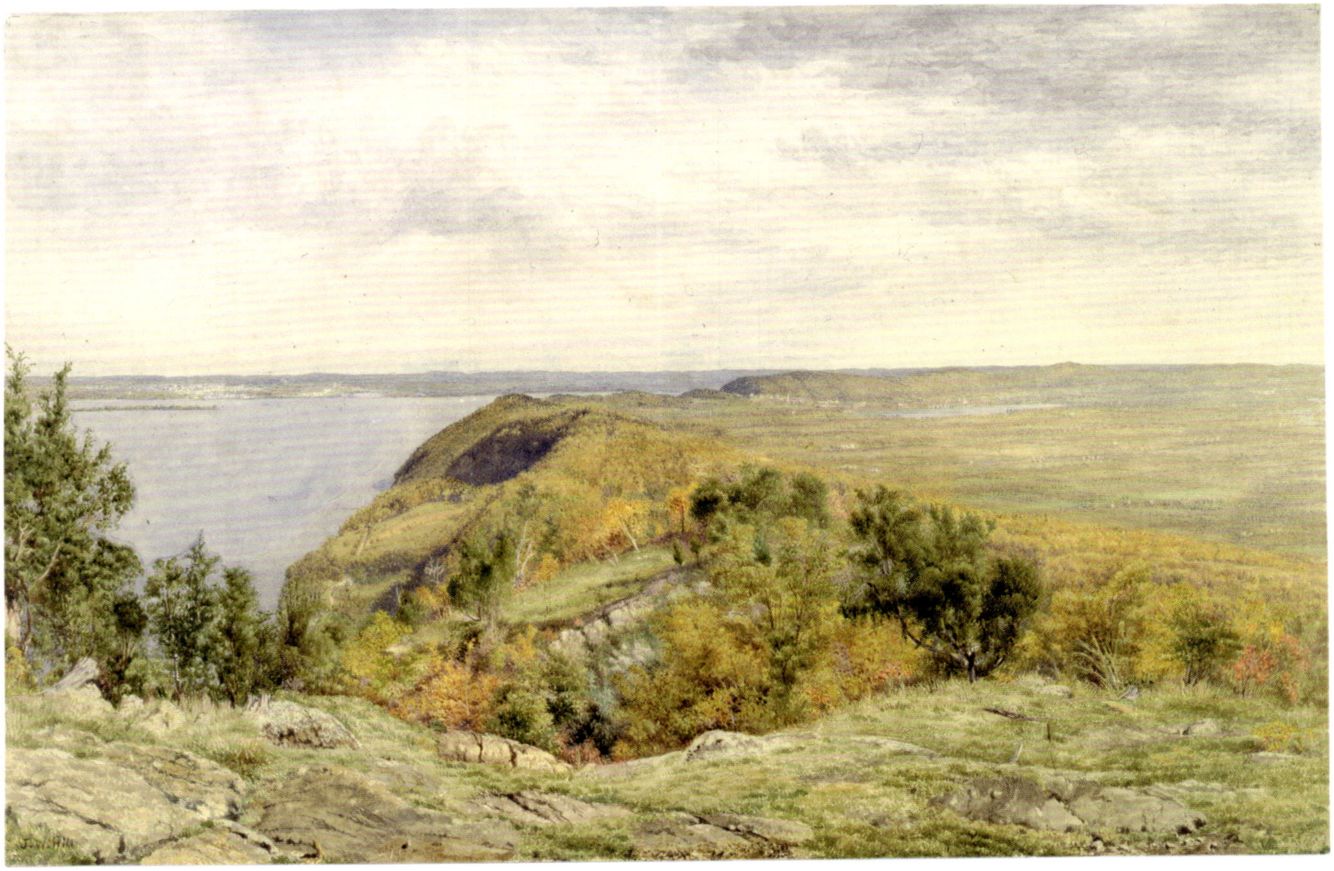

44
JOHN WILLIAM HILL
View from High Tor, Haverstraw, New York, c. 1866

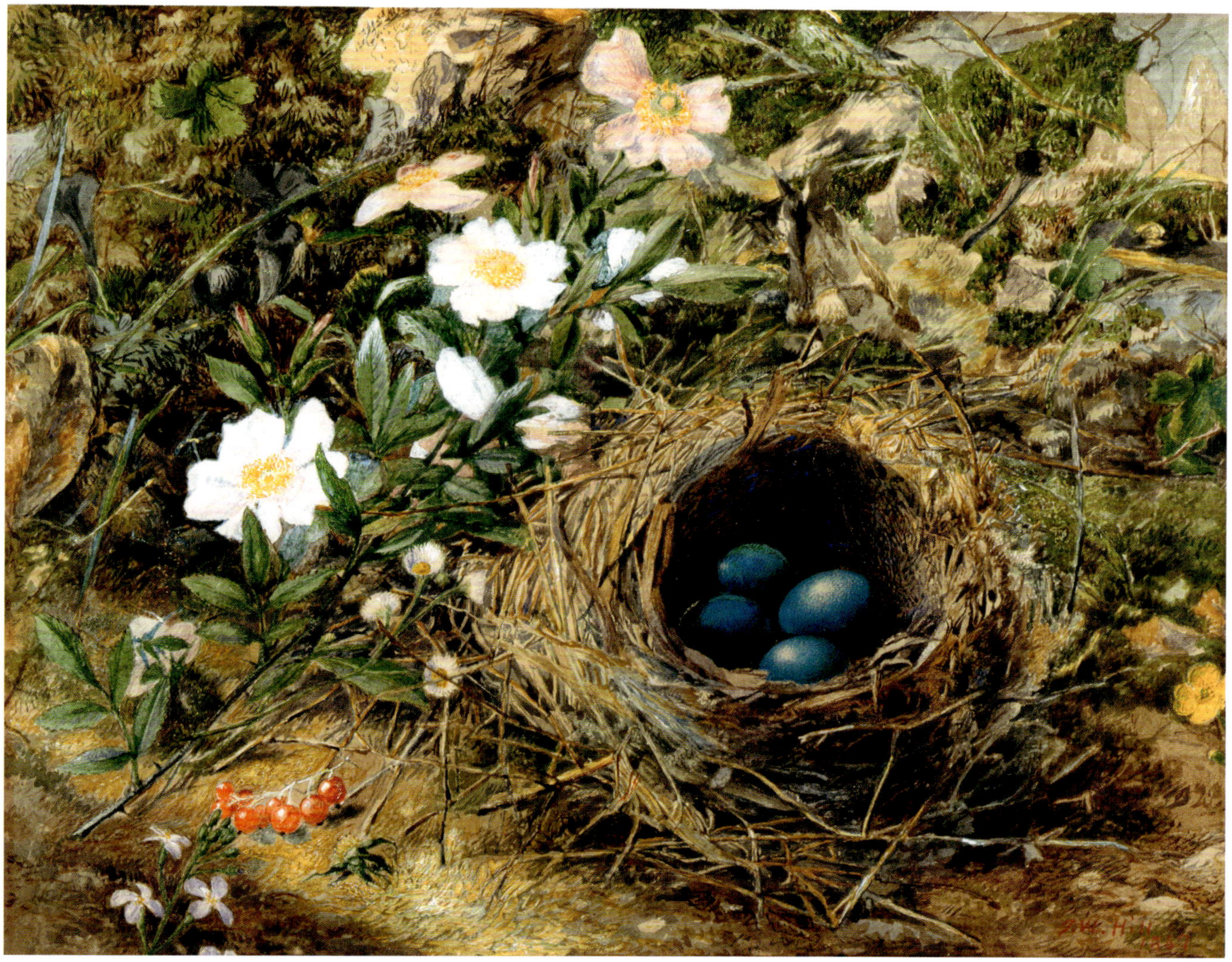

45
JOHN WILLIAM HILL
Bird's Nest and Dog Roses, 1867

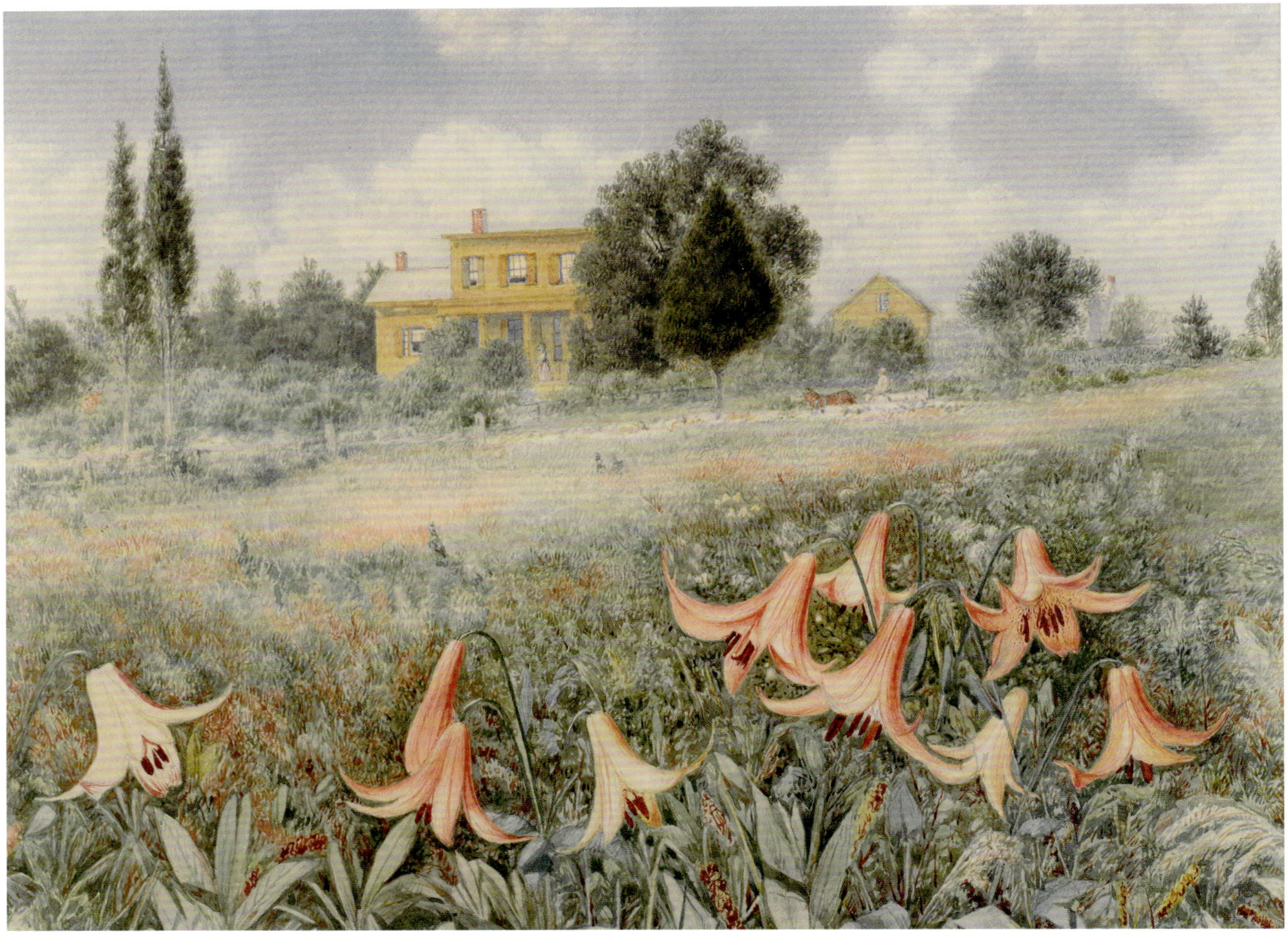

46
JOHN WILLIAM HILL
West Nyack, New York (The Lilies of the Field), 1868

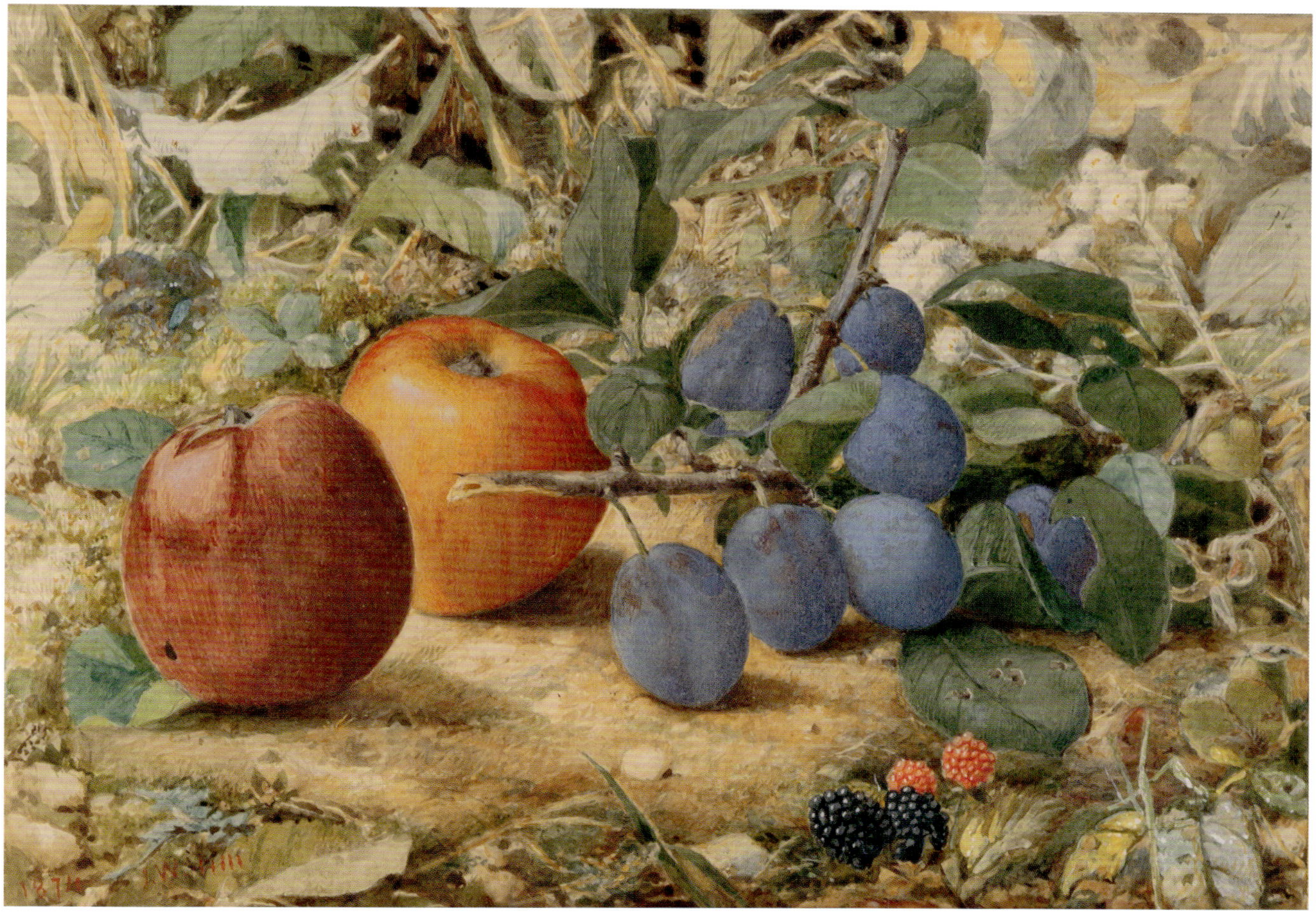

47
JOHN WILLIAM HILL
Apples and Plums, 1874

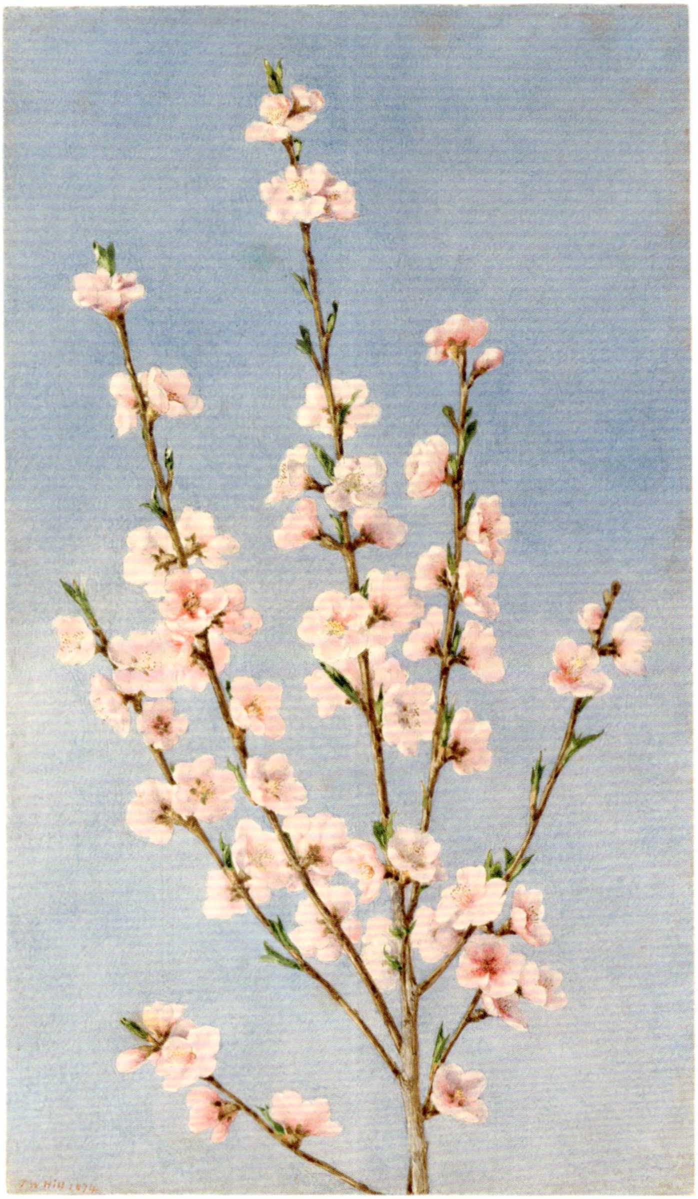

48
JOHN WILLIAM HILL
Peach Blossoms, 1874

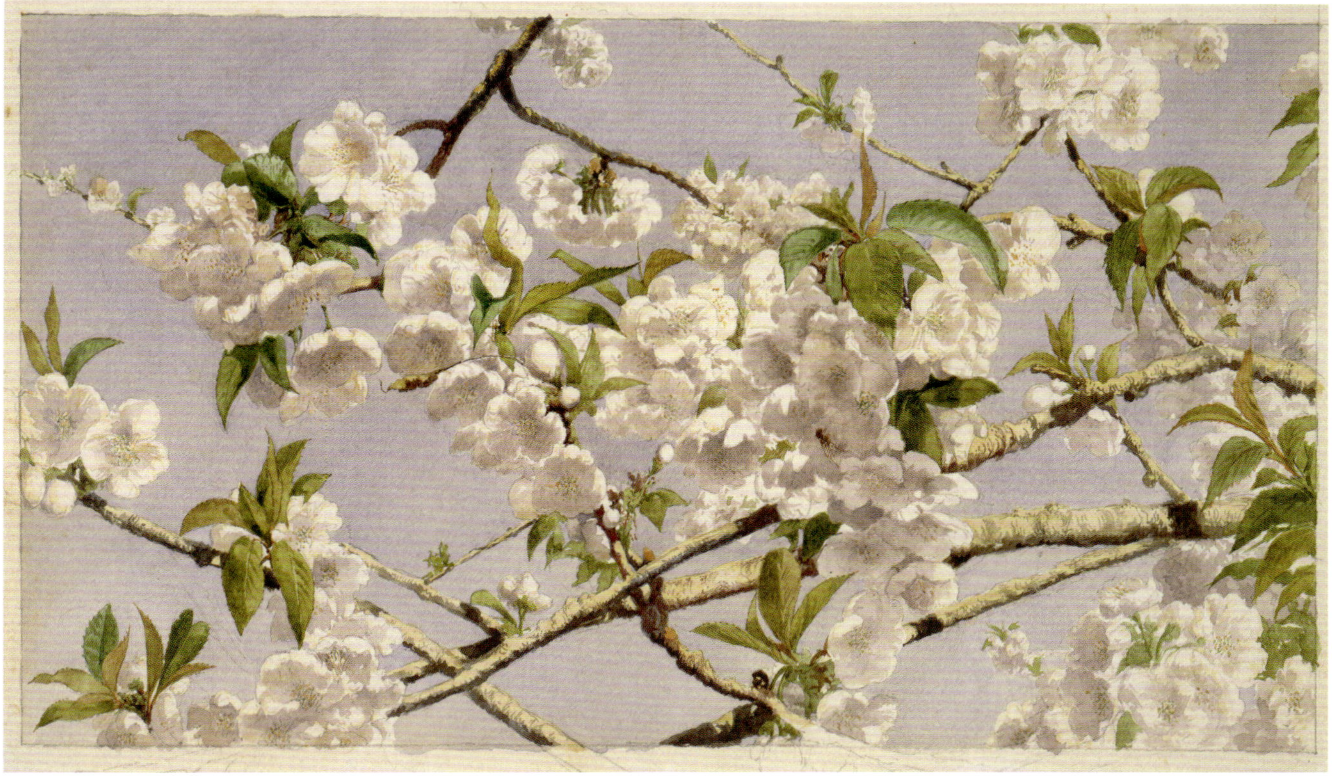

49
JOHN WILLIAM HILL
Apple Blossoms, c. 1874

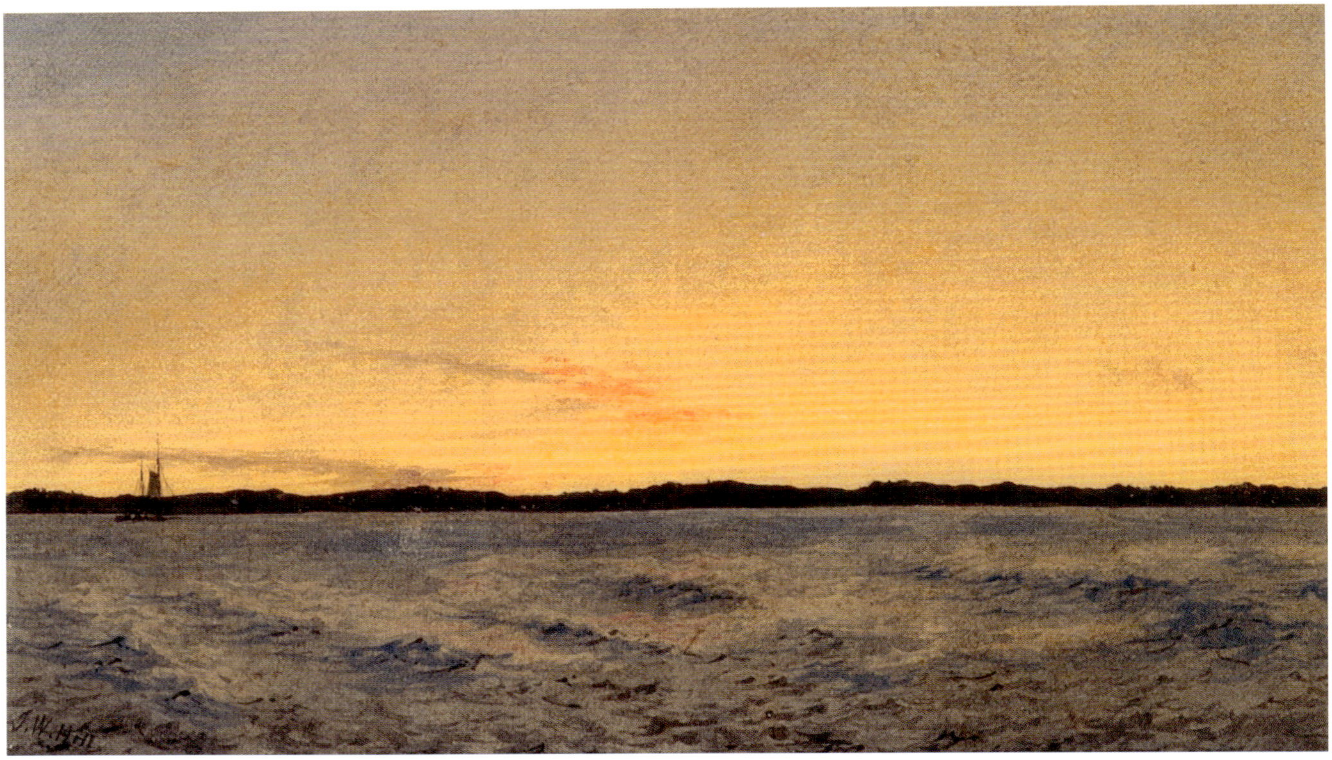

50
JOHN WILLIAM HILL
Afterglow, c. 1875

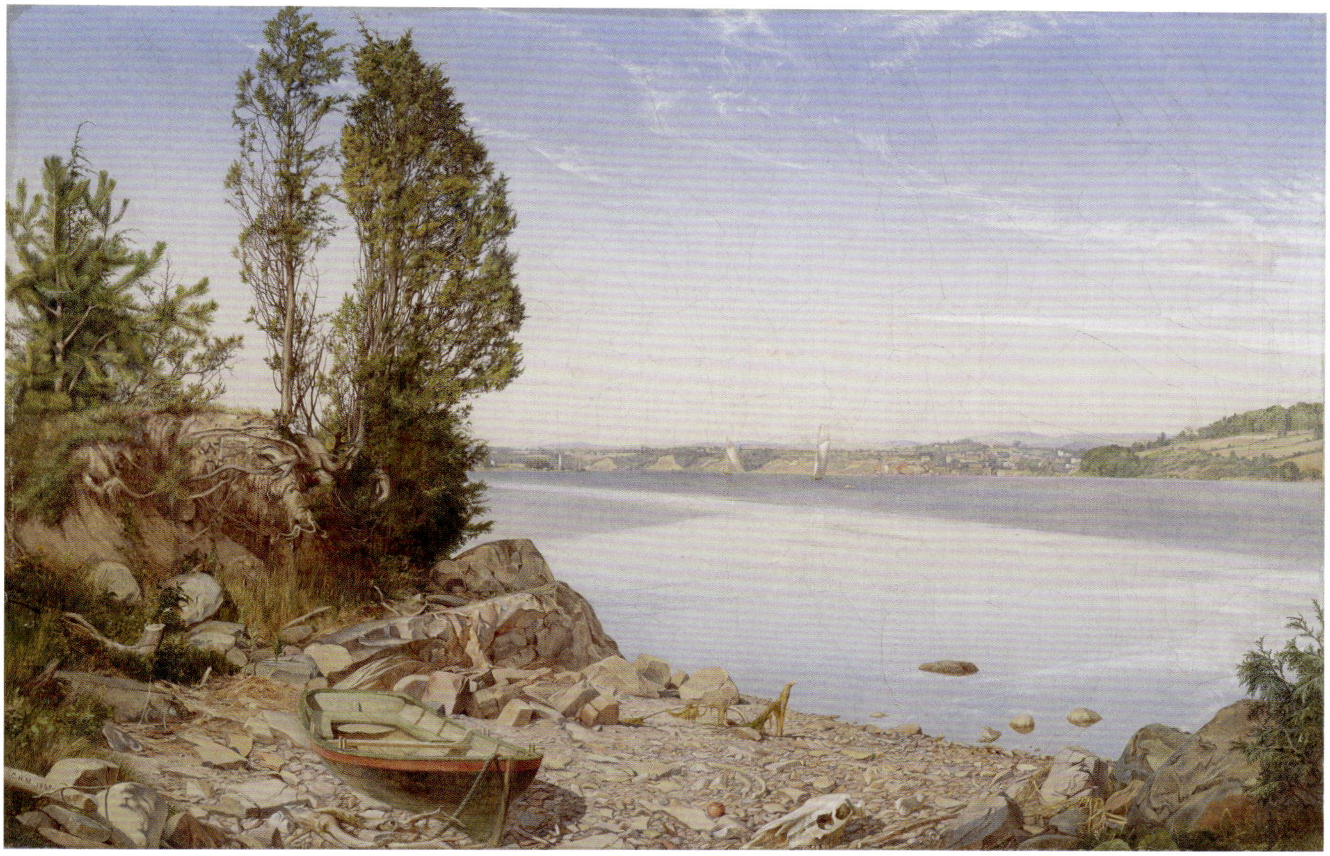

51
CHARLES HERBERT MOORE
Hudson River, Above Catskill, 1865

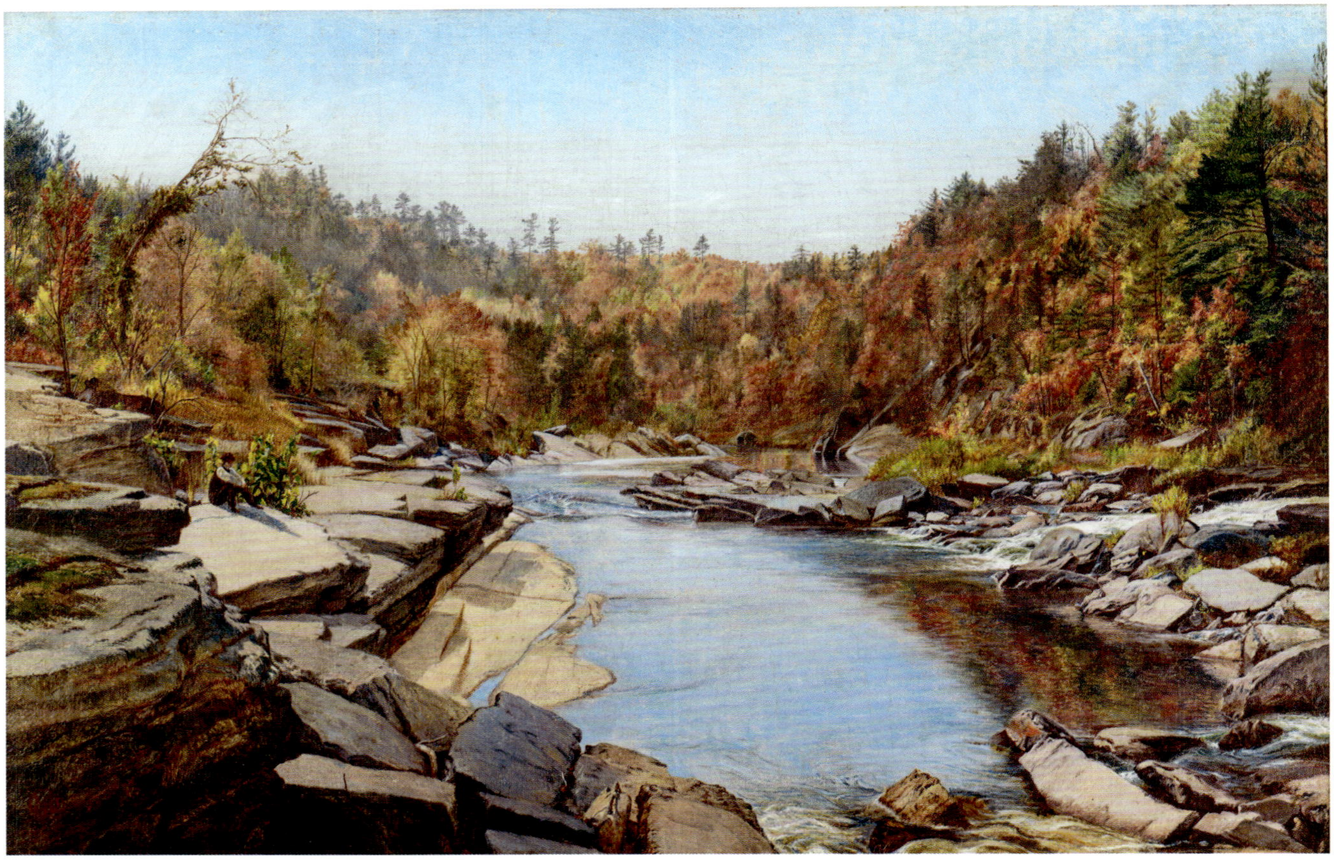

52

CHARLES HERBERT MOORE

Autumn Landscape, 1865 – 1868

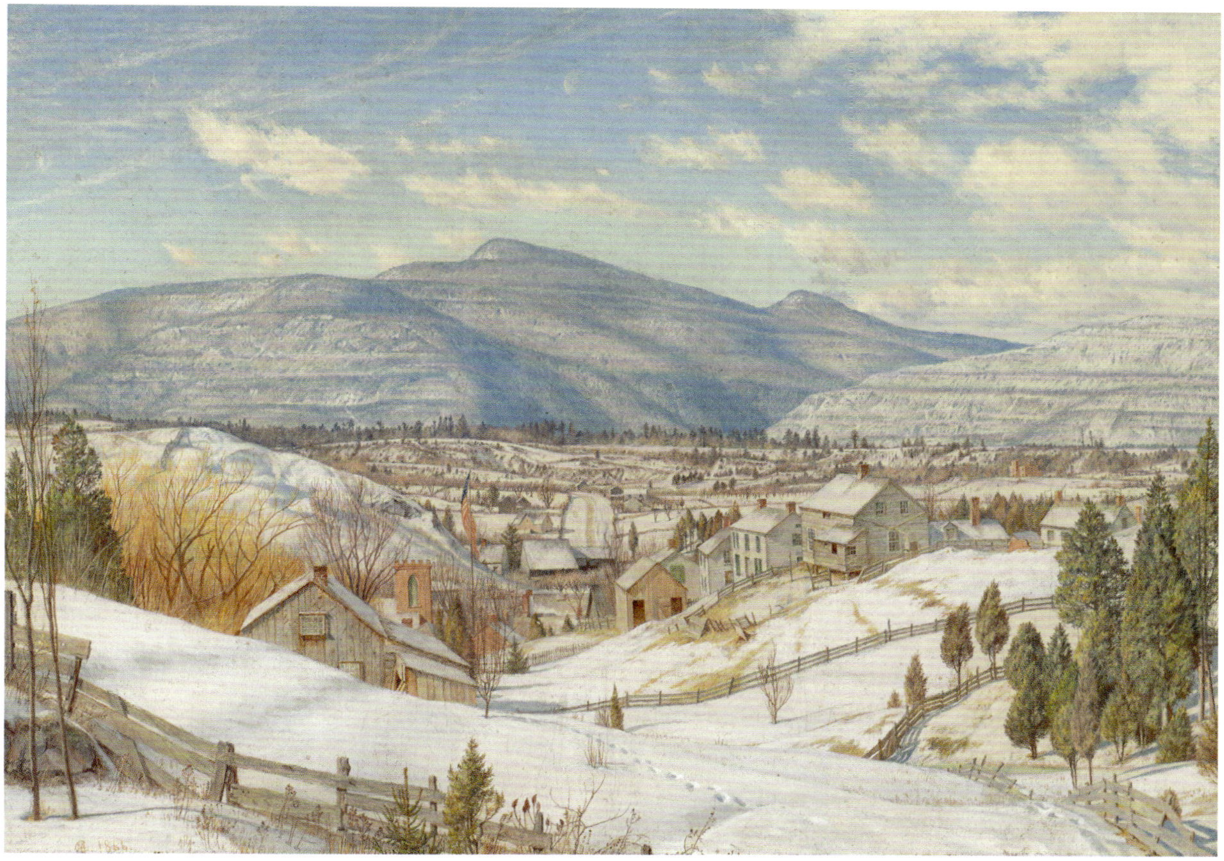

53
CHARLES HERBERT MOORE
High Peak and Round Top (Catskill) in Winter, 1866

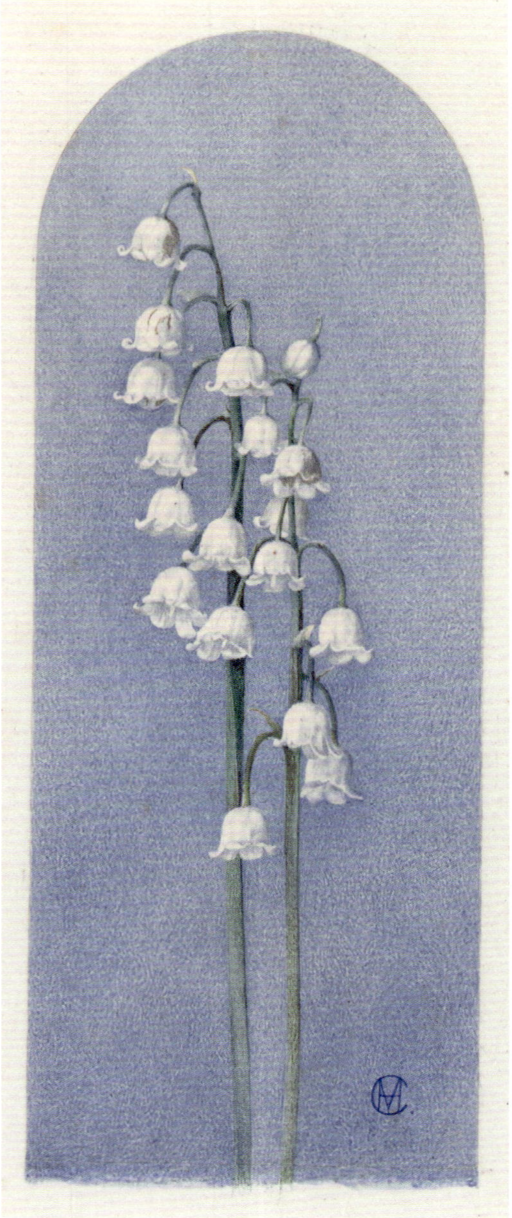

54
CHARLES HERBERT MOORE
Lilies of the Valley, 1861

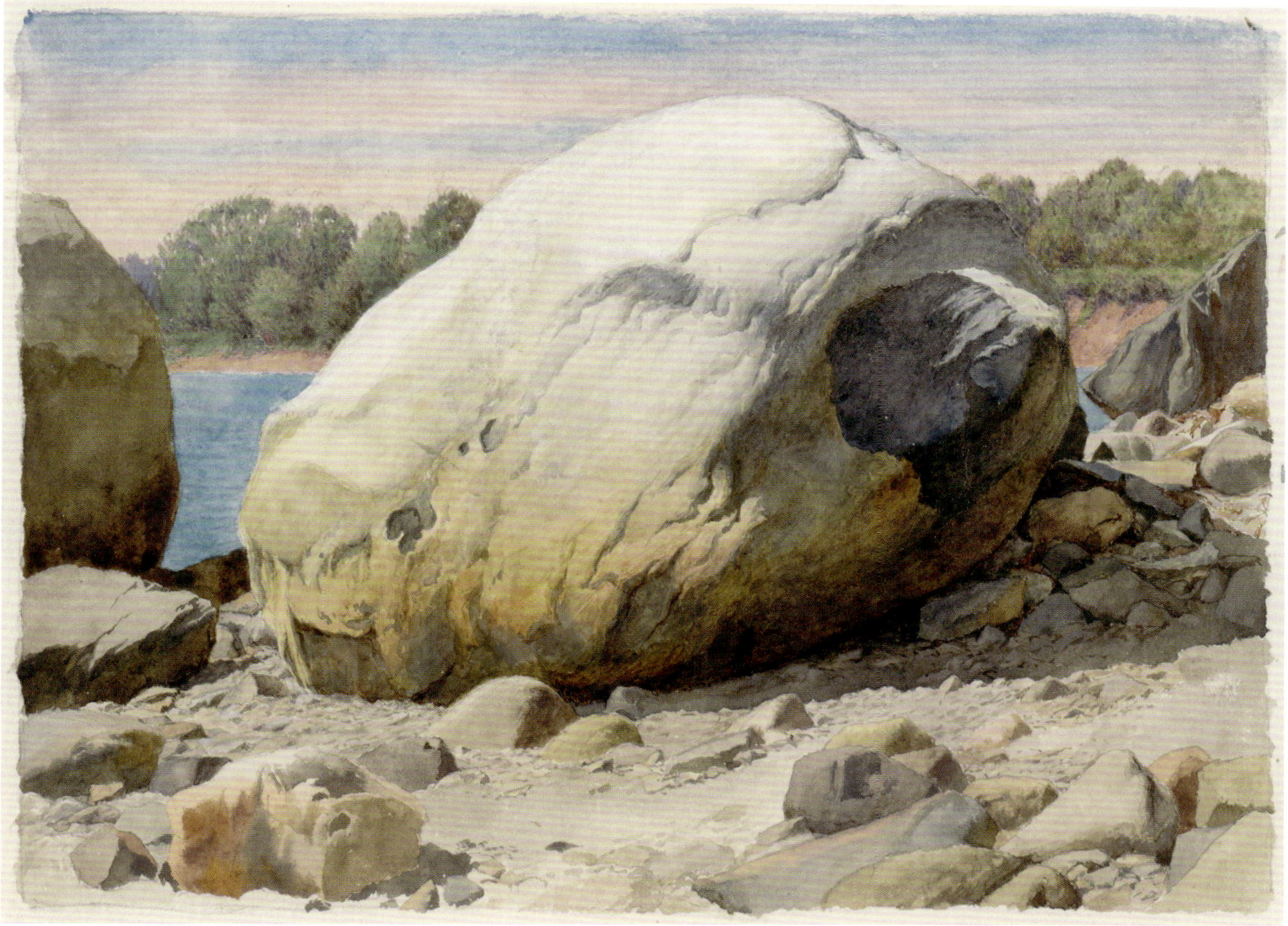

55
CHARLES HERBERT MOORE
Rocks by the Water, c. 1865 – 1872

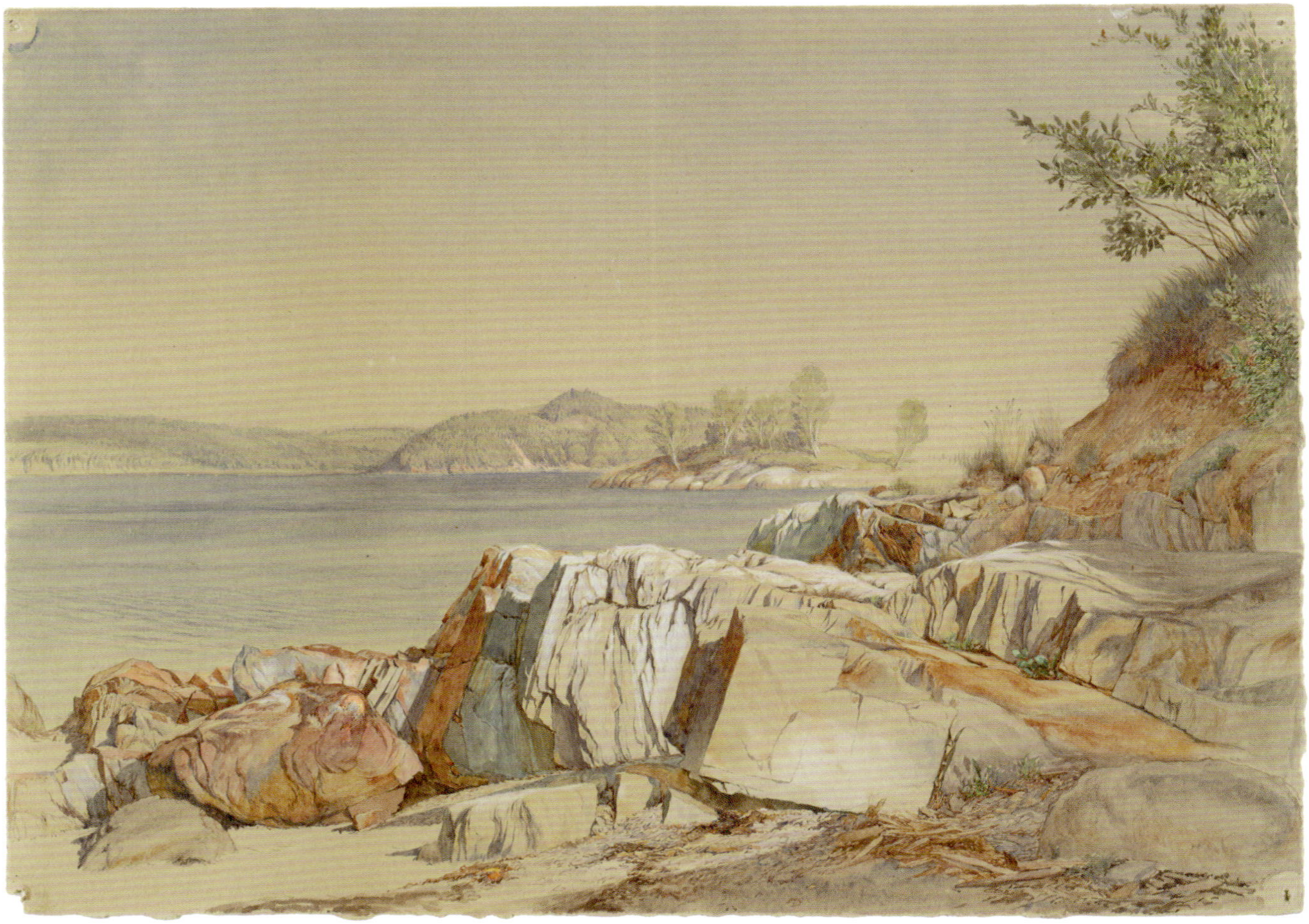

56
CHARLES HERBERT MOORE
Landscape: Rocks and Water, c. 1865–1872

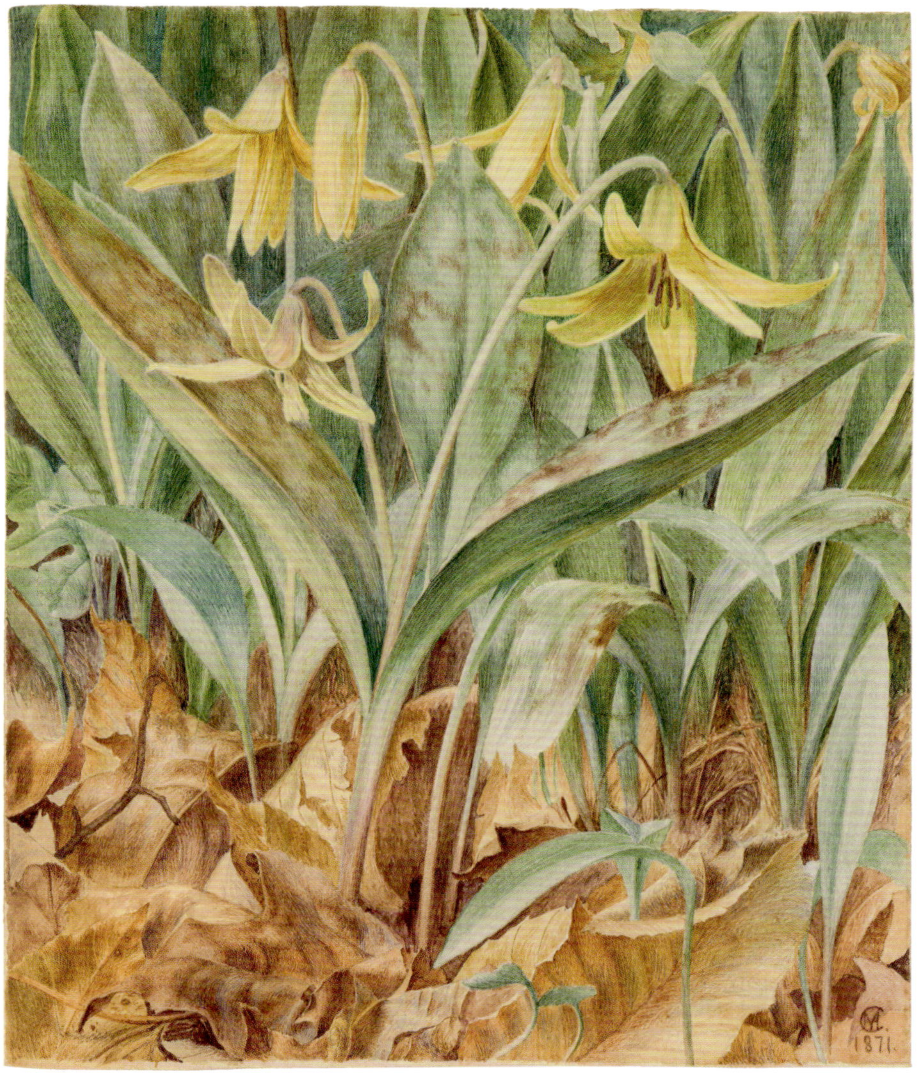

57
CHARLES HERBERT MOORE
Dog Tooth Violet, 1871

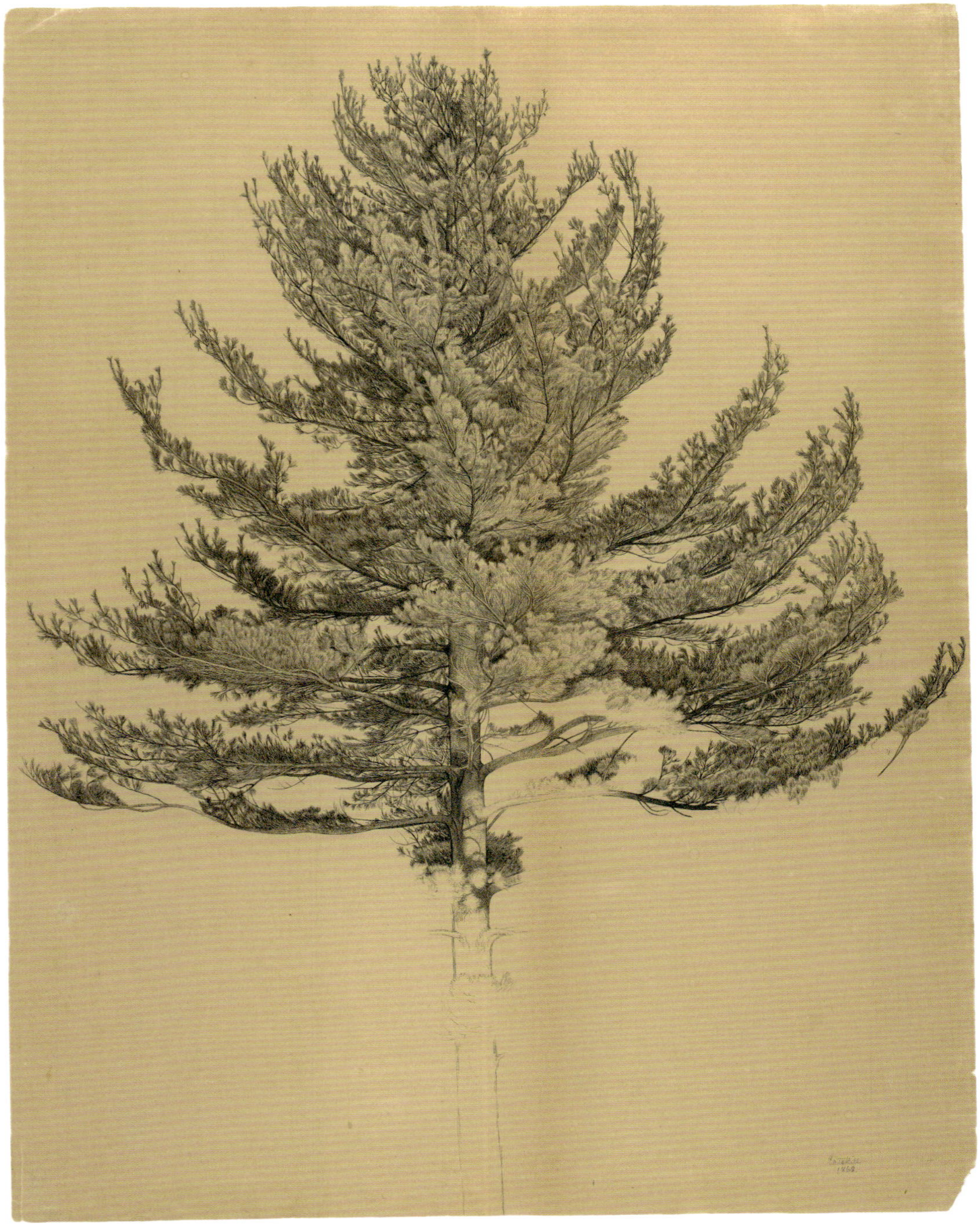

58
CHARLES HERBERT MOORE
Pine Tree, 1868

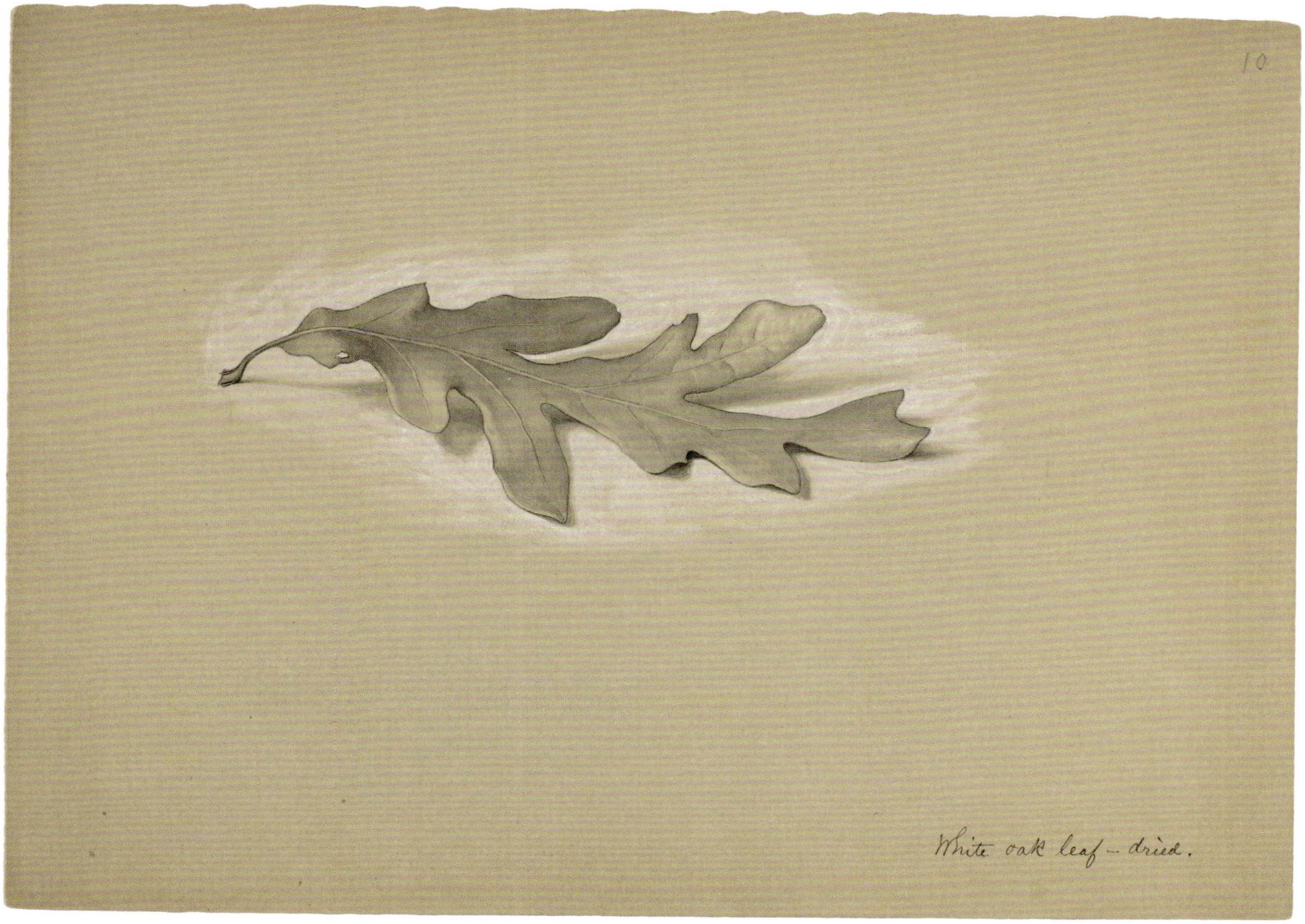

59
CHARLES HERBERT MOORE
Dried White Oak Leaf, c. 1871–1874

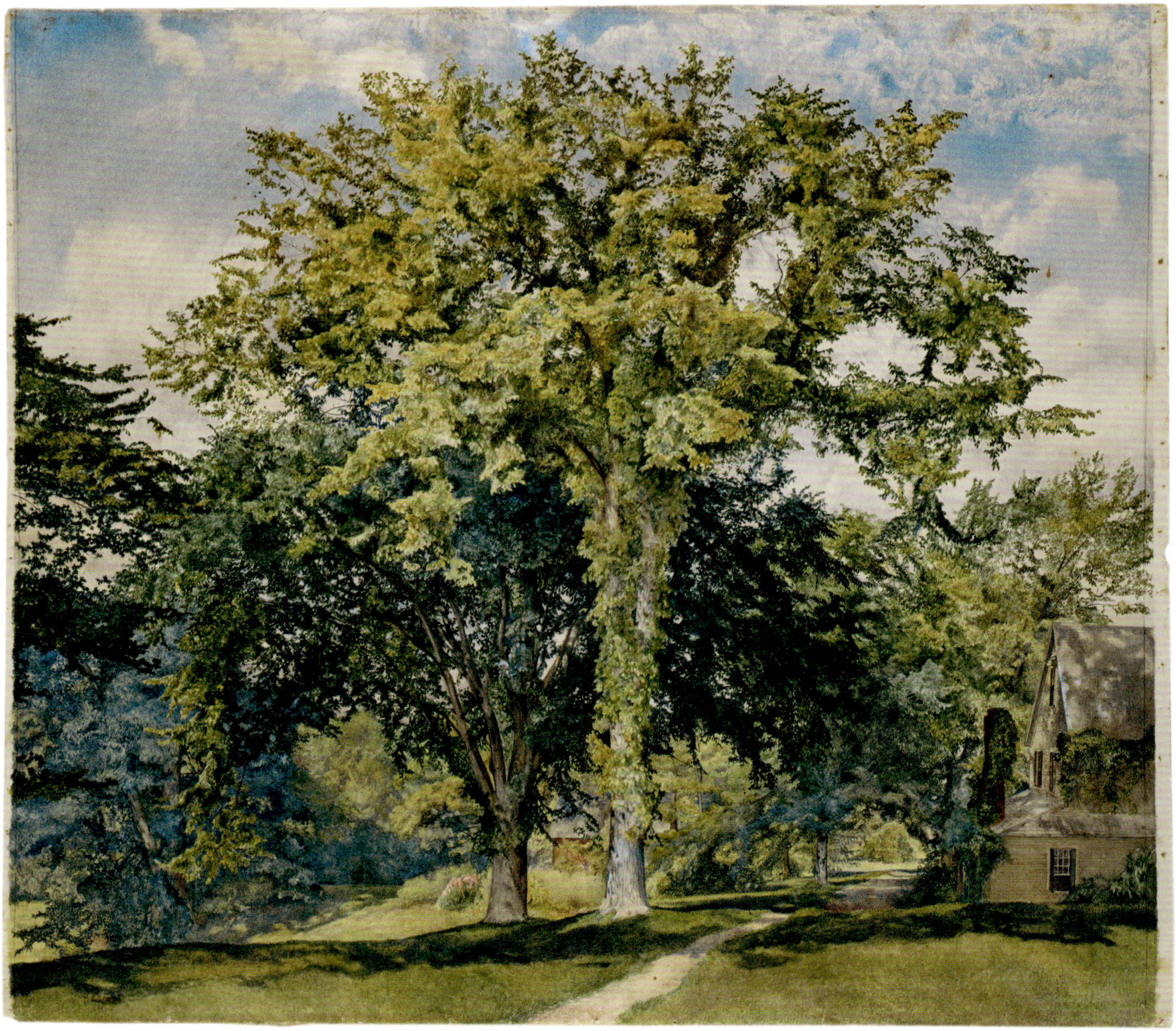

60
HENRY RODERICK NEWMAN
Study of Elms, 1866

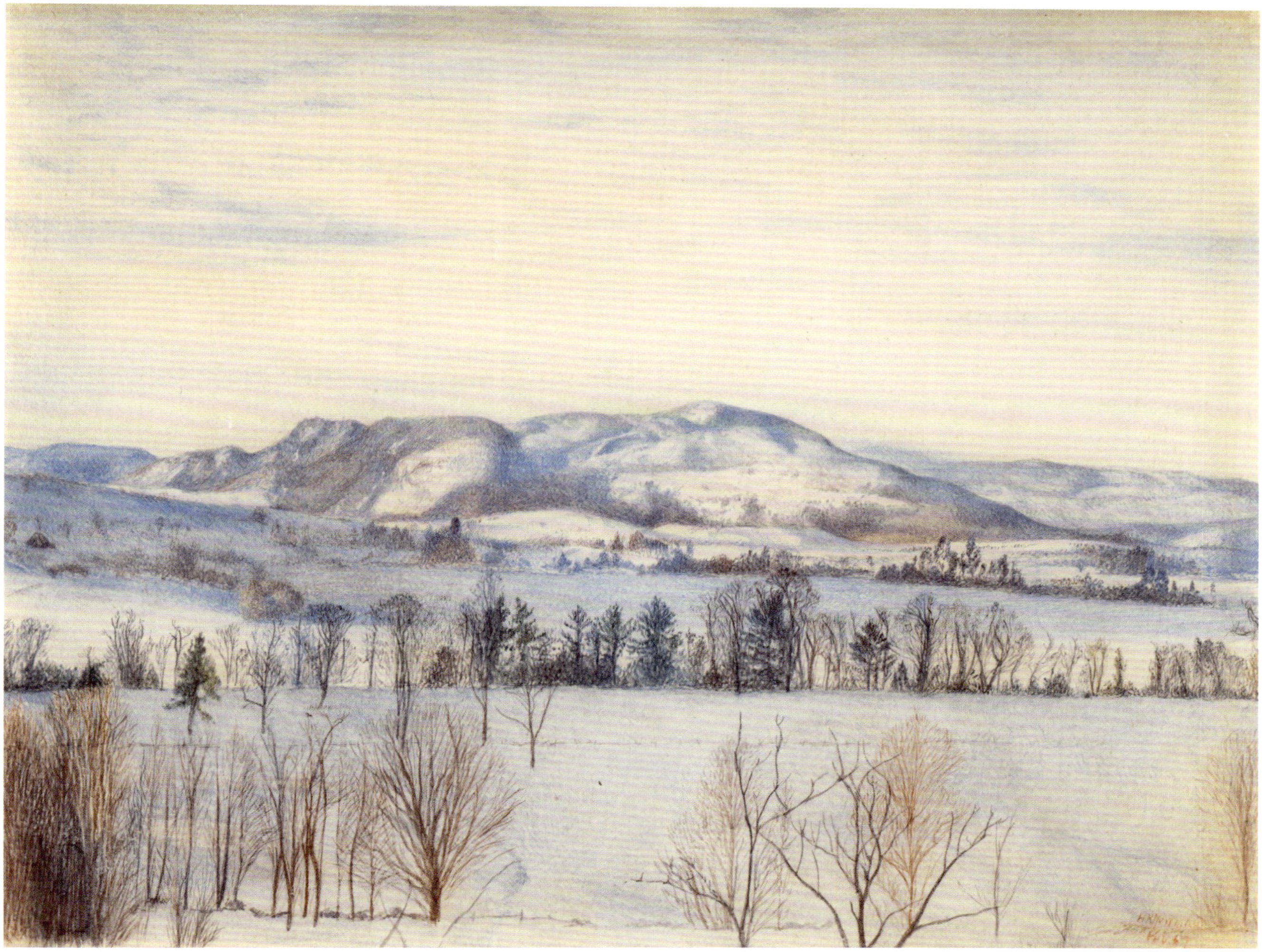

61
HENRY RODERICK NEWMAN
Monument Mountain, 1867

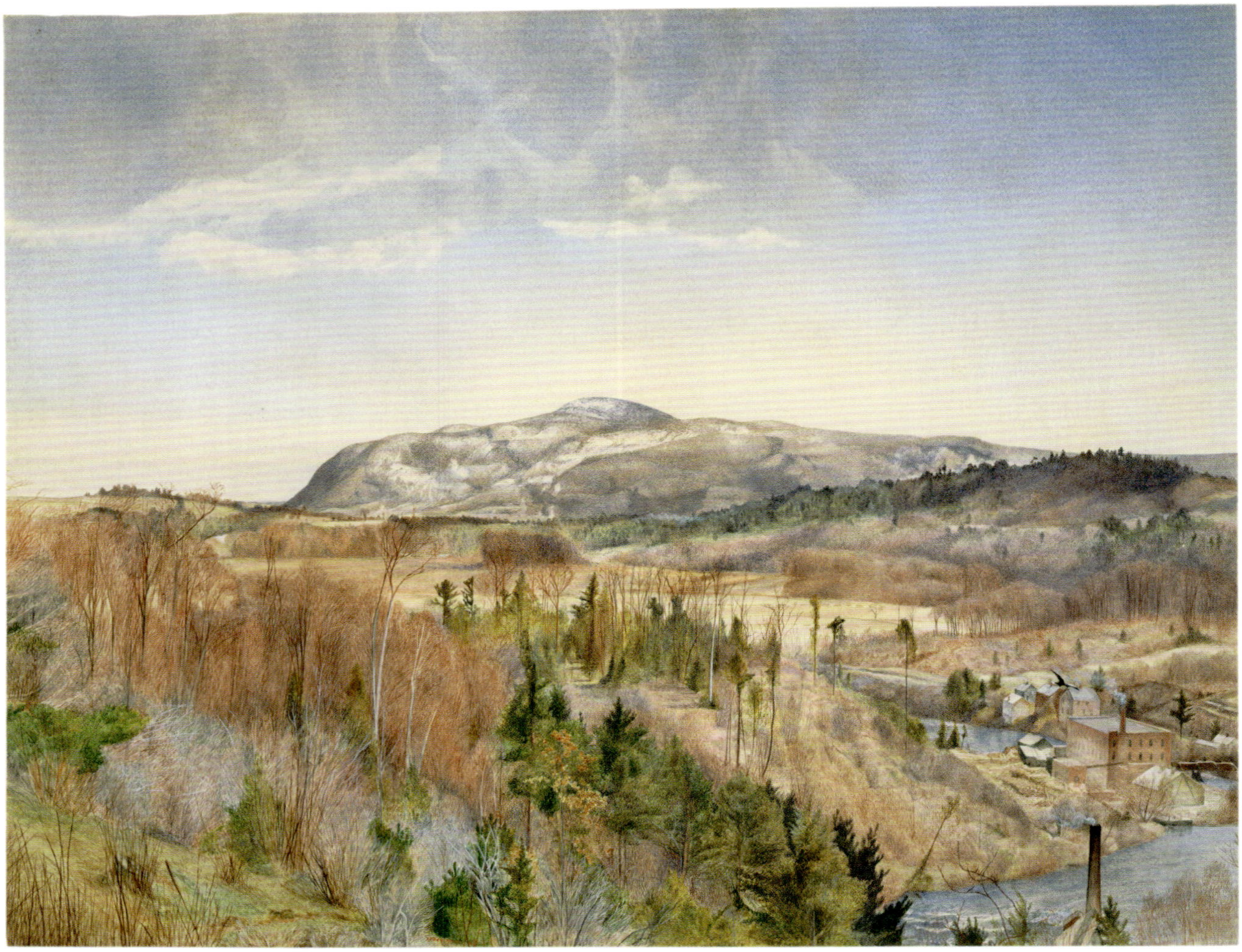

62

HENRY RODERICK NEWMAN

Mt. Everett from Monument Mountain in April, 1867

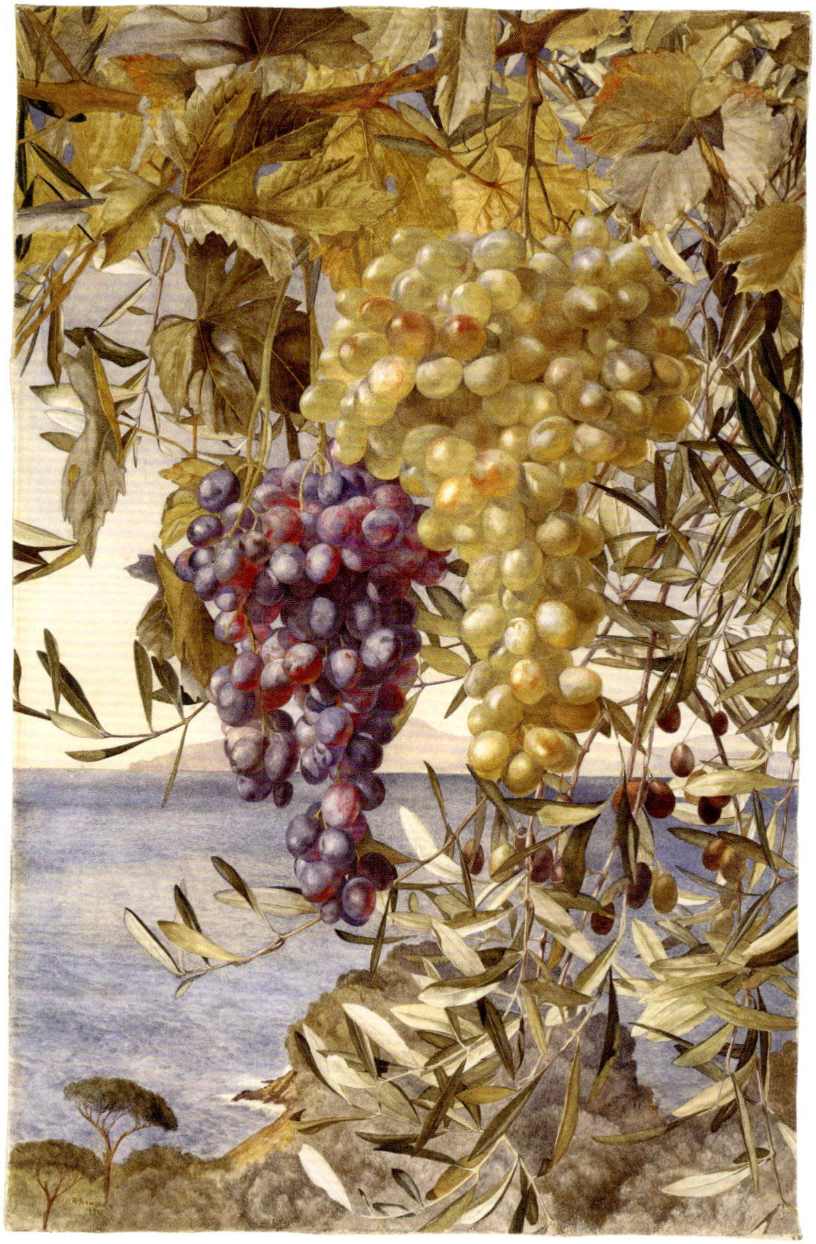

63
HENRY RODERICK NEWMAN
Grapes and Olives, 1878

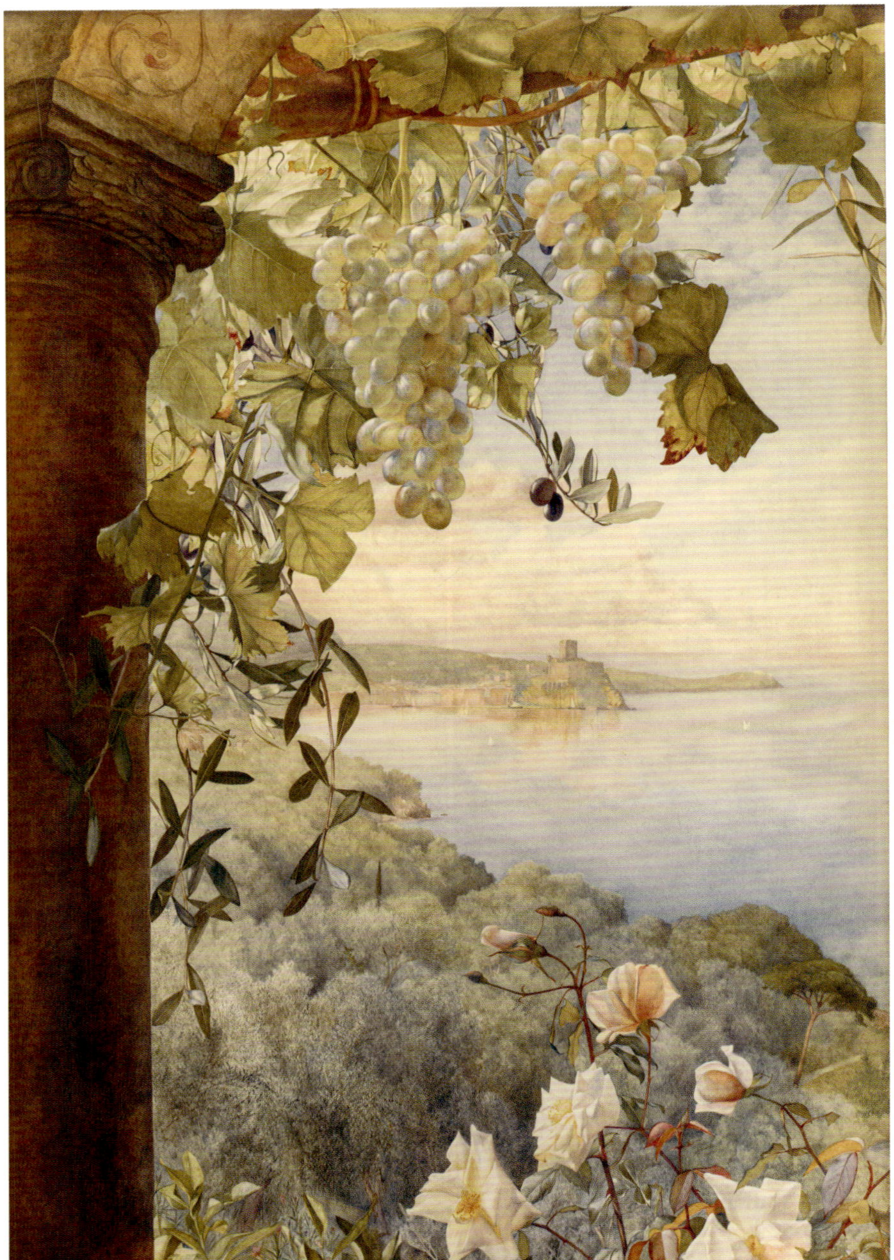

64
HENRY RODERICK NEWMAN
Italy, 1883

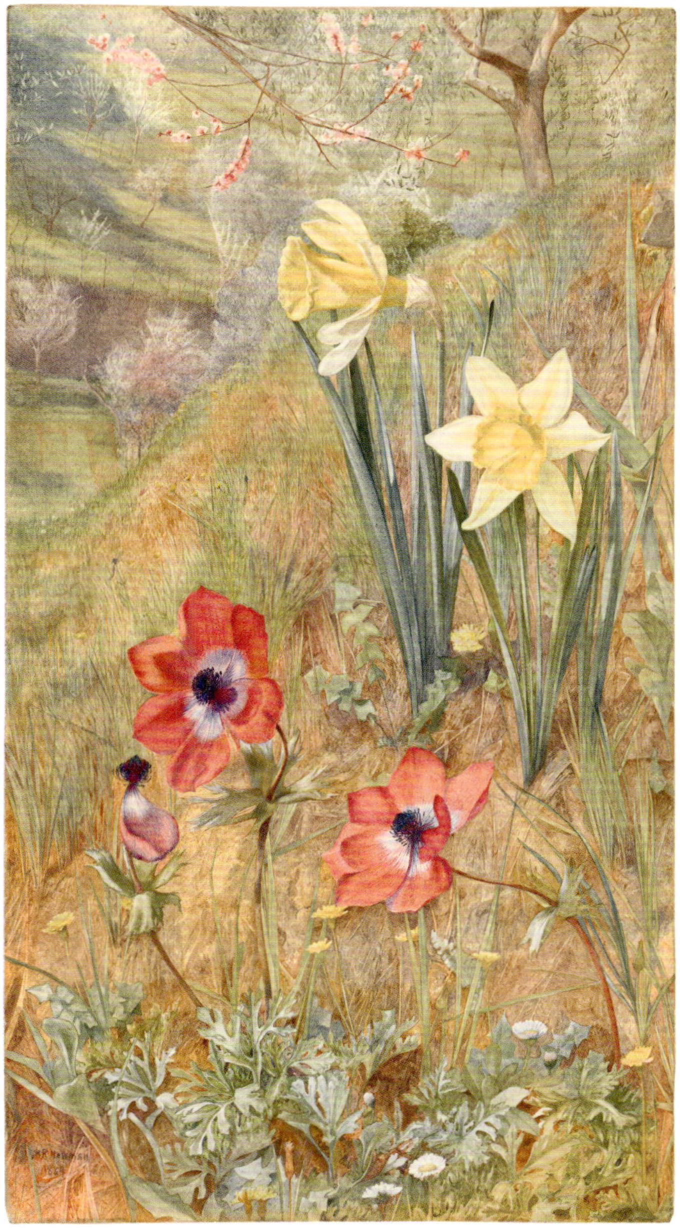

65
HENRY RODERICK NEWMAN
Anemones and Daffodils, 1884

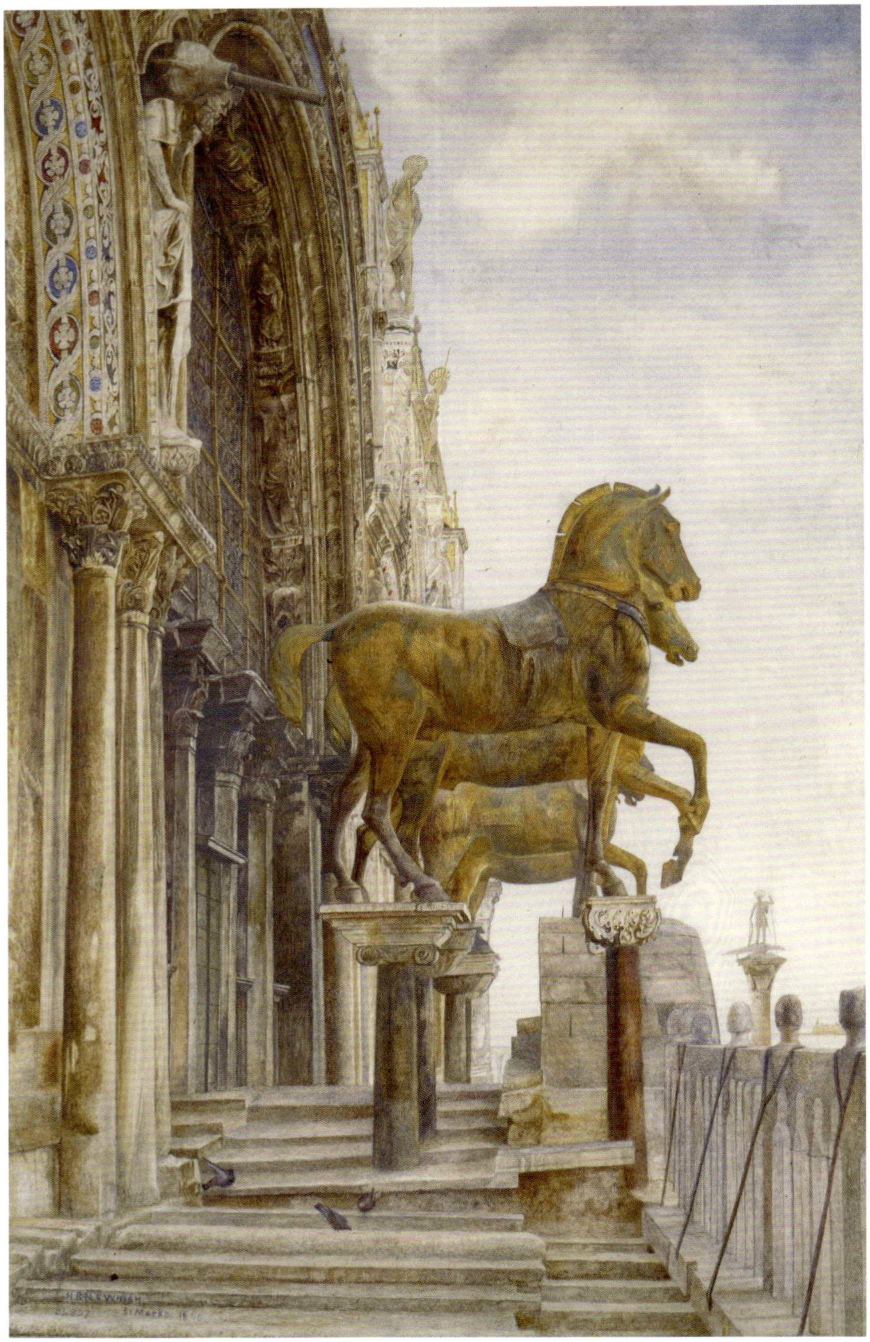

66

HENRY RODERICK NEWMAN

The Horses of St. Marks, 1890

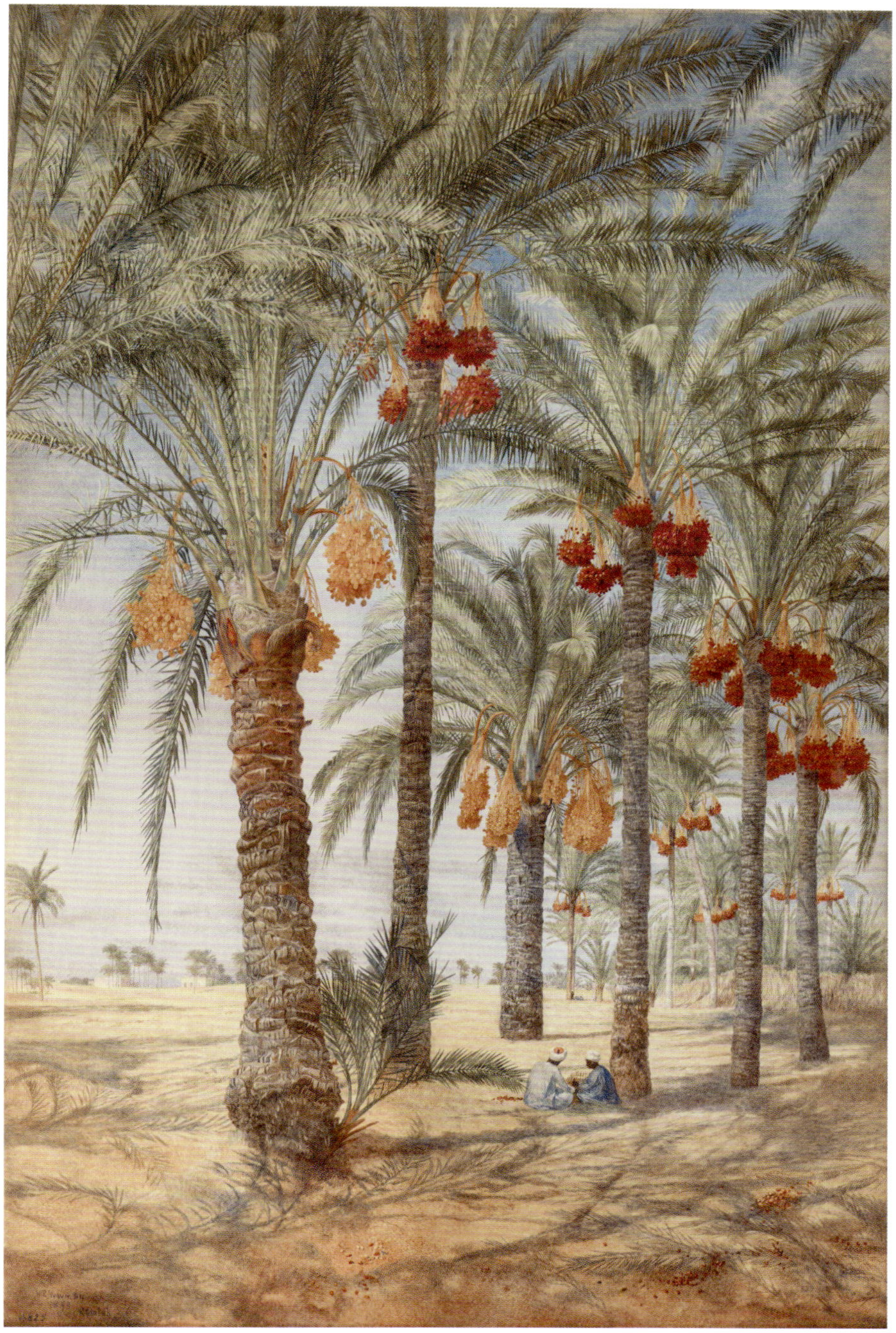

67
HENRY RODERICK NEWMAN
Ramleh, 1893

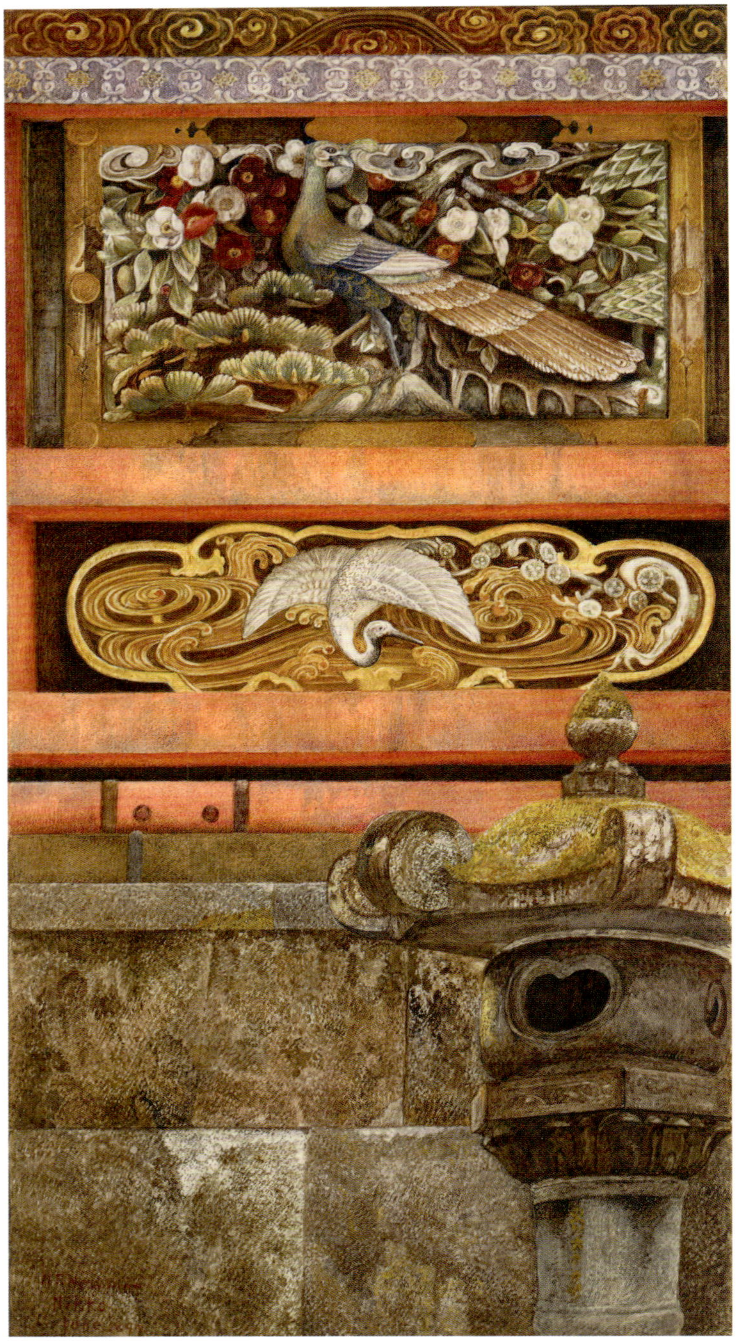

68

HENRY RODERICK NEWMAN

Wall Enclosing the Mausoleum of Ieyasu at Nikko, Japan, 1897

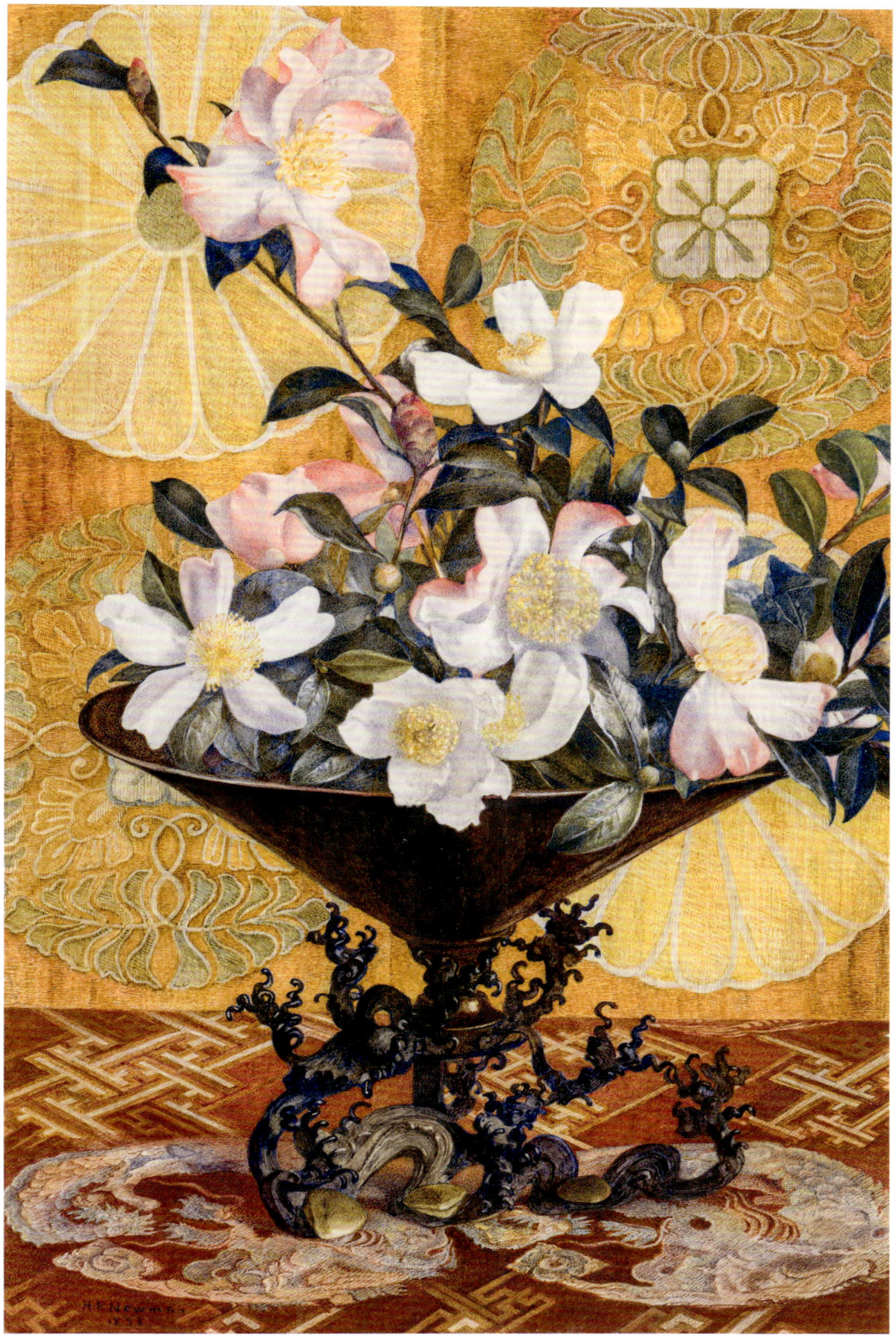

69
HENRY RODERICK NEWMAN
Sasanqua, Wild Tea, Yokohama, 1898

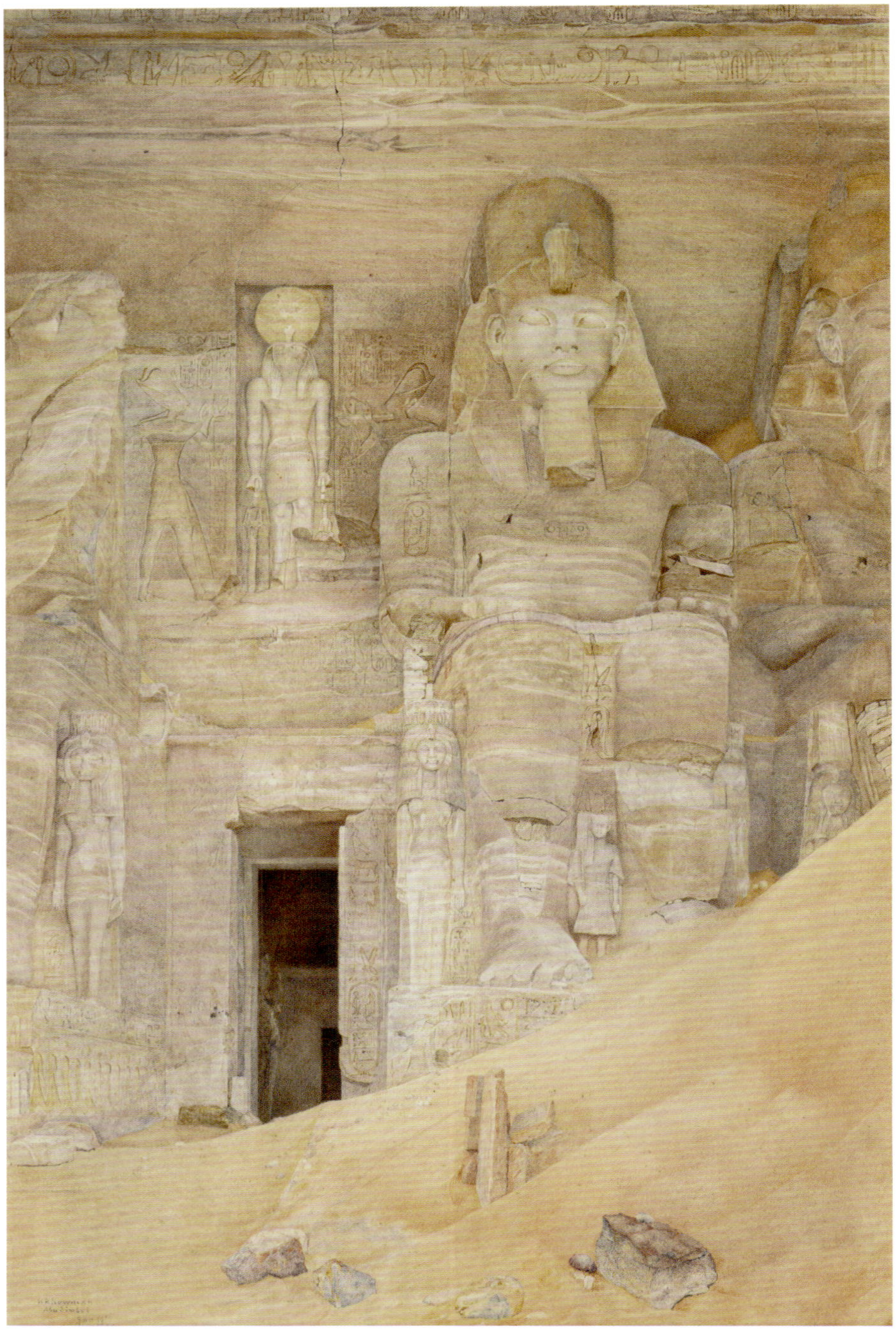

70
HENRY RODERICK NEWMAN
The Temple Door at Abu Simbel, 1900

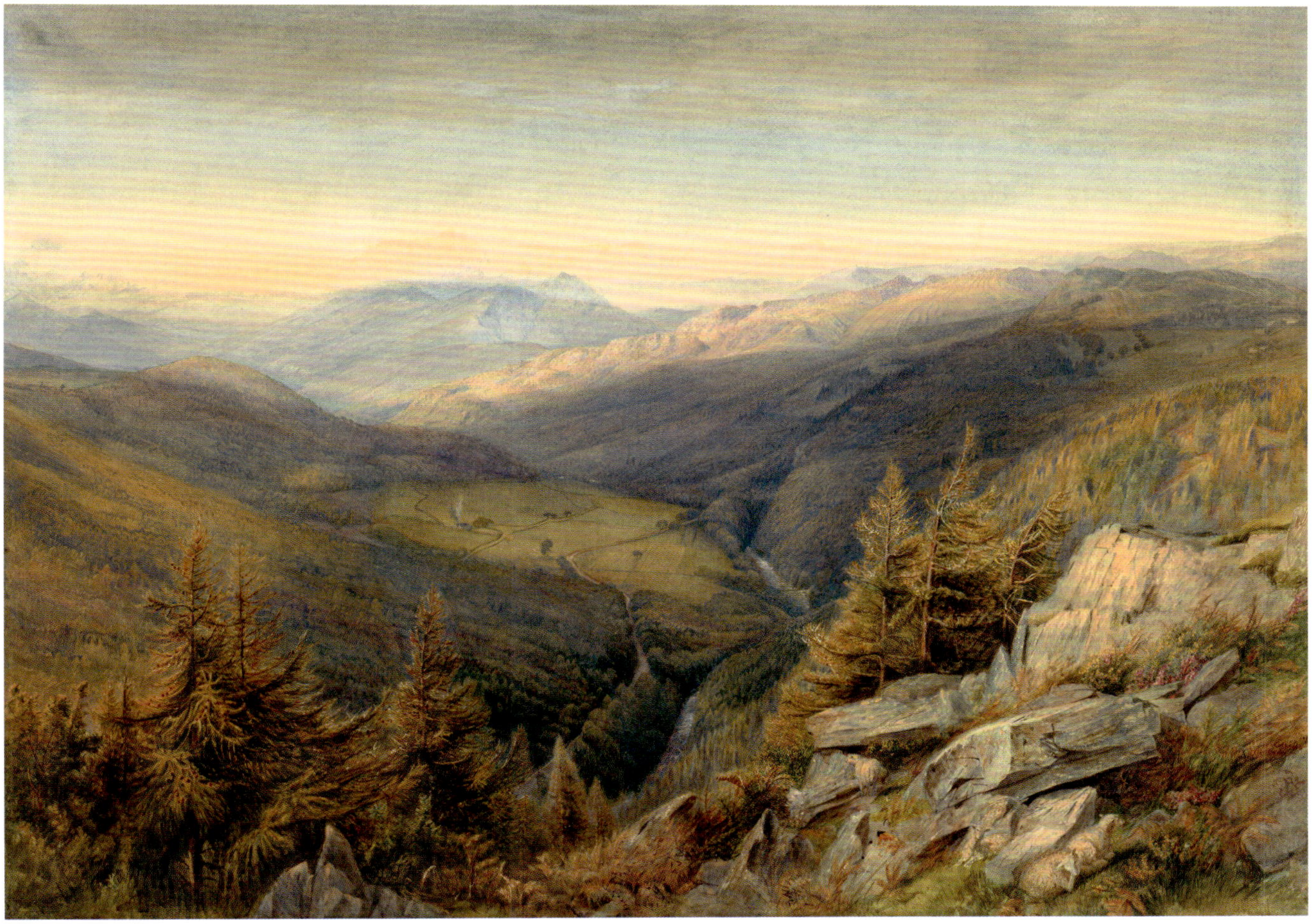

71
ROBERT J. PATTISON
Mountain View, c. 1867

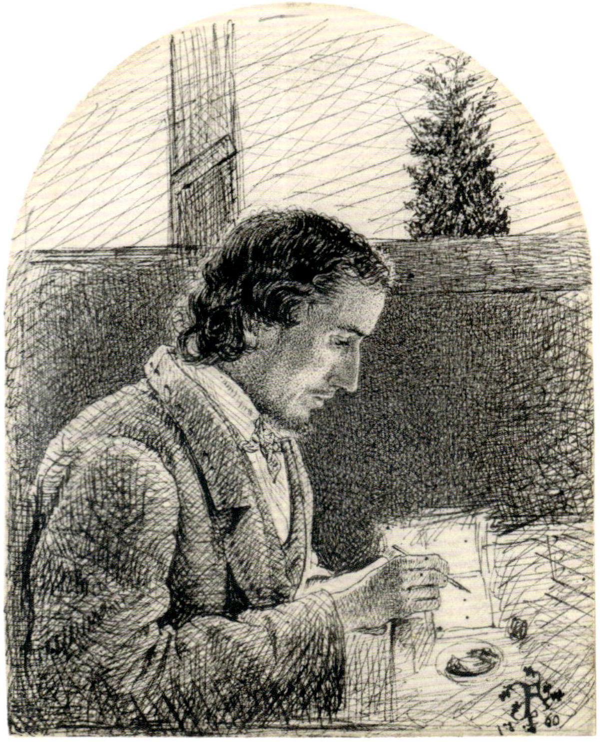

72
ROBERT J. PATTISON
Portrait of John Henry Hill, 1860

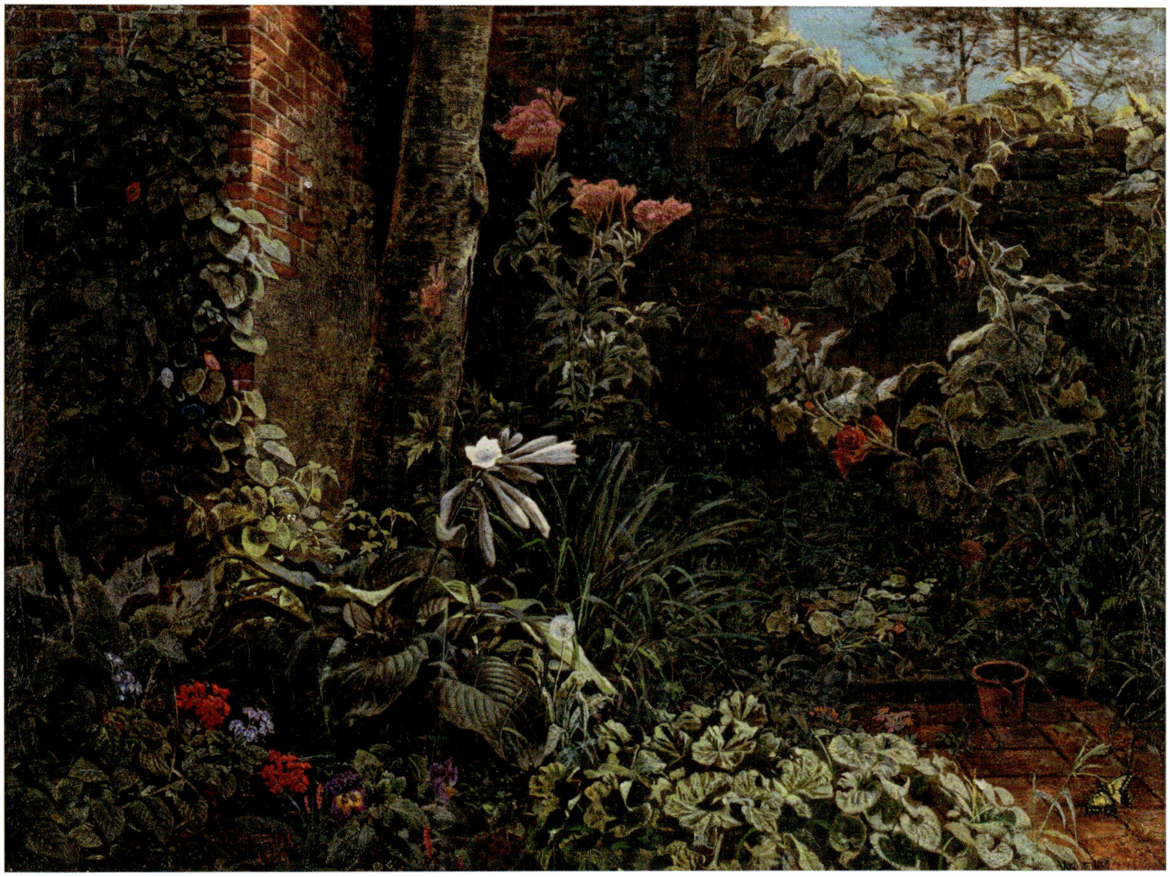

73
WILLIAM TROST RICHARDS
A Neglected Garden, 1859

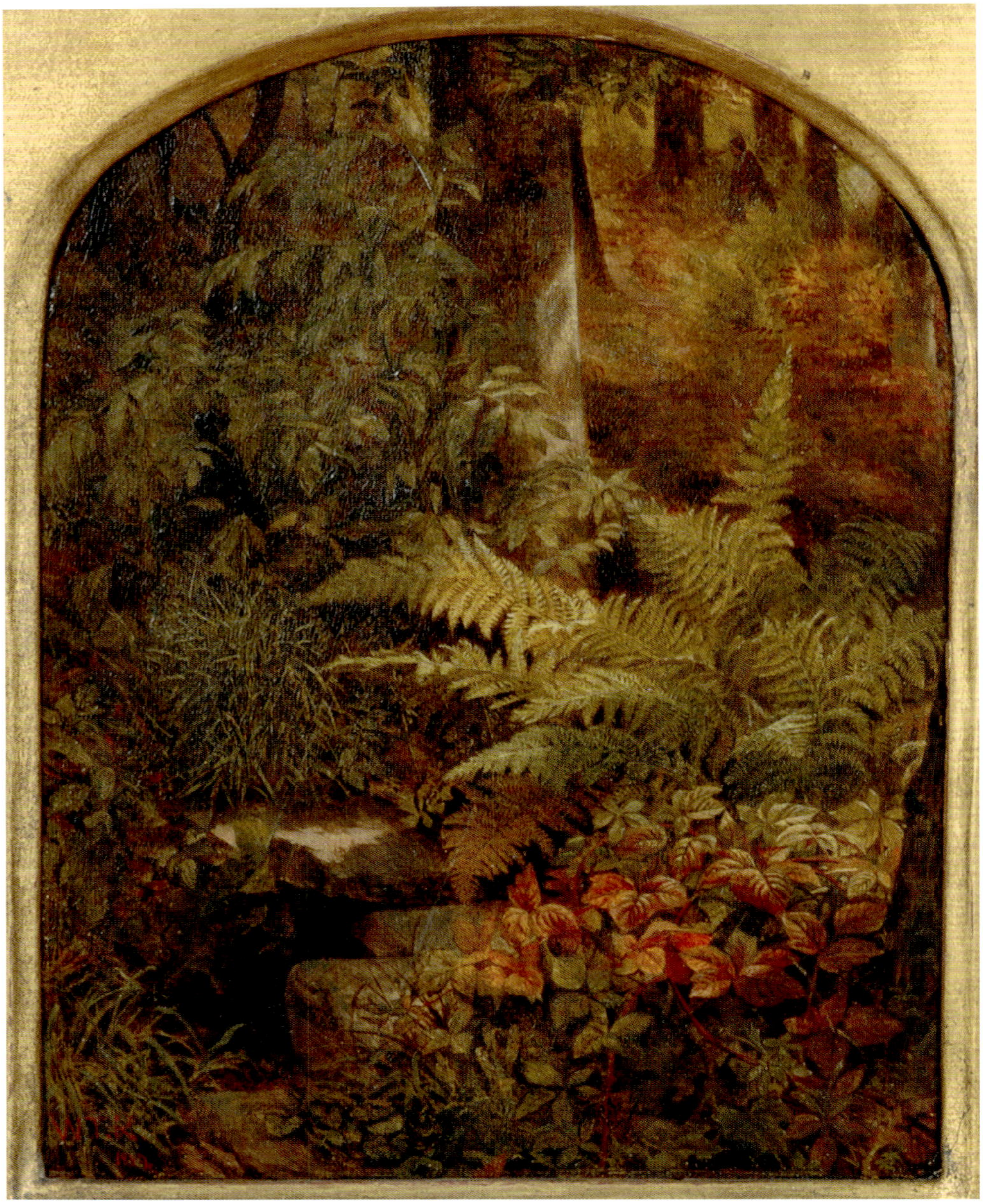

74
WILLIAM TROST RICHARDS
Ferns in a Glade, 1859

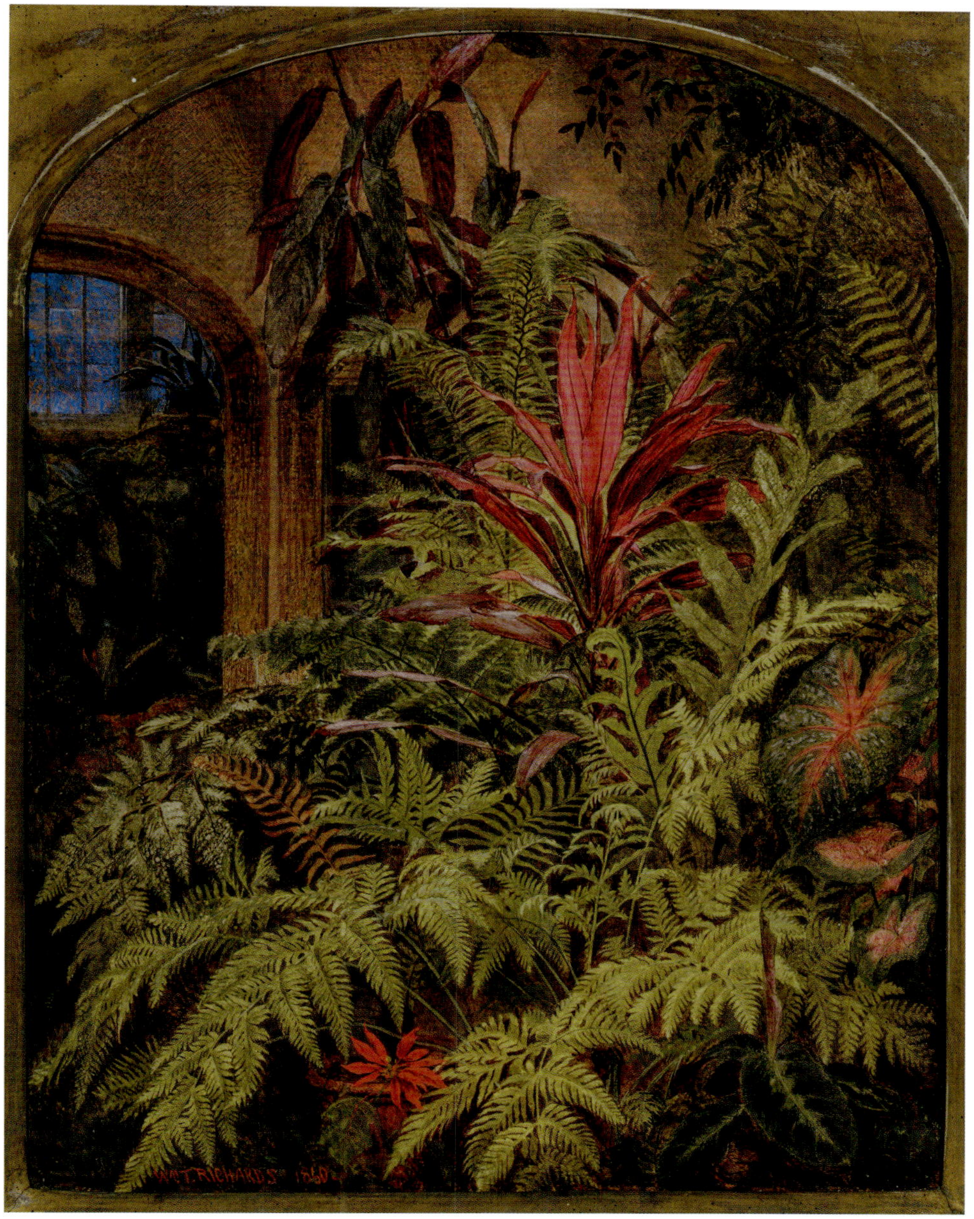

75
WILLIAM TROST RICHARDS
The Conservatory, 1860

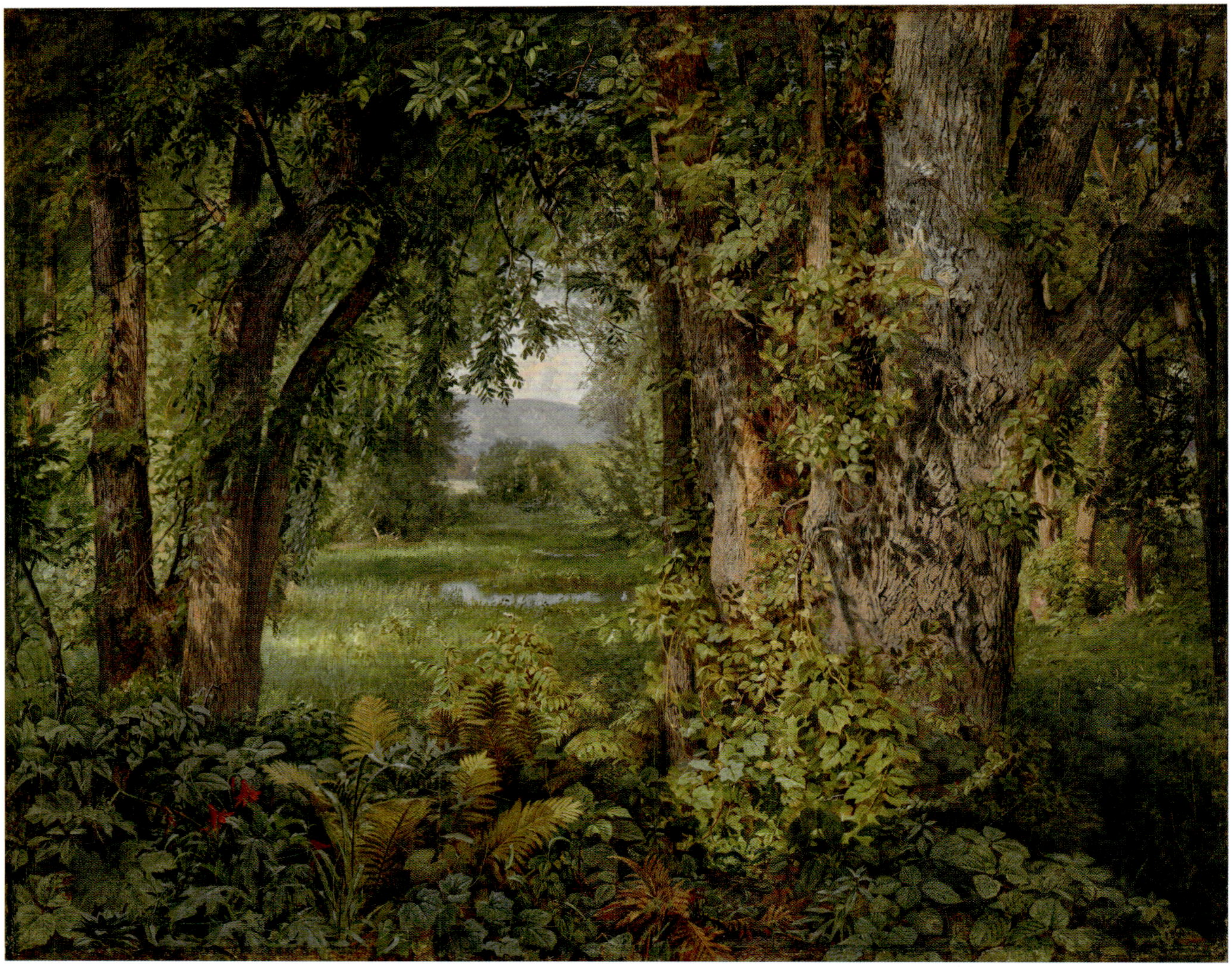

76

WILLIAM TROST RICHARDS

In the Woods, 1860

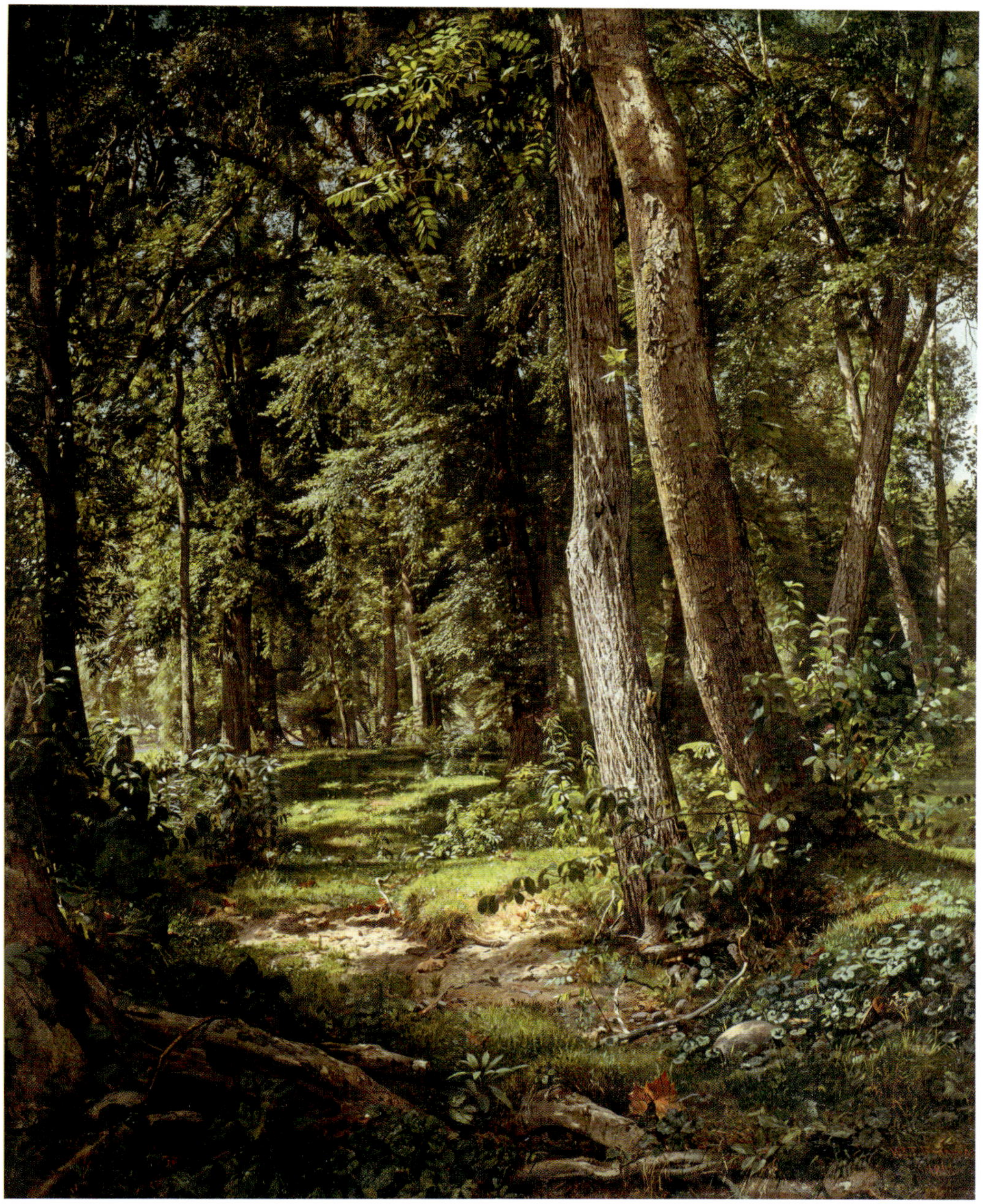

77
WILLIAM TROST RICHARDS
Path in the Woods, 1861

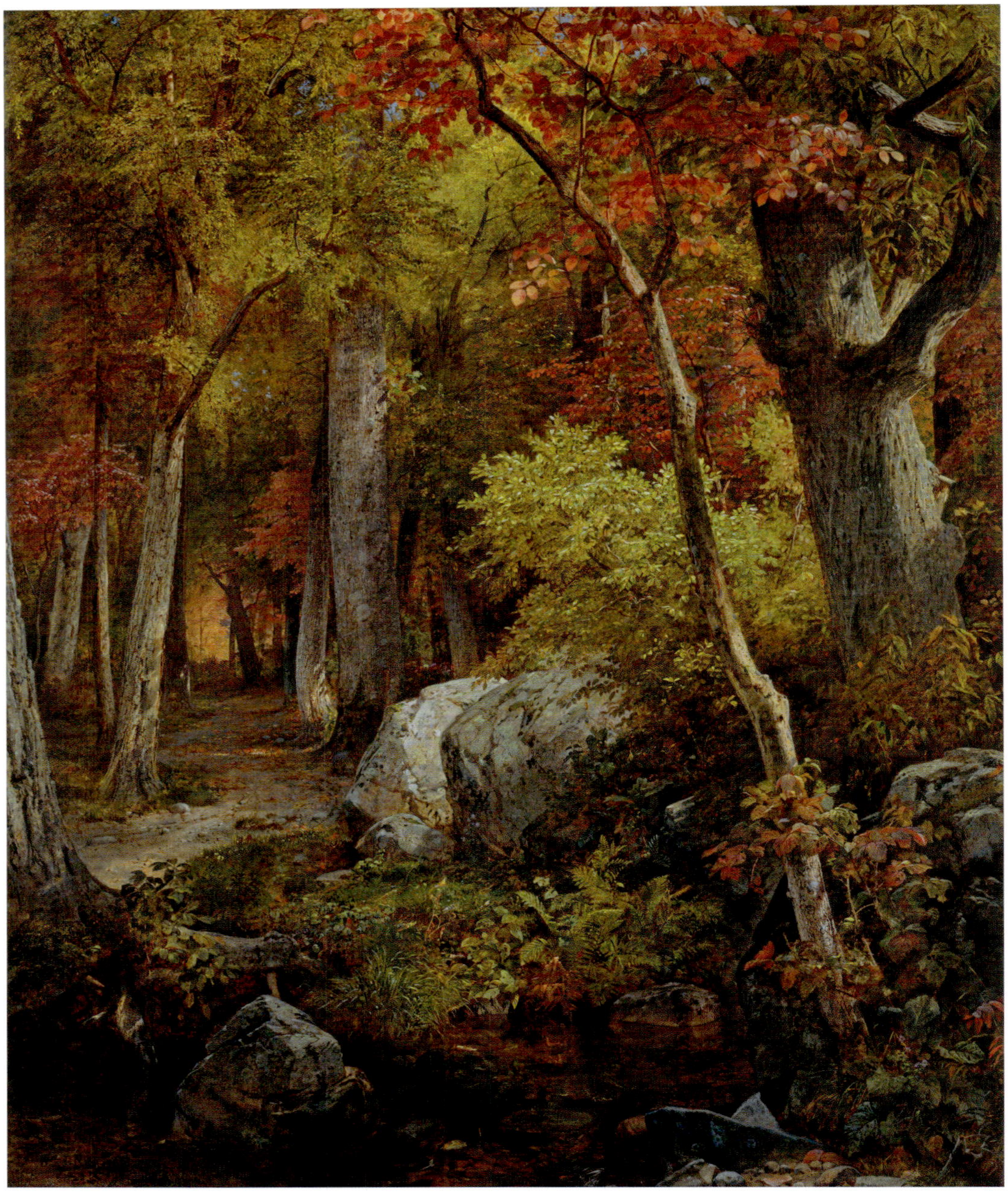

78
WILLIAM TROST RICHARDS
October, 1863

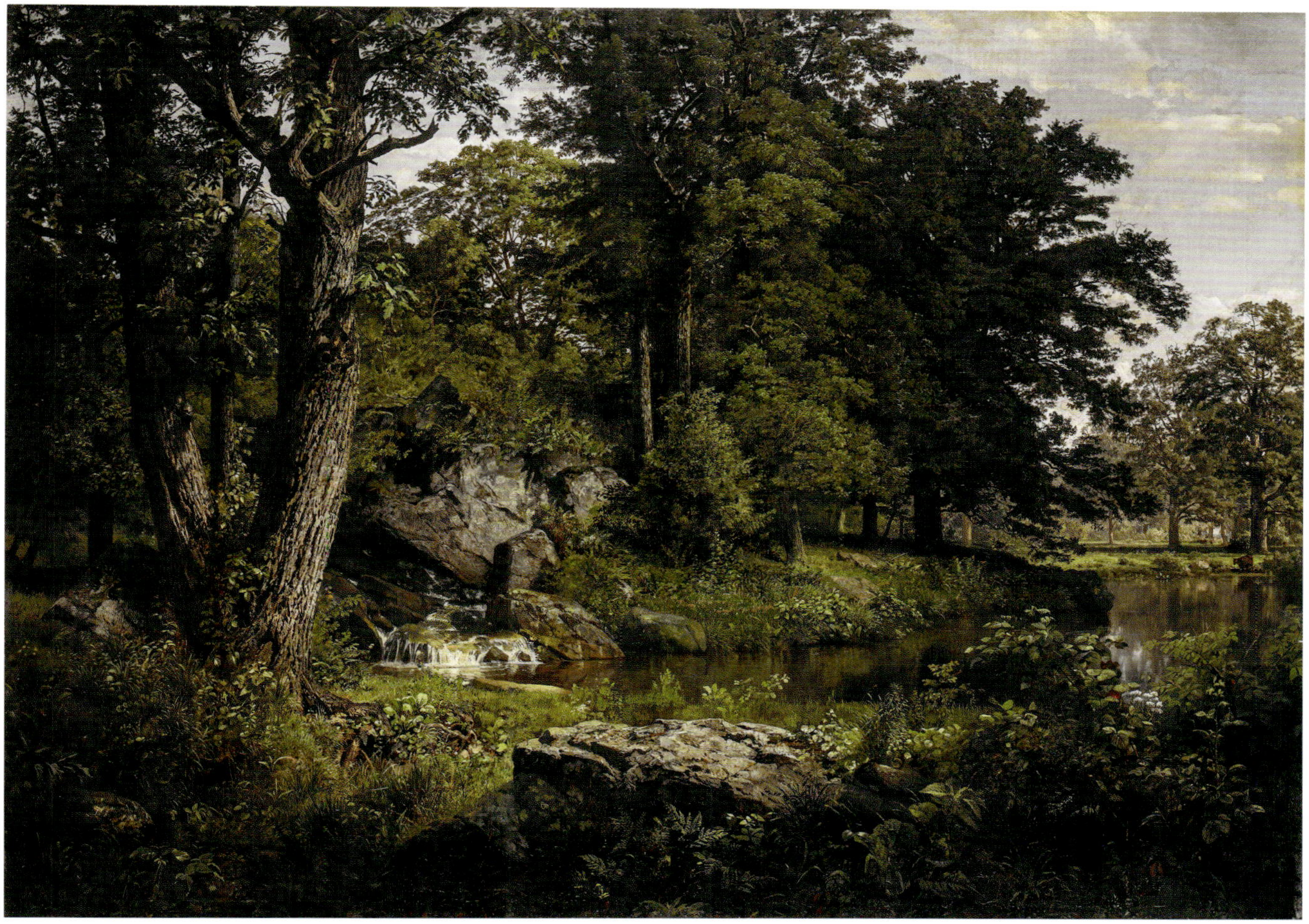

79
WILLIAM TROST RICHARDS
Landscape, c. 1863–1864

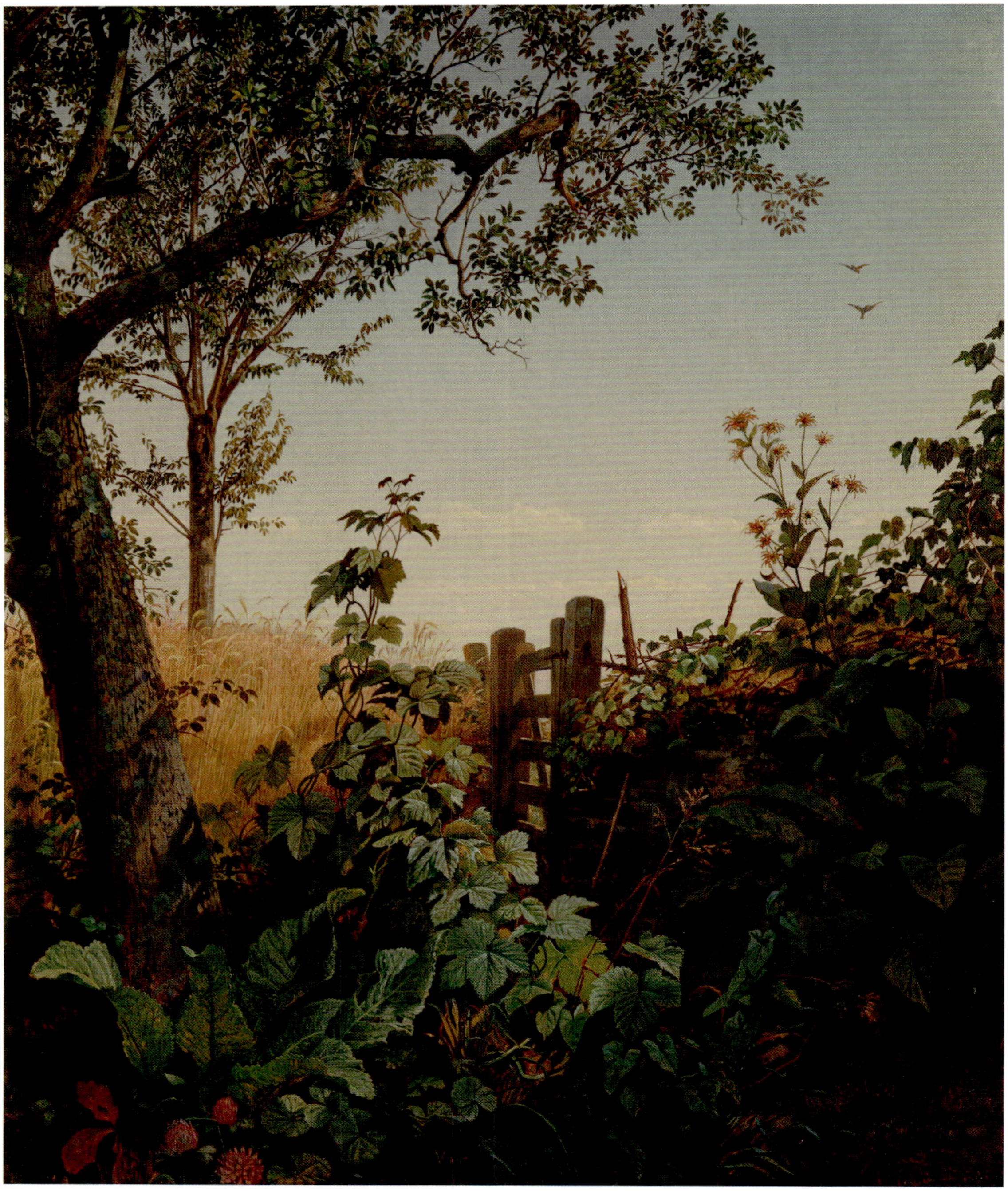

80

WILLIAM TROST RICHARDS

A Neglected Corner of the Wheatfield, 1865

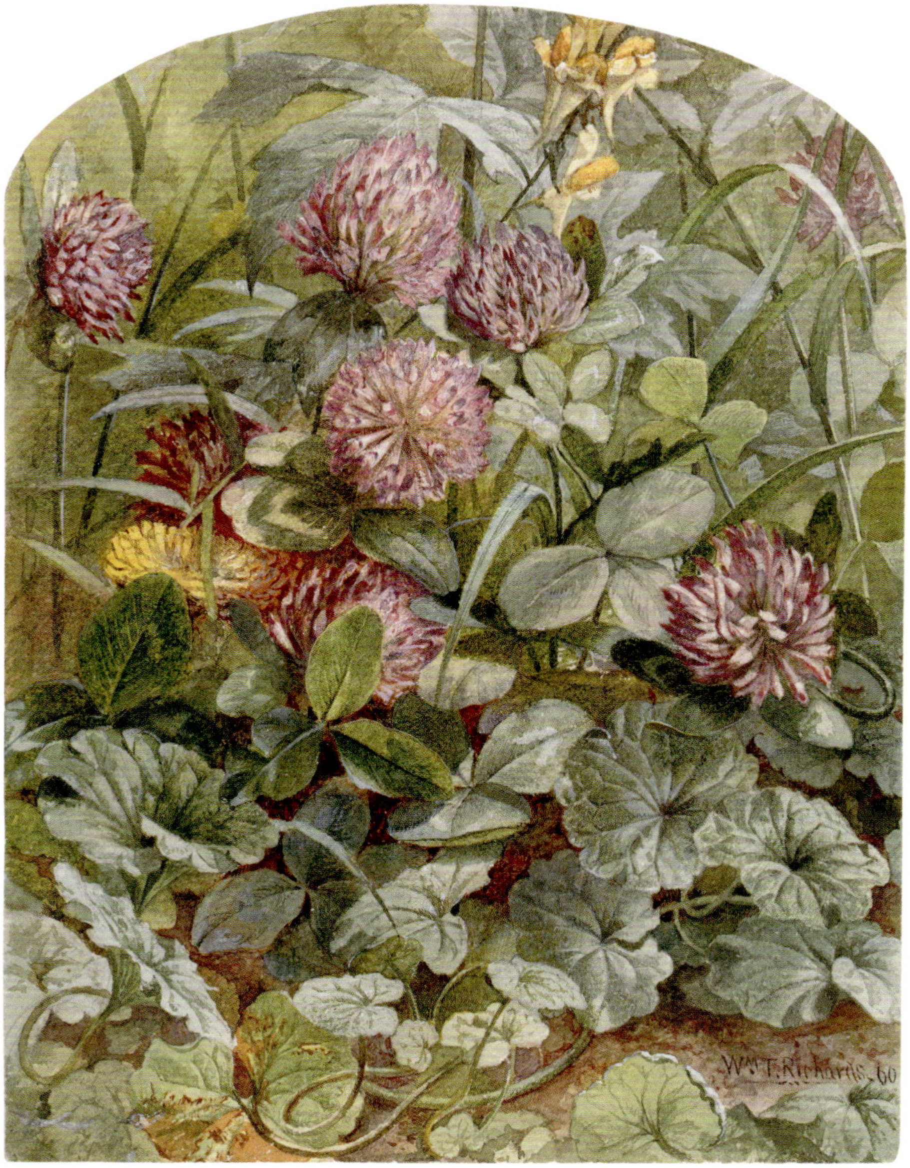

81
WILLIAM TROST RICHARDS
Red Clover with Butter-and-Eggs, and Ground Ivy, 1860

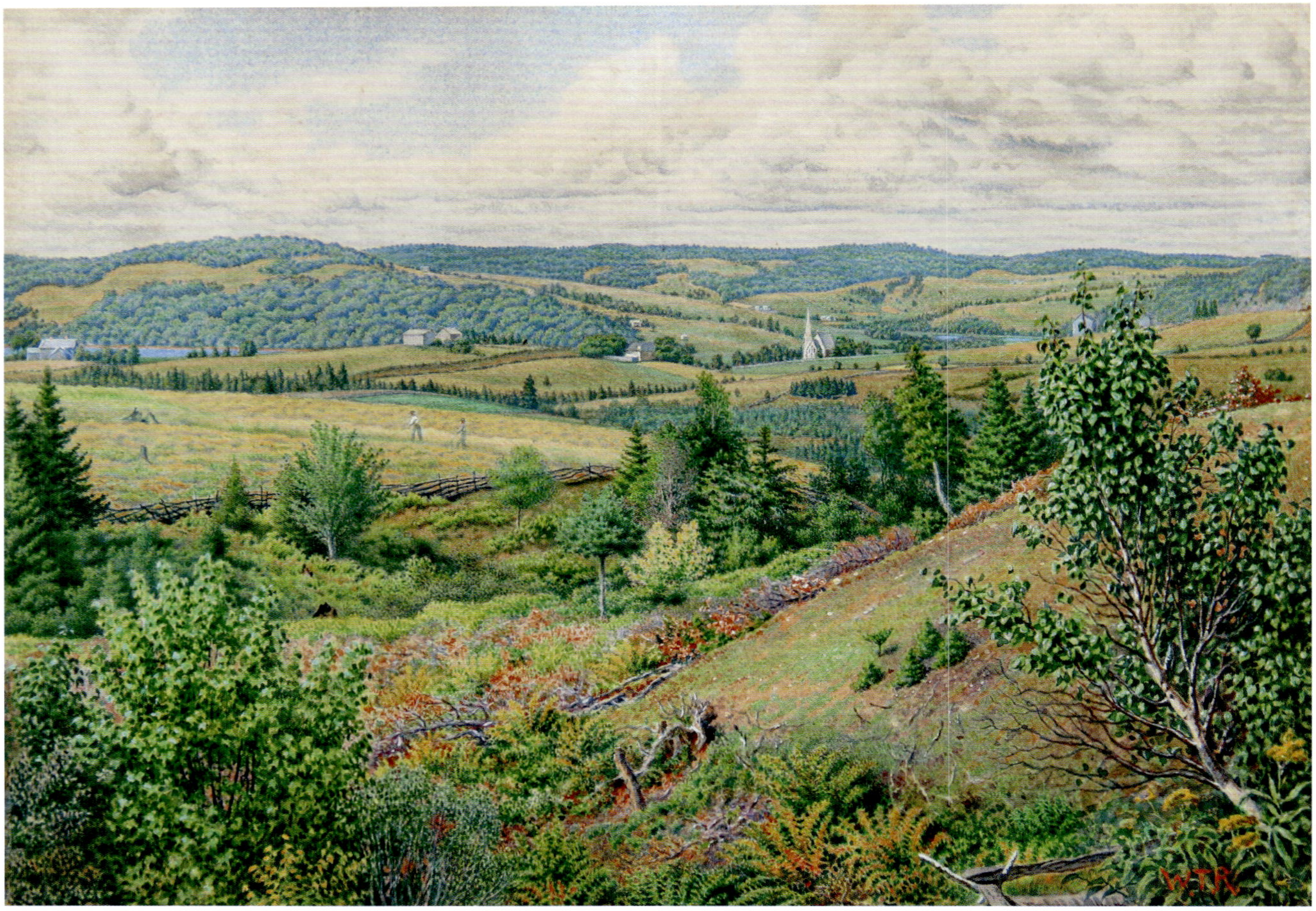

82

WILLIAM TROST RICHARDS

Landscape, c. 1863–1864

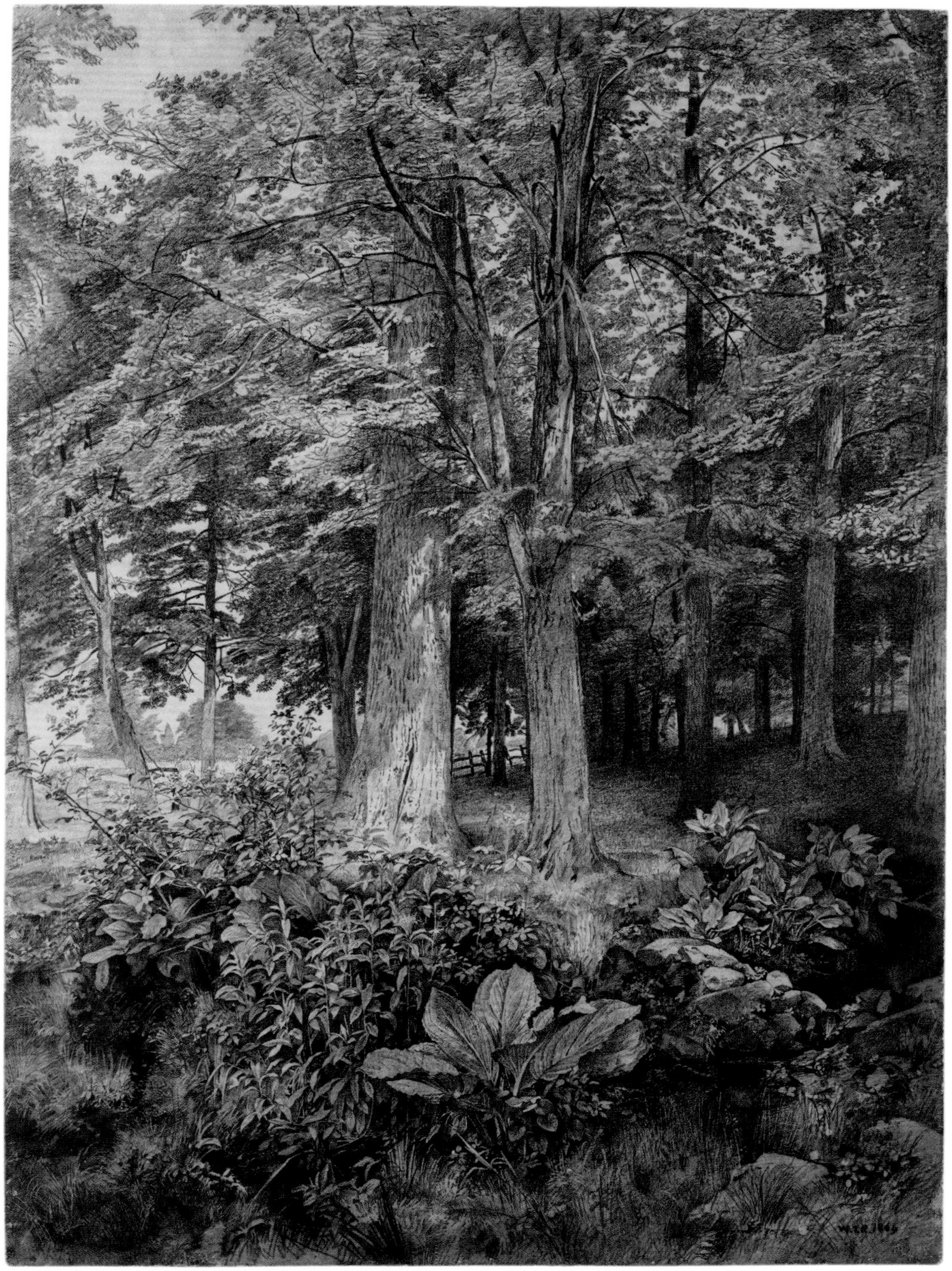

83
WILLIAM TROST RICHARDS
Corner of the Woods, 1864

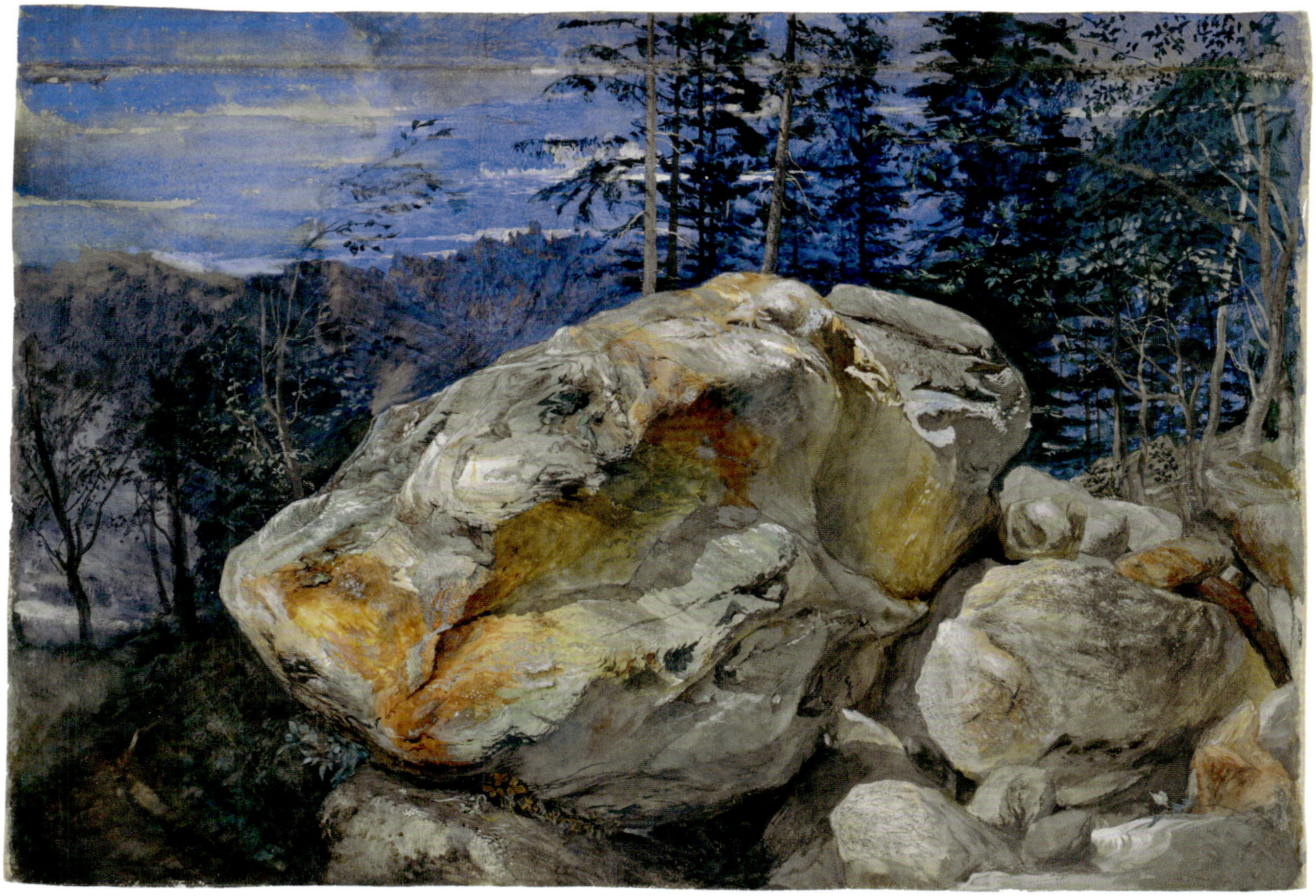

84

JOHN RUSKIN

Fragment of the Alps, c. 1854–1856

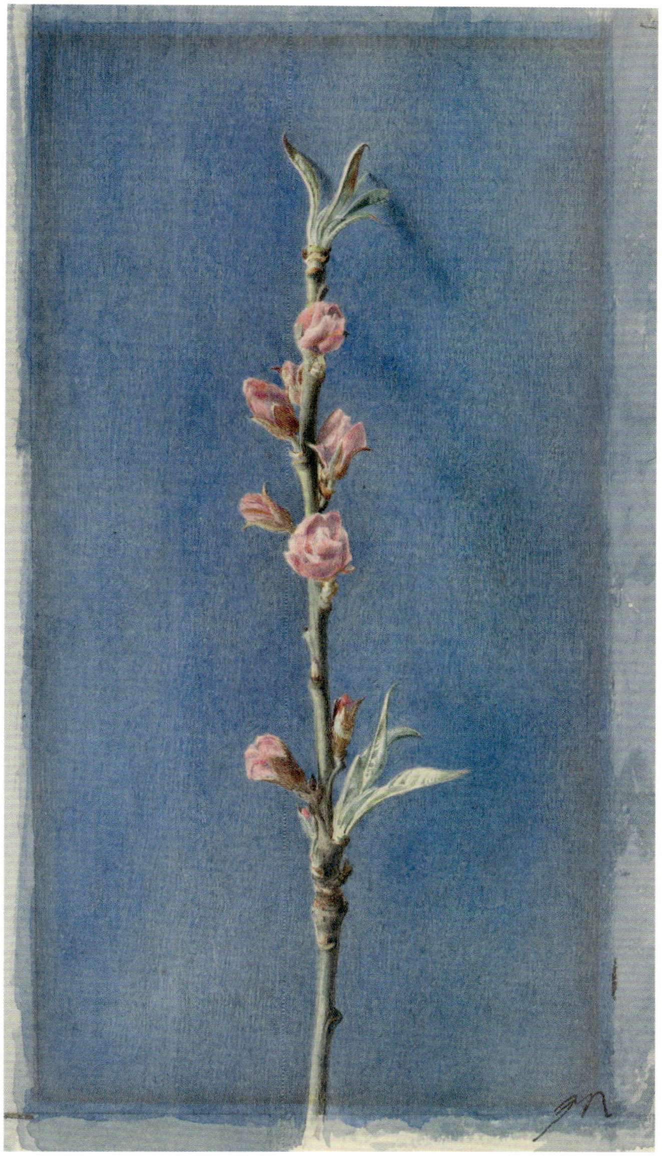

85
JOHN RUSKIN
Twig of Peach Bloom, c. 1874

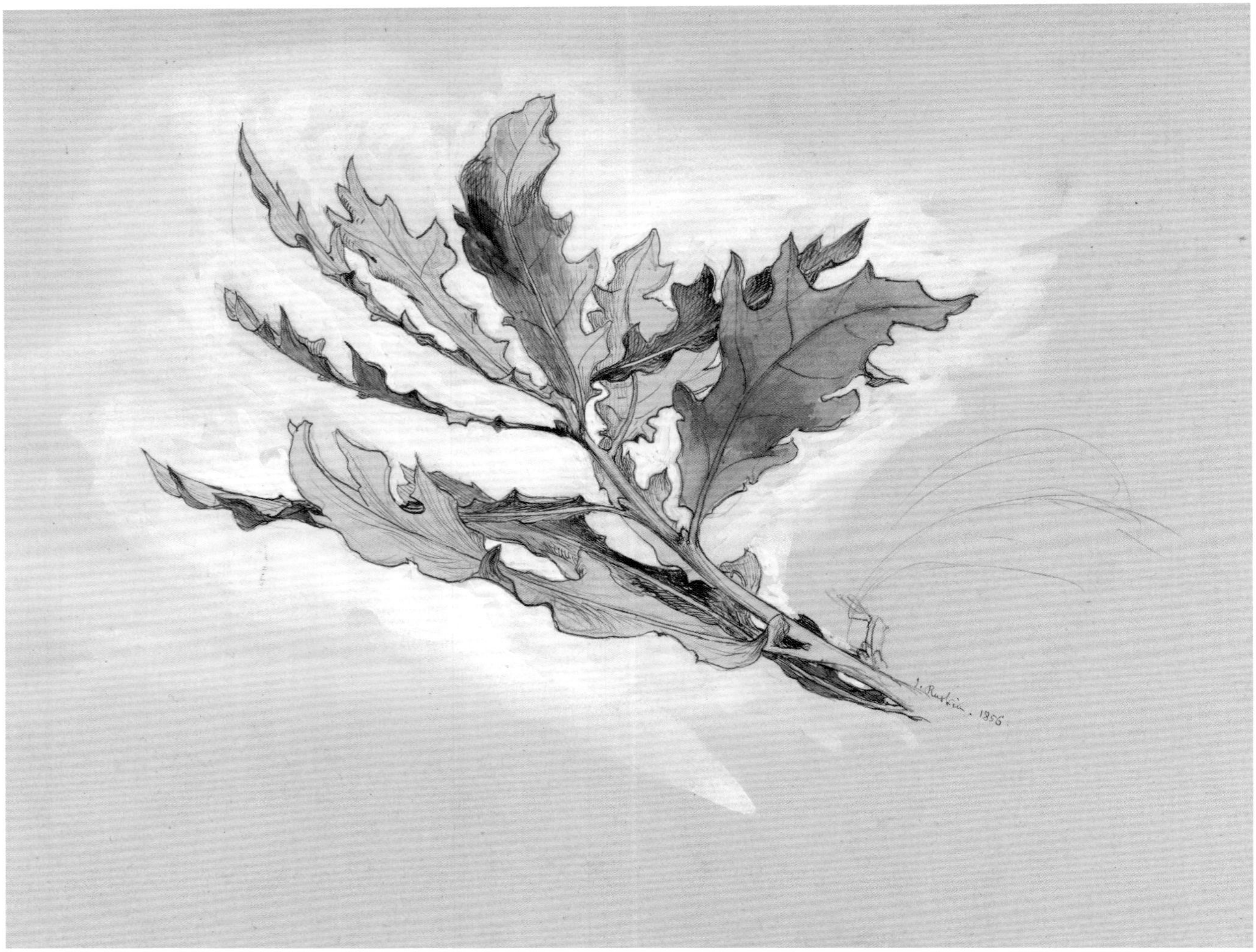

86

JOHN RUSKIN

A Cluster of Oak Leaves, 1856

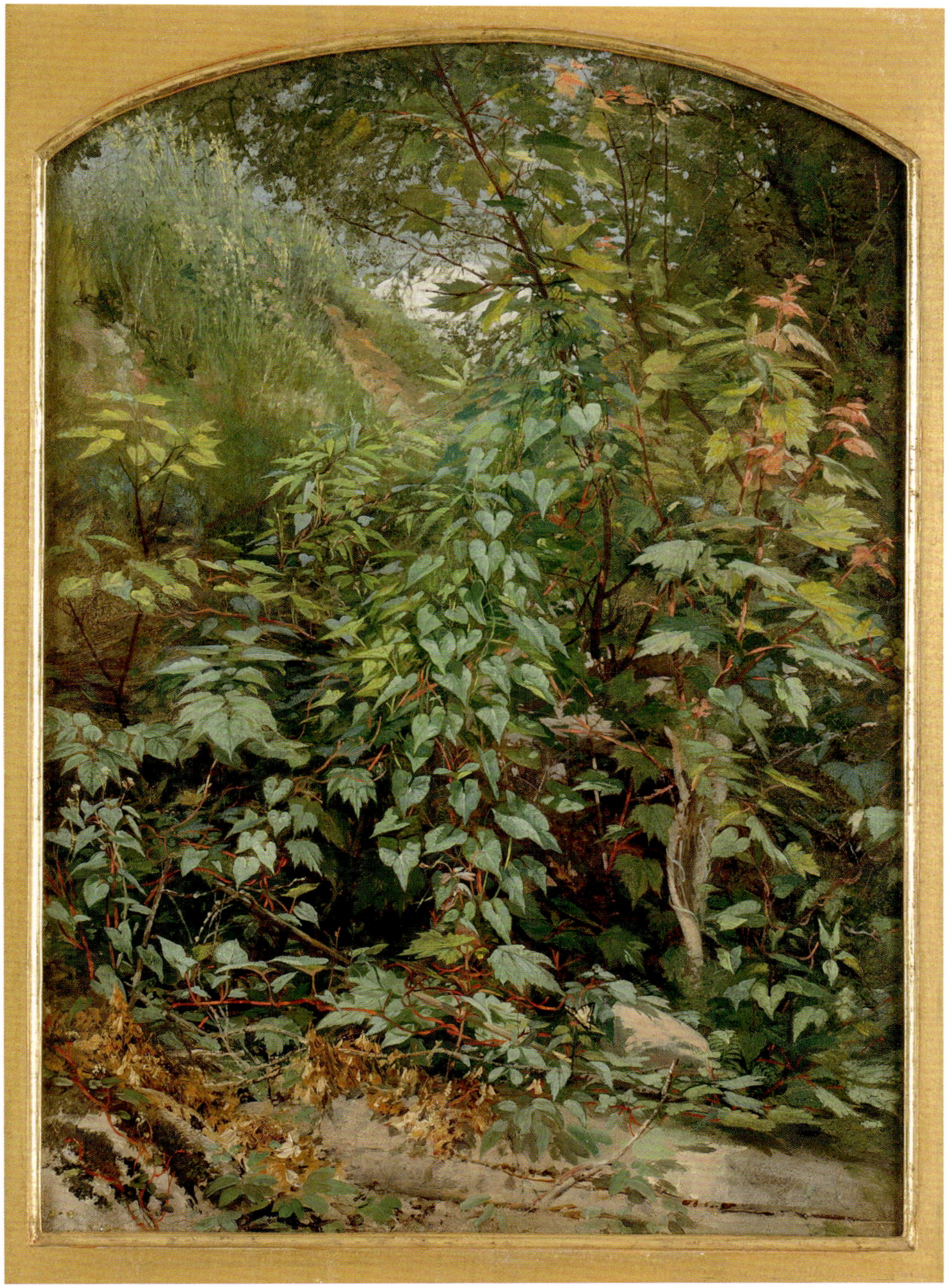

87
AARON DRAPER SHATTUCK
Leaf Study with Yellow Swallow Tail, c. 1859

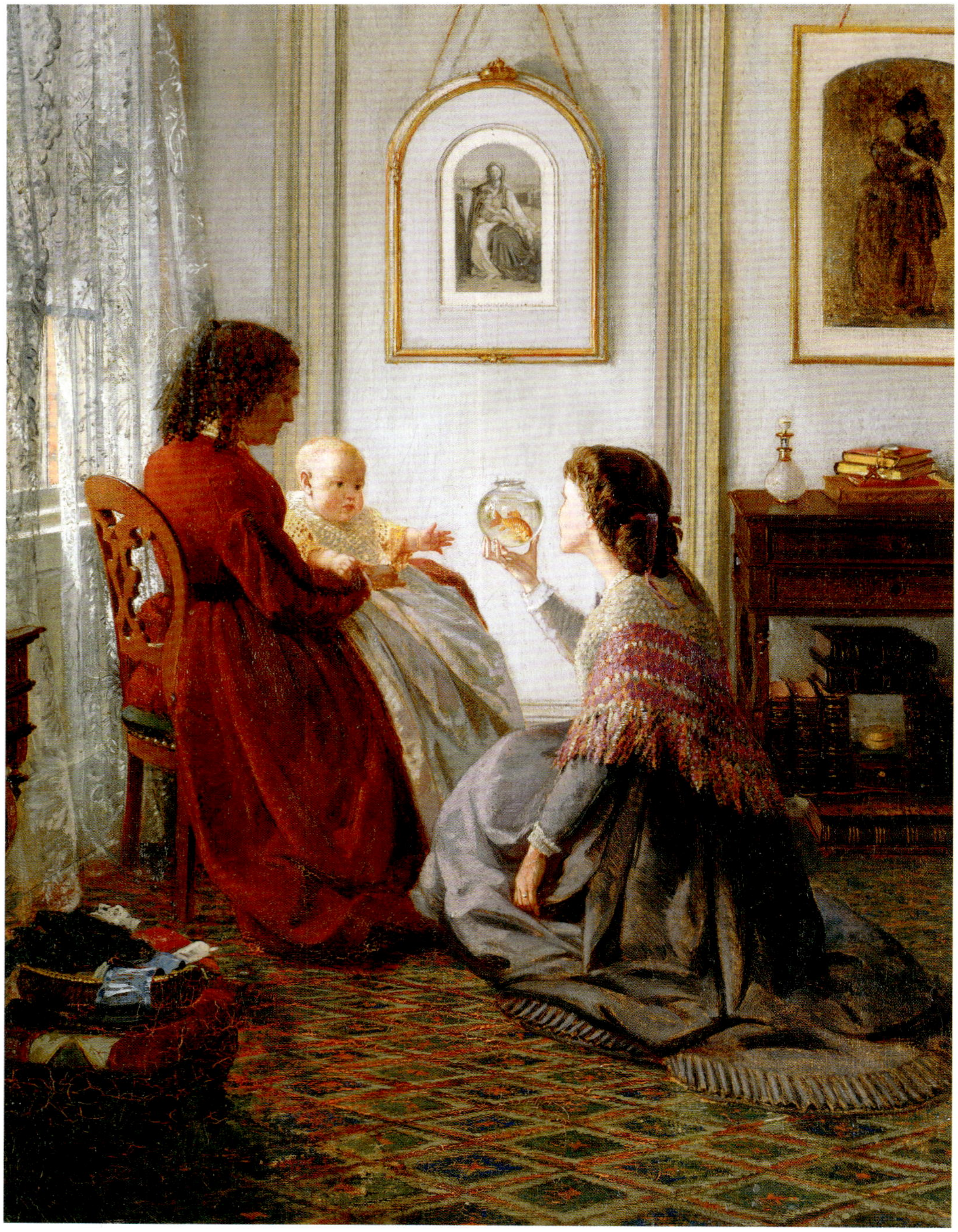

88

AARON DRAPER SHATTUCK

The Shattuck Family, with Grandmother, Mother and Baby William, 1865

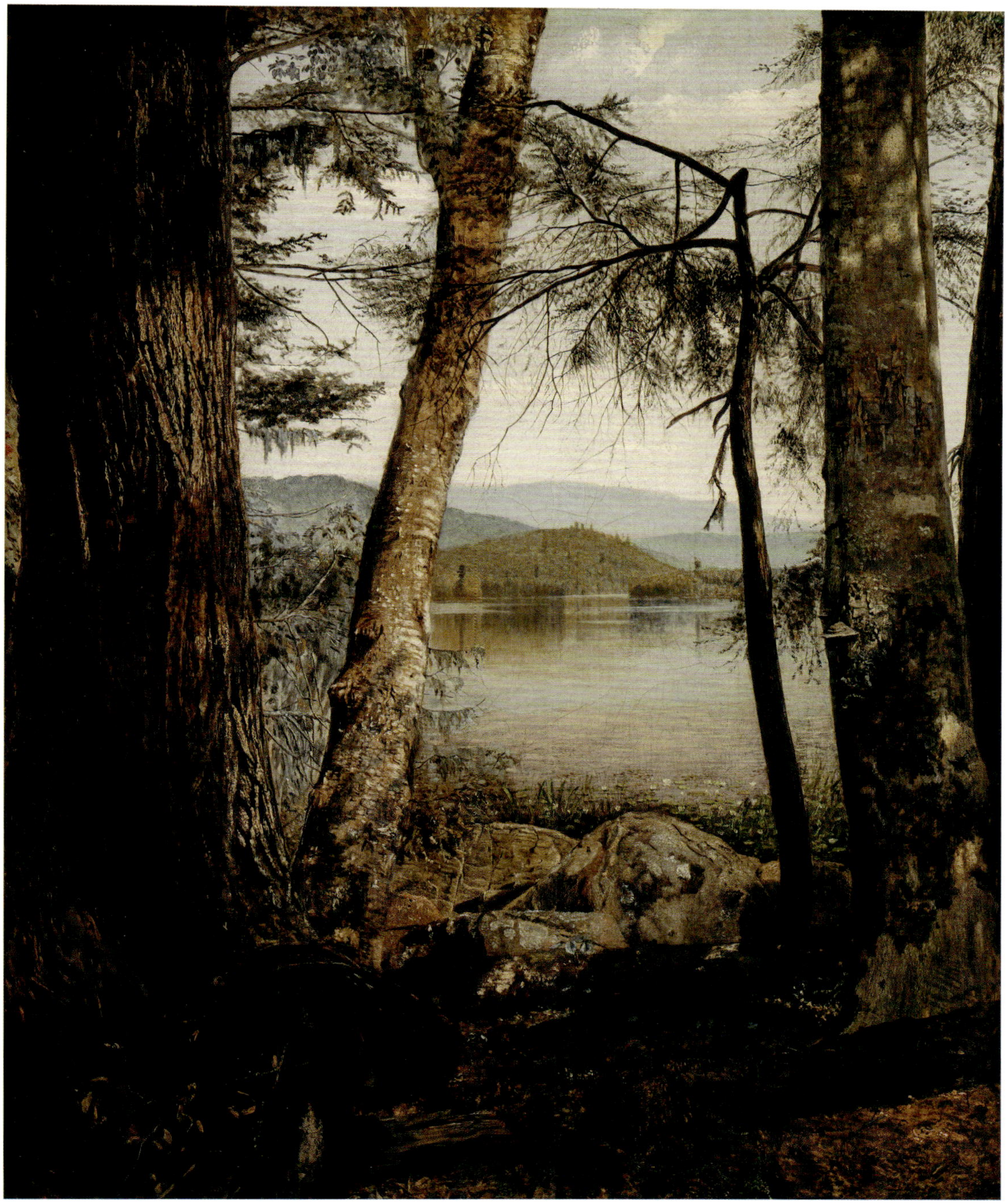

89
WILLIAM JAMES STILLMAN
Saranac Lake, Adirondack Mountains (Study on Upper Saranac Lake), 1854

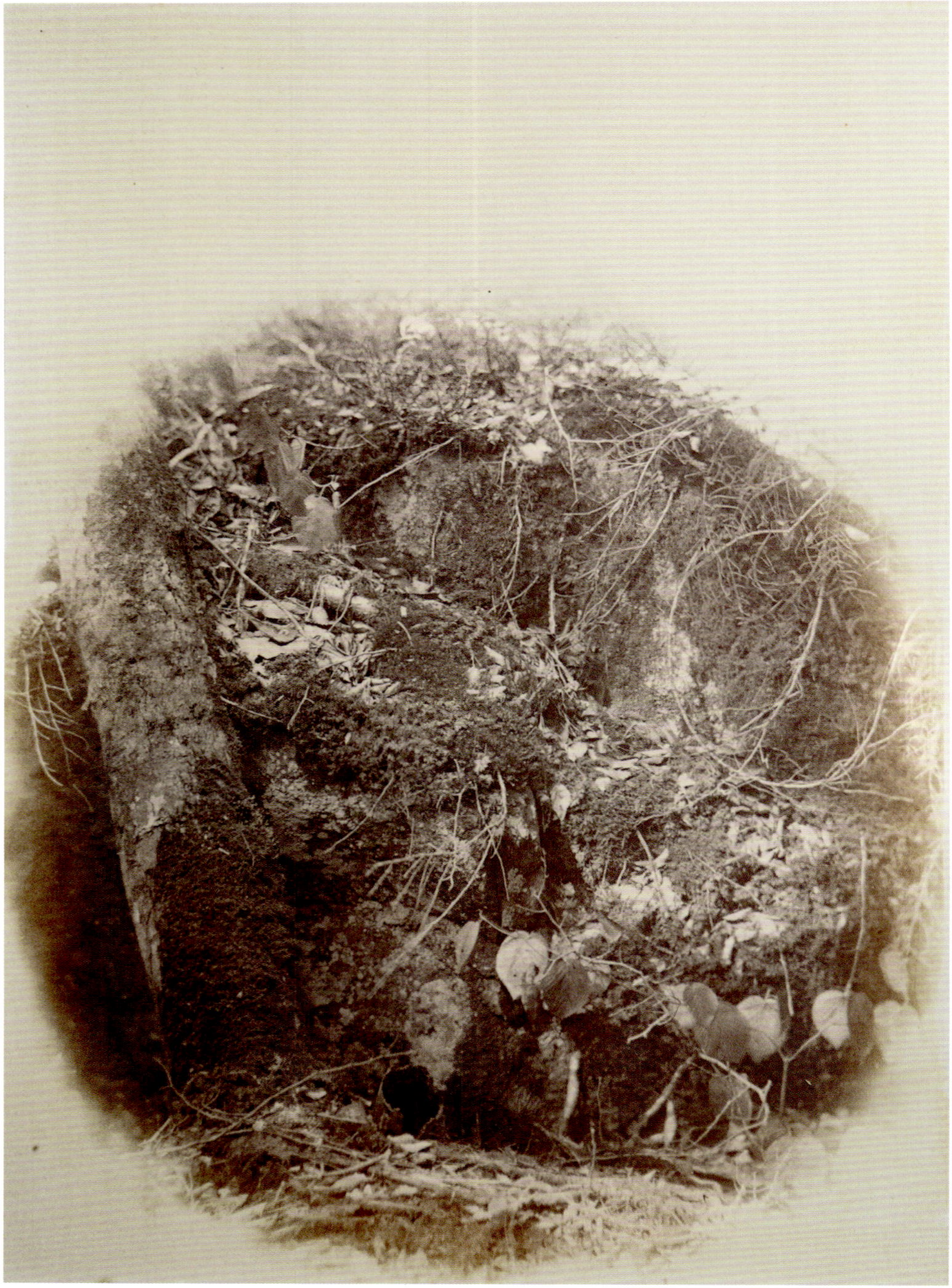

90
WILLIAM JAMES STILLMAN
Photographic Study, 1859

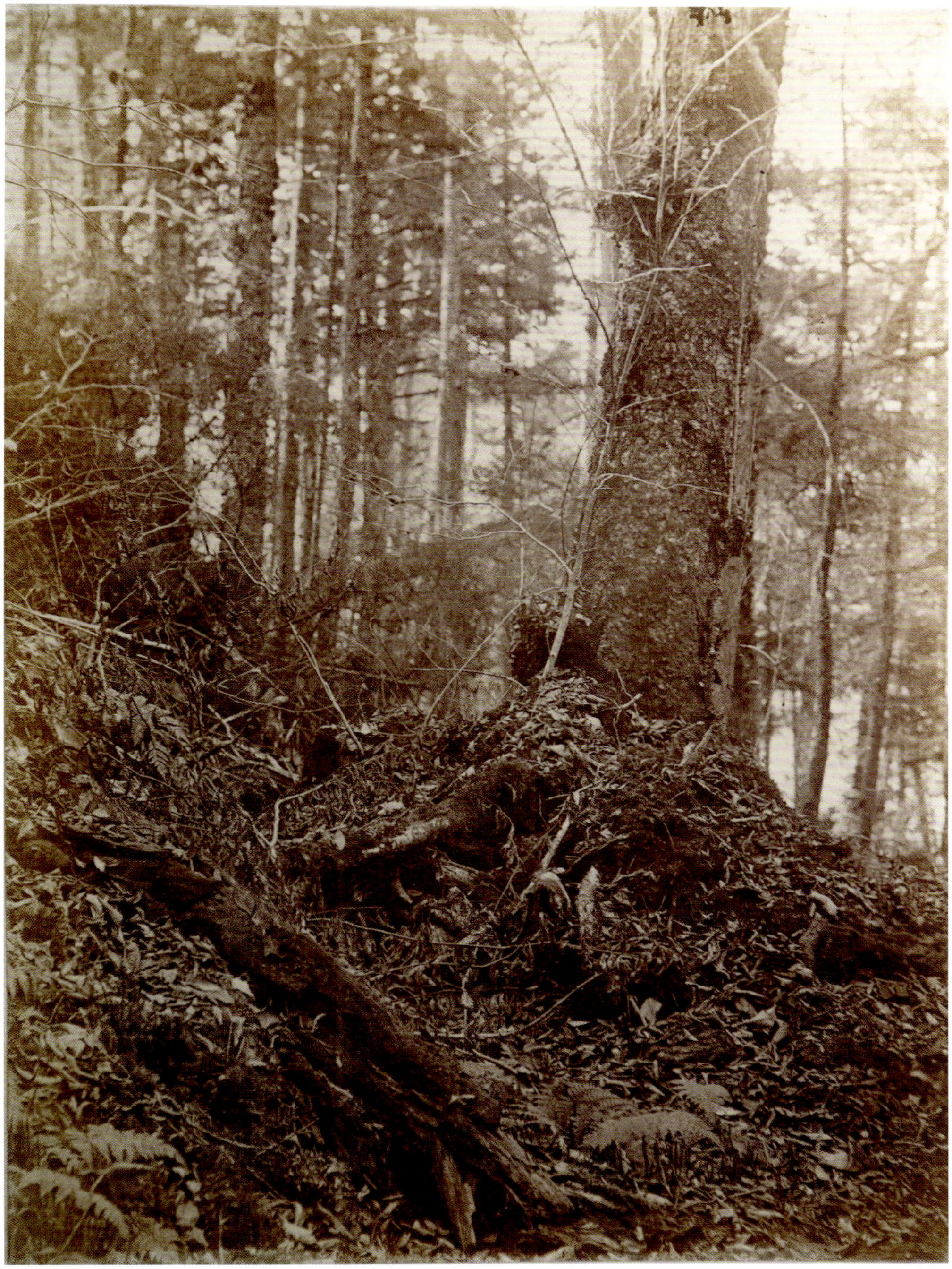

91
WILLIAM JAMES STILLMAN
Photographic Study, 1859

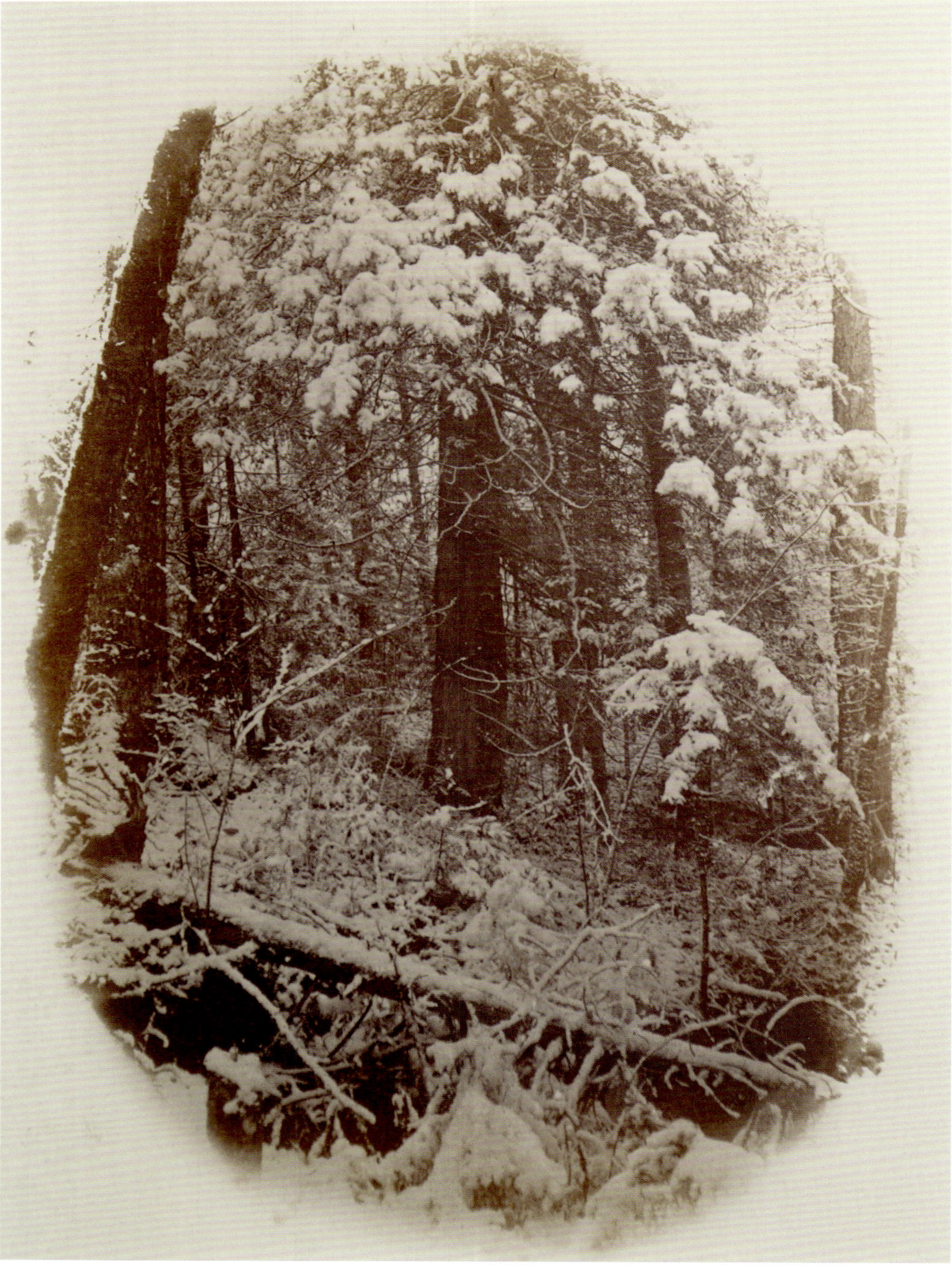

92
WILLIAM JAMES STILLMAN
Photographic Study, 1859

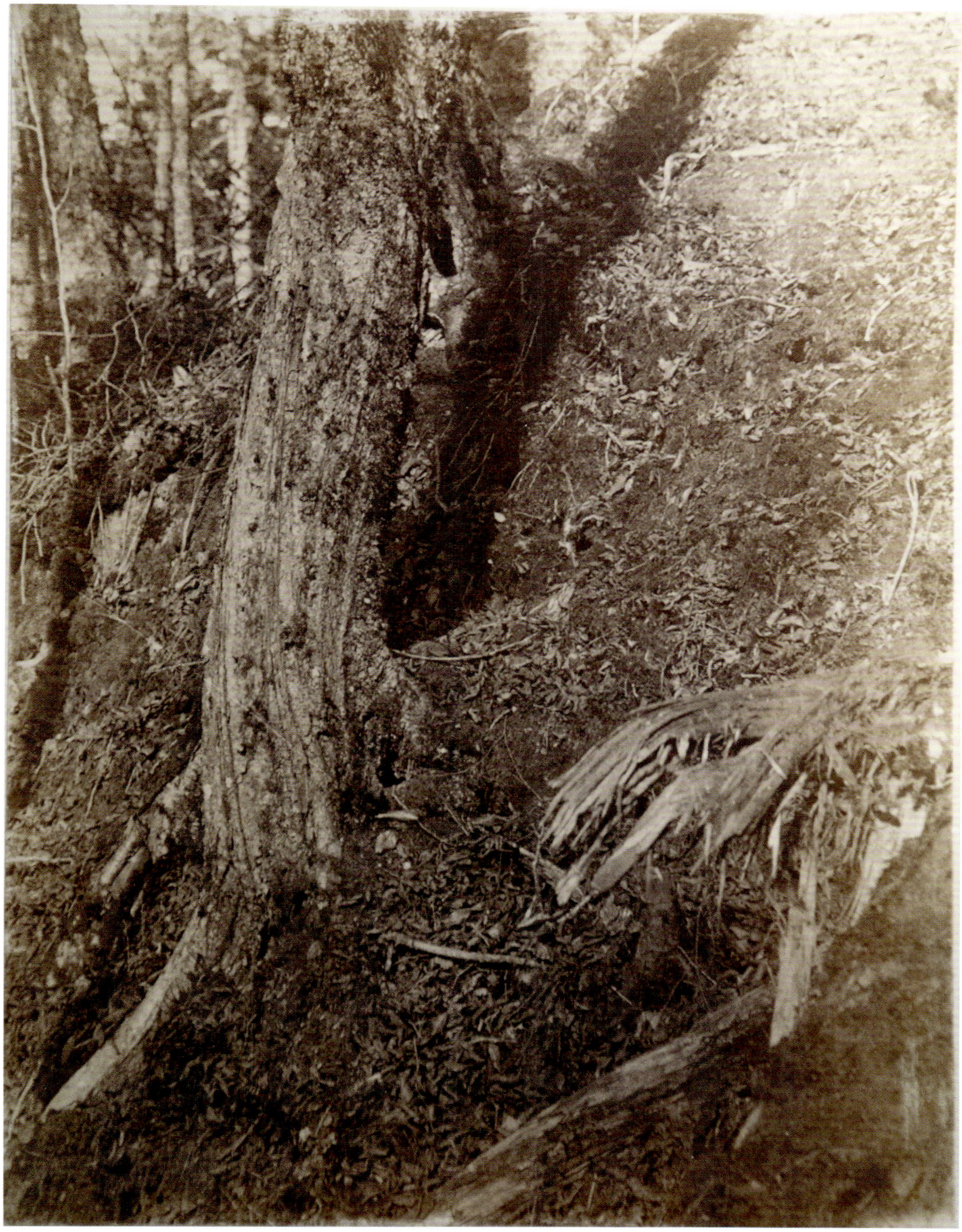

93
WILLIAM JAMES STILLMAN
Photographic Study, 1859

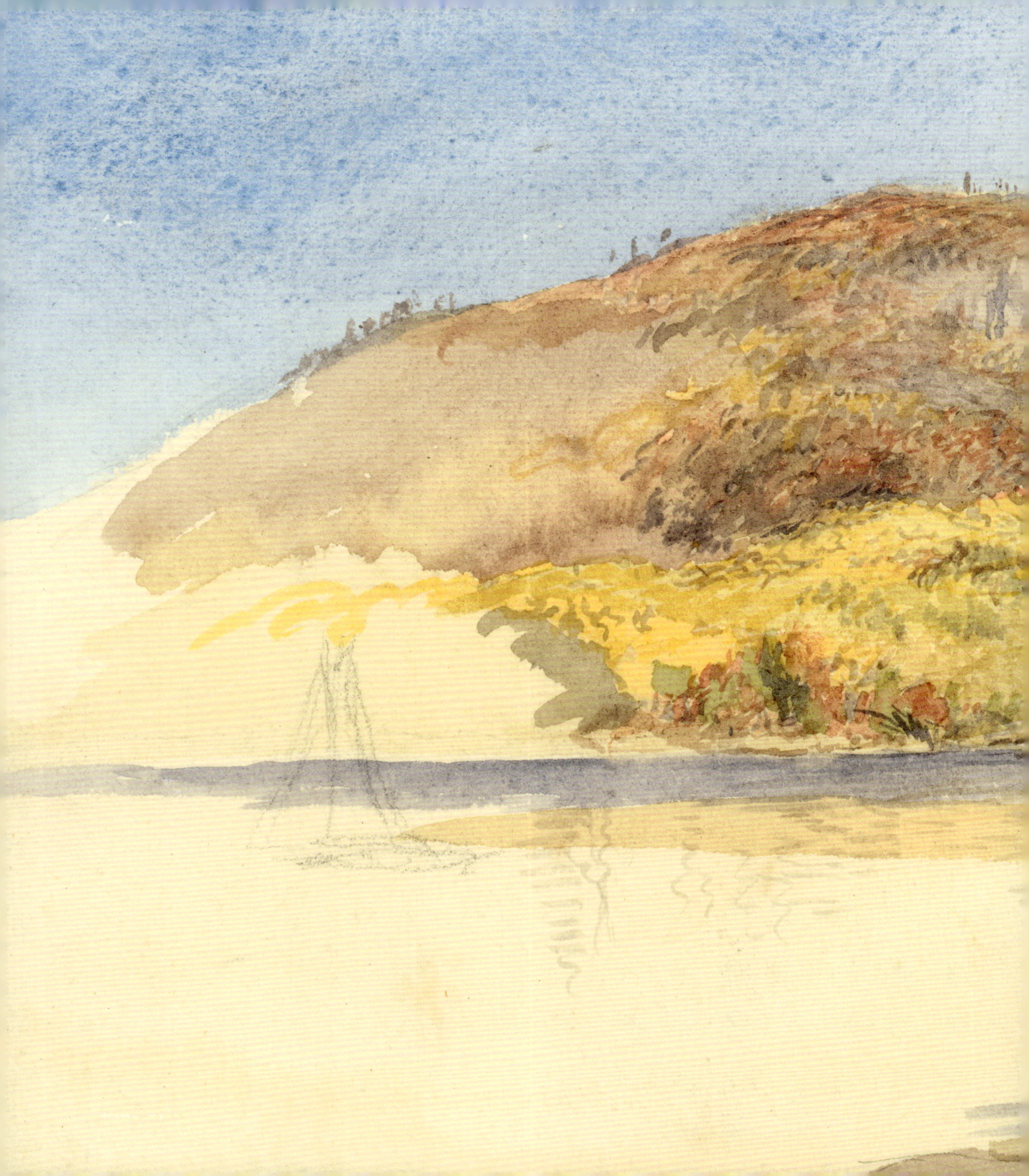

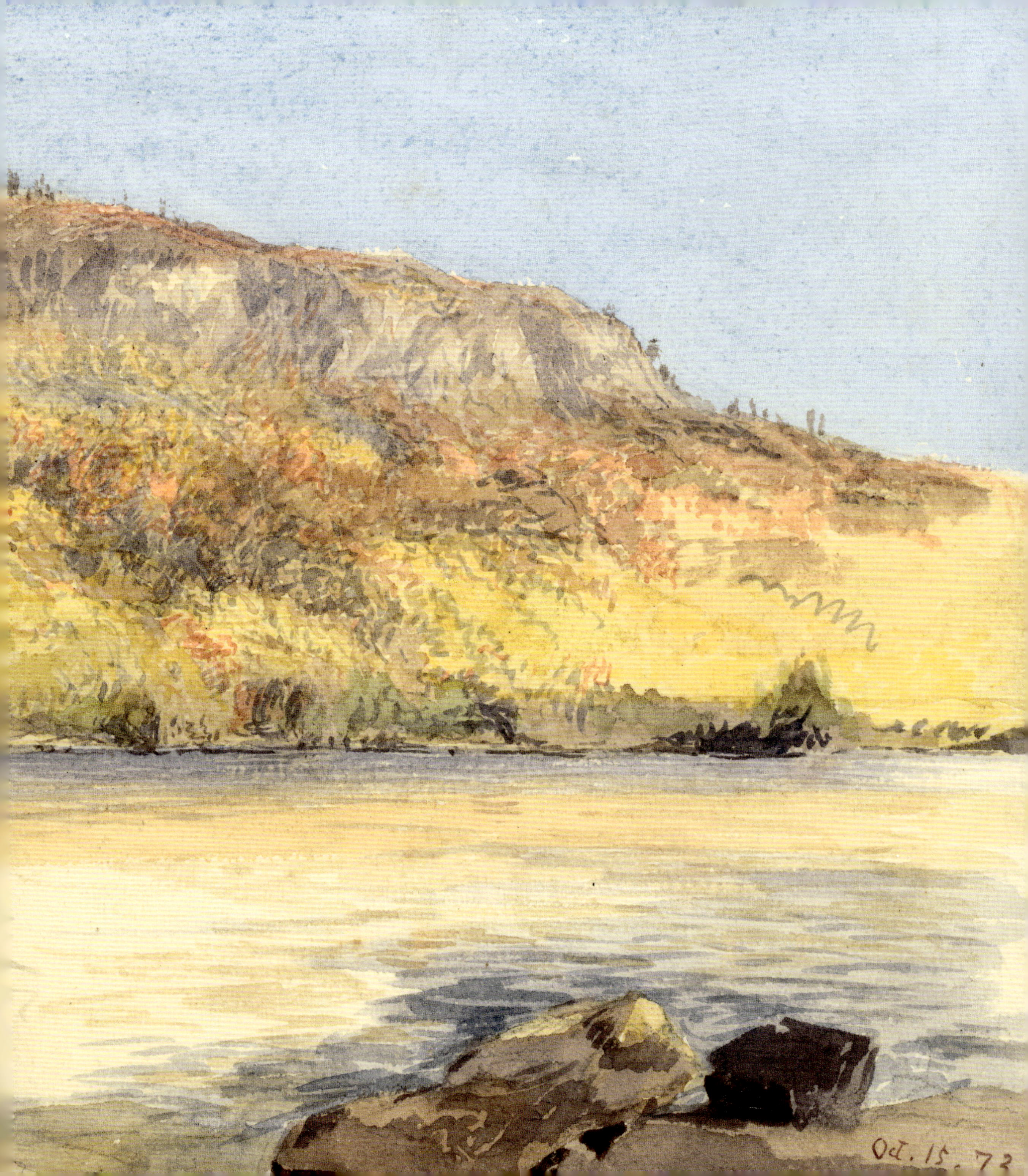
Oct. 15. 72

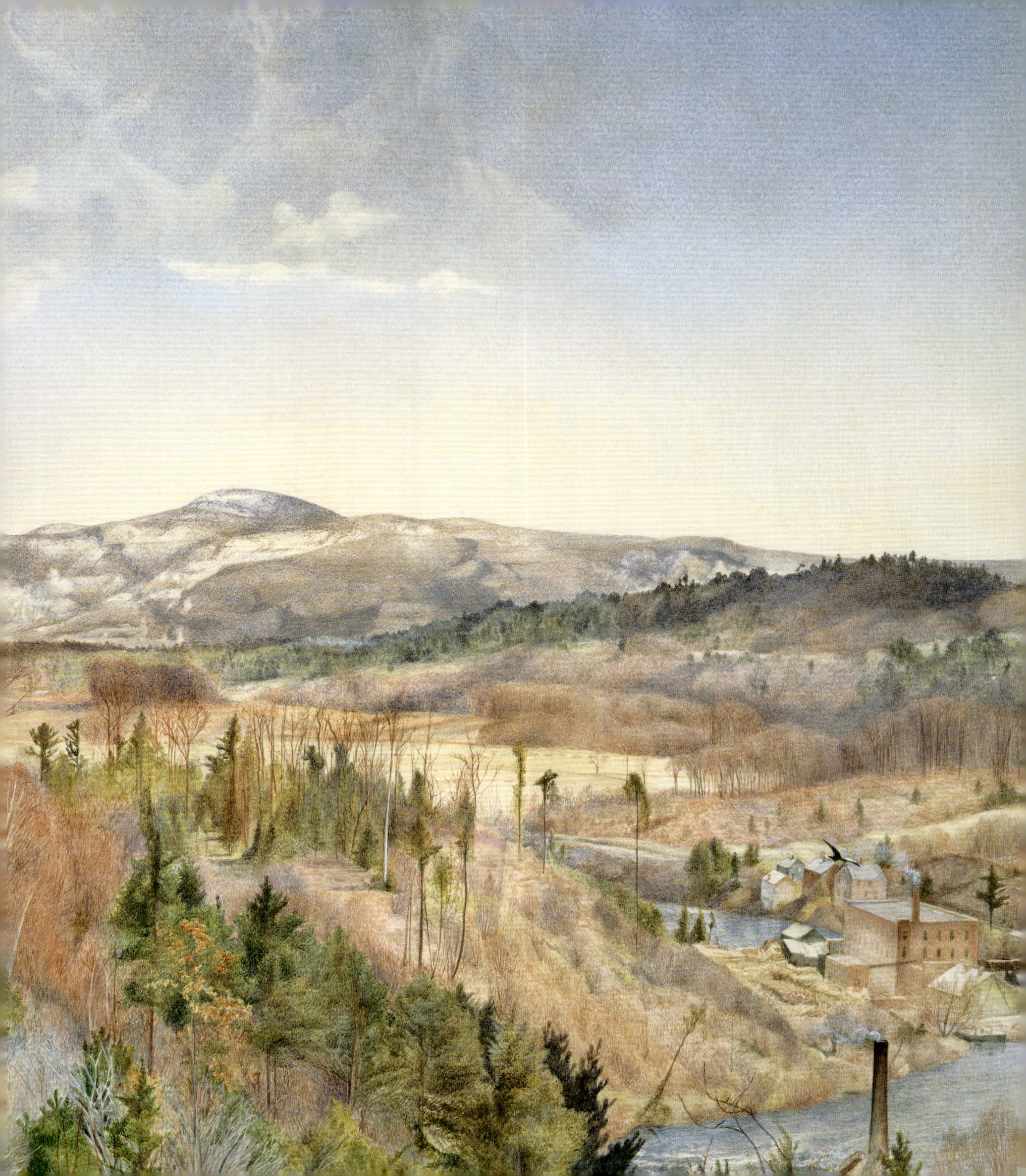

Checklist of the Exhibition

ROBERT BOLLING BRANDEGEE (1849–1922)

Plate 1
Writing to Mother, 1869
watercolor on paper
9 3⁄8 × 8 7⁄8 in. (23.81 × 22.54 cm)
Brooklyn Museum, New York, Charles Stewart Smith Memorial Fund

FIDELIA BRIDGES (1834–1923)

Plate 2
Study of Ferns, 1864
oil on board
10 × 12 in. (25.4 × 30.48 cm)
New Britain Museum of American Art, Gift of Jean E. Taylor

Plate 3
Laura Brown in a Wingchair, 1867
oil on canvas
21 × 18 in. (53.34 × 45.72 cm)
High Museum of Art, Atlanta, Purchase with American Art Acquisitions Fund

Plate 4
Pink Roses, 1875
watercolor on wove paper
14 × 10 in. (35.56 × 25.4 cm)
National Gallery of Art, Washington, Gift of William and Abigail Gerdts

Plate 5
Calla Lily, 1875
watercolor on paper
14 × 10 in. (35.56 × 25.4 cm)
Brooklyn Museum, New York, Museum Collection Fund

Plate 6
Milkweeds, 1876
watercolor on paper
17 1⁄4 × 13 in. (43.82 × 33.02 cm)
Proctor Collection, Munson-Williams-Proctor Arts Institute, Museum of Art, Utica

Plate 7
Wisteria on a Wall, 1870s
watercolor on paper
14 × 10 1⁄16 in. (35.56 × 25.56 cm)
Brooklyn Museum, New York, Gift of Mr. and Mrs. O. Kelley Anderson, Jr.

HENRY FARRER (1844–1903)

Plate 8
Two Birds: Canary and Robin, 1867
watercolor on paper
7 3⁄8 × 5 13⁄16 in. (18.73 × 14.76 cm)
Lent by Mr. and Mrs. Stuart P. Feld

Plate 9
Winter Scene in Moonlight, 1869
watercolor and gouache on white wove paper
11 7⁄8 × 15 3⁄16 in. (30.2 × 38.6 cm)
Lent by The Metropolitan Museum of Art, Purchase, Morris K. Jessup Fund, Martha and Barbara Fleischman, and Katherine and Frank Martucci Gifts, 1999

Plate 10
Pink Rose, 1874
watercolor on paper
4 5⁄8 × 10 1⁄4 in. (11.75 × 26.04 cm)
Elizabeth Feld-Herzberg

Plate 11
On Whitehead, Coast of Maine, 1875
watercolor on paper
12 × 18 1⁄2 in. (30.48 × 46.99 cm)
Leonard and Ellen Milberg

THOMAS CHARLES FARRER (1839–1891)

Plate 12
Gone! Gone!, 1860
oil on canvas
20 × 14 in. (50.8 × 35.56 cm)
The Hon. William Gibson

Plate 13
A Buckwheat Field on Thomas Cole's Farm, 1863
oil on canvas
11 ¾ × 25 ¼ in. (29.85 × 64.14 cm)
Museum of Fine Arts, Boston, Gift of Maxim Karolik for the M. and M. Karolik Collection of American Paintings

Plate 14
Mount Tom, 1865
oil on canvas
16 × 24 ¼ in. (40.6 × 61.6 cm)
National Gallery of Art, Washington, John Wilmerding Collection, Promised Gift

Plate 15
View of Northampton from the Dome of the Hospital, 1865
oil on canvas
28 ½ × 26 in. (72.39 × 66.04 cm)
Smith College Museum of Art, Northampton, Purchased

Plate 16
June, 1867
oil on board
9 ½ × 6 ½ in. (24.13 × 16.51 cm)
Private Collection

Plate 17
Three Eggs, 1868
watercolor on paper
5 × 10 in. (12.7 × 25.4 cm)
Lent by Elizabeth Feld-Herzberg and Peter A. Feld

Plate 18
Woman Sewing, 1859
graphite heightened with white gouache on cream paper
11 15⁄16 × 9 ¼ in. (30.32 × 23.5 cm)
Princeton University Art Museum, Gift of Professor Charles Ryskamp, in memory of Mr. Gerard B. Lambert, Class of 1908

Plate 19
Practicing Her Lesson, 1859
pencil, heightened with tempera, on wove paper, prepared with a cream ground
11 ⅞ × 9 ¼ in. (30.16 × 23.5 cm)
The Morgan Library & Museum, New York, Gift of Mr. Charles Ryskamp

Plate 20
The Fiddler, 1859
graphite and opaque watercolor on paper
11 ¾ × 9 ⅛ in. (29.85 × 23.18 cm)
Amon Carter Museum of American Art, Fort Worth

Plate 21
John Henry Hill in the Studio Etching, 1859
pencil on paper
6 ¼ × 5 ¾ in. (15.89 × 14.61 cm)
Paul Worman Fine Art, Worcester

Plate 22
Self-Portrait, Sketching, c. 1859
pencil on tan paper with Chinese white
10 ½ × 7 ⅝ in. (26.67 × 19.37 cm)
Lent by Mr. and Mrs. Stuart P. Feld

Plate 23
Portrait of John William Hill, c. 1859
graphite and gouache on paper
4 ¾ × 4 ½ in. (12.1 × 11.4 cm)
New-York Historical Society, Gift of Samuel V. Hoffman

Plate 24
Sketching from Nature, 1861
pen and black and brown ink on paper cut into the shape of an arch
7 ⅞ × 5 ½ in. (20 × 13.9 cm)
National Gallery of Art, Washington, John Davis Hatch Collection

WILLIAM JOHN HENNESSY (1839–1917)

Plate 25
Mon Brave, 1870
oil on board
11 15⁄16 × 8 15⁄16 in. (30.32 × 22.7 cm)
Brooklyn Museum, New York, Purchased with funds given by the Rembrandt Club

JOHN HENRY HILL (1839–1922)

Plate 26
A Study of Trap Rock (Buttermilk Falls), 1863
oil on canvas
24 × 20 in. (60.96 × 50.8 cm)
Lent by The Metropolitan Museum of Art, Gift of the artist, 1882

Plate 27
Fringed Gentians, c. 1867
oil on board
10 × 7 in. (25.4 × 17.78 cm)
Private Collection

Plate 28
Golden Robin (Northern Oriole), 1866
watercolor on paper
5 × 8 ⅞ in. (12.7 × 22.5 cm)
National Gallery of Art, Washington, Gift of William and Abigail Gerdts

Plate 29
Fringed Gentians, c. 1867
watercolor on paper
10 1/8 × 7 1/8 in. (25.72 × 18.1 cm)
Brooklyn Museum, New York, Purchased with funds given by Mr. and Mrs. Leonard L. Milberg

Plate 30
Gentians, 1870
watercolor heightened with gum glaze over graphite on paper
13 1/8 × 15 1/2 in. (33.34 × 39.37 cm)
Amon Carter Museum of American Art, Fort Worth

Plate 31
Waterlilies, c. 1870
watercolor on paper
5 1/16 × 7 9/16 in. (12.86 × 19.21 cm)
Lent by Mr. and Mrs. Stuart P. Feld

Plate 32
Lake George, 1873
watercolor on paper
6 3/4 × 9 3/4 in. (17.15 × 24.77 cm)
Washburn Gallery, New York

Plate 33
Autumn on Lake George, 1873
watercolor and graphite on paper
6 × 8 3/4 in. (15.24 × 22.23 cm)
Leonard and Ellen Milberg

Plate 34
Lake George, 1875
watercolor on paper
10 7/16 × 14 in. (26.51 × 35.56 cm)
Brooklyn Museum, New York, Gift of Mrs. Mary Stewart Bierstadt, by exchange

Plate 35
Natural Bridge, Virginia, 1876
watercolor on paper
21 1/4 × 14 1/8 in. (53.98 × 35.88 cm)
Brooklyn Museum, New York, Gift of Mr. and Mrs. Leonard L. Milberg

Plate 36
Thrush's Nest, 1866
pen and ink on paper
16 × 12 1/2 in. (40.64 × 31.75 cm)
Leonard and Ellen Milberg

JOHN WILLIAM HILL
(1812–1879)

Plate 37
Hunter and Dog, c. 1867
oil on canvas mounted on board
10 × 16 in. (25.4 × 40.64 cm)
Private Collection

Plate 38
Fawn's Leap, Catskill Mountains, 1868
oil on canvas
30 × 38 in. (76.2 × 96.52 cm)
Museum Purchase, Munson-Williams-Proctor Arts Institute, Museum of Art, Utica

Plate 39
Mountain Stream (Catskill Creek), 1863
watercolor on paper
13 1/16 × 17 1/16 in. (33.18 × 43.34 cm)
Brooklyn Museum, New York, Gift of Mary Stewart Bierstadt, by exchange

Plate 40
Grapes, 1864
watercolor on paper
8 1/4 × 7 1/2 in. (20.96 × 19.05 cm)
Leonard and Ellen Milberg

Plate 41
Plums, Pears, Peaches, and a Grape, 1864
watercolor on paper
8 9/16 × 13 1/16 in. (21.75 × 33.18 cm)
Lent by Mr. and Mrs. Stuart P. Feld

Plate 42
Pineapples, c. 1864
watercolor on paper
10 1/2 × 15 1/8 in. (26.67 × 38.42 cm)
Brooklyn Museum, New York, Purchased with funds given by Mr. and Mrs. Leonard L. Milberg

Plate 43
Dead Blue Jay, c. 1865
watercolor and graphite with selective light glazing on paper, mounted on card
5 7/8 × 12 in. (14.92 × 30.48 cm)
New-York Historical Society, Gift of Mrs. Charlan Whiteley Plummer Gellatly

Plate 44
View from High Tor, Haverstraw, New York, c. 1866
watercolor on paper
11 3/4 × 18 in. (29.85 × 45.72 cm)
New-York Historical Society, Foster-Jarvis Fund

Plate 45
Bird's Nest and Dog Roses, 1867
watercolor, gouache, graphite, and selective glazing with scratching out on paper
10 13/16 × 14 in. (27.46 × 35.56 cm)
New-York Historical Society, Gift of Mrs. Roswell Skeel, Jr.

Plate 46
West Nyack, New York (The Lilies of the Field), 1868
watercolor on paper
12 × 16 3/8 in. (30.48 × 41.59 cm)
Brooklyn Museum, New York, Gift of George J. Arden, Carroll J. Dickson, Mrs. Alfred T. Dillhoff, the Estate of Emil Fuchs, Mrs. Willis Reese, and Dr. Ben Shenson, by exchange, and the Dick S. Ramsay Fund

Plate 47
Apples and Plums, 1874
watercolor on paper
7 7/8 × 11 3/8 in. (20 × 28.89 cm)
Lent by Susan and Ted Stebbins

Plate 48
Peach Blossoms, 1874
watercolor and graphite on off-white wove paper
16 1⁄16 × 9 5⁄8 in. (40.8 × 24.4 cm)
Lent by The Metropolitan Museum of Art, Gift of J. Henry Hill, 1882

Plate 49
Apple Blossoms, c. 1874
watercolor on paper
8 13⁄16 × 15 1⁄2 in. (22.38 × 39.37 cm)
Brooklyn Museum, New York, Designated Purchase Fund

Plate 50
Afterglow, c. 1875
watercolor on paper
4 1⁄4 × 8 1⁄4 in. (10.8 × 20.96 cm)
Lent by Susan and Ted Stebbins

CHARLES HERBERT MOORE (1840–1930)

Plate 51
Hudson River, Above Catskill, 1865
oil on canvas
10 1⁄8 × 16 in. (25.72 × 40.64 cm)
Amon Carter Museum of American Art, Fort Worth

Plate 52
Autumn Landscape, 1865–1868
oil on canvas
8 3⁄4 × 13 3⁄4 in. (22.23 × 34.93 cm)
Leonard and Ellen Milberg

Plate 53
High Peak and Round Top (Catskill) in Winter, 1866
oil on canvas
7 1⁄16 × 10 1⁄4 in. (18 × 26 cm)
Princeton University Art Museum, Gift of Frank Jewett Mather Jr.

Plate 54
Lilies of the Valley, 1861
watercolor on cream wove paper
8 1⁄4 × 4 1⁄4 in. (20.9 × 10.8 cm)
Princeton University Art Museum, Gift of Frank Jewett Mather Jr.

Plate 55
Rocks by the Water, c. 1865–1872
watercolor and white gouache over graphite on cream wove paper
5 5⁄8 × 7 3⁄4 in. (14.3 × 19.7 cm)
Harvard Art Museum/Fogg Museum, Cambridge, Transfer from the Fine Arts Department, Harvard University

Plate 56
Landscape: Rocks and Water, c. 1865–1872
watercolor and gouache on paper
7 1⁄2 × 10 3⁄4 in. (19.05 × 27.31 cm)
Harvard Art Museum/Fogg Museum, Cambridge, Transfer from the Fine Arts Department, Harvard University

Plate 57
Dog Tooth Violet, 1871
graphite and watercolor on paper
7 7⁄8 × 6 7⁄8 in. (20 × 17.46 cm)
Private Collection

Plate 58
Pine Tree, 1868
pen and black ink with touches of graphite on tan board
23 7⁄8 × 19 3⁄4 in. (60.6 × 50.2 cm)
Princeton University Art Museum, Gift of Miss Elizabeth Huntington Moore, the artist's daughter

Plate 59
Dried White Oak Leaf, c. 1871–1874
pen and black ink, gray wash, and white gouache over graphite on beige wove paper
7 1⁄2 × 10 13⁄16 in. (19.1 × 27.4 cm)
Princeton University Art Museum, Gift of Miss Harriet Dyer Adams

HENRY RODERICK NEWMAN (1843–1917)

Plate 60
Study of Elms, 1866
watercolor on paper
16 3⁄4 ×19 1⁄4 in. (42.55 × 48.9 cm)
Museum of Fine Arts, Boston, Bequest of Maxim Karolik for the M. and M. Karolik Collection of American Watercolors and Drawings

Plate 61
Monument Mountain, 1867
watercolor on paper
4 3⁄4 × 6 1⁄4 in. (12.07 × 15.88 cm)
Lent by Amy and Robert Poster

Plate 62
Mt. Everett from Monument Mountain in April, 1867
watercolor on paper
10 7⁄16 × 13 3⁄4 in. (26.51 × 34.93 cm)
Museum of Fine Arts, Boston, Gift of Mrs. Harriet Ropes Cabot

Plate 63
Grapes and Olives, 1878
watercolor on paper
26 × 18 13⁄16 in. (66.04 × 47.78 cm)
Brooklyn Museum, New York, Purchased with funds given by Sol Schreiber in memory of Rose Schreiber, and with funds given by Joanne Witty and Eugene Keilin, Dick S. Ramsay Fund and Designated Purchase Fund

Plate 64
Italy, 1883
watercolor on paper
39 1⁄2 × 26 3⁄8 in. (100.33 × 66.99 cm)
Leonard and Ellen Milberg

Plate 65
Anemones and Daffodils, 1884
watercolor on paper
21 ¼ × 12 in. (53.98 × 30.48 cm)
Virginia Museum of Fine Arts, Richmond, Museum Purchase, The J. Harwood and Louise B. Cochrane Fund for American Art

Plate 66
The Horses of St. Marks, 1890
watercolor on paper
25 ½ × 16 ⅝ in. (64.77 × 42.23 cm)
Rob and Mary Joan Leith

Plate 67
Ramleh, 1893
watercolor on paper
39 ½ × 26 ½ in. (100.33 × 67.31 cm)
Private Collection

Plate 68
Wall Enclosing the Mausoleum of Ieyasu at Nikko, Japan, 1897
watercolor on paper
16 ½ × 9 in. (41.91 × 22.86 cm)
Museum of Fine Arts, Boston, General Funds

Plate 69
Sasanqua, Wild Tea, Yokohama, 1898
watercolor on paper
20 × 14 in. (50.8 × 35.56 cm)
Lent by Mr. and Mrs. Stuart P. Feld

Plate 70
The Temple Door at Abu Simbel, 1900
watercolor on paper
39 ½ × 26 ½ in. (100.33 × 67.31 cm)
Private Collection

ROBERT J. PATTISON
(1838–1903)

Plate 71
Mountain View, c. 1867
watercolor on paper with graphite, touches of gouache and scraping
20 13⁄16 × 29 13⁄16 in. (52.86 × 75.72 cm)
The Cleveland Museum of Art, Dudley P. Allen Fund

Plate 72
Portrait of John Henry Hill, 1860
pen and ink on paper
4 × 3 ⅛ in. (10.16 × 7.94 cm)
Leonard and Ellen Milberg

WILLIAM TROST RICHARDS
(1833–1905)

Plate 73
A Neglected Garden, 1859
oil on canvas
9 × 12 in. (22.86 × 30.48 cm)
Leonard and Ellen Milberg

Plate 74
Ferns in a Glade, 1859
oil on panel
7 ¼ × 6 in. (18.42 × 15.24 cm)
Lent by Susan and Ted Stebbins

Plate 75
The Conservatory, 1860
oil on wood panel
10 ⅞ × 8 9⁄16 in. (27.62 × 21.75 cm)
Lent by Mr. and Mrs. Stuart P. Feld

Plate 76
In the Woods, 1860
oil on canvas
16 × 20 ⅛ in. (40.64 × 51.12 cm)
Bowdoin College Museum of Art, Brunswick, Gift of Miss Mary T. Mason and Miss Jane Mason

Plate 77
Path in the Woods, 1861
oil on canvas
28 × 23 in. (71.12 × 58.42 cm)
Private Collection

Plate 78
October, 1863
oil on canvas
28 ⅛ × 24 in. (71.4 × 61 cm)
National Gallery of Art, Washington, The William Stamps Farish Fund

Plate 79
Landscape, c. 1863–1864
oil on canvas
23 ½ × 33 ½ in. (59.69 × 85.09 cm)
Crystal Bridges Museum of American Art, Bentonville

Plate 80
A Neglected Corner of the Wheatfield, 1865
oil on canvas
14 × 17 in. (35.56 × 43.18 cm)
Private Collection

Plate 81
Red Clover with Butter-and-Eggs, and Ground Ivy, 1860
watercolor with selectively applied glaze over graphite on paper
6 13⁄16 × 5 5⁄16 in. (17.3 × 13.49 cm)
The Walters Art Museum, Baltimore

Plate 82
Landscape, c. 1863–1864
watercolor and gouache on paper
6 ⅝ × 9 ⅝ in. (16.83 × 24.45 cm)
Jeff and Betsey Cooley

Plate 83
Corner of the Woods, 1864
graphite on paper
23 ¼ × 17 ½ in. (59.06 × 44.45 cm)
Museum of Fine Arts, Boston, Gift of Maxim Karolik for the M. and M. Karolik Collection of American Watercolors and Drawings

JOHN RUSKIN
(1819–1900)

Plate 84
Fragment of the Alps, c. 1854–1856
watercolor and gouache over graphite on cream wove paper
13 3⁄16 × 19 7⁄16 in. (33.5 × 49.3 cm)
Harvard Art Museums/Fogg Museum, Cambridge, Gift of Samuel Sachs

Plate 85
Twig of Peach Bloom, c. 1874
watercolor and gouache on cream wove paper
8 1⁄4 × 6 5⁄16 in. (20.9 × 16.1 cm)
Harvard Art Museums/Fogg Museum, Cambridge, Bequest of Mrs. Alfred Mansfield

Plate 86
A Cluster of Oak Leaves, 1856
ink, pencil, wash, and tempera on blue paper
8 1⁄4 × 11 in. (21 × 27.9 cm)
The Morgan Library & Museum, New York, Purchased on the E. J. Rousuck Fund

AARON DRAPER SHATTUCK
(1832–1928)

Plate 87
Leaf Study with Yellow Swallow Tail, c. 1859
oil on canvas
18 × 12 3⁄4 in. (45.72 × 32.39 cm)
Private Collection

Plate 88
The Shattuck Family, with Grandmother, Mother and Baby William, 1865
oil on canvas
20 × 15 7⁄8 in. (50.8 × 40.32 cm)
Brooklyn Museum, New York, Given in memory of Mary and John D. Nodine, by Judith and Wilbur Ross

WILLIAM JAMES STILLMAN
(1828–1901)

Plate 89
Saranac Lake, Adirondack Mountains (Study on Upper Saranac Lake), 1854
oil on canvas
30 1⁄2 × 25 1⁄2 in. (77.47 × 64.77 cm)
Museum of Fine Arts, Boston, Gift of Dr. J. Sydney Stillman

Plate 90
Photographic Study from *Photographic Studies by W. J. Stillman. Part 1. The Forest. Adirondac Woods*, 1859
albumen print
8 × 5 3⁄4 in. (20 × 15 cm)
Milne Library Special Collections, State University of New York at Geneseo

Plate 91
Photographic Study from *Photographic Studies by W. J. Stillman. Part 1. The Forest. Adirondac Woods*, 1859
albumen print
7 1⁄4 × 5 3⁄4 in. (18 × 15 cm)
Milne Library Special Collections, State University of New York at Geneseo

Plate 92
Photographic Study from *Photographic Studies by W. J. Stillman. Part 1. The Forest. Adirondac Woods*, 1859
albumen print
8 1⁄4 × 6 1⁄4 in. (21 × 15.75 cm)
Milne Library Special Collections, State University of New York at Geneseo

Plate 93
Photographic Study from *Photographic Studies by W. J. Stillman. Part 1. The Forest. Adirondac Woods*, 1859
albumen print
7 1⁄4 × 5 1⁄2 in. (18 × 14.25 cm)
Milne Library Special Collections, State University of New York at Geneseo

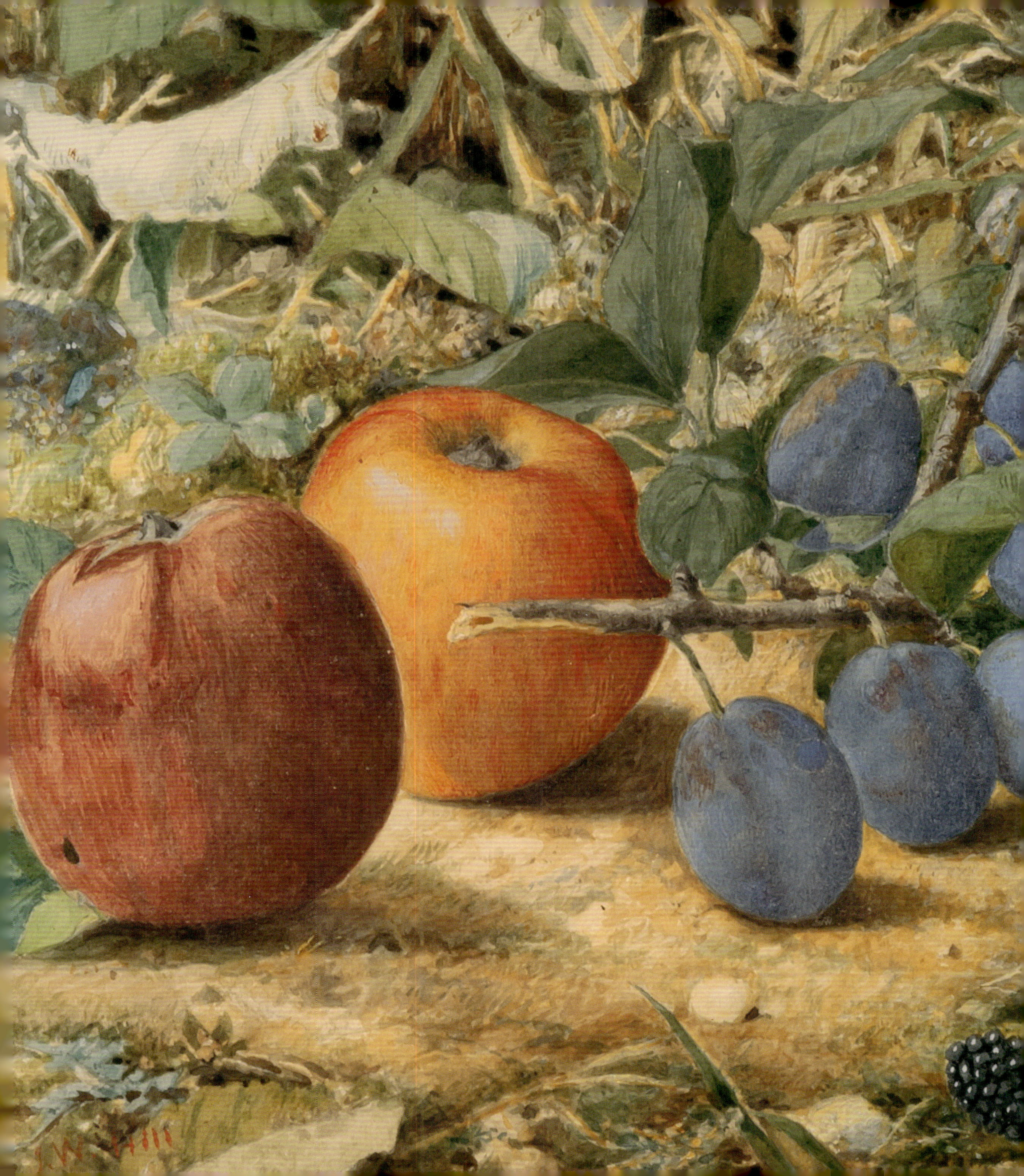

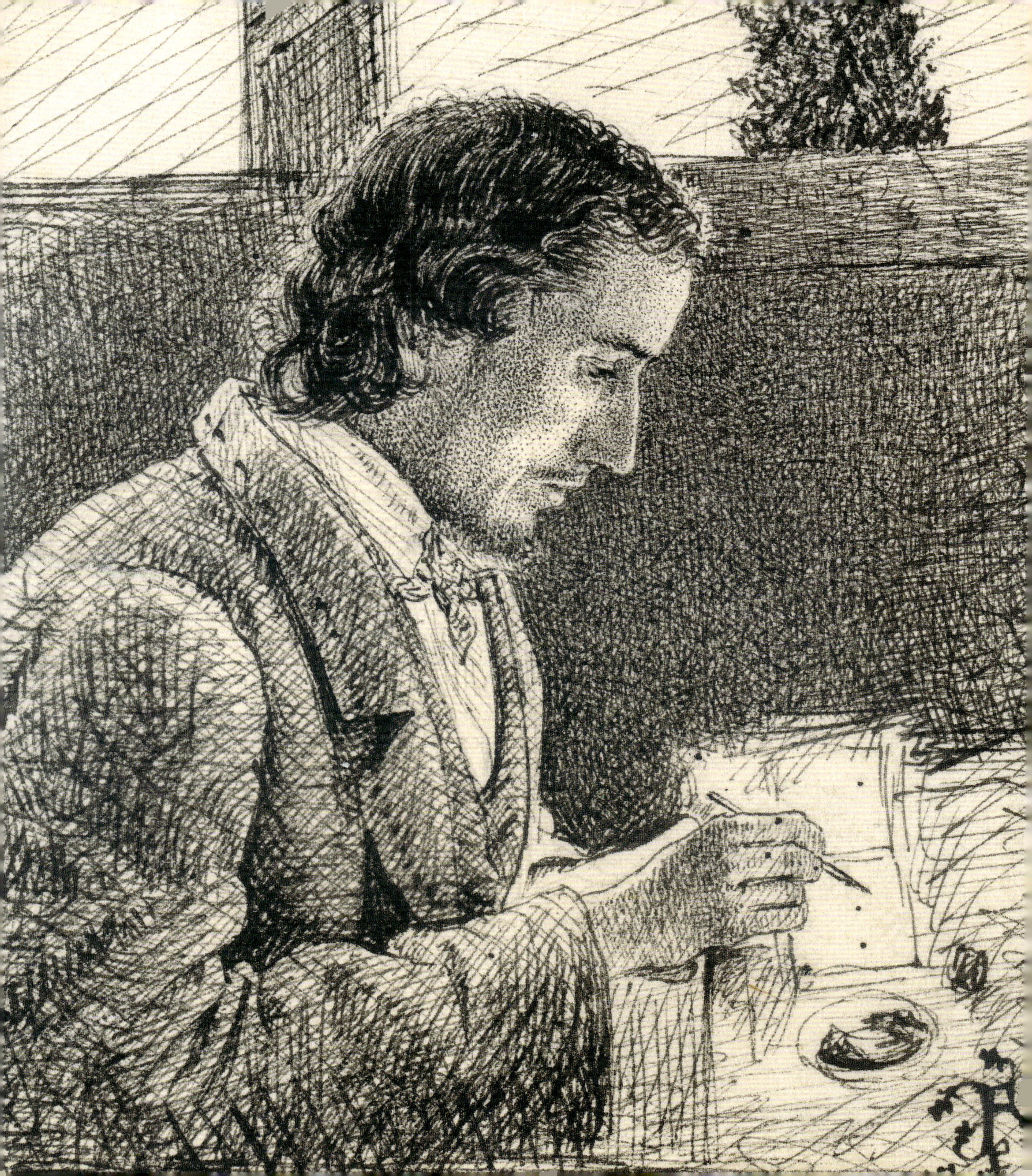

Association for the Advancement of Truth in Art Timeline (1863–1865)

ABBY ERON
LINDA S. FERBER
NANCY K. ANDERSON
MARGARET R. LASTER

Abbreviations

AATA Association (Society) for the Advancement of Truth in Art

AFS Artists' Fund Society (exhibition listings from Pre-1877 Art Exhibition Catalogue Index, Smithsonian Institution Research Information System)

BAA Brooklyn Art Association (exhibition listings and dates from Marlor 1970)

BT *Daily Evening Transcript*, Boston

DT *New-York Daily Tribune*

EP *Evening Post*, New York

GLF Gordon Lester Ford Papers, 1828–1889, New York Public Library

MMA Metropolitan Museum of Art, New York

NAD National Academy of Design, New York (exhibition listings from Cowdrey 1943/Naylor 1973)

NYT *New York Times*

PAFA Pennsylvania Academy of the Fine Arts, Philadelphia (exhibition listings from Falk 1988)

* Object in 2019 exhibition at National Gallery of Art, Washington

Unless otherwise noted, all information about AATA meetings and membership is derived from the Minutes of the Meetings, Society for the Advancement of Truth in Art (Peter Bonnett Wight Papers, Ryerson & Burnham Libraries, The Art Institute of Chicago).

Prologue: 1858

Thomas Charles Farrer emigrates to New York from London. A student of John Ruskin and Dante Gabriel Rossetti, he will play a key role in the establishment of a formal organization of Ruskin acolytes in America.

1863

January 27
Against a background of ongoing civil war, and just days after Abraham Lincoln issues the Emancipation Proclamation on January 1, a group of young men gather at Thomas Charles Farrer's 32 Waverly Place studio to found an organization to promote "the cause of 'truth in Art.'" Present are Eugene T. Gardner, James T. Gardner (later spelled Gardiner), Clarence R. King, Farrer, Charles H. Moore, James E. Munson, Russell Sturgis Jr., and Peter B. Wight. Sturgis "present[s]

in written form, a scheme of a proposed organization." J. T. Gardner moves that a committee (Sturgis, Farrer, and King) prepare Articles of Organization and report at the next meeting.

February 4
The group gathers again in Farrer's studio, joined by John Henry Hill, John Matthews Jr., and Carl Muller. Sturgis reports on the Articles of Organization; each article is voted on separately. A final version with suggested amendments is presented at the next meeting.

February 11
Farrer's studio is again the meeting venue at which "the Articles of Organization of the 'Association for the Advancement of the Cause of Truth in Art'" (hereafter the Association) are reviewed by Clarence Cook, E. Gardner, J. T. Gardner, Farrer, John William Hill, King, Matthews, Moore, Sturgis, and James Lyman Van Buren. A final draft is presented to members for signatures at the next meeting.

February 18
Wight's rooms at 241 Fourth Avenue are the venue for the first regular meeting of the Association attended by Cook, E. Gardner, J. T. Gardner, Farrer, Eastburn Hastings, J. H. Hill, King, Matthews, Moore, Robert J. Pattison, and Wight to sign the Articles and hold elections. J. W. Hill (although absent) is elected president; Cook, vice president; King, secretary; Wight, treasurer. William Doughty of Troy, NY, is nominated for honorary membership by E. Gardner. At the meeting, the Articles are signed by all in attendance, plus Munson. On February 23, Sturgis, Van Buren, and Eugene Schuyler sign. On April 10, Mary L. Booth, Louisa W. Cook, and Sarah M. Barney sign.

February 25
The Association's second regular meeting is held at Matthews's residence, First Avenue. Cook, Farrer, Hastings, Matthews, Moore, Pattison, Sturgis, and Wight attend. Doughty is elected as an honorary member.

March 5
Association holds its third regular meeting at Cook's residence where Farrer, E. Gardner, J. T. Gardner, Hastings, King, Matthews, Moore, Sturgis, and Wight hear Cook's report on Pre-Raphaelite works seen on a visit to England. Farrer proposes William Trost Richards for membership. Moore reads a letter from John Ruskin's father, John James Ruskin, acknowledging receipt of Moore's letter regarding "allegations" made by G. W. Nichole concerning Ruskin's views on J. M. W. Turner and the Pre-Raphaelites. Sturgis reads Dante Gabriel Rossetti's poem "The Blessed Damozel."

March 10
The Association meets at Farrer's studio. J. T. Gardner, Matthews, Moore, Pattison, Sturgis, Wight, and "some visitors" are present. Richards's nomination is called up and tabled until next meeting. Seven women are nominated for membership: "Mrs. D. N. Barney of Irvington; Mrs. Clarence Cook, of N.Y.; Mrs. Howland, of Irvington; Miss S. M. Barney, of Irvington; Miss Mary L. Booth, of N.Y., Miss Annie R. McLane, of Brooklyn; Miss S. S. Tuthill, of Brooklyn." An informal discussion of photography takes place. Funds are approved to print two hundred copies of the First and Second Articles of Organization. Elections are held; Cook will fill vacant presidency (J. W. Hill having declined to serve); Farrer is elected vice president; Moore replaces King as secretary.

March 17
The Association convenes its fifth regular meeting at Mrs. Henriette Desportes Field's residence. Present are Booth, Farrer, Matthews, McLane, Moore, Pattison, Sturgis, Van Buren, Wight, and "a number of friends invited by Mrs. Field to meet the 'association.'" Sturgis presents a paper titled "Our Articles" addressing "Architecture of the past." Farrer also presents a paper and reads an unpublished poem, "Work." The "seven ladies" nominated on March 10 are elected.

March 25
At Samuel P. Avery's house in Brooklyn, "a number of the members and friends of the cause met...and passed a pleasant evening. The meeting was not called to order, and no business was done."

March 28
A special meeting called by the president (Cook) is held at Farrer's studio and attended by Farrer, Hastings, Matthews, Moore, Munson, Sturgis, and Wight, who reads a "communication" from J. W. Hill. Members vote to distribute ten copies of the Articles of Organization to each member; discussion of scheduling alternate business and literary meetings as well as "beginning the publication of a Journal." Richards's nomination is tabled once again. It is decided that, hereafter, no meetings will be held at private houses other than those of the members.

March 31
Association meets at Miss S. M. Hitchcock's residence, East Twenty-Ninth Street, where Farrer reads "A Few Questions Answered" (*The New Path*, June 1863).

April 3
Sixth regular meeting convenes at Wight's rooms to discuss the journal *The New Path*. In attendance are Cook,

Farrer, Moore, Pattison, Wight, and Sturgis. "The Society does hereby establish a [monthly] Journal of general publication. . . . The Journal shall contain: 1st. Articles on Art, having for their principal purpose the education of the public to the true perception of Nature, and understanding of Art. 2d. Criticisms of existing works of Art. 3d. Poems or such other matter. . . . 4th. Such correspondence as may seem desirable to print. 5th. Such extracts from the Journal [probably the Minutes] of the Society as it may seem desirable to publish." Cook is unanimously elected editor.

April 7
The Association meets at Clarence and Louisa Cook's house with Pattison, Farrer, Matthews, and Wight in attendance. Wight reads a letter from W. T. Richards and recommends his election, as had Farrer in the past. Richards is elected. After much discussion of names for the journal, members adopt Louisa Cook's suggestion, *The New Path*.

April 14
The Association meets at Matthews's residence with Barney, Clarence and Louisa Cook, (probably J. H.) Hill, Farrer, Moore, Pattison, Schuyler, Sturgis, and Wight in attendance. A room is rented at 32 Waverly Place to serve as editorial office for *The New Path*. The Home Printing Office is contracted to print the journal.

April 28
Association meets (venue and attendance unrecorded but probably their room at 32 Waverly Place). Members vote to assess dues of one dollar a month. (Wight, June 1, 1863, GLF)

April 30–May 6
Battle of Chancellorsville, Virginia. Confederate victory; Stonewall Jackson is mortally wounded.

May 1863–July 1864
The New Path is issued monthly.

July 1–3
Battle of Gettysburg, Pennsylvania. Union victory; bloodiest battle of the Civil War, with an estimated 51,000 casualties.

July
J. H. Hill spends "nearly every afternoon in the month while our civil war [is] going on" painting *A Study of Trap Rock (Buttermilk Falls)*.* (J. H. Hill to MMA, May 14, 1911. MMA Archives, quoted in Spassky 1985, 538)

July 13–16
New York City draft riots erupt as a violent protest against new conscription regulations.

July 18
Battle of Fort Wagner, South Carolina. The Fifty-Fourth Massachusetts Volunteer Infantry, one of the first African American regiments formed during the Civil War, is defeated; Colonel Robert Gould Shaw is killed. (In 1864 Farrer would exhibit a portrait drawing of another casualty of the battle, titled *Captain Cabot Russel, 54th Massachusetts Regiment, Killed at Fort Wagner*.) (Wiles 2001, 441, there incorrectly dated 1865)

August 11
Wight writes to T. C. Farrer that he'd heard "Miss Maclean [McLane] had gone to Catskill on a *Sketching Expedition*, with a Mr. Farrer." He urges Farrer: "You must hurry up those subscriptions from the Catskillers, or we shall carry out the threat I made to Cook, and the journal [*The New Path*] will appear as 'Wight & Sturgis' magazine of Art, Architecture, Literature, Abolition and Spiritualism', and the subscription will be raised to ten dollars a year." Wight mentions the visit of Henry Farrer, Thomas's brother, who had also immigrated to the United States. As a pupil of Thomas, Wight reports, "[Henry] used a point[?], and worked with *painful fidelity*." (GLF)

August 15
Regarding "the whereabouts of our [AATA] artists this summer. . . . The Hills (father and son) have been at Portland, Me., and are now near Shelburne N.H. . . . W. T. Richards, of Philadelphia, is among the Adirondacks. . . . Shattuck is among the elms and meadows of Great Barrington, Mass. . . . [William J.] Hennessy is yet at his studio, finishing numerous genre pictures. . . . Stillman is residing at Rome, having been for some time the American Consul there." (BT)

August 19
Wight declares in a letter to T. C. Farrer: "I believe that upon you and I more than any others depends the success of our crusade." (GLF)

August 20
Hennessy is drafted into the Union army. (EP, August 21, 1863)

August 30
On steamboat to San Francisco, King and J. T. Gardner meet William Henry Brewer, who takes them to the California Geological Survey offices, where King volunteers for survey duty. Brewer later recalls finding King "saturated chiefly with Ruskin and [scientist John] Tyndall." Gardner stays in San Francisco, joining the survey in May 1864 as volunteer assistant topographer. (Raymond 1903, 623–624; Sandweiss 2009, 34, 39)

September 26
Viewing Mount Shasta from Lassen Peak, California, as a storm approaches, King wonders aloud, "What would Ruskin have said, if he had seen *this*!" (Raymond 1903, 625)

October 13
T. C. Farrer is in correspondence with H. R. Newman, who writes from Factory Point, Vermont, that he is "completely stirred" by *The New Path*. He requests back numbers and "all the art news concerning the P. R. B. and otherwise." (GLF)

October 20
After a six-month hiatus, the Association meets, probably at their 32 Waverly Place editorial office. The Cooks, T. C. Farrer, McLane, Schuyler, Sturgis, and Wight gather to consider contributions to the November issue of *The New Path* and to vote on appropriations for the magazine. The meeting seems to have been stormy. Cook reads submissions. One article is accepted—Wight's "What Can Be Done"—while debate and criticism ensue on the others. Schuyler resigns as editor and secretary, but his resignation is not accepted.

October 21
Cornerstone ceremonies for Wight's National Academy of Design building: "Gothic renaissance will be the chief style of architecture, with some florid adaptations of the still more modern day." Wight's design is drawn from Venetian Gothic models reflecting the Association's championship of Ruskin's endorsement of Gothic architecture as the ideal style for buildings. (NYT, October 22, 1863; Landau 1981, 18–21)

October 22
Newman sends T. C. Farrer drawings, explaining: "I have this summer got so far in the 'agonizing' business [of making Ruskinian studies from nature] that I don't think I can very well do any other way." (GLF)

October 23
Association meeting with no quorum, so Schuyler adjourns. No further meetings held until March 1864.

November 19
Lincoln delivers Gettysburg Address.

1864

January
Two important reviews of *The New Path* appear in influential journals with opposing positions. *The North American Review*, published in Boston and coedited at the time by Charles Eliot Norton and James Russell Lowell, is most optimistic about the magazine's propsects:

"By far the most interesting and noteworthy American publication concerning Art, during the past year, is the little journal called by the somewhat vague and inappropriate name of 'The New Path.'...[T]here has been no discourse or criticism upon matters of Art in America so valuable as its pages contain, since the essays by Mr. Stillman in the earlier volumes of 'The Crayon.'...There is occasionally in its papers a tone of dogmatism and self-sufficiency, occasionally also a crudity and want of completeness, which being combined with singular sincerity and simplicity, not unpleasantly reveal the youth while indicating the capacity for growth of the writers....'The New Path' may not gain a wide and general success, but it gives happy promise for the future of Art in America, by giving proof of the increase and ability of the school of thinkers and artists to whom the truth-seeking reformers who contribute to its pages belong. It is a small school as yet, but it includes the most genuine artistic aspirations and most ardent feeling of the times. Its influence is already deeply felt, and if its leaders hold firm to their own principles, they will finally be recognized as the redeemers of American Art from its present servitude to tradition and falsehood, and its subserviency [*sic*] to the popular preference for what is showy and admired to what is intrinsically worthy of admiration." ("Reviewed Work(s): 'The New Path,'" *The North American Review* 98, no. 202: 303–304)

The Round Table's critique is less sanguine: "The pre-Raphaelite movement [was] begun some ten or fifteen years past in England, and...gave [us] the most powerful art-writer and the truest and loveliest art-work that England can show. The same principle commenced its action in American art about seven years since....Now seven years afterward with such men as W. T. Richards and 'the two Hills' as its representatives....we find a society organized and a journal published for the exposition of pre-Raphaelitism!...With the purposes of the Society and journal we have no quarrel, but we must express our surprise that both have ignored the existence here of that with which they intend to inoculate the body of American art." Irked by these omissions, as well as by the overall pugnacious stance of the magazine, the review closes on an unfriendly note: "We believe in Ruskin's pre-Raphaelitism, and that of Millais, Holman Hunt, and Rossetti; but it does not follow that we believe in that of the critics of the *New Path*." ("Recent Art Criticism," *The Round Table*, January 2, 1864: 42)

February 13
Clarence Cook writes of Willam T. Walters's collection on exhibition at Düsseldorf Gallery in New York City, describing Richards's *A Neglected Garden**: "It is a most careful, pains-taking piece of painting...but the result is more scientific than beautiful." (DT)

February 13 and 20
Eugene Benson in *The Round Table* comments on several landscapes by Richards seen at the Century and at Goupil & Co.: "These pictures are remarkable examples of certain tendencies in modern art. They evince a spirit of such laborious

earnestness, such unshrinking persistency of purpose, such capacity for labor, that they almost take the rank of works of genius; certainly win from the most unsympathetic critic respect and reverence. They represent realism in landscape painting, and can lay no claim to the imaginative . . . These pictures show that Mr. Richards is remarkable for two things — a slow, keen vision, and a slow, sure hand. . . . He painted what he saw. . . . He forgot that seeing nature as a botanist is not seeing nature as a poet." (139, 153)

March 29

Association members Barney, the Cooks, Farrer, McLane, Moore, Munson, Pattison, Schuyler, Sturgis, Van Buren, and Wight gather for what is their last formal meeting, at which Newman is elected to membership. *The New Path* is turned over to Cook, Sturgis, and Wight. Members are taxed equally to pay debts incurred in publishing the magazine. A partial list is compiled of "members of the Association at its demise": Sarah M. Barney; Mary L. Booth, writer; Clarence Cook, writer and teacher; Louisa W. Cook; Thomas C. Farrer, painter; Eugene T. Gardner, lawyer; James T. Gardner, geologist; Eastburn Hastings, architect; J. Henry Hill, painter; Clarence R. King, geologist; John Matthews Jr., manufacturer; Annie R. McLane; Charles H. Moore, painter; James E. Munson, lawyer and reporter; R. J. Pattison, painter; Eugene Schuyler, lawyer; Russell Sturgis Jr., architect; J. Lyman Van Buren, lawyer and soldier; and P. B. Wight, architect.

April 4–23

Metropolitan Fair in Aid of the US Sanitary Commission (to support sick and wounded soldiers) opens in New York; the art exhibition includes Richards's *October*,* as well as works by T. C. Farrer, Hennessy, Moore, Newman, and Shattuck. The Union Square Branch Exhibition Pavilion annexed to the main building is designed

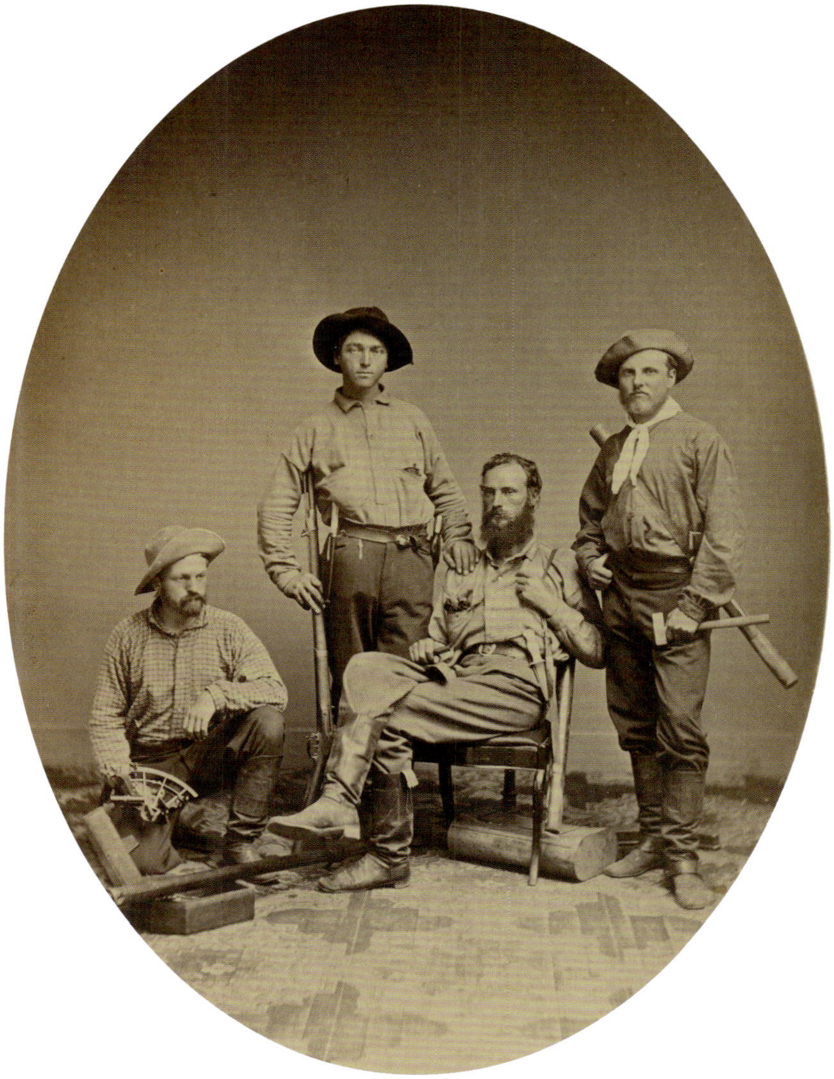

Silas Selleck, *Clarence King and the Field Party of 1864*, albumen print, National Portrait Gallery, Smithsonian Institution. From left: James Terry Gardner, Richard D. Cotter, William Henry Brewer, and Clarence King.

and managed by Wight. (Metropolitan Fair 1864; Metropolitan Fair 1867, 4, 222; Landau 1981, 77)

April 9
In two infamous DT reviews, Clarence Cook severely critiques the Metropolitan Fair's loan exhibition of mainstream American paintings while defending works by the American Pre-Raphaelites. Of the survey of American paintings on loan from major collectors and institutions, Cook observes, "We are in the midst of a great revolution; that 'The old order changeth, yielding place to new.'"

April 16
In his second review, Cook defends Farrer's small painting *Twilight (An Hour after Sunset in the Catskills)* (fig. 7 in Ferber essay), lamenting that the work is "laughed at, sneered at, and quizzed." In opposition, Cook declares: "To our mind, in spite of marked defects which we shall not fail to notice, few pictures have been painted in America more true, more solemn, or more earnest."

April 30
Daily Evening Bulletin (Philadelphia) reviews PAFA exhibition over two issues. In the first: "It is one of the peculiar features of this time of war, the fine arts are flourishing unusually"; "Mr. W. T. Richards, who has made the paintings of leaves a special study, and has brought pre-Raphaelite perfection, has gone further in the two pictures he contributes to this exhibition [*Bouquet Valley, Adirondack Mountains*; *Landscape*]."

May
The May issue of *The New Path* is published without the Association's name on the masthead.

May 7
Daily Evening Bulletin publishes second PAFA exhibition review: "We may watch the attitude of any chance spectator; he is sure to give the preraphaelite [*sic*] a frank tribute of wonder; these leaves that you could pluck, these fissures in which you could pinch your fingers, . . . the connoisseur is invariably observed in the posture of entomologist searching for very small insects among the weeds."

May 21
Clarence Cook writes ambivalent review considering T. C. Farrer at NAD exhibition: "This artist, though strong to point out the way, has not the power to climb himself to a higher ground than this of accurate copyism. . . . The mountain landscape, No. 143 [*A Buckwheat Field on Thomas Cole's Farm**], would be at once admitted by every candid, unprejudiced person to be a picture bearing the evident marks of hard study, patient labor, and a strong desire to record just what the artist saw. . . . As it was Ruskin who moved Farrer—so it was Ruskin who moved us." (DT)

July 10
Moore writes from Catskill to T. C. Farrer reflecting on the laborious Pre-Raphaelite painting process: "I cover about as much canvass [*sic*] as I could cover with the end of my thumb in a forenoon of three hours work." (GLF)

August 1864–March 1865
Publication of *The New Path* is suspended.

August 7
Moore writes T. C. Farrer: "The picture of the valley (the one I commenced when you were here), is now not more than *half* done. . . . It is *faithful*, but I am not sure that it is *successful*. Dr. Lauer likes it however & offers me $200 if I can't get more. This is a good price for 10 × 17 inches of canvass [*sic*], but does not pay me for the labor." He also reports that John H. Hill's younger brother, James Henry Hill (1845–1864) has "died in the Army." (GLF)

August 21
Cook writes to T. C. Farrer. While praising Ruskin's genius, he laments "the difference between Ruskin's words which are read by two nations, and teach two . . . and my six or seven articles in the Tribune which were scarcely read out of New York City." He hopes Farrer will visit the scholar Charles Eliot Norton in Cambridge, Massachusetts, to see works by D. G. Rossetti in his collection. (GLF)

September 11
Newman writes to T. C. Farrer that potential patrons find his portfolio "*to* [*sic*] *Pre Raphaelite*," explaining, "I find that Pre Raphs are not fashionable here 'they are so ultra [extreme].'" (GLF)

October 5
Association members King and J. T. Gardner arrive at edge of Yosemite, where they undertake a boundary survey for the park commission. (King 1872, 133; Moore 2006, 109)

November 8
President Lincoln is elected to a second term.

1865

January 31
The Thirteenth Amendment abolishes slavery.

February 23
Cook, Sturgis, and Wight call a meeting at Schuyler's rooms, 32 Waverly Place, to form the New Path Association—to which they intend to transfer *The New Path* ownership—and to raise funds to complete the second volume of the journal. Members/subscribers are Cook, Annie R. McLane, T. C. Farrer, William

C. Gilman, Francis Lathrop (T. C. Farrer's student), Munson, Newman, Sturgis, Van Buren, and Wight. Additional subscribers are George P. Philes & Co., Josiah Cleaveland Cady (architect), James J. Jarves, Dr. John E. Lauer, Mrs. J. L. Little, Matthews, Benjamin Richards Jr., T. N. Rooker, and R. H. Smith. Munson is elected treasurer; Cook, editor.

April–December
The New Path resumes publication on monthly basis.

April 9
General Robert E. Lee's surrender to General Ulysses S. Grant at Appomattox ends the Civil War.

April 15
President Lincoln is assassinated.

April 27
Wight's NAD building opens, draped in mourning for Lincoln. (Landau 1981, 18; National Academy of Design 1865, 47–48)

June 7
X.'s "Artistic Growls, Pre-Raphaelite Pictures at the Academy" ridicules the American Pre-Raphaelites: "Moore's organs of vision, we presume, are not entomological, nor in any way different in kind from those of other Americans. But he professes in [*Study in the Catskill Valley*] to see in nature much that has escaped the acutest vision of ordinary mortals.... In [T. C. Farrer's *April, 1861*] the artist has represented a lady in a violently blue silk dress, and with an intensely miserable and cadaverous expression, standing near a window, from which we catch a glimpse of a troop of soldiers marching along the street. The title of the picture intimates that she has parted with her soldier-lover, whom she has probably seen pass with his regiment.... We presume that this little study [Pattison's *Study by a Brook*] is held in high esteem among that small sect of mutual admirationists who devote their time to microscopic studies of foregrounds (and whom we might term the Myopian Club), from the fact that it is reproduced on an easel in Mr. Farrer's tea-table picture [*Home Scenes—Morning*].... If we had the slightest hope that our advice could influence the extreme P. R. brethren, we should recommend them to leave for a while their dry sticks and stones and botanical specimens, throw by their magnifiers, and try to look at Nature as if she had a beautiful and divine soul." (EP)

July 3/13
Clarence Cook (DT) and Sturgis (writing for the *Nation*), defend the truthfulness of Moore's *Study in the Catskill Valley* at NAD exhibition.

August 29
Northampton Free Press reports that T. C. Farrer has completed two landscapes (*Mount Tom** and *View of Northampton from the Dome of the Hospital**). (NP, 165; Wiles 2001, 428–449)

November 18
Albion's review of AFS exhibition, focusing on Fidelia Bridges's *September Afternoon,* cautions the artist "to observe that it is an exceedingly clever imitation of Mr. Farrar [*sic*], and also to ask the young lady, in all kindliness, whether Mr. Farrar be worth imitating."

November 30
Sturgis reviews AFS exhibition in the *Nation*: "We conclude, after long consideration, and careful re-examination of all Mr. Farrer's work that is within our reach, that he has up to this time shown no power to combine local with general truth.... Pattison, in his little picture No. 277, has grappled with a tremendous subject, a 'View of the White Mountains and Androscoggin Valley.'... yet rather beyond his powers."

December
Final issue of *The New Path* is published.

December 1865–January 1866
T. C. Farrer exhibition of eighteen watercolors and four pencil drawings at M. Knoedler & Co. (Foster 2017, 54, 400n7; Wiles 2001, 79; NYT, December 19, 1865; NYT, January 3, 1866)

December 16, 28
Both Cook (DT) and Sturgis (*The Nation*) offer mixed reviews of Farrer's Knoedler exhibition, extolling his small still-life watercolors but lamenting the artist's inability to work successfully on a larger scale. Both critics and fellow members offer the example of Farrer's *Northampton**, then in the AFS exhibition, to support their opinions. Farrer responded to *The Nation*'s critique in a letter published in the January 11, 1866, issue.

Epilogue: 1871

May 25 and 26
T. C. Farrer "contemplating a prolonged absence in Europe" auctions his entire collection at Mr. Schenck's at 60 Liberty Street. This 1871 sale marks the close of the artist's residence in America. He and his family settle in England. His brother Henry remains in America. (DT, May 23, 1871; Wiles 2001, 33)

American Pre-Raphaelites:
Participants, Patrons, Advocates

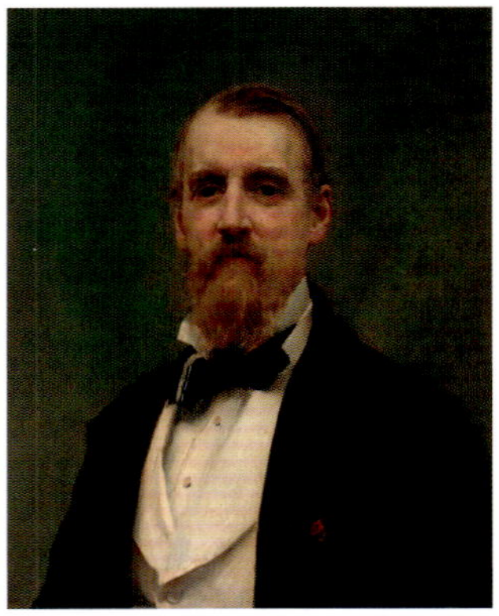

SAMUEL PUTNAM AVERY
(1822–1904)

Engraver, dealer, collector; hosted Association meeting on March 25, 1863, at his home in Brooklyn.

(Raimundo de Madrazo y Garreta, *Samuel P. Avery*, 1876. The Metropolitan Museum of Art, Gift of the family of Samuel P. Avery, 1904) (See also fig. 3 in Ferber essay.)

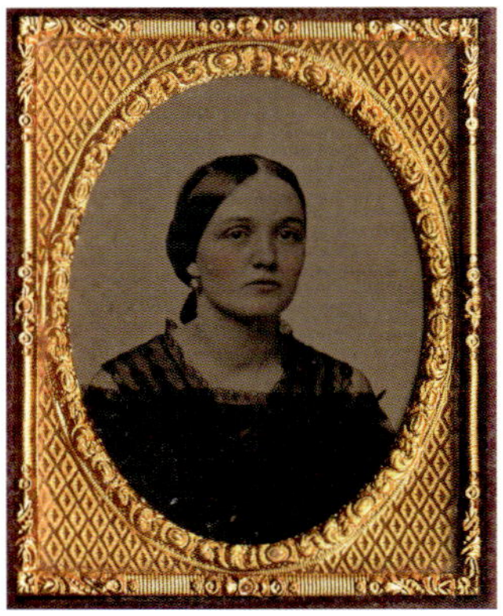

SARAH MARIA BARNEY
(1836–1910)

Association member, wife of Russell Sturgis Jr.

(*Sarah M. Barney, age 21*, c. 1858. Russell Sturgis, Jr., Family Papers, Manuscripts and Archives, Yale University Library)

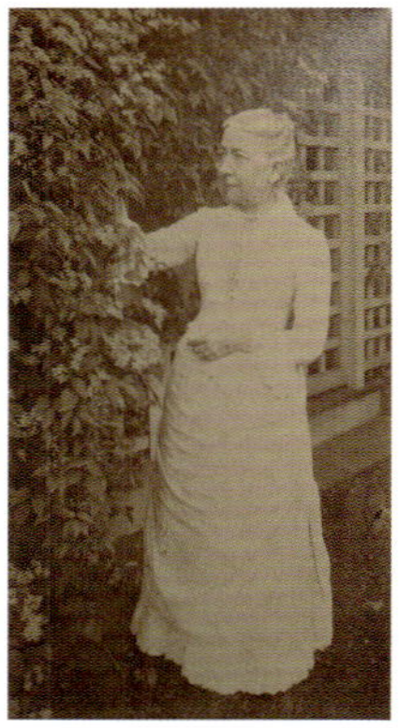

SARAH BRANDEGEE BARNEY
(1833–1908)

Association member, sister-in-law of Sarah Maria Barney and Russell Sturgis Jr., aunt of artist Robert Bolling Brandegee.

(Private Collection)

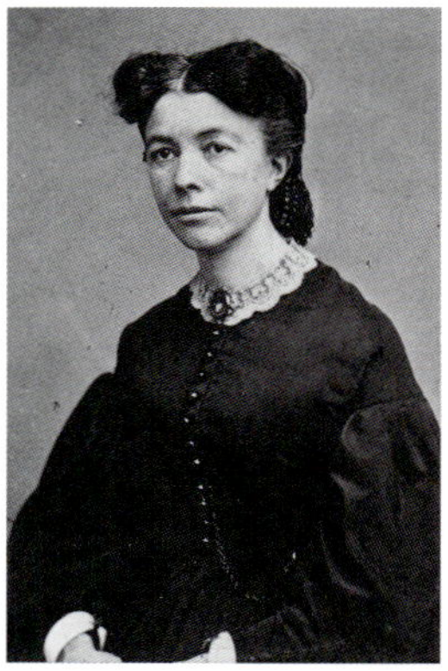

MARY LOUISE BOOTH
(1831–1889)

Association member, journalist, advocate for abolition and women's rights. First female writer for the *New-York Daily Tribune* and founding editor of *Harper's Bazar* [*sic*] (1867–1889). Held salons at family home in Brooklyn. Her circle included T. C. and Annie Farrer, Sarah Strong Tuthill, and the Fords.

(*Mary L. Booth*, 1855–1865. Brady-Handy Photograph Collection, Library of Congress, Prints and Photographs Division)

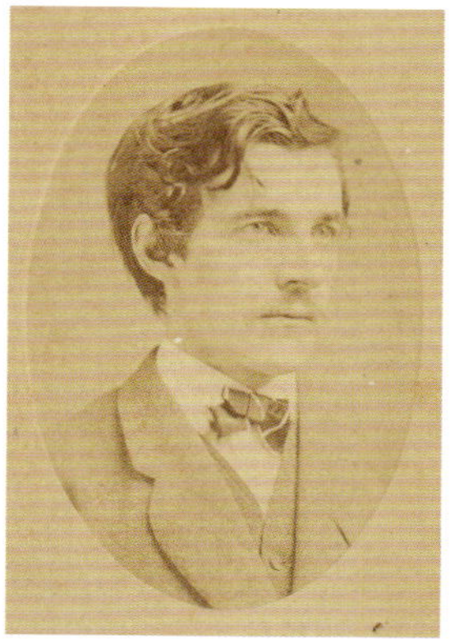

ROBERT BOLLING BRANDEGEE
(1849–1922)

Artist in oil and watercolor; student of T. C. Farrer and Sarah Strong Tuthill, his aunt, whom he succeeded as art teacher at Miss Porter's School in Farmington, CT.

(Paul Worman Fine Art, Worcester)

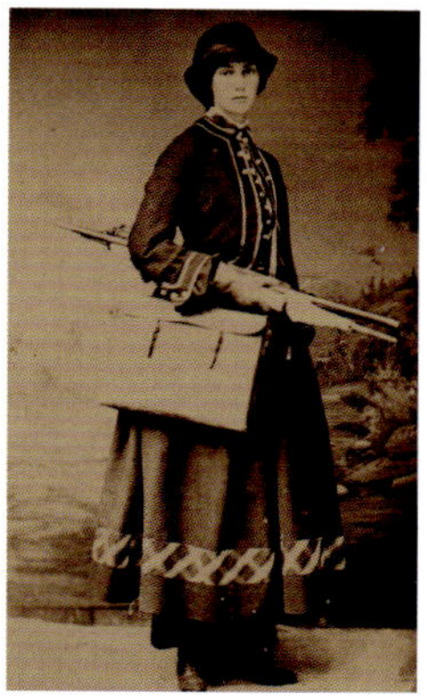

FIDELIA BRIDGES
(1834–1923)

Artist, student of W. T. Richards. A watercolor specialist who also provided images for chromolithographs published by Louis Prang & Co.

(*Fidelia Bridges*, c. 1864. Oliver Ingraham Lay, Charles Downing Lay, and Lay Family Papers, Archives of American Art, Smithsonian Institution)

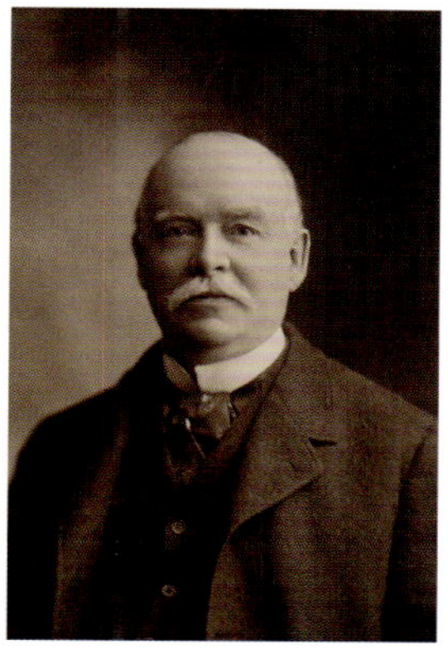

J. CLEAVELAND (CLEVELAND) CADY
(1837–1919)

Subscriber to *The New Path*, architect, designer of the Brooklyn Art Association building in modern Gothic style (1872), Peabody Museum of Natural History, Yale (1876), and American Museum of Natural History, south façade (1899).

(Courtesy of the Watkinson Library, Trinity College, Hartford)

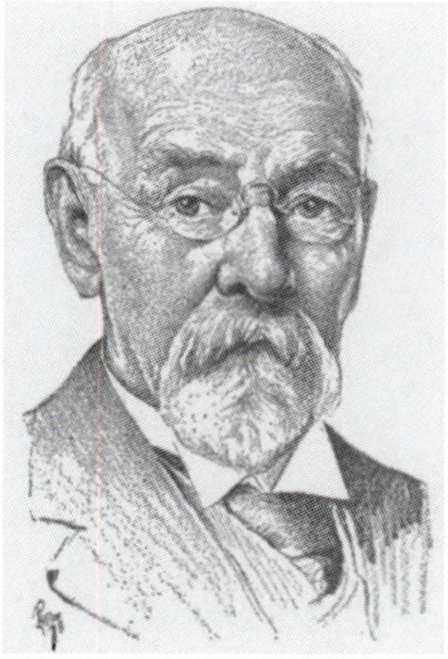

EDWARD CARY
(1840–1917)

Journalist, editor, and American Pre-Raphaelite collector. Staunch abolitionist, editor of the *Brooklyn Union*, and later member, editorial staff of the *New York Times*.

(Reproduced in obituary, *The Fourth Estate*, May 26, 1917: 30)

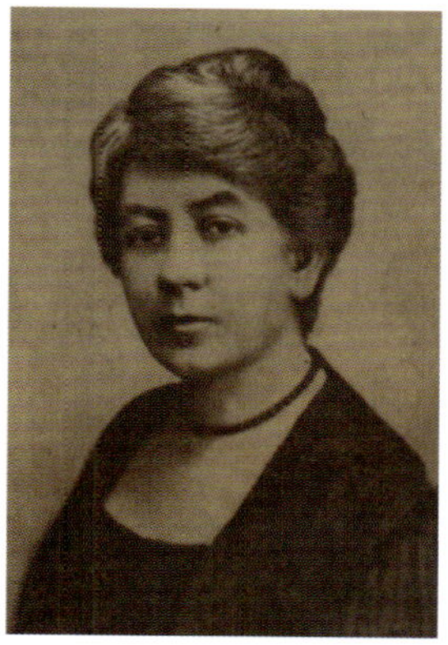

ELISABETH LUTHER CARY
(1867–1936)

Editor, art critic, author, and American Pre-Raphaelite collector; daughter of Edward Cary. Began publishing the journal *The Scrip* in 1905; first full-time art editor of the *New York Times* (1908–1936).

(Print Collection, Miriam and Ira D. Wallach Division of Art, Prints and Photographs, The New York Public Library)

CLARENCE COOK
(1828–1900)

Association member, editor of *The New Path*, critic, poet. Architectural drawing instructor at the Cooper Union. Editor of *The Independent*, then *The New Path*, and in 1864 became art critic for the *New-York Daily Tribune*. Published *The House Beautiful* (1878) and *What Shall We Do with Our Walls?* (1881), central texts of the American Aesthetic movement.

(See fig. 1 in Gallati essay.)

LOUISA DE WINDT WHITTEMORE COOK
(1821–1908)

Association member, wife of Clarence Cook. Suggested the title for *The New Path*. Clarence Cook dedicated *The House Beautiful* to her; she published a volume of his poems two years after his death.

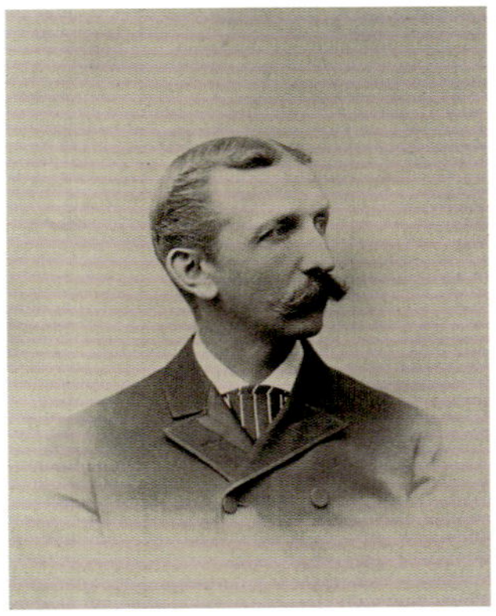

WILLIAM DOUGHTY
(1837/8–1909)

Honorary Association member (nominated by Eugene T. Gardner at meeting on February 18, 1863). Civil engineer and prominent figure in Troy, NY; trustee of Rensselaer Polytechnic Institute.

(Reproduced in George Baker Anderson, *Landmarks of Rensselaer County New York*, Syracuse, NY, 1897)

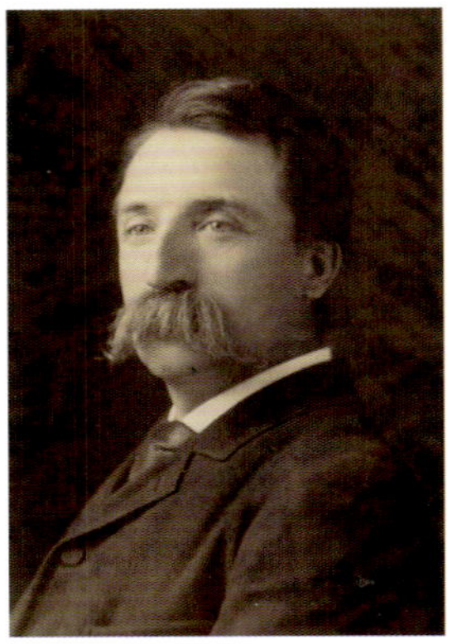

HENRY FARRER
(1844–1903)

Printmaker and watercolor artist; younger brother and pupil of T. C. Farrer who emigrated about 1862 (after T. C., who emigrated in 1858). A founder of and longtime exhibitor at the American Watercolor Society.

(Farrer Family Archives)

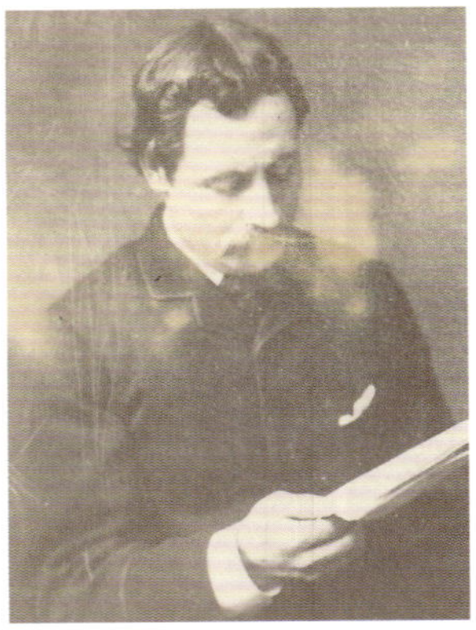

THOMAS CHARLES FARRER
(1839–1891)

Association founder, contributor to *The New Path*, artist in oil, watercolor, and later a printmaker. Studied in London with John Ruskin and Dante Gabriel Rossetti at the Working Men's College. In the United States from late 1858 to 1871, when he returned to England; served in Union army in spring/summer 1862; instructor at Cooper Union School of Design for Women, 1861–1865.

(Farrer Family Archives)

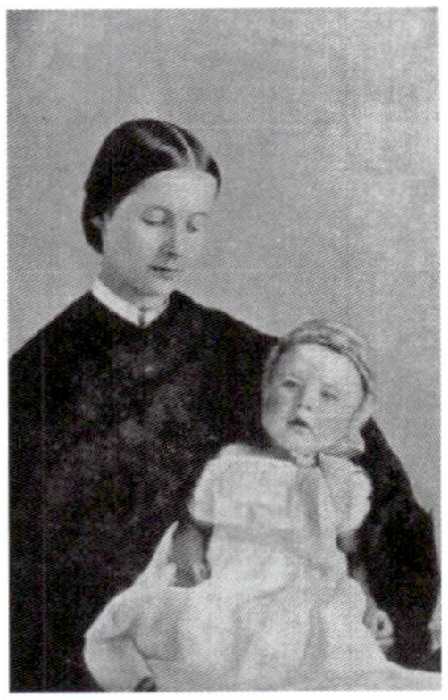

ANNIE R. MCLANE FARRER
(1836–1933)

Association member, wife of T. C. Farrer. Graduated from Rutgers Female Institute in 1855, where she may have taken drawing classes. Moved to England with Farrer around 1871.

(*Annie R. McLane Farrer with son Charles Moore Farrer.* Farrer Family Archives)

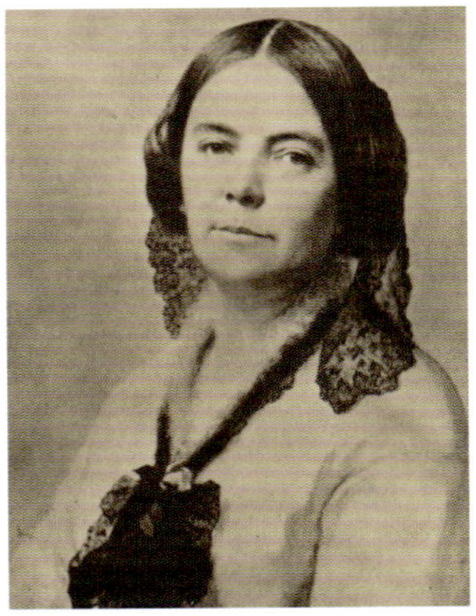

HENRIETTE DESPORTES FIELD
(1813–1875)

Crayon artist; principal of Cooper Union School of Design for Women and hired T. C. Farrer as drawing instructor in 1861. Married to Henry M. Field, Presbyterian minister and abolitionist. Her salon at their Gramercy Park residence attracted artists (Eastman Johnson was a friend) and literati. Hosted Association meeting on March 17, 1863.

(Courtesy of the Frick Art Reference Library)

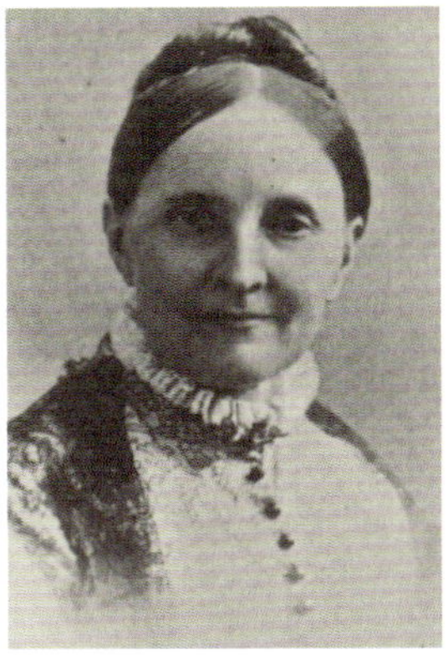

EMILY ELLSWORTH FOWLER FORD
(1826–1893)

Poet and childhood friend of Emily Dickinson, American Pre-Raphaelite collector, granddaughter of Noah Webster, and wife of Gordon Lester Ford.

(Reproduced in *Notes on the Life of Noah Webster*, vol. 1, comp. Emily Ellsworth Fowler Ford, ed. Emily Ellsworth Ford Skeel, New York, 1912)

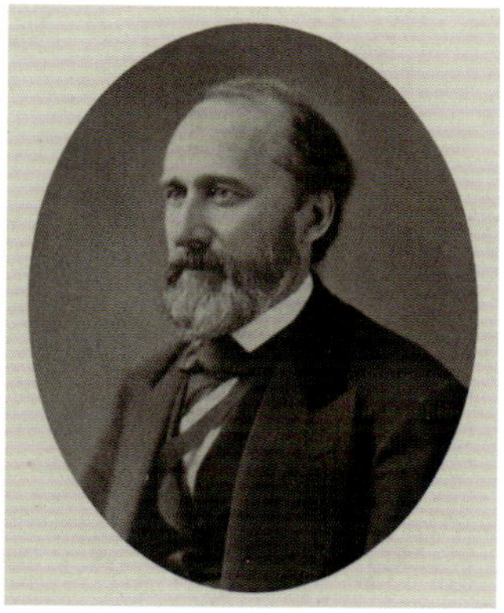

GORDON LESTER FORD
(1823–1891)

Newspaperman, bibliophile, lawyer, American Pre-Raphaelite collector, philanthropist. Business manager of *New York Tribune.* In 1863, became publisher of the *Brooklyn Union,* an abolitionist pro-Union paper. Helped found Brooklyn Art Association.

(Print Collection, Miriam and Ira D. Wallach Division of Art, Prints and Photographs, The New York Public Library)

EUGENE TERRY GARDNER
(1840–1910)

Association member, lawyer, brother of James Terry Gardner.

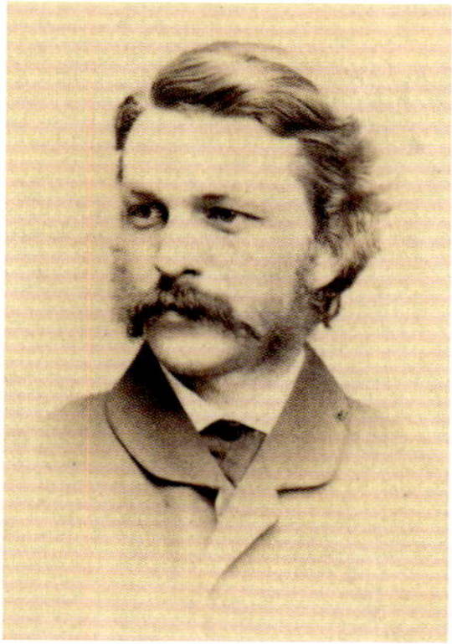

JAMES TERRY GARDNER
(1842–1912) (later spelled Gardiner)

Association member, topographer, civil engineer. Friend and Yale classmate of Clarence King. Traveled west with King, joined US Engineer Corps; surveyed Yosemite Valley in 1864. Appointed chief topographer of Fortieth Parallel Survey; later director of New York State [Geological] Survey.

(Rockwood, *James Terry Gardiner, age 21,* May 6, 1863. James Terry Gardiner Papers, Manuscript and Special Collections, New York State Library, Albany. See also Silas Selleck, *Clarence King and the Field Party of 1864,* in Timeline, p. 239.)

WILLIAM C. GILMAN
(1833–1922)

Subscriber to *The New Path,* insurance broker, American Pre-Raphaelite collector. Helped support publication of second volume of *The New Path.*

EASTBURN HASTINGS
(1833–1884)

Association member, architect; served in the Seventh Regiment, New York State Militia, Company H, during its one-month activation in 1861.

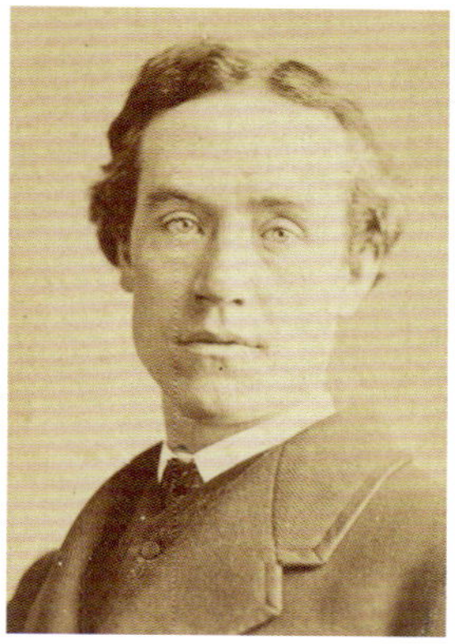

WILLIAM JOHN HENNESSY
(1839–1917)

Artist and illustrator; neighbor of T. C. Farrer in the University Building, NY. Left the United States to settle abroad in 1870.

(Paul Worman Fine Art, Worcester)

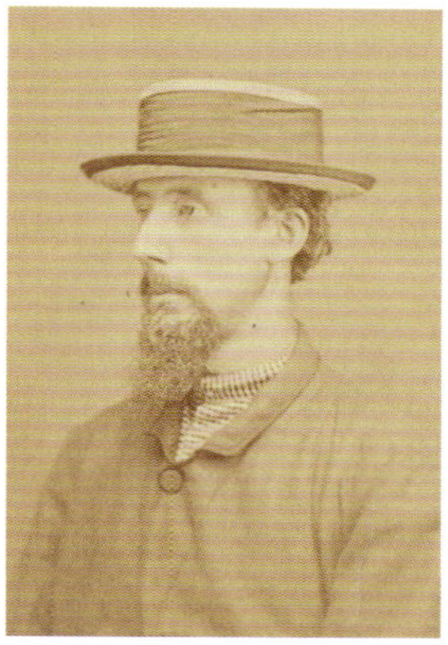

JOHN HENRY HILL
(1839–1922)

Association member, contributor to *The New Path,* artist in oil and watercolor and printmaker. Son of John William Hill. Like his father, an early convert to Ruskinian "truth to nature." In 1868 traveled west as staff artist for fellow member Clarence King's geological survey expedition. Sojourned at Lake George in the early 1870s, returning to the family homestead at West Nyack, NY, upon the death of his father in 1879.

(G. S. Irish, *John Henry Hill,* c. 1870s. Paul Worman Fine Art, Worcester)

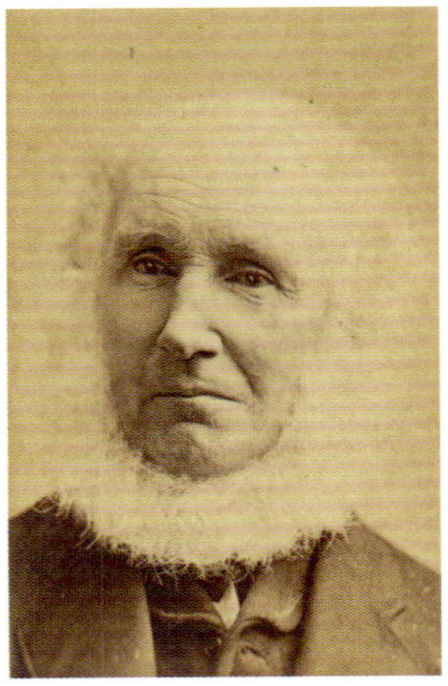

JOHN WILLIAM HILL
(1812–1879)

Association member and first president, artist in oil and watercolor and printmaker. Father of John Henry Hill and known as "Poppy" Hill. Topographical approach and technique of father and son transformed following the publication of Ruskin's *Modern Painters*. They welcomed T. C. Farrer to their West Nyack homestead shortly after his arrival in the United States.

(Paul Worman Fine Art, Worcester)

SARAH M. HITCHCOCK
(c. 1836–1891)

Art collector, philanthropist. Hosted Association's literary meeting on March 31, 1863.

FLORENCE HOWLAND
(1825–1911)

Association member, mother of Clarence King. From a Rhode Island family with strong abolitionist and temperance leanings. After the death of her husband (Clarence King's father), she married Brooklyn merchant George S. Howland, who supported King at the Sheffield Scientific School at Yale.

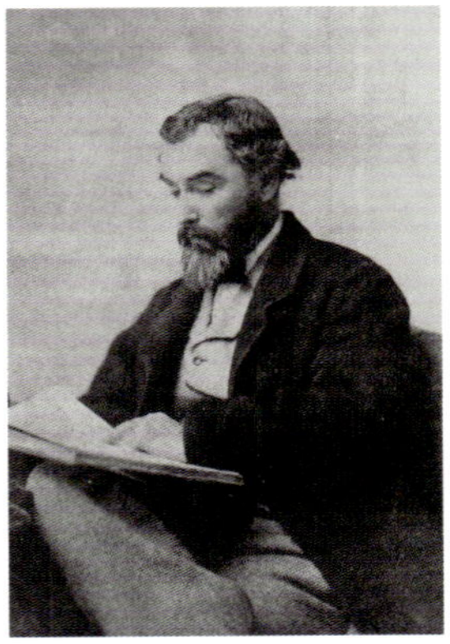

JAMES JACKSON JARVES
(1818–1888)

Subscriber to *The New Path*; writer and critic often at odds with the editorial slant of both *The Crayon* and *The New Path*. Nonetheless, an ardent Ruskinian and a prominent early collector of early Italian paintings (sold to Yale in 1871).

(James Jackson Jarves Papers, Manuscripts and Archives, Yale University Library)

CLARENCE R. KING
(1842–1901)

Association member, geologist. Headed Fortieth Parallel Survey from 1867 to 1872. Became director of the US Geological Survey in 1879. Met John Ruskin in England in 1883 and reportedly purchased two J. M. W. Turner paintings from Ruskin.

(See Silas Selleck, *Clarence King and the Field Party of 1864*, in Timeline, p. 239.)

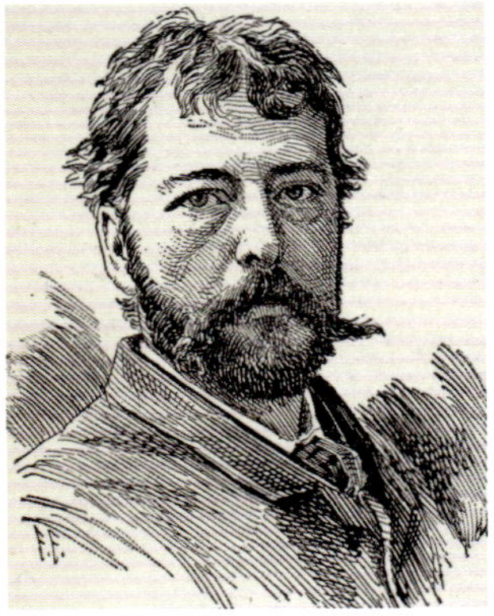

FRANCIS LATHROP
(1849–1909)

Subscriber to *The New Path,* decorative painter. Attended Association meeting on February 23, 1865. Student of T. C. Farrer and later of Ford Madox Brown, and Edward Burne-Jones in London. Member, National Society of Mural Painters; assisted John La Farge with wall paintings for Trinity Church, Boston. Selected by Clarence Cook to illustrate *The House Beautiful.*

(Reproduced in "Francis Lathrop," *The National Cyclopedia of American Biography*, vol. 9. New York, 1901: 292)

DR. JOHN E. LAUER
(Dates unknown)

Subscriber to *The New Path;* collector.

J. L. LITTELL (LITTLE?) (MISS OR MRS.)
(Dates unkown)

Subscriber to *The New Path.*

JOHN MATTHEWS JR.
(1832–1883)

Association member, brother-in-law of Carl Muller, manufacturer of soda fountains (invented by his father) famous for their elaborate ornamentation.

MARGARET J. MCDONALD
(1839–1881)

Artist in watercolor and decorative painting, teacher. Student of T. C. Farrer. Attended Cooper Union School of Design for Women and member, American Watercolor Society.

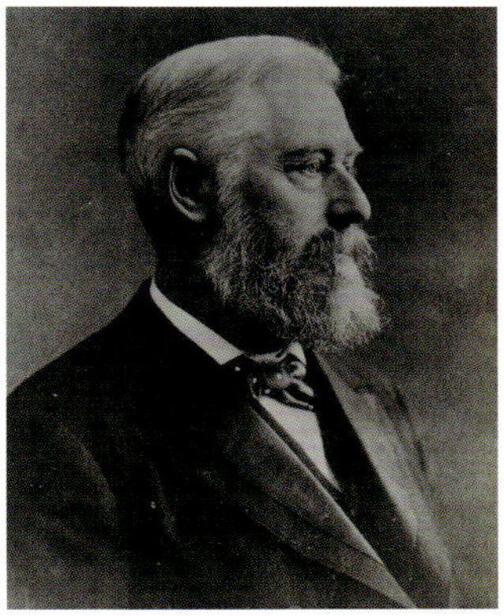

CHARLES HERBERT MOORE
(1840–1930)

Association member, artist in oil and watercolor and printmaker, contributor to *The New Path*. In 1871 accepted Charles Eliot Norton's invitation to teach drawing at Lawrence Scientific School at Harvard; in 1875, transferred to Harvard College faculty to teach art history with Norton. First curator and director of the Fogg Art Museum. On his retirement in 1909, settled in England.

(Harvard Art Museums/Harvard Art Museums Archives, Fogg History Photographs)

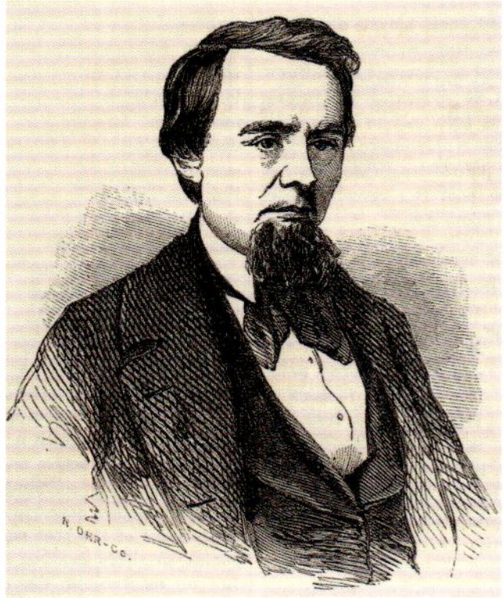

CARL MULLER
(c. 1820–1887)

Attended Association meeting on February 4, 1863, with member and brother-in-law John Matthews Jr.; sculptor and designer for Union Porcelain Works in Brooklyn.

(Reproduced in "Masters of Art and Literature," *Cosmopolitan Art Journal* 1, no. 3 [March 1857]: 84)

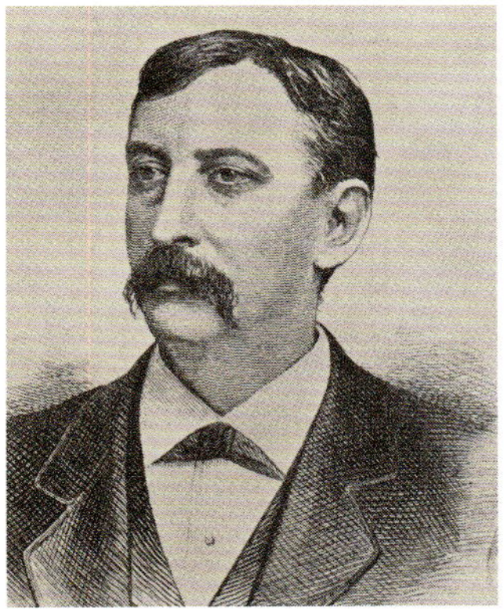

JAMES E. MUNSON
(1835–1906)

Association member, court stenographer, lawyer.

(Reproduced in Myron A. Munson, *The Munson Record: A Genealogical and Biographical Account of Captain Thomas Munson [A Pioneer of Hartford and New Haven] and His Descendants*, vol. 2. New Haven, CT, 1895: 871)

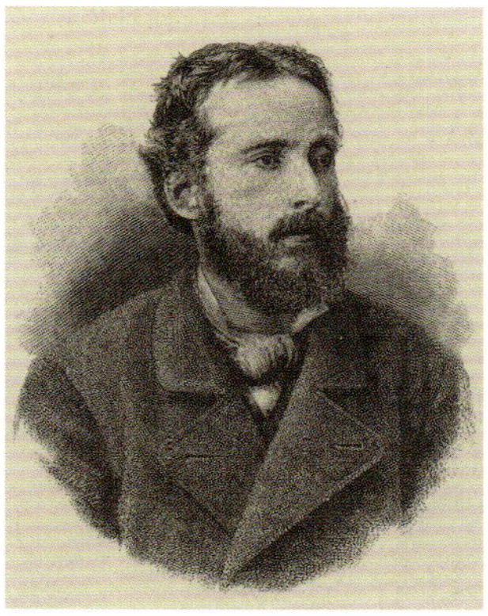

HENRY RODERICK NEWMAN
(1843–1917)

Association member, artist (specialist in watercolor); mentored by T. C. Farrer; taught at Cooper Union, 1864–1866. In 1870, traveled to Europe; settled in Florence in 1874. In 1877, Charles Herbert Moore introduced his work to Ruskin, who became a patron. Made first trip to Egypt in 1887–1888, returning nearly every winter thereafter; traveled to Japan in 1896–1897.

(*Henry Roderick Newman*, after F. Guidi. Reproduced in Forman 1884: 527)

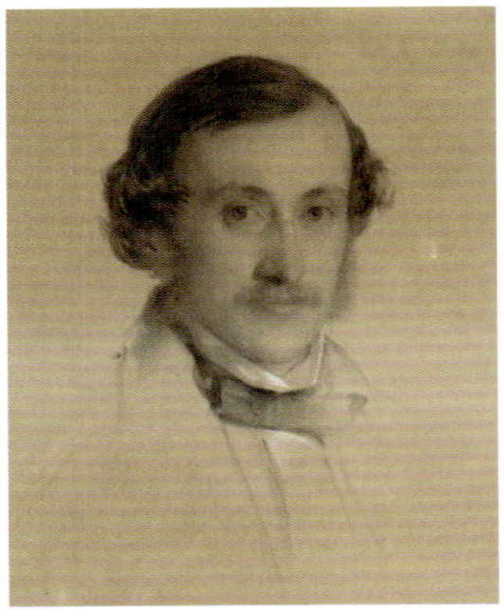

CHARLES ELIOT NORTON
(1827–1908)

Ruskin's literary executor and a lifetime friend. Used his positions as editor of *The North American Review* and founder of *The Nation* to promote the American Pre-Raphaelite movement. In 1871 Norton enlisted Charles Herbert Moore to teach drawing at Harvard's Lawrence Scientific School.

(Samuel W. Rowse, *Charles Eliot Norton*, 1858. Harvard University Portrait Collection, Bequest of Susan Norton to Harvard University, 1989)

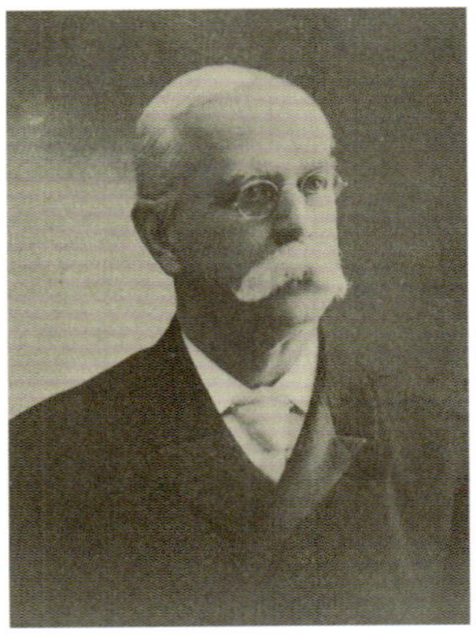

ROBERT J. PATTISON
(1838–1903)

Association member, artist in oil and watercolor, partner in the firm of V. G. Stiepevich and Company, Mural Decorators, drawing teacher in New York and Brooklyn.

(Collection of the Brooklyn Historical Society)

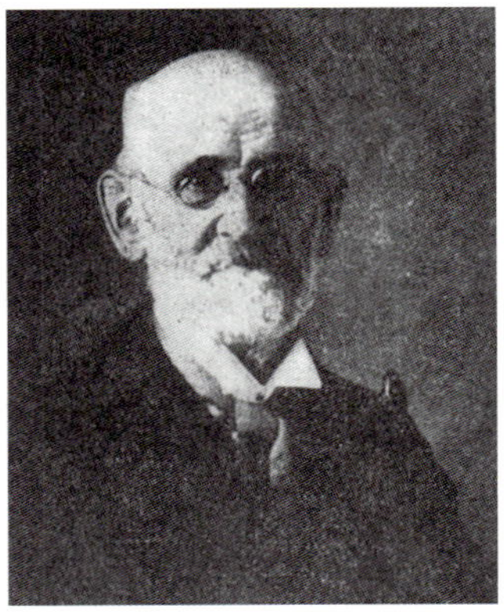

GEORGE PHILIP PHILES
(1828–1913)

Subscriber to *The New Path*, publisher, bibliophile, and book dealer.

(Reproduced in Lydenberg 1954: 5)

BENJAMIN RICHARDS JR.
(Dates unknown)

Subscriber to *The New Path*.

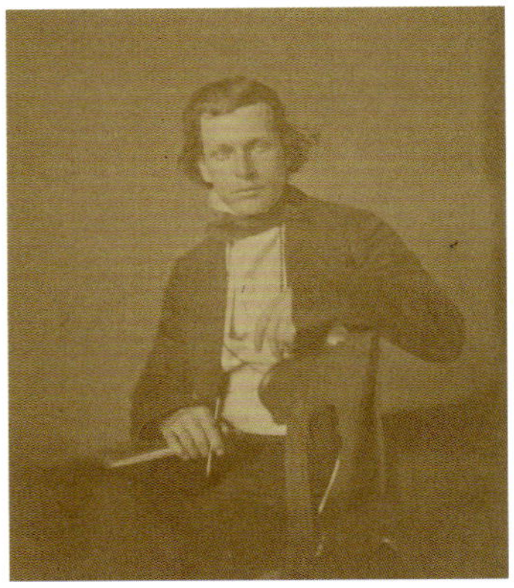

WILLIAM TROST RICHARDS
(1833–1905)

Association member, artist in oil and watercolor. Pursued Ruskinian realism from 1858 until the late 1860s, when he turned from landscapes to marine subjects in both oil and watercolor.

(*William Trost Richards*, c. 1855. William Trost Richards Papers, Archives of American Art, Smithsonian Institution)

T. N. ROOKER
(Dates unknown)

Subscriber to *The New Path*.

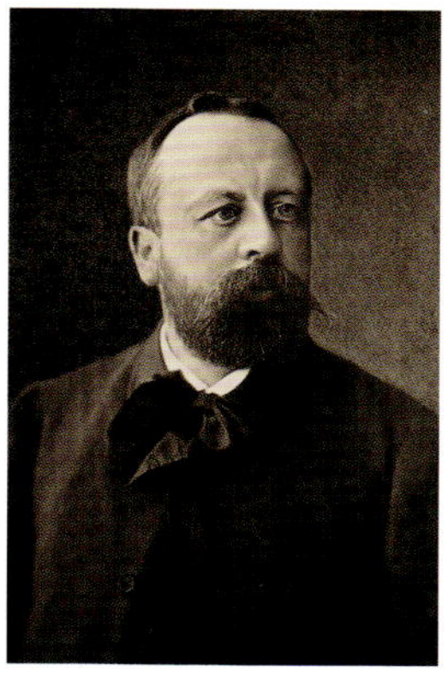

EUGENE SCHUYLER
(1840–1890)

Association member, diplomat, historian. Gifted linguist and translator; earned PhD and law degrees. Held consular posts in Russia, Romania, Constantinople, Greece.

(Reproduced as frontispiece in Schuyler and Schaeffer 1901)

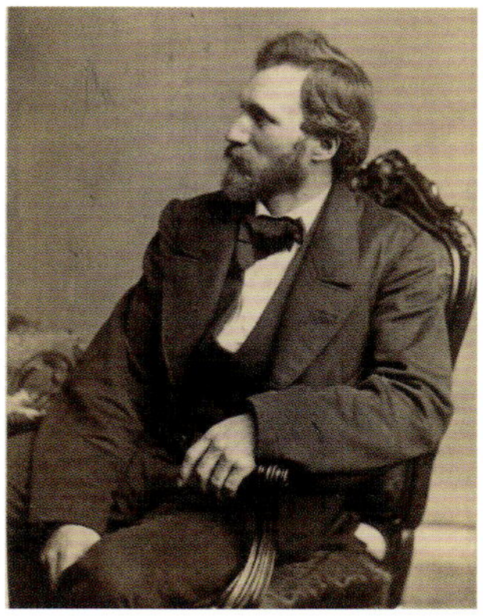

AARON DRAPER SHATTUCK
(1832–1928)

Artist admired by the American Pre-Raphaelites. His landscapes displayed Ruskinian influence from the late 1850s to c. mid-1860s.

(George Gardner Rockwood, *Aaron Draper Shattuck*, 1860s. The Metropolitan Museum of Art, The Albert Ten Eyck Gardner Collection, Gift of the Centennial Committee, 1970)

R. H. SMITH
(Dates unknown)

Subscriber to *The New Path*.

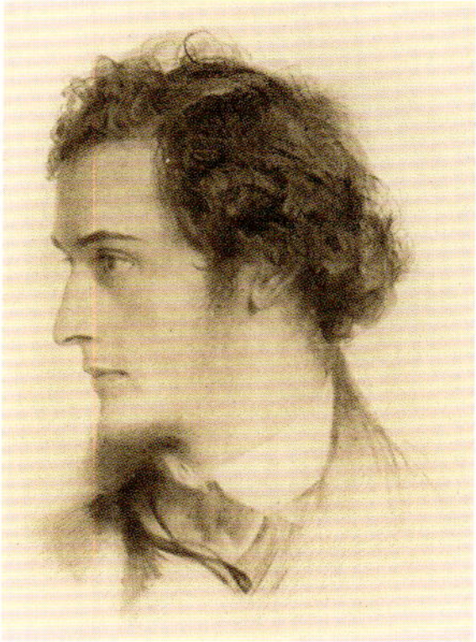

WILLIAM JAMES STILLMAN
(1828–1901)

Painter, photographer, writer, editor, diplomat. Met Ruskin in 1850 and became familiar with the British Pre-Raphaelites. Cofounder of *The Crayon* in 1855; contributor to *The New Path*. Keen woodsman and associate of Ralph Waldo Emerson. Following the death of his first wife, married Pre-Raphaelite artist and model Marie Spartali in 1871; settled in England.

(Samuel W. Rowse, *William James Stillman*, c. 1858. Reproduced in Stillman 1901: frontispiece)

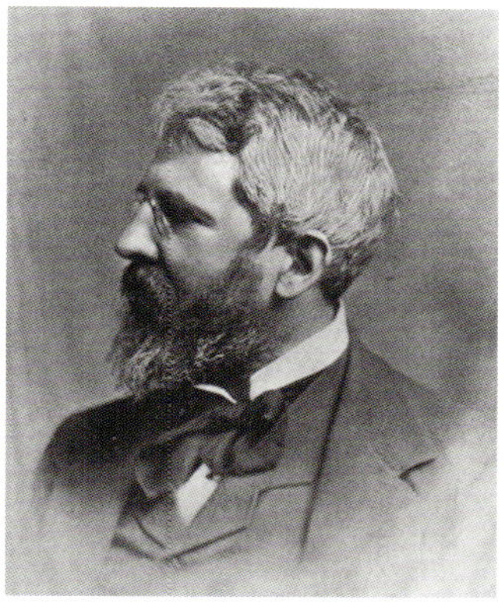

RUSSELL STURGIS JR.
(1836–1909)

Association member, architect, critic, contributor to *The New Path*. Attended the Free Academy (later City College) of New York with James Lyman Van Buren and close friend Peter Wight. Strong proponent of Gothic architecture; designed Battell Chapel and Durfee Hall at Yale. Appointed professor of architecture at City College and in 1893, awarded university's first honorary doctorate. Art critic of *The Nation* and contributor to *The North American Review*.

(*Russell Sturgis Jr.*, 1880. Reproduced in Everett P. Wheeler, "Russell Sturgis," *The City College Quarterly* 5 [1909]: 12–13)

SARAH STRONG TUTHILL
(1830–1882)

Association member, art teacher. Graduate of Mount Holyoke Seminary. Taught in Chicago, Bridgeport, CT, and at a women's college in Alabama at the start of the Civil War. In 1863, began long tenure as art teacher at Miss Porter's School in Farmington, CT. Taught nephew Robert Brandegee, who succeeded her at Miss Porter's School. Joined Mary L. Booth and others in advocating for women's rights. Exhibited at American Watercolor Society, 1867–1868.

(See fig. 4 in Ferber essay.)

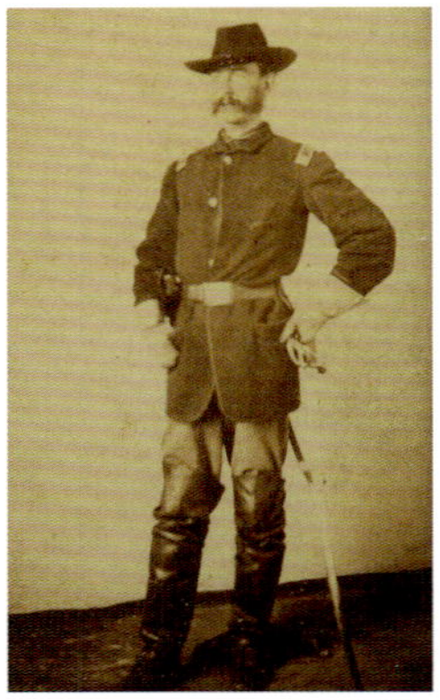

JAMES LYMAN VAN BUREN
(1837–1866)

Association member, lawyer, soldier. Cousin of President Martin Van Buren. Scholar of modern languages. Second lieutenant and later brigadier general in Union army; fought alongside General Grant in the Richmond campaign. Sturgis signed for him at last AATA meeting. Died in 1866 of illnesses contracted during his military service.

(Courtesy Heritage Auctions)

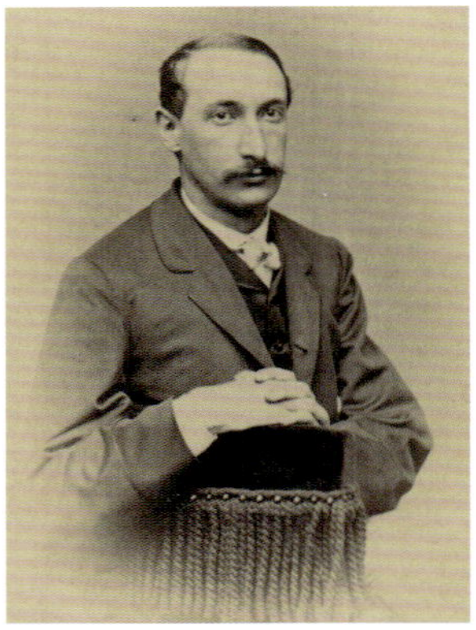

PETER BONNETT WIGHT
(1838–1925)

Association member, architect, critic, contributor to *The New Path*. Proponent of Ruskin's polychromatic Italianate Gothic architectural style. Won competition for first permanent building of the National Academy of Design (1865), architect for the Yale School of Fine Arts building (1867). Rebuilt residences and commercial buildings after Great Chicago Fire (1871), developing fireproofing construction technology. Published a memoir of the American Pre-Raphaelite movement in *The Development of Fine Arts in America* in 1884.

(J. Gurney & Son, *Peter Bonnett Wight*, 1860s. The Metropolitan Museum of Art, The Albert Ten Eyck Gardner Collection, Gift of the Centennial Committee, 1970)

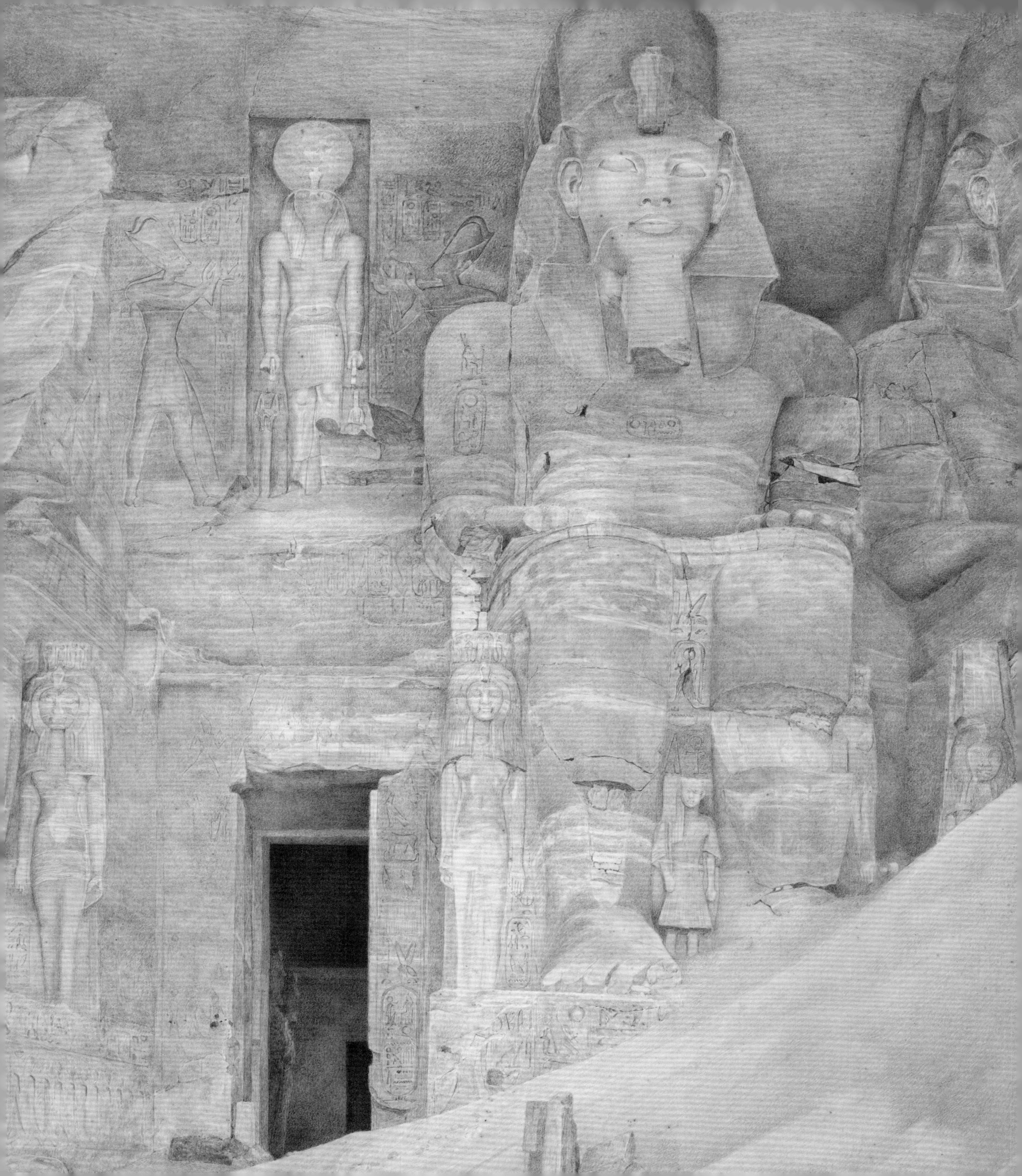

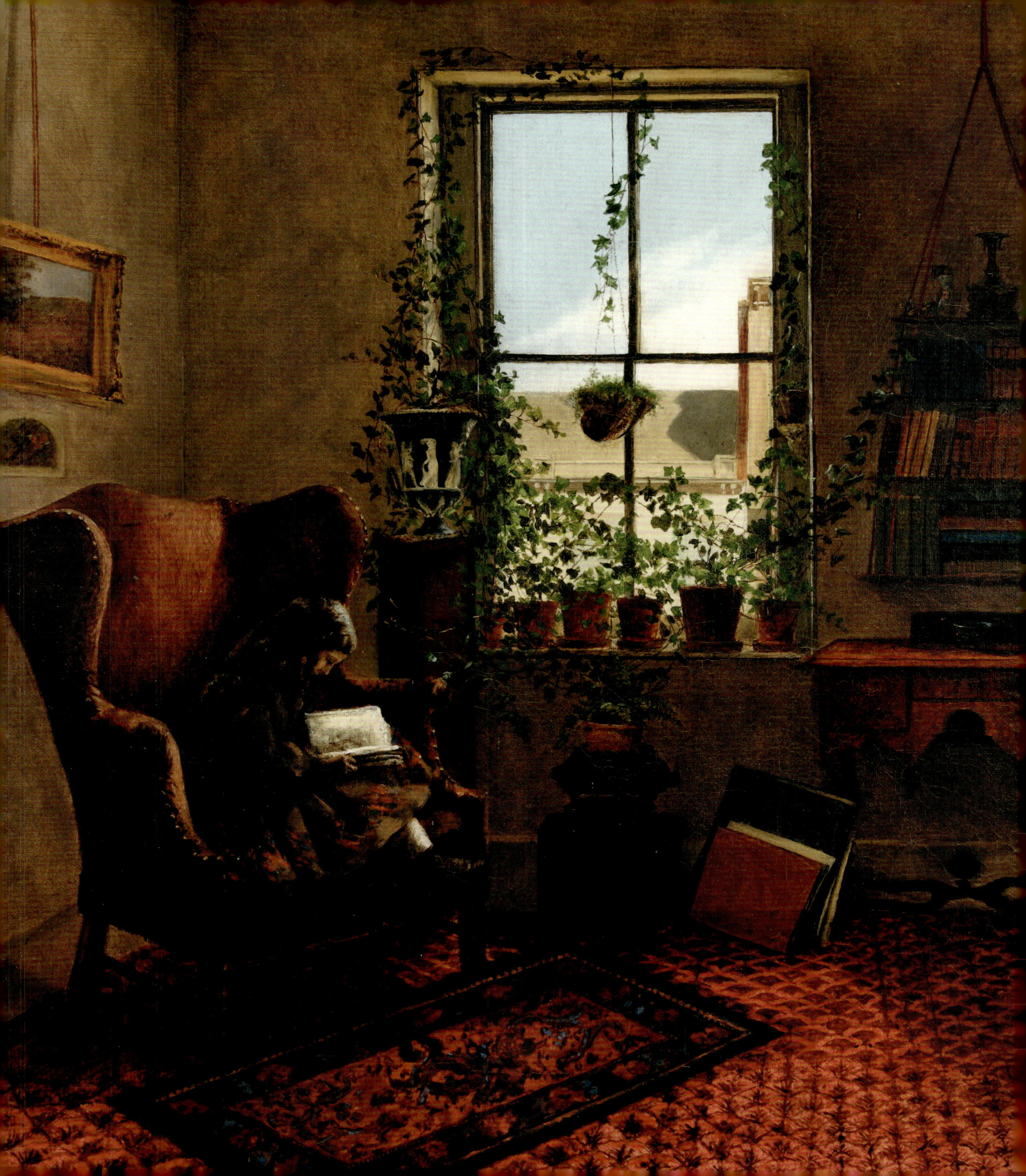

Notes

Who Were the American Pre-Raphaelites?

LINDA S. FERBER

I am deeply grateful to my cocurator, Nancy Anderson, who has flawlessly guided our team through the complexities of organizing the exhibition and writing this book and for her critical role in shaping the Timeline. My personal thanks go to Nancy, Sophie Lynford, and Caroline Weaver for advice and generous support when I was writing the introduction.

1 John Ruskin, preface to *Modern Painters*, 2nd ed. (1844), 1:lii.

2 Any investigation of Ruskin and the American Pre-Raphaelite movement, including this one, builds upon the pioneering studies of William H. Gerdts in Gerdts 1969 and "Through a Glass Brightly: The American Pre-Raphaelites and Their Still Lifes and Nature Studies" in Ferber and Gerdts 1985.

3 Ruskin, *Modern Painters*, vol. 1 (1843).

4 For discussions of the political and social implications of the Gothic revival style, see Tim Barringer's and Sophie Lynford's essays in this volume.

5 Stein 1967, 41.

6 Clarence Cook, "The Modern Architecture of New York," *The New York Quarterly* 4, no. 1 (April 1855): 106, cited in Simoni 1952, 434.

7 Linda S. Ferber, "Asher B. Durand, American Landscape Painter," in Linda S. Ferber, ed., *Kindred Spirits: Asher B. Durand and the American Landscape* (Brooklyn Museum, New York, 2007), 171, 174, 181; Linda S. Ferber, *The Hudson River School: Nature and the American Vision* (New-York Historical Society, 2009), 82.

8 John Ruskin to William J. Stillman, Denmark Hill, March 28, 1855, published in "Sketchings," *The Crayon* 1 (May 2, 1855): 288. See Sophie Lynford's essay in this volume for Ruskin's ambivalent attitudes toward social and political matters in the United States, especially regarding the American Civil War.

9 Norton's watercolor was acquired in 1858 from the important American Exhibition of British Art. Although Ruskin wrote to Norton in October 1858 expressing dissatisfaction with the drawing, by 1886 he had changed his mind and concluded, "There is no drawing of stone by my hand as good as your boulder." Ruskin's correspondence is cited in Rachel Rosenfield, cat. 53 in Marjorie B. Cohn, *Wash and Gouache: A Study of the Development of the Materials of Watercolor* (Center for Conservation and Technical Studies, Fogg Art Museum, Cambridge, MA, 1977), 107–108; Ferber and Gerdts 1985, cat. 125, 284–285.

10 Farrer's studio at 32 Waverly Place was located in a wing on the north side of the New York University Building. An early landmark of the collegiate Gothic style, the University Building also housed many artists. Their studio addresses were customarily listed in National Academy of Design (NAD) records as "N. Y. University"; nevertheless, Farrer's name is on the 1859 university rent rolls for a studio whose address he listed in 1863 and 1864 as 32 Waverly Place. His neighbors included Winslow Homer, William J. Hennessy, and Eugene Benson. (Dr. Margaret R. Laster and I thank New York University Archives for assistance in her research.)

11 See also Gerdts, "Through a Glass Brightly," in Ferber and Gerdts 1985, 40.
12 Lynford 2019.
13 For an annotated list of all individuals in the "Minutes of the Association for the Advancement of Truth in Art," see pp. 242–250.
14 For further information about affiliated and unaffiliated artists, see Timeline.
15 "The Yale Art Exhibition," *New Haven Daily Palladium*, July 12, 1867, 2.
16 Cohn Rosenfield 1977, 50–52; Foster, "The Pre-Raphaelite Medium," in Ferber and Gerdts 1985, 79–105; Ferber and Gallati 1998, 24–27, 60–62, 70–71; Foster 2017, 45–57.
17 See also Gerdts, "Through a Glass Brightly," in Ferber and Gerdts 1985, 40–41.
18 "The Yale Exhibition," *Hartford Daily Courant*, July 12, 1867, 4; Tuckerman 1867, 524. Ferber 2008 includes an excerpt from a review by Eugene Benson of Richards's *Path in the Woods* (plate 77), as well as Clarence Cook's comments on his *October* (plate 78).
19 For Wight and Sturgis, see Pearson 1999; for Wight, see Landau 1981; for Sturgis, see Alexis 1986.
20 Sturgis, "An Important Gothic Building," *The New Path* 2, no. 2 (June 1864): 17–32.
21 Peter B. Wight, "Reminiscences of the Building of the Academy of Design," *New York Times*, April 22, 1900, 25. Sophie Lynford discusses the project in her essay in this volume.
22 For an examination of the American Pre-Raphaelites' involvement in the building of Street Hall and the mounting of the inaugural exhibition in its galleries, see Lynford 2019.
23 Sturgis, "Mr. Street's Gift to Yale College," *The New Path* 2, no. 9 (September 1865): 146–149; Sturgis, "Fine Arts: The Yale College Art Building and Exhibition," *The Nation* 5, no. 110 (August 8, 1867): 115–116.
24 Sturgis's buildings at Yale are Farnham Hall, 1868; Durfee Hall, 1870; Battell Chapel, 1872–1873; Lawrance Hall, 1884.
25 Sturgis, "Art Criticism," *The New Path* 2, no. 12 (April 1864): 154–155.
26 Sturgis, "Our Artists and Their Critics," *The New Path* 2, no. 1 (May 1864): 3.
27 "Articles of Organization," in Wight Papers. The manifesto that opened "Articles of Organization" was published in Wight 1884, 14–16.
28 Cook, "Introductory," *The New Path* 1, no. 1 (May 1863): 1. For *The New Path* and Cook see also Gerdts, "Through a Glass Brightly," in Ferber and Gerdts 1985, 39.
29 These memorable remarks (vintage Cook) reached a much wider readership because, by February 1864, Horace Greeley had engaged Cook to write for the *New-York Daily Tribune*. In 1865, Sturgis was appointed as art critic for the newly founded progressive journal *The Nation*. (Cook, "Exhibition of Pictures at the Sanitary Fair," *New-York Daily Tribune*, April 16, 1864, 12, quoted in Simoni 1952, 250.)
30 "Notices of the Press" were regularly published in *The New Path*; these are from the *Springfield Republican* (September 1865) and the *Hartford Evening Press* (August 1865). The strongest opinion in print came from artist-critic Eugene Benson, the ablest of the Association's critical opponents. Cook and Sturgis consistently (and cruelly) panned his paintings, possibly because Benson had exhibited a parody of Farrer's *Gone! Gone!* (plate 12) at the 1863 NAD annual titled *Coming Tears* (unlocated). The heat of the culture wars fueled Benson's protest in 1865 that "we are overrun by the maggots that have crawled out of the literary body of John Ruskin." See "A New Art Critic," *Atlantic Monthly* 16, no. 95 (September 1865): 325.
31 Sturgis, "Art Criticism," *The New Path* 2, no. 12 (April 1864): 153–157.
32 Cook, part 1: "Art: The Cooper Institute 'School of Design for Women,'" *The Round Table* 2, no. 5 (October 7, 1865), 71; part 2: *The Round Table* 2, no. 6 (October 14, 1865): 92–93. See also Gerdts, "Through a Glass Brightly," in Ferber and Gerdts 1985, 61–62, for Farrer's methods at Cooper Union; Wiles 2001, 38–40; Masten 2008, 91–128.
33 Ruskin 1857, 48–49.
34 "Articles of Organization," Wight 1884, 15. The Articles mention mentoring "the class of mechanics" as well as "meritorious artists," 14. Both were to be served by *The New Path*'s series of ten photographs "from original drawings and paintings" by member artists recalled by Wight (20) and discussed by Diane Waggoner in this volume. Cook himself was especially passionate about the benefits of Farrer's Ruskinian regimen at Cooper Union to prepare women for careers. Farrer's departure and the discontinuance of his program for conventional methods infuriated Cook ("the present head of the school [has] thrown Mr. Farrer's plants and flowers, and lichened rocks and birds, out a window"), inspiring the two-part critique of Cooper Union's founders and managers cited in note 29.
35 After receiving a drawing from Margaret McDonald, the elder Hill invited her "to spend a week or two with us this season... when we will try and do something out of doors." J. W. Hill to Miss McDonald, March 26, 1867, "Hill, John W.," Ford Papers, quoted in Masten 2008, 113, 280n80.
36 Hill 1867, 1. Several other Association artists were also active in the rise of the American etching revival, a development that paralleled the rise of the American watercolor movement and the later nineteenth century's reassessment of these so-called minor mediums. Printmaking members included the Hills (originally trained in the medium as topographical draftsmen), both Farrer brothers, and Moore. Richards was not a printmaker but produced designs and drawings for engravers early in his career. See Gerdts, "Through a Glass Brightly," in Ferber and Gerdts 1985, 41. For the American etching revival see S. R. Koehler, "The Works of the American Etchers: XII. J. Henry Hill," *The American Art Review* 1, no. 10 (August

1880): 429–430; Francine Tyler, *American Etchings of the Nineteenth Century* (New York, 1984); Phyllis Peet, *American Women of the Etching Revival* (High Museum of Art, Atlanta, 1988); Rona Schneider, "The American Etching Revival: Its French Sources and Early Years," *The American Art Journal* 14, no. 4 (Autumn 1982): 40–65; Rona Schneider, *American Painter Etchings, 1853–1908* (New York, 1989); Nancy Finlay, "The Hermit of Phantom Island: John Henry Hill's Etchings of Lake George," in *Adirondack Prints and Printmakers: The Call of the Wild*, ed. Caroline M. Welsh (Syracuse, NY, 1998), 105–124.

37 For the dead bird motif see also Gerdts, "Through a Glass Brightly," in Ferber and Gerdts 1985, 50–53, and Mark Mitchell's essay in this volume.

38 Leith 1996, 12. Much later in Florence, Newman mentored a number of young artists from Harvard recommended by Moore, including Harold Broadfield Warren, Denman Ross, and Joseph Lindon Smith (Leith 1996, 31–37; Stebbins and Anderson 2007, 100, 101); Sarah Strong Tuthill graduated from Mount Holyoke College in 1850 as an art teacher. She taught at several posts during the 1850s (leaving her position at a girls' school in Alabama as the Civil War began). In 1863, she began her long tenure as art teacher at Miss Porter's School. A family member's diary recalls that, as "an accomplished artist, [she] strove to record natural objects as they truly were. Still lifes, especially birds, were her specialty. She displayed her work at national exhibitions and achieved renown as a practitioner of the 'Pre-Raphaelite' art style." Tuthill's later sojourn in Paris (seemingly a sabbatical "to perfect her technique") from 1877 to 1880 ended with illness, as did her career at Miss Porter's. She died of cancer in Brooklyn in 1883 (White 2003, 17–18). Fidelia Bridges, Richards's best-known student, recalled: "In the year 1860, I went to Philadelphia to study art. Mr. Richards who was ever ready to render help, especially to women, kindly proposed my coming to paint in his studio where there were some half-dozen pupils" (quoted in Hill 1981, 10). Pattison's 1903 eulogy noted that he had taught "a long while in private academies in New York" before moving to Brooklyn (*The High School Recorder*, 1903, n.p.).

39 Mather 1957, 57–63; Stebbins and Anderson 2007; Renn 2012.

40 Cook, "Another Artists' Reception," *New-York Daily Tribune*, April 14, 1863, 2 (quoted in Simoni 1952, 240).

41 For Wight's war services see Landau 1981, 5, and Sophie Lynford's essay in this volume as well as Lynford 2019.

42 The American Pre-Raphaelites were represented. Richards's *October* (plate 78) was loaned by Marshall O. Roberts. Three works by Association members were included among the nearly two hundred donated for the "Pro Patria" benefit sale: Moore's *Landscape* (cat. 227); Newman's *Study from Nature* (cat. 330); and T. C. Farrer's *Twilight* (cat. 349, fig. 7 in this essay) (see Metropolitan Fair 1864 in Bibliography). Thanks to Sophie Lynford for bringing these to my attention. For the Sanitary Fair exhibitions see Evdokia Savidou-Terrono "For 'The Boys in Blue': The Art Galleries of the Sanitary Fairs" (PhD diss., City University of New York, 2002) and Charlotte Emans Moore, "Art as Text, War as Context: The Art Gallery at the Metropolitan Fair, New York City's Artistic Community, and the Civil War" (PhD diss., Boston University, 2009).

43 Cook, "The Exhibition of Pictures at the Sanitary Fair," *New-York Daily Tribune*, April 9, 1864, 12, and April 16, 1864, 12. Farrer's *Twilight* (fig. 7) is a reprise (moved outdoors) of his earlier and larger treatment in 1860 of this poignant wartime theme, *Gone! Gone!* (plate 12). *Twilight* was likely displayed again in 1867 at Yale, loaned by William Gilman, the premier private collector of American Pre-Raphaelites.

44 Kevin Avery notes that Worthington Whittredge was undoubtedly referring to Cook in his 1905 *Autobiography* when he recalled the "savage critic in the New York Tribune" who may also have coined the then-pejorative term Hudson River School. Kevin J. Avery, "A Historiography of the Hudson River School," in Howat 1987, 3–4.

45 Foster 2017, 56–57.

46 Street Hall: Kenny 2011, 153; Lynford 2019.

47 Gerdts, "Through a Glass Brightly," in Ferber and Gerdts 1985, 70–71; Lynford 2019. Thanks to May Brawley Hill and Thomas Parker for allowing me to read their individual unpublished works on this topic.

48 *First Annual Exhibition of the Yale School of the Fine Arts, Founded as a Department of Yale College, by the Late Augustus Russell Street* (New Haven, CT, 1867), hereafter Yale 1867.

49 Clarence Cook, "Fine Arts in New-Haven," *New-York Daily Tribune*, August 14, 1867, 2.

50 "The Yale Art Exhibition," *Hartford Daily Courant*, July 12, 1867, 4.

51 For the post-1870 aftermath of the movement, see also Gerdts, "Through a Glass Brightly," in Ferber and Gerdts 1985, 70–73.

52 In 1884 Wight did not include Richards in his reprise of former members, but instead singled him out as one of the "realists . . . who were opposed both to criticism and association" (23). In fact, T. C. Farrer and Richards were in touch by late 1862 and the founder nominated him for membership at the March 5 Association meeting. After delays in voting, during which a letter seemed to have been solicited from the candidate, he was elected on April 7. An educated guess suggests that Cook delayed the vote given his harsh treatment of Richards in his notorious review of the Metropolitan Fair. Despite a nod to the "naturalism" of Richards's *October* (plate 78), Cook maliciously declared that the artist was not in fact a

Pre-Raphaelite. "It is from Dusseldorf, not from London that he draws his inspiration." Richards may have resigned in protest. His name is not on the final roll call of "members of the Association at its demise" (Minutes, March 1864). Cook's vendetta continued into the next decade; in 1877, Richards seems to have been deliberately excluded from membership or exhibition privileges by the Society of American Artists. In 1878, Richards lamented, surely with Cook in mind, "the unreasonableness and malignity of Art Critics!!" (Ferber 1980, 302, 304).

53 Pattison loaned five paintings, all displayed in the South Gallery: 179, *Winter Scene near Harlem*; 180, *Baltimore Oriole*; 181, *Dandelion*; 183, *White Mountains from Shelbourne*; 191, *Study of a Turtle*. Yale 1867, 12–13.

54 Wight 1884, 23–24.

55 Hill, "John Henry Hill," in Ferber and Gerdts 1985, 174–175; Joni Kinsey, "Shoshone Falls: The Niagara of the West," *SiteLines* 10, no. 2 (Spring 2015): 16–18.

56 Cook, "Art in America in 1883," *Princeton Review* 2 (May 1883): 311–320. For the Society of American Artists see Jennifer A. Bienenstock, "The Formation and Early Years of the Society of American Artists: 1877–1884" (PhD diss., The City University of New York, 1983).

57 Doreen Bolger Burke, et al., *In Pursuit of Beauty: Americans and the Aesthetic Movement* (Metropolitan Museum of Art, New York, 1986): 133–134, 327–329, 412–413, 476, 486.

58 The Brooklyn Art Association's 1879 Fall Exhibition included a memorial exhibition of some nineteen watercolors by J. W. Hill. Most were loaned by Gordon L. Ford, Alexander Forman, and Edward Cary (Marlor 1970, 227, 400). Hill also loaned fourteen of his father's works to the 1880 American Watercolor Society exhibition (Foster 2017, 409n2).

59 Hill 1888, 4–10.

60 Samuel Isham, *The History of American Painting* (New York, 1905), 243.

61 Cary 1906.

62 Cary 1900, 52. William Gerdts first recognized the Carys as the keepers of the American Pre-Raphaelite flame (Gerdts, "Through a Glass Brightly," in Ferber and Gerdts 1985, 75).

A Radical Legacy: The British Pre-Raphaelites and Global Pre-Raphaelitism

TIM BARRINGER

1 For a belated reassertion of this twentieth-century critique, see Roberta Smith, "Blazing a Trail for Hypnotic Hyper-Realism: 'Pre-Raphaelites' at National Gallery of Art," *New York Times*, March 23, 2013.

2 Augustus Welby Northmore Pugin, *Contrasts, or A Parallel between the Noble Edifices of the Fourteenth and Fifteenth Centuries, and Similar Buildings of the Present Day; Shewing the Present Decay of Taste*, 2nd ed. (London, 1841).

3 Charles Dickens, "Old Lamps for New Ones," *Household Words* 12 (June 15, 1850): 265.

4 Charlotte Brontë to W. S. Williams, *Macmillan's Magazine*, August 1891, vol. 64, 280, quoted in "Introduction," in Ruskin 1903–1912, vol. 3, xxxix.

5 William James Stillman, "Modern Painters, Volume 5 by J. Ruskin," *Atlantic Monthly* 6, no. 34 (August 1860): 239.

6 Ruskin 1903–1912, vol. 12, 339.

7 Ruskin 1903–1912, vol. 12, 339.

8 Ruskin 1850–1852, vol. 1; Ruskin 1903–1912, vol. 3, 623, 624.

9 For a discussion of Stillman, see Diane Waggoner's essay in this volume.

10 Ferber and Gallati 1998, 24–25, 210; Foster 2017, 51–55.

11 Quoted in Alastair Grieve, "Ruskin and Millais at Glenfinlas," *The Burlington Magazine* 138, no. 1117 (April 1996): 229.

12 Ruskin 1903–1912, vol. 12, xxiv.

13 Ruskin 1903–1912, vol. 14, 237.

14 Ruskin 1903–1912, vol. 10, 459.

15 William Michael Rossetti, ed., *The Germ, Thoughts towards Nature in Poetry, Literature and Art, Being a Facsimile Reprint of the Literary Organ of the Pre-Raphaelite Brotherhood, Published in 1850* (London, 1901), 121.

16 "The Author of 'Modern Painters'" [John Ruskin], Letter to *The Times*, May 25, 1854, in Ruskin 1903–1912, vol. 12, 334.

17 "A Working Parson" [Charles Kingsley], "Address to the Working Men of England," *Politics for the People*, 1848, reprinted in Frances Eliza Grenfell Kingsley, *Charles Kingsley: His Letters and Memories of His Life, Edited by His Wife* (London, 1894), 1:118.

18 Brown was on the staff from October 1857 until the spring of 1861; see [Ford Madox Brown], "Copy of a Letter from Ford Madox Brown," *The Working Men's College Journal* 23 (1923): 50–51.

19 Nikolaus Pevsner, *Pioneers of Modern Design* (1936; New Haven, CT, 2005), 13–15.

Abolitionism and the American Pre-Raphaelite Experiment

SOPHIE LYNFORD

1 The "New Path," "A Letter to a Subscriber," *The New Path* 1, no. 9 (January 1864): 117–118. While many of the unsigned articles in *The New Path* contain content that reveals the identity of their authors as members of the Association for the Advancement of Truth in Art, "A Letter to a Subscriber" is the only piece in *The New Path* to be signed "The 'New Path'" and should thus be read as a collaborative and collective statement made by the Association.

2 The minutes of the Association for the Advancement of Truth in Art list at least twenty-five members who were elected into the Association or signed the group's Articles of Organization between its founding on January 27, 1863, and its disbandment on March 29, 1864. In 1884, Peter Bonnett Wight published *The*

Development of New Phases of the Fine Arts in America, in which he records a reminiscence of the early days of the Association: "The original society numbered nineteen persons, mostly residing in New York and vicinity. But there were eleven subscribers to the publication fund who were not original members" (Wight 1884, 20–21). Using either the contemporary account or Wight's recollection, one can conclude that there were approximately thirty individuals directly involved in the activities of the Association between 1863 and 1864.

3 Russell Sturgis Jr., "Our 'Articles' Examined. An Essay Read before the Association, at the Regular Meeting, Tuesday, March 17th, 1863," *The New Path* 1, no. 1 (May 1863): 6.

4 The "New Path," "A Letter to a Subscriber," *The New Path*, 118; Peter Bonnett Wight, "What Has Been Done and What Can Be Done. I," *The New Path* 1, no. 5 (September 1863): 52.

5 Wight, "What Has Been Done and What Can Be Done. I," *The New Path*, 52.

6 Ruskin 1903–1912, vol. 5, *Modern Painters III* (1856), 212.

7 For an examination of the American Pre-Raphaelites' involvement in each of these cultural spheres, see Lynford 2019.

8 "Introductory," *The New Path* 1, no. 1 (May 1863): 3, 4.

9 Ray Haslam, "Looking, Drawing and Learning with John Ruskin at the Working Men's College," *Journal of Art & Design Education* 7, no. 1 (1988): 66.

10 Harrison 1954, 49–50.

11 Clarence Cook, "Farrer (Thomas Charles)," *Johnson's New Universal Cyclopaedia: F. Lichens* (New York, 1875), 36.

12 The Abolition Act of 1833 came into effect in 1834, with a transitional period leading to full emancipation in 1838.

13 John Guille Millais, *The Life and Letters of Sir John Everett Millais*, vol. 1 (London, 1899), 350.

14 Millais, *The Life and Letters of Sir John Everett Millais*, vol. 1, 148.

15 *Gone! Gone!* is close in composition to another British painting of the period, *Thoughts of the Past*, by John Roddam Spencer Stanhope (Tate, Britain), which was exhibited at the Royal Academy in 1859. Farrer may have also seen this painting in London. See May Brawley Hill, "*Gone! Gone!*," in Ferber and Gerdts 1985, 162.

16 W., "Sketchings," *The Crayon* 8, no. 4 (April 1861): 94.

17 Ford Madox Ford, *Ford Madox Brown: A Record of His Life and Work* (London, 1895), 184, 314.

18 Ferber 2002, 77. Farrer pictured a third contemporary abolitionist in *Captain Cabot Russel, Fifty-Fourth Massachusetts Regiment, Killed at Fort Wagner* (1864, also unlocated), with a portrait of William Garrison hanging on the wall in the background. The Fifty-Fourth Massachusetts Volunteer Infantry was the first African American regiment raised in the North, commanded by Colonel Robert Gould Shaw, scion of a Boston abolitionist family. Both Shaw and Russel were killed at the Second Battle of Fort Wagner on July 18, 1863.

19 Louisa Cook to Thomas Farrer, May 18, 1861, Ford Autograph Collection.

20 George Wood Wingate, *History of the Twenty-Second Regiment of the National Guard of the State of New York, from Its Organization to 1895* (New York, 1895), 34–35.

21 Russell Sturgis Jr., "National Academy of Design—Fortieth Anniversary Exhibition," *The New Path* 2, no. 6 (June 1865): 93.

22 David Blight, "When This Cruel War Is Over," in *A Place Called Paradise: Culture and Community in Northampton, Massachusetts, 1654–2004*, ed. Kerry Wayne Buckley (Historic Northampton Museum and Education Center, Amherst, 2004), 370.

23 "Art Matters," *New York Times*, April 3, 1867, 8.

24 Deborah Chotner, "Mount Tom," in *American Masters from Bingham to Eakins: The John Wilmerding Collection*, ed. Franklin Kelly (National Gallery of Art, Washington, 2004), 64.

25 Everett P. Wheeler, "Russell Sturgis," *The City College Quarterly* 5 (1909): 6. The Free Academy later became City College in New York.

26 Gill G. Cockram, *Ruskin and Social Reform: Ethics and Economics in the Victorian Age* (London, 2007), 18–21.

27 Peter Bonnett Wight, "Reminiscences of Russell Sturgis," *Architectural Record* 26 (August 1909): 123.

28 Dowling 2007, 24.

29 Peter Bonnett Wight, "What Has Been Done and What Can Be Done. II," *The New Path* 1, no. 7 (November 1863): 81.

30 Landau 1981, 17.

31 Henry W. Acland and John Ruskin, *The Oxford Museum* (London, 1859), 52.

32 "The National Academy of Design," *Harper's Weekly*, June 3, 1865, 348.

33 Peter Bonnett Wight, *National Academy of Design. Photographs with an Introductory Essay and Description by P. B. Wight, Architect* (New York, 1866), 9.

34 T. Addison Richards, *The National Academy of Design. Ceremonies on the Occasion of the Laying the Corner-stone, October 21st, 1863. Inauguration of the Building, April 27th, 1865* (New York, 1865), 47.

35 Wight unsuccessfully attempted to secure a position as a voluntary military engineer at the start of the war. See Landau 1981, 15. He also managed to avoid the draft, likely by paying the $300 fee that covered the cost of a "substitute" enlisting in his place.

36 [Russell Sturgis Jr.], "An Important Gothic Building," *The New Path* 2, no. 2 (June 1864): 18.

37 [Sturgis], "An Important Gothic Building," 17–18.

38 Landau 1981, 19.

39 Landau 1981, 19.

40 Wight, *National Academy of Design*, 9.

41 Wight, *National Academy of Design*, 9.

42 Ruskin 1903–1912, vol. 9, *The Stones of Venice* (1851–1853), 182–184. For a reception of Ruskin's architectural methods in America, see Michael Walter Brooks, *John Ruskin and Victorian Architecture*

(London, 1989); Stein 1967; and Lauren S. Weingarden, *Louis H. Sullivan and a Nineteenth-Century Poetics of Naturalized Architecture* (Farnham, 2009).

43 Peter Anthony, *John Ruskin's Labour: A Study of Ruskin's Social Theory* (Cambridge, 1983), 56–57.

44 [Sturgis], "An Important Gothic Building," 26; Wight, *National Academy of Design*, 6.

45 Wight, *National Academy of Design*, 6.

46 "Association for the Advancement of Truth in Art," *The New Path* 1, no. 1 (May 1863): 12.

47 Clarence Cook, "National Academy of Design, Annual Exhibition," *New-York Daily Tribune*, June 23, 1865, 6.

48 "Art: American Art and Artists," *The Round Table. A Saturday Review of Politics, Finance, Literature, Society and Art*, September 23, 1865, 36.

49 [Sturgis], "An Important Gothic Building," 25; Charles Eliot Norton, "Wight's National Academy of Design," *North American Review* (October 1866): 586; [Russell Sturgis Jr.], "Mr. Street's Gift to Yale College," *The New Path* 2, no. 9 (September 1865): 149.

50 "The Work of the True and the False Schools," *The New Path* 1, no. 7 (November 1863): 84; "Association for the Advancement of Truth in Art," 11.

51 David C. Miller, "The Iconology of Wrecked or Stranded Boats in Mid to Late Nineteenth-Century American Culture," in *American Iconology: New Approaches to Nineteenth-Century Art and Literature*, ed. David C. Miller (New Haven, CT, 1993), 81.

52 *Hudson River, Above Catskill* is signed at the lower left "C. H. M. 1865," but an inscription on the tacking edge of the stretched canvas, otherwise concealed by the frame, reads "April." This inscription suggests that Moore may have begun this work in April that year, following Lincoln's assassination.

53 Patricia Junker, "Sacred to the Memory of Thomas Cole: Charles Herbert Moore and His Views of Cedar Grove" (lecture, Thomas Cole National Historic Site, January 10, 2010).

54 "Association for the Advancement of Truth in Art," 11.

55 John Henry Hill to Bryson Burroughs, May 14, 1911, The Metropolitan Museum of Art Archives, New York.

56 Although the title of Hill's painting does not identify Farrer as the figure sketching, Hill notes in his diary that the engraving of the same composition, which apppears in Hill's *Sketches from Nature* (1867), is titled "Trap Rock, Mr. T. C. Farrer sketching." Hill's diary is housed in the collection of the Adirondack Museum, Blue Mountain Lake, New York.

57 May Brawley Hill, "Landscapes of Rockland County and the Hudson by three generations of artists who resided in West Nyack" (unpublished manuscript, 1991), 35–36.

58 Ferber 2002, 74.

59 Ruskin 1903–1912, vol. 16, "Cambridge School of Art: Inaugural Address" (1858), 181.

60 Ruskin 1903–1912, vol. 3, *Modern Painters I* (1843), 345. Ruskin is paraphrasing the Old Testament passage 1 Kings 19:11–12. For a discussion of American "grand manner" landscape painting and the more modestly scaled works executed in response by such artists as John Kensett, Martin Johnson Heade, and Fitz Henry Lane, see Novak 1980, 15–28.

61 Elizabeth Mankin Kornhauser, "Manifesto for an American Sublime: Thomas Cole's Oxbow," in *Thomas Cole's Journey: Atlantic Crossings*, ed. Elizabeth Mankin Kornhauser and Tim Barringer (The Metropolitan Museum of Art, New York, 2018), 47–89.

62 In 1862 *The American Traveller* reported that local hospitals for the insane had received patients suffering from a "new cause": "Excitement of Camp." "Insanity in Massachusetts: Remarkable Cases in Boston," *The American Traveller*, January 11, 1862, 2.

Thought on Canvas: American Pre-Raphaelite Iconography

BARBARA DAYER GALLATI

1 "Pictures and Studies," *The New Path* 2, no. 3 (July 1864): 39, 44. The author, who has been identified as Russell Sturgis Jr. by Sophie Lynford, outlined the distinctions between "pictures" and "studies," and implied that the American Ruskinians were merely making studies.

2 Jarves 1869, 294.

3 Jarves 1864, 245.

4 "National Academy of Design [Fifth and Last Notice.]," *New-York Daily Tribune*, May 10, 1856, 10.

5 Farrer's pen-and-ink portrait of Clarence Cook is known only through reproduction as the frontispiece in Cook 1902.

6 An itemized assessment of the significant objects portrayed is found in Wiles 2001, 408.

7 Farrer apparently based his portrait of Brown on an 1859 daguerreotype attributed to Martin M. Lawrence (Library of Congress Prints and Photographs Division, Washington).

8 W., "Sketchings. National Academy of Design," *The Crayon* 8, no. 4 (April 1861): 94.

9 Farrer delivered a paper and read the poem "Work" at the Association's meeting on March 17, 1863.

10 John Ruskin, *The Stones of Venice*, vol. 2, 2nd ed. (London, 1867), 169.

11 Farrer probably met Avery through John William and John Henry Hill and doubtless cemented their friendship at the numerous gatherings that Avery held starting about 1857. Dated 1860, Farrer's unlocated portrait of Avery shows the engraver at work in his studio. There is no record of its having been exhibited until 1873, when it was displayed as *An Engraver on Wood* at the American Society of Painters in Water Colors under Avery's ownership. By that time Avery was on the

cultural map as one of the most astute dealers in contemporary European art and Farrer likely realized that the display of his portrait of this easily recognized art expert would link the two men in the eyes of the public at a time when his style was shifting to a more painterly facture. Like many of the core members of the Association, Avery was sympathetic to the Union cause. At one point he owned Farrer's *Gone! Gone!* (plate 12) and a number of works by William Trost Richards, John William Hill, and John Henry Hill.

12 John William Hill's portrait of his daughter sewing in the out-of-doors (*Portrait of the Artist's Daughter*, 1868, watercolor on cardboard, 15 × 13 inches) is now in a private collection.

13 The studio was the site of artistic creation for three generations of the Hill family. It was frequented early on by other key figures of the American Ruskinian group, as documented in Thomas Farrer's portraits of John William and John Henry Hill (plates 23, 21), in which they are portrayed in the studio.

14 Foster 2017, 68.

15 Stillman S. Conant, "The Exhibition of Water Colors," *The Galaxy* 3, no. 1 (January 1, 1867): 57.

16 See, for example, Sarah C. Edgarton Mayo, *The Flower Vase; Containing the Language of Flowers and Their Poetic Sentiments* (Lowell and Boston, 1844); Frederick Marryat, *The Floral Telegraph: or, Affection's Signals* (London, [1850]); and Lucy Hooper, ed., *The Lady's Book of Flowers and Poetry* (New York, 1860).

17 C. C. [Clarence Cook], "Sonnet. To the Fringed Gentian," *The New Path* 2, no. 10 (October 1865): 165. Yet another poem, "Fringed Gentians" by T. W. Parsons, situated the flower as a symbol of remembrance for the dead. The poem was published in *The Galaxy* 2, no. 6 (November 15, 1866): 539. Poetry often inspired the American Pre-Raphaelites, as witnessed again by T. C. Farrer's *June* (plate 16), the frame of which bears lines from James Russell Lowell's 1848 poem "The Vision of Sir Launfal." ("There is no price set on the lavish summer, / And June may be had by the poorest comer.")

18 *Prang's Chromo* 1868, 1.

19 Newman expert Royal W. Leith notes that Newman's earliest-known anemone subjects date to 1875. See Leith 1996, 113.

20 George Ferguson, *Signs and Symbols in Christian Art* (London, 1961), 27.

21 Leith 1996, 24.

22 John Ruskin, letter to the *Times* (London), May 5, 1854. Farrer attended the Working Men's College in London, where he was taught by John Ruskin and Dante Gabriel Rossetti. It is highly unlikely that Farrer would not have seen the painting or paid attention to his instructors' opinions.

23 "The Light of the World" was written by the minor English Pre-Raphaelite John Lucas Tupper, who was incorrectly recorded as John Lionel Tupper when the poem was published in *The Crayon* 2, no. 6 (August 8, 1855): 87. "The Two Pre-Raphaelites. Third Article (Concluded)," *The Crayon* 3, no. 12 (December 1856): 354.

24 For a fine study of the reception of William Holman Hunt's art in nineteenth-century America, see Casteras 1990, 102–120. Regarding provenance and exhibition histories for Hunt's paintings, see Judith Bronkhurst, *William Holman Hunt: A Catalogue Raisonné*, 2 vols. (New Haven, CT, 2006).

25 "The Two Pre-Raphaelites. Third Article (Concluded)," *The Crayon* 3, no. 12 (December 1856): 354.

26 Linda S. Ferber was the first to observe this in Ferber 1980, 157.

27 Shakespeare's plays enjoyed immense popularity in eighteenth- and nineteenth-century America. See Lawrence Levine, "William Shakespeare in America," in *Highbrow Lowbrow: The Emergence of Cultural Hierarchy in America* (Cambridge, MA, 1988), 13–81.

28 See May Brawley Hill's entry for the drawing in Ferber and Gerdts 1985, 156–157.

29 Amelia Farrer's death was reported in *Brooklyn Daily Eagle*, July 12, 1904. The sitter in *Practicing Her Lesson* (plate 19) has been identified as either Amelia or Maria Meek; see Hill in Ferber and Gerdts 1985, 156–157. Wiles has identified the sitter as Maria Meek, having based her opinion on a comparison with the figure in *Portrait of Maria L. Meek*, an 1859 drawing by Farrer now in the collection of the Columbus Museum of Art (see Wiles 2001, 395–396). Amelia would have been nineteen and Maria would have been seventeen in 1859, but the figure in the drawing appears to be older. A Henrietta Meek (possibly a sister of Edward) was also living at the Meek home in 1855 and would have been approximately thirty-three years old at the time the drawing was made. (See New York State Census, 1855, Household Number 775, New York City, Ward 22, New York, NY, Head of Household, Edward Meek.)

30 See David Kimbell, *Vincenzo Bellini: Norma* (Cambridge, UK, 1998).

31 See Alison Smith, Caroline Bugler, Susan Foister, and Anna Koopstra, *Reflections: Van Eyck and the Pre-Raphaelites* (National Gallery, London, 2017).

32 As a dedicated realist, Farrer was bound to have explored and questioned the nature of reality itself, a philosophical inquiry that extends beyond the idea of truth.

33 May Brawley Hill first made the connection between Van Eyck and Farrer's *Woman Sewing* in Ferber and Gerdts 1985, 157.

34 Farrer's use of the picture-within-a-picture device was already well established in his *portraits d'apparat*. His portrait of John William Hill (plate 23), although unfinished, demonstrates the importance of the landscape hanging adjacent to Hill's head in the early phase of the drawing process. Identified as

either a watercolor or a print after a work by J. M. W. Turner, the prominent image in the composition reinforces the sitter's identity by announcing his artistic preferences. Then, too, Farrer likely exploited the imagery of famous works to validate his own artistic aims by association.

35 Among the many articles that devoted lengthy discussion specific to *The Huguenot Lover* were "The Two Pre-Raphaelitisms. Third Article. The Modern Pre-Raphaelites," *The Crayon* 3, part 11 (November 1856): 321–324; J. S. [William James Stillman], "Naturalism and Genius," *The New Path* 1, no. 6 (October 1863): 64–70; and especially "Art. Three Representative Pictures," *The Round Table* 2, no. 31 (July 16, 1864): 74.

36 Thomas Oldham Barlow's mezzotint after the Millais painting was available by 1857.

37 See Alison Smith's entry for the painting in Jason Rosenfeld and Alison Smith, *Millais* (London: Tate, 2007), 94.

38 The inscription reads, "Come unto me, all ye that labor and are heavy laden, and I will give you rest. Take my yoke upon you and learn of me; for I am meek and lowly in heart: and ye shall find rest unto your souls."

39 See Sophie Lynford's additional comments regarding this interpretation of *Gone! Gone!* in this volume.

40 *The Shattuck Family, with Grandmother, Mother and Baby William* (also known as *The Shattuck Family*, plate 88) is an extremely rare genre subject in Shattuck's oeuvre and he may have been directly influenced by Farrer's *Gone! Gone!*, a work that was owned by Samuel Putnam Avery, a staunch Shattuck supporter. In the late 1850s and early 1860s Shattuck's landscapes revealed his deep regard for Ruskinian aesthetics (see, for example, *Leaf Study with Yellow Swallow Tail*, plate 87), but despite his continued admiration for the English critic, Shattuck subsequently avoided the exacting facture prescribed by Ruskinian theory and appears not to have created genre subjects after 1865. For a detailed analysis of the painting, see Gallati 1988, 36–47.

41 Shattuck owned a Martinet engraving of the *Virgin and Child* that is now in the collection of the Brooklyn Museum, a gift of a Shattuck descendant. It may be safely assumed that the artist also owned a print after Millais's *The Huguenot Lover*.

42 Shattuck did not join the military during the Civil War and it is highly likely that he paid for the services of another to fight in his place (a lawful practice at the time).

43 Paletta, "Art Matters," *The American Art Journal* 5, no. 26 (October 18, 1866): 408. An image of what might be the "American" *Mon Brave* has turned up on Pinterest. Lacking information about its location, measurements, and the opportunity to examine it, however, there is no way to determine its authenticity. It is assumed here that the Pinterest image is either the original or based on the original. No exhibition history for this painting has been established; it was also mentioned in Henry T. Tuckerman, *Book of the Artists* (New York, 1867), 454.

44 Hennessy reportedly went to his native Ireland before settling in London. Tracing his movements during this period is problematic.

45 For additional comments linking Hennessy's iconography with the Keats poem, see my entry for the painting in Teresa A. Carbone, Barbara Dayer Gallati, and Linda S. Ferber, *American Paintings in the Brooklyn Museum, Artists Born by 1876*, vol. 2 (London, 2006): 627–628. See also Sarah Wooten, "Keats's Poetry as a Common Thread in English and American Pre-Raphaelitism," in Tobin 2005, 279–301.

46 Bedell 2001, 8. Although Rebecca Bedell provides an excellent history of the relationship of geology and art in nineteenth-century America, she does not discuss or reproduce works by the American Pre-Raphaelites, and mentions the group only in passing. The group is similarly ignored (with the exception of comments regarding Richards's fascination with geology) in Virginia L. Wagner, "John Ruskin and Artistical Geology in America," *Winterthur Portfolio* 23, no. 2/3 (Summer–Autumn 1988): 151–167. Forthcoming at this writing are Patricia Phagan, with Jill S. Schneiderman, *Past Time: Geology in European and American Art* (Poughkeepsie, NY: Frances Lehman Loeb Art Center, 2018) and John Holmes, *The Pre-Raphaelites and Science* (New Haven, CT, 2018).

47 See Anthony Lacy Gully, "Sermons in Stone: Ruskin and Geology," in Casteras 1993, 158–183.

48 "Exhibition of British Art," *Boston Daily Courier*, May 15, 1858, quoted in Casteras 1990, 65. Only a short time passed after the Boston venue closed before visual testimony to the confluence of art, science, philosophy, and literature emerged in Stillman's *Philosophers' Camp in the Adirondacks* (1858, Concord Free Public Library, fig. 1 in Waggoner essay), in which the artist portrayed a group of Bostonian intellectuals on a camping expedition in upstate New York. Among the group were poets Ralph Waldo Emerson and James Russell Lowell and renowned scientists Louis Agassiz and Jeffries Wyman. By that time Stillman was already an avid Ruskinian, having met the critic in England in 1850, and the American's artistic aims were shaped by the injunction that true art required the intense—even scientific—study of nature.

49 John Henry Hill's *Shoshone Falls* is illustrated in Ferber and Gerdts 1985, 175, plate 22.

50 Ruskin 1903–1912, vol. 6, *Modern Painters IV* (1856), 132.

51 Ruskin 1903–1912, vol. 6, *Modern Painters IV* (1856), 133.

52 Ruskin 1857, 121.

53 In a letter written to his sister dated November 30, 1862, Moore referred to Farrer as "the greatest gentleman friend I have in the world" (quoted in Mather

1957, 17). Although Moore was probably familiar with Ruskin's writings prior to meeting Farrer, his paintings do not reflect strict Pre-Raphaelite technique until the early 1860s.

54 C. H. M. [Charles Herbert Moore], "Fallacies of the Present School," *The New Path* 1, no. 6 (October 1863): 61–64.

55 J. S. [William James Stillman], "Naturalism and Genius," *The New Path* 1, no. 6 (October 1863): 66. For an explanation of the attribution of "Art as a Record" and "Naturalism and Genius" to Stillman, see Lynford 2019.

56 See Robert G. Watts, "Global Warming and the Future of the Earth," *Synthesis Lectures on Energy and the Environment: Technology, Science, and Society* 1, no. 1 (January 2007): 19.

57 Quoted in Gully, "Sermons in Stone: Ruskin and Geology," in Casteras 1993, 168.

58 Patricia Junker, "Sacred to the Memory of Thomas Cole: Charles Herbert Moore and His Views of Cedar Grove" (paper presented at Cedar Grove, Catskill, New York, January 10, 2010). I am grateful to Dr. Junker for allowing me to read her paper. See also Sophie Lynford's discussion of the painting in this volume.

A Knowing Look: The American Pre-Raphaelite Still Life

MARK D. MITCHELL

1 Such heterogeneity contradicts the revolutionary language embraced by the group in their journal, *The New Path,* and follows similar complexity in their practice of the genre of landscape, manifested in the unevenly critical language toward artists of the previous generation, including leading figure Asher B. Durand but not John F. Kensett, both of whom embraced Ruskin's influence. For further discussion, see Linda S. Ferber, "'Determined Realists': The American Pre-Raphaelites and the Association for the Advancement of Truth in Art," in Ferber and Gerdts 1985, 13–14. On Kensett's sympathy with Pre-Raphaelitism, see Henry T. Tuckerman, *Book of the Artists,* reprint ed. (New York, 1966), 511, and note 12 below.

2 Publications illustrating Ruskin's own works included his *Modern Painters* (1843–1860), *The Stones of Venice* (1851–1853), and *The Elements of Drawing* (1857).

3 "The word 'Blue,' say certain philosophers, means the sensation of colour which the human eye receives in looking at the open sky, or at a bell gentian." John Ruskin, "Of the Pathetic Fallacy," in *Modern Painters,* 5 vols., new ed. (London, 1873), 3:157. William H. Gerdts observes a similar effect in American depictions of burdocks, by John Henry Hill and others, including Jasper Cropsey, John F. Kensett, Jervis McEntee, and Stephen Shaughnessey, following Ruskin's admiration for their "framework of extending ribs like a Gothic roof." Gerdts, "Through a Glass Brightly: The American Pre-Raphaelites and Their Still Lifes and Nature Studies," in Ferber and Gerdts 1985, 44.

4 John Henry Hill to Thomas Charles Farrer, July (n.d.) 1860, Ford Papers, microfilm reel N14, frame 1145.

5 Pre-Raphaelite critic Clarence Cook would also write a sonnet on this subject in 1849—"To the Fringed Gentian"—shortly after the release of *Modern Painters* in the United States, writing, "Oft had I heard thy beauty praised, dear flower," in Cook 1902, 60.

6 Ferber 1985, 882.

7 John Ruskin, *The Elements of Drawing,* reprint ed. (New York, 1971), 109.

8 Ruskin 1873, 3:231.

9 The watercolor's reattribution was derived from a contemporary published description of a watercolor of the same subject by Thomas Charles Farrer (see Timeline, December 1865, p. 241). This watercolor's signature and date by his brother Henry, and also the consistency with Henry's known practice, sustain the possibility that this work is simply related to the better-documented earlier work by Thomas Charles, in whose surviving work no still lifes are known with which to compare this one. Thomas Charles Farrer was nevertheless a prolific still-life painter, and the dearth of surviving examples presents a considerable challenge to the fuller appreciation of Pre-Raphaelite still-life painting in the United States because of his formative influence on the wider group of artists, including his brother. Ferber in Ferber and Gerdts 1985, 16; Wiles 2002, 318.

10 Moore also benefited from a uniquely early, sympathetic, and extensive study of his career—at least as a landscape painter—by art historian Frank Jewett Mather Jr. See Mather 1957.

11 Mather 1957, 21.

12 On Moore's financial struggles, see Kenneth Myers and Margaret Favretti, "'In Most Extreme Need': Correspondence of C. H. Moore with J. F. Kensett," *Archives of American Art Journal* 26, no. 1 (1986): 11–12, and note 1 above.

13 On the widely mixed reviews of Ruskin's watercolor, exhibited as *Study of a Block of Gneiss,* see Susan P. Casteras, "The 1857–58 Exhibition of English Art in American and Critical Responses to Pre-Raphaelitism," in Ferber and Gerdts 1985, 128–130. On Norton's friendships with the Pre-Raphaelites, see Theodore E. Stebbins Jr. with Susan C. Ricci, "Charles Eliot Norton: Ruskin's Friend, Harvard's Sage," in Stebbins and Anderson 2007, 16–17.

14 Ruskin 1971, 91.

15 Notably, Ruskin solicited a similar exercise, also using granite, from William Henry Hunt: "'A Bit of Mont Blanc'—a piece of granite brought thence by Mr. Ruskin and painted for him." William Collingwood, "Reminiscences: William Hunt," *Magazine of Art* 21 (January 1898):

504. The work was exhibited in 1856 at the Society of Painters in Water-Colours exhibition in London.

16 Mather calls Moore's watercolor a "valedictory" of his career as a Pre-Raphaelite painter; see Mather 1957, 40–42. See also Melissa Renn, "Charles Herbert Moore and the Teaching of Art at Harvard," in Stebbins and Anderson 2007, 45–52.

17 John Witt, *William Henry Hunt (1790–1864), Life and Work* (London, 1982), 52.

18 Ruskin 1971, 220n.

19 Hill "stands aloof from any school of artists feeling that there is a higher or at least more delicate and spiritual conception of art than finds expression in the columns of *The New Path*," in "Art in Brooklyn," *Brooklyn Daily Union* 2, no. 1 (May 14, 1864): 4. See also the *New York Times* obituary reprinted in Hill 1888, 11. Although Hill was the first president of the Association of the Advancement of Truth in Art, his tenure was brief. Moreover, the group self-identified as "young" men, which would not easily have encompassed the fifty-one-year-old Hill, who was actually the father of another member of the group and by all accounts an earnest, patient, and generous man—no firebrand.

20 *Hedge-Sparrow's Nest with Primroses and Violets* (c. 1840–1850), reproduced in Ferber and Gerdts 1985, 283, no. 124.

21 Charles Herbert Moore, "An Artist's Memorial," in Hill 1888, 7.

22 According to William Collingwood, "if [Hunt] painted a bank of primroses, or anything in his background, it must be there before his eyes, the piece of the bed dug out and brought to him in a barrow just as it stood." See William Collingwood, "Reminiscences: William Hunt," *Magazine of Art* 21 (January 1898): 504.

23 Hunt quoted in Craig W. England, "Constructed Naturalism in the Watercolors of William Henry Hunt," *Huntington Library Quarterly* 53, no. 1 (Winter 1990): 79.

24 Gerdts, "Through a Glass Brightly," in Ferber and Gerdts 1985, 46.

25 "But admiration excited by the budding of a flower is a poetical feeling, because it is impossible that this manifestation of spiritual power and vital beauty can ever be enough admired." Ruskin 1873, 3:11.

26 Ruskin 1971, 115.

27 Hill 1981, 17.

28 Lambdin's work was known and admired by the New York artists, including John William Hill, who wrote to collector Gordon Lester Ford in 1875 that he was "glad to hear that Lambdin has done some nice naturalistic work" in that year's annual American Watercolor Society exhibition. Ford Papers, microfilm reel N14, frame 1237.

29 William H. Gerdts was the first to acknowledge the potential impact of Preyer on the American Pre-Raphaelites, calling for further study of the subject at the end of his pioneering 1969 article "The Influence of Ruskin and Pre-Raphaelitism on American Still-Life Painting," *The American Art Journal* 1, no. 2 (Autumn 1969): 97n41.

30 The other primary German academy, in Munich, favored history painting in an Italian Renaissance–inspired mode during the period. See Marion F. Deshmukh, "Between Tradition and Modernity: The Düsseldorf Art Academy in Early Nineteenth Century Prussia," *German Studies Review* 6, no. 3 (October 1983): 442–445.

31 Still-life painters were one class of the artisans who immigrated and formed close-knit cultural communities, especially on New York City's Lower East Side. Most prominent, perhaps, among these were the cabinetmakers, whose practice shared attributes with still-life painters in their "reputation for excellent craftsmanship, if not for original design." See Emily Eerdmans, "German Cabinet-Makers in New York, c. 1825–c. 1850," *Furniture History* 40 (2004): 99–101, 104.

32 William H. Gerdts, "'Good Tidings' to the Lovers of the Beautiful: New York's Düsseldorf Gallery, 1849–1862," *The American Art Journal* 30, no. 1/2 (1999): 51. As Ruskin confessed, "I never speak of German art, or German philosophy, but in depreciation . . . because I . . . feel that the immediate tendency of the English mind is to rate them too highly." See Ruskin 1873, 3:343.

33 Stein 1967, 151. Notably, however, even William Henry Hunt would create works around midcentury that resembled the mainstream taste for the vibrant, sensual, continental tradition of which Ruskin vigorously disapproved.

34 "The Dusseldorf Gallery," *Cosmopolitan Art Journal* 2, no. 1 (December 1857): 43.

35 Russell Sturgis argued aggressively against such accommodations to remove flowers or fruits from their natural contexts as "not dignified" offerings and "poor subjects," favoring instead what May Brawley Hill terms "orthodox Ruskinianism." Hill in Ferber and Gerdts 1985, 188.

36 Mitchell 2015, 170–171.

37 He thereby circumvented Ruskin's lament: "Sometimes I have really thought her miserliness intolerable: in a gentian, for instance, the way she economizes her ultramarine down in the bell is a little too bad." Ruskin 1971, 153.

38 "Good Work in the Academy Exhibition," *The New Path* 1, no. 2 (June 1863): 22.

39 On Moore's introduction of Newman's work to Ruskin, see Forman 1884, 530.

40 "Articles of Organization," *The New Path* 1, no. 1 (May 1863): n.p.

41 Gerdts, "Through a Glass Brightly," in Ferber and Gerdts 1985, 42.

"The Perfect Observance of Truth": Photography and American Pre-Raphaelitism

DIANE WAGGONER

1 See Diane Waggoner, *The Pre-Raphaelite Lens: British Photography and Painting, 1848–1875* (National Gallery of Art,

Washington, 2010), and Tim Barringer, Jason Rosenfeld, and Alison Smith, *Pre-Raphaelites: Victorian Avant-Garde* (Tate Britain, London, 2012).

2 *The New Path* 1, no. 1 (May 1863): 1.

3 *The New Path* 1, no. 1 (May 1863): 2.

4 See Diane Waggoner, *East of the Mississippi: Nineteenth-Century American Landscape Photography* (National Gallery of Art, Washington, 2017).

5 For example, John William Hill's drawing "On the Hackensack" was described as so faithful to its subject that it "is as true as a photograph." See "Good Work in the Academy Exhibition," *The New Path* 1, no. 2 (June 1863): 24.

6 "Our Illustrations," *Photographic and Fine Art Journal* 9, no. 11 (December 1856): 380.

7 For more on Stillman, see Stillman 1988; Dyson 2014; Elliot 2006; Simon 2013.

8 "The Work of the True and the False Schools," *The New Path* 1, no. 7 (November 1863): 87.

9 W. J. Stillman, *The Autobiography of a Journalist* (Boston and New York, 1901), 222.

10 Stillman, *Autobiography*, 138.

11 Stillman, *Autobiography*, 140.

12 Stillman, *Autobiography*, 177.

13 Stillman, *Autobiography*, 178.

14 "Sketchings," *The Crayon* 1, no. 7 (February 14, 1855): 107.

15 "Recreation and Solitude," *Atlantic Monthly* 40, no. 237 (July 1877): 10.

16 Stillman, *Autobiography*, 280–281.

17 Norton Papers, William J. Stillman to Charles Eliot Norton, Belmont, October 6, 1858.

18 See Stillman, *Autobiography*, 283. "Being advised not to occupy myself with painting while there, I bought a photographic apparatus, and learned photography as it was practiced in 1857,—a rude, inefficient, and cumbersome apparatus and process for field work, of which few amateurs nowadays can conceive the inconveniences." He also wrote to Norton, who funded his trip: "I am very glad that I have brought my photographic apparatus as much of what is most peculiar and charming in the scenery here is from its situation and the difficulty of getting at it, scarcely paintable while as a whole it is rather curious and delightful from its novelty than beautiful as compared with northern scenery. A Floridian creek stands no chance in a comparison with a mountain brook at home." Norton Papers, William J. Stillman to Charles Eliot Norton, Hibernia, Florida, April 1859.

19 Norton Papers, William J. Stillman to Charles Eliot Norton, Ampersand Pond, September 30, 1859. The Adirondack Club built a lodge at Ampersand Pond and gathered there in 1860, but Stillman had already gone abroad and visits ceased after the outbreak of the Civil War. Stillman returned to the site in 1883 to find the camp in bad shape. By that time, all the other attendees had died and Stillman recalled "among the memories which are the only realities left to it, this image of Emerson claiming kinship with the forest stands out alone, and I feel as if I had stood for a moment on a mount of transfiguration, and seen, as if in a vision, the typical American, the noblest in the idealization of the American, of all the race" (Stillman, *Autobiography*, 256).

20 Stillman's other major photography projects included *The Acropolis of Athens* and *Poetic Localities of Cambridge Illustrated* (Boston, 1876), a compendium of photographs by Stillman and poems by Lowell, Holmes, and Longfellow made during visits back to America.

21 Stillman mentions a visit to the White Mountains in 1870, which was the last time he met with Agassiz (Stillman, *Autobiography*, 465–466). It is certainly possible he also went back to the White Mountains earlier, as Stillman wrote to Albert Bierstadt from Saranac Lake during one of his trips back to America, likely in 1861, offering his services as a guide in the Adirondacks and encouraging him to come there and make photographs: "Would you not like to come and take some Adirondack photographs? I shall be here for some two or three weeks and would like to join you in doing so and will furnish the necessary outfit for the woods, boat, tent &c and go as assistant and guide. I can show you some magnificent bits of virgin forest, probably the last remaining this side the Mississippi, lake and mountain just as nature finished them. . . .We are just in the first flush of autumn and in a week or two there will be light enough in the forest to get some good wood views, and by the first of Oct we shall have snow." Though Bierstadt evidently did not take Stillman up on the offer, his letter suggests he was still considering the wooded landscapes of the Adirondacks or the White Mountains as photographic subjects. (Bierstadt Papers, Winterthur Library, William J. Stillman to Albert Bierstadt, Saranac Lake, September 16, no year.) See also Schlett 2015, 146, 227.

22 Another view in the same album shows a closer view of the tent, revealing a small clearing around it and an additional rough lean-to shelter.

23 Other photographs in the album include similar views of Naushon Island, Massachusetts, the woods of Maine, and the Adirondacks.

24 Stillman, *Autobiography*, 250.

25 "Forest Photographs," *Atlantic Monthly* 5, no. 27 (January 1860): 109.

26 Stillman, *Autobiography*, 141.

27 The ten works listed as "Photographs of Studies from Nature" are as follows: Thomas Charles Farrer, *Spring Weeds*, pencil drawing; Charles Herbert Moore, *Mandrakes*, pencil drawing; Robert Pattison, *Dog's Head*, painting; Henry Roderick Newman, *Ferns*, pencil drawing; Thomas Charles Farrer, *Yellow Water Lily*, sepia drawing; John Henry Hill, *Mulleins*, pen drawing; Charles Herbert Moore, *Cedar Tree*, pen drawing; Thomas Charles Farrer, *Gone! Gone!* (plate 12), painting; Thomas Charles Farrer, *May in the Woods*, pencil drawing; Thomas Charles Farrer, *Pumpkin Vine*, pencil drawing. Farrer's *May in the*

Woods, though unlocated, was illustrated in Edward Cary, "Some American Pre-Raphaelites: A Reminiscence," *The Scrip* 2 (October 1906): 1–7, and also reproduced in Ferber and Gerdts 1985, 30.

28 "Pictures and Studies," *The New Path* 2, no. 3 (July 1864): 42.

29 "Pictures and Studies," 44.

30 "Pictures and Studies," 45.

31 A notice in the Philadelphia *Daily Evening Bulletin* stated: "Mr. John Moran is about starting upon a tour through this State for the purpose of obtaining photographic views of its mountain scenery. Mr. M. will visit and transfer to the magic plate the scenic glories of Kittaning point, and other romantic spots among the Alleghenies." See "Photographic Novelties," *Daily Evening Bulletin* 1, no. 2 (June 5, 1862). The two albums, "Alleghany Mountains," are housed at the William L. Clements Library, University of Michigan, Ann Arbor.

32 Coleman Sellers, "Foreign Correspondence," *British Journal of Photography* 9, no. 176 (October 15, 1862): 398.

33 Quoted in Ferber and Gerdts 1985, 215.

34 Tuckerman 1867, 254.

35 Coleman Sellers, "Foreign Correspondence," *British Journal of Photography* 9, no. 165 (May 1, 1862): 177.

36 John Henry Hill exhibited an oil of Shoshone Falls at the National Academy of Design in 1871 and noted in his diary that "a friend to whom I showed the study made on the spot from which the picture is painted and a photograph taken from nature said I am astonished, they are identical." Quoted in Ferber and Gerdts 1985, 175.

37 *Special Report of New York State Survey on the Preservation of the Scenery of Niagara Falls and Fourth Annual Report on the Triangulation of the State for the Year 1879, James T. Gardner, Director* (Albany, 1880).

38 "Art and Photography," *The New Path* 2, no. 12 (December 1865): 198–199.

The New Path 1863–1865: "He Serves All, Who Dares Be True"

JANICE SIMON

I would like to thank Linda Ferber and Nancy Anderson for inviting me to write on *The New Path* and for their wonderful editorial support. Caroline Weaver of the National Gallery of Art clarified my essay appreciably with her knowing editorial eye. This essay is dedicated to Phylis Floyd, whose long friendship since our years in graduate school at the University of Michigan and shared interest in nineteenth-century art criticism I have greatly treasured.

1 William Michael Rossetti, "Introduction, July 1899," *The Germ: Thoughts towards Nature in Poetry, Literature and Art* (1850; repr., New York, 1965), 15–16.

2 Rossetti 1965, 9–10. William Michael Rossetti credited the subtitle to his poet brother, Dante Gabriel Rossetti.

3 John Ruskin, *Modern Painters*, vol. 2 (New York, 1852), 98.

4 The official name of the group was altered for the journal to Society for the Advancement of Truth in Art, and beginning with the second meeting on February 20, 1863, Association and Society alternately appeared. Society became the preferred term especially in relation to the journal and the holding of meetings. In addition to the February 11 meeting in which the governing articles of the association were adopted, it was only on April 7, 1863, that the Association for the Advancement of the Cause of Truth in Art appeared in the minutes. When, in February 23, 1865, the proprietors of *The New Path*—Clarence Cook, Russell Sturgis Jr., and Peter B. Wight—called a meeting regarding the publication of the second volume of the journal (which had been suspended since July 1864), they employed a shortened name, the Association for the Advancement of Truth in Art. Their ending resolution to secure funds for continuing publication of the second volume created the New Path Association—those willing to contribute to the $800 needed. They proposed that the record of the meeting "be placed in the book of the Society for the Advancement of Truth in Art." By March 29, 1864, the Association as originally conceived had folded, with the three aforementioned editors of *The New Path* taking control. To publish nine additional numbers, the editors put the responsibilities of printing, advertising, distribution, and sale of current and back issues and volumes into the hands of James Miller of Broadway. Nineteen subscribers to support the remaining issues of the second volume were listed in the minutes. See Wight Papers.

5 Linda Ferber, "'Determined Realists': The American Pre-Raphaelites and the Association for the Advancement of Truth in Art," in Ferber and Gerdts 1985, 36n52.

6 John Ruskin, *The Two Paths: Being Lectures on Art, and Its Application to Decoration and Manufacture, Delivered in 1858–59* (New York, 1872), v, viii.

7 [Russell Sturgis Jr.], "Association for the Advancement of Truth in Art," *The New Path* 1, no. 1 (May 1863): 11.

8 The "New Path," "A Letter to a Subscriber," *The New Path* 1, no. 9 (January 1864): 114–115. The second volume incorporates many more excerpts from other publications, letters from friends, and—beginning in the ninth issue (September 1865)—includes a closing section, "Notes Here and There," of various ruminations. *The New Path* even included the arrival of works of art at Knoedler's gallery, the type of notice Cook once said the journal would not do. The articles are almost all unsigned in the second volume and appear to be written primarily by Cook, Sturgis, and Wight, with an increasing burden placed on Sturgis from May 1864. For attribution of articles to Sturgis and Wight, see Pearson 1999, 434–435, 439. The question of the extent

of Cook's involvement in writing for *The New Path* after he became an art critic for the *New-York Daily Tribune* in the spring of 1864 is one of speculation. Certainly, his involvement with the *Tribune* led to the hiatus of *The New Path* from July 1864 (when issue 3 of volume 2 was published) until April 1865, when issue 4 appeared. Linda Ferber does quote Cook on the hiatus in a letter to Farrer in August 1864: "I have not seen nor heard anything of the men since I came down... you know I am not in love with any of them. How the 'New Path' fares, I am entirely ignorant. I cannot write for it anymore than for anything else, and I dare say they are very willing I should not." See Ferber and Gerdts 1985, 23. However, Cook doesn't say he will stop writing for *The New Path* just that he won't privilege it above other assignments. Cook's attitudes toward various artists seem to be voiced in the journal's pages during its last year of publication, suggesting that he still had a hand in its drafting or at the very least, an influence on the point of view of its authors, especially in the art reviews. According to Jo Ann Weiss, Sturgis replaced Cook as editor in 1864: in correspondence with Farrer dated July 11, 1864, Cook wrote how Sturgis had written the whole of the May number and wondered how the journal could survive especially with the price still being a dollar for an annual subscription. See Weiss 1977, 218n29.

9 For a thoughtful analysis of Cook's art criticism throughout his career and its consistency as social critique against capitalist consumerism, see Georgi 2013.

10 [Clarence Cook], "Introductory," *The New Path* 1, no. 1 (May 1863): 1–4.

11 [Cook], "Introductory," 3.

12 Oliver Wendell Holmes Sr., *Ralph Waldo Emerson* (Boston, 1885), 115.

13 Kenneth S. Sacks, *Understanding Emerson: "The American Scholar" and His Struggle for Self-Reliance* (Princeton, NJ, 2003), 1–20, 121–128.

14 Ralph Waldo Emerson, "The American Scholar," in *Ralph Waldo Emerson: Essays and Lectures*, ed. Joel Porte (New York, 1983), 54, 57, 70, 57, 71, 56.

15 J. S., "Art as a Record," *The New Path* 1, no. 4 (August 1863): 37–44.

16 J. S., "Naturalism and Genius," *The New Path* 1, no. 6 (October 1863): 65, 66, 70.

17 See Lynford 2019 for references to Stillman's own experiences creating art under Ruskin's tutelage. Although Cook was a published poet and studied with Longfellow at Harvard (which explains the poetic excerpts and references that pepper the pages of the journal), he did not have the close connections with Holmes or the Browning family (Robert and Elizabeth Barrett), the Rossetti brothers, and John Everett Millais that characterized Stillman's time in England and Italy, and which are essential references in the articles by J. S. In his essay "The Work of the True and False Schools," published the month after Stillman's "Naturalism and Genius" appeared, Cook directly credits Stillman with acknowledging the importance of the Pre-Raphaelites and alluding to his writings in *The Crayon*: "Less than ten years ago there was but one man in America, W. J. Stillman, who practically understood and believed in the new art." See [Clarence Cook], *The New Path* 1, no. 7 (November 1863): 87. One should note, however, that Russell Sturgis Jr. refers to poetry in his articles for *The New Path* as well.

William H. Gerdts has attributed "Art as a Record" to Thomas Farrer; Farrer's "A Few Questions Answered" appeared with full byline in issue 2 of *The New Path* (June 1863) and it has none of the references to poets who were intimates of Stillman or even of Cook. See Gerdts, "Through a Glass Brightly: The American Pre-Raphaelites and Their Still Lifes and Nature Studies," in Ferber and Gerdts 1985, 41, 76n7.

18 For a recent discussion of the Philosophers' Camp see Schlett 2015. For a close reading of Stillman's experiences as a member of the Philosophers' Camp and the implications of Emerson's philosophy on Stillman's photographs of the Adirondacks, see Janice Simon, "William James Stillman's Photographic Turn: The *Adirondac Woods* as Transcendental Experience," in *The Photograph and the Collection*, ed. Graeme Farnell (Edinburgh, 2013), 96–124.

19 [William James Stillman], "The Art of the Present," *The Crayon* 1, no. 19 (May 9, 1855): 289–290. Stillman opens this essay with Longfellow's line from his 1838 "Psalm of Life": "Act, act in the living present." Stillman's emphasis on the reality of the moment and obsession with the artist's duty to reveal the truth, both material and spiritual, in this and other articles for *The Crayon* (see also "Duty in Art," *The Crayon* 1, no. 4 [January 24, 1855]: 49–50 and "The Position of the Artist," *The Crayon* 1, no. 13 [March 28, 1855]) are reiterated in his two articles for *The New Path*. Stillman used several pseudonyms in his journal, including a series of essays ("The Landscape Element in American Poetry") discussing the poetry of Bryant, Alfred B. Street, and Lowell, which he signed as "G. M. James." See *The Crayon* 1, no. 1 (January 3, 1855): 3–4; *The Crayon* 1, no. 3 (January 17, 1855): 39–40; and *The Crayon* 1, no. 12 (March 21, 1855): 179–180. "W. Sylvester" was Stillman's pseudonym for his poetry in the journal.

20 *The New Path* 2, no. 12 (December 1865): 200; Ralph Waldo Emerson, "Initial, Daemonic, and Celestial Love," in *Ralph Waldo Emerson: Collected Poems and Translations*, ed. Harold Bloom and Paul Kane (New York, 1994), 90.

21 "Art and Photography," *The New Path* 2, no. 12 (December 1865): 198–199. For a thorough discussion of the American Pre-Raphaelite attitude toward photography, see Diane Waggoner's contribution to the present volume, "'The Perfect

Observance of Truth': Photography and American Pre-Raphaelitism."

22 [William J. Stillman and John Durand], "Introductory," *The Crayon* 1, no. 1 (January 3, 1855): 1. Stillman and Durand's introductory essay advocated ordinary nature's power to elevate the common individual, even the rowdy urban urchin, to a harmonized spirit. Using the metaphors of "the little blue flower," the liverleaf, that blooms in early spring as well as common flowers tossed on the street as embodiments of "Art, which is Beauty's gospel," the *Crayon* editors argued that contemplation of nature and art would redeem the nation from its commercial crises and individuals like the Bowery boys from their rollicking ways. As *The Crayon* ended its first essay with the declaration that "flowers" "seemed texts dropped from the Evangel of Art" so *The New Path* concluded its journal with the natural revelations of Emerson's "Celestial Love." For a discussion of the metaphoric elements of this introductory essay and its connections to the goals of *The Crayon,* see Simon 1990, 84–86. For an extended analysis of Stillman's use of metaphor and metonymy in his art criticism, see Georgi 2013, 92–107.

23 Another borrowing from *The Crayon* involved poetry. As the editors announced: "There are several poems by D. G. Rossetti, the head of the English Pre-Raphaelites, very much loved by those who know them, but very little known in this country, although three of them were printed some years ago in 'The Crayon.' In compliance with numerous requests, we reprint, from the Crayon, one of the finest." D[ante]. G. Rossetti, "The Blessed Damosel," *The New Path* 1, no. 8 (December 1863): 103–104.

24 The "New Path," "A Letter to a Subscriber," 117.

25 Russell Sturgis Jr., "Our 'Articles' Examined," *The New Path* 1, no. 3 (July 1863): 31.

26 [Russell Sturgis Jr.], "Pictures and Studies," *The New Path* 2, no. 3 (July 1864): 39–40. For attribution of article to Sturgis, see Ferber 1985, 32; Pearson 1999, 435.

27 J. S. [William James Stillman], "Naturalism and Genius," 66–68.

28 "In Memory of Abraham Lincoln," *The New Path* 2, no. 5 (May 1865): 80.

29 [William Wordsworth], ["Lines Written a Few Miles above Tintern Abbey on Revisiting the Banks of the Wye During a Tour, July 13, 1798"], *The New Path* 1, no. 5 (September 1863): 60; C. [Clarence Cook], "Advance," *The New Path* 1, no. 5 (September 1863): 59.

30 John Keats, ["Endymion"], *The New Path* 1, no. 6 (October 1863): 76; C. H. M. [Charles Herbert Moore], "Fallacies of the Present School," *The New Path*, 1, no. 6 (October 1863): 64.

31 John Ruskin, "Mount Blanc Revisited. July, 1845," *The New Path* 1, no. 10 (February 1864): 135–136; C. C. [Clarence Cook], "Sonnet. To the Fringed Gentian," *The New Path* 2, no. 10 (October 1865): 165.

32 [Clarence Cook], "The Humorous in Art," *The New Path* 1, no. 10 (February 1864): 133–135; [Russell Sturgis Jr.], "Pictures and Studies," 46–47.

33 Lionel [Clarence Cook?], "The Artist's Fund Society, Fourth Annual Exhibition," *The New Path*, 1, no. 8 (December 1863): 98.

34 [Clarence Cook?], "Notices of Recent Pictures," *The New Path* 1, no. 12 (April 1864): 163; [Russell Sturgis Jr.], "National Academy of Design—Thirty-Ninth Annual Exhibition," *The New Path* 2, no. 1 (May 1864): 9.

35 [Russell Sturgis Jr.], "National Academy of Design—Thirty-Ninth Annual Exhibition," 10, 13.

36 [Russell Sturgis Jr.], "National Academy of Design—Thirty-Ninth Annual Exhibition," 12.

37 [Clarence Cook?], "Notices of Recent Pictures," 161–162; [Russell Sturgis Jr.], "Recent Exhibitions, Sales, Etc.," *The New Path* 2, no. 5 (May 1865): 75–77.

38 [Russell Sturgis Jr.?], "The Sixth Annual Exhibition of the Artist's Fund Society," *The New Path* 2, no. 12 (December 1865): 192–193.

39 C. H. M. [Charles Herbert Moore], October 1863, 61.

40 M. [Charles Herbert Moore], "The Office of Imagination," *The New Path* 1, no. 7 (November 1863): 77–80. In a letter to Farrer dated November 15, 1863, from his Catskill home, Moore asks, "How do you like my second article for the Path?" He then mentions Sturgis writing him, "pointing out some faults that I see plainly now. His suggestions are invaluable." He also mentions asking Wight for copies and says he would like to have six so he could keep one for himself and requests a copy of the October number. Moore Letters.

41 J. S. [William James Stillman], "Naturalism and Genius," 66–69.

42 M. [Charles Herbert Moore], "The Office of Imagination," 77.

43 M. [Charles Herbert Moore], "The Office of Imagination," 78.

44 M. [Charles Herbert Moore], "The Office of Imagination," 80.

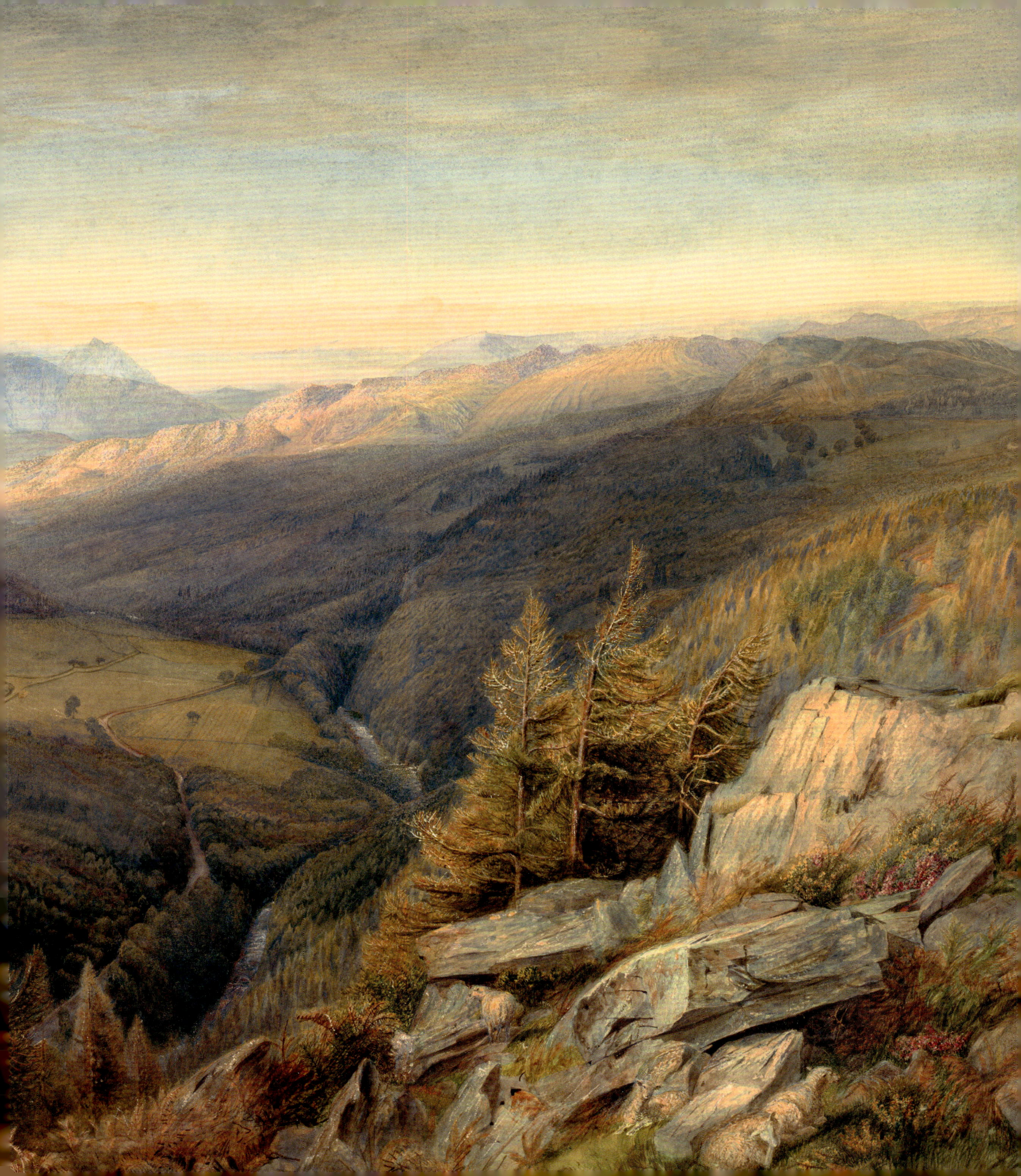

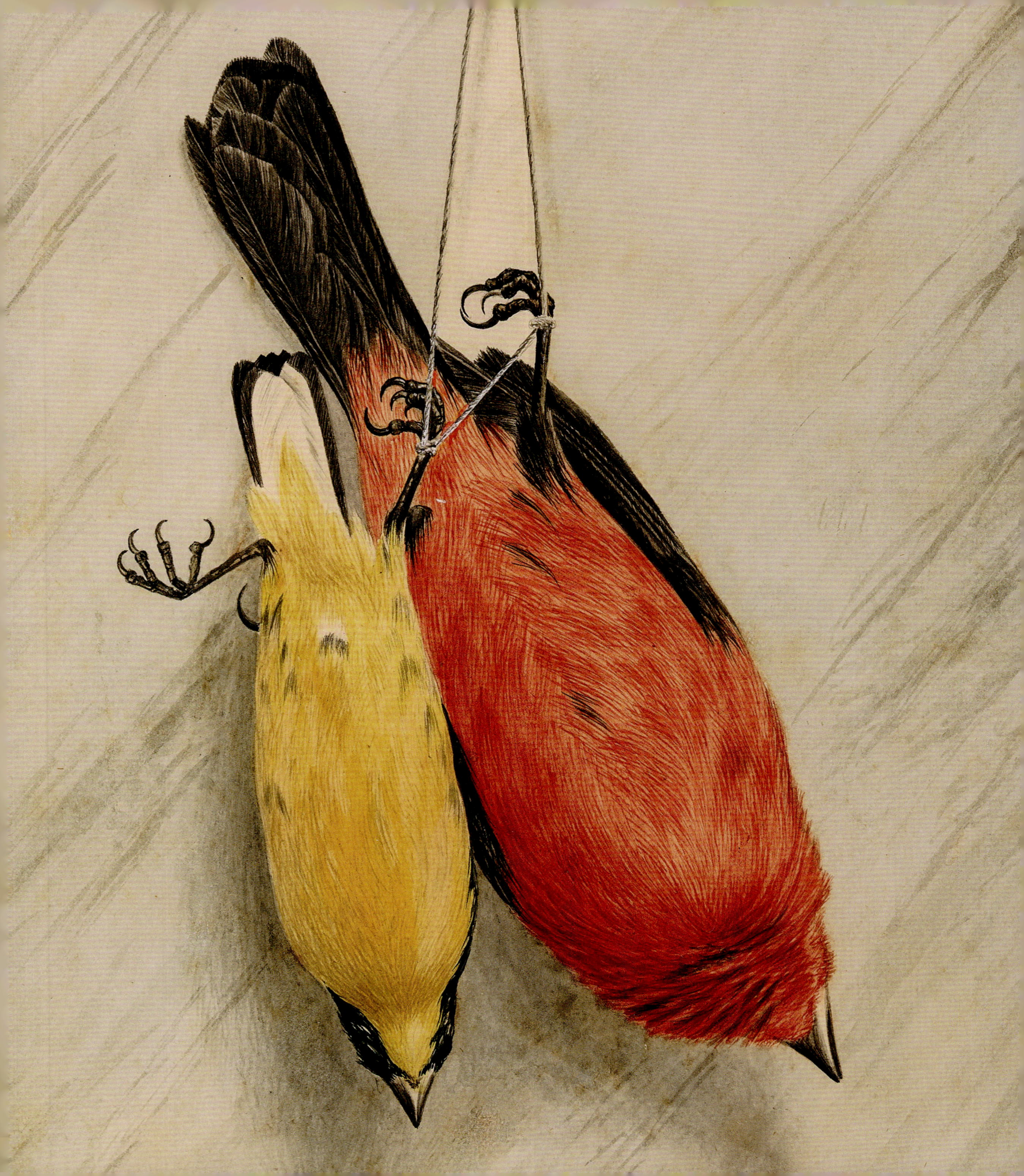

Selected Bibliography

Archival Sources

COOK LETTERS
Clarence Chatham Cook Letters, 1855–1891. Manuscripts and Archives Division, New York Public Library.

FARQUHAR COLLECTION
Francis P. Farquhar Papers, 1912–1968 (including material relating to Clarence King). The Bancroft Library, University of California, Berkeley.

FORD AUTOGRAPH COLLECTION
Ford Autograph Collection, 1589–1898. Manuscripts and Archives Division, New York Public Library.

FORD PAPERS
Gordon Lester Ford Papers, 1828–1889. Archives of American Art, Smithsonian Institution, Washington, DC.

FOWLER FORD PAPERS
Emily Fowler Ford Papers, 1744–1893. Manuscripts and Archives Division, New York Public Library.

GARDINER PAPERS
James Terry Gardiner Papers, 1776–1927. New York State Library, Albany. As the NYSL notes, "The family name historically had been spelled with an 'i' until his [James Terry's] grandfather, George, dropped the 'i.' James returned to the original spelling in his middle years" (*http://www.nysl.nysed.gov/msscfa/sc11835a.htm*). The present volume uses the spelling Gardner.

GARDINER PAPERS B
James Terry Gardiner Papers, 1860–1896. New York State Library, Albany.

HILL CORRESPONDENCE AND MISCELLANY
John William Hill Correspondence and Miscellany, 1854–1879. Manuscripts and Archives Division, New York Public Library.

HILL PRINT COLLECTION
John Hill Print Collection, [1799]–1836. New-York Historical Society, Department of Prints, Photographs, and Architectural Collections.

KING PAPERS
Clarence King Papers, 1873–1894. American Philosophical Society, Philadelphia.

LAY PAPERS
Oliver Ingraham Lay, Charles Downing Lay, and Lay Family Papers, 1789–2000. Archives of American Art, Smithsonian Institution, Washington, DC.

MISS PORTER'S FACULTY AND OTHERS COLLECTION
Miss Porter's Faculty and Others Collection. M. Burch Tracy Ford Library, Miss Porter's School, Farmington, MA.

MOORE LETTERS
Charles Herbert Moore Letters, 1860–1905. Manuscripts and Archives Division, New York Public Library.

MOORE PAPERS
Charles Herbert Moore Papers, 1894–1910. Harvard Art Museums Archives, Harvard University, Cambridge, MA.

NEWMAN MANUSCRIPT MATERIAL 1880
Henry Roderick Newman Manuscript Material, 1880. Manuscripts and Archives Division, New York Public Library.

NORTON PAPERS
Charles Eliot Norton Papers, c. 1845–1908. Houghton Library, Harvard College Library, Cambridge, MA.

RICHARDS PAPERS
William Trost Richards Papers, 1848–1920. Archives of American Art, Smithsonian Institution, Washington, DC.

ROSSETTI PAPERS
Dante Gabriel Rossetti Collection of Papers, 1855–1941. Manuscripts and Archives Division, New York Public Library.

SHATTUCK PAPERS
Aaron Draper Shattuck Papers, 1810–1983. Archives of American Art, Smithsonian Institution, Washington, DC.

STURGIS FAMILY PAPERS
Russell Sturgis Jr. Family Papers, 1808–c. 1940. Manuscripts and Archives, Sterling Memorial Library, Yale University, New Haven, CT.

STURGIS PAPERS
Russell Sturgis Architectural Drawings and Papers, 1847–1932. Columbia University Libraries, NY.

STURGIS PHOTOGRAPH COLLECTION
Russell Sturgis Photograph Collection, 1853–1903. Washington University in St. Louis University Library Archives, St. Louis, MO.

VAN BUREN COLLECTION
James Lyman Van Buren Collection. Special Collections Research Center, Syracuse University Libraries, NY.

WIGHT PAPERS
"Minutes of the Society for the Advancement of Truth in Art," Peter Bonnett Wight Papers. Ryerson & Burnham Libraries, The Art Institute of Chicago.

Books and Articles

ACKERMAN 1994
Ackerman, Gerald M. *American Orientalists*. Paris, 1994.

AHRENS 1976
Ahrens, Kent. "Pioneer Abroad, Henry R. Newman (1843–1917): Watercolorist and Friend of Ruskin." *The American Art Journal* 8, no. 2 (November 1976): 85–98.

ALEXANDER 1884
Alexander, Francesca. *Roadside Songs of Tuscany*. Parts 1 and 2. Translated and illustrated by Francesca Alexander. Edited by John Ruskin. Boston, 1884.

ALEXANDER 1885
Alexander, Francesca. *Roadside Songs of Tuscany*. Translated and illustrated by Francesca Alexander. Edited by John Ruskin. Orpington, Kent, UK, 1885.

ALEXIS 1986
Alexis, Karin May Elizabeth. "Russell Sturgis, Critic and Architect." PhD diss., University of Virginia, 1986.

ANDERSON 1997
Anderson, Nancy K. *Thomas Moran*. National Gallery of Art, Washington, DC, 1997.

ANDERSON AND FERBER 1990
Anderson, Nancy K., and Linda S. Ferber. *Albert Bierstadt: Art and Enterprise*. Brooklyn Museum, New York, 1990.

ATHENAEUM 1857
"Fine-Art Gossip." *Athenaeum*, June 20, 1857: 796.

ATHENAEUM 1858
Catalogue of the American Exhibition of British Art, at the Athenaeum Gallery. Boston, 1858.

AVERY 2002
Avery, Kevin J., Marjorie Shelley, Claire A. Conway, Carrie Rebora Barratt, Elliot Bostwick Davis, Tracie Felker, Stephanie L. Herdrich, and Karl Kusserow. *American Drawings and Watercolors in the Metropolitan Museum of Art*. Vol. 1, *A Catalogue of Works by Artists Born before 1835*. Metropolitan Museum of Art, New York, 2002.

BAILEY 2017
Bailey, Colin B., Michael Kelly, Carolyn Vega, Marta Werner, and Susan How. *The Networked Recluse: The Connected World of Emily Dickinson*. Amherst, MA, 2017.

BARR AND TABOR 2005
Barr, Sheldon, and Paul Tabor. "A Pre-Raphaelite Gem in New York City." *Magazine Antiques* 167, no. 4 (April 2005): 116–125.

BARRINGER 1999
Barringer, Tim. *Reading the Pre-Raphaelites*. New Haven, CT, 1999.

BARRINGER 2012
Barringer, Tim. *Reading the Pre-Raphaelites*. Rev. ed. New Haven, CT, 2012.

BARRINGER AND FAIRCLOUGH 2014
Barringer, Tim, and Oliver Fairclough. *Pastures Green & Dark Satanic Mills: The British Passion for Landscape*. American Federation of Arts, 2014.

BARTLETT 2011
Bartlett, Rosamund. *Tolstoy: A Russian Life*. New York, 2011.

BEDELL 2001
Bedell, Rebecca. *The Anatomy of Nature: Geology and American Landscape Painting, 1825–1875*. Princeton, NJ, 2001.

BEECHER AND STOWE 1969
Beecher, Catharine Esther, and Harriet Beecher Stowe. *The American Woman's Home: Or, Principles of Domestic Science*. New York, 1969.

BICKFORD 1982
Bickford, Christopher P. *Farmington in Connecticut*. Canaan, NH, 1982.

BOOTH 1867
Booth, Mary Louise. *History of the City of New York*. New York, 1867.

BOOTH AND ZAKRZEWSKA 1862
Booth, Mary L., and Marie E. Zakrzewska. *Prospectus of the Woman's Journal*. Boston, May 15, 1862.

BRADLEY AND OUSBY 1987
Bradley, John Lewis, and Ian Ousby, eds. *The Correspondence of John Ruskin and Charles Eliot Norton*. New York, 1987.

BRANDEGEE 1901
Brandegee, Robert B. *From the Open Book of Nature*. N.p., 1901.

BREWER 1930
Brewer, William Henry, and Francis P. Farquhar, eds. *Up and Down California in 1860–1864: The Journal of William H. Brewer*. 1st ed. New Haven, CT, 1930.

BRIDGES 2005
Bridges, Peter. "Eugene Schuyler: The Only Diplomatist." *Diplomacy and Statecraft* 16, no. 1 (2005): 13–22.

BROOKLYN AND LONG ISLAND 1864
Executive Committee, Brooklyn and Long Island Fair in Aid of the United States Sanitary Commission. *History of the Brooklyn and Long Island Fair*. Brooklyn, 1864.

BURKE AND GERDTS 1971
Burke, Russell E., and William H. Gerdts. *American Still-Life Painting*. New York, 1971.

BURNS AND DAVIS 2009
Burns, Sarah, and John Davis. *American Art to 1900: A Documentary History*. Berkeley, 2009.

CALIANDRI, JACOBS, AND MORAN 2012
Caliandri, Sarah M., Lisa M. Jacobs, and Nancy A. Moran. *Field Music: From Antietam to Andersonville—The Civil War Letters of Lyman B. Wilcox*. Kensington, CT, 2012.

CARY 1900
Cary, Elisabeth Luther. *The Rossettis, Dante Gabriel and Christina*. New York, 1900.

CARY 1906
Cary, Edward. "Some American Pre-Raphaelites: A Reminiscence." *The Scrip* 2, no. 1 (October 1906): 1–7.

CARY 1932A
Cary, Elisabeth Luther. "Art Trends: the Years Between." *New York Times*, January 31, 1932, X13.

CARY 1932B
Cary, Elisabeth Luther. "Art Trends: More Ancestors." *New York Times*, February 7, 1932, X11.

CASSEDY 1999
Cassedy, David. *A Civil War Album: Works by Twenty Artists Exhibited at the Great Central Fair in Philadelphia, June 1864 and Sold to Benefit the U.S. Sanitary Commission*. Schwarz Gallery, Philadelphia, 1999.

CASTERAS 1990
Casteras, Susan P. *English Pre-Raphaelitism and Its Reception in America in the Nineteenth Century*. Rutherford, NJ, 1990.

CASTERAS 1993
Casteras, Susan P. *John Ruskin and the Victorian Eye*. Phoenix Art Museum, 1993.

CIKOVSKY AND KELLY 1995
Cikovsky, Nicolai Jr., and Franklin Kelly. *Winslow Homer*. National Gallery of Art, Washington, DC, 1995.

COCHIN 1863
Cochin, Augustin. *The Results of Slavery*. Translated by Mary L. Booth. Boston, 1863.

COOK 1863
Cook, Clarence C. "Introductory." *The New Path* 1, no. 1 (May 1863): 1–4.

COOK 1902
Cook, Clarence C. *Poems by Clarence Cook*. Edited by Louisa W. Cook. New York, 1902.

COOPER UNION 1864
Cooper Union for the Advancement of Science and Art. "Fifth Annual Report of the Trustees of the Cooper Union for the Advancement of Science and Art." New York, 1864.

COOPER UNION 1866
Cooper Union for the Advancement of Science and Art. "Seventh Annual Report of the Trustees of the Cooper Union for the Advancement of Science and Art." New York, 1866.

CORTISSOZ 1911
Cortissoz, Royal. *John La Farge: A Memoir and a Study*. New York, 1911.

COWDREY 1943
Cowdrey, Mary Bartlett, ed. *National Academy of Design Exhibition Record, 1826–1860*. 2 vols. New York, 1943.

THE CRAYON
The Crayon 1, no. 1 (1855)–*The Crayon* 8, no. 7 (1861).

CURRAN 1993
Curran, Kathleen. "A Forgotten Architect of the Gilded Age: Josiah Cleaveland Cady's Legacy." *Watkinson Exhibition Catalogs* (1993).

DEARDEN 1999
Dearden, James S. *John Ruskin: A Life in Pictures*. Sheffield, UK, 1999.

DE KAY 1887
De Kay, Charles. "Movements in American Painting." *Magazine of Art* 10 (1887): 37–42.

DEXTER 1848
Dexter, Franklin B. "Modern Painters." *North American Review* 66, no. 138 (January 1848): 110–145.

DICKASON 1953
Dickason, David Howard. *The Daring Young Men: The Story of the American Pre-Raphaelites*. Bloomington, IN, 1953.

DOUGHTY AND WAHL 1965–1967
Doughty, Oswald, and John Robert Wahl, eds. *The Letters of D. G. Rossetti*. 4 vols. Oxford, UK, 1965–1967.

DOWLING 2007
Dowling, Linda. *Charles Eliot Norton: The Art of Reform in Nineteenth-Century America*. Durham, NH, 2007.

DUYCKINCK AND DUYCKINCK 1881
Duyckinck, Evert Augustus, and George Long Duyckinck. *Cyclopædia of American Literature*. Vol. 2, edited by Michael Laird Simons. Philadelphia, 1881.

DYSON 2014
Dyson, Stephen L. *The Last Amateur: The Life of William J. Stillman*. Albany, 2014.

EDWARDS 1988
Edwards, Gary. *International Guide to Nineteenth-Century Photographers and Their Works*. Boston, 1988.

ELLIOTT 2006
Elliott, David B. *A Pre-Raphaelite Marriage: The Lives and Works of Marie Spartali Stillman and William James Stillman*. Easthampton, MA, 2006.

ELZEA 1984
Elzea, Rowland. *The Samuel and Mary R. Bancroft, Jr. and Related Pre-Raphaelite Collections*. Rev. ed. Delaware Art Museum, 1984.

EMMONS 1907
Emmons, Samuel Franklin. *Biographical Memoir of Clarence King*. Washington, DC, 1907.

ESKIND 1995
Eskind, Andrew H. *Index to American Photographic Collections*. 3rd enlarged ed. New York, 1995.

EVENING POST 1857
"The American Exhibition of British Art." *Evening Post*, October 20, 1857, 2.

FALK 1988/1989
Falk, Peter Hastings, ed. *The Annual Exhibition Record of the Pennsylvania Academy of the Fine Arts.* 3 vols. Madison, CT, 1988–1989.

FARR 1992
Farr, Judith. *The Passion of Emily Dickinson.* Cambridge, MA, 1992.

FARR AND CARTER 2004
Farr, Judith, with Louise Carter. *The Gardens of Emily Dickinson.* Cambridge, MA, 2004.

FAVRETTI AND MYERS 1986
Favretti, Margaret, and Kenneth Myers. "'In Most Extreme Need': Correspondence of C. H. Moore with J. F. Kensett." *Archives of American Art Journal* 26, no. 1 (1986): 11–17.

FERBER 1973
Ferber, Linda S. *William Trost Richards: American Landscape & Marine Painter.* Pennsylvania Academy of Fine Arts, Philadelphia, 1973.

FERBER 1980
Ferber, Linda S. *William Trost Richards (1833–1905): American Landscape and Marine Painter.* New York, 1980.

FERBER 1982
Ferber, Linda S. *Tokens of Friendship: Miniature Watercolors by William T. Richards.* Metropolitan Museum of Art, New York, 1982.

FERBER 1985
Ferber, Linda S. "An Introduction to the American Pre-Raphaelites." *Magazine Antiques* 127, no. 4 (April 1985): 878–887.

FERBER 1986
Ferber, Linda S. *"Never at Fault": The Drawings of William Trost Richards.* Hudson River Museum of Westchester, Yonkers, NY, 1986.

FERBER 2001
Ferber, Linda S. *Pastoral Interlude: William T. Richards in Chester County.* Brandywine River Museum, Chadds Ford, PA, 2001.

FERBER 2002
Ferber, Linda S. "John Brown's Grave and Other Civil War Themes in William T. Richards's Adirondack Landscapes." *Magazine Antiques* 162, no. 1 (July 2002): 72–81.

FERBER 2008
Ferber, Linda S. "An American Pre-Raphaelite in New York: William Trost Richards." *Archives of American Art Journal* 47, nos. 1–2 (2008): 4–15.

FERBER 2012
Ferber, Linda S. *A Mine of Beauty: Landscapes by William Trost Richards.* Pennsylvania Academy of the Fine Arts, Philadelphia, 2012.

FERBER AND GALLATI 1998
Ferber, Linda S., and Barbara Dayer Gallati. *Masters of Color and Light: Homer, Sargent, and the American Watercolor Movement.* Brooklyn Museum of Art, New York, 1998.

FERBER AND GERDTS 1985
Ferber, Linda S., and William H. Gerdts. *The New Path: Ruskin and the American Pre-Raphaelites.* Brooklyn Museum, New York, 1985.

FERGUSON 1970
Ferguson, Charles B. *Aaron Draper Shattuck, N.A., 1832–1928: A Retrospective Exhibition.* New Britain Museum of American Art, CT, 1970.

FERGUSON 1971
Ferguson, Charles B. *An Exhibition of the Work of Robert Bolling Brandegee, A. N. A.* New Britain Museum of American Art, CT, 1971.

FINLAY 1998
Finlay, Nancy. "The Hermit of Phantom Island: John Henry Hill's Etchings of Lake George." In *Adirondack Prints and Printmakers: The Call of the Wild,* edited by Caroline M. Welsh, 105 – 124. Syracuse, NY, 1998.

FOLEY AND MOUZAKES 2012
Foley, Tricia, and Karen Mouzakes. *Images of America: Yaphank.* Charleston, 2012.

FORMAN 1884
Forman, Henry Buxton. "An American Studio in Florence." *The Manhattan* 3, no. 6 (June 1884): 525–539.

FOSHAY 1984
Foshay, Ella M. *Reflections of Nature.* New York, 1984.

FOSTER 2017
Foster, Kathleen A. *American Watercolor in the Age of Homer and Sargent.* Philadelphia Museum of Art, 2017.

FREDERICK AND MARSH 2015
Frederick, Margaretta S., and Jan Marsh. *Poetry in Beauty: The Pre-Raphaelite Art of Marie Spartali Stillman.* Delaware Art Museum, Wilmington, 2015.

GALLATI 1988
Gallati, Barbara Dayer. "The Shattuck Family: Aaron Draper Shattuck's Experiment in Narrative Content." *The American Art Journal* 20, no. 3 (1988): 36–47.

GARRISON 1893
Garrison, Wendell P. "William James Stillman." *Century* 46, no. 5 (September 1893): 656–658.

GEORGI 2013
Georgi, Karen L. *Critical Shift: Rereading Jarves, Cook, Stillman, and the Narratives of Nineteenth-Century American Art.* University Park, PA, 2013.

GERDTS 1969
Gerdts, William H. "The Influence of Ruskin and Pre-Raphaelitism on American Still-Life Painting." *The American Art Journal* 1, no. 2 (Fall 1969): 80–97.

THE GERM 1859/1979
The Germ: The Literary Magazine of the Pre-Raphaelites. Preface by Andrew Rose. Oxford, UK, 1979.

GOLDYNE 1975
Goldyne, Joseph R. *J. M. W. Turner: Works on Paper in American Collections.* University Art Museum, Berkeley, 1975.

GOLDYNE 1981
Goldyne, John. *Francesca Alexander (1837–1917)—Drawings for the "Roadside Songs of Tuscany."* Sven A. Bruntjen Fine Arts, Woodside, CA, 1981.

GOODYEAR 2011
Goodyear, Frank H., III. "An Early Photograph of Shoshone Falls: Uncovering a Network of Communities in 1870s Idaho." *History of Photography* 35, no. 3 (2011): 269–280.

GREAT CENTRAL FAIR 1864
Catalogue of Paintings, Drawings, Statuary Etc. of the Art Department in the Great Central Fair. 2nd rev. ed. US Sanitary Commission, Philadelphia, June 1864.

HAGUE 1904
Hague, James, ed. *Clarence King Memoirs: The Helmet of Mambrino*. New York, 1904.

HARDING 1996
Harding, Ellen, ed. *Re-Framing the Pre-Raphaelites: Historical and Theoretical Essays*. Brookfield, VT, 1996.

HARRISON 1954
Harrison, John Fletcher Clews. *A History of the Working Men's College 1854–1954*. London, 1954.

HARRISON AND NEWALL 2010
Harrison, Colin, and Christopher Newall. *The Pre-Raphaelites and Italy*. Ashmolean Museum, Oxford, UK, 2010.

HERRON 2010
Herron, John P. *Nature, Culture, and Community, 1865–1965*. New York, 2010.

HILL 1867
Hill, John Henry. *Sketches from Nature*. New York, 1867.

HILL 1888
Hill, John Henry. *John William Hill: An Artist's Memorial*. New York, 1888.

HILL 1981
Hill, May Brawley. *Fidelia Bridges: American Pre-Raphaelite*. New Britain Museum of Art, CT, 1981.

HILL 1991
Hill, May Brawley. "Landscapes of Rockland County and the Hudson by Three Generations of Artists Who Resided in West Nyack." Unpublished manuscript, 1991.

HOPPIN 1981
Hoppin, Martha J., ed. *Arcadian Vales: Views of the Connecticut River Valley*. George Walter Vincent Smith Art Museum, Springfield, MA, 1981.

HOWAT 1987
Howat, John K. *American Paradise: The World of the Hudson River School*. The Metropolitan Museum of Art, New York, 1987.

HUTCHESON 1993
Hutcheson, Katurah. *Determined Realists: The American Pre-Raphaelites*. Richard York Gallery, New York, 1992.

IKIN 2012
Ikin, Caroline. *The Victorian Garden*. Oxford, UK, 2012.

JACKSON 2010
Jackson, Kevin. *The Worlds of John Ruskin*. Pallas Athene & the Ruskin Foundation, 2010.

JARVES 1864
Jarves, James Jackson. *The Art-Idea*. 2nd ed. New York, 1864.

JARVES 1869
Jarves, James Jackson. *Art Thoughts: The Experiences and Observations of an American Amateur in Europe*. New York, 1869.

JONES 1958
Jones, Agnes Halsey. *Rediscovered Painters of Upstate New York, 1700–1875*. New York State Historical Association, Cooperstown. Utica, NY, 1958.

KELLY 1985
Kelly, James C. *The South on Paper: Line, Color, and Light*. Spartanburg, SC, 1985.

KEMP 1990
Kemp, Wolfgang. *The Desire of My Eyes: The Life and Work of John Ruskin*. Translated by Jan van Heurck. New York, 1990.

KENNEY 2008
Kenney, Elise K. "From the Archives: The Patrons/Benefactors of the School of the Fine Arts at Yale College." *Yale University Art Gallery Bulletin* (2008): 152–160.

KENNEY 2011
Kenney, Elise K. "From the Archives: The Yale School of the Fine Arts First Exhibition of 1867." *Yale University Art Gallery Bulletin* (2011): 86–90.

KING 1872
King, Clarence. *Mountaineering in the Sierra Nevada*. Boston, 1872.

KIRCHHOFF 1984
Kirchhoff, Frederick. *John Ruskin*. Boston, 1984.

KOEHLER 1880
Koehler, S. R. "The Works of the American Etchers: XII—J. Henry Hill." *American Art Review* 1, no. 10 (August 1880): 429–430.

LANDAU 1981
Landau, Sarah B., and John Zukowsky. *P. B. Wight: Architect, Contractor, and Critic, 1838–1925*. Burnham Library of Architecture, Art Institute of Chicago, 1981.

LEITH 1994
Leith, Royal W. *Ruskin and His American Followers in Tuscany: A Historical Study*. St. Albans, Herts, UK, 1994.

LEITH 1996
Leith, Royal W. *A Quiet Devotion: The Life and Work of Henry Roderick Newman*. Jordan-Volpe Gallery, New York, 1996.

LEITH 2007
Leith, Royal W. "New Light on Henry Roderick Newman as an Oil Painter: Recent Discoveries." *Magazine Antiques* 172 (October 2007): 98–105.

LILLIE 1890
Lillie, Lucy Cecil White. "Two Phases of American Art." *Harper's New Monthly Magazine* 80, no. 476 (January 1890): 206–216.

LIONEL 1863
Lionel [but probably Clarence Cook; see Simon note 33, p. 266]. "The Artists' Fund Society, Fourth Annual Exhibition." *The New Path* 1, no. 8 (December 1863): 92–98.

LYDENBERG 1954
Lydenberg, Harry Miller. "George Philes: Bookman." *The Papers of the Bibliographical Society of America* 48, no. 1 (First Quarter, 1954): 1–48.

LYNFORD 2019
Lynford, Sophie. "Painting Dissent: The Pre-Raphaelite Experiment in America." PhD diss., Yale University, 2019.

MANTHORNE 2012
Manthorne, Katherine E. "'The Voice of Nature': The Art of Fidelia Bridges in the 1870s." *American Arts Quarterly* 29, no. 1 (Winter 2012): 27–34.

MARLOR 1970
Marlor, Clark S. *Brooklyn Art Association. A History of the Brooklyn Art Association with an Index of Exhibitions*. New York, 1970.

MARSH 1998
Marsh, Jan. *The Pre-Raphaelites*. National Portrait Gallery, London, 1998.

MARTIN 1865
Martin, Henri. *Martin's History of France: The Age of Louis XIV*. 2 vols. Translated by Mary L. Booth. Boston, 1865.

MARYANSKI 2012
Maryanski, Maureen. "A Different Booth: William Henry Seward Corresponds with Mary L. Booth." *From the Stacks* (blog). New-York Historical Society Museum & Library. November 7, 2012. *http://blog.nyhistory.org/a-different-booth-william-henry-seward-corresponds-with-mary-l-booth/*.

MASTEN 2008
Masten, April F. *Art Work: Women Artists and Democracy in Mid-Nineteenth-Century New York*. Philadelphia, 2008.

MATHER 1957
Mather, Frank Jewett. *Charles Herbert Moore: Landscape Painter*. Princeton, NJ, 1957.

MCCLINTON 1973
McClinton, Katharine (Morrison). *The Chromolithographs of Louis Prang*. New York, 1973.

METROPOLITAN FAIR 1864
Catalogue of the Art Exhibition at the Metropolitan Fair, in Aid of the U. S. Sanitary Commission. New York, 1864.

METROPOLITAN FAIR 1867
A Record of the Metropolitan Fair: In Aid of the United States Sanitary Commission, Held at New York in April, 1864. New York, 1867.

MILLER 1993
Miller, Angela. *Empire of the Eye*. Ithaca, NY, 1993.

MITCHELL 2015
Mitchell, Mark D., Bill Brown, Katie A. Pfohl, and Carol Troyen. *The Art of American Still Life: Audubon to Warhol*. Philadelphia Museum of Art, 2015.

MOORE 1900
Moore, Charles H. "John Ruskin as an Art Critic." *Atlantic Monthly* 86, no. 516 (October 1900): 438–449.

MOORE 2006
Moore, James Gregory. *King of the 40th Parallel: Discovery in the American West*. Stanford, CA, 2006.

MORRIS 1912
Morris, Harrison S. *Masterpieces of the Sea: William T. Richards, A Brief Outline of His Life and Art*. Philadelphia, 1912.

MOSENTHAL AND HORNE 1907
Mosenthal, Philip J., and Charles F. Horne, eds. *The City College: Memories of Sixty Years, Edited for the Associate Alumni of the College of the City of New York*. New York, 1907.

MUNSON 1894–1895
Munson Phonographic News and Teacher 9 (April 1894–March 1895).

MUNSON 1895
Munson, Myron A. *The Munson Record: A Genealogical and Biographical Account of Captain Thomas Munson (A Pioneer of Hartford and New Haven) and His Descendants*. Vol. 2. New Haven, CT, 1895.

MURRAY 2004
Murray, Christopher John, ed. *Encyclopedia of the Romantic Era, 1760–1850*. Vol. 2. New York, 2004.

MYERS 1981
Myers, John Walker. "Aaron Draper Shattuck, 1832–1928: Painter of Landscapes and Student of Nature's Charms." PhD diss., University of Delaware, 1981.

MYERS 1987
Myers, Kenneth. *The Catskills: Painters, Writers, and Tourists in the Mountain, 1820–1895*. Hudson River Museum of Westchester, Yonkers, New York, 1987.

NAEF AND WOOD 1975
Naef, Weston J., and James N. Wood. *Era of Exploration: The Rise of Landscape Photography in the American West, 1860–1885*. Albright-Knox Art Gallery and Metropolitan Museum of Art, 1975.

THE NATION 1865
"The Sixth Annual Exhibition of the Artists' Fund Society of New York." *The Nation* 1, no. 21 (November 1865): 663–664.

NATIONAL ACADEMY OF DESIGN 1857
American Exhibition of British Art: Oil Pictures and Water Colours. New York, 1857.

NATIONAL ACADEMY OF DESIGN 1865
Ceremonies on the Occasion of the Laying the Corner-Stone, October 21, 1863, and the Inauguration of the Building, April 27, 1865. National Academy of Design, New York, 1865.

NATIONAL ACADEMY OF DESIGN 1867–1868
Catalogue of the First Winter Exhibition of the National Academy of Design Including the First Annual Collection of the American Society of Painters in Water Colors and the Works from the American Art Department of the Paris Universal Exposition. National Academy of Design, New York, 1867–1868.

NATIONAL ACADEMY OF DESIGN 1868–1869
Catalogue of the Second Winter Exhibition of the National Academy of Design Including the Second Annual Collection of the American Society of Painters in Water Colors and the Works from the American Art Department of the Paris Universal Exposition. National Academy of Design, New York, 1868–1869.

NAYLOR 1973
Naylor, Maria. *The National Academy of Design Exhibition Record 1861–1900*, 2 vols. New York, 1973.

NAYLOR 2012
Naylor, Natalie A. *Women in Long Island's Past: A History of Eminent Ladies and Everyday Lives*. Charleston, 2012.

NEW YORK TIMES 1924
"The World of Art: The New Path a Byway." *New York Times*, September 7, 1924, 35, 131.

NEWALL 2014
Newall, Christopher. *John Ruskin: Artist and Observer*. National Gallery of Canada, Ottawa, 2014.

NEWALL 2016
Newall, Christopher. *Pre-Raphaelites: Beauty and Rebellion*. Liverpool, 2016.

THE NEW PATH
The New Path 1, no. 1 (May 1863)–*The New Path* 2, no. 12 (December 1865).

NORTON 1879
Norton, Charles Eliot. *Notes on Drawings by Mr. Ruskin, Placed on Exhibition by Professor Norton, of Harvard College*. Museum of Fine Arts, Boston, 1879.

NOVAK 1980
Novak, Barbara. *Nature and Culture: American Landscape and Painting, 1825–1875*. New York, 1980.

PEARSON 1999
Pearson, Marjorie. "The Writings of Russell Sturgis and Peter B. Wight: The Victorian Architect as Critic and Historian." PhD diss., City University of New York, 1999.

PENNSYLVANIA ACADEMY OF THE FINE ARTS 1858
Catalogue of the American Exhibition of British Art at the Pennsylvania Academy of the Fine Arts: Oil Pictures and Water Colors. Philadelphia, 1858.

PHILLIPS 1988
Phillips, Sandra S. *Charmed Places: Hudson River Artists and Their Houses, Studios, and Vistas*. New York, 1988.

PHISTERER 1912
Phisterer, Frederick. *New York in the War of the Rebellion, 1861 to 1865*. Vol. 1. Albany, 1912.

PRANG'S CHROMO 1868
Prang's Chromo: A Journal of Popular Art 1, no. 2 (April 1868).

RAYMOND 1903
Raymond, R. W. "Biographical Notice of Clarence King." *Transactions of the American Institute of Mining Engineers* 33 (1903): 619–650.

REED AND TROYEN 1993
Reed, Welsh, and Carol Troyen. *Awash in Color: Homer, Sargent, and the Great American Watercolor*. Boston, 1993.

RENN 2013
Renn, Melissa. "Deep Seers: John Ruskin and the Teaching of Art at Harvard." In *Persistent Ruskin: Studies in Influence, Assimilation, and Effect*. Edited by Keith Hanley and Brian Maidment. Burlington, VT, 2013.

RINALDUCCI 2000
Rinalducci, Jennifer. "The 1857–58 American Exhibition of British Art: Critical Reactions in the Cultural Context of New York." MA thesis, Florida State University, 2000.

RINALDUCCI 2002
Rinalducci, Jennifer. "The 1857–58 American Exhibition of British Art: Critical Reactions in the Cultural Context of New York." *Athanor* 20 (2002): 77–83.

ROSENBERG 1962
Rosenberg, Ralph P. "Eugene Schuyler's Doctor of Philosophy Degree: A Theory concerning the Dissertation." *Journal of Higher Education* 33, no. 7 (October 1962): 381–386.

ROSSETTI 1895
Rossetti, Dante Gabriel, and William Michael Rossetti. *Dante Gabriel Rossetti: His Family Letters with a Memoir by William Michael Rossetti*. Vol. 1. London, 1895.

ROSSETTI 1906
Rossetti, William Michael. *Some Reminiscences*. Vol. 1. New York, 1906.

RUSKIN 1848
Ruskin, John. *Modern Painters*. Vol. 1. 4th ed. London, 1848.

RUSKIN 1849
Ruskin, John. *The Seven Lamps of Architecture*. New York, 1849.

RUSKIN 1850–1852
Ruskin, John. *Modern Painters*. 1st American ed. from 3rd London ed., rev. by author. New York, 1850–1852.

RUSKIN 1851 NY
Ruskin, John. *Pre-Raphaelitism*. New York, 1851.

RUSKIN 1857
Ruskin, John. *Elements of Drawing*. New York, 1857.

RUSKIN 1885
Ruskin, John. *Arrows of the Chace: A Collection of Scattered Letters Published Chiefly in the Daily Newspapers, 1840–1880*. New York, 1885.

RUSKIN 1895
Ruskin, John. *The Ruskin Reader: Being Passages from Modern Painters, the Seven Lamps of Architecture, and the Stones of Venice*. London, 1895.

RUSKIN 1903–1912
Ruskin, John. *The Works of John Ruskin*. Edited by E. T. Cook and Alexander Wedderburn. 39 vols. London, 1903–1912.

RUSKIN AND SWAN 1888
Ruskin, John, and Howard Swan. *Preliminary Catalogue of the St. George's Museum, Walkley, Sheffield*. Sheffield, UK, 1888.

RUTLEDGE 1955
Rutledge, Anna Wells, ed. *Cumulative Record of Exhibition Catalogues: the Pennsylvania Academy of the Fine Arts, 1807–1870; the Society of Artists, 1800–1814; the Artists' Fund Society, 1835–1845*. Philadelphia, 1955. Rev. ed. Madison, CT, 1988.

SACHS 2006
Sachs, Aaron. *The Humboldt Current: Nineteenth-Century Exploration and the Roots of American Environmentalism*. New York, 2006.

SANDWEISS 2009
Sandweiss, Martha A. *Passing Strange: A Gilded Age Tale of Love and Deception Across the Color Line*. New York, 2009.

SCHLETT 2015
Schlett, James. *A Not Too Greatly Changed Eden: The Story of the Philosophers' Camp in the Adirondacks*. Ithaca, NY, 2015.

SCHUYLER AND SCHAEFFER 1901
Schuyler, Eugene, and Evelyn Schuyler Schaeffer. *Eugene Schuyler: Selected Essays with a Memoir by Evelyn Schuyler Schaeffer*. New York, 1901.

SCOTT 1975
Scott, John. "The Hill Family of Clarksville." *South of the Mountains* 19, no. 1 (January–March 1975): 5–18.

SHARF 1968
Sharf, Frederic A. "Fidelia Bridges, Painter of Birds and Flowers." *Essex Institute Historical Collections* 104, no. 3 (July 1968): 217–238.

SHELDON 1879
Sheldon, George William. *American Painters: With Eighty-Three Examples of Their Work Engraved on Wood*. New York, 1879.

SHELDON 1881
Sheldon, George William. *American Painters: With One Hundred and Four Examples of Their Work Engraved on Wood*. New York, 1881.

SHELDON 1972
Sheldon, George William. *American Painters: With One Hundred and Four Examples of Their Work Engraved on Wood*. New York, 1972, reprint of 1881 ed.

SHI 1995
Shi, David. *Facing Facts: Realism in American Thought and Culture, 1850–1920*. New York, 1995.

SIDDALL 2012
Siddall, Lawrence. "Thomas Farrer and the Pre-Raphaelite Movement in America." *Review of the Pre-Raphaelite Society* 20, no. 1 (Spring 2012): 1–14.

SIMON 1990
Simon, Janice. "'*The Crayon*,' 1855–1861: The Voice of Nature in Criticism, Poetry, and the Fine Arts." PhD diss., University of Michigan, 1990.

SIMON 2013
Simon, Janice. "William James Stillman's Photographic Turn: The Adirondac Woods as Transcendental Experience." In *The Photograph and the Collection*, edited by Graeme Farnell, 96–124. Edinburgh, 2013.

SIMONI 1952
Simoni, John Peter. "Art Critics and Criticism in Nineteenth Century America." PhD diss., Ohio State University, 1952.

SPARLING 1985
Sparling, Tobin Andrews. *American Scenery: The Art of John & John William Hill*. Print Gallery, New York Public Library, 1984.

SPASSKY 1985
Spassky, Natalie. *American Paintings in the Metropolitan Museum of Art*. Vol. 2. New York, 1985.

STALEY 1973
Staley, Allen. *The Pre-Raphaelite Landscape*. Oxford, UK, 1973.

STEBBINS AND ANDERSON 2007
Stebbins, Theodore E., and Virginia Anderson. *The Last Ruskinians: Charles Eliot Norton, Charles Herbert Moore, and Their Circle*. Fogg Art Museum, Cambridge, MA, 2007.

STEIN 1967
Stein, Roger B. *John Ruskin and Aesthetic Thought in America, 1840–1900*. Cambridge, MA, 1967.

STEPHANIC 1997
Stephanic, Barbara Jean. "Clarence Cook's Role as Art Critic, Advocate for Professionalism, Educator, and Arbiter of Taste in America." PhD diss., University of Maryland, 1997.

STILLMAN 1860
Stillman, William James. "*Modern Painters*. By J. Ruskin. Vol. V. Smith, Elder, & Co. London." *Atlantic Monthly* 6, no. 34 (August 1860): 239–242.

STILLMAN 1900
Stillman, William James. "Art as a Means of Expression." *International Monthly* 1 (February 1900): 133–161.

STILLMAN 1901 LONDON
Stillman, William James. *The Autobiography of a Journalist*. Vol. 1. London, 1901.

STILLMAN 1901 NEW YORK
Stillman, William James. *The Autobiography of a Journalist*. Vol. 1, 2nd impression. New York, 1901.

STILLMAN 1988
Stillman, William James. *Poetic Localities: Photographs of Adirondacks, Cambridge, Crete, Italy, Athens*. With essays by Anne Ehrenkranz, Colin Eisler, Linda S. Ferber, and Andre Jammes. Aperture and International Center of Photography, New York, 1988.

STULA 2007
Stula, Nancy. *At Home and Abroad: The Transcendental Landscapes of Christopher Pearse Cranch (1813–1892)*. Lyman Allyn Art Museum, New London, CT, 2007.

STURGIS 1866
Sturgis, Russell, Jr. "Obituary: J. L. Van Buren, Major and A. D. C. and Brevet Brigadier-General, U.S. Vols." *United States Service Magazine* 5, no. 6 (June 1866): 565–566.

STURGIS 1905
Sturgis, Russell. *The Interdependence of the Arts and Design: A Series of Six Lectures Delivered at the Art Institute of Chicago*. Chicago, 1905.

SWETT 1931
Swett, Lucia Gray. *John Ruskin's Letters to Francesca and Memoirs of the Alexanders*. Boston, 1931.

TOBIN 2005
Tobin, Thomas J., ed. *Worldwide Pre-Raphaelitism*. Albany, 2005.

TROY YOUNG MEN'S ASSOCIATION 1861
Catalogue of the Fourth Annual Art Exhibition of the Troy Young Men's Association. Troy, NY, 1861.

TUCKERMAN 1867
Tuckerman, Henry S. *The Book of the Artists*. New York, 1867.

TURNER 1999
Turner, James. *The Liberal Education of Charles Eliot Norton*. Baltimore, 1999.

VALENTINE 1866
Valentine, David T. *Obsequies of Abraham Lincoln, in the City of New York*. New York, 1866.

WAERN 1896
Waern, Cecilia. *John La Farge: Artist and Writer*. New York, 1896.

WASHBURN GALLERY 1976
Drawings and Watercolors: John William Hill, John Henry Hill. Washburn Gallery, New York, 1976.

WEISS 1977
Weiss, Jo Ann W. "Clarence Cook: His Critical Writings." PhD diss., Johns Hopkins University, 1977.

WEITKAMPF 1901
Weitkampf, Frank. “A Hackensack Ruskin Disciple.” *New York Times*, December 8, 1901, Magazine Supplement, 15.
WHITE 2003
White, Willis H. “Using Uncommon Sources to Illuminate Family History: A Long Island Tuthill Example.” *National Genealogical Society Quarterly* 91, no. 1 (March 2003): 17–18.
WHITNEY 1868
Whitney, J. D. *The Yosemite Book: A Description of the Yosemite Valley and the Adjacent Region of the Sierra Nevada, and of the Big Trees of California*. New York, 1868.
WIGHT 1884
Wight, Peter Bonnett. *The Development of the New Phases of the Fine Arts in America (From the Inland Architect and Builder of November and December 1884)*. Chicago, 1885.
WIGHT 1890
Wight, Willliam Ward. *The Wights: A Record of Thomas Wight of Dedham and Medfield and of His Descendants 1635–1890*. Milwaukee, 1890.
WIGHT 1925
Wight, Peter B. “A Portrait Gallery of Chicago Architects: IV. Asher Carter, F. A. I. A.” *The Western Architect* 34, no. 1 (January 1925): 10–13.
WILES 2001
Wiles, Stephanie. “Between England and America: The Art of Thomas Charles Farrer and Henry Farrer.” PhD diss., City University of New York, 2001.
WILES 2002
Wiles, Stephanie. “A Survey of Watercolors by Henry Farrer.” *Master Drawings* 40, no. 4 (Winter 2002): 317–331.
WILKINS 1958
Wilkins, Thurman. *Clarence King: A Biography*. New York, 1958.
WILKINS 1988
Wilkins, Thurman. *Clarence King: A Biography*. Rev. ed. Albuquerque, 1988.
WILSON 2006
Wilson, Robert. *The Explorer King: Adventure, Science, and the Great Diamond Hoax—Clarence King in the Old West*. New York, 2006.
WODEHOUSE 1966
Wodehouse, Lawrence. “‘New Path’ and the American Pre-Raphaelite Brotherhood.” *Art Journal* 25, no. 4 (Summer 1966): 351–354.
WOOTTON 2005
Wootton, Sarah. “Keats’s Poetry as a Common Thread in English and American Pre-Raphaelitism.” In *Worldwide Pre-Raphaelitism*, edited by Thomas J. Tobin, 279–302. Albany, 2005.
YALE 1867
First Annual Exhibition of the Yale School of the Fine Arts: Founded as a Department of Yale College by the Late Augustus Russell Street. New Haven, CT, 1867.
YARNALL 1986
Yarnall, James L. “John La Farge’s *Portrait of the Painter* and Use of Photography in His Work.” *The American Art Journal* 18, no. 1 (Winter 1986): 4–20.
YARNALL 2012
Yarnall, James L. *John La Farge, A Biographical and Critical Study*. Burlington, VT, 2012.
YATES 2006
Yates, Donald. “John Matthews: Father of the Soda Fountain.” *Bottles and Extras* (Summer 2006): 72–75.
ZIMMERN 1890
Zimmern, Helen. “An American Watercolorist in Paris.” *The Sun*, September 7, 1890, 15.

Additional Newspaper and Journal Articles Related to Timeline

“Art: The Cooper Institute ‘School of Design’ for Women [II].” *The Round Table,* n.s., 1, no. 6 (October 14, 1865): 92–93.
“Art: Exhibition at the National Academy of Design [III].” *The Round Table* 1, no. 21 (May 7, 1864): 326–327.
Benson, Eugene (Sordello). “Foreign and American Art: Pictures at the Artist Fund Society Exhibition [Concluding Article].” *Evening Post*, New York, November 29, 1865.
Benson, Eugene. “A New Art Critic.” *Atlantic Monthly* 16, no. 95 (September 1865): 325–330.
Boston Transcript. “Art Intelligence.” May 24, 1860, 2:3.
Conant, S. S. “Fine Arts.” *Putnam’s Magazine* 1, no. 2 (February 1868): 257–259.
[Conant, S. S.(?)]. “Literary and Art Notes.” *The Galaxy* 8, no. 5 (November 1869): 717–720.
Cook, Clarence. “The New American Art.” *Daily Evening Transcript*, Boston. February 16, 1882.
[Cook, Clarence]. “Fine Arts: Mr. Farrer’s Water-Color Drawings.” *New-York Daily Tribune*. December 16 1865, 4.
[Cook, Clarence]. “Fine Arts in New-Haven.” *New-York Daily Tribune*. August 14, 1867, 2.
[Cook, Clarence]. “National Academy of Design: Fortieth Annual Exhibition [Sixth Article].” *New-York Daily Tribune*. July 3, 1865, 6.
[Cook, Clarence]. “Mr. Walters’s Collection of Pictures.” *New-York Daily Tribune*. February 13, 1864, 12.
[Cook, Clarence]. “The National Academy of Design: Forty-First Annual Exhibition.” *New-York Daily Tribune*. July 14, 1867, 2.
[Cook, Clarence]. “The Thirty-Ninth Exhibition [Fifth Article].” *New-York Daily Tribune*. May 21, 1864, 3.
Daily Evening Bulletin, Philadelphia. “The Academy of Fine Arts.” May 7, 1864, 6.
Daily Evening Bulletin, Philadelphia. “The Fine Arts, Annual Exhibition of the Pennsylvania Academy.” April 30, 1864, 6.
“Editor’s Easy Chair.” *Harper’s New Monthly Magazine* 32, no. 190 (March 1866): 519–524.
Evening Post, New York. “City Intelligence: Nine Artists Drafted.” August 21, 1863.
Evening Post, New York. “Paintings in Water Colors: The New Water-Color Society.” March 19, 1867.

Farrer, Thomas C. "Art Criticism," letter to the editor. *New-York Tribune*. June 8, 1867.
Farrer, Thomas C. "Correspondence: Farrer's Water-Colors." *The Nation* 2, no. 28 (January 11, 1866): 48–49.
"Fine Arts: The Artists' Fund Society." *Albion: A Journal of News, Politics, and Literature*. November 18, 1865.
Gasparin, Agénor. "Letter from the Count Agenor de Gasparin on the Presidential Election, translated by Mary L. Booth." *New York Times*. October 21, 1864.
Harper's Weekly. "United States Sanitary Commission." April 9, 1864, 228.
Home Journal, New York. "Fine Arts: National Academy of Design." June 25, 1859.
Home Journal, New York. "Personal." November 3, 1860.
National Republican, Washington, DC. "Extensive Hospital Buildings." January 7, 1862.
"The New Path." *The North American Review* 98, no. 202 (January 1864): 303–304.
New-York Daily Tribune. "The Fine Arts: Exhibition of the National Academy [Second Article]." April 22, 1854, 6.
New York Herald. "National Academy of Design," December 20, 1867.
New York Times. "Amusements This Evening." January 3, 1865.
New York Times. "Amusements This Evening." December 19, 1865.
New York Times. "Art Matters." April 3, 1867, 8.
New York Times. "Art in New York." March 14, 1867, 8.
New York Times. "Art Notes: The Artists' Fund Exhibition." November 24, 1864.
New York Times. "Fine Arts." November 14, 1864.
New York Times. "Fine Arts." December 17, 1867.
New York Times. "Fine Arts." December 20, 1867.
New York Times. "Married." June 6, 1864.
New York Times. "National Academy of Design East Room." June 7, 1865.
New York Times. "New Publications." March 14, 1872.
New York Times. "Passengers Sailed." July 1, 1869, 8.
New York Times. "What Our Artists Are Doing." January 14, 1858.
Oscuro. "The Fine Arts: The Exhibition at Yale College," Correspondence of the New-York Times, *New York Times*. July 22, 1867, 3.
Paletta. "Art Matters: Artists' Fund Society Exhibition—Water-Color Room." *The American Art Journal* 6, no. 6 (November 29, 1866): 87–88.
Paletta. "Art Matters: Artists' Fund Society Exhibition—South Room." *The American Art Journal* 6, no. 7 (December 8, 1866), 102–103.
"Recent Art Criticism." *The Round Table* 1, no. 3 (January 2, 1864): 42.
"Reviews: Minor Notices." *The Critic* vol. 2, no. 44 (November 1, 1884): 208.
S. "Notes at Art Museum." *Daily Evening Transcript*, Boston. November 23, 1883.
[Sturgis, Russell]. "Fine Arts: American Pictures on Exhibition." *The Nation* 1, no. 26 (December 28, 1865): 819–820.
[Sturgis, Russell]. "Fine Arts: The Sixth Annual Exhibition of the Artists' Fund Society [III]." *The Nation* 1, no. 22 (November 30, 1865): 692–693.
[Sturgis, Russell]. "Fine Arts: The Seventh Annual Exhibition of the Artists' Fund Society of New York [III]." *The Nation* 3, no. 74 (November 29, 1866): 435.
[Sturgis, Russell]. "The Fortieth Annual Exhibition of the National Academy of Design [Second Notice]." *The Nation* 1, no. 2 (July 13, 1865): 56–59.
[Sturgis, Russell(?)]. "Fine Arts: Seventh Annual Exhibition of the Artists' Fund Society of New York [I]." *The Nation* 3, no. 72 (November 15, 1866): 395–396.
X. "Pre-Raphaelite Pictures at the Academy [To the Editors of the Evening Post]." *Evening Post*. June 7, 1865.

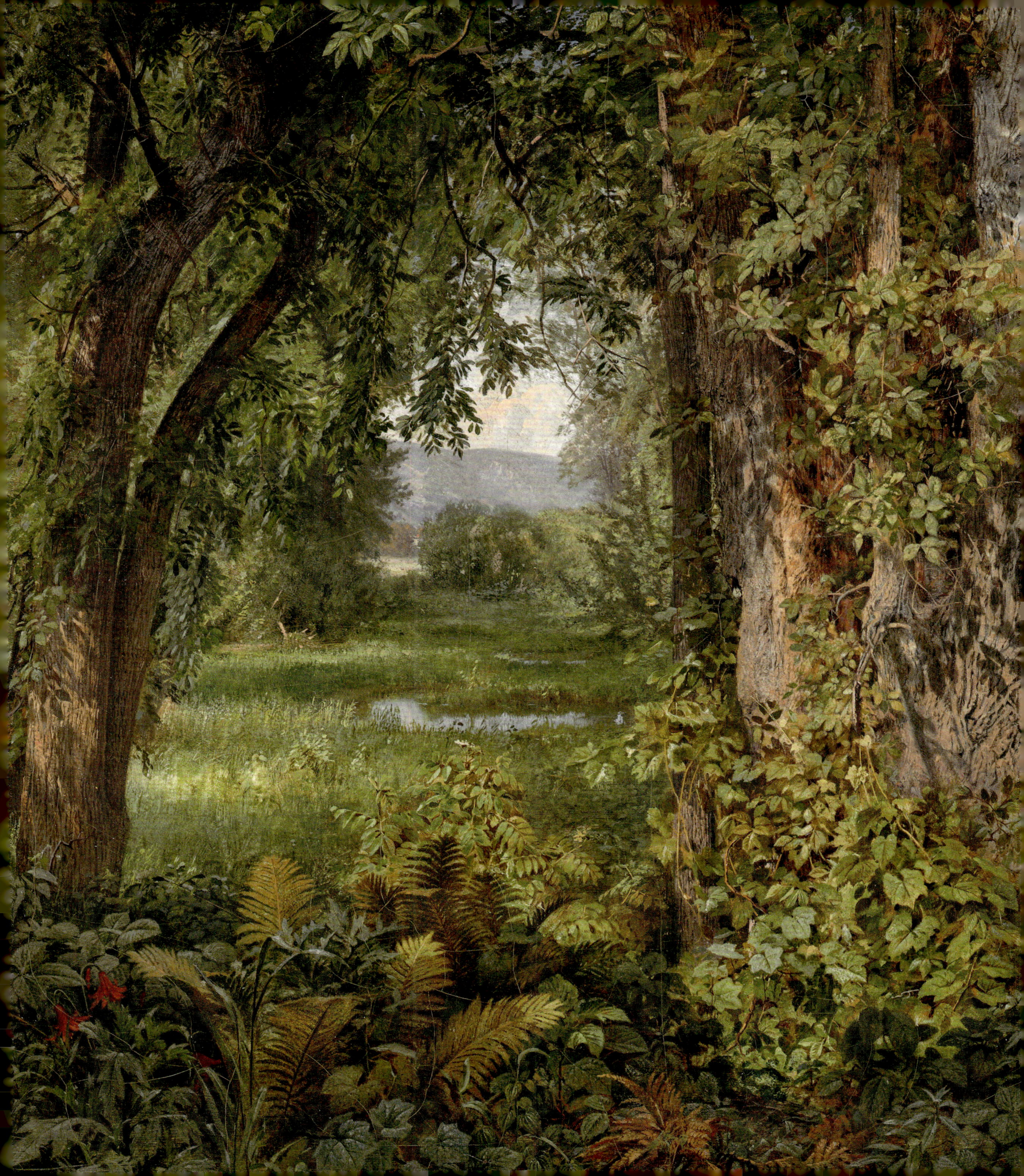

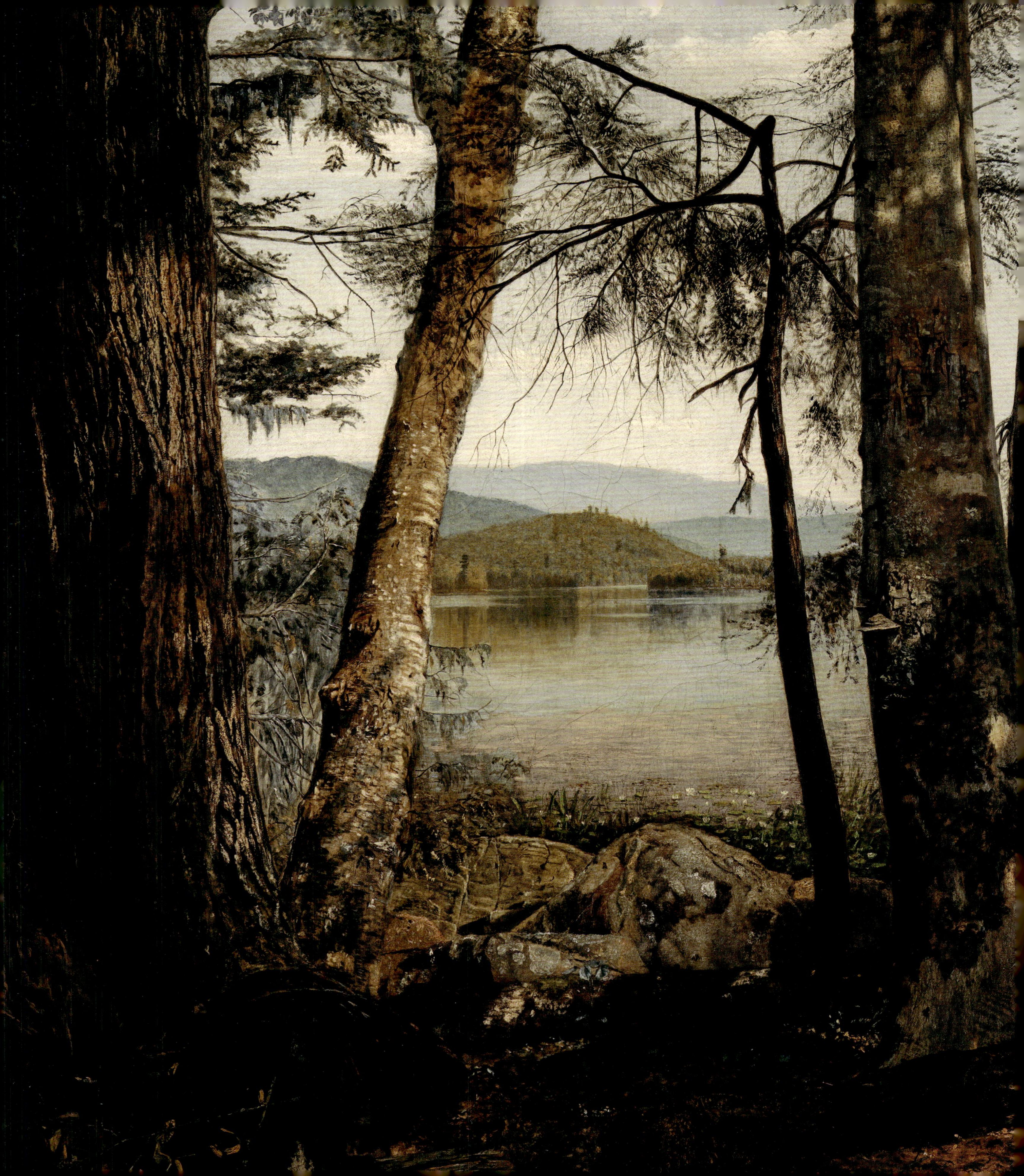

Acknowledgments

From the outset, *The American Pre-Raphaelites: Radical Realists* has been a collaborative project enriched by the combined efforts of many curators, collectors, scholars, and museum colleagues who joined together to examine in depth the works of a select group of artists, architects, scientists, photographers, collectors, and critics—all admirers of John Ruskin—who briefly banded together in a concerted effort to change the direction of art in America. This overlooked chapter of American art history was initially explored in 1985 by Linda S. Ferber and William H. Gerdts, who organized *The New Path: Ruskin and the American Pre-Raphaelites*, the first exhibition of works by this forgotten group. More than thirty years have passed since that landmark show at the Brooklyn Museum. In the interim, many additional works by members of the group have come to light and scholarship on nineteenth-century American art has advanced significantly. An updated and fresh look at the American Pre-Raphaelites is long overdue.

Early in the project we were fortunate to have the good counsel of eminent art historian William H. Gerdts (now retired) who, along with Linda Ferber, introduced the subject through the Brooklyn Museum exhibition. All the contributors to this publication benefited from Professor Gerdts's pioneering work on the American Pre-Raphaelites.

Special acknowledgment is due as well for the contributions made by Yale University doctoral candidate Sophie Lynford, whose essay has sharpened our focus on crucial political dimensions of the topic. She has also shared significant new documentary discoveries with fellow authors and cocurators throughout the process of the research and writing of this volume.

We are enormously grateful to Tim Barringer, Paul Mellon Professor of the History of Art, Yale University; Barbara Dayer Gallati, curator emerita of American painting and sculpture, Brooklyn Museum; Mark D. Mitchell, Holcombe T. Green Curator of American Paintings and Sculpture, Yale University Art Gallery; Sophie Lynford, Yale University; Janice Simon, Josiah Meigs Distinguished Teaching Associate Professor of Art History, University of Georgia; and Diane Waggoner, curator of nineteenth-century photographs, National Gallery of Art, for their eloquent and insightful essays.

Several individuals who provided critical assistance deserve special recognition. Abby Eron, University of Maryland Museum Fellow (2016–2017) at the National Gallery of Art, created a comprehensive chronology documenting the key dates and varied activities of the many figures associated with the Pre-Raphaelite cause. Abby's remarkable timeline was shared with all the catalog authors in advance of their initial essay drafts, thus ensuring factual consistency. Margaret R. Laster, independent art historian, went to extraordinary lengths to locate information and photographs of the men—and the often-overlooked women—associated with the group. These images appear in the Timeline in this volume, and many are published here for the first time.

At the National Gallery, Earl A. Powell III, director, and Franklin Kelly, deputy director and chief curator, have been supportive of the project since its inception. D. Dodge Thompson, chief of exhibitions, and his staff, especially Naomi Remes, exhibition officer, with associates Olivia Wood and Elizabeth Dent, skillfully coordinated the organization of the exhibition with the department of American and British paintings curatorial associates Zoë Samels and Catherine Southwick conducted research, tracked images, created spreadsheets, assembled databases, and assisted in countless other ways.

In the publishing office, both former editor in chief, Judy Metro, and current editor in chief, Emiko Usui, assisted by Chris Vogel, deputy publisher, skillfully guided production of the catalog at every stage. Brad Ireland, senior designer, designed the handsome catalog; Sara Sanders-Buell, photography rights coordinator, and Barbara Wood, image permission coordinator, secured images and reproduction rights. With patience and grace, Caroline Weaver edited contributions from multiple authors, combining individual voices into a seamless whole. We are all deeply indebted to her for expertise, guidance, and unfailing good cheer.

Mark Leithauser, senior curator and chief of design; Gordon Anson, deputy chief of design/head of exhibition production/chief lighting designer; Donna Kirk, senior architect and designer; Deborah Kirkpatrick, design coordinator; Elizabeth Parr, production coordinator; Jeffrey Wilson, head of silkscreen; Lisa Farrell, graphic designer; and Bethann Heinbaugh, head of preventive conservation, prepared individual works and the exhibition space with special care, ensuring that every object in the exhibition was shown to advantage. Kimberly Schenck, head of paper conservation, and Shan Linde, matting and framing specialist, oversaw the matting and framing of a number of works included in the exhibition with extraordinary attention to the details of presentation.

Educational materials and programs were prepared by Susan Arensberg, head of the department of exhibition programs, and Margaret Doyle, deputy head and associate curator of exhibition programs. Allison Peil, acting head of academic programs, and Sarah Battle, program assistant for lectures, arranged for a series of public lectures in conjunction with the exhibition. Eric Denker, senior lecturer and manager of gallery talks and lectures for adults, and David Gariff, senior lecturer, administered exhibition tours. Anabeth Guthrie, chief of communications, assisted by Laurie Tylec, oversaw publicity and responded to press inquiries. Special events associated with the exhibition were expertly arranged by Carol Kelley, chief of protocol and special events.

The coordinated efforts of several additional divisions within the Gallery ensured the success of the exhibition. Christine Myers, chief development and corporate relations officer, Patricia Donovan, senior development officer for major gifts and foundation giving, and Kate Conrad, development officer for foundation giving, worked to secure critical funding. Michelle Fondas, chief registrar and head of the division of registration and loans, and Theresa Beall, registrar for exhibitions, arranged for the transportation of the works included in the exhibition. William McClure, treasurer, assisted by Nancy Hoffmann, manager of fine arts risk and special projects, arranged for insurance. Nancy Breuer, secretary and general counsel, advised on legal matters. Roger Lawson, executive librarian; John Hagood, head of reader services; Tessa Brawley-Barker, interlibrary loan librarian; Faye Karas, interlibrary loan assistant; Anne Simmons, reference librarian; and Yuri Long, rare book librarian, offered indispensable assistance in procuring books, articles, and other critical research materials.

We also wish to express our gratitude to a number of colleagues, collectors, librarians, archivists, and dealers who graciously offered their assistance: Brett Abbott, Eric W. Baumgartner, Katie Blumenkrantz, Bernard Brown, Janet Bunde, Elisar Cabrera, Teresa A. Carbone, Kerry Dean Carso, David Chenkin, Allison Chomet, Mark Cole, Thomas Colville, Margaret Conrads, Jeff Cooley, Patrick Crowley, Kathleen A. Curran, Anna Tobin D'Ambrosio, Elliot Bostwick Davis, Samantha Deutch, Sally S. Dickinson, Mary Adair Dockery, John Driscoll, Cecily Dyer, Judith Farr, Stuart P. Feld, Madeleine Fidell-Beaufort, Nancy Finlay, Tricia Foley, Todd Forrest, Brandon Fortune, Kathleen A. Foster, Hugh Gibson, William Gibson, Laura M. Giles, Anne Collins Goodyear, Frank H. Goodyear, Stephanie Heydt, May Brawley Hill, Patricia Hills, Erica Hirshler, Miranda Hofelt, Margaret Hofer, Laura A. Horn, Shirley Reese Hughes, Jay Johnston, Patricia Junker, Margarita Karasoulis, Eugene Keilin, Christopher Kennedy, Elaine Komorowski, Elizabeth Kornhauser, Beth Kushner, Marilyn Satin Kushner, Karl Kusserow, Deirdre Lawrence, Royal W. Leith, Heather Lemonedes, Anastasia Levadas, Eunice Liu, Melanie Locay, Mary Lublin, Abigael MacGibeny, Catherine Mackay, David Mandel, Katherine Manthorne, Clark Marlor, Julie I. May, John F. McLaughlin, Andrew Melville-Smith, Susan Menconi, Leonard and Ellen Milberg, Louise Mirrer, Heidi Nakashima, M. P. Naud, Jennifer Neal, Terri O'Hara, Roberta M. Olson, Kimberly Orcutt, Angie Park, Thomas B. Parker, Emily Peters, Patricia Phagan, Ellen Prokop, Jill Reichenbach, William B. Rhoads, Jeff Richmond, Peter B. Sand, Andrew Schoelkopf, David P. Schuyler, Megan Schwenke, Marjorie Shelley, Deborah Smith, Sarah B. Snook, Sandra Solof, Gail Stavitsky, Kevin L. Stayton, Theodore E. Stebbins Jr., Barbara J. Stephanic, Patricia Svoboda, Diana Thompson, Amy Torbert, Andrew Walker, Sandy Wallace, Alice Walton, Joan Washburn, Caroline M. Welsh, Stephanie Wiles, Patrick Wilmerding, Joanne Witty, Paul Worman, Fiona York, and Sylvia Yount.

To all those who helped bring the project to fruition and especially to the many generous lenders to the exhibition, we extend our deepest gratitude.

LINDA S. FERBER AND NANCY K. ANDERSON

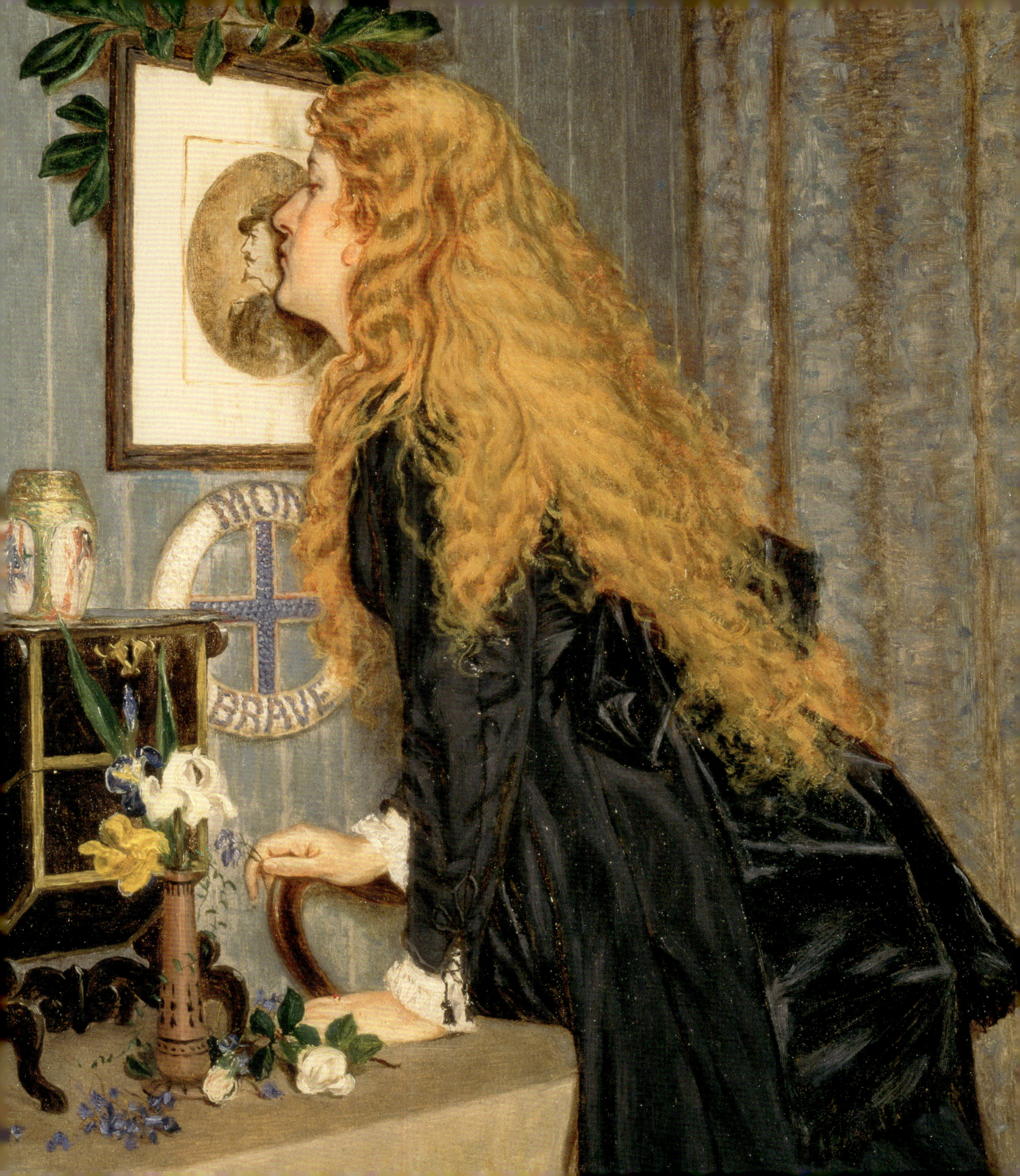
MON
BRAVE

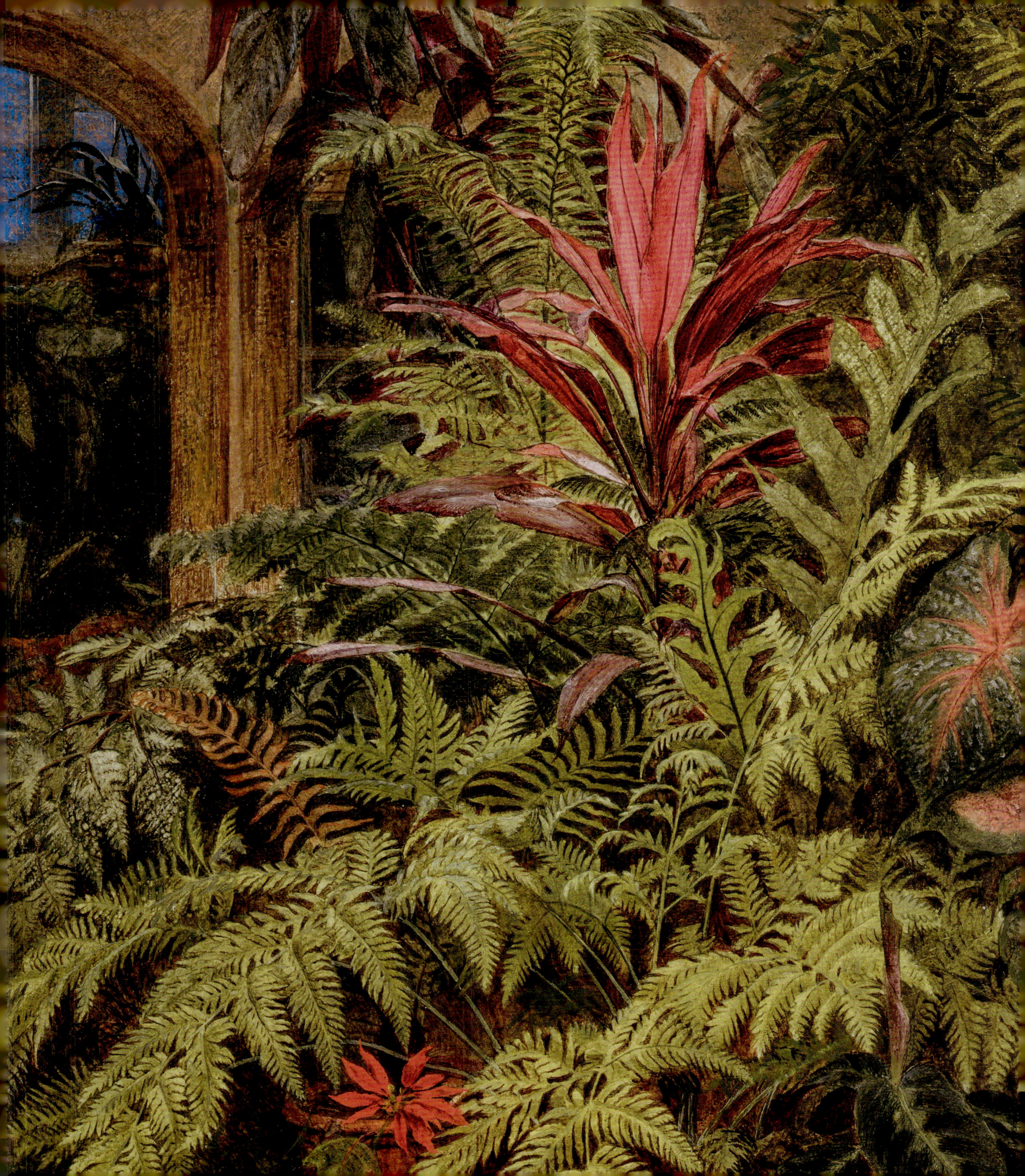

Index

Note: Page numbers in italic type indicate illustrations.

A

B

C

D

E

F

G

H

Display Illustrations (Details)

Photography Credits

Every effort has been made to locate the copyright holders for the reproductions used in this book. Any omissions will be corrected in subsequent editions.

PLATES

Plate 3: High Museum of Art, Atlanta; plates 4, 14, 24, 28, 78: Image courtesy of the Board of Trustees, National Gallery of Art, Washington; plates 6, 38: Munson-Williams-Proctor Arts Institute/Art Resource, NY; plates 8, 10, 17, 22, 31, 41, 57, 69, 75, 77: Photography by Eric W. Baumgartner; plates 13, 60, 62, 68, 83, 89: Photograph © 2019 Museum of Fine Arts, Boston; plates 18, 53, 54, 58, 59: Princeton University Art Museum/Art Resource, NY; plates 19, 86: The Pierpont Morgan Library, New York; plates 23, 43–45: Photography © New-York Historical Society; plates 55, 56, 84, 85: Imaging Department © President and Fellows of Harvard College; plate 65: © Virginia Museum of Fine Arts, photography by Travis Fullerton; plate 71: © The Cleveland Museum of Art; plate 79: Photography by Dwight Primiano; plate 87: Photography by Laura Wulf

COMPARATIVE ILLUSTRATIONS

Who Were the American Pre-Raphaelites?
Fig. 1: The Morgan Library & Museum, New York; fig. 7: Photograph © 2019 Museum of Fine Arts, Boston

A Radical Legacy: The British Pre-Raphaelites and Global Pre-Raphaelitism
Fig. 1: Royal Collection Trust/© Her Majesty Queen Elizabeth II 2018; figs. 2, 5, 8: © Tate, London 2019; fig. 4: © National Gallery, London/Art Resource, NY; fig. 6: © Ashmolean Museum, University of Oxford; fig. 9: Manchester Art Gallery, UK/Bridgeman Images; fig. 10: © The Henry Barber Trust, The Barber Institute of Fine Arts, University of Birmingham

Abolitionism and the American Pre-Raphaelite Experiment
Fig. 2: The Metropolitan Museum of Art, Libary; fig. 3: The Art Institute of Chicago/Art Resource, NY

Thought on Canvas: American Pre-Raphaelite Iconography
Fig. 2: Manchester Art Gallery, UK/Bridgeman Images; fig. 4: © National Gallery, London/Art Resource, NY; fig. 5: The Makins Collection/Bridgeman Images; fig. 6: © Tate, London 2018

A Knowing Look: The American Pre-Raphaelite Still Life
Fig. 2: Yale Center for British Art; figs. 3, 4: © 2019 Board of Trustees, National Gallery of Art, Washington; fig. 7: Yale University Art Gallery; fig. 8: Brooklyn Museum, 83.33.1

Timeline
James Terry Gardner (p. 245): From the collections of the New York State Library, Manuscript and Special Collections, Albany, New York; Charles Herbert Moore (p. 247) and Charles Eliot Norton (p. 248): Imaging Department © President and Fellows of Harvard College

The exhibition is organized by the National Gallery of Art, Washington.

EXHIBITION DATES
April 14–July 21, 2019

The exhibition and catalog are made possible through support from the Terra Foundation for American Art.

Major support for the exhibition and catalog is provided by the Henry Luce Foundation.

Produced by the Publishing Office, National Gallery of Art, Washington
www.nga.gov

Emiko Usui, editor in chief
Chris Vogel, deputy publisher
Wendy Schleicher, design manager

Edited by Caroline Weaver
Designed by Brad Ireland

Sara Sanders-Buell, image manager
John Long, print and digital production associate
Mariah Shay, production assistant

Typeset in TEFF Lexicon No. 2

Printed in Italy by Conti Tipocolor on Condat matt Périgord

Published in association with
Yale University Press
302 Temple Street
P.O. Box 209040
New Haven, CT 06520-9040
www.yalebooks.com/art

Library of Congress Control Number: 2018054932
Library of Congress Cataloging-in-Publication Data is on file.

ISBN 978-0-300-24252-2

10 9 8 7 6 5 4 3 2 1